Research Anthology on Big Data Analytics, Architectures, and Applications

Information Resources Management Association
USA

Volume III

Published in the United States of America by
    IGI Global
    Engineering Science Reference (an imprint of IGI Global)
    701 E. Chocolate Avenue
    Hershey PA, USA 17033
    Tel: 717-533-8845
    Fax: 717-533-8661
    E-mail: cust@igi-global.com
    Web site: http://www.igi-global.com

Library of Congress Cataloging-in-Publication Data

Names: Information Resources Management Association, editor.
Title: Research anthology on big data analytics, architectures, and
  applications / Information Resources Management Association, editor.
Description: Hershey, PA : Engineering Science Reference, an imprint of IGI
  Global, [2022] | Includes bibliographical references and index. |
  Contents: Overview of big data and its visualization / Richard S.
  Segall, Arkansas State University, USA, Gao Niu, Bryant University, USA
  -- Big data analytics and visualization of performance of stock exchange
  companies based on balanced scorecard indicators / Iman Raeesi Vanani,
  Allameh Tabataba'i University, Iran, Maziar Shiraj Kheiri, Allameh
  Tabataba'i University, Iran. | Summary: "This complete reference source
  on big data analytics that offers the latest, innovative architectures
  and frameworks, as well as explores a variety of applications within
  various industries offering an international perspective on a variety of
  topics such as advertising curricula, driven supply chain, and smart
  cities"-- Provided by publisher.
Identifiers: LCCN 2021039213 (print) | LCCN 2021039214 (ebook) | ISBN
  9781668436622 (h/c) | ISBN 9781668436639 (eisbn)
Subjects: LCSH: Big data. | Quantitative research.
Classification: LCC QA76.9.B45 .R437 2022 (print) | LCC QA76.9.B45
  (ebook) | DDC 005.7--dc23/eng/20211019
LC record available at https://lccn.loc.gov/2021039213
LC ebook record available at https://lccn.loc.gov/2021039214

British Cataloguing in Publication Data
A Cataloguing in Publication record for this book is available from the British Library.

The views expressed in this book are those of the authors, but not necessarily of the publisher.

For electronic access to this publication, please contact: eresources@igi-global.com.

List of Contributors

Table of Contents

Section 2
Development and Design Methodologies

Volume II

Section 3
Tools and Technologies

Section 4
Utilization and Applications

Volume IV

Section 5
Organizational and Social Implications

Section 6
Managerial Impact

Section 7
Critical Issues and Challenges

Preface

Society is now completely driven by data with many industries relying on data to conduct business or basic functions within the organization. With the efficiencies that big data bring to all institutions, data are continuously being collected and analyzed. However, data sets may be too complex for traditional data processing, and therefore, different strategies must evolve to solve the issue. For managers, data management can be particularly overwhelming as businesses sift through information and determine how to utilize it. Thus, investigating the current architectures and applications of data analytics is integral for achieving efficient and productive processes. The field of big data works as a valuable tool for many different industries.

Staying informed of the most up-to-date research trends and findings is of the utmost importance. That is why IGI Global is pleased to offer this four-volume reference collection of reprinted IGI Global book chapters and journal articles that have been handpicked by senior editorial staff. This collection will shed light on critical issues related to the trends, techniques, and uses of various applications by providing both broad and detailed perspectives on cutting-edge theories and developments. This collection is designed to act as a single reference source on conceptual, methodological, technical, and managerial issues, as well as to provide insight into emerging trends and future opportunities within the field.

The *Research Anthology on Big Data Analytics, Architectures, and Applications* is organized into seven distinct sections that provide comprehensive coverage of important topics. The sections are:

1. Fundamental Concepts and Theories;
2. Development and Design Methodologies;
3. Tools and Technologies;
4. Utilization and Applications;
5. Organizational and Social Implications;
6. Managerial Impact; and
7. Critical Issues and Challenges.

The following paragraphs provide a summary of what to expect from this invaluable reference tool.

Section 1, "Fundamental Concepts and Theories," serves as a foundation for this extensive reference tool by addressing crucial theories essential to understanding the concepts and uses of big data in multidisciplinary settings. Opening this reference book is the chapter "Understanding Big Data" by Profs. Naciye Güliz Uğur and Aykut Hamit Turan of Sakarya University, Turkey, which defines big data basically and provides an overview of big data in terms of status, organizational effects (technology, healthcare, education, etc.), implementation challenges, and big data projects. This first section ends with the chapter "A Brief Survey on Big Data in Healthcare" by Prof. Ebru Aydindag Bayrak of Istanbul University-Cerrahpaşa, Turkey and Prof. Pinar Kirci of Bursa Uludağ University, Turkey, which presents a brief introduction to big data and big data analytics and their roles in the healthcare system.

Section 2, "Development and Design Methodologies," presents in-depth coverage of the design and development of big data architectures for their use in different applications. This section starts with "Big Data Analytics and Models" by Prof. Ferdi Sönmez of Istanbul Arel University, Turkey; Prof. Ziya Nazım Perdahçı of Mimar Sinan Fine Arts University, Turkey; and Prof. Mehmet Nafiz Aydın of Kadir Has University, Turkey, which explores big data analytics as a comprehensive technique for processing large amounts of data to uncover insights. This section ends with the chapter "Big Data Analytics and Visualization for Food Health Status Determination Using Bigmart Data" by Profs. Sumit Arun Hirve and Pradeep Reddy C. H. of VIT-AP University, India, which elaborates on pre-processing a commercial market dataset using the R tool and its packages for information and visual analytics.

Section 3, "Tools and Technologies," explores the various tools and technologies used in the implementation of big data analytics for various uses. This section begins with "Big Data and Advance Analytics: Architecture, Techniques, Applications, and Challenges" by Prof. Surabhi Verma of National Institute of Industrial Engineering, Mumbai, India, which investigates the characteristics of big data, processes of data management, advance analytic techniques, applications across sectors, and issues that are related to their effective implementation and management within broader context of big data analytics. This section ends with the chapter "Big Data for Satellite Image Processing: Analytics, Tools, Modeling, and Challenges" by Prof. P. Swarnalatha of Vellore Institute of Technology, Vellore, India and Prof. Prabu Sevugan of VIT University, India, which presents an introduction to the basics in big data including architecture, modeling, and the tools used.

Section 4, "Utilization and Applications," describes how big data is used and applied in diverse industries for various technologies and applications. The opening chapter in this section, "An Analysis of Big Data Analytics," by Profs. Vijander Singh, Amit Kumar Bairwa and Deepak Sinwar of Manipal University Jaipur, India, explains that the immense measure of organized, unstructured, and semi-organized information is produced each second around the cyber world, which should be managed efficiently. This section ends with the chapter "Computational and Data Mining Perspectives on HIV/AIDS in Big Data Era: Opportunities, Challenges, and Future Directions" by Prof. Ali Al Mazari of Alfaisal University, Saudi Arabia, which provides a review on the computational and data mining perspectives on HIV/AIDS in big data era.

Section 5, "Organizational and Social Implications," includes chapters discussing the ways in which big data impacts society and shows the ways in which big data is used in different industries and how this impacts business. The chapter "Big Data and IoT Applications in Real Life Environment" by Prof. Anjali Chaudhary of Noida International University, India and Pradeep Tomar of Gautam Buddha University, India, discusses various applications of big data and IoT in detail and discusses how both the technologies are affecting our daily life and how it can make things better. This section ends with the chapter "Cloud Computing Big Data Adoption Impacts on Teaching and Learning in Higher Education: A Systematic Review" by Prof Fahad Nasser Alhazmi of King Abdulaziz University, Saudi Arabia, which evaluates and assesses the impact of big data and cloud computing in higher education.

Section 6, "Managerial Impact," presents coverage of academic and research perspectives on the way big data analytics affects management in the workplace. Starting this section is "Big Data Technologies and Management" by Profs. Jayashree K. and Abirami R. of Rajalakshmi Engineering College, India, which discusses the background of big data. It also discusses the various application of big data in detail. This section ends with the chapter "Exploring Big Data Analytic Approaches to Cancer Blog Text Analysis" by Prof. Viju Raghupathi of Koppelman School of Business, Brooklyn College of the City University of New York, Brooklyn, USA and Profs. Yilu Zhou and Wullianallur Raghupathi of Gabelli School of Business, Fordham University, New York, USA, which establishes an exploratory approach to involving big data analytics methods in developing text analytics applications for the analysis of cancer blogs.

Section 7, "Critical Issues and Challenges," highlights current problems within the field and offers solutions for future improvement. Opening this final section is the chapter "A Survey on Comparison of Performance Analysis on a Cloud-Based Big Data Framework" by Profs. Krishan Tuli and Amanpreet Kaur of Chandigarh University, India and Prof. Meenakshi Sharma of Galgotias University, India, which discusses the survey on the performance of the big data framework based on a cloud from various endeavors which assists ventures to pick a suitable framework for their work and get a desired outcome. This section ends with the chapter "How Big Data Transforms Manufacturing Industry: A Review Paper" by Profs. Victor I. C. Chang and Wanxuan Lin of Xi'an Jiaotong-Liverpool University, Suzhou, China, which defines what big data means for the manufacturing industry. It explains four advantages about big data analytics and their benefits to manufacturing.

Although the primary organization of the contents in this multi-volume work is based on its seven sections, offering a progression of coverage of the important concepts, methodologies, technologies, applications, social issues, and emerging trends, the reader can also identify specific contents by utilizing the extensive indexing system listed at the end of each volume. As a comprehensive collection of research on the latest findings related to big data, the *Research Anthology on Big Data Analytics, Architectures, and Applications* provides data scientists, data analysts, computer engineers, software engineers, technologists, government officials, managers, CEOs, professors, graduate students, researchers, and academicians with a complete understanding of the application and impact of big data. Given the vast number of issues concerning usage, failure, success, strategies, and applications of big data in modern technologies and processes, the *Research Anthology on Big Data Analytics, Architectures, and Applications* encompasses the most pertinent research on its uses and impact on global institutions.

Chapter 47
Big Data Analytics in Healthcare Sector

Sheik Abdullah A.
Thiagarajar College of Engineering, India

Selvakumar S.
G. K. M. College of Engineering and Technology, India

Parkavi R.
Thiagarajar College of Engineering, India

Suganya R.
Thiagarajar College of Engineering, India

Abirami A. M.
Thiagarajar College of Engineering, India

ABSTRACT

The importance of big data over analytics made the process of solving various real-world problems simpler. The big data and data science tool box provided a realm of data preparation, data analysis, implementation process, and solutions. Data connections over any data source, data preparation for analysis has been made simple with the availability of tremendous tools in data analytics package. Some of the analytical tools include R programming, python programming, rapid analytics, and weka. The patterns and the granularity over the observed data can be fetched with the visualizations and data observations. This chapter provides an insight regarding the types of analytics in a big data perspective with the realm in applicability towards healthcare data. Also, the processing paradigms and techniques can be clearly observed through the chapter contents.

DOI: 10.4018/978-1-6684-3662-2.ch047

DATA ANALYTICS AN OVERVIEW

There are different types of analytics. They are Predictive analytics, Descriptive analytics, Diagnostic analytics and Prescriptive analytics. Among these predictive analytics is very useful to predict the future events. Predictive analytics uses many techniques such as statistical learning, machine learning, data mining a nd artificial intelligence. The patterns found in past and transactional data can recognize risks opportunities for future. Applications of predictive analytics are as follows; Customer Relationship Management (CRM), Fraud Detection in Banking sectors, Risk Management, Direct Marketing, Healthcare, etc. The following Figure 1 depicts the types of data analytics.

Figure 1. Types of analytics

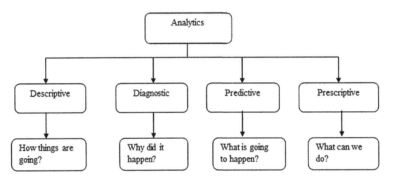

APPLICATIONS OF DATA ANALYTICS

Data analytics has its applications towards diverse fields in real time perspective. The major domain includes search engine, weather forecasting, medical informatics, recommender systems, image and speech recognition, risk analysis and logistic support recognition. Let's discuss the application of analytics over health care sector.

Data analytics plays a major role with an adherent potential to improve the notion of healthcare system. Patient monitoring system with improvement over care and cost reduction factor plays a major role towards the betterment of patient health. Monitoring and managing the risk behavior of patients also plays a significant role for the determination of risk corresponding to specific disease. Approaches, in machine learning, mathematical statistics, and soft computing paradigms plays a major role in data classification and prediction.

Systematic process in data analytics and data models enhances prediction over medical data with the target that the patients receive right direction to diagnosis in right time. Algorithms in analytics can also serve to detect fraud and abuse over medical informatics.

ANALYTICS IN HEALTHCARE

The healthcare community is changing from huge volume-base data to value-based data that is designed to achieve higher quality, lower costs and a better patient knowledge. To succeed, healthcare contributors are forming Accountable Care Organizations (ACOs) and restructuring their care delivery system. The healthcare industry is evolving at rapid speed. At the front of this transformation is big data, creating giant opportunities for companies to develop patient outcomes while managing costs. Healthcare Analytics & Care Delivery controls data-driven transformations.

PREDICTIVE ANALYTICS IN HEALTHCARE

Mainly Predictive analytics are used by healthcare professionals to process patient's data, forecast the potential for illness, identify high-risk patient, reduce hospital readmission rates and so on. Risk stratification evaluation will facilitate in prioritizing clinical progress, reducing system waste, and make financially efficient population management. Well-established risk stratification includes low-risk, high-risk, and rising-risk will play a key role in some health care situations. For instance, a calculated risk score will facilitate decrease system waste by setting progress priorities for patient follow-up in patient populations. Using this predictive risk score ranking, care managers are prompted to concentrate on those patients at highest risk and preemptively get involved with medication reconciliation, planning home visits, or follow-up appointments. The following Figure 2 describes the workflow of predictive analytics.

Figure 2. Predictive analytics process

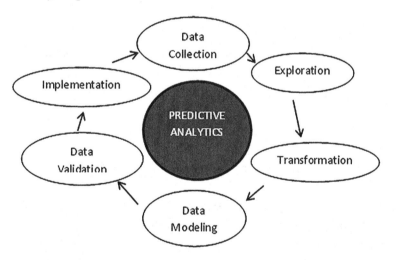

The major application of predictive analytics in health care is predicting the risk factors related to diabetic condition among patients. Now a day, Diabetes is the most common disease among adults and old age people. In 1980, the number of people suffered from diabetes is 108 million but in 2014, the number of people rises to 422 million. Among these 8.5% are adults who are suffering from diabetes. There are types of diabetes Type 1 diabetes and Type 2 diabetes. Type 1 diabetes is deficient insulin production, but Type 2 diabetes caused by the most of the people around the world. It is due to the body's inefficient use of insulin. Diabetes causes half of the death due to high blood glucose level. World Health Organization predicts that in 2030 the diabetes will be the 7th leading cause of death. So, make predictive analytics in Diabetes will be more useful to prevent more deaths in future due to this disease.

CASE STUDY DEPICTING THE APPLICATION OF PREDICTIVE ANALYTICS IN HEALTHCARE

1. Data Description

Data records of various Heart Disease patients from the UCI machine learning repository has been taken for the evaluation of the model. The record related to each patient should have at least one of the following in their history: Percutaneous Coronary Intervention (PCI), Angina, Acute Myocardial Infarction (AMI), and Coronary Artery Bypass Graft (CABG). The predominant risk factors is of Clinical factors such as age, trestbps,sex, chest pain type and Biochemical factors such as serum cholesterol (TC) mg/dL, fasting blood sugar (FBS) mg/dL, thalach, exang, old peak, restecg, slope, the number of vessels colored by fluoroscopy and thal. . The flowchart below depicts the evaluation and prediction of HD and its associated events.

The evaluation proceeds by normalizing the input data set by means of Min-Max normalization. This technique performs a linear transformation and preserves the relationship among the original data values (Sheik Abdullah et al., 2012). The retrieved data is sorted with respect to the specified age related to each patient. This is a form of data coding by which the prediction can be effectively made if the age group is classified with respect to each of the event in predicting Coronary Heart Disease. Table 1 provides the clustering scheme of data records.

Table 1. Clustering of data records

Risk Factor	Cluster 1	Cluster 2	Cluster 3	Cluster 4
AGE	34-50	51-60	61-70	71-85
SEX	MALE	FEMALE		

2. Data Classification Using Neural Network Classifier

Neural Network refers to the information processing paradigm inspired by biological nervous systems, such as our brain. The general structure of the Neural Network refers to the large number of highly interconnected processing elements (neurons) working together. Neural networks are configured for a specific application, such as pattern recognition or data classification, through a learning process (Asdrubal Lopez chau et al., 2014). The operations performed in the learning process are,

- Fixing the Weight.
- Simulating the Network which equals the input signal flow through network to the outputs.
- The output is manipulated which is often a binary representation.
- Based upon simple operations and threshold the network formulates fast decisions and real time response.

3. Mathematical Representation of a Neural Network

The basic architecture consists of three types of neuron layers such as the input, hidden and the output layer. The signal flow is from the input to the output units, strictly in a feed-forward direction. The user can define the structure of the neural network with the parameter list "hidden layers". Each list entry describes a new hidden layer. Each entry key must correspond to the layer name. The value of each entry must be a number defining the size of the hidden layer. The neuron calculates a weighted sum of inputs and compares it to a threshold. If the threshold is lower than the sum, the output is set to 1, otherwise to-1. The data processing can extend over multiple layers of units, the activation values of the units undergo a relaxation process such that the network will evolve to a stable state in which these activations do not change anymore (Sheik Abdullah 2012). The strength of connection between the neurons is stored for the specific connection. Learning the solution to a problem equals to changing the connection weights. The following Figure 3 depicts the mathematical representation of a neural network.

Figure 3. Mathematical representation of a neural network

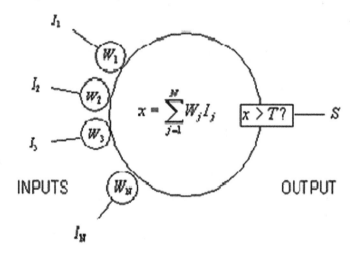

4. Models Investigated

- **AMI:** Myocardial infarction (MI) or acute myocardial infarction (AMI), commonly known as a heart attack, results from the interruption of blood supply to a part of the heart, causing heart cells to die. This is due to occlusion of a coronary artery following the rupture of a vulnerable atherosclerotic plaque, which is an unstable collection of cholesterol and fatty acids which are lipids and white blood cells in the wall of an artery.
- **PCI:** Percutaneous coronary intervention (PCI), commonly known as coronary angioplasty or simply angioplasty is one therapeutic procedure used to treat the stenotic (narrowed) coronary arteries of the heart found in coronary heart disease. These stenotic segments are due to the buildup of cholesterol-laden plaques that form due to atherosclerosis.
- **CABG:** Coronary artery bypass surgery, also coronary artery bypass graft surgery, and colloquially heart bypass or bypass surgery is a surgical procedure performed to relieve angina and reduce

the risk of death from coronary artery disease. Arteries or veins from elsewhere in the patient's body are grafted to the coronary arteries to bypass atherosclerotic narrowing's and improve the blood supply to the coronary circulation supplying the heart muscle.

5. Results and Discussion

The use of Neural Network models lies in the fact that they can be used to infer a function from observations and also to use it. Unsupervised neural networks can also be used to learn representations of the input that capture the salient characteristics of the input distributions. The entire information is contained in the overall activation 'state' of the network. 'Knowledge' is represented by the network itself, which more than the sum of its individual components. The performance analysis of the algorithms is illustrated in Table 2.

Table 2. Performance analysis

Performance Measures	Decision Tree	Neural Network
Accuracy (%)	85.55	89.63
Precision (%)	77.04	80.58
Recall (%)	72.06	78.87
Classification Error (%)	14.44	10.37
Kappa Statistics	0.794	0.830
RMS Error	0.420	0.315
Correlation	0.782	0.867

Meanwhile, Decision trees are constructed in a top-down recursive divide-and-conquer manner and the compatibility of Decision trees degrades because the output is limited to one attribute. Trees created from the numeric datasets seems to be more complex and also when the database is large the complexity of the tree increases.

DATABASES USED IN HEALTHCARE

Big data differs from a typical relational database. The biggest difference between big data and relational databases is that big data doesn't have the traditional table-and-column structure that relational databases have. In classic relational databases, a schema for the data is required (for example, demographic data is housed in one table joined to other tables by a shared identifier like a patient identifier). Every piece of data exists in its well-defined place. In contrast, big data has hardly any structure at all. Data is extracted from source systems in its raw form stored in a massive, somewhat chaotic distributed file system. The Hadoop Distributed File System (HDFS) stores data across multiple data nodes in a simple hierarchical form of directories of files. Conventionally, data is stored in 64MB chunks (files) in the data nodes with a high degree of compression.

BIG DATA AND ITS CHARACTERISTICS

By convention, big data is typically not transformed in any way. Little or no "cleansing" is done and generally, no business rules are applied. Some people refer to this raw data in terms of the "Sushi Principle" (i.e. data is best when it's raw, fresh, and ready to consume). This approach doesn't transform data, apply business rules, or bind the data semantically until the last responsible moment–in other words, bind as close to the application layer as possible (Barbierato et al., 2014).

Due to its unstructured nature and open source roots, big data is much less expensive to own and operate than a traditional relational database (Chakraborty & MK Pagolu, 2014). A Hadoop cluster is formed by master / slave architecture and it is built by several commodity hardware, and it typically runs on traditional disk drives in a direct-attached (DAS) configuration rather than an expensive storage area network (SAN). Most relational database engines are proprietary software and require expensive licensing and maintenance agreements. There are different types of NoSql database that fit into this category, such as key-value stores and document stores in MongoDB, which focus on the storage and retrieval of large volumes of unstructured, semi-structured, or even structured data. They achieve performance gains by doing away with some (or all) of the restrictions traditionally associated with conventional databases, such as read-write consistency, in exchange for scalability and distributed processing.

Relational databases also require significant, specialized resources to design, administer, and maintain. In contrast, big data doesn't need a lot of design work and is fairly simple to maintain. A lot of storage redundancy allows for more tolerable hardware failures. Hadoop clusters are designed to simplify rebuilding of failed nodes.

The lack of pre-defined structure means a big data environment is cheaper and simpler to create. The difficulty with big data is not in storing huge data in large storage devices, processing big data is the most challenging task. A structured relational database essentially comes with a roadmap—an outline of where each piece of data exists. On the big data side, there are no traditional schemas, and therefore not much guidance. With a relational database, a simple, structured query language (i.e. SQL) pulls the needed data using a sophisticated query engine optimized for finding data.

With big data, the query languages are much more complicated. A sophisticated data user—such as a data scientist—is needed to find the subset of data required for applications. Creating the required Map Reduce algorithms for querying big data instances isn't for the faint of heart. In short, big data is cheap but more difficult to use (Lin et al., 2014). Relational databases are expensive but very usable (Cho, 1999). The maturity level of big data technology is low–after all the big data journey only began a few short years ago. So, as the tooling and security catches up with its potential, health systems will be able to do exciting things with it.

Both hadoop and map reduce plays a significant role in medical data prediction and analysis. The impact of big data in hadoop platform serves to compute larger volume of medical data in a shorter period of time and analysis. Even though hadoop has its various eco system tools and service it offers a wide range of flexible opportunities for medical data in data analysis. The realm of data integrity and security has to be considered to be as the major consequence in big data platform and services.

IMPORTANCE OF BIG DATA IN HEALTH CARE ANALYTICS

Big data technologies are progressively more used for biomedical and health – care informatics research. Large amounts of biological and clinical data have been generated and collected at an exceptional speed and scale. A number of scenarios in healthcare are well suited for a big data solution (Das et al., 2016). In 2001, Doug Laney, now at Gartner, coined the term "the 3 V's" to define big data–Volume, Velocity, and Variety. Other analysts have argued that this is too simplistic, and there are more things to think about when defining big data. They suggest more V's such as Variability and Veracity, and even a C for Complexity (Paulcheung 2012).

Modern years have seen an escalating volume of medical image data and observations being gathered and accumulated. Collaborative, global ideas have begun the acquisition of hundreds of terabytes / petabytes of data to be made accessible to the medical and scientific community. For example, the new generation of sequencing technologies enables the dispensation of billions of DNA sequence data per day, and the application of Electronic Health Records (EHRs) is documenting large amounts of patient data (Fatos & Leonard, 2014). Handling out these large datasets and processing is a challenging task. Together with the new medical opportunities arising, new image and data processing algorithms are required for functioning with, and learning from, large scale medical datasets. This book aims to scrutinize recent progress in the medical imaging field, together with new opportunity stemming from increased medical data availability, as well as the specific challenges involved. "Big Data" is a key word in medical and health care sector for patient care. NASA researchers coined the term big data in 1967 to describe the huge amount of information being generated by supercomputers. It has evolved to include all data streaming from various sources – cell phones, mobile devices, Satellites, Google, Amazon and Twitter. The impact of big data may be deep, and it will have in-depth implications for medical imaging as healthcare tracks, handles, exploits and documents relevant patient information (kambatla et al., 2014).

Medical Data collection can necessitate an incredible amount of time and effort once collected; the information can be utilized in several ways:

- To improve early detection, diagnosis, and treatment
- To predict patient diagnosis; aggregated data are used to speck early warning symptoms and mobilize resources to proactively address care
- To increase interoperability and interconnectivity of healthcare (i.e., health information exchanges)
- To enhance patient care via mobile health, telemedicine, and self-tracking or home devices (Sheik Abdullah et al., 2017)

Storing patient health information and managing is a challenging task. Big data in medical field is crucial one (Christian et al., 2014). Ensuring patient data privacy and security is a significant challenge for any healthcare organization seeking to fulfil with the new rule. Any individual or organization that uses Protected Health Information (PHI) must comply, and this includes employees, physicians, vendors or other business associates, and other covered entities.

Consider also that your compliance for data (small or big) must cover the following systems, processes, and policies:

- Registration systems
- Patient portals

- Patient financial systems
- Electronic medical records
- E-prescribing
- Business associate and vendor contracts
- Audits
- Notice of privacy practice

REAL-TIME LOCATING SYSTEMS

Increasingly, hospitals and large healthcare organizations are investing in systems that provide the real-time location of assets (e.g., intravenous pumps) and/or people (e.g., staff and patients) in order to better manage operations. These systems locate the asset or person through some combination of wireless technologies, such as RFID, Wi-Fi, ultrasound, infrared, and GPS. Combined with management front-ends, these technologies can reduce loss and theft of assets and improve the situational awareness of staff who direct workflow (Daewoo et al., 2014).

VISUALIZATION AND REPORTING

Traditionally, healthcare has used business data far less regularly and comprehensively than most other industries. It has underinvested in advanced managerial technologies like reporting systems and data visualization. This may be partly due to some healthcare providers viewing investments in managerial and operational information systems as less important than investments in clinical information systems.

Whereas many organizations outside healthcare have developed or purchased real-time reporting systems that push targeted updates to specific end users, healthcare has typically relied on centralized production of static, undifferentiated report documents that provide the same view of historical performance to all recipients (Philip et al., 2014). Contemporary reporting systems often incorporate features such as interactive dashboards that provide customized, up-to-the-minute (or at least frequently updated) graphical displays of critical performance metrics, historical trends, and reference benchmarks or goals. These dashboards are designed to help the end user focus on those data that are most informative about how their systems are performing. In healthcare, decision-support dashboards are increasingly common on the clinical side, especially in EHR environments, but far less so when it comes to supporting managerial or operational decisions.

REFERENCES

Barbierato, E. (2014). *Performance Evaluation of NoSQL big-data applications using multi-formalism models. In Future Generation Computer Systems* (vol. 37, pp. 345–353). Elsevier.

Chakraborty & Pagolu. (2014). *Analysis of Unstructured Data: Applications of Text Analytics and Sentiment Mining*. Academic Press.

Chau, Li, & Yu. (2014). Supportvector machine classification for large datasets using Decision Tree and fisher linear discriminant. *Future Generation Computer Systems, 36*, 80–90.

Cho, Y. E. (1999). Efficient Resource Utilization for parallel I/O in cluster environments. U. Illinois.

Christian, E., Massimo, F., Francesco, P., & Aniello, C. (2014). *A Knowledge-based Platform for Big Data analytics based on publish/subscribe services ans stream processing, Knowledge based systems.* Elsevier.

Daewoo, L., Jin-Soo, K., & Seungryoul, M. (2014). *Large-scale Incremental Processing with MapReduce. In Future Generation Computer Systems* (Vol. 36, pp. 66–79). Elsevier.

Das & Mohan Kumar. (2016). *BIG Data Analytics: A Framework for Unstructured Data Analysis.* Academic Press.

Fatos, X., & Leonard, B. (2014). Semantics, intelligent processing and services for big data. *Future Generation Computer Systems, 37*, 201–202. doi:10.1016/j.future.2014.02.004

Kambatla, K, K, & G. (2014). Trends in Big Data Analytics. *Journal of Parallel Distributed Computing, 74*, 2561 – 2573.

Lin, X.-Y., & Chung, Y.-C. (2014). Master-worker model for map reduce paradigm on the TILE64 many-core platform. *Future Generation Computer Systems, 36*, 19–30. doi:10.1016/j.future.2013.05.001

Paulcheung. (2012). *Big data official statistics and social science research – Emerging Data Challenges.* United Nations Statistics Division.

Philip, C. L. (2014). Data-Intensive applications, Challenges, techniques and Technologies: A survey on big data. *Journal of Information Science, 275*, 314–347. doi:10.1016/j.ins.2014.01.015

Sheik Abdullah. (2012a). A Data mining Model for predicting the Coronary Heart Disease using Random Forest Classifier. *International Journal of Computer Applications*, (3).

Sheik Abdullah. (2012b). A Data Mining Model to predict and analyze the events related to Coronary Heart Disease using Decision Trees with Particle Swarm Optimization for Feature Selection. *International Journal of Computer Applications, 55*(8). DOI: . doi:10.5120/8779-2736

Sheik Abdullah, A., Gayathri, N., & Selvakumar, S. (2017). *Determination of the Risk of Heart Disease using Neural Network Classifier.* National Conference on Big Data Analytics and Mobile Technologies (NCBM 2017) at Thiagarajar College of Engineering, Madurai, India.

Sheik Abdullah, A., Selvakumar, S., Karthikeyan, P., & Venkatesh, M. (2017, May). Comparing the Efficacy of Decision Tree and its Variants using Medical Data. *Indian Journal of Science and Technology, 10*(18). doi:10.17485/ijst/2017/v10i18/111768

This research was previously published in Machine Learning Techniques for Improved Business Analytics; pages 94-106, copyright year 2019 by Business Science Reference (an imprint of IGI Global).

Chapter 48
Big Data Applications in Healthcare Administration

Joseph E. Kasten
Pennsylvania State University, York, USA

ABSTRACT

The healthcare industry has a growing record of using big data-related technologies such as data analytics, internet of things, and machine learning, especially in the clinical areas. However, healthcare institutions must also perform all of the administrative processes just as any other organization. Thus, like many other industries, healthcare has begun to apply these same technologies to improve their understanding of these internal operations and use them to make better decisions and run a more effective operation. This study takes a structured literature review approach to describe the current state of this literature and identify the major themes and priorities of both the research community and the healthcare industry as a whole. The contribution made by this study is to provide a comprehensive analysis of the state of the literature to use as a foundation for the future research opportunities noted in the paper.

INTRODUCTION

As the concept of big data and the tools that surround it have matured, the world of business has witnessed an inexorable migration of these tools from the financial sector to other areas of commerce such as transportation and insurance. Shortly into this transition, these tools made their way to the healthcare industry. Some of the first areas within healthcare that big data techniques first appeared were in the clinical areas such as oncology, radiology, and genetics (Chang & Choi, 2016). However, healthcare organizations are also businesses with the same internal and external processes as any other business. These include the hiring of staff, the procuring of supplies, and the running of sometimes vast physical plant installations. So, it is not surprising that the healthcare industry has begun using big data techniques to improve their ability to perform these important, yet often out of the spotlight, activities.

There is a large and enthusiastic literature surrounding the clinical uses of big data in healthcare and there have been a number of reviews in these various areas (Pashazadeh & Navimpour, 2018; Otokiti, 2019). However, there is a much smaller, but still important, literature that describes the uses of big

DOI: 10.4018/978-1-6684-3662-2.ch048

data in the administration of healthcare and hospital activities. The purpose of this paper is to review the literature regarding the uses of big data and its ancillary tools and processes in the improvement of healthcare processes. The term improvement can, of course, encompass many different aspects of healthcare and hospital administration. Improvement can involve the reduction of costs, the improvement of patient care and experience, the prediction of patient admission or readmission, and the allocation and management of hospital resources. In these and many other cases the use of big data techniques and tools has provided many options and opportunities for hospitals, healthcare systems, and other parts of the overall healthcare industry to create more effective and efficient methods for providing quality healthcare to their community and the nation.

BACKGROUND

When most people encounter the healthcare industry, they see mostly the clinical side of the process (except when it comes time to pay the bill). Many do not consider that healthcare is an industry and even if the facility they are using for provision of healthcare services is a non-profit organization, the business side of the healthcare equation is a crucial part of the overall system. Hospitals depend on well-trained and experienced personnel to perform their essential services, thus human resources is a critical activity. Even if they do not have shareholders to answer to, though many healthcare systems in the US are publicly traded companies, they still must monitor costs and revenues just as any other organization and therefore the financial processes of the organization is just as important as for any Fortune 500 firm. Issues of workflow streamlining, document management, and technology selection and implementation have very important roles in healthcare just as they do in any other organization.

Healthcare as a Business

Healthcare organizations face many of the same challenges as other firms. Cost reduction is a constant process. Large healthcare bureaucracies are inherently expensive to run, and with the high level of expertise in the clinical side of the organization and very expensive equipment to purchase and operate, cost reduction processes often take center stage. This is vitally important not just for the success of the enterprise, but for the healthcare system writ large. Workflow analysis allows the reduction of delays for patients to receive care and also reduce the overall complexity of the organization (Wolf, Herrmann & Rothermel, 2013). Increasing accuracy is a fundamental objective of healthcare administration as it is closely related to not just patient outcomes, but also the areas of cost reduction, asset utilization, and continuous process improvement (Cutler, Wikler & Basch, 2012).

Big Data Related Technologies

When organizations say they are using "big data," it also means they are using some other tools to utilize that large collection of data. The simple collection of data, even in large amounts, is of little value unless actionable information can be extracted from them. Therefore, when reviewing the literature on the use of big data in the administration arm of healthcare, these ancillary but closely related technologies and tools must be included in the analysis. In the current study, the search for literature of big data in healthcare administration was combined with the following technologies to provide a more robust view of the literature:

- **Internet of Things (IoT):** The proliferation of sensors attached to machines, monitoring a process, and even measuring a patient's vital signs, is the basis of much of the huge datasets that organizations are using to create new understandings of their processes. Therefore, even if big data is not explicitly mentioned, they are implicitly creating a big data environment;
- **Deep Learning:** A branch of machine learning that leads to tools such as Artificial Neural Networks (ANN) that can be trained to make decisions such as classifications or speech recognition. Related to big data because the datasets required to train and verify the algorithms are typically very large and commonly fall into the general definition of big data;
- **Machine Learning:** A broader category of algorithms that use training data to create the ability to make decisions. Included in this are many different types of training methods and architectures, which are out of the scope of this paper but can be reviewed in (ref);
- **Data Analytics:** A broad term covering all of the statistical and mathematical tools and techniques commonly used to analyze and draw meaningful information from big data repositories.

There are, of course, many other terms that can be associated with big data – based technologies, but these terms are some of the more commonly used and therefore make a good starting point for the literature examination process. In the rest of the paper, this grouping of technologies and tools will be referred to as Big Data technologies.

METHODOLOGY

As this study is a structured review of the literature, it is important that the methodology used is both transparent and easily replicated. Briner & Denyer (2012) provide an easily implemented and repeatable approach to the completion of a systematic literature review:

- Identify the research question(s);
- Locate and select relevant studies;
- Critically appraise the studies;
- Analyze and synthesize the findings;
- Disseminate the findings.

There are two research questions driving this study:

- For which healthcare administrative processes are big data technologies (as defined in this study) being used to improve or analyze?
- For how long have big data technologies been used to improve or analyze healthcare administrative processes?

In order to perform a structured literature review properly, a set of ground rules must be established to ensure consistency and validity of the study protocol. This study limits the review to peer reviewed academic journals, conference proceedings, dissertations, and edited book chapters. This removes the professional journals, unpublished papers, white papers, and other sources of information from the study. This is not to say that they are not sources of valid information, only that the study is centered on the research efforts that have resulted in either specific tools to be used in healthcare administration tasks or big data tools that are being used to research these activities. Future research will be necessary to unearth whether the directions of researchers are aligned with the concerns and ideas of the practitioner literature.

Searches were carried out in many of the major electronic databases that provide coverage for the vast majority of scholarly journals in the field. The databases analyzed were ABI/Informs, Emerald, IEEE Explore, JSTOR, Science Direct, Scopus, Springer, Taylor & Francis, Web of Science, Google Scholar, PubMed, CINAHL, and ACM. The searches were conducted by searching the metadata (title, abstract, keywords) using the following search terms in all combinations: big data, Internet of Things (IoT), deep learning, machine learning, and analytics along with healthcare and hospital. To center on the administrative aspects of the industry, administration and management were also included. This study does not claim to be exhaustive, but the wide selection of databases combined with the increased rate of result duplication as the study progressed, provides evidence that a reasonable coverage of the topic has been achieved. There was no temporal restriction placed upon the searches so that the full scope of relevant research might be discovered.

This search protocol retrieved thousands of initial results, but the vast majority of them were focused on the clinical side of the healthcare industry. This is partially because of the use of the search term management (i.e. "*disease* management"), partially because of the automatic use of synonyms in many search protocols, and probably because the exclusion of purely clinical systems is very difficult to do in many situations. In the case of many of these returned articles, the title was sufficient to classify them as clinical in nature. However, that still left a list of over a thousand articles to deal with. After reading the abstract of these articles to gain more insight into their core topic, the final list of 227 articles remained to begin the actual analysis.

For those papers accepted into the study, the next step was to use the abstract, introduction, and conclusion sections to gain a more complete understanding of the topic being addressed by the author(s). Using a technique known as open coding, which is a qualitative research method of identifying the set of concepts within a document, the papers were sorted into sets of major themes that represent the focus of the author(s). As these themes were defined and refined, it became apparent that the complexity of the topics being studied required a more subtle approach. Therefore, a set of sub-themes were developed under the major topic headings to provide a better understanding of the scope of the research being undertaken. As these themes and sub-themes took shape, the last task was to categorize each paper into the theme and sub-theme that fit them most accurately. It should be noted that a significant number of studies could have been slotted into multiple categories. These papers required a deeper analysis to discern their main contribution. This involved a close reading of the entire paper, not just the introductory and concluding sections, to make that determination based on the author's stated goals, outcomes, and methodologies. The interdisciplinarity inherent in the healthcare and many other industries makes this overlap unavoidable.

To complete the structured review protocol, the findings of the literature analysis are presented and discussed in the following section. The complete literature review process followed in this project is depicted in Figure 1.

Figure 1. Literature review process

RESULTS

The findings section is divided into two sections. The first contains an overview of the descriptive statistics of the sample. The second section describes the various research themes and sub-themes contained in the sample.

Descriptive Statistics

The documents included in this study come from only three sources: journals, conference proceedings, and book chapters. The searches did not uncover any theses, dissertations, or books on the topics listed in the methodology section. The breakdown among these three forms is shown in Table 1.

Table 1. Types and quantity of article types uncovered in the literature review

Article Type	Quantity Found
Journal Articles	121
Conference Proceedings	94
Book Chapters	12

The proportions of each format given above held relatively constant for each of the themes discussed below except for the technology theme, which had almost twice as many conference proceedings as journal articles. Most of these articles discussed a framework or architecture for a proposed system or tool, which is a common topic at many technology-related conferences and workshops.

There were no time boundaries placed upon the searches so that the full range of activity in the field could be captured. The searches were all completed by May 1, 2020 and the temporal results of those searches are shown in Figure 2. The search results show that there were very few articles published on Big Data – type processes or tools in healthcare administration prior to 2014, with the earliest occurring in 2007. However, in 2014 the level of activity began to increase significantly with an exponential growth displayed through 2019. Since the data for 2020 represents only a third of the year, it appears that the trajectory points to at least as many publications in the field for the current year.

Research Themes

There are four research themes identified in the literature: resource management, technology, hospital management, and patient outcomes. These themes are expanded on in the following paragraphs. However,

Figure 2. Number of publications in Big Data / Healthcare administration by year (as of 1 May, 2020)

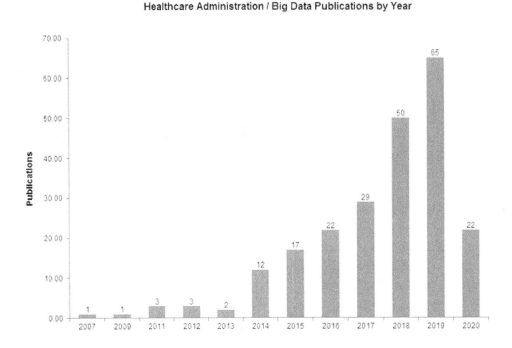

within each theme there are sub-themes that serve to better focus the analysis of the papers within each theme. To assist in understanding how these various sub-themes organize to support the major themes, Figure 3 provides a graphical representation of these themes and sub-themes.

Three of the four themes identified in this analysis are of very similar size, which suggests an even spread of importance for these various topics. The Information Management theme will be discussed first. The papers that fall into this theme are centered on the use of Big Data technologies to assist in the handling and application of organizational data and information to improve, or in some cases enable, certain functions. As will be true of most of these research themes, a number of authors provide very important overview papers that help to orient those readers who are relatively new to the topic. Such overviews can be found in Robinson, Presskila & Lawrence (2020) who discuss the Internet of Things, Alsinglawi & Mubin (2019) who explore predictive analytics and deep learning, and Menasalvas, Rodriguez-González & Gonzalo (2018) who look into the mining of electronic health records.

Of the three sub-themes in this grouping, by far the largest is that of data management (35 papers). These authors develop mechanisms and tools that use Big Data technologies to improve the movement and analysis of healthcare information. Some examples of these efforts include the team of Redfield et al (2020) who develop a machine learning record linkage mechanism to improve information flow between emergency services and the emergency department and Mehmood, Mehmood & Song (2019) who look at the use of IoT mechanisms to improve e-prescription processes. Perdana et al (2019) link Big Data with knowledge management tools to increase the efficiency of hospital inpatient services and Silvestri et al. (2019) describe a Big Data architecture that improves the extraction of actionable information from Electronic Health Records (EHR).

Figure 3. Breakdown of themes and sub-themes within the Big Data/Healthcare Administration Literature

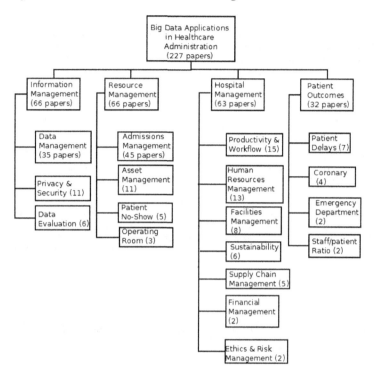

The privacy and security of patient and hospital data is of prime importance and eleven author teams addressed this imperative. Some excellent examples of these efforts include Xu et al's (2019) design of a blockchain-based privacy preserving mechanism for large health data depositories, Martinez's (2018) approach to securing IoT-based medical device systems, and Yoon-Su and Seung-Soo (2019) who consider virtual reality to help professionals secure multimedia healthcare information.

The last sub-theme (6 papers) includes those papers using Big Data technologies to assist in the evaluation of some aspect of healthcare data. Some examples include the use of data analytics to assess the level of medication requirements using EHR data (Xu et al, 2019), the use of data analytics to detect anomalies in many areas such as cardiac monitoring (Ukil et al, 2016), and the evaluation and monitoring of data quality in multisite EHR systems (Nobles et al, (2015). Table 2 lists the works in the Information Management theme.

The second, and equally large, theme has to do with the use of Big Data technologies to manage hospital resources. The literature reviewed uncovered four classes of asset management tasks addressed by these researchers and they form the four sub-themes. Two of these deal with the utilization of general resources in terms of admisssions and, in the converse, no-shows. More specific asset management activities center on the operating room and the medical equipment used throughout the organization, which will be grouped under the sub-theme of asset management. A good overview of the science of medical asset management can be found in Cui et al (2018) and Pollom, Balvach & Jones (2007).

The ability to understand and predict the rate of admissions to a specific practice, department, or the hospital in general is the key to being able to predict and control asset allocation, and thus costs. The largest sub-theme in this grouping (45 papers) centers on the use of Big Data technologies to enable healthcare organizations to regulate and predict the flow of patients into the various areas of treatment

Table 2. Papers focused on the use of big data technologies to promote information management

Sub-Theme	Author(s)
Overview	Alsinglawi & Mubin (2019); Chauhan et al (2019); Ghosh & Scott (2011); Halder & Pan (2018); Liu & Park (2014); Mathew & Pillai (2015); Menasalvas, Rodriguez-González & Gonzalo (2018); Mohamed et al (2020); Nithya & Ilango (2017); Patel & Gandhi (2018); Robinson, Presskila & Lawrence (2020);Thangaraj, Ponmalar & Anuradha (2015); Woodside (2014); Zhu & Hou (2018)
Data Management	Azaria et al (2016); Celesti et al (2016); Chennamsetty, Chalasani & Riley (2015); Cronin et al (2017); Hong, Morris & Seo (2017); Ivan et al (2016); Khazaei et al (2014); Khennou, Khamlichi & Chaoui (2016); Lauría & March (2011); Liu et al (2019); Liu, Zhang & Xing (2017); Lu & Feng (2018); Ma et al (2018); Mamoon et al (2018); Maria, Sever & Carlos (2018); Mehmood, Mehmood & Song (2019); Mian et al (2014); Nammour, Danas & Mansour (2016); Nicolau, Alexandru & Ianculescu (2019); Nouraei et al (2015a,b); Noussa-Yao, Heudes & Degoulet (2018); Perdana et al (2019); Pir, Akram & Khan (2015a,b); Rathee et al (2019); Redfield et al (2020); Silvestri et al (2019); Stadler et al (2016); Sudarto et al (2018); Wilder et al (2020); Weng et al (2017); Ye et al (2018); Zhang et al (2018); Zhang et al (2017)
Privacy/Security	He & Zeadally (2015); Elhoseny et al (2018); Maheswari & Vasanthanayaki (2020); Martinez (2018); Mavroeidakos, Tsolis & Vergados (2016); Nortey et al (2019); Patil & Seshadri (2014); Shi et al (2019); Tang et al (2019); Xu et al (2019); Yoon-Su & Seung-Soo (2019)
Data Evaluation	Carvalho et al (2019); Nobles et al (2015); Solangi, Aziz & Asadullah (2015); Ukil et al (2016); Woodbridge et al (2015); Xu et al (2019)

within the healthcare system. Some examples of these efforts include the use of semi-supervised machine learning models to predict the length of stay of hospitalized patients (Livieris et al, (2018), the readmission of diabetic patients using neural networks (Chopra et al, 2017), and the use of machine learning models for the prediction of peak emergency department visit times (Peng et al, 2020). The literature suggests that machine learning has applicability in many areas of patient activity prediction such as predicting the admission of patients with Chronic Obstructive Pulmonary Disease (Orchard et al, 2018), asthma (Luo et al, 2020), and elective spine surgery (Stopa et al, 2019). This is but a sample of how machine learning tools (and others) can be used to help level the demand profile and reduce the level of uncertainty for hospital planners.

The management of medical assets such as IV machines and ventilators has long been an area of concern due to the high cost of these items and their importance in the healing of patients. The eleven articles in this sub-theme look specifically at the use of Big Data technologies to improve the availablility and utilization of these important assets. Some studies provide approaches to IoT-based systems that help to locate and manage the usage of wheelchairs (Kurita, Matsuo & Barolli, 2019), incubators (Kovačević et al, 2019), and rehabilitation equipment (Meng, Zhang & Yu, 2018). Others apply these tools to the need for predicting maintenance (Shamayleh, Awad & Farhat, 2020) or monitoring performance (Gurbeta, Badnjević & Kurta, 2020) of medical equipment.

Certain areas of the hospital have much more specific needs in terms of asset management, such as operating rooms (OR). These are often in short supply and therefore highly sought after, so their proper management is literally a life or death challenge. Three papers examine this problem specifically. Bellini et al (2020) review the use of artificial intelligence and machine learning in OR organization including the prediction of care of perioperative patients with impacts on OR scheduling. Schneider & Brandeau (2017) use machine learning to improve surgical case length estimation and Fairley, Scheinker & Brandeau (2019) use machine learning tools to estimate post-anesthesia care of surgical patients to remove patient-flow bottlenecks.

Last, the bane of effective hospital administration is patients that do not show up for scheduled meetings or procedures. This phenomenon is studied by five research teams. Luo et al (2018) use machine learning to identify surgeries with a high risk of cancellation, while no-shows at a community health center are modeled by Mohammadi et al (2018). Levy (2013) uses a predictive tool to understand nonattendance at a specialty clinic. Table 3 displays the papers in this study that focus on resource management.

The third theme is only slightly smaller (63 papers) and consists of those papers highlighting Big Data technologies in the management of the hospital or healthcare facility. Once the healing processes are stripped away, the hospital is much like any other business and the same opportunities for improvements in the organizational processes exist. A number of authors have provided useful overviews of the application of Big Data technologies in this realm, including Juswishin (2019), Kane et al (2019), and Kumar & Suresh (2019). The sub-themes that support a more specific application of these technologies are detailed in the following paragraphs.

As with any other organization, productivity and efficiency are of vital importance. The papers in the largest sub-theme are all related in that they discuss some way in which these technologies might either improve or analyze a hospital's productivity. Fizgerald & Dadich (2009) use visual analytics to improve hospital scheduling. Xu et al (2017) use machine learning to predict the length of patient stay and time to transition for a specific care unit in a hospital. Gattner, Ekinci & Schneider (2016) point out the clinical, operational, and financial improvements brought about by the implementation of workflow analytics in healthcare.

Human resources are a critical component of any knowledge-based operation and healthcare is at the top of any list of knowledge-intensive industries. Ouyang, Shan & Bui (2016) design a RF-based sensor network that provides for the tracking of essential personnel within the hospital for ease of contact. Mesabbah, Abo-Hamad & McKeever (2019) discuss a hybrid process mining framework that will support complex decision-making during hospital staff planning, and Fischer et al (2020) use IoT and data analytics to support the flexible management of human resources in a smart hospital.

Facilities management processes are often overlooked and more complex than first understood, and they represent a fertile opportunity for these technologies to improve. Ramanathan et al (2020) use IoT to control access to the hospital through its various apertures. Facility layout planning is improved through the use of clinical pathway mining by Arnolds & Gartner (2018), and Guo et al (2016) use IoT technologies to monitor temperature and humidity in the key areas of a hospital.

When discussing hospital facilities, the conversation often turns to sustainability. This turns out to be another sub-theme of hospital management addressed by researchers. For example, Sahni, Arora & Dubey (2017) and Golbaz, Nabizadeh & Sajadi (2019) both take on the management of medical waste, Bacon (2014) addresses the low-carbon hospital design problem using what he calls "occupancy analytics," and Ruiz, Pacheco-Torres & Casillas (2017) use machine learning to model energy consumption by a hospital.

A few very small sub-themes emerged, as well. Supply chain management using datamining (Hussein et al, 2018) and IoT (Kakkar & Farshori, 2019) are two examples. A data-driven marketing analysis tool is proposed by Lee et al (2019) to improve pricing and resource allocation. Lastly, two single paper sub-themes on vitally important topics are Mittlestadt's (2017) review of the ethical dimensions of IoT devices and Peng et al's (2017) discussion of an IoT-based risk management system. Table 4 displays the papers that address various hospital management issues using Big Data technologies.

Table 3. Papers focused on the use of big data technologies to promote resource management

Sub-Theme	Author(s)
Overview	Cui et al (2018); Pollom, Balbach & Jones (2007)
Admissions	Allam et al (2019); Alloghani et al (2019); Artetxe et al (2017); Baechle et al (2020); Barnes et al (2016); Belderrar & Hazzab (2017); Benbelkacem et al (2019); Berger et al (2020); Cho et al (2019); Chopra et al (2017); Daghistani et al (2019); Grana et al (2019);Golas et al (2018); Gowsalya, Krushitha & Valliyammai (2014); Helm et al (2016); Hendri & Sulaiman (2018); Inibhunu et al (2017); Jeong, Kim & Shin (2019); Kadri, Baraoui & Nouaouri (2019); Karhade et al (2018); Kong et al (2020); Li et al (2014); Lin et al (2019); Livieris et al (2018a,b); Luo et al (2020); McCoy & Das (2017); Moyo et al (2018); Mtonga et al (2019); Nas & Koyuncu (2019); Nelson et al (2019); Orchard et al (2018); Peng et al (2020); Roy & Chin (2014); Shams, Ajorlou & Yang (2015); Silva et al (2018); Tesfaye et al (2019); Tideman et al (2019); Turgeman, May & Aciulli (2017); Raluy-Callado et al (2018); Stopa et al (2019); Vargheese & Viniotis (2014); Wojtusiak, Elashkar & Nia (2018); Zhang (2019); Zhu, Akkati & Hongwattanakul (2016)
Asset Management	Çoban et al (2018); Chai et al (2018); Gurbeta, Badnjeić & Kurta (2020); Karthikeyan, Devi & Valarmathi (2015); Kovačević et al (2019); Kurita, Matsuo & Barolli (2019); Meng, Zhang & Yu (2018); Nutdanai, Pornthip & Sanpanich (2016); Patil et al (2016); Ranjbar et al (2019); Shamayleh, Awad & Farhat (2020)
Operating Room Mgmt.	Bellini et al (2020); Fairley, Scheinker & Brandeau (2019); Scheinker & Brandeau (2017)
No Show Mgmt	Harris, May & Vargas (2016); Levy (2013); Luo et al (2018); Mohammadi et al (2018); Simsek, Tiahrt & Dag (2020)

The last theme (32 papers) evident in the literature centers on the impact that Big Data technologies have on patient outcomes. This encompasses the disposition of a patient's medical problem but also the factors that affect these outcomes. There are a number of papers that provide a comprehensive discussion of how Big Data and patient outcomes are related such as Tan et al (2016), Lee et al (2011), and Kachroo, Melek & Kurian (2013). However, the improvement of patient outcomes has been applied to more specific medical conditions as well as specific areas within the hospital. These applications form the basis of the following sub-themes.

The largest of the sub-themes in this category focuses on patient delay. In this paper, the term patient delay is taken in its broadest sense, encompassing any delay in the movement, treatment, or discharge of a patient from a medical department or facility. It is a clear case of research topics taking root in multiple themes, since this could also be examined through an organizational process lens. In these papers, the thrust was more technical, rather than organizational, hence a different theme. While not a patient outcome per se, it does impact the swiftness of the application of medical activities to the patient and is a strong influencer of patient satisfaction (Price & Lauffer, 2014). A study using datamining methods to create simulations of coronary patient flows provides a framework within which to improve decision making and training methods (Kovalchuk et al, 2018). Perimal-Lewis and King (2018) describe the process of making data ready for a simulation study of the movement of patients from the ED to the various wards in the hospital. Jiang, Abouee-Mehrizi & Diao (2020) explore the use of data analytics to support scheduling of patients with complicated conditions based on their clinical priorities.

Because coronary disease is such a large contributor to the total patient load, there have been a number of studies directed at the management of these patients and because it appears as more of a focus than other maladies, it is provided its own sub-theme. For example, Delen, Oztekin, and Tomak (2012) use a data analytic approach to study and predict the complex medical interventions necessary for a successful outcome. A number of supervised machine learning models that help predict the risk of heart disease are compared and verified by Krishnani et al (2019) and Jain and Kaur (2018).

A few minor sub-themes also emerged from the overall category of patient outcomes. The emergency department is the focus of one of them. Raita et al (2019) uses machine learning to predict clinical outcomes and Hu et al (2017) use it to select patients for more intense case management. Another sub-theme centers on the relationship between staffing and patient outcomes. Leary et al (2016) use datamining to unearth the nonlinear relationship between nurse staffing levels and outcomes while Intensive Care Unit (ICU) staffing is examined to understand how specific staffing characteristics help predict certain patient results.

A significant number of papers addressed very compelling issues having to do with patient outcomes, but there were not enough of them on any particular topic to create even a very small sub-theme. Hopefully, these topics will be expanded upon. Some examples of the "miscellaneous" papers in this theme include the use of machine learning to reduce the number of false alarms in the ICU (Hever et al, 2020), the creation of an in-hospital IoT-based infection management system (Yamashita et al, 2019), and the prediction of hospital-acquired pneumonia (Kuo et al, 2019). Table 5 displays the papers that center on the relationship between Big Data technologies and patient outcomes.

Table 4. Papers focused on the use of big data technologies to improve hospital management

Sub-Theme	Author(s)
Overview	Couturier et al (2012); Dhanvijay & Patil (2019); Erickson & Rothberg (2017); Guha & Kumar (2017); Habibzadeh et al (2020); Juswishin (2019); Kane et al (2019); Kumar & Suresh (2019); Rathore, Panwar & Soral (2014); Ratia, Myllärniemi & Helander (2019); Stephens (2018); Wills (2014)
Productivity/Workflow	Agnihothri, Banderjee & Thalacker (2015); Ali, Salehnejad & Mansur (2018); Almeida (2016); Biehl, Girgensohn & Patel (2019); Gattner, Ekinci & Schneider (2016); Hall & Partyka (2012); Firzgerald & Dadich (2009); Katrakazas et al (2018); Koufi et al (2017); Lee & Lee (2020); Nukavarapu & Durbha (2017); Safdar, Khan & Shaukat (2019); Sousa et al (2019); Xu et al (2017); Yip et al (2016)
Human Resources	Bala & Venkatesh (2017); Berkowitz (2017); Cheng & Kuo (2016); Fischer et al (2020); Foster et al (2017); Kushniruk & Borycki (2019); Mesabbah, Abo-Hamad & McKeever (2019); Meskó, Hetényi & Győrffy (2018); Ouyang, Shan & Bui (2016); Packianather et al (2019); Rashwan, Fowler & Arisha (2018); Verma, Xavier & Agrawal (2016); Ye et al (2019)
Facilities Management	Arnolds & Gartner (2018); Fatema, Malik & Iqbal (2020); Gartner & Padman (2017); Guo et al (2016); Iqbal, Dar & Bukhari (2018); Marques, Ferreira & Pitarma (2019); Ramanathan et al (2020); Yang et al (2019)
Sustainability	Bacon (2014); Baghapour et al (2018); Godpole & Lamb (2015); Golbaz, Nabizadeh & Sajadi (2019); uiz, Pacheco-Torres & Casillas (2017); Sahni, Arora & Dubey (2018)
Supply Chain Management	Alotaibi, Mehmood & Katib (2020); Feng et al (2018); Hussein et al (2019); Jordan, Dossou & Chang Jr. (2019); Kakkar & Farshori (2019)
Financial Management	Lee et al (2019); Rivera & DeLaney (2015)
Ethics & Risk Mgmt	Mittelstadt (2017); Peng et al (2017)

DISCUSSION

A number of interesting insights can be drawn from the documents analyzed for this project. The first is driven by the types of studies published. Overall, 77 papers in the sample were strickly theoretical or prescriptive in nature, in that the purpose of the study is to either describe an opportunity, describe a need, or to provide an overall description of some aspect of the topic at hand. This means that the remaining papers fell into one of three categories (again, with some overlap):

- Papers that provide a design, framework, or model for a proposed system or tool (62 papers);
- Papers that describe the implementation of a system or tool, either at a prototype or production level of development (27 papers);
- Papers that perform some form of empirical analysis (61 papers).

Table 5. Papers focused on the use of big data technologies to promote patient outcomes

Sub-Theme	Author(s)
Overview	AbdulGhaffer et al (2020), Atoum & Al-Jarallah (2019); Krishnan & Kamath (2019); Kachroo, Melek & Kurian (2013); Lee et al (2011); Phillips-Wren & McKniff (2019); Sahoo, Mohapatra & Wu (2017); Seng et al (2016)
General Patient Delays	Cáceres, Rosário & Amaya (2019); Jiang, Abouee-Mehrizi & Diao (2020); Kolesnichenko et al (2017); Kovalchuk et al (2018); Niu et al (2019); primal-Lewis & King (2018); Sumarsono, Anshari & Almunawar (2019)
Coronary Patient Outcomes	Delen, Oztekin & Tomak (2012); Jain & Kaur (2018); Krishnani et al (2019); Rajiwall, Chetty & Davey (2017)
Emergency Department	Hu et al (2017); Raito et al (2019)
Staffing Levels/Patient Outcomes	Leary et al (2016); Zampieri et al (2019)
Miscellaneous	Chu et al (2018); Chung & Jung (2019); Hever et al (2020); Kuo et al (2019); Khaldi et al (2017); Martinez-Millana et al (2019); Parisi, RaviChandran & Manaog (2018); Yamashita et al (2019); Zachariadis et al (2018)

The high number of design-based papers displays the level of energy being applied to creating systems and tools to improve the administration of healthcare organizations. More importantly, 27 papers discuss the actual implementation of some of these designs so that they can be evaluated for effectivenenss and demonstrated to the key stakeholders in the medical fields. There are a number of implemented systems that provide key capabilities. These include a tool to increase accuracy and efficiency of medical coding using MongoDB (Noussa-Yao et al, 2018), a cloud-based medical equipment management tool that has been implemented in a number of Greek hospitals (Katrakazas et al, 2018), and Rivera and Delaney's (2015) description of a performance management tool at an Orlando hospital. Each of these implementation descriptions provide valuable insight into what has already been done in this field and provide a guide as to what can be done with future research.

The amount of empirical papers included in the study largely consists of analyses of various aspects of healthcare management (e.g. patient stay prediction) that have been completed using some form of machine learning. In many cases, these studies center on the comparison of multiple machine learning models to see which one created a more accurate prediction. In very view of these papers do the authors apply empirical methods to study the actual usage of Big Data tools in the healthcare administration.

There was an almost even split between papers that centered on technology solutions, resource management, and hospital management. Those efforts regarding patient outcomes showed a relatively distant fourth. This might be due to a lack of interest in the topic, but more likely it has other roots. First, many systems that seek to improve patient outcomes would have been excluded from the study because they would have been primarily clinical in nature, which was one of the gates used to define this particular study. The papers included in the study were focused on management processes that influence patient outcomes, but it is possible that the clinically-focused papers would also have some management themes within them. Also, since the overall reason for the application of Big Data technologies is to improve the services provided to patients, it is entirely reasonable that the papers ending up in the other three categories could also be considered to be "patient outcomes" papers, as well.

The last point to be considered in this body of literature is that while the technological and analytical aspects of healthcare administration have been well covered, there has been relatively little discussion of any changes in organizational processes to adapt to these new tools or to take advantage of them. Many authors discussed the organizational issues at hand when providing justification of their new systems or analyses, but the repercussions for the organization were seldom fully considered. Thus, there appears to be much opportunity for fruitful research to consider how these, and other, data-centric tools might be reflected in the personnel and procedures in the organization.

CONCLUSION

This analysis provides a detailed overview of the literature surrounding the application of Big Data Technologies, as defined in the beginning of the paper, to the administrative functions of the healthcare industry. By completing this review, the paper makes two contributions to the literature. First, it should serve as a starting point for future researchers to select the organizational area to address as well as lending assistance in the selection of methodology and approach. As noted above, there is a need for a deeper look into the inner workings of the organization as these tools are implemented, including an analysis of implementation techniques to understand the level of involvement of the clinical and administration staff, as well as developing a deeper understanding of the changes in information flow, usage, and control as this new paradigm continues to mature. Moreover, because of the scale of the present study, there was not sufficient space to provide any significant level of detail regarding the strengths and contributions of each paper or a more indepth analysis of those papers that could have been categorized into multiple themes. These, and other research questions such as the contributions of Big Data technologies to the improvement of healthcare performance or the reduction of healthcare costs are fruitful areas for future research that the present paper forms a foundation for.

The second contribution of this study is to inform practitioners and administrators in the healthcare industry of the areas of emphasis that are consuming research resources. In some cases, we see significant involvement by clinical and administrative staff in these papers as coauthors and sources of information, but there is always room for more interdisciplinary research and hopefully studies such as this will provide a strong foundation for those efforts.

REFERENCES

AbdulGhaffar, A. A., Mostafa, S. M., Alsaleh, A., Sheltami, T., & Shakshuki, E. M. (2020). Internet of things based multiple disease monitoring and health improvement system. *Journal of Ambient Intelligence and Humanized Computing*, *11*(3), 1021–1029. doi:10.100712652-019-01204-6

Agnihorthri, S., Banerjee, A., & Thalacker, G. (2015). Analytics to improve service in a pre-admission testing clinic. *Proceedings of the 2015 48th Hawaii International Conference on System Sciences.* 10.1109/HICSS.2015.162

Al Mamoon, I., Islam, M. A. K. M., Haque, A. L. M. S., Zeb, A., & Ahmed, A. (2018). Cognitive radio enabled biomedical and non-medical hospital device communication protocols for cogmed. *Proceedings of the 10th International Conference on Electrical and Computer Engineering.*

Ali, M., Salehnejad, R., & Mansur, M. (2018). Hospital productivity: The role of efficiency drivers. *The International Journal of Health Planning and Management, 34*(2), 806–823. doi:10.1002/hpm.2739 PMID:30729610

Allam, A., Nagy, M., Thoma, G., & Krauthammer, M. (2018). Neural networks versus logistic regression for 30 days all-cause readmission prediction. *Nature,* 1–11. doi:10.103841598-019-45685-z

Alloghani, M., Aljaaf, A., Hussain, A., Baker, T., Mustafina, J., Al-Jumeily, D., & Khalaf, M. (2019). Implementation of machine learning algorithms to create diabetic patient re-admission profiles. *BMC Medical Informatics and Decision Making, 19*(253), 1–16. doi:10.118612911-019-0990-x PMID:31830980

Almeida, J. P. (2016). A disruptive big data approach to leverage the efficiency in management and clinical decision support in a hospital. *Porto Biomedical Journal, 1*(1), 40–42. doi:10.1016/j.pbj.2015.12.001 PMID:32258546

Alotaibi, S., Mehmood, R., & Katib, I. (2020). The role of big data and twitter data analytics in healthcare supply chain management. In Smart infrastructure and applications (pp. 267-278). Springer Nature Switzerland AG. doi:10.1007/978-3-030-13705-2_11

Alsinglawi, B., & Mubin, O. (2019). Predictive analytics and deep learning techniques in electronic medical records: recent advancements and future direction. *Proceedings of the WAINA 2019.* 10.1007/978-3-030-15035-8_89

Arnolds, I. V., & Gartner, D. (2018). Improving hospital layout planning through clinical pathway mining. *Annals of Operations Research, 263*(1-2), 453–477. doi:10.100710479-017-2485-4

Artetxe, A., Grana, M., Beristain, A., & Rios, S. (2017). Emergency department readmission risk prediction: a case study in Chile. *Proceedings of the IWINAC 2017.* 10.1007/978-3-319-59773-7_2

Atoum, I., & Al-Jarallah, N. A. (2019). Big data analytics for value-based care: challenges and opportunities. *International Journal of Advanced Trends in Computer Science and Engineering, 8*(6), 3012-3016. doi:10.30534-ijatcse/2019/558622019

Azaria, A., Ekblaw, A., Thiago, V., & Lippman, A. (2016). Medrec: using blockchain for medical data access and permission management. *Proceedings of the 2016 2nd International Conference on Open and Big Data.* 10.1109/OBD.2016.11

Bacon, M. (2014). Occupancy analytics: a new basis for low-energy-low-carbon hospital design and operation in the UK. *Architectural Engineering and Design Management, 10*(1-2), 146-163. doi:10.1080-17452007.2013.837254

Baechle, C., Huang, C. D., Agarwal, A., Behara, R. S., & Goo, J. (2020). Latent topic ensemble learning for hospital readmission cost optimization. *European Journal of Operational Research*, *281*(3), 517–531. doi:10.1016/j.ejor.2019.05.008

Baghapour, M. A., Shooshtarian, M. R., Javaheri, M. R., Dehghanifard, S., Sefidkar, R., & Nobandegani, A. F. (2018). A computer-based approach for data analyzing in hospital's health- care waste management sector by developing an index using consensus-based fuzzy multi- criteria group decision-making models. *International Journal of Medical Informatics*, *118*, 5–15. doi:10.1016/j.ijmedinf.2018.07.001 PMID:30153921

Bala, H., & Venkatesh, V. (2017). Employees' reactions to it-enabled process innovations in the age of data analytics in healthcare. *Business Process Management Journal*, *23*(3), 671–702. doi:10.1108/BPMJ-11-2015-0166

Barnes, S., Hamrock, E., Toerper, M., Siddiqui, S., & Levin, S. (2015). Real-time prediction of inpatient length of stay for discharge prioritization. *Journal of Medical Informatics Association*, *23*(e1), e2–e10. doi:10.1093/jamia/ocv106 PMID:26253131

Belderrar, A., & Hazzab, A. (2017). Hierarchical genetic algorithm and fuzzy radial basis function networks for factors influencing hospital length of stay outliers. *Healthcare Informatics Research*, *23*(3), 226–232. doi:10.4258/hir.2017.23.3.226 PMID:28875058

Bellini, V., & Guzzon, M., Bigliardi, B., Mordonini, M., Filippelli, S., & Bignami, E. (2020). Artificial intelligence: A new tool in operating room management. Role of machine learning models in operating room optimization. *Journal of Medical Systems*, *44*(20), 1–10. doi:10.100710916-019-1512-1 PMID:31823034

Benbelkacem, S., Kadri, F., Atmani, B., & Chaabane, S. (2019). Machine learning for emergency department management. *International Journal of Information Systems in the Service Sector*, *11*(3), 19–36. doi:10.4018/IJISSS.2019070102

Berger, J. S., Haskell, L., Ting, W., Lurie, F., Chang, S.-C., Mueller, L. A., Elder, K., Rich, K., Crivera, C., Schein, J. R., & Alas, V. (2020). Evaluation of machine learning methodology for the prediction of healthcare resource utilization and healthcare costs in patients with critical limb ischemia—Is preventive and personalized approach on the horizon. *The EPMA Journal*, *11*(1), 53–64. doi:10.100713167-019-00196-9 PMID:32140185

Berkowitz, B. (2017). Quality outcomes and credentialing: implication for informatics and big data science. In Big data-enabled nursing (pp. 399-406). Springer International Publishing AG. doi:10.1007/978-3-319-53300-1_20

Biehl, J. T., Girgensohn, A., & Patel, M. (2019). Achieving accurate room-level indoor location estimation with emerging iot networks. *Proceedings of the IoT 2019*. 10.1145/3365871.3365875

Briner, R. B., & Denyer, D. (2012). Systematic review and evidence synthesis as a practice and scholarship tool. In D. M. Rousseau (Ed.), *The Oxford Handbook of Evidence-Based Management*. Oxford University Press.

Caceres, C., Rosario, J. M., & Amaya, D. (2018). Proposal of a smart hospital based on internet of things (iot) concept. *Proceedings of the SaMBa 2018*.

Carvalho, J. V., Rocha, A., Vasconcelos, J., & Abreu, A. (2019). A health data analytics maturity model for hospitals information systems. *International Journal of Information Management*, *46*, 278–235. doi:10.1016/j.ijinfomgt.2018.07.001

Celesti, A., Fazio, M., Romano, A., & Villari, M. (2016). A hospital cloud-based archival information system for the efficient management of hl7 big data. *Proceedings of the MIPRO*. 10.1109/MIPRO.2016.7522177

Chai, P. R., Zhang, H., Baugh, C. W., Jambaulikar, G. D., McCabe, J. C., Gorman, J. M., Boyer, E. W., & Landman, A. (2018). Internet of things buttons for real-time notifications in hospital operations: Proposal for hospital implementation. *Journal of Medical Internet Research*, *20*(8), 1–9. doi:10.2196/jmir.9454 PMID:30097420

Chang, H., & Choi, M. (2016). Big data and healthcare: Building an augmented world. *Healthcare Informatics Research*, *22*(3), 153–155. doi:10.4258/hir.2016.22.3.153 PMID:27525155

Chauhan, S. S., Sharma, I., Kanungo, I., & Singh, G. (2019). Healthcare data management and analytics using big data tools. *International Journal of Innovative Technology and Exploring Engineering*, *8*(12), 3725–3728. doi:10.35940/ijitee.L2658.1081219

Cheng, C.-H., & Kuo, Y.-H. (2016). Rfid analytics for hospital ward management. *Flexible Services and Manufacturing Journal*, *28*(4), 593–616. doi:10.100710696-015-9230-6 PMID:32288935

Chennamsetty, H., Chalasani, S., & Riley, D. (2015). Predictive analytics on electronic health records (ehrs) using hadoop and hive. *Proceedings of the IEEE International Conference on Electronics, Computer, and Communication Technologies*. 10.1109/ICECCT.2015.7226129

Cho, J., Alharin, A., Hu, Z., Fell, N., & Sartipi, M. (2019). Predicting post-stroke hospital discharge disposition using interpretable machine learning approaches. *Proceedings of the 2019 IEEE International Conference on Big Data*. 10.1109/BigData47090.2019.9006592

Chopra, C., Sinha, S., Jaroli, S., Shukla, A., & Maheshwari, S. (2017). Recurrent neural networks with non-sequential data to predict hospital readmission of diabetic patients. *Proceedings of the ICCBB 2017*. 10.1145/3155077.3155081

Chu, J., Dong, W., He, K., Duan, H., & Huang, Z. (2018). Using neural attention networks to detect adverse medical events from electronic health records. *Journal of Biomedical Informatics*, *87*, 118–130. doi:10.1016/j.jbi.2018.10.002 PMID:30336262

Chung, K., & Jung, H. (2019). Knowledge-based dynamic cluster model for healthcare management using a convolutional neural network. *Information Technology and Management*, 1-10. doi:10.1007/s10799-019-00304-1

Coban, S., Gokalp, M. O., Gokalp, E., Eren, P. E., & Kocyigit, A. (2018). Predictive maintenance in healthcare services with big data technologies. *Proceedings of the 2018 IEEE 11th International Conference on Service-Oriented Computing and Applications*. 10.1109/SOCA.2018.00021

Couturier, J., Sola, D., Borioli, G. S., & Raiciu, C. (2012). How can the internet of things help to overcome current healthcare challenges. *Digiworld Economic Journal,* (87), 67-180.

Cronin, R. M., Fabbri, D., Denny, J. C., Rosenbloom, S. T., & Jackson, G. P. (2017). A comparison of rule- based and machine learning approaches for classifying patient portal messages. *International Journal of Medical Informatics, 105,* 110–120. doi:10.1016/j.ijmedinf.2017.06.004 PMID:28750904

Cui, L., Xie, X., Shen, Z., Lu, R., & Wang, H. (2018). Prediction of the healthcare resource utilization using multi-output regression models. *IISE Transactions on Healthcare Systems Engineering, 8*(4), 291-302. doi:10.1080/24725579.2018.1512537

Cutler, D., Wikler, E., & Basch, P. (2012). Reducing administrative costs and improving health care system. *The New England Journal of Medicine, 367*(20), 1875–1878. doi:10.1056/NEJMp1209711 PMID:23150956

Daghistani, T. A., Elshawi, R., Sakr, S., Ahmed, A. M., Al-Thwayss, A., & Al-Mallah, M. H. (2019). Predictors of in-hospital length of stay among cardiac patients: A machine learning approach. *International Journal of Cardiology, 288,* 140–147. doi:10.1016/j.ijcard.2019.01.046 PMID:30685103

Delen, D., Oztekin, A., & Tomak, L. (2012). An analytic approach to better understanding and management of coronary surgeries. *Decision Support Systems, 12*(3), 698–705. doi:10.1016/j.dss.2011.11.004

Dhanvijay, M., & Patil, S. C. (2019). Internet of things: A survey of enabling technologies in healthcare and its applications. *Computer Networks, 153,* 113–131. doi:10.1016/j.comnet.2019.03.006

Elhoseny, M., Shankar, K., Lakshmanaprabu, S. K., Maseleno, A., & Arunkumar, N. (2018). *Hybrid optimization with cryptography encryption for medical image security in internet of things.* doi:10.1007/s00521-018-3801-x

Erickson, G. S., & Rothberg, H. N. (2017). Healthcare and hospitality: Intangible dynamics for evaluation industry sectors. *Service Industries Journal, 37*(9-10), 589–606. doi:10.1080/02642069.2017.1346628

Fairley, M., Scheinker, D., & Brandeau, M. L. (2019). Improving the efficiency of the operating room environment with an optimization and machine learning model. *Health Care Management Science, 22*(4), 756–767. doi:10.1007/10729-018-9457-3 PMID:30387040

Feng, Y., Chai, L., Li, X., Zhang, S., & Song, B. (2018). A distributed procurement cost control scheme of medical material for regional medical consortiums. *Proceedings of the MOBIMEDIA 2018.* 10.4108/eai.21-6-2018.2276581

Fischer, G. S., da Rosa Righi, R., de Oliveira Ramos, G., de Costa, C. A., & Rodrigues, J. J. P. C. (2020). Elhealth: Using internet of things and data prediction for elastic management of human resources in smart hospitals. *Engineering Applications of Artificial Intelligence, 87,* 1–14. doi:10.1016/j.engappai.2019.103285

Fitzgerald, J. A., & Dadich, A. (2009). Using visual analytics to improve hospital scheduling and patient flow. *Journal of Theoretical and Applied Electronic Commerce Research, 4*(2), 20–30.

Foster, K., Penninti, P., Shang, J., Kekre, S., Hegde, G. G., & Venkat, A. (2018). Leveraging big data to balance new key performance indicators in emergency physician management networks. *Production and Operations Management, 27*(10), 1795-1815. doi:10.1111-poms.12835

Gartner, D., & Padman, R. (2017). E-hospital-a digital workbench for hospital operations and services planning using information technology and algebraic languages. *Proceedings of the MEDINFO 2017.*

Gattnar, E., Ekinci, O., & Schneider, J. (2016). Leveraging the value for health care providers using clinical workflow analytics. In Boundaryless hospital (pp. 201-209). Springer-Verlang Berlin Heidelberg. doi:10.1007/978-3-662-49012-9_11

Ghosh, B., & Scott, J. E. (2011). Antecedents and catalysts for developing a healthcare analytic capability. *Communications of the Association for Information Systems, 29*, 395–410. doi:10.17705/1CAIS.02922

Godbole, N. S., & Lamb, J. (2015). Using data science & big data analytics to make healthcare green. *Proceedings of the 12th International Conference & Expo on Emerging Technologies For a Smarter World.* 10.1109/CEWIT.2015.7338161

Golas, S. B., Shibahara, T., Agboola, S., Otaki, H., Sato, J., Nakae, T., ... Jethwani, K. (2018). A machine learning model to predict the risk of 30-day readmissions in patients with heart failure: A retrospective analysis of electronic medical records data. *BMC Medical Informatics and Decision Making, 18*(44), 1–17. doi:10.118612911-018-0620-z PMID:29929496

Golbaz, S., Nabizadeh, R., & Sajadi, H. S. (2019). Comparative study of predicting hospital solid waste generation using multiple linear regression and artificial intelligence. *Journal of Environmental Health Science & Engineering, 17*(1), 41–51. doi:10.100740201-018-00324-z PMID:31297201

Gowsalya, M., Krushitha, K., & Valliyammai, C. (2014). Predicting the risk of readmission of diabetic patients using MapReduce. *Proceedings of the 2014 Sixth International Conference on Advanced Computing (ICoAC).* 10.1109/ICoAC.2014.7229729

Grana, M., Lopez-Guede, J. M., Irazusta, J., Labayen, I., & Besga, A. (2019). Modelling hospital readmissions under frailty conditions for healthy aging. *Expert Systems: International Journal of Knowledge Engineering and Neural Networks*, 1–10. doi:10.1111/exsy.12437

Guhu, S., & Kumar, S. (2018). Emergence of big data research in operations management, information systems, and healthcare: Past contributions and future roadmap. *Production and Operations Management, 27*(9), 1724–1735. doi:10.1111/poms.12833

Guo, B., Wang, X., Zhang, X., Yang, J., & Wang, Z. (2016). Research on the temperature & humidity monitoring system in the key areas of the hospital based on the internet of things. *International Journal of Smart Home, 10*(7), 205–2016. doi:10.14257/ijsh.2016.10.7.21

Gurbeta, L., Badnjevic, A., & Kurta, E. (2019). Everlab: Software tool for medical device safety and performance inspection management. *Proceedings of the CMBEBIH 2019.*

Habibzadeh, H., Dinesh, K., Shishvan, O. R., Boggio-Dandry, A., Sharma, G., & Soyata, T. (2020). A survey of healthcare internet of things (HIoT): A clinical perspective. *IEEE Internet of Things Journal, 7*(1), 53–71. doi:10.1109/JIOT.2019.2946359

Halder, P., & Pan, I. (2018). Role of big data analysis in healthcare sector: a survey. *Proceedings of the 2018 Fourth International Conference on Research in Computational Intelligence and Communications Networks (ICRCICN)*. 10.1109/ICRCICN.2018.8718684

Hall, R., & Partyka, J. (2012). How analytics and o.R. Driven tools help healthcare organizations move from "Tracking" Mentality to "Delivery and logistics." *Informs*, *39*(3), 1–8.

Harris, S. L., May, J. H., & Vargas, L. G. (2016). Predictive analytics model for healthcare planning and scheduling. *European Journal of Operational Research*, *253*(1), 121–131. Advance online publication. doi:10.1016/j.ejor.2016.02.017

He, D., & Zeadally, S. (2015). An analysis of RFID authentication schemes for internet of things in healthcare environment using elliptic curve cryptography. *IEEE Internet of Things Journal*, *2*(1), 72–83. doi:10.1109/JIOT.2014.2360121

Helm, J. E., Alaeddini, A., Stauffer, J. M., Bretthauer, K. M., & Skolarus, T. A. (2016). Reducing hospital readmissions by integrating empirical prediction with resource optimization. *Production and Operations Management*, *25*(2), 233–257. doi:10.1111/poms.12377

Hendri, H. J. M., & Sulaiman, H. (2018). Predictive modeling for dengue patient's length of stay (los) using big data analytics (bda). In Recent trends in information and communication technology (pp. 12-19). Springer International Publishing.

Hever, G., Cohen, L., O'Connor, M. F., Matot, I., Lerner, B., & Bitan, Y. (2020). Machine learning applied to multi-sensor information to reduce false alarm rate in the icu. *Journal of Clinical Monitoring and Computing*, *34*(2), 339–352. doi:10.100710877-019-00307-x PMID:30955160

Hong, J., Morris, P., & Seo, J. (2017). Interconnected personal health record ecosystem using iot cloud platform and hl7 fhir. *Proceedings of the 2017 IEEE International Conference on Healthcare Informatics*. 10.1109/ICHI.2017.82

Hu, X., Barnes, S., Bharnadottir, M., & Golden, B. (2017). Intelligent selection of frequent emergency department patients for case management: A machine learning framework based on claims data. *IISE Transactions on Healthcare Systems Engineering*, *7*(3), 130–143. doi:10.1080/24725579.2017.1351502

Hussein, B. R., Kasem, A., Omar, S., & Siau, N. Z. (2019). A data mining approach for inventory forecasting: a case study of medical store. *Proceedings of the CIIS 2018*. 10.1007/978-3-030-03302-6_16

Inibhunu, C., Schauer, A., Redwood, O., Clifford, P., & McGregor, C. (2017). Predicting hospital admissions and emergency room visits using remote home monitoring data. *Proceedings of the IEEE Life Sciences Conference*. 10.1109/LSC.2017.8268198

Iqbal, U., Dar, M. A., & Bukhari, S. N. (2018). Intelligent hospitals based on iot. *Proceedings of the 4th International Conference on Advances in Electrical, Electronics, Information, Communication and Bio-Informatics (AEEICB-18)*. 10.1109/AEEICB.2018.8480947

Ivan, M.-L., Velicanu, M., Trifu, M. R., & Ciurea, C. (2016). Using business intelligence tools for predictive analytics in healthcare system. *(IJACSA). International Journal of Advanced Computer Science and Applications*, *7*(5), 178–182. doi:10.14569/IJACSA.2016.070527

Jain, P., & Kaur, A. (2018). Big data analysis for prediction of coronary artery disease. *Proceedings of the 2018 4th International Conference on Computing Sciences*. 10.1109/ICCS.2018.00038

Jeong, Y.-S., Kim, D.-R., & Shin, S.-S. (2019). An efficient patient information transmission and receiving scheme using cloud h-IoT system. *International Journal of Recent Technology and Engineering, 8*(2S6), 180-184. doi:10.35940/ijrte.B1034.0782S619

Jiang, Y., Abouee-Mehrizi, H., & Diao, Y. (2020). Data-driven analytics to support scheduling of multi-priority multi-class patients with wait time targets. *European Journal of Operational Research, 281*(3), 597–611. doi:10.1016/j.ejor.2018.05.017

Jordan, K., Dossou, P.-E., & Chang, J. Jr. (2019). Using lean manufacturing and machine learning for improving medicines procurement and dispatching in a hospiital. *Procedia Manufacturing, 38*, 1034–1041. doi:10.1016/j.promfg.2020.01.189

Juzwishin, D. W. M. (2019). Big data challenges from a healthcare administration perspective. In Big data, big challenges: a healthcare perspective (pp. 55-67). Springer Nature Switzerland. doi:10.1007/978-3-030-06109-8_5

Kachroo, S., Melek, W. W., & Kurian, C. J. (2013). Evaluation of predictive learners for cancer incidence and mortality. *Proceedings of the 4th IEEE International Conference on E-Health and Bioengineering*. 10.1109/EHB.2013.6707388

Kadri, F., Baraoui, M., & Nouaouri, I. (2019). An LSTM-based deep learning approach with application to predicting hospital emergency department admissions. *Proceedings of the International Conference on Industrial Engineering and Systems Management*. 10.1109/IESM45758.2019.8948130

Kakkar, A., & Farshori, A. (2019). Collaborative medical inventory resources using edge computing-a solution to serve critical healthcare requirements at public hospitals. *Proceedings of the Amity International Conference on Artificial Intelligence*. 10.1109/AICAI.2019.8701242

Kane, E. M., Scheulen, J. J., Puttgen, A., Martinez, D., Levin, S., Bush, B. A., . . . Efron, D. T. (2019). Use of systems engineering to design a hospital command center. *Joint Commission Journal on Quality and Patient Safety, 45*, 370–379. doi:10.1016/j.jcjq.2018.11.006 PMID:30638974

Karhade, A. V., Ogink, P., Thio, Q., Broekman, M., Cha, T., Gormley, W. B., Hershman, S., Peul, W. C., Bono, C. M., & Schwab, J. H. (2018). Development of machine learning algorithms for prediction of discharge disposition after elective inpatient surgery for lumbar degenerative disc disorders. *Neurosurgical Focus, 45*(5), E6. Advance online publication. doi:10.3171/2018.8.FOCUS18340 PMID:30453463

Karthikeyan, S., & Devi, K. V. (2015). Internet of things: hospice appliances monitoring and control system. *Proceedings of the Online International Conference on Green Engineering and Technologies*. 10.1109/GET.2015.7453776

Katrakazas, P., Costarides, V., Tarousi, M., Christodoulakis, M., Tournpaniaris, P., Pavlopoulos, S., . . . Koutsouris, D. (2018). Business process modeling for a Greek hospitals' medical equipment data center. *Proceedings of the 2018 IEEE 31st International Symposium on Computer-Based Medical Systems*.

Khaldi, R., El Afia, A., Chiheb, R., & Ensias, R. F. (2017). Artificial neural network based approach for blood demand forecasting: fez transfusion blood center case study. *Proceedings of the BDCA 2017.* 10.1145/3090354.3090415

Khazaei, H., McGregor, C., Eklund, M., El-Khatib, K., & Thommandram, A. (2014). Toward a big data healthcare analytics system: a mathematical modeling perspective. *Proceedings of the 2014 IEEE 10th World Congress on Services.* 10.1109/SERVICES.2014.45

Khennou, F., Khamlichi, Y. I., & Chaoui, N. E. H. (2016). Designing a health data management system based hadoop-agent. *Proceedings of the 4th IEEE International Colloquium on Information Science and Technology.* 10.1109/CIST.2016.7804983

Kolesnichenko, O., Smorodin, G., Mazelis, A., Nikolaev, A., Mazelis, L., Martynov, A., ... Kolesnichenko, Y. (2017). Ipatient in medical informations systems and future of internet of health. *Proceedings of the The 20th Conference of FRUCT Association.* 10.23919/FRUCT.2017.8071308

Kong, G., Xu, D.-L., Yang, J.-B., Wang, T., & Jiang, B. (2020). Evidential reasoning rule-based decision support system for predicting icu admission and in-hospital death of trauma. *IEEE Transactions on Systems, Man, and Cybernetics. Systems*, 1–12. doi:10.1109/TSMC.2020.2967885

Kovacevic, Z., Pokvic, L. G., Spahic, L., & Badnjevic, A. (2019). Prediction of medical device performance using machine learning techniques: Infant incubator case study. *Health and Technology*, *1-5*. Advance online publication. doi:10.100712553-019-00386-5

Kovalchuk, S. V., Funkner, A. A., Metsker, O. G., & Yakovlev, A. (2018). Simulation of patient flow in multiple healthcare units using process and data mining techniques for model identification. *Journal of Biomedical Informatics*, *82*, 128–142. doi:10.1016/j.jbi.2018.05.004 PMID:29753874

Krishnan, G. S., & S., S. K. (2019). A novel GA-ELM model for patient-specific mortality prediction over large-scale lab event data. *Applied Soft Computing*, *80*, 525–533. doi:10.1016/j.asoc.2019.04.019

Krishnani, D., Kumari, A., Dewangan, A., Singh, A., & Naik, N. S. (2019). Prediction of coronary heart disease using supervised machine learning algorithms. *Proceedings of the IEEE Region 10 Conference.* 10.1109/TENCON.2019.8929434

Kumar, N. A. J., & Suresh, S. (2019). A proposal of smart hospital management using hybrid cloud, IoT, ML, and AI. *Proceedings of the Fourth International Conference on Communication and Electronics Systems (ICCES 2019).*

Kuo, K. M., Talley, P. C., Huang, C. H., & Cheng, L. C. (2019). Predicting hospital-acquired pneumonia among schizophrenic patients: A machine learning approach. *BMC Medical Informatics and Decision Making*, *19*(42), 1–8. doi:10.118612911-019-0792-1 PMID:30866913

Kurita, T., Matsuo, K., & Barolli, L. (2019). A wheelchair management system using iot senors and agile-kanban. *Proceedings of the INCoS 2019.*

Kushniruk, A. W., & Borycki, E. M. (2019). Big data challenges from a human factors perspective. In Big data, big challenges: a healthcare perspective (pp. 91-99). Springer Nature Switzerland. doi:10.1007/978-3-030-06109-8_8

Lauria, E. J. M., & March, A. D. (2011). Combining bayesian text classification and shrinkage to automate healthcare coding: A data quality analysis. *ACM Journal of Data and Information Quality, 2*(3), 1–22. doi:10.1145/2063504.2063506

Leary, A., Cook, R., Jones, S., Smith, J., Gough, M., Maxwell, E., Punshon, G., & Radford, M. (2016). Mining routinely collected acute data to reveal non-linear relationships between nurse staffing levels and outcomes. *BMJ Open, 6*(12), 1–7. doi:10.1136/bmjopen-2016-011177 PMID:27986733

Lee, C. S., Tiong, A., Tang, W. L., & Yap, K. H. (2019). Data-driven "Market basket"-pricing and personalized health information services using salesforce's model-driven systems service design. *Proceedings of the IEEE International Conference on Industrial Engineering and Engineering Management.* 10.1109/IEEM44572.2019.8978835

Lee, N., Laine, A. F., Hu, J., Wang, F., Sun, J., & Ebadollahi, S. (2011). Mining electronic medical records to explore the linkage between healthcare resource utilization and disease severity in diabetic patients. *Proceedings of the 2011 First IEEE International Conference on Healthcare Informatics, Imaging and Systems Biology.* 10.1109/HISB.2011.34

Lee, S., & Lee, Y. H. (2020). Improving emergency department efficiency by patient scheduling using deep reinforcement learning. *Health Care*, 1–17. doi:10.3390/healthcare8020077 PMID:32230962

Levy, V. (2013). A predictive tool for nonattendance at a specialty clinic. *Proceedings of the 10th International Conference and Expo on Emerging Technologies for a Smarter World.*

Li, Y., Sun, N., Wu, F., Zheng, C., & Li, Y. (2014). Predictive analysis of outpatient visits to a grade 3, class a hospital using arima model. *Proceedings of the 2014 International Symposium on Information Technology (ISIT 2014).*

Lin, Y.-W., Zhou, Y., Faghri, F., Shaw, M. J., & Campbell, R. H. (2019). Analysis and prediction of unplanned intensive care unit readmission using recurrent neural networks with long short-term memory. *PLoS One, 14*(7), e0218942. Advance online publication. doi:10.1371/journal.pone.0218942 PMID:31283759

Liu, J., Zhang, Y., & Xing, C. (2017). Medical big data web service management platform. *Proceedings of the 2017 IEEE 11th International Conference on Semantic Computing.* 10.1109/ICSC.2017.69

Liu, W., & Park, E. K. (2014). Big data as an e-health service. *Proceedings of the International Conference on Computing, Networking and Communications.*

Liu, Y., Zhang, L., Yang, Y., Zhou, L., Ren, L., Wang, F., Liu, R., Pang, Z., & Deen, M. J. (2019). A novel cloud-based framework for the elderly healthcare services using digital twin. *IEEE Access: Practical Innovations, Open Solutions, 7*, 49088–49101. doi:10.1109/ACCESS.2019.2909828

Livieris, I. E., Dimopoulos, I. F., Kotsilieris, T., & Pintelas, P. (2018). Predicting length of stay in hospitalized patients using ssl algorithms. *Proceedings of the DSAI 2018.* 10.1145/3218585.3218588

Livieris, I. E., Kotsilieris, T., Dimopoulos, I., & Pintelas, P. (2018). Decision support software for forecasting patient's length of stay. *Algorithms, 11*(199). Advance online publication. doi:10.3390/a11120199

Lu, C., & Feng, L. (2018). Design and implementation of resident health record management system based on big data technology. *Proceedings of the 2018 11th International Conference on Intelligent Computation Technology and Automation.* 10.1109/ICICTA.2018.00073

Luo, G., He, S., Stone, B. L., Nkoy, F. L., & Johnson, M. D. (2020). Developing a model to predict hospital encounters for asthma in asthmatic patients: Secondary analysis. *JMIR Medical Informatics, 8*(1), 1–16. doi:10.2196/16080 PMID:31961332

Luo, L., Zhang, F., Yao, Y., & Gong, R. (2018). Machine learning for identification of surgeries with high risks of cancellations. *Health Informatics Journal,* 1–15. doi:10.1177/1460458218813602 PMID:30518275

Ma, X., Wang, Z., Zhou, S., Wen, H., & Zhang, Y. (2018). Intelligent healthcare systems assisted by data analytics and mobile computing. *Proceedings of the 14th International Wireless Communications and Mobile Computing Conference.* 10.1109/IWCMC.2018.8450377

Maria, A. R., Sever, P., & Carlos, V. (2018). Cloud computing for big data from biomedical sensors monitoring, storage and analyze. *Proceedings of the Conference on Grid, Cloud, & High Performance Computing in Science.*

Marques, G., Ferreira, C. R., & Pitarma, R. (2019). Indoor air quality assessment using a co2 monitoring system based on internet of things. *Journal of Medical Systems, 43*(67), 1–10. doi:10.100710916-019-1184-x PMID:30729368

Martinez, J. B. Medical device security in the iot age. *Proceedings of the 9th IEEE Annual Ubiquitous Computing, Electronics and Mobile Communication Conference.* 10.1109/UEMCON.2018.8796531

Martinez-Millana, A., Lizondo, A., Gatta, R., Traver, V., & Fernandez-Llatas, C. (2018). Expectations from a process mining dashboard in operating rooms with analytic hierarchy process. *Proceedings of the BPM 2018 Workshops.*

Mathew, P. S., & Pillai, A. S. (2015). Big data solutions in healthcare: problems and perspectives. *Proceedings of the IEEE Sponsored 2nd International Conference on Innovations in Information Embedded and Communications Systems.* 10.1109/ICIIECS.2015.7193211

Mavroeidakos, T., Tsolis, N., & Vergados, D. D. (2016). Centralized management of medical big data in intensive care unit: a security analysis. *Proceedings of the 3rd Smart Cloud Networks & Systems.* 10.1109/SCNS.2016.7870557

McCoy, A., & Das, R. (2017). Reducing patient mortality, length of stay and readmissions through machine learning-based sepsis prediction in the emergency department, intensive care unit and hospital floor units. *BMJ Open Quality, 6*(2), 1–7. doi:10.1136/bmjoq-2017-000158 PMID:29450295

Mehmood, A., Mehmood, F., & Song, W.-C. (2019). Cloud based e-prescription management system for healthcare services using IoT devices. *Proceedings of the International Conference on Information and Communication Technology Convergence.* 10.1109/ICTC46691.2019.8939916

Menasalvas, E., Rodriguez-Gonzalez, & Gonzalo, C. (2018). Mining electronic health records: challenges and impact. *Proceedings of the 2018 14th International Conference on Signal-Image Technology & Internet-Based Systems (SITIS).*

Meng, Q., Zhang, H., & Yu, H. (2018). The internet of things-based rehabilitation equipment monitoring system. *Proceedings of the AIAAT 2018*. 10.1088/1757-899X/435/1/012015

Mesabbah, M., & Abo-Hamad, w. (2019). A hybrid process mining framework for automated simulation modelling for healthcare. *Proceedings of the 2019 Winter Simulation Conference*. 10.1109/WSC40007.2019.9004800

Mesko, B., Hetenyi, G., & Gyorffy, Z. (2018). Will artificial intelligence solve the human resource crisis in healthcare? *BMC Health Services Research*, *18*(545), 1–5. doi:10.118612913- 018-3359-4 PMID:30001717

Mian, M., Teredesai, A., Hazel, D., Pokuri, S., & Uppala, K. (2014). Work in progress-in- memory analysis for healthcare big data. *Proceedings of the 2014 IEEE International Congress on Big Data*. 10.1109/BigData.Congress.2014.119

Mittelstadt, B. (2017). Ethics of the health-related internet of things: A narrative review. *Ethics and Information Technology*, *19*(3), 157–175. doi:10.100710676-017-9426-4

Mohamed, A., Najafabadi, M. K., Wah, Y. B., Zaman, E. A. K., & Maskat, R. (2020). The state of the art and taxonomy of big data analytics: View from new big data framework. *Artificial Intelligence Review*, *53*(2), 989–1037. doi:10.100710462-019-09685-9

Mohammadi, I., Wu, H., Turkcan, A., Tocos, T., & Doebbeling, B. N. (2018). Data analytics and modeling for appointment no-show in community health centers. *Journal of Primary Care & Community Health*, *9*, 111. doi:10.1177/2150132718811692 PMID:30451063

Mtonga, K., Kumaran, S., Mikeka, C., Jayavel, K., & Nsenga, J. (2019). Machine learning-based patient load prediction and IoT integrated intelligent patient transfer systems. *Future Internet*, *11*(236), 1–24. doi:10.3390/fi11110236

Nammour, F., Danas, K., & Mansour, N. (2016). CorporateMeasures: A clinical analytics framework leading to clinical intelligence. *Proceedings of the 2016 IEEE 18th international conference on e-health networking, applications and services*. 10.1109/HealthCom.2016.7749451

Nas, S., & Koyuncu, M. (2019). Emergency department capacity planning: A recurrent neural network and simulation approach. *Computational and Mathematical Methods in Medicine*, *2019*, 1–13. doi:10.1155/2019/4359719 PMID:31827585

Nelson, A., Herron, D., Rees, G., & Nachev, P. (2019). Predicting scheduled hospital attendance with artificial intelligence. *Digital Medicine*, 1-7. doi:10.1038/s41746-019-0103-3

Nicolau, D. N., Alexandru, A., & Ianculescu, M. (2019). An iot, virtual machines and cloud computing-based framework for an optimal management of healthcare cata collected from a smart environment. A case study: Ro-smart ageing project. *Informações Econômicas*, *23*(3), 72–83. doi:10.12948/issn14531305/23.3.2019.07

Nithya, B., & Ilango, V. (2017). Predictive analytics in health care using machine learning tools and techniques. *Proceedings of the International Conference on Intelligent Computing and Control Systems ICICCS 2017*. 10.1109/ICCONS.2017.8250771

Niu, W., Huang, J., Xing, Z., & Chen, J. (2019). Knowledge spillovers of medical big data under hierarchical medical system and patients' medical treatment decisions. *IEEE Access: Practical Innovations, Open Solutions, 7*, 55770–55779. doi:10.1109/ACCESS.2019.2908440

Nobles, A. L., Vilankar, K., Wu, H., & Barnes, L. E. (2015). Evaluation of data quality of multisite electronic health record data for secondary analysis. *Proceedings of the 2015 IEEE International Conference on Big Data.* 10.1109/BigData.2015.7364060

Nortey, R. N., Yue, L., Agdedanu, P. R., & Adjeisah, M. (2019). Privacy module for distributed electronic health records (EHRS) using the blockchain. *Proceedings of the 2019 The 4th IEEE International Conference on Big Data Analytics.* 10.1109/ICBDA.2019.8713188

Nouraei, S. A. R., Hudovsky, A., Frampton, A. E., Mufti, U., White, N. B., Wathen, C. G., Sandhu, G. S., & Darzi, A. (2015). A study of clinical coding accuracy in surgery. *Annals of Surgery, 261*(6), 1096–1107. doi:10.1097/SLA.0000000000000851 PMID:25470740

Nouraei, S. A. R., Virk, J. S., Hudovsky, A., Wathan, C., Dari, A., & Parsons, D. (2015). Accuracy of clinician-clinical coder information handover following acute medical admissions: Implication for using administrative datasets in clinical outcomes management. *Journal of Public Health, 38*(2), 352–362. doi:10.1093/pubmed/fdv041 PMID:25907271

Nukavarapu, N., & Durbha, S. (2017). Geo-visual analytics for healthcare critical infrastructure simulation model. *Proceedings of the IGARSS 2017.* 10.1109/IGARSS.2017.8128402

Nutdanai, S., & Sanpanich, A. (2016). Development of an information system for medical equipment management in hospitals. *Proceedings of the 2016 Biomedical Engineering International Conference (BMEiCON-2016).* 10.1109/BMEiCON.2016.7859583

Nuzhat, F., Hasmat, M., & Atif, I. (2020). Big-data analytics based energy analysis and monitoring for multi-storey hospital buildings: case study. In H. Malik (Ed.), *Soft computing in condition monitoring and diagnostics of electrical and mechanical systems, advances in intelligent systems* (pp. 325–343). Springer Nature Singapore Pte.

Orchard, P., Agakova, A., Pinnock, H., Burton, C. D., Sarran, C., Agakov, F., & McKinstry, B. (2018). Improving prediction of risk of hospital admission in chronic obstructive pulmonary disease: Application of machine learning to telemonitoring data. *Journal of Medical Internet Research, 20*(9), 1–11. doi:10.2196/jmir.9227 PMID:30249589

Otokiti, A. (2019). Using informatics to improve healthcare quality. *International Journal of Health Care Quality Assurance, 32*(2), 425–430. doi:10.1108/IJHCQA-03-2018-0062 PMID:31017059

Ouyang, Y., Shan, K., & Bui, F. M. (2016). An rf-based wearable sensor system for indoor tracking to facilitate efficient healthcare management. *Proceedings of the 38th Annual International Conference of the IEEE Engineering in Medicine.* 10.1109/EMBC.2016.7591808

Packianather, M. S., Munizaga, N. L., Zouwail, S., & Saunders, M. (n.d.). Development of soft computing tools and iot for improving the performance assessment of analysers in a clinical laboratory. *Proceedings of the 14 Annual Conference of Systems Engineering.*

Parisi, L., RaviChandran, N., & Manaog, M. L. (2018). Decision support system to improve postoperative discharge: A novel multi- class classification approach. *Knowledge-Based Systems*, *152*, 1–10. doi:10.1016/j.knosys.2018.03.033

Pashazadeh, A., & Navimipour, N. J. (2018). Big data handling mechanisms in the healthcare applications: A comprehensive and systematic literature review. *Journal of Biomedical Informatics*, *82*, 47–62. doi:10.1016/j.jbi.2018.03.014 PMID:29655946

Patel, H. B., & Gandhi, S. (2018). A review on big data analytics in healthcare using machine learning approaches. *Proceedings of the 2nd International Conference on Trends in electronics and Informatics (ICOEI 2018)*. 10.1109/ICOEI.2018.8553788

Patil, H. K., & Seshadri, R. (2014). Big data security and privacy issues in healthcare. *Proceedings of the 2014 IEEE International Congress on Big Data*. 10.1109/BigData.Congress.2014.112

Patil, M. A., Patil, R. B., Krishnamoorthy, P., & John, J. (2016). A machine learning framework for auto classification of imaging system exams in hospital setting for utilization optimization. *Proceedings of the 38th Annual International Conference of the IEEE Engineering in Medicine and Biology Society*. 10.1109/EMBC.2016.7591219

Peng, J., Chen, C., Zhou, M., Xie, X., Zhou, Y., & Luo, C.-H. (2002). Peak outpatient and emergency department visit forecasting for patients with chronic respiratory diseases using machine learning methods: Retrospective cohort study. *JMIR Medical Informatics*, *8*(8), 1–8. doi:10.2196/13075

Peng, S., Su, G., Chen, J., & Du, P. (2017). Design of an iot-bim-gis based risk management system for hospital basic operation. *Proceedings of the 2017 IEEE Symposium on Service-Oriented System Engineering*. 10.1109/SOSE.2017.22

Perdana, T. R., Mujiatun, S., Sfenrianto, S., & Kaburuan, E. R. (2019). Designing knowledge management system with big data for hospital inpatient services (case study at Islamic hospital xyz pekanbaru). *Proceedings of the 2019 International Conference on Information and Communications Technology (ICOIACT)*. 10.1109/ICOIACT46704.2019.8938469

Perimal-Lewis, L., & King, B. (2018). Patient journey modelling: is a single continuous clinical care venue essential to good patient outcomes? A retrospective analysis of administrative data enhanced with detailed clinical care review. *Proceedings of the ACSW*. 10.1145/3167918.3167957

Phillips-Wren, G., & McKniff, S. (2019). Aligning operational benefits of big data analytics and organizational culture at Wellspan health. In T. D. M. Anandarajan (Ed.), *Aligning business strategies and analytics* (pp. 115–131). Springer International Publishing. doi:10.1007/978-3-319-93299-6_8

Pir, A., Akram, M. U., & Khan, M. A. (2015a). Internet of things based context awareness architectural framework for HMIS. *Proceedings of at the 2015 IEEE 17th International Conference on e-Health Networking, Applications and Services*. 10.1109/HealthCom.2015.7454473

Pir, A., Akram, M. U., & Khan, M. A. (2015b). Survey based analysis of internet of things based architectural framework for hospital management system. *Proceedings of the 2015 13th International Conference on Frontiers of Information Technology*.

Pollom, R. K., Balbach, J., & Jones, K. A. (2007). Clinical analytics equal better systemwide outcomes. *Nursing Management*, 44–48. PMID:18188008

Price, S., & Lauffer, V. (2014). Increasing patient satisfaction by empowering staff to manage delays. *Journal of Perianesthesia Nursing*, 29(5), e25. doi:10.1016/j.jopan.2014.08.085

Raita, Y., Goto, T., Faridi, M. K., Brown, D. F. M., Camargo, C. A. Jr, & Hasegawa, K. (2019). Emergency department triage prediction of clinical outcomes using machine learning models. *Critical Care (London, England)*, 23(64), 1–13. doi:10.118613054-019-2351-7 PMID:30795786

Rajliwall, N. S., Girija, C., & Davey, R. (2017). Chronic disease risk monitoring based on an innovative predictive modelling framework. *Proceedings of the IEEE Symposium Series on Computational Intelligence*. 10.1109/SSCI.2017.8285257

Raluy-Callado, M., Cox, A., MacLachlan, S., Bakheit, A. M., Moore, A. P., Dinet, J., & Gabriel, S. (2018). A retrospective study to assess resource utilization and costs in patients with post- stroke spasticity in the united kingdom. *Current Medical Research and Opinion*, 34(7), 1317–1324. doi:10.1080/0300799 5.2018.1447449 PMID:29490512

Ramanathan, L., Swarnalatha, P., Ramani, S., Prabakaran, N., Phogat, P. S., & Rajkumar, S. (2020). Secured smart hospital cabin door knocker using internet of things (iot). In Smart healthcare analytics in IoT enabled environment (pp. 77-89). Springer Nature Switzerland.

Ranjbar, E., Sedehi, G., Rashidi, M., & Suratgar, A. A. (2019). Design of an iot-based system for smart maintenance of medical equipment. *Proceedings of the Third International Conference on Internet of Things and Applications*. 10.1109/IICITA.2019.8808841

Rashwan, W., Fowler, J., & Arisha, A. (2018). A multi-method scheduling framework for medical staff. *Proceedings of the 2018 Winter Simulation Conference*. 10.1109/WSC.2018.8632247

Rathee, G., Sharma, A., Saini, H., Kumar, R., & Iqbal, R. (2019). A hybrid framework for multimedia data processing in IoT-healthcare using blockchain technology. *Multimedia Tools and Applications*, 1–23. doi:10.100711042-019-07835-3

Rathore, S., Panwar, A., & Soral, P. (2014). Critical factors for successful implementation of business analytics: Exploratory findings from select cases. *International Journal of Business Analytics and Intelligence*, 2(2), 11–23.

Ratia, M., Myllarniemi, J., & Helander, N. (2019). The potential beyond IC 4.0: The evolution of business intelligence towards advanced business analytics. *Measuring Business Excellence*, 23(4), 396–410. doi:10.1108/MBE-12-2018-0103

Redfield, C., Tlimat, A., Haplern, Y., Schoenfeld, D. W., Ullman, E., Sontag, D. A., ... Horng, S. (2020). Deriviation and validation of a machine learning record linkage algorithm between emergency medical services and the emergency department. *Journal of the American Medical Informatics Association*, 27(1), 147–153. doi:10.1093/jamia/ocz176 PMID:31605488

Rivera, J., & Delaney, S. (2015). Using business analytics to improve outcomes. *Healthcare Financial Management*, 69(2), 64–67. PMID:26665541

Robinson, Y. H., Presskila, A., & Samraj, L. T. (2020). Utilization of internet of things in health care information system. In Internet of things and big data applications (pp. 35-46). Springer Nature Switzerland.

Roy, S. B., & Chin, S.-C. (2014). Prediction and management of readmission risk for congestive heart failure. *Proceedings of the Health Informatics (HEALTHINF-2014)*.

Ruiz, E., Pacheco-Torres, R., & Casillas, J. (2017). Energy consumption modeling by machine learning from daily activity metering in a hospital. *Proceedings of the 22nd IEEE International Conference on Emerging Technologies and Factory Automation*. 10.1109/ETFA.2017.8247667

Safdar, S., Khan, S. A., & Shaukat, A. (2019). Customer experience management (CEM) for automation, data collection and methodology. *Proceedings of the ICTC 2019*. 10.1109/ICTC46691.2019.8939860

Sahni, P., Arora, G., & Dubey, A. K. (2017). Healthcare waste management and application through big data analytics. *Proceedings of the REDSET 2017*.

Sahoo, P. K., Mohapatra, S. K., & Wu, S.-L. (2017). Analyzing healthcare big data with prediction for future health condition. *IEEE Access: Practical Innovations, Open Solutions*, *4*, 9786–9799. doi:10.1109/ACCESS.2016.2647619

Sangiwe, M., Doan, T. N., Yun, J. A., & Tshuma, N. (2018). Application of machine learning models in predicting length of stay among healthcare workers in underserved communities in South Africa. *Human Resources for Health*, *16*(68), 1–9. doi:10.118612960-018-0329-1 PMID:29301559

Scheinker, D., & Brandeau, M. L. (2017). Analytical approaches to operating room management. In Health care systems engineering (pp. 17-26). Springer International Publishing. doi:10.1007/978-3-319-66146-9_2

Shamayleh, A., Awad, M., & Farhat, J. (2020). IoT based predictive maintenance management of medical equipment. *Journal of Medical Systems*, *42*(72), 1–12. doi:10.100710916-020-1534-8 PMID:32078712

Shams, I., Ajoriou, S., & Yang, K. (2015). A predictive analytics approach to reducing 30-day avoidable readmissions among patients with heart failure, acute myocardial infarction, pneumonia, or copd. *Health Care Management Science*, *18*(1), 19–34. doi:10.100710729-014-9278-y PMID:24792081

Shi, M., Jiang, R., Hu, X., & Shang, J. (2019). A privacy protection method for health care big data management based on risk access control. *Health Care Management Science*, 1–16. doi:10.100710729-019-09490-4 PMID:31338637

Silva, C., Oliveira, D., Peixoto, H., Machado, J., & Abelha, A. (2018). Data mining for prediction of length of stay of cardiovascular accident inpatients. *Proceedings of the DTGS*. 10.1007/978-3-030-02843-5_43

Silvestri, S., Esposito, A., Garguilo, F., Sicuranza, M., Ciampi, M., & De Pietro, G. (2019). A big data architecture for the extraction and analysis of ehr data. *Proceedings of the 2019 IEEE World Congress on Services*. 10.1109/SERVICES.2019.00082

Simsek, S., Tiahrt, T., & Dag, A. (2020). Stratifying no-show patients into multiple risk groups via a holistic data analytics-based framework. *Decision Support Systems*, 1–11. doi:10.1016/j.dss.2020.113269

Solangi, Z. A., Abd. Aziz, M. S., & Asadullah. (2015). The study of internet of things (iot)-based healthcare acceptance in Pakistan. *Proceedings of the IEEE International Conference on Engineering Technologies and Social Science.*

Sousa, M. J., Pesqueira, A. M., Lemos, C., Sousa, M., & Rocha, A. (2019). Decision-making based on big data analytics for people management in healthcare organizations. *Journal of Medical Systems*, *43*(290), 1–10. doi:10.100710916-019-1419-x PMID:31332535

Stadler, J. G., Donlon, K., Siewert, J. D., Franken, T., & Lewis, N. E. (2016). Improving the efficiency and ease of healthcare analysis through use of data visualization dashboards. *Big Data*, *4*(2), 129–135. doi:10.1089/big.2015.0059 PMID:27441717

Stephens, E. (2018). Patient-centered analytics. *OR-MS Today*, *45*(6). Advance online publication. doi:10.1287/orms.2018.06.09

Stopa, B. M., Robertson, F. C., Karhade, A. V., Chua, M., Broekman, M. L. D., Schwab, J. H., Smith, T. R., & Gormley, W. B. (2019). Predicting nonroutine discharge after elective spine surgery: External validation of machine learning algorithms. *Journal of Neurosurgery. Spine*, *31*(5), 742–747. doi:10.3171/2019.5.SPINE1987 PMID:31349223

Sudarto, F., Kristiadi, D. P., Warnars, H. L. H. S., Ricky, M. Y., & Hashimoto, K. (2018). Developing of Indonesian intelligent e-health model. *Proceedings of the 1st 2018 INAPR International Conference.*

Sumarsono, A. M., & Almunawar, M. N. (2019). Big data in healthcare for personalization & customization of healthcare services. *Proceedings of the 2019 International Conference on Information Management and Technology (ICIMTech).* 10.1109/ICIMTech.2019.8843822

Tan, C. S., Deng, X., Tai, E. S., Khoo, Y. H. E., Toh, E. S., Salloway, M. K., . . . Wee, H. L. (2016). Predicting high cost patients with type 2 diabetes mellitus using hospital databases in a multi-ethnic Asian population. *Proceedings of the IEEE-EMBS International Conference on Biomedical and Health Informatics.*

Tang, W., Ren, J., Deng, K., & Zhang, Y. (2019). Secure data aggregation of lightweight e- healthcare iot devices with fair incentives. *IEEE Internet of Things Journal*, *6*(5), 8714–8726. doi:10.1109/JIOT.2019.2923261

Tesfaye, B., Atique, S., Azim, T., & Kebede, M. M. (2019). Predicting skilled delivery service use in Ethiopia: Dual application of logistic regression and machine learning algorithms. *BMC Medical Informatics and Decision Making*, *19*(209), 1–10. doi:10.118612911-019-0942-5 PMID:31690306

Thangaraj, M., Ponmalar, P. P., & Anuradha, S. (2015). Internet of things (iot) enabled smart autonomous hospital management system-a real world health care use case with the technology drivers. *Proceedings of the IEEE International Conference on Computational Intelligence and Computing Research.* 10.1109/ICCIC.2015.7435678

Tideman, S., Santillana, M., Bickel, J., & Reis, B. (2019). Internet search query data improve forecasts of daily emergency department volume. *Journal of the American Medical Informatics Association*, *26*(12), 1574–1583. doi:10.1093/jamia/ocz154 PMID:31730701

Turgeman, L., May, J. H., & Scuilli, R. (2017). Insights from a machine learning model for predicting the hospital length of stay (LoS) at the time of admission. *Expert Systems with Applications*, *78*, 376–385. doi:10.1016/j.eswa.2017.02.023

Ukil, A., Bandyoapdhyay, S., Puri, C., & Pal, A. (2016). IoT healthcare analytics: The importance of anomaly detection. *Proceedings of the 2016 IEEE 30 the International Conference on Advanced Networking and Applications*. 10.1109/AINA.2016.158

Uma, M. S., & Thanayaki, C. V. (2020). Secure medical health care content protection system (SMCPS) with watermark detection for multi cloud computing environment. *Multimedia Tools and Applications*, *79*(5-6), 4075–4097. doi:10.100711042-019-7724-z

Van Wilder, A., Spriet, I., Van Eldere, J., Peetermans, W. E., Vanhaecht, K., Vandersmissen, J., Artois, M., Gilis, K., Vanautgaerden, P., Balcaen, K., Rademakers, F. E., & Bruyneel, L. (2020). Translating data from an electronic prescribing and medicines administration system into knowledge. *Medical Care*, *58*(1), 83–89. doi:10.1097/MLR.0000000000001222 PMID:31584461

Vargheese, R., & Viniotis, Y. (2014). Influencing data availability in iot enabled cloud based e- health in a 30 day readmission context. *Proceedings of the 10th IEEE International Conference on Collaborative Computing: Networking, Applications and Worksharing*. 10.4108/icst.collaboratecom.2014.257621

Verma, N., Xavier, T., & Agrawal, D. (2016). Biometric attendance and big data analysis for optimizing work processes. *Proceedings of the Nursing Informatics 2016*.

Weng, W.-H., Wagholikar, K. B., McCray, A. T., Szolovits, P., & Chueh, H. C. (2017). Medical subdomain classifications of clinical notes using a machine learning-based natural language processing approach. *BMC Medical Informatics and Decision Making*, *17*(155), 1–13. doi:10.118612911-017-0556-8 PMID:29191207

Wills, M. J. (2014). Decisions through data: Analytics in healthcare. *Journal of Healthcare Management*, *59*(4), 254–262. doi:10.1097/00115514-201407000-00005 PMID:25154123

Wojtusiak, J., Elashkar, E., & Nia, R. M. (2018). C-lace2: Computational risk assessment tool for 30-day post hospital discharge mortality. *Health and Technology*, *8*(5), 341–351. Advance online publication. doi:10.100712553-018-0263-1

Wolf, H., Herrmann, K., & Rothermel, K. (2013). Dealing with uncertainty: Robust workflow navigation in the healthcare domain. *ACM Transactions on Intelligent Systems and Technology*, *4*(4), 65. doi:10.1145/2508037.2508046

Woodbridge, D. M.-k., Wilson, A. T., Rintoul, M. D., & Goldstein, R. H. (2015). Time series discord detection in medical data using a parallel relational database. *Proceedings of the 2015 IEEE International Conference on Bioinformatics and Biomedicine (BIBM)*. 10.1109/BIBM.2015.7359885

Woodside, J. M. (2014). Virtual health management. *Proceedings of the 2014 11th International Conference on Information Technology: New Generations*.

Xu, E., Mei, J., Li, J., Yu, Y., Huang, S., & Qin, Y. (2019). From EHR data to medication adherence assessment: a case study on type 2 diabetes. *Proceedings of the IEEE International Conference on Healthcare Informatics*. 10.1109/ICHI.2019.8904786

Xu, H., Wu, W., Nemati, S., & Zha, H. (2017). Patient flow prediction via discriminative learning of mutually-correcting processes. *IEEE Transactions on Knowledge and Data Engineering*, *29*(1), 157–171. doi:10.1109/TKDE.2016.2618925

Xu, J., Xue, K., Li, S., Tian, H., Hong, J., Hong, P., & Yu, N. (2019a). Healthchain: A blockchain-based privacy preserving scheme for large-scale health data. *IEEE Internet of Things Journal*, *6*(5), 8770–8781. doi:10.1109/JIOT.2019.2923525

Yamashita, Y., Iwasaki, H., Muroi, Y., Hida, M., & Shigemi, H. (2019). Development of in- hospital infection management using iot. *Proceedings of the MEDINFO 2019: Health and Wellbeing e-Networks for All*.

Yang, L., Yao, T., Liu, G., Sun, L., Yang, N., Zhang, S., ... Hou, X. (2019). Monitoring and control of medical air disinfection parameters of nosocomial infection system based on internet of things. *Journal of Medical Systems*, *43*(126), 1–7. doi:10.100710916-019-1205-9 PMID:30919075

Ye, B., Basdekis, I., Smyrlis, M., Spanoudakis, G., & Koloutsou, K. (2018). A big data repository and architecture for managing hearing loss related data. *Proceedings of the 2018 IEEE EMBS International Conference on Biomedical & Health Informatics*. 10.1109/BHI.2018.8333397

Ye, Y., Zhao, Y., Shang, J., & Zhang, L. (2019). A hybrid it framework for identifying high- quality physicians using big data analytics. *International Journal of Information Management*, *47*, 65–75. doi:10.1016/j.ijinfomgt.2019.01.005

Yip, K., Pang, S.-K., Chan, K.-T., Chan, C.-K., & Lee, T.-L. (2016). Improving outpatient phlebotomy service efficiency and patient experience using discrete-event simulation. *International Journal of Health Care Quality Assurance*, *29*(7), 733–743. doi:10.1108/IJHCQA-08-2015-0093 PMID:27477930

Yoon-Su, J., & Seung-Soo, S. (2019). Staganography-based healthcare model for safe handling of multimedia health care information using vr. *Multimedia Tools and Applications*, 1–15. doi:10.100711042-019-07833-5

Zachariadis, C., Velivassaki, T. H., Zahariadis, T., Railis, K., & Leligou, H. C. (2018). Matisse: A smart hospital ecosystem. *Proceedings of the 2018 21st Euromicro Conference on Digital System Design*.

Zampieri, F. G., Salluh, J. I. F., Azevedo, L. C. P., Kahn, J. M., Damiani, L. P., Borges, L. P., Viana, W. N., Costa, R., Corrêa, T. D., Araya, D. E. S., Maia, M. O., Ferez, M. A., Carvalho, A. G. R., Knibel, M. F., Melo, U. O., Santino, M. S., Lisboa, T., Caser, E. B., Besen, B. A. M. P., ... Soares, M. (2019). ICU staffing feature phenotypes and their relationship with patients' outcomes: An unsupervised machine learning analysis. *Intensive Care Medicine*, *45*(11), 1599–1607. doi:10.100700134-019-05790-z PMID:31595349

Zhang, H., Li, J., Wen, B., Xun, Y., & Liu, J. (2018). Connecting intelligent things in smart hospitals using nb-iot. *IEEE Internet of Things Journal*, *5*(3), 1550–1560. doi:10.1109/JIOT.2018.2792423

Zhang, Y. (2019). Patient-specific readmission prediction and intervention for health care. *International Journal of Prognostics and Health Management, 10*, 1-5.

Zhang, Y., Qiu, M., Tsai, C.-W., Mehedi, M., & Alamri, A. (2017). Health-cps: Healthcare cyber-physical system assisted by cloud and big data. *IEEE Systems Journal, 11*(1), 88–95. doi:10.1109/JSYST.2015.2460747

Zhu, H., & Hou, M. (2018). Research on an electronic medical record system based on the internet. *Proceedings of the 2018 2nd International Conference on Data Science and Business Analytics.* 10.1109/ICDSBA.2018.00106

Zhu, Q., Akkati, A., & Hongwattanakul, P. (2016). Risk feature assessment of readmission for diabetes. *Proceedings of the 2016 IEEE International Conference on Bioinformatics and Biomedicine (BIBM).*

Chapter 49
Big Data, Data Mining, and Data Analytics in IoT-Based Healthcare Applications

Isakki Alias Devi P

Ayya Nadar Janaki Ammal College, India

ABSTRACT

IoT seriously impacts every industry. The healthcare industry has experienced progression in digitizing medical records. Healthcare services are costlier than ever. Data mining is one of the largest challenges to face IoT. Big Data is an accumulation of data. IoT devices receive lots of data. Big data systems can do a lot of data analytics. The tools can also be used to perform these operations. The big health application system can be built by integrating medical health resources using intelligent terminals, internet of things (IoT), big data, and cloud computing. People suffer from many diseases. A big health system can be applied to scientific health management by detecting risk factors for the occurrence of diseases. Patients can have special attention to their health requirements and their devices can be tuned to remind them of their appointments, calorie count, exercise check, blood pressure variations, symptoms of any diseases, and so much more.

INTRODUCTION

The global population is aging and the chronic diseases are growing day by day. While technology can't stop the population from ageing, it can make healthcare easier in terms of ease of use. The combination of latest information technology with healthcare system will diminish the problems. A new paradigm, known as the Internet of Things (IoT), is an extensive applicability in healthcare industry also. Big data and data analytics are the in-demand. IoT devices collect lots of data. It is not possible for queries. If IoT devices collect data, Big data will analyze data. The information can be measured faster.

According to S. Haller et al. "A world where physical objects are seamlessly integrated into the information network, and where the physical objects can become active participants in business pro-

DOI: 10.4018/978-1-6684-3662-2.ch049

cesses. Services are accessible to interact with these 'smart object' over the Internet, query their state and information associated with them, account security and privacy issues."

IoT is the next generation of Internet which will contain trillions of nodes representing various objects from many ubiquitous sensor devices to large web servers (Dey et al., 2018). IoT incorporates the classical networks with the emerging technologies such as ubiquitous computing, cloud computing, data mining, sensor networks, RFID technology, etc. From the perspective of technology, IoT is an integration of sensor networks, which include RFID, and ubiquitous network (Lee & Yoon, 2017). From the perspective of economical view, IoT integrates new related technologies and applications, productions and services, R. & D., industry and market. Convenience, efficiency and automation are the goals of IoT.

Needs of IoT

- Quantified health will be the future of healthcare. The data affect the performance, and so that IoT is needed for better outcomes with respect to health tracking.
- IoT ensures that all information is considered to make better decisions for patients. It is possible by updating the health information of patients on the cloud.
- The primary area of focus is prevention because health care expenses are very high.
- Patient satisfaction is possible by IoT. Through internet-connected devices, valuable patient's data will be gathered.
- IoT allows care teams to collect various data points on personal fitness like heart-rate, temperature, sleep routine etc.,

Challenges to Adopt IoT in Healthcare

The challenges are storage, security and data management (Pang, 2013). There are reliability and security issues with data along with the lack of infrastructure and training among providers. Another problem is the poor internet access. The medical resources are limited. The development of medical resources is not balanced. 80% people are living in areas with limited medical resources but 80% medical resources are provided to the big cities only. One third of diseases could be completely prevented, one third could be detected early and one third could be done with regular treatment to save people. In general, the status of health is from health to low-high risk status. The application of this paradigm in healthcare industry is a mutual hope because it allows medical centers to function proficiently and patients to obtain better treatment. With the help of this technology-based healthcare method, there are unique benefits which improve the quality and efficiency of healing and accordingly the patient's health will be improved.

Internet-connected devices have been used for patients in various forms. Data comes from fetal monitors, electrocardiograms, temperature monitors or blood glucose levels, health information is essential for patients. These measures are needed follow-up interaction with a healthcare professional. The smart technology quickly became an asset in healthcare is when linked with home medication dispensers. These dispensers routinely upload data to the cloud when medication is not taken.

Internet-of-things technology implementations have issues about personal data privacy and security. IoT devices can be used to save the patient's life. IoT in healthcare may be life threatening if not secured. In 2012, an episode of *Homeland* demonstrated a hacked pacemaker inducing a heart attack. Former Vice President Dick Cheney subsequently asked that the wireless capabilities of his pacemaker be disabled.

In 2016, Johnson & Johnson notified one of its connected insulin pumps was susceptible to attack. "In 2017, St. Jude released patches for weak remote monitoring system of implantable pacemakers".

U.S. Food and Drug Administration (FDA) have published lots of guidelines for establishing end-to-end security for the connected medical devices. "In late 2018, the FDA signed a memorandum of agreement with the Department of Homeland Security to implement a new medical device cyber security framework to be established by both agencies".

- Uses of IoT for Business
  - 53% of IoT projects are used for optimizing current businesses and 47% is used for business investment.
  - Target audiences are consumers (42%), business (54%) and internal use by employees (5%) .
- Challenges in IoT Projects
  - 96% of developers faced challenges with their IoT projects
  - IoT does not deliver full potential due to data challenges.
  - Only 8% are able to analyze IoT data in a timely manner.
  - 86% of stakeholders in business roles say that data is important to their IoT projects.
  - 94% face challenges to collect IoT data.
- Better IoT data collection and analysis
  - 70% developers make better, meaningful decisions with improved data
  - 86% can report faster and flexible analytics and increase the ROI of their IoT investments.

BIG DATA

Big data is defined as huge sets of data that can only be analyzed by computers to reveal patterns (Doukas & Maglogiannis, 2012), trends and associations, mainly with regards to human behavior. The term "big data", with regards to healthcare, is the intersection of mathematics, statistics, computer science and healthcare. The adoption of this expertise is not only about quality care for patients, but the sustainability of healthcare systems on the whole. It also raises the issues such as data privacy, data discrimination and data security (Ali & Ebu-Elkheir, 2012).

Big health is an industry which characterized by people-center, managing a person's health from birth to death. The domain of big health covers health products, health service, health finance field.

Big Data is defined in terms of 3V's:

1. Volume (how much data)
2. Velocity (how fast the data is processed)
3. Variety (different formats of data).

A small volume of complex data, a huge volume of simple data, or sophisticated analytics and predictions from any of the data benefits from the Big Data technology modernization. Big Data is classified into three main types:

Structured Data

Structured Data refers to the data which is already stored in databases. It reports about 20% of total existing data. It is used in computer-related activities. There are two sources of structured data which are machines and humans (Raghupathi & Raghupathi, 2014). All the data received from sensors, web logs and financial systems can be classified under machine-generated data. Human-generated structured data includes all the data as human input into a computer, such as his demographic details. When the user surfs on the internet, or even makes a game movement, data is created. This can be used by companies to predict their customer behavior and take the necessary decisions.

Unstructured Data

The structured data exists in the traditional row-column databases. But the unstructured data is opposite to structured data. These do not have any clear format in storage. The remaining data are created, about 80% of the total account for unstructured big data. Most of the data belongs to this category.

Unstructured data are also categorized based on its source into machine generated and human generated. Machine generated data contains all the satellite images, the scientific data from various experiments captured by different technology. Human generated unstructured data is resided enormously on the internet, since it contains social media data, mobile data and lot of website content.

Semi-Structured Data

Information that is not in the traditional database format as structured data, but contain some organizational properties which make it easier to process, are included in semi-structured data. NoSQL documents are semi structured, since they contain keywords that can be used to process the document effectively.

VARIETIES OF BIG DATA

Big Data is focused on three main varieties:

1. Transactional data—these include data from invoices, payment orders, delivery records, claim activities and cost data. These are useful for payers and providers in healthcare.
2. Machine or clinical data—this can be data gathered from industrial equipments, real-time data from sensors and wearable techs as well as web logs that track user behaviors online.
3. Social data—this can be coming from social media services, such as Facebook Likes, Tweets and YouTube views which gives insights on patients behavior.

Original business value comes from combining these big data with traditional data such as patient records, medical history, location details, and medication management to generate new decisions. In the healthcare arena, the amount of patient and consumer health data has grown largely because of computer-based information systems. In recent years, the adoption of wearable technology, biosensors and mHealth increase the amount of biological data being captured. In a clinical setting, these data include details which come from electronic patient records outcomes (ePRO), electronic health records

(EHR) and other software sources. It is calculated that there are over 10.7 billion objects and devices connected to the internet today. It is expected to cultivate to 50 billion by 2020 according to a recent report by Cisco and DHL.

Big Data Value Chain

Big data value chain contains 6 phases such as:

1. Collection
2. Ingestion
3. Discovery & Cleansing
4. Integration
5. Analysis
6. Delivery

Figure 1 shows big data value chain with 6 phases.

1. **Collection**: Structured, unstructured and semi-structured data from multiple sources.
2. **Ingestion**: Loading vast amounts of data onto a single data store.
3. **Discovery & Cleansing:** Understanding format and content; clean up and formatting.
4. **Integration**: Linking, entity extraction, entity resolution, indexing and data fusion.
5. **Analysis**: Intelligence, statistics, predictive and text analytics, machine learning.
6. **Delivery**: Querying, visualization, real time delivery in enterprise-class availability.

Figure 1. Big data value chain

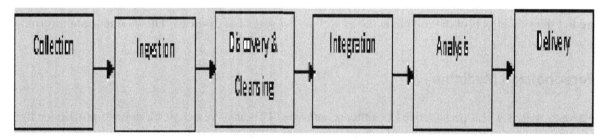

BIG DATA AND INTERNET OF "MEDICAL" THINGS

Big data become valuables to healthcare industry in what's known as the internet of things (IoT). Data scientist uses big data to reorganize healthcare of patients. The diseases can be detected and treated by algorithms. Devices are helpful for human health. This data will be checked against genetic profile. Death rates will be reduced. Any device which generates data about a person's health and sends that data into the cloud, will be part of IoT. This data also has lot of variations and in terms of huge amount of medical data from different age groups, or high variability of veracity in terms of incomplete patient records and so on (Dey et al., 2018).

Medical big data has different features compared to big data from other fields. It is hard to frequently access. It is structured in comparison and has legal complications associated with its use (Doukas & Maglogiannis, 2012).In order to get value from the connected digital health environments, it is important to have a platform on which to create and manage applications, to run analytics, to receive, store and secure data. The term "connected health" is described that how healthcare is connecting in the digital health industry. Health information systems confirm great potential in improving the efficiency in the delivery of care, a reduction in overall costs to the health care system. It is necessary to organize and process the ever-increasing quantity of data which is digitally collected and stored within the health care organizations.

Many patients are using mobile applications (apps) to manage their health needs. The devices and mobile apps are now progressively used and integrated with telemedicine via the medical Internet of Things (mIoT). mIoT is a very tedious way of the digital transformation in healthcare industry. It allows new business paradigms to emerge changes. Wearables and mobile apps support fitness, health education, tracking of symptom, etc. All those platform analytics can raise the relevancy of data interpretations together data outputs.

Applications of Big Data in Healthcare

Big data is the collection of data sets. It is very tedious to process using hand database management tools or traditional data processing applications. Companies utilize big data to ensure higher profitablility.

Early Disease Detection

Big data analytics can guess the start of epidemics. It goes one step ahead and predicts the location of carriers. This was happened in the issue of Ebola to negate its spread. The body composition data can predict the side effects of certain medicine as well as the spread of diseases. This is important information for doctors.

Personalized Medicine

Big data makes a real personalized healthcare industry. This involves creating genetic profile for the patients based on which perfect healthcare plan is created. The plan is also collaborated with social and lifestyle habits. This helps to predict the issues of diseases as well as provides recommendations for better treatment.

Clinical Trials

Big data can be used for on-scale clinical trials. This can be started with the selection of a sample set, The doctors can scan through medical profiles which meet their requirements. Then, Big data can enable to track which was not happened earlier. The trial success rate has increased.

Increased Profits Via High Cost Patients

A minority group of patients report for major healthcare spending. The high cost patients never bother about money and they used to do master check up twice in a year.

Loss of Privacy Because of Big Data

Healthcare transformation comes with many challenges.

1. Access to healthcare
2. Consumer Engagement
3. Cost efficiency
4. Levels and quality of care

Fortunately, companies taking advantage of big data are gaining deeper insights into patient health and creating exceptional customer experiences. Suppose, for example, Linda is seeing her physician for her annual physical checkup. She has the problems such as diabetic, stress, irritable, low blood pressure. In a big data world, Linda's physician has a 360 degree view of her healthcare history. Her appointments, diets, exercise, labs, vitals, prescriptions, treatments, allergies, etc., will be recorded.

Big Data Standardization Challenges

- Big Data use cases, definitions, vocabulary and reference architectures (e.g. system, data, plat-forms, online/offline)
- Specifications and standardization of metadata including data provenance
- Application models (e.g. batch, streaming)
- Query languages including non-relational queries to support diverse data types (XML, RDF, JSON, multimedia) and Big Data operations
- Domain-specific languages
- Semantics of eventual consistency
- Advanced network protocols for efficient data transfer
- General and domain specific ontology and taxonomies for describing data semantics including interoperation between ontology
- Big Data security and privacy access controls
- Remote, distributed, and federated analytics (taking the analytics to the data) including data and processing resource discovery and data mining
- Data sharing and exchange
- Data storage, e.g. memory storage system, distributed file system, data warehouse, etc.
- Human consumption of the results of big data analysis (e.g. visualization)
- Interface between relational (SQL) and non-relational (NoSQL)
- Big Data Quality and Veracity description and management

DATA MINING AND DATA ANALYTICS IN IoT

Many data mining tools are useful to face those challenges effectively. So the propagation of the IoT would be the next stage of the big data concept. Big data analysis can drive the digital interruption of the healthcare industry, business processes and decision making. Data mining is used to extract targeted data from a very large dataset. The technique involves traversing through the huge volume of data using data mining methods of association, classification, compilation and so on (Imadali, 2012).

Association is used to create interrelationships between two or more data sets to identify a pattern. It enables the deduction of general tendencies among data sets. Other significant part of data mining techniques is classification and clustering. Classification is used to assign data into particular target classes to precisely predict what will occur within the class (Jara, Zamora-Izquierdo, & Skarmeta, 2012, 2013; Jiawei & Kamber, 2011). Clustering is the process of grouping similar data records.

Role of Data Analytics in Internet of Things (IoT)

IoT and big data are linked together to perform various operations. Data which is consumed and produced in IoT keep growing at an expanding rate. This incursion of data is increasing rapidly. In 200, there will be approximately 30.73 billion IoT connected devices. The data generated from IoT devices will turn as value. If it subjects to analysis, data analytics will bring into the picture. Data analytics can be used to examine big and small data sets with varying data properties to extract meaningful conclusions. These conclusions are in the form of trends, patterns, and statistics. It helps for the organization to make good and effective decisions in business.

Merging Data Analytics and IoT for the Businesses

Data Analytics are useful for the growth of IoT applications. An analytics tools will allow an organization to make use of their variety of dataset. The following lists must be considered:

- **Volume:** There are huge amount of clusters of data sets. IoT applications can make use of those data sets. The organizations are needed to manage these data and analyze the same for extracting required patterns. These datasets along with real time data must be analyzed effectively with the help of data analytics software.
- **Structure:** IoT applications contain data sets that have a structure as unstructured, semi-structured and structured data sets.
- **Driving Revenue:** The data analytics in IoT investments will allow organizations to gain an detailed approach into customer preferences. This leads to the development of offers as per the customer's expectations. It will improve the revenues of the organizations in an effective manner.

Optimize the Processes With Data

There are different types of data analytics that can be applied in the IoT investments. Some of these types have been described below:

- **Streaming Analytics:** This form of data analytics refers as event stream processing and it analyzes huge in-motion data sets. Real-time data streams are analyzed in this process to detect urgent situations and immediate actions. IoT applications based on financial transactions, air fleet tracking, traffic analysis etc. can benefit from this method.
- **Spatial Analytics:** This data analytics method is used to analyze geographic patterns to determine the spatial relationship between the physical objects. Location-based IoT applications, such as smart parking applications can benefit from this form of data analytics.
- **Time Series Analytics:** This form of data analytics is based upon the time-based data which is analyzed to reveal associated patterns and trends. IoT applications, such as weather forecasting applications and health monitoring systems can benefit from this form of data analytics method.
- **Prescriptive Analysis:** This form of data analytics is the combination of descriptive and predictive analysis. It is applied to comprehend the best steps of action which can be taken in a particular situation. Commercial IoT applications can make use of this form of data analytics to gain better conclusions.

Healthcare is one of the leading sectors of every country. The utilization of data analytics in IoT based healthcare applications can provide breach in this area. The reduction of the healthcare costs, enhancement of telehealth monitoring, and remote health services, increased diagnosis and treatment can be achieved using the same. The utilization of data analytics shall be promoted in the area of IoT to gain improved revenues, competitive gain, and customer engagement.

DATA MINING PROCESSES

IoT data mining processes are divided into multiple stages, as follows:

- Data is integrated according to different data sources.
- Data is cleaned, so it can be easily extracted and processed.
- Some parts of data are extracted and prepared for future processing.
- Sophisticated algorithms are used to identify patterns.
- Data is restructured and presented to the users in a articulate way.

The enormous amount of data produced by IoT devices can be converted into knowledge using data mining techniques. Technologies are used to mine certain useful trends and patterns which are unknown, to enhance the performance of the organizations. All the organizations are growing rapidly with the help of data mining functionalities. Data mining helps to find out something in the huge data which is profitable to the organization. The primary aim of knowledge discovery in databases is to discover the novel patterns in the large data sets. It is the blend of artificial intelligence, machine learning and statistics. Data mining transforms a data set into meaningful structure and extracts information which helps to gain deep knowledge into the raw data collected from various IoT applications.

But there also are challenges that need to be overcome such as issues related to data structure, security, standardization, storage and transfer. With the use of technology and potential data mining tools like Hadoop, big data can be investigated more quickly and in a less cumbersome way. With the large quantities of medical data available, we feel confident that we can uncover important and solid information regarding people's health. If this presumption is valid and the analysis outcomes are dependable, this could be the start of a new phase of total illnesses prevention or even eradication.

Therefore, IoT forms a network of physical objects or things which might be embedded with electronics, sensor and network connectivity by which the devices can collect and exchange data (Höller et al., 2014). The perfect association between IoT and Data Mining result into a new emerging technology which benefits to the society. Different applications generate huge amount of heterogeneous data. As the data in IoT application is generated continuously from different sources like wireless sensor networks, RFID etc.

Imadali (2012) differentiated types of data from IoT into "data about things" and "data generated by things". Data about things refers to data that describe things themselves and data generated by things refers to data generated by things. This new type of data (i.e., data captured by sensor or RFID) has been defined as a kind of "big data" (Jara, Zamora-Izquierdo, & Skarmeta, 2012). The huge amount of data generated by IoT applications and potential of KDD motivated us to analyze a data mining framework for IoT applications.

Clustering for IoT

Clustering algorithms (Raghupathi & Raghupathi, 2014) divide data into meaningful groups. The patterns in the same group are similar in some sense and patterns in different group are dissimilar in the same sense. This is an unsupervised learning technique. For example, search engine uses clustering method to group web pages into different groups like news, videos, images, blogs etc.

Clustering is an efficient way to enhance the performance of IoT on the integration of identification, sensing, and actuation. New clustering algorithms are developed for the WSNs that are found on IoT (Uttarkar & Kilkarni, 2014). One of the clustering algorithms which considers the energy conservation of WSN is the low-energy adaptive clustering hierarchy (LEACH) (Zhang & Zhang, 2011).

Classification for IoT

Classification is an important technique in data mining. It predicts the output based on the given training data. This is called supervised learning technique. In this technique, a training data is given by the use of which a classifier model is build and based on this model the future pattern is predicted.

For IoT applications, classification algorithms are divided into 2 types – outdoor and indoor. The example for the outdoor IoT is traffic jam problem. The smart phones and other smart devices are used to predict the traffic situations and communicate them to the users. Some classification algorithms are there to solve the traffic jam problem, where the classifiers predict and suggest the less jammed route to the driver based on the previous traffic conditions.

DATA MINING CHALLENGES WITH THE IoT

In healthcare industry, lots of data mining challenges exist. Enormous numbers of patients, doctors, and other details are to be maintained.

Increasingly Large Volumes of Data

As new applications become progressively more complex, developers are facing pressure to process large data sets. Certain applications require data scientists to extract and analyze plenty of petabytes of data. According to EMC, IT support companies are under pressure to facilitate their customers for better solutions and manage huge data.

Data Sets Aren't Homogenous

Before the IoT comes, most applications received data from a single source. Since data were already structured in the same format, data scientists rarely encountered compatibility issues. The IoT has introduced a new layer of complexity for data analysis. Data is created from many different sources in multiple formats, such as web documents, CSV sheets, and SQL tables. Before big data analytics tools can process it, data must be cleaned and convert it into a single structure.

Integrity of Different Sources

Each system uses its own methodology to develop data, which will always introduce some level of uncertainty. Unfortunately, a feasible solution to this challenge has yet to present itself, but the barriers should be nominal for most real-world applications.

Need for Real-Time Analysis

Some applications need data to be extracted and processed in real time. This can be a challenge when analyzing data sets that are petabytes in size.

Solutions to These Challenges

If data mining problems have surfaced with the IoT, new solutions have been developed to solve them. Hadoop and big data extraction tools are important to make it easier. Many companies are expected to get the advantage of Hadoop as IoT becomes widely implemented.

Big Data Hadoop Architecture

Big Data Hadoop Architecture supports for analytic solution using open source Apache Hadoop framework. In Big Data Hadoop architecture, big volumes, variety, and velocity of data are collected from online and stored in HDFS file system. Hadoop architecture also provides HBase and RDBMS for processing and storing big data in the traditional format and useful for users on Big Data Architectures.

Hadoop acts like an information coordinator. It enables specialists to discover relationships in informational indexes with numerous factors. This is the reason for using Hadoop with healthcare information. The big data landing zone can be set up on Hadoop cluster to collect huge data which are stored in HDFS file system (Jara, Zamora-Izquierdo, & Skarmeta, 2012). Map Reduce programming is for online marketing analysts and various algorithms in Hadoop cluster to perform Big data analysts and core java programming language is implemented for Algorithms. The data regarding the previous medical history of patients provide better service from hospitals.

Big Data Hadoop Challenges

The major Big Data Challenges are associated with as follows:

- Capturing data
- Storage
- Cure
- Sharing
- Searching
- Transfer
- Analysis

To fulfill the all above challenges, organizations get help from enterprise servers.

Health Cloud and Health Big Data

Big health system is required to create health IoT. The quantity of networking devices is more nowadays and the enormous amount of data increases much faster. Traditional computing models and data analysis techniques are far from satisfying the massive concurrent user's demands and wobbly growth of data. Therefore, the combination of cloud computing and big data is used to build a platform for big health services. The health big data based on mobile health cloud must have the following features:

- **Heterogeneity**: This is mainly reflected in two aspects: the different parts of the body, different categories of different organizations and different countries and regions can store health data with different medical standards with different storage format. There is a possibility of structured relational data and semi-structured data. CDA (Clinical Document Architecture) is one of the examples. There are text, images, video, audio, and other unstructured data, such as medical records, X-ray, ultrasound, cardiac EEG. With the development of new technology, same kinds of data can be changed in the structure: for example, with the development of medical technology, complete blood test indicators can be measured. It will predictably lead to inconsistent format of historical data.
- **High Correlation**: Medical health data include the body's vital signs which are closely linked and related each other. Small portions of the data, does not accurately identify the function of the body. For example, human leukocyte data which are high and not able to determine the illness. Its causes are acute infection, tissue injuries, hepatitis, and leukemia. However, if the white blood cells in urine is high, the patients may be affected by renal disease.

In addition to the above two basic features, mobile medical big data has the following three characteristics:

- **Real-Time**: The detected data must be real-time due to the nature of health care. It also requires timely treatment.
- **Time and Space Correlation**: Healthcare has important time and space characteristics which manifested in two aspects: First, the different regions people have certain differences. For example, the range of hemoglobin of the persons at high altitude is usually higher than others. In addition, the same physiological parameters of the human body at different times will have certain variations. For example, the blood pressure is relatively high during day time. It is relatively low at night. The human adrenal cortex hormone is high during the day and low at night. With mobile smart devices and sensing devices, the data with time and space properties can be collected.
- **Low Proportion of Valid Data**: Mobile smart devices and conventional sensing devices cannot provide accurate test results like professional medical devices. For example, in the collection process of heart rate data, only the heart rate beyond the normal range will attract patients and medical personnel's attention.

IoT-BASED APPLICATIONS

As per the reports submitted by the P&S Market Research, there will be a compound annual growth rate (CAGR) of 37.6% in the healthcare Internet of Things industry between the years 2015 and 2020. People can enjoy personalized attention for their health requirements and their devices can be tuned to remind them of their appointments, calorie count, exercise check, blood pressure variations and so much more.

The patient medical record (MR) contains emergency data and medical case profiles. The clinical documentation (CD) is a digital or analog record which tracks all the treatment related activities. MR and CD are important for hospital information system (HIS). The clinical documentation serves as the benchmark medical information document for further clinical activities. It must be accurate. It further can serve to generate complete patient medical records. A hospital information system (HIS) must ensure that the patient's health records, as well as the clinical documentation, are always available. They must be reliable, and ensure data privacy.

Furthermore, remote monitoring of patient's health helps to reduce the length of hospital stay. IoT has applications in healthcare that benefit patients, families, physicians, hospitals, and healthcare related organizations. Devices in the form of wearables like fitness bands, wirelessly connected devices like blood pressure and heart rate monitoring cuffs, glucometer etc. provide patients access to personalized attention. These devices are tuned to remind calorie count, exercise check, appointments, blood pressure variations and much more. If any disturbances produced in the routine activities of a person, alert mechanism will send signals to family members and concerned health providers. IoT devices tagged with sensors are used to track real time location of medical equipment like wheelchairs, defibrillators, nebulizers, oxygen pumps and other monitoring equipment. Deployment of medical staff at different locations can also be analyzed in real time.

There are plenty of opportunities for health insurers with IoT-connected intelligent devices. Insurance companies can leverage data captured through health monitoring devices for their underwriting and claims operations. This data will enable them to detect fraud claims and identify prospects for underwriting. IoT devices bring transparency between insurers and customers in the underwriting, pricing, claims handling, and risk assessment processes. In the light of IoT-captured data-driven decisions in all operation processes, customers will have adequate visibility into underlying thought behind every decision made and process outcomes.

Insurers can offer incentives to their customers for sharing health data generated by IoT devices. They can reward customers for using IoT devices to keep track of their routine activities and adherence to treatment plans and precautionary health measures. This will help insurers to reduce claims significantly. IoT devices can enable insurance companies to validate claims through the data captured by these devices. The proliferation of healthcare-specific IoT products opens up immense opportunities. And the huge amount of data are generated by these connected devices hold the potential to transform healthcare.

IoT has a four-step architecture which are basically four stages process (See Figure 2). All four stages are connected in a mode that data is processed at one stage and yield the value to the next stage. Integrated values in the process deliver dynamic business prospects.

Step 1: It consists of deployment of interconnected devices such as sensors, actuators, monitors, detectors, camera systems etc. These devices are used to collect the data.
Step 2: Data received from sensors and other devices are in analog form and need to be aggregated and converted to the digital form for further data processing.
Step 3: Once the data is digitized and aggregated, this is pre-processed, standardized and moved to the data center or Cloud (El-Sayed, 2018).
Step 4: Final data is managed and analyzed at the required level. Advanced Analytics can be applied and gives business insights for effective decision-making.

Figure 2. Four step IoT architecture

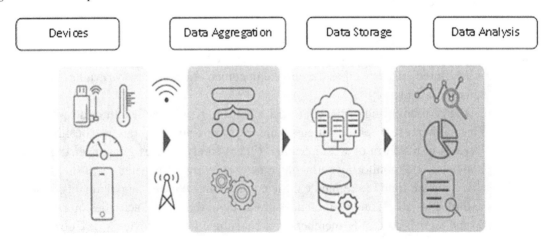

IoT is redefining healthcare by ensuring better care, improved treatment outcomes and reduced costs for patients, and better processes and workflows, improved performance and patient experience for healthcare providers.

The major advantages of IoT in healthcare include:

- **Cost Reduction**: IoT enables patient monitoring in real time. It significantly avoids unnecessary visits to doctors and hospital stays.
- **Future Treatment:** It enables physicians to make evidences based decisions and brings absolute transparency
- **Faster Diagnosis:** Continuous patient monitoring and real time data helps in diagnosing diseases at an early stage.
- **Proactive Treatment**: Continuous health monitoring provides proactive medical treatment.
- **Drugs and Equipment Management:** Management of drugs and medical equipment is a major challenge in a healthcare industry. Through connected devices, these are managed and utilized effectively with less costs
- **Error Reduction:** Data generated through IoT devices not only help in effective decision making but also make sure smooth healthcare operations with less errors and system costs.

Healthcare IoT is not without challenges. IoT-enabled connected devices capture huge amounts of data, including sensitive information, giving rise to concerns about data security. Implementing apt security measures is crucial. IoT explores new dimensions of patient care through real-time health monitoring and access to patients' health data. This data is a goldmine for healthcare stakeholders to improve patient's health and experiences while making revenue opportunities and improving healthcare operations. Being prepared to harness this digital power would prove to be the differentiator in the increasingly connected world.

Wearables and mobile applications support fitness, health education, disease's symptoms tracking, and care coordination (El-Sayed, 2018). All these platform analytics can raise the relevancy of data interpretations, reducing the amount of time that end users spend piecing together data outputs. The details are gained from big data analysis and will drive the digital disruption of the healthcare world and useful to make real time decisions. The applications of IoT in the healthcare industry are numerous:

1. Real Time Location Services

The doctors can use real time location services and track the devices to treat patients and give medications. Medical devices like wheelchairs, scales, defibrillators, nebulizers, pumps or monitoring equipment can be tagged with sensors and located with IoT. Apart from real time location services, there are IoT devices which help in environmental monitoring (Imadali, 2012). The system with IoT sensors are designed to track the moments of caretaking and care giving process. This provides to track locations of patients and medical equipment. It is called as location-as-a-service. The system is designed to improve the satisfaction of staffs and patients. Ex: AwarePoint.

2. Prediction of the Patients in PACU

With the help of Internet of Things, clinicians can predict the arrival of patients who are located in the Post-Anesthesia Care Unit (PACU). Doctors can also monitor the status of patients in real time.

3. Hand Hygiene Compliances

There is a hand hygiene monitoring system that would identify the degree of cleanliness. According to the Center for Disease Control and Prevention in United States, about one patient out of every 20 gets infections due to lack of hand hygiene in hospitals. Many patients lose their lives because of infections.

The communications in the hand hygiene monitoring systems can be done in real time. If a clinician comes closer to a patient's bed without washing his hands, the device will start buzzing. The information about the healthcare worker, his/her ID, time and location will all be fed into a database and this information would be forwarded to the concerned authorities.

4. Tighten Budgets and Improve Patient Journey

The healthcare industry must keep a watchful eye on the budget and at the same time have updated infrastructure to provide better patient experiences. It is now possible for the medical staff to access patient information from the cloud.

The goal is to give quality medical care to patients, and by spending a small amount on IT infrastructure. The hospitals can provide high quality care to patients at affordable rates. IoT aims to give better treatment for patients by:

- Room lighting through personal control
- Communicate with family and friends through email services
- Immediate attention to patient needs

5. Remote Monitoring

Remote health monitoring is significant in the application of Internet Of Things. Through monitoring, adequate healthcare can be given to people who need help. Lots of people die daily, because of not getting timely medical attention. With IoT, devices fit with sensors will notify the healthcare providers about the changes in the functions of body.

These devices are capable of handling complex algorithms and analyzing them. So, the patients can be able to receive proper attention and medical care. The collected patient information would be stored in the cloud. The patients do not need to stay in the hospitals continuously. If there are any variations in the daily activity of a person, alerts will send to the family members and their health providers immediately. These monitoring devices are provided in the form of wearables too.

6. Glucose Level Monitoring Scheme

Glucose Level Sensing Diabetes is a metabolic disease that increases the blood glucose level for a certain amount of time. The monitoring of glucose shows variations in blood patterns, activities and in the formation of meal. A real-time glucose level monitoring scheme was introduced in Istepanian et al. (Uttarkar & Kulkarni, 2014).

7. ECG Monitoring

An electrocardiogram (ECG) monitors the electrical movement of the human heart, determining the heart rate, QT intervals, myocardial ischemia, and diagnosis of arrhythmias (Zhang & Zhang, 2011).

8. Body Temperature Monitoring

Body Temperature Monitoring of human body temperature is an essential measure of medical services since it may be considered a vital indication of preservation of homeostasis (Kamal, Dey, Ashour, 2017). Istepanian et al. (Uttarkar & Kulkarni, 2014) verified the m-IoT strategy using body temperature sensors located in TelosB motes.

9. Medical Alert System

The medical alert system can be worn by a patient as clothing or jewelry. It feeds into a series of connected sensors. Those are useful to measure the health and welfare of the wearer. If a patient falls out of bed, or unconscious for too long period, an alert will be sent to family or friends who can help. Ex: Zanthion.

- **Medication Dispensing Device by Philips**: The patients will not miss a dose anymore. It is suitable for elderly patients.
- **Niox Mino by Aerocrine**: It measures Intric Oxide in a patient's breath.
- **Uro Sense by Future Path Medical**: It is for catheterized patients to check their body temperature and urine results.
- **GPS SmartSole**: This is a shoe-tracking wearable device for dementia patients who used to forget.

Benefits of IoT in Healthcare

a. Research

The resources in the current medical research have lack of real-world information. It uses controlled environments. IoT opens lot of ways to a variety of data and information through analysis and real time data. IoT can deliver data that is far better to standard analytics through making use of instruments. It helps in healthcare by providing more reliable data, which provides better solutions.

b. Devices

The current devices are improving with more power and precision (Jara, Zamora, & Skarmeta, 2012). IoT has the potential to unlock existing technology. It leads us towards better solutions. It fills the gap between the way which deliver healthcare and the equipment. It then detects errors and try to reveal the patterns and missing elements in healthcare.

c. Care

IoT empowers the professionals to use their knowledge and the proper training in a better way to crack the problems. It helps to utilize better data and equipment. Finally, better actions can be happened. IoT allows the professionals to exercise their talents.

d. Medical Information Distribution

This is a most significant innovation of IoT applications in healthcare. The distribution of accurate information to patients remains one of the challenges in medical care. IoT devices can not only improved health in the patient's life but also to facilitate the professional practice.

e. Emergency Care

The emergency services are suffered by the limited resources and sometimes disconnected also. The effective automation and analytics is the best solution in the healthcare industry. An emergency situation can be analyzed from a long distance (Uttarkar & Kulkarni, 2014). The providers can access the profiles of the patients during their arrival at hospitals. It is very essential care to the patients for their life. The losses can be reduced and emergency healthcare is well-improved.

CONCLUSION

With the help of big data, data mining and data analytics, IoT is really helpful for the patients and doctors. IoT will attain the goals of reduced costs and better health once it fully gets adopted the healthcare industry.

A new revolution of personalized preventative health coaches will emerge in this health industry. They are digital health advisors. These workers will possess the skills and the ability to manipulate the medical data. The coaches will help their clients to resolve chronic illness, improve cognitive function and achieve improved mental health.

REFERENCES

Ali, N., & Abu-Elkheir, M. (2012). Data management for the internet of things: Green directions. In *Proc. IEEE Globecom Workshops*, pp. 386–390. 10.1109/GLOCOMW.2012.6477602

Dey, N., Hassanien, A. E., Bhatt, C., Ashour, A., & Satapathy, S. C. (2018). Internet of Things and Big Data Analytics toward Next Generation Intelligence (pp. 3–549). Berlin, Germany: Springer International Publishing. doi:10.1007/978-3-319-60435-0

Doukas, C. & Maglogiannis, I. (2012). Bringing IoT and cloud computing towards pervasive healthcare. *Sixth international conference on innovative mobile and internet services in ubiquitous computing (IMIS)*. Piscataway, NJ: IEEE. 10.1109/IMIS.2012.26

El-Sayed, H., Sankar, S., Prasad, M., Puthal, D., Gupta, A., Mohanty, M., & Lin, C.-T. (2018). Edge of Things: The Big Picture on the Integration of Edge, IoT and the Cloud in a Distributed Computing Environment. *IEEE Access: Practical Innovations, Open Solutions, 6,* 1706–1717. doi:10.1109/AC-CESS.2017.2780087

Höller, J., Tsiatsis, V., Mulligan, C., Karnouskos, S., Avesand, S., & Boyle, D. (2014). *From machine-to-machine to the internet of things: Introduction to a new age of intelligence.* Amsterdam, The Netherlands: Elsevier.

Imadali, S., Karanasiou, A., Petrescu, A., Sifniadis, I., Vèque, V., & Angelidis, P. (2012, October). eHealth service support in IPv6 vehicular networks. In *2012 IEEE 8th International Conference on Wireless and Mobile Computing, Networking and Communications (WiMob)* (pp. 579-585). Piscataway, NJ: IEEE.

Jara, A. J., Zamora, M. A., & Skarmeta, A. F. (2012). Knowledge acquisition and management architecture for mobile and personal health environments based on the internet of things. *IEEE 11th international conference on trust, security and privacy in computing and communications (TrustCom).* 10.1109/TrustCom.2012.194

Jara, A. J., Zamora-Izquierdo, M. A., & Skarmeta, A. F. (2013). Interconnection framework for mHealth and remote monitoring based on the internet of things. *IEEE Journal on Selected Areas in Communications, 31*(9), 47–65. doi:10.1109/JSAC.2013.SUP.0513005

Jiawei, H., & Kamber, M. (2017). *Data Mining: Concepts and Techniques.* Morgan Kaufmann.

Kamal, M. S., Dey, N., & Ashour, A. S. (2017). Large scale medical data mining for accurate diagnosis: A blueprint. In S. U. Khan, A. Y. Zomaya, & A. Abbas (Eds.), *Handbook of Large-Scale Distributed Computing in Smart Healthcare* (pp. 157–176). Cham: Springer. doi:10.1007/978-3-319-58280-1_7

Lee, H. C., & Yoon, H.-J. (2017). Medical big data: Promise and challenges. *Kidney Research and Clinical Practice, 36*(1), 3–11. doi:10.23876/j.krcp.2017.36.1.3 PMID:28392994

Pang, Z. (2013). Ecosystem analysis in the design of open platform-based in-home healthcare terminals towards the internet-of-things. In *15th international conference on advanced communication technology (ICACT).* IEEE.

Raghupathi, W., & Raghupathi, V. (2014). Big data analytics in healthcare: Promise and potential. *Health Information Science and Systems, Springer, 2*(3), 2–10. PMID:25825667

Uttarkar, R., & Kulkarni, R. (2014). Internet of Things: Architecture and Security. *International Journal of Computers and Applications, 3*(4).

Zhang, X. M., & Zhang, N. (2011). An open, secure and flexible platform based on internet of things and cloud computing for ambient aiding living and telemedicine. In *2011 international conference on computer and management (CAMAN).* IEEE.

Chapter 50
Remote Patient Monitoring for Healthcare:
A Big Challenge for Big Data

Andrew Stranieri

ⓘ https://orcid.org/0000-0002-4415-5771
Federation University, Australia

Venki Balasubramanian
Federation University, Australia

ABSTRACT

Remote patient monitoring involves the collection of data from wearable sensors that typically requires analysis in real time. The real-time analysis of data streaming continuously to a server challenges data mining algorithms that have mostly been developed for static data residing in central repositories. Remote patient monitoring also generates huge data sets that present storage and management problems. Although virtual records of every health event throughout an individual's lifespan known as the electronic health record are rapidly emerging, few electronic records accommodate data from continuous remote patient monitoring. These factors combine to make data analytics with continuous patient data very challenging. In this chapter, benefits for data analytics inherent in the use of standards for clinical concepts for remote patient monitoring is presented. The openEHR standard that describes the way in which concepts are used in clinical practice is well suited to be adopted as the standard required to record meta-data about remote monitoring. The claim is advanced that this is likely to facilitate meaningful real time analyses with big remote patient monitoring data. The point is made by drawing on a case study involving the transmission of patient vital sign data collected from wearable sensors in an Indian hospital.

DOI: 10.4018/978-1-6684-3662-2.ch050

INTRODUCTION

Continuous remote monitoring of patients using wearable sensors and Cloud processing is emerging as a technology that promises to lead to new ways to realize early detection of conditions and increased efficiency and safety in health care systems (Chan, Estève, Fourniols, Escriba, & Campo, 2012). The approach combines body area wireless sensor networks (BSN) with systems that are designed to process and store the data for the purpose of raising alarms immediately or for data analytics exercises at a later point in time (Balasubramanian, Stranieri, & Kaur, 2015). Real time remote monitoring systems have been described for a number of remote monitoring applications including: continuous vital signs monitoring (Balasubramanian & Stranieri, 2014; Catley, Smith, McGregor, & Tracy, 2009), arrhythmia detection (Kakria, Tripathi, & Kitipawang, 2015), regulating oxygen therapy (Zhu et al., 2005), monitoring of pregnant women (Balasubramanian, Hoang, & Ahmad, 2008), fall detection (Thilo et al., 2016), chemotherapy reaction (Breen et al., 2017) and glucose monitoring(Klonoff, Ahn, & Drincic, 2017). Ultimately, a multitude of condition specific applications, each using different subsets of each patient's health data commissioned by diverse healthcare practices can be expected to emerge in the near future. For instance, a rehabilitation clinic may be interested in tracking a patient's gait, while a counselling service may be interested in tracking heart rate variability to detect suicidal depression (Carta & Angst, 2016) and a hospital may be interested in detecting post-operative sepsis (Brown et al., 2016).

Remote patient monitoring (RPM) applications often generate high volumes of data with great velocity and variety to produce valuable diagnostic information. For instance an ECG wearable sensor alone can produce 125 to 8000 samples per second (Shimmer, 2018), that can be used to predict various heart conditions in real time. In many occasions, a RPM application uses more than one wearable sensor to monitor vital signs, such as ECG, body temperature, blood pressure, oxygen saturation (SpO_2) and respiratory rate, to analyze and predict the health condition of the patient. This leads to large data repositories that present serious challenges for Big Data analytics algorithms (Kalid et al., 2018). A review by (Mikalef, Pappas, Krogstie, & Giannakos, 2017) reveals that Big Data is characterized in terms of the five main 'Vs:' volume, velocity, variety, veracity and value. Although a great deal has been written about the Big Data explosion, little is known of the conditions under which Big Data Analysis (BDA) leads to the generation of value for an organization (Wang, Kung, & Byrd, 2018).

In this chapter, the observation is first made that BDA for remote patient monitoring is difficult to perform due to the volume, velocity, veracity and diversity of data. Consequently, few electronic health records include RPM data despite the increasing prevalence of data from continuous monitors because electronic health records were designed for structured and less variable health data. In addition, explicit decisions about the way in which RPM data is collected, processed and interpreted in practice are rarely made by analysts acting in isolation in health care, but by diverse stakeholders working in teams in sociopolitical contexts. For instance, in the data analytics exercise with an Australian hospital described by (Sharma, Stranieri, Ugon, Vamplew, & Martin, 2017), the problem, and interpretation of analytics results depended on stakeholder priorities at the executive, management and operational levels of the hospital. The data analytics process model CRISP-DM (Shearer, 2000) cannot readily accommodate diverse stakeholder priorities and also cannot easily be adapted for continuous analytics with RPM data.

The openEHR (open Electronic Health Record pronounced open A'yr) standard that depicts the pragmatics of health care concepts described by (Kalra, Beale, & Heard, 2005) provides an important precursor to facilitate the application of Big Data analytics for RPM data. The use of openEHR has the potential to ensure data is correctly interpreted in analytics exercises and facilitate diverse stakeholder priorities and views. The next section in this chapter outlines the background literature, describes RPM research and provides an overview of the openEHR standard. Following that, the way in which openEHR can facilitate RPM Big Data analytics is described.

BACKGROUND

In general, an application system consists of a group of related application programs designed to perform certain functions. The RPM is an application system made up of two related applications, the healthcare application (HA) and the body area wireless sensor network (BAWSN), the monitoring application component. A BAWSN consists of a number of wireless sensors located on or in close proximity to the human body, such as on the clothing. The low-power sensors, such as medical sensors, wearable sensors, mobile sensors and fixed sensors, depending on the disease or needs of those aged and other patients, are equipped with a wireless interface and are capable of sensing the required intrinsic health data of that person over an extended period of time. In addition, these sensors can transmit the data to a monitoring application in a Local Processing Unit (LPU), generally a smartphone, for pre-processing. The distinct functions of a BAWSN are to authenticate the patient for continuous monitoring, to sense the vital health data from the patient, to pre-process the health data of the patient for sending any alert messages in the case of an emergency and to send the pre-processed data to the HA for further medical diagnoses. The HA is a sophisticated application assisting the doctors/care staff to monitor the patients' health condition and consult with the patient 'on the fly', regardless of where they are located. It is evident from early work by (Soini, Nummela, Oksa, Ukkonen, & Sydänheimo, 2008; Van Halteren et al., 2004; Van Laerhoven et al., 2004; Venkatasubramanian et al., 2005), the HA depends heavily on its monitoring component, the BAWSN, for the continuous generation of the health data. One of the pioneer RPM applications by (Balasubramanian et al., 2008), Active Care Loop Framework consist of Assistive Maternity Care application and a BAWSN capable of continuously monitor the Blood Pressure of a pregnant women and raise alarms using an SMS gateway is shown in Figure 1.

Figure 1. Active care loop framework for monitoring pregnant women

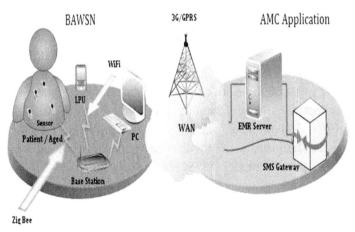

Although the BAWSN achieves the critical function of gathering trustworthy health data from the patient, the HA provides the visualisation of the patients' progress to the doctor and can have many functionalities. Examples are maintaining the electronic health records (EHR) in the database, alerting the concerned clinicians about the condition of the patients, the ability to provide a common ground for the patients and the care staff to discuss their needs in detail and in private; it can have an intelligent algorithm to predict any forthcoming emergency.

The general functionalities mentioned above are under the perspective of the user of this application. However, from the application developers' perspective, the specific implementation of these functionalities differs considerably depending on the health care requirements. For instance, the design of the electronic health records differs considerably for patients who are suffering from lymphoma and heart disease, and for those with other functionalities associated with an intelligent algorithm to predict any situation(Balasubramanian Appiah, 2012).

Therefore, the development of electronic health records requires a very high level of interoperability between diverse computer systems and extensive use of standards (Sitton & Reich, 2016). Government led electronic health record systems development tends to be enormously expensive and few countries have successfully implemented EHR systems despite the promise of potential efficiency gains and healthcare improvements that arise from access to so much data (Séroussi & Bouaud, 2016)(Garavand, Samadbeik, Kafashi, & Abhari, 2016). (Allen-Graham et al., 2018) outline the benefits and deficiencies of an electronic health record system introduced by the Australian government for a cost of well over $AUD 1 billion.

The standards essential for electronic health records include Open Systems Interconnection (OSI) network communication standards, messaging standards such as HL7 (Schloeffel, Beale, Hayworth, Heard, & Leslie, 2006) and medical vocabulary standards such as SNOMET-CT ((IHTSDO), 2018). Each standard maintained and kept up to date by worldwide communities engaging thousands of contributors. A great deal of importance on the benefits of having standardized terminologies for data mining exercises some years ago was emphasized by (Ramakrishnan, Hanauer, & Keller, 2010), when SNOMED-CT and Big Data were in their infancy. However, perhaps contrary to early expectations, the emergence of SNOMED-CT has not automatically facilitated Big Data analytics (BDa) (Benson & Grieve, 2016).

Reasons for this include the observation that coding of conditions, events, and test results to the appropriate SNOMED-CT code requires expertise and, in practice is often not done precisely or consistently, resulting in ambiguous data. For example: a variable "systolic blood pressure" may appear in a dataset with no indication of whether this refers to inter-arterial blood pressure measured with an intravenous device or the more common, around the cuff blood pressure. Relating blood pressures measures over time for the same patient is likely to result in very misleading analyses if the different kinds of blood pressure measures are confused. In addition, as (Matney et al., 2017) found, physiological variables used by diverse providers needed to be manually mapped to SNOMED-CT concepts in order to create a minimum data set of variables that could be used for data mining exercises. The concept of "patient height" may appear to be terminologically unique and well defined as the distance between the top of the head and the bottom of the feet, however this concept is inappropriate if the patient cannot stand straight or is an infant. Height data collected inappropriately is likely to hamper analytics exercises. Issues related to understanding the data is recognized as critical for BDa or Data mining exercise and is a key phase of the CRISP-DM reference model used to guide the execution of Data Mining exercises (SmartVision, Accessed 2017).

The CRISP-DM standard sets out six phases illustrated in *Figure 2*.

Figure 2. The CRISP-DM process model (adapted from (Chapman et al., 2000)

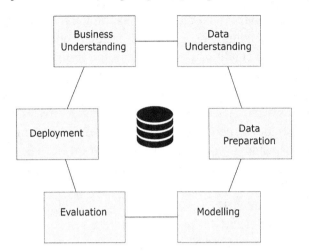

The first CRSIP-DM phase, *business understanding* focuses on understanding organizational objectives and identifying a data mining problem that is in alignment with the business objectives. The outcome is a preliminary plan designed to achieve project objectives. The next phase is the *data understanding* phase which provides understanding of the data that needs to be analysed. In the understanding phase, the data mining expert becomes familiar with the meaning and quality of the data. Following that phase, data needs to be prepared for modelling. The *data preparation* phase includes deciding what needs to be included in the dataset, cleaning the data and all other activities that need to be done to process the data, which serves as an input to the modelling step. In the *modelling* phase, a classification, prediction, association or clustering technique is applied on the data set and a model is generated. In the evaluation phase, the model is evaluated and results are analysed in relation to the business success criterion. If the model and the results are not in alignment with the organisational objectives, a new cycle of CRISP-DM is initiated otherwise, the model is deployed.

CRISP-DM has limited applicability for remote patient monitoring data because the temporal nature of RPM data requires additional abstraction as noted in (Catley et al., 2009). A patient's blood pressure measured continuously every 20 minutes over 24 hours may fluctuate between 140/70 mmHg and 110/90 mmHg for a particular patient. This level of fluctuation is not usually clinically significant so can be abstracted to a label like "Normal blood pressure". Conversely, a sudden drop in blood pressure from 150/80 mmHg to 90/60 mmHg in minutes warrants concern even if both measures are not clinically concerning in their own right.

Another limitation inherent in the CRISP-DM approach was raised in (Sharma et al., 2017). In their case study of a data analytics exercise in a hospital setting, they report that every aspect of the exercise required decisions and collaboration amongst groups of stakeholders within the organization. However, the way in which groups reason toward making decisions in an analytics exercise is not described or prescribed in the CRISP-DM process. This is paradoxical because major decisions including the specification of business objectives, the selection of a problem to focus on, the identification of relevant variables, and the ultimate interpretation of Big Data Analysis findings are rarely made by a single decision maker but involve a complex interplay between and within staff at operational, management and executive levels.

This chapter outlines challenges for Big Data Analytics that specifically arise in the presence of Remote Patient Monitoring data. *Table 1* provides an outline of the main challenge which are elaborated on in subsequent sections. A key feature of the chapter involves the assertion that many Big Data challenges inherent in remote patient monitoring can be reduced with the use of standards. The openEHR standard outlined in the next section, is sufficiently expressive for this.

Table 1. Overview of big data analysis challenges for remote patient monitoring

Phenomena	Challenge
The interpretation of Big Data Analyses in health requires input from many individuals across multiple disciplines	Decision making techniques designed to support groups to reach decisions are rarely used to facilitate consensus between stakeholders interpreting Big Data Analytics exercises in healthcare
The extent to which Big Data Analyses realise business objectives is a recommended evaluation criteria by CRISP-DM, however this is not an effective criteria to evaluate BDA using RPM data.	The challenge is to discover criteria for the evaluation of BDA exercises on RPM data that do not rely on abstract statements of business objectives.
BDA is difficult to perform live on RPM because few analytics algorithms can operate on streams of data in real time	The challenge is to discover analytics algorithms that can operate quickly on partial data, then revise analyses as new data streams in.
RPM data cannot easily be integrated into electronic health records.	The challenge is for RPM developers and EHR developers to use common standards to encode meta-data that will facilitate inter-operability of health information.
Existing standards for inter-operability of health data including HL7 are not well suited to encoding meta-data from RPM datasets.	The challenge is to adapt the openEHR standard so that RPM data can be readily encoded. The openEHR standard requires minor modification to existing archetypes compared with HL7 which would need major adjustments.
The meaning of each variable in an RPM exercise is often difficult to ascertain	The challenge is to collect meta-data that describes each variable with sufficient detail to enable Analysts to correctly interpret RPM data.

Outline of openEHR

The demands of interoperability between health care provider computer systems has driven the development of standards in addition to OSI network standards. The openEHR standard (Kalra et al., 2005) (www.openehr.org) was proposed over a decade ago as an attempt to model the pragmatics of health care knowledge. This was considered to be critical for the design of electronic health records systems and the achievement of the interoperability required.

The archetype is a core primitive in the openEHR standard. An archetype models a concept in use within health care with the following elements: concept name, description, purpose, use and misuse. For example, the archetype named "Blood pressure" listed in the openEHR clinical knowledge base (http://openehr.org/ckm/) is linked to SNOMED-CT Concept 16307200007. In the "Blood pressure" openEHR archetype, the blood pressure concept is described as the local measurement of arterial pressure as a surrogate for pressure in systemic circulation. The purpose of the concept is to record an individual's blood pressure. The appropriate use and misuse are listed. For instance, the concept is not to be used to refer to intravenous blood pressure. The openEHR archetype for "Blood pressure" also includes a description of the data associated with the measurement of blood pressure. This includes definitions and units of measure for systolic, diastolic, mean arterial pressure and pulse pressure. The state of the individual when the "Blood pressure" is measures is also specified in the archetype; for instance the assumed position is sitting but "Blood pressure" can also be taken standing or reclining. Descriptors relevant for a protocol for the measure of "Blood pressure" including cuff size, location on the body, various formulas and the type of device used are also specified in the archetype. Version 1.1.1 of the "Blood pressure" archetype was attributed to an originator, Sam Heard in 2006 (openEHR, 2018). A community comprised of over 30 contributors whose names are listed in the archetype is also included.

In the next section of this chapter, the way in which the openEHR standard can facilitate data analytics with Big Data that derives from remote patient monitoring will be outlined. The approach accommodates the group reasoning amongst diverse stakeholders inherent in most data mining exercises despite not being made explicit in the CRSIP-DM process model. The innovations will be described with reference to a case study involving remote monitoring of vital signs amongst patients in an Indian Hospital.

OPENEHR FOR RPM ANALYTICS

RPM Trial

An architecture was designed and implemented by (Balasubramanian & Stranieri, 2014) that enables the transmission of patient data to Cloud-based repositories, as shown in Figure 3, where software services invoked by health care providers can be instantiated, executed and terminated readily to securely and efficiently process all or part of a patient's data collected continuously with wearable sensors. The prototype of the architecture was trialed in a Medical College Hospital, Coimbatore, India in 2016. Consenting patients in a general medical ward at the hospital were fitted with wearable sensors capable of monitoring ECG, blood pressure, temperature, respiratory rate and heart rate. The sensors were con-

Figure 3. Architecture Design for Assistive Patient monitoring cloud Platform for active healthcare Applications (AppA)

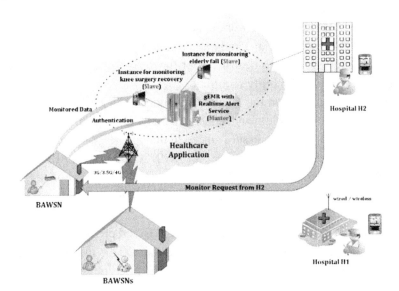

figured to continuously transmit data to a nearby Android Tablet running prototype software developed by (Balasubramanian & Stranieri, 2014).

Twelve patients were selected to participate in the trial over a three-week period. The data was streamed by room and bed number only so that the patient privacy was maintained. Nurses who volunteered for the trial were trained to recharge sensors, locate them on the patients, and check that data transmission had commenced. *Table 2* illustrates sample raw data for blood oxygen (SPO2), diastolic blood pressure (DiaPress), systolic blood pressure (SysPress), pulse rate and respiratory rate. *Table 1* presents data collected from one patient for 27 seconds during the trial. A "0" was entered into the array between sensed episodes. The device did not broadcast any meta-data so the units of measurement for each variable were only understood from the manufacturer's technical manuals. A value for the body temperature seemed to be included in every second's transmission except when the SPO2 and pulse was recorded.

During the trial, the nurses had to remove the sensors an average of two times per day per patient, to help the patient to use the restroom or to have lunch. States such as active, paused, disconnected, are not identified in a standard way and rarely captured in RPM devices but become very important for RPM Analytics exercises.

The transfer of data from the tablet to the cloud server used a TCP/IP connection with the total payload of 26 Bytes, the TCP packet sent every second from a sensor will be less than 100 Bytes which includes the maximum TCP header size of 60 Bytes. Therefore, the total amount of data produced for one patient will not be more than 300 Megabytes every month. However, one hundred patients monitored in this way generates 360 Gbytes of data per year. The vast majority of this data is not of direct clinical interest for treating physicians, however once collected in digital form, health record legislation in most jurisdictions mandate that digital health data be stored and only deleted following onerous procedures. Most hospital information systems are not designed to store RPM data so storage must be done outside these systems with safeguards in place to ensure privacy and security.

The data was processed in real time by software executing on the Tablet and in the Cloud to raise SMS alarms to nurses and doctors mobile phones during the trial. Data regarding the status of the messages was not captured for the trial however this can be regarded as useful data for future data analysis exercises as discussed further below. Data relating to remote physician login such as the login duration, delays, and outcomes was not collected but can also be expected to be useful for future analyses.

The Trial illustrated that remote and continuous patient monitoring can be seen as technology that has recently arisen that enables a great deal of data to be generated continuously. However, as RPM continues to be adopted by healthcare systems, problems for data analytics exercises can be expected to emerge that dramatically reduce the utility of the data. Two challenges include:

- **Meta-Data:** Describing the data generated, on the fly, that includes units of measure needs to be associated with each bucket of data collected. For interoperability with other systems such as hospital information systems, the meta-data needs to be expressed using the openEHR standard though some extensions are required to accommodate RPM.
- **Real Time Analytics:** The incremental acquisition of data from real time sensors raises the possibility of real time analytics. Automated raising of alarms is an obvious application of real time analytics for RPM.

Table 2. Sample data for 27 seconds RPM

SPO2	SysPress	DiaPress	PulseRate	RespRate	Temp1	SensorId	PatientId	CreatedDate
0	0	0	0	0	37.1	5	4	17/10/2016 4:22
0	0	0	0	0	37.1	5	4	17/10/2016 4:22
0	0	0	0	0	37.1	5	4	17/10/2016 4:22
95	0	0	80	0	37.1	5	4	17/10/2016 4:22
0	0	0	0	0	37.1	5	4	17/10/2016 4:22
0	0	0	0	0	37.1	5	4	17/10/2016 4:22
0	0	0	0	0	37.1	5	4	17/10/2016 4:22
0	0	0	0	0	37.1	5	4	17/10/2016 4:22
0	0	0	0	0	37.1	5	4	17/10/2016 4:22
0	0	0	0	0	37.1	5	4	17/10/2016 4:22
0	0	0	0	0	37.1	5	4	17/10/2016 4:22
0	0	0	0	0	37.1	5	4	17/10/2016 4:22
0	0	0	0	0	37.1	5	4	17/10/2016 4:22
95	0	0	81	0	0	5	4	17/10/2016 4:22
0	0	0	0	0	37.0	5	4	17/10/2016 4:22
0	0	0	0	0	37.0	5	4	17/10/2016 4:22
0	0	0	0	0	37.0	5	4	17/10/2016 4:22
0	0	0	0	0	37.0	5	4	17/10/2016 4:22
0	0	0	0	0	37.0	5	4	17/10/2016 4:22
0	0	0	0	0	37.0	5	4	17/10/2016 4:22
0	0	0	0	0	37.0	5	4	17/10/2016 4:22
0	0	0	0	0	37.0	5	4	17/10/2016 4:22
95	0	0	81	0	0	5	4	17/10/2016 4:22
0	0	0	0	0	37.1	5	4	17/10/2016 4:22
0	0	0	0	0	37.1	5	4	17/10/2016 4:22
0	0	0	0	0	37.1	5	4	17/10/2016 4:22
0	140	90	0	0	37.1	5	4	17/10/2016 4:22

SOLUTIONS AND RECOMMENDATIONS

Meta-Data

The sample data illustrated in *Table 2* can be imagined to be useful for real time processing to raise alarms that the patient is deteriorating. If the vitals signs are not alarming, the data does not need to be stored beyond its collection. Indeed, the vast majority of static patient monitoring devices currently in use in hospitals do not store data after its collection and simply provide an optional print out facility. However, RPM data is collected digitally so there is a legislative requirement in most jurisdictions to store the data

(Swire, 2013). For instance, the Health Records Act in Victoria, Australia prescribes detailed processes for the archiving of health records and deletion is only permissible to correct errors.

The storage of RPM data such as that in *Table 2* can be seen to be of use for future, off-line analytics purposes in addition to real time purposes. For example, associations between features can be used for predictions, particularly if linked with other data. Lee et al (2010) present an example of the potential that data mining can bring to monitoring by integrating environmental data including weather information with patient bio-data to predict an asthma attack. Data such as that presented in *Table 2* can be linked to medication and demographic information about patients across multiple hospitals for outcomes such as the early detection of adverse reactions to medications. If the data was linked to staffing data in hospital information systems, a raft of analyses to do with workplace efficiencies can be readily imagined.

Linking data collected at different times and places across diverse repositories becomes extremely labor intensive unless meta-data describing the data collected is included with the data. Without the meta-data, the "Understanding Data" phase in the CRISP-DM process involves discovering what each feature is, the unit of measure, the collection method and many more meta-data concepts. This kind of exercise with RPM data cannot be imagined to be successfully performed by data analysts without clinical knowledge. For example, in *Table 2* the temperature occasionally drops from 37.1 degrees to 0 degrees for a second then returns to 37.0 degrees. Clinical knowledge is required to understand that this is not a real drop in body temperature but an indication that the temperature was not sensed at that instance. Similarly, clinical knowledge is required to know that the temperature feature may refer to surface temperature, core temperature, temperature at extremities or other commonly used temperature measures and that each measure of temperature ought not be confused with other measures.

Meta-data stored with the RPM data enables the "Understanding Data" phase to be performed far more easily. However, this is likely to be the case only to the extent that the Meta-data conforms to a common standard. The contention advanced here is that the openEHR standard is sufficiently expressive to capture the semantics and pragmatics of RPM data with some expansion. An archetype currently exists for each feature listed in *Table 2* such as the blood pressure archetype described above. That archetype clearly distinguishes between systolic and diastolic blood pressure and defines units of measure. An archetype can be used as a rich template whenever RPM data is initialized for storage to enable clear and comparable descriptions of the data later when RPM Analytics exercises are performed.

Additional fields that are required for RPM include the status of the monitoring (e.g. active, off, paused), the status and history of the remote access, and feature based interpretation (e.g. 0 means no data is sensed). (Robles-Bykbaev, Quisi-Peralta, López-Nores, Gil-Solla, & García-Duque, 2016) demonstrate that meta-data expressed as openEHR archetypes can lead to a great deal of automation in the development of decision support system knowledge bases from data mining.

Real Time Analytics

Data streams pose unique space and time constraints on the computation process (Aggarwal & Philip, 2007). Unlike conventional data mining, stream mining approaches must occur in real time, which challenges computational processing efficiency. Further, most machine learning algorithms have been developed assuming all data is available to the algorithm. (Sanila, Subramanian, & Sathyalakshmi, 2018) reviews real time mining techniques to reveal the adaptation of algorithms for use when data streams incrementally in, is a pressing research problem. One approach to deal with this involves data summarisation where data is typically segmented into windows and reduced using filters. For instance,

(Allami, Stranieri, Balasubramanian, & Jelinek, 2016) presents a low computational resource algorithm for reducing ECG data without losing key data points critical for diagnoses. Another approach involves incrementing subsequence counts (Abadia, Stranieri, Quinn, & Seifollahi, 2011) as each new data streams in. Sub-sequence counts can be directly used in classification algorithms advanced by (Quinn, Stranieri, Yearwood, Hafen, & Jelinek, 2008). Frequency counts profiles of interbeat heart rate variability has been shown by (Allami, Stranieri, Balasubramanian, & Jelinek, 2017) to predict future heart rate variability and some heart conditions.

Real time analytics with data streams is enhanced when it is linked with other data. The data stream exemplified in *Table 2* can be enhanced with links to the patient's conditions, medication, demographic or other relevant data. However, accessing static data stored in other repositories during a real time analysis of the stream presents severe computational complexity challenges. Setting up processes to perform analyses that link stream data with static data requires a great deal of labor intensive work and challenges in the "Understanding Data" phase as alluded to above.

Analytics with Big Data in practice requires that many decisions in the analytics process be made by a group of stakeholders who often have competing priorities. This is particularly the case in the business understanding, data understanding and evaluation phases of a CRISP-DM process. The pilot study (Sharma et al., 2017) revealed three main categories of decisions that were made by groups in a hospital data mining exercise; decisions about what problem to focus on, how to interpret data, and how to resource the data mining exercise.

Decision made by groups involve characteristics that render the decision making process quite different than decisions made by individuals. A group, deliberating toward a decision has been called a Reasoning Community by (Yearwood & Stranieri, 2010) who advance a process for ensuring that some of the deficiencies of group reasoning including groupthink (Janis, 1972), shared information bias (Wittenbaum, 2000) and argument fallacies are contained. A Reasoning Community refers to any group of participants that reason individually, communicate with each other, and attempt to coalesce their reasoning in order to reason collectively to perform an action or solve a problem. Reasoning communities are viewed as broader and more encompassing than communities of practice(Lave & Wenger, 1998).

The process for ideal deliberation advanced by (Yearwood & Stranieri, 2010) includes tasks to be performed in four key phases illustrated in *Figure 4* and include: Engagement, Individual reasoning, Coalesced Reasoning and Decision making described below.

Figure 4. Group reasoning in the CRISP-DM process

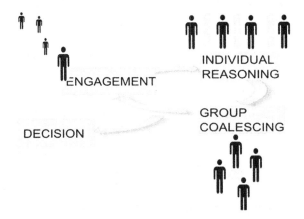

The Engagement phase for an RPM Analytics exercise involves the selection and recruitment of the people who participate in the decision making process. An RPM Analytics process can be expected to involve clinicians along with data analysts but may also require Internet of Things (IOT) experts. This phase also involves the articulation of the issue to be resolved. RPM Analytics is new and emerging, so articulating the issue that could be resolved except at a very high and abstract level such as "increase efficiency" may be difficult.

In the individual reasoning phase of a Reasoning Community process, each participant establishes facts, makes inferences from facts to draw conclusions and, by so doing contributes reasons to a pool of reasons for the community. A key part of individual reasoning involves an individual's coalescing of reasoning. This is the process of juxtaposing background knowledge with reasons advanced by other participants in order to understand the issue and position his or her claims amidst the others. A participant's coalescing of reasoning involves making sense of reasons in order to assert their own claims or to understand the claims of others. Following the Reasoning Community model, each participant of an RPM Analytics process will initially analyse the data independently from others. Initially, there is no interaction or exchange of thoughts/ideas between the group members in order to avoid negative consequences of group interactions such as groupthink (Janis, 1972).

Group coalescing of reasoning involves organizing the analyses advanced by each participant into an explicit, coherent representation. This is important for shared and democratic decision-making where decisions are made on the basis of reasoned debate. Further, group coalescing enables communities in the future to adopt coalesced reasoning as a starting point for their own deliberations in what Stranieri and Yearwood (Stranieri & Yearwood, 2012) call re-use of reasoning. Most analytics exercises perform individual reasoning but do not systematically perform group coalescing.

Finally, the decision making phase of a Reasoning Community depicts the stage when participants must decide on an ultimate interpretation from the RPM Analyses. Many patterns noticed in an analytics exercise are deemed to be spurious or uninteresting. Conclusions that are reached as a result of the RPM Analytics are typically determined to be worthwhile by the entire team including clinicians, data analyst and management.

The recognition that any Analytics exercise is not performed in isolation by an analyst but occurs in a socio-political context where a group of interacting individuals performs at each phase of the CRISP-DM process. RPM Analytics exercises, currently in their infancy, are likely to require a more diverse group of stakeholders that each initially arrive at diverse conclusions that must be assimilated into an agreed analytics outcome.

FUTURE RESEARCH DIRECTIONS

Future research is required to explore how RPM endeavors are actually established and conducted as their prevalence emerges. Work is also required to validate the difficulties inherent in the use of the openEHR standard to specify meta-data needs of RPM data.

CONCLUSION

Remote patient monitoring systems collect data from patients, typically with wearable sensors, and transfer the data to servers so that health care professionals can remotely log in to view the data in real time. Although these systems are emerging, to date little attention has been placed on the challenges inherent in analyzing data collected from remote patient monitoring systems. In this chapter, the openEHR standard was presented as an important standard for specifying the variables and context for the data collected so that data collected from diverse RPM systems or at different times can be more readily compared and analysed. The view that *openEHR* can be used to describe meta-data inherent in collecting RPM data. The chapter also advanced the notion that RPM analytics exercises, like any analytics process is not performed by an analyst in isolation but involves a group of stakeholders who have diverse interests, expertise and background. Real time analytics is challenging because data streams need to be analysed in real time and ideally linked with static data stored in electronic health records. Analyses reached by individuals need to be validated and confirmed by stakeholders for analyses to be accepted. Remote patient monitoring in a Big Data era has the potential to add another dimension to health care, however many technical, organizational and clinical challenges need to be addressed before useful outcomes of analyses emerge.

ACKNOWLEDGMENT

This research received no specific grant from any funding agency in the public, commercial, or not-for-profit sectors.

REFERENCES

Abadia, R., Stranieri, A., Quinn, A., & Seifollahi, S. (2011). Real time processing of data from patient biodevices. *Proceedings of the Fourth Australasian Workshop on Health Informatics and Knowledge Management-Volume 120.*

Aggarwal, C. C., & Philip, S. Y. (2007). *A survey of synopsis construction in data streams. In Data Streams* (pp. 169–207). Springer.

Allami, R., Stranieri, A., Balasubramanian, V., & Jelinek, H. F. (2016). *ECG Reduction for Wearable Sensor.* Paper presented at the Signal-Image Technology & Internet-Based Systems (SITIS), 2016 12th International Conference on. 10.1109/SITIS.2016.88

Allami, R., Stranieri, A., Balasubramanian, V., & Jelinek, H. F. (2017). A count data model for heart rate variability forecasting and premature ventricular contraction detection. *Signal, Image and Video Processing*, 1–9.

Balasubramanian, V., Hoang, D. B., & Ahmad, N. (2008). *SOAP based Assistive Care Loop using wireless sensor networks.* Paper presented at the IT in Medicine and Education, 2008. ITME 2008. IEEE International Symposium on. 10.1109/ITME.2008.4743897

Balasubramanian, V., & Stranieri, A. (2014). *A scalable cloud Platform for Active healthcare monitoring applications*. Paper presented at the e-Learning, e-Management and e-Services (IC3e), 2014 IEEE Conference on. 10.1109/IC3e.2014.7081248

Balasubramanian, V., Stranieri, A., & Kaur, R. (2015). AppA: assistive patient monitoring cloud platform for active healthcare applications. *Proceedings of the 9th International Conference on Ubiquitous Information Management and Communication*. 10.1145/2701126.2701224

Balasubramanian Appiah, V. (2012). *Dependability of body area wireless sensor networks in assistive care loop framework (PhD)*. University Technology Sydney.

Breen, S., Kofoed, S., Ritchie, D., Dryden, T., Maguire, R., Kearney, N., & Aranda, S. (2017). Remote real-time monitoring for chemotherapy side-effects in patients with blood cancers. *Collegian (Royal College of Nursing, Australia)*, *24*(6), 541–549. doi:10.1016/j.colegn.2016.10.009

Brown, S. M., Jones, J., Kuttler, K. G., Keddington, R. K., Allen, T. L., & Haug, P. (2016). Prospective evaluation of an automated method to identify patients with severe sepsis or septic shock in the emergency department. *BMC Emergency Medicine*, *16*(1), 31. doi:10.118612873-016-0095-0 PMID:27549755

Carta, M., & Angst, J. (2016). Screening for bipolar disorders: A public health issue. *Journal of Affective Disorders*, *205*, 139–143. doi:10.1016/j.jad.2016.03.072 PMID:27442457

Catley, C., Smith, K., McGregor, C., & Tracy, M. (2009). *Extending CRISP-DM to incorporate temporal data mining of multidimensional medical data streams: A neonatal intensive care unit case study*. Paper presented at the Computer-Based Medical Systems, 2009. CBMS 2009. 22nd IEEE International Symposium on. 10.1109/CBMS.2009.5255394

Chan, M., Estève, D., Fourniols, J.-Y., Escriba, C., & Campo, E. (2012). Smart wearable systems: Current status and future challenges. *Artificial Intelligence in Medicine*, *56*(3), 137–156. doi:10.1016/j.artmed.2012.09.003 PMID:23122689

Chapman, P., Clinton, J., Kerber, R., Khabaza, T., Reinartz, T., Shearer, C., & Wirth, R. (2000). *CRISP-DM 1.0 Step-by-step data mining guide*. Academic Press.

IHTSDO. (2018). *SNOMED-CT*. Retrieved from https://www.snomed.org

Janis, I. L. (1972). *Victims of groupthink: a psychological study of foreign-policy decisions and fiascoes*. Academic Press.

Kakria, P., Tripathi, N., & Kitipawang, P. (2015). A real-time health monitoring system for remote cardiac patients using smartphone and wearable sensors. *International Journal of Telemedicine and Applications*, *2015*, 8. doi:10.1155/2015/373474 PMID:26788055

Kalid, N., Zaidan, A. A., Zaidan, B. B., Salman, O. H., Hashim, M., & Muzammil, H. (2018). Based Real Time Remote Health Monitoring Systems: A Review on Patients Prioritization and Related "Big Data" Using Body Sensors information and Communication Technology. *Journal of Medical Systems*, *42*(2), 30. doi:10.100710916-017-0883-4 PMID:29288419

Kalra, D., Beale, T., & Heard, S. (2005). The openEHR foundation. *Studies in Health Technology and Informatics*, *115*, 153–173. PMID:16160223

Klonoff, D. C., Ahn, D., & Drincic, A. (2017). Continuous glucose monitoring: A review of the technology and clinical use. *Diabetes Research and Clinical Practice, 133*, 178–192. doi:10.1016/j.diabres.2017.08.005 PMID:28965029

Lave, J., & Wenger, E. (1998). *Communities of practice*. Academic Press.

Matney, S. A., Settergren, T., Carrington, J. M., Richesson, R. L., Sheide, A., & Westra, B. L. (2017). Standardizing Physiologic Assessment Data to Enable Big Data Analytics. *Western Journal of Nursing Research, 39*(1), 63–77. doi:10.1177/0193945916659471 PMID:27435084

Mikalef, P., Pappas, I. O., Krogstie, J., & Giannakos, M. (2017). Big data analytics capabilities: A systematic literature review and research agenda. *Information Systems and e-Business Management*, 1–32. doi:10.100710257-017-0362-y

openEHR. (2018). *Clinical Knowledge Manager*. Retrieved from http://openehr.org/ckm/

Quinn, A., Stranieri, A., Yearwood, J., Hafen, G., & Jelinek, H. F. (2008). AWSum-Combining Classification with Knowledge Aquisition. *Int. J. Software and Informatics, 2*(2), 199–214.

Robles-Bykbaev, V., Quisi-Peralta, D., López-Nores, M., Gil-Solla, A., & García-Duque, J. (2016). *SPELTA-Miner: An expert system based on data mining and multilabel classification to design therapy plans for communication disorders*. Paper presented at the Control, Decision and Information Technologies (CoDIT), 2016 International Conference on.

Sanila, S., Subramanian, D. V., & Sathyalakshmi, S. (2018). Real-Time Mining Techniques: A Big Data Perspective for a Smart Future. *Indian Journal of Science and Technology, 10*(42), 1–7. doi:10.17485/ijst/2017/v10i42/120344

Schloeffel, P., Beale, T., Hayworth, G., Heard, S., & Leslie, H. (2006). The relationship between CEN 13606, HL7, and openEHR. *HIC 2006 and HINZ 2006: Proceedings, 24*.

Sharma, V., Stranieri, A., Ugon, J., Vamplew, P., & Martin, L. (2017). An Agile Group Aware Process beyond CRISP-DM: A Hospital Data Mining Case Study. *Proceedings of the International Conference on Compute and Data Analysis*. 10.1145/3093241.3093273

Shearer, C. (2000). The CRISP-DM model: The new blueprint for data mining. *Journal of Data Warehousing, 5*(4), 13–22.

Shimmer. (2018). Retrieved from http://www.shimmersensing.com/products/shimmer3-ecg-sensor#specifications-tab

Sitton, M., & Reich, Y. (2016). Enterprise Systems Engineering for Better Operational Interoperability. *Systems Engineering*.

SmartVision. (n.d.). *CRSP-DM*. Retrieved from http://crisp-dm.eu

Soini, M., Nummela, J., Oksa, P., Ukkonen, L., & Sydänheimo, L. (2008). Wireless body area network for hip rehabilitation system. *Ubiquitous Computing and Communication Journal, 3*(5), 42–48.

Stranieri, A., & Yearwood, J. (2012). The Case for a Re-Use of Community Reasoning. In J. Yearwood & A. Stranieri (Eds.), *Approaches for Community Decision Making and Collective Reasoning* (pp. 237–249). IGI Global.

Swire, P. (2013). Finding the best of the imperfect alternatives for privacy, health it, and cybersecurity. *Wisconsin Law Review*, (2): 649–669.

Thilo, F. J., Hürlimann, B., Hahn, S., Bilger, S., Schols, J. M., & Halfens, R. J. (2016). Involvement of older people in the development of fall detection systems: A scoping review. *BMC Geriatrics*, *16*(1), 42. doi:10.118612877-016-0216-3 PMID:26869259

Van Halteren, A., Bults, R., Wac, K., Konstantas, D., Widya, I., Dokovsky, N., ... Herzog, R. (2004). Mobile patient monitoring: The mobihealth system. *The Journal on Information Technology in Healthcare*, *2*(5), 365–373.

Van Laerhoven, K., Lo, B. P., Ng, J. W., Thiemjarus, S., King, R., Kwan, S., ... Needham, P. (2004). Medical healthcare monitoring with wearable and implantable sensors. *Proc. of the 3rd International Workshop on Ubiquitous Computing for Healthcare Applications.*

Venkatasubramanian, K., Deng, G., Mukherjee, T., Quintero, J., Annamalai, V., & Gupta, S. K. (2005). Ayushman: A wireless sensor network based health monitoring infrastructure and testbed. *Proceedings of the First IEEE international conference on Distributed Computing in Sensor Systems.* 10.1007/11502593_39

Wang, Y., Kung, L., & Byrd, T. A. (2018). Big data analytics: Understanding its capabilities and potential benefits for healthcare organizations. *Technological Forecasting and Social Change*, *126*, 3–13. doi:10.1016/j.techfore.2015.12.019

Wittenbaum, G. M. (2000). The bias toward discussing shared information: Why are high-status group members immune. *Communication Research*, *27*(3), 379–401. doi:10.1177/009365000027003005

Yearwood, J., & Stranieri, A. (2010). *Technologies for Supporting Reasoning Communities and Collaborative Decision Making: Cooperative Approaches: Cooperative Approaches*. IGI Global.

Zhu, Z., Barnette, R. K., Fussell, K. M., Michael Rodriguez, R., Canonico, A., & Light, R. W. (2005). Continuous oxygen monitoring—A better way to prescribe long-term oxygen therapy. *Respiratory Medicine*, *99*(11), 1386–1392. doi:10.1016/j.rmed.2005.03.010 PMID:15878655

ADDITIONAL READING

Stranieri, A., & Yearwood, J. (2012). The Case for a Re-Use of Community Reasoning. In J. Yearwood & A. Stranieri (Eds.), *Approaches for Community Decision Making and Collective Reasoning* (pp. 237–249). IGI Global Press.

KEY TERMS AND DEFINITIONS

CRISP-DM: A process model for performing data mining exercises.

Electronic Health Record: A virtual record of major health related events for an individual from before birth to after death.

openEHR: A standard that describes clinical concepts and their use.

Reasoning Community: A model of how individuals reason together to solve a problem. This model can be applied to describe how analysts and other stakeholders interact to analyze data from remote patient monitoring systems.

Remote Patient Monitoring: Monitoring patients physiological signs. This is typically performed with wearable, implantable or digestible sensors but may be done at a distance with camera surveillance.

Chapter 51
ANT Perspective of Healthcare Big Data for Service Delivery in South Africa

Tiko Iyamu
https://orcid.org/0000-0002-4949-094X
Cape Peninsula University of Technology, Cape Town, South Africa

Sibulela Mgudlwa
Cape Peninsula University of Technology, South Africa

ABSTRACT

In South Africa, there has been for many years challenges in how healthcare big data are accessed, used, and managed by facilities, particularly the small health facilities. The challenges arise from inaccuracy and inconsistency of patients' data and have impact on diagnoses, medications, and treatments, which consequently contributes to fatalities in South Africa, particularly in the rural areas of the country. The problem of inaccuracy and inconsistency of patients' data is often caused by lack of or poor analysis (or analytics) of data. Thus, the objective of this research was to understand the factors that influence the use and management of patients' big data for healthcare service delivery. The qualitative methods were applied, and a South African healthcare facility was used as a case in the study. Actor network theory (ANT) was employed as a lens to guide the analysis of the qualitative data. Based on the findings from the analysis, a model was developed, which is intended to guide analytics of big data for healthcare purposes, towards improving service delivery in the country.

1. INTRODUCTION

Due to the essentiality of healthcare, delivery of quality service is always crucial (Cresswell, Worth & Sheikh, 2010). However, there have been many cases of wrong diagnosis and prescribed medications by health facilities in many countries, including South Africa (Lewandowski et al., 2017; Fico et al., 2016). The problems are linked to many factors including analysis of patients' big data (Sacristán & Dilla, 2015).

DOI: 10.4018/978-1-6684-3662-2.ch051

From a healthcare standpoint, the characteristics of big data are volume, variety, and velocity (Priyanka & Kulennavar, 2014). The unprecedented types, speed, and sources of patients' big data do sometimes create challenges and limitations in its accessibility, quality, use, and management in providing and receiving healthcare services (Ganjir, Sarkar & Kumar, 2016; Nativi et al., 2015).

Big data that are for specific purpose and usefulness require harnessing its capabilities, from both technological and human standpoints. Thus, analytics tools are needed to analyse diverse big data types, at velocity, and real-time (Priyanka & Kulennavar, 2014). However, big data analytics can be a disruptive phenomenon, from privacy and standardisation perspectives (Bello-Orgaz, Jung & Camacho, 2016). This is attributed to largeness and complexity of big data, which analytics tools have so far found difficult to address at socio-technical levels (Ularu et al., 2012). In South Africa, this has been a serious challenge for many health facilities (Ruxwana, Herselman & Conradie, 2010).

There have been gaps in patients' data which impedes progress in the South Africa healthcare environment (Coovadia et al., 2009). Thus, Mgudlwa and Iyamu (2018) suggest that the integration of various datasets is essentially relevant and useful to healthcare service providers. From South Africa viewpoint, Mayosi et al. (2012) argue that good-quality data in a timely manner is always needed due to the rapid changes that happen in the health environment. This is contrast with the on-going improper coordination and management of patients' data, which leads to incorrect diagnoses and treatments (Ruxwana et al., 2010).

Based on the challenges established above, this study attempts to answer the question: What are the factors that influence access, use, and management of healthcare big data in the South African health facilities? In answering this question, it was necessary to examine the actors (personnel and technologies) that are involved, their roles in accessing healthcare big data, and how the activities involving big data are translated or manifested. Thus, moments of translation from actor-network theory (ANT) (Callon, 1986) was selected to guide the analysis. The core tenets of ANT are actor, network, and translation (Latour 2005). Iyamu and Roode (2012) describe ANT as a theory which focuses on the interaction between humans and technology.

This article is structured into seven main sections. The first section introduces the entire article, followed by sections covering review of literature about actor-network theory and big data, respectively. The research methodology is discussed in the fourth section. The fifth and sixth sections present the data analysis and discussion of the results, respectively. The conclusion is drawn in the last section.

2. ACTOR-NETWORK THEORY

Actor-network theory (ANT) focuses on how human and nonhuman actors form stable, heterogeneous networks of aligned interests through processes of translations and negotiations (Callon, 1986; Law, 1992). According to Latour (2005), ANT is holistic in its incorporation of humans and non-human into actor-network. This means that human and nonhuman actors have relationship, which ultimately shapes each other (Law, 1992). Despite possible human actors' different understandings and intentions, they are able to associate and influence each other (Latour, 2005). In ANT, translations are the interactions that happen between actors and their many manifestations (Callon, 1986). Translations entails four moments: problematization, interessement, enrolment and mobilisation (Callon, 1986). Accessing, use and management of healthcare big data involve processes of interaction and negotiations between: humans, human and nonhuman, and nonhumans.

Accessing, using and managing patient' big data for healthcare service delivery are stages influenced by various factors, which manifest from translations during interactions between actors. Problematization is to initiate an idea, foster relationships, and allocate and reallocate power between the involved actors (Akrich, 1992). Each or a combination of the stages is a situation that has to happen in order to provide healthcare services. Callon (1986) refers to such situation as Obligatory Passage Point (OPP), which has to occur in order for all the actors to satisfy the interests that have been attributed to them by the focal actor. At the stage of interessement, the focus is to understand how healthcare practitioners became interested in accessing, use and management of patients' big data for healthcare service delivery. Interessement is the set of actions by which an entity attempts to impose and stabilise the identity of other actors in the same network for the cause of problematization (Akrich, Callon & Latour, 2002).

The third, enrolment stage involves the consolidation of alliances through bargaining and mutual concessions (Law, 1992). This helps to examine and understand various roles in accessing, use and management of patients' big data. Callon (1986) explains that actors accept the roles defined for them when enrolling in the network. ANT proposes that enrolling allies creates aligned interests and the translation of their interests must be such that participation will lead to the network's maintenance (Latour, 2005). Enrolment can be seen as a successful outcome of the *'problematization'* and the *'interessement'* processes. Finally, actor represents the network (Callon, 1986). Some actors are used as (new) initiators. They become delegates or spokespersons for the focal actor. The new network starts to operate in a target-oriented approach to implement the solution proposed.

Actor-work theory (ANT) is sociotechnical theory that focuses on actors, networks, and the relationship and interaction that take place between actors within heterogeneous networks (Latour, 2005). The relationship and interaction between actors passes through translation from the perspective of ANT (Calon, 1986). Many studies have been conducted in the field of ICT and healthcare, where the four moments of translation from the perspective of ANT were employed as a lens in the analysis of the data (Mauthe & Webb, 2013; Cresswel et al., 2010; Heeks & Stanforth, 2007). According to Iyamu (2018), ANT is appropriate for gaining better understanding, formulation, and stabilisation of groupings, referred to as networks of data sets, in the analytics of big data.

3. LITERATURE REVIEW

Healthcare data includes personal medical records, radiology images, clinical trial data, FDA submissions, human genetics and population (Feldman, Martin & Skotnes, 2012), which Hansen et al. (2014) classified as big data because of its size, variety and velocity nature. Big data in healthcare challenges relates to its characteristics, which include volume, variety, velocity, and veracity (Acharjya & Kauser, 2016; Asri et al., 2015). Wang and Krishnan (2014) state that the size of data sets within healthcare affects important aspects, such as storing, processing, and analysing of data. Mancini (2014) explains that these challenges call for new approaches to big data. Peisker and Dalai (2015) are of the view that the integration and analysis of health data can actually address many persistent problems within the healthcare sector.

In addition to size, another description of big data is that it is also unstructured in nature, thus adding to its complexity. According to Gulamhussen et al. (2013), the healthcare sector produces thousands of unlinked data which is classed in multiple categories such as clinical data, claims, pharmaceuticals, medical products, research and development data, patient behaviour, and sentiment data. Based on

Priyanka and Kulennavar's (2014) description, big data in healthcare is the result of digitization of healthcare data, which had already accumulated over the years but in paper form. However, generally speaking, the term Big Data is defined as a tool and technique which contains information of value but for that information to be uncovered, innovative integration has to be in place (Sathiyavathi, 2015). This definition leads to the description of healthcare big data. These are large and complex data sets, which cannot be handled with traditional systems and which consists of data such as patient information (Ganjir, Sakar & Kumar, 2016). Raghupathi and Raghupathi (2014) state that healthcare big data can easily be defined with 4 Vs of big data.

There are points of importance to highlight the issues and challenges that persist in the use of big data. Augustine (2014) points out that the biggest challenge seems to be that big data exists within legacy systems which makes it hard to relate to other data. Furthermore, Archenaa and Anita (2015) suggest that the challenge is no longer just a lack of information but rather lack of information which can lead to better decision making in healthcare. In addition, Chen and Zhang (2014) purport that these challenges may result in big data becoming a gold mine that we cannot extract any value from because we lack the means to explore it. In support of this Kankanhalli et al. (2016) state that challenges in analysing data stem from the variety within healthcare, implying that the data is both structured and unstructured since it appears in various formats and from various sources. The type of data set, whether structured and unstructured, influences disparity especially in developing countries (Ruxwana et al., 2010).

Evidently, some of the diagnoses within the South African healthcare are caused by disparities in existing data and records of patients (Benatar, 2013). Leon, Schneider and Daviaud (2012) argue that some of the disparities in South African primary health care are influenced by culture and capacity, as well as the poor availability and use of ICT. According to Mayosi et al. (2012), data system in the South African healthcare is a challenge, which affects national distribution of patients information. Mgudlwa and Iyamu (2018) therefore suggest that big data analytics can help to integrate and harness healthcare data for more purposefulness. It is within this context that actor-network theory was selected to examine the interactions that happen among actors, which manifest to factors that influence various stages in gathering, accessing, use and management of patients' big data for healthcare service delivery in South Africa.

4. RESEARCH METHODOLOGY

To fulfil the objectives of this study, qualitative research methods were followed. This is mainly because the methods place emphasis on highlighting and explaining human experiences (Chinedu et al., 2014), through which factors that influence access, use, and management of big data can be identified. The case study approach was employed in the design of the research, primarily because it allows investigation of an entity, in a natural setting (Yin, 2017). A healthcare facility, Salem Clinic in Eastern Cape of South Africa was used in the research. Salem Clinic participated in the research for two main reasons: accessibility and it fulfils the criteria needed. Eight facilities were contacted and requested to participate in the research, but declined. The Salem Clinic fulfilled the requirements for a healthcare facility, which was the criteria for this research. The facility attends to over 6000 patients per month.

The semi-structured interview technique was used to collect qualitative data. This is because the technique allows for conversation between interviewer and interviewee, which helps to provide clarifications during the process (Cohen et al., 2013). A total of ten participants were interviewed. This includes doctor (x2); nurse (2); clerk (x1); data capturer (x1); pharmacist (x2); and radiographer(x2). With permission, the interviews were tape recorded and transcribed. Each participant was assigned a name-code: SC_P1 to SC_P10. This was purposeful in order to protect the identities of the participants as well to adhere to ethical considerations of the facility. A format was applied in accessing the data for analysis purposes: *Participant, Page number, line number*. For example, SC_P1, Pg 1, 102-103.

The four moments of translation are problematization, interessement, enrolment and mobilisation from Actor-Network Theory (ANT) (Callon, 1996) was selected and used as a lens to guide the analysis of the data. The focus was to determine the factors that influence access, use and management of patients' big data for healthcare service delivery in South Africa.

5. ANALYSIS OF DATA: ANT VIEW

In the use of ANT, first, the actors that exist in the environment was established. This is followed by understanding the types of networks within the healthcare facility. These help to gain a better understanding of the various roles as well as the relationship and interactions that happened. The moments of translation cover how patients' big data are consciously or unconsciously accessed, used or managed in the process of providing or receiving healthcare services.

5.1. Actors

As in the norm, there were different actors, human and non-human within Salem clinic. The health facility consists of many different employees, divided into two main groups, namely, medical and administrative personnel. The human actors were medical and administrative personnel. The non-human actors include processes, big data, IS/IT solutions, and medical apparatus. The medical employees included doctors, nurses, radiographers, and pharmacists. The other group which were non-medical personnel consists of counsellors and administrative staff. The actors play critical roles in how big data were collected, accumulated, utilized, and managed at the facility.

In Salem Clinic, the data was gathered included voice, text, and images. The voice data was particularly derived from staff interaction with patients through telephonic conversations. Text data were gathered from the administrative and medical part of the facility through notarizes of patient visits and their details, while the medical staff were responsible for writing notes on the reason for visit and other information. The X-Ray machines produce image data, which the medical staff then use for activities such as conducting diagnosis. A radiographer at the facility briefly describes the process as follows:

The result of patient's x-ray goes to the doctor, who carries out the review, and confirm the diagnosis. (SC_P6, pg 20:998-999)

Salem Clinic employs different technological artefacts, which included medical apparatus and IS/IT solutions. The medical apparatus were used to examine patients' health condition through diagnoses and X-Rays. While the IS/IT solutions were used for activities such as collection and storage of patients' medical records, interactions, and events. One participant indicates:

There are computers used by the manager, clerks, doctors and the pharmacy (SC_P1, Pg 6: 280-281). There is a certain software used to capture that information, not one software but there is one which integrates all services. It is called District Health Information System (DHIS). (SC_P5, Pg 13: 638-640)

In the process of healthcare service delivery, the employees worked in isolation. Similarly, the apparatus or data were not applied in a vacuum. The human actors operated in groups (networks) as they access and applied various tools (big data and medical apparatus), making the nonhuman actors part of the networks.

5.2. Networks

Networks are formed through a linkage of actors with similar interests or qualities as argued by Borgatti and Halgin (2011). At Salem Clinic, there were three main networks, which consisted of healthcare practitioners, IT and administrative personnel. The networks of healthcare practitioners included doctors, counsellors, radiographers, pharmacists, and nurses. Another group of people were the patients. The patients were unconsciously divided into groups based on their health conditions and purpose of visits to the facility.

Despite the use of technology within the facility, there was no designated IT department within the facility. However, there was availability of IT artefacts, which constitute a network of its own. On the administrative side, Salem Clinic employs data capturers and clerical assistants. This group of administrative staff share a common goal which was to capture patient information. One of the administrative staff describes her job role as follows:

We as admin clerks register patients, whether first-time or regular clients. For children below the age of 12 years, we always advise them to bring a clinic card. Thereafter, we create a file, before sending them to the respective medical personnel (SC_P2, Pg 6: 299-303).

The medical and administrative staff both interact with the data using the different sources. Through their different contributions, data is accumulated, processed, and stored. The set of data was used for different purposes within the facility, but the end goal was to enable decision-making. The data goes through different stages until it reaches a point of usefulness to the organization and the body that conducts decision-making.

5.3. Moments of Translation: Problematization

Like other healthcare service providers, Salem Clinic collects and accumulates data from patients on a daily basis, as patients visit the facility. The accumulation of data begins from two main sources, namely patients' walk-in and via technology devices, which include telephone conversations and email. The data is used to diagnose the health conditions and trace medical conditions and history of the patients. Therefore, it is critical that the patients provide enough and accurate information about themselves. On a patient's visit at Salem Clinic, consultation takes place, which follows two main steps: (1) inquiring whether it is the patient's first visit, or he/she is a returning patient; and (2) a nurse determines the patient's purpose of visit.

Both steps are parts of problematizing a patient's presence at the facility. The patients provide information about themselves based on their knowledge. Many patients sometimes struggle to express themselves or articulate their condition clearly enough for the medical personnel to understand them. At Salem Clinic, there has been cases of a patients presenting inaccurate information about their condition or purpose of visit. This was common among the youths that visit the Salem Clinic. One of the experienced (having served for over ten years) nurses explained as follows:

The information that the patients provide is often influenced by the type of disease they had. Especially the youth, we had cases where a patient had STI, which he was fully aware of, but decide to offer unrelated information because he was shy. (SC_P1, Pg 2: 76-78)

The initial incorrect information that some of the patients provide about themselves was influenced by culture and understanding. Culture may affect a patient's willingness to disclose information, for instance, some male patients do not think that a person of the opposite sex needs to know about their private medical conditions. Furthermore, the patients are not always well educated to understand that medical conditions do not have boundaries of gender affiliation.

Additionally, the patients provide information based on how they are guided or the type of questions that were asked of them by the medical personnel. This is the primary reason that personnel require intensive training as an administrator or first aid personnel to the patients. Another critical aspect is how the administrative and medical personnel gather information from the patients. This include what tools, such as language, automated system, or manual process, are used to gather information from the patients. At Salem Clinic, the majority of the patients were isiXhosa speaking Africans. However, some of the nurses and other personnel were people of other races, such as Coloured. Even though some of the personnel sometimes spoke in isiXhosa, it was never the same, in that there are always cultural differences. One of the nurses shared her experience:

I am not a Xhosa speaking person, even though I do understand a bit of the language. As a result, I'd rather prefer to consult in English language, to avoid complication. (SC_P1, Pg 1: 3)

Based on the information that is provided by the patient, medical personnel, from general practitioners to specialists, including nurses, are assigned to carry out further checks and diagnosis. Even though the medical practitioners are assigned, different factors influence their interest in the patients' health conditions.

5.4. Moments of Translation: Interessement

For each patient's condition, there were different stakeholders: the patients themselves, patient's relations, support (IT), medical personnel at the Salem Clinic, and the South Africa Department of Health (DoH). Each of these stakeholders have interest of consciousness and unconsciousness in patients' health conditions.

Patients visit Salem Clinic with the intention of receiving medical treatment. Their interest stems from their need for healthcare services that the facility offers, in order to better their state of health. The services are offered in different forms, which include referrals to specialists, prescriptions for medication, and actual medical care to patients with less serious conditions. These services are captured and documented by using IS/IT artefacts. The documentation enables follow-up, tracking and tracing of individual patients. Parents or relations' interest was evident in their efforts leading up to, or during, the treatment process, with some acting as patient escorts/porters.

The DoH formulates policies to guide health services in South Africa. Based on some of the policies, technological solutions, such as the District Health Information System (DHIS), Tier.Net, and the Electronic TB Register (ETR.NET) were implemented. One of the medical personnel at Salem facility explains as follows:

A report is compiled monthly and submitted to sub-district level, and escalated to provincial and national levels. Using DHIS, the department is able to identify gaps, in improving performance. (SC_P1, Pg 13: 655-661)

The various interests on patients' care are influenced by different factors, which include care, availability of medications and medical apparatus, availability of qualified medical personnel, and the use of IS/IT artefacts to enable and support the activities. These interests only become materialised, produce care if put to use through participation of the associated and affected actors.

5.5. Moments of Translation: Enrolment

In Salem Clinic, participation of stakeholders in the process of patients' care was determined by different factors, which include roles and responsibilities, and rules and regulations that were put in place by the management. The medical and administrative staff of Salem Clinic take part in the process of patient care within the facility through offering their services. As medical staff, doctors within Salem Clinic are available daily to conduct their duty towards the patient by providing medical treatment to them. This starts with consultation, wherein they check the patients' complaints and weigh it against their medical history presented in the folder. Thereafter, a doctor is able to conduct a diagnosis, provide treatment, and advise the patient based on their findings. These activities show participation from this category of medical staff. Individually, these doctors have their roles and responsibilities; however, they are still required to work jointly with other staff within the facility. Consequently, nurses are second order to the doctors.

The different roles and responsibilities of medical staff do not mean that they work in isolation. There is a systematic process that happens with patient care and this tightly links the medical staff of Salem clinic. Following this process, nurses are responsible for sending patients to the pharmacy within the facility to receive their medications. As one participant points out:

In accordance to the process, everyone that has been seen or first-aid examined by the nurses still have to visit the pharmacy. (SC_P1, pg 1: 19-20)

Pharmacists at Salem Clinic were at the end of the patient care process at the facility. However, they were pivotal to the process because medications were administered by them to patients, as per the doctor's or nurses' instruction. Moreover, they were responsible for ensuring that patients receive the correct medications as stated in their prescriptions. As a primary stakeholder, their participation was driven by their job role. Another factor that motivates participation in the pharmacy department was auditing that takes place. The DoH ensures that the medications that were administered by the facility pharmacy was recorded. An interviewee states as follows:

The nurses and pharmacists who are responsible for dispensing medications were also obligated to record what medications has been administered to patients. (SC_P5, pg 18:869-870)

In addition, the administrative personnel of Salem Clinic were responsible for ensuring that the medical staff were able to conduct these activities in a systematic manner. Patients follow a particular process from the moment that they enter the facility. Their responsibilities were centred around the medical unit, as they have to guide the patients through the different activities that occur while receiving treatment. Their participation in patient care was measured by how smooth the process was, starting from registration to the moment they receive medication. However, the process was challenged, in that some patients were not able to provide sufficient documentation and information, for efficient service.

The other group of stakeholders, DoH, actively contributes to the activities and processes of healthcare in the country. Some of the key areas of participation; training of nurses and health workers; provision of medical equipment; formulation of policies that govern for both private and public health practice; and formulation of policies that govern health professionals. Like any other organization, the availability of equipment was valuable to Salem Clinic. With proper equipment, medical and administration staff are able to conduct their duties with ease. This also contributes to the quality of care, which was influenced by existing patients' data.

However, monitoring and evaluation become challenging, especially to those who were responsible for ensuring that they were carried out correctly. This includes data capturers of Salem clinic. In their participation with regards to providing care to patients, they have to ensure that the correct information was captured on the systems, which forms the types of patients' data. The patients of Salem Clinic, both chronic and acute, have had to adapt to the processes imposed on them by the facility. Due to their need for medical care, they were required to follow these processes and to make use of the solutions introduced by the facility, specifically the chronic patients, who were registered under programs such as Tier.NET and ETR.net. Through these processes, big data were collected and stored. An interview provides an example of the type of information patients would have to give out:

Programs such as Tier.Net, it's all about the patients. You capture their names, addresses, HIV status, ARV treatment and how well controlled they were. (SC_P5, Pg 17: 679:681)

There were different stakeholders enrolled in the process of patient care at Salem clinic. The medical staff and administrative staff contribute through providing a service, while the DoH enables this through providing support, both financially and with technological resources. The patients of Salem Clinic stand to gain medical assistance; therefore, they were obligated to comply with the processes put in place by the facility. Patients' participation did not guarantee success and functionality of these processes and systems of Salem Clinic. Therefore, for them to be considered successful, mobilisation needs to take place.

5.6. Moments of Translation: Mobilisation

Salem Clinic encounters multiple spokespersons at various stages of each patient' care duration. Some of these spokespersons were representatives of the facility, while others were self-appointed. The spokespersons responsible for mobilising other actors into participating in activities surrounding patient health were both internal and external to the organization. Internally, the elected representatives included management. As the decision makers, they can enforce participation from the different departments within Salem Clinic. A participant states the following:

Everything is dependent on management. This is because, as the verification committee we can only do so much. We are restricted in many areas. (SC_P5, Pg.16: 787-789)

This may affect the facility both positively and negatively. From a positive perspective, a single point of power of authority regulates the operation of the facility. This happens in two ways: (1) employees know their reporting lines; and (2) the DoH is aware of structure and accountability of the facility. However, having a single point of power can also negatively affect productivity within the organisation. Decisions regarding the facility could only be undertaken and implemented by the management. Therefore, in its absence, certain decisions and actions cannot be made, which can result in delays of the patient care process. Furthermore, the DoH that governs the facility places all responsibility upon this section of Salem Clinic. This means that accountability was not shared across the organisation and this could negatively impact those who constitute management in the facility.

Like any other health facility, Salem clinic encounters emergency situations. In such cases, doctors were the representative of the patients in need of urgent medical care. As a smaller scale healthcare facility, there were cases they had to escalate to bigger facilities that were equipped with more tools and resources. Also, the facility encounters cases of patients who were unable to communicate their problem as they wait to be attended. This requires another party to act as proxy to the medical staff. The facility refers to those people as patient escorts. These can be relatives or friends to the patient. Views from some medical personnel are as follows:

If our doctors feel it's a case that needs emergency medical attention or a theatre, then it is referred to nearby facility, a hospital. (SC_P1, Pg.6: 290-292)

An escort was given the responsibility to articulate the patient's case as best as they can for them to get treated. This requires them to know the patient well so that they can give information to the medical practitioner. This was critical, especially in the absence of a patient file. With no view of the patient's history, doctors or nurses at Salem Clinic were unable to give prognosis and the treatment process was delayed. This becomes even more challenging when a patient was brought into the facility by someone who has no knowledge of them and was just there to assist. A doctor in the facility states:

It was often difficult to obtain information from some patients during an emergency situation. It gets more difficult when a stranger brings a patient who desperately needed medical attention, because no one can offer information about the patient. (SC_P4, Pg.12:562-563)

Clearly, the level of familiarity between the patients and their representative is crucial in the treatment process. Failure to thoroughly communicate the case endangers the patients as this requires doctors to treat patients without thorough background knowledge. Furthermore, this contributes to misdiagnosis and dispensing of wrong medication. The DoH also had representatives that visit Salem Clinic to ensure that the resources they provide were utilised efficiently. These resources included the medication they dispense to the organisation. This was done through the evaluation of data collected by the facility.

Mobilisation of stakeholders could be carried out by anyone. However, due to the sensitive nature of the health environment in South Africa, there were restrictions. Thus, only persons with legal authority could speak on behalf of the patient of the health facility, Salem Clinic. This had both negative and positive influence in the activities of the Clinic. For example, there was no firm solution because some patients do not insert their correct addresses on their folders, leading to the facility being unable to track them, in that it could not be interrogated by unauthorised persons.

6. RESULTS AND DISCUSSION

From the above analysis, there were five main factors that influence access, use and management of big data, therefore, determine the selection of analytics, for the analysis of healthcare data. The factors are: common health facility requirements, structure of the big data, integration of healthcare systems, availability of skilled personnel, and the availability of patients' data sets. These factors are all interconnected in one way or another, as shown in Figure 1.

Figure 1. Health facility influencing factors

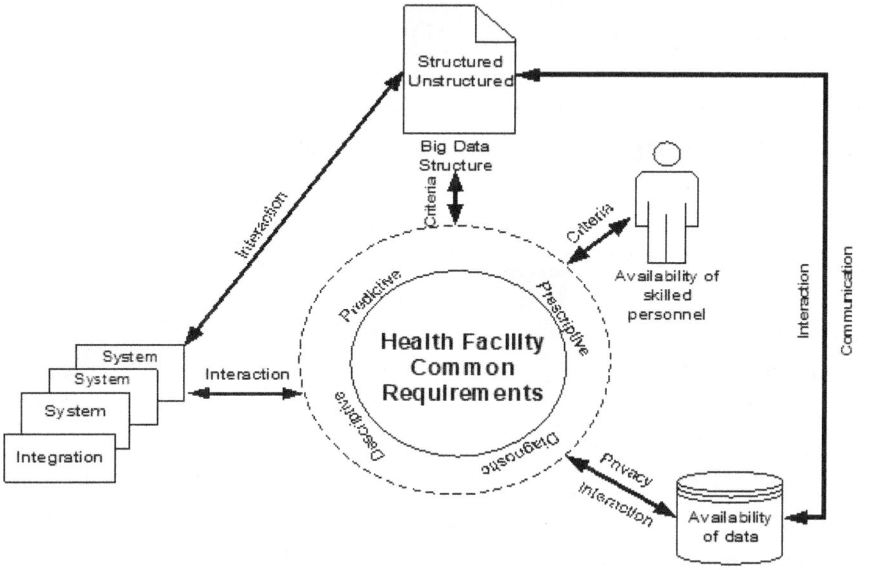

6.1. The Source and Structure of the Big Data

Salem Clinic has been in existence for many years and they have evolved in their way of handling data. However, they still use traditional methods in conjunction with technology and both contribute equally to gathering and management of their big data. This has resulted in structured and unstructured data. The structured data is sourced from their traditional filing systems. Their files contain textual data of the patient and these are all placed in their suitable fields. These fields contain data such as the individual's demographics and their reasons for visit. The technological tools used to capture this data were centred around these traditional systems. They were similar, but one was manual while the other was computerised; however, both generate structured data.

On the subject of technology, the facility uses different tools to carry out the patient care process. This includes computers, telephones, and x-ray machines. These tools generate unstructured data which comprises of voice, image, and video data. These sets of data were equally as important as structured, but it often goes unattended to. This was attributed to the facility's data tools giving no consideration to them. This impacts Salem Clinic's data analytics, in the sense that there is a fundamental part of data that was not being included. This brings to question the completeness of data and its impact on the results that were yielded when it's analysed.

6.2. The Availability of Suitable Big Data Manipulation Tools

At Salem Clinic there were systems (tools), which were used to gather and store patients' data. These systems were provided by the South African Department of Health (DoH). The systems included Tier. Net, ETR.Net, and the District Health Information System (DHIS). These tools were designed mainly to store patients' data. However, the tools differ in terms of their criteria and requirements that were needed in deploying them.

Tier.Net was specifically designed to store data of patients who have been diagnosed with HIV/AIDS. This was due to the high influx of HIV/AIDS patients in facilities. The lack of infrastructure led to the facility being unable to handle patient data using only a paper-based system. However, before deploying the system, Salem Clinic had to fulfil certain criteria. These criteria included serving more than 600 patients and being unable to accommodate patient data using only a paper-based filing system. Considering that this was a technological solution, the facility had to migrate to using computers as a requirement.

The ETR.Net is a smaller system created specifically for patients who have been diagnosed with TB, and needed treatment. The system was designed to capture patient data from the diagnosis stage until treatment was successful. Since this is not a lifelong disease, specifications and requirements stated that a patient may only exist on the system for six months, as this was the TB treatment period. Thereafter, they would be removed from the system unless they relapse. From the facility's perspective, it was meant to improve data coordination with regards to TB patients. Therefore, the only criteria were facilities who diagnose and treat patients diagnosed with TB.

The DHIS was designed to store data for all patients who visit the facility. The purpose of this system was to collect statistical data of the facility's therefore, the criteria was location based. The system encompasses data of patients who reside in that catchment area. Therefore, the only requirement was that the patient seeks treatment from the facility. The same patient can also exist in the facility database (DHIS). This brings about issues of duplication and this has not been fully explored by the facility at the time of this study. These issues relate to lack of integration between the databases. Another issue was failure in establishing common requirements with regards to data analytics. The facility has not explicitly stated what they would like to gain from the data.

6.3. The Availability of Standardized Big Data Interpretation Criteria

The existence of big data is futile to the organisation unless they know what they seek to gain from the data. The facility has tools at their disposal; however, they have not considered the potential of their data. There were no standardized requirements stated with regards to big data and how it can improve the quality of healthcare in the facility. There were various options available that could be of benefit to their cause. However, the choice was dependent on the facility's common requirements, which they have not yet established at the time of this study. These options include (1) prescriptive; (2) predictive; (3) diagnostic; and (4) descriptive big data analytics.

As a healthcare facility, Salem Clinic lacks the necessary tools to determine which illnesses mostly affect patients that visit the clinic. Therefore, they have no knowledge on what areas to prioritise in an attempt to reduce the number of patients visiting the clinic with the same problem. There were only two areas of focus in the facility, namely HIV/AIDS and Tuberculosis. These diseases were only prioritised under the DoH's command. However, with the help of prescriptive analytics, the facility could find out what health issues are prevalent in the community. These would be specific to their patients and they would know which areas to mostly focus on.

Additionally, Salem Clinic was situated in an area of Eastern Cape of South Africa that is prone to health outbreaks. This is due to the living conditions of people and lifestyle. However, the facility has no foresight on these outbreaks due to insufficient use of their big data. With the use of predictive analytics, they could view patterns based on past occurrences. These could give them a view of what could most likely happen in the future with regards to patient treatment. Similarly, diagnostic analytics would be highly beneficial to the facility, mainly because it serves a big part of their purpose. The facility would be able to uncover the reasons behind occurrences; thus, enabling them to prevent its repetition.

Mining the data through descriptive analytics would help the facility gain knowledge on rampant issues affecting patients. Further investigation into these problems would help in improving the patient care process and standard of the facility. However, these tools can only be of use once the facility uncovers its purpose for big data. That would help in determining which data analytics tools suit the facility's goals, and this requires an explicit communication of their requirements. This brings about the issue of integration within the facility. The type of data analytics tool to use is most likely to be determined by the medical personnel of the facility. The medical personnel know what issues they face due to lack of foresight and insight. Therefore, they should be working jointly with those who handle data in order to find a data analytics solution best suited for the facility. However, that is not possible unless integration of different units in the facility takes place.

6.4. The Degree of Big Data Integration of the In-House Healthcare Information Systems

Several issues affect Salem Clinic. These were rooted in the dispersion of resources meant to serve patients visiting the clinic. This includes the staff and technological resources of the facility. Salem Clinic lacks a properly coordinated patient care system. There were five different departments, all operating under the same facility but somehow, they were still disintegrated. This was from the perspective of operations within the facility and the process that data goes through.

The facility has five different departments and they all have the same purpose of serving the patient. In all these departments, a report has to be written on the patient's file and it has to indicate what was conducted and the next step in treatment. In that process, the data was prone to error because many people were involved in carrying it out. By the time all data has been collected, it was difficult to trace where errors occurred.

These errors decrease the quality of data being collected in the facility. Thus, leading to analysis being conducted on data that were not up to par. This could be avoided if integration was in place because data would be collected and updated in real time. The issue also relates to level of knowledge around data analytics in the facility. These problems cannot be raised, because no skilled personnel were available to provide input regarding data, its importance, and how it can be analysed.

6.5. The Availability of Medical Personnel Skilled in Big Data

The facility, Salem Clinic, has been in operation for a decade. Even though the health clinic has been in operation for many years, it continues to use the same manual systems to capture and store patients' data. This was irrespective of the fact that the DoH has provided technology solutions (systems) to health facilities in the country, including Salem Clinic. The non-use of the technologies was attributed to lack of knowledge and know-how, which results to unavailability of skilled personnel.

The facility was also lacking in terms of skilled personnel to handle the data that accumulates daily in the facility. This brings the facility's management into question as they were responsible for decision making in the facility. Management has failed to address skills acquisition for data analytics. This includes education, training, and retention of staff who specialise in data analytics. This has led to the neglect of data analytics, which would help in improving the healthcare standard of Salem Clinic.

6.6. The Availability of Relevant Big Data Sets

At Salem Clinic, patients' data were accessed by different personnel. This includes clerks, nurses, doctors, radiographers, pharmacists, and data capturers. As a result, patients' data were split into sets in accordance to area of specialisation and responsibilities. For example, the clerk can only have access to patient data which relates to administration, such as contact details and bio-data. This makes certain sets of data unavailable to some personnel. The unavailability of the entire data makes it difficult or challenging for the analytics approach, which somehow affects the completeness of results that were obtained from big data analysis. However, at the same time, it must be noted that the unavailability of complete data is often justified from privacy and security perspectives.

The availability of patients' data requires policy and regulation in order to manage and maintain the privacy and security. Privacy was a valued element in patient information. It creates a sense of trust between the patient and medical caregiver. This was based on the sensitivity of information shared during the treatment process. It ensures that a patient knows that any information they divulge was kept between them and the person treating them. However, this affects the completeness of data based on the fact that some information regarding the patient is only limited to certain people within the facility. This brings about the aspect of security as well. Patient information requires a high level of security. The facility has to ensure that information shared by a patient was not accessible to anyone unless consent was given by the patient. This requires regulation, and was done by limiting access only to those who are treating the patient. This was to avoid cases, such as patient data being used for malice or a data leak that could have legal consequences. Therefore, the facility can only make certain sets of data available for consumption.

There were other issues that contribute to incomplete data, such as missing or incomplete patients' medical reports. In addition, the facility lets patients keep their own files and this leads to damage of patient files and loss of information. This also affects data analytics of the facility negatively as they were now required to conduct analysis on incomplete data. These issues stem from a lack of integration within the facility. Data was only prioritised by one part of the facility, namely the data capturers, whereas, the different departments should be working in conjunction as they all contribute to big data. The facility lacks an integrated data process from the beginning of patient treatment until the last stage.

7. CONCLUSION

This study highlights the factors that influence access, use and management of patients' big data for healthcare service delivery. The factors directly or indirectly impact the quality of healthcare services being provided within South African healthcare facilities. The factors exist because many of the facilities are often challenged with analysis of their patients' big data. Thus, the study can be of benefit to South African health practitioners primarily because some of the factors can influence and how they manifest in the activities and process of healthcare services.

The contribution of this study extends further in two ways: theoretically and methodologically. Theoretically, this study adds to the existing body of knowledge within IS and Healthcare fields. Methodologically, the use of ANT as a guide through analysis provides a fresh perspective to analysing IS related phenomena. Further studies can also be conducted on this research, through the application of different theories that are commonly used in social science.

REFERENCES

Acharjya, D. P., & Kauser Ahmed, P. (2016). A Survey on Big Data Analytics: Challenges, Open Research Issues and Tools. *International Journal of Advanced Computer Science and Applications, 7*(2), 511–518.

Akrich, M. (1992). The de-scription of technical objects. In Shaping Technology/Building Society: Studies in Sociotechnical Change. Cambridge, MA: the MIT Press.

Akrich, M., Callon, M., Latour, B., & Monaghan, A. (2002). The key to success in innovation part I: The art of interessement. *International Journal of Innovation Management, 6*(02), 187–206. doi:10.1142/S1363919602000550

Archenaa, J., & Mary Anita, E. A. (2015). A survey of big data analytics in healthcare and government. *Procedia Computer Science, 50*(1), 408–413. doi:10.1016/j.procs.2015.04.021

Augustine, D. P. (2014). Leveraging big data analytics and hadoop in developing India's healthcare services. *International Journal of Computers and Applications, 89*(16), 44–50. doi:10.5120/15719-4622

Bates, D. W., Saria, S., Ohno-Machado, L., Shah, A., & Escobar, G. (2014). Big data in healthcare: Using analytics to identify and manage high-risk and high-cost patients. *Health Affairs, 33*(7), 1123–1131. doi:10.1377/hlthaff.2014.0041 PMID:25006137

Bello-Orgaz, G., Jung, J. J., & Camacho, D. (2016). Social big data: Recent achievements and new challenges. *Information Fusion, 28*, 45–59. doi:10.1016/j.inffus.2015.08.005 PMID:32288689

Benatar, S. (2013). The challenges of health disparities in South Africa. *SAMJ: South African Medical Journal, 103*(3), 154–155. doi:10.7196/SAMJ.6622 PMID:23472690

Callon, M. (1986). Some elements of a sociology of translation: domestication of the scallops and the fishermen of St Brieuc Bay. In J. Law (Ed.), *Power, Action & Belief: A New Sociology of Knowledge?* (pp. 196–229). Routledge.

Chandarana, P., & Vijayalakshmi, M. (2014). Big Data analytics frameworks. *2014 International Conference on Circuits, Systems, Communication and Information Technology Applications (CSCITA)*, 430–434. 10.1109/CSCITA.2014.6839299

Chawla, N. V., & Davis, D. A. (2013). Bringing big data to personalized healthcare: A patient- centered framework. *Journal of General Internal Medicine*, *28*(S3, Suppl.3), 660–665. doi:10.100711606-013-2455-8 PMID:23797912

Chen, C. P., & Zhang, C. Y. (2014). Data-intensive applications, challenges, techniques and technologies: A survey on Big Data. *Information Sciences*, *275*, 314–347. doi:10.1016/j.ins.2014.01.015

Chinedu Eze, S., Duan, Y., & Chen, H. (2014). Examining emerging ICT's adoption in SMEs from a dynamic process approach. *Information Technology & People*, *27*(1), 63–82. doi:10.1108/ITP-03-2013-0044

Cohen, L., Manion, L., & Morrison, K. (2013). *Research methods in education*. Routledge. doi:10.4324/9780203720967

Coovadia, H., Jewkes, R., Barron, P., Sanders, D., & McIntyre, D. (2009). The health and health system of South Africa: Historical roots of current public health challenges. *Lancet*, *374*(9692), 817–834. doi:10.1016/S0140-6736(09)60951-X PMID:19709728

Cresswell, K. M., Worth, A., & Sheikh, A. (2010). Actor-Network Theory and its role in understanding the implementation of information technology developments in healthcare. *BMC Medical Informatics and Decision Making*, *10*(1), 67–78. doi:10.1186/1472-6947-10-67 PMID:21040575

Dwiartama, A., & Rosin, C. (2014). Exploring agency beyond humans: The compatibility of Actor-Network Theory (ANT) and resilience thinking. *Ecology and Society*, *19*(3), 28–38. doi:10.5751/ES-06805-190328

Esposito, C., Ficco, M., Palmieri, F., & Castiglione, A. (2015). A knowledge-based platform for Big Data analytics based on publish/subscribe services and stream processing. *Knowledge-Based Systems*, *79*, 3–17. doi:10.1016/j.knosys.2014.05.003

Feldman, B., Martin, E.M. & Skotnes, T. (2012). Big Data in Healthcare - hype and hope. *Dr. Bonnie 360 degree (Business Development for Digital Health)*, *2013*(1), 122-125.

Fico, G., Fioravanti, A., Arredondo, M. T., Gorman, J., Diazzi, C., Arcuri, G., Conti, C., & Pirini, G. (2016). Integration of Personalized Healthcare Pathways in an ICT Platform for Diabetes Management: A Small-Scale Exploratory Study. *IEEE Journal of Biomedical and Health Informatics*, *20*(1), 29–38. doi:10.1109/JBHI.2014.2367863 PMID:25389246

Ganjir, V., Sarkar, B. K., & Kumar, R. R. (2016). Big data analytics for healthcare. *International Journal of Research in Engineering. Technology and Science*, *6*, 1–6.

Giambrone, G. P., Hemmings, H. C., Sturm, M., & Fleischut, P. M. (2015). Information technology innovation: The power and perils of big data. *British Journal of Anaesthesia*, *115*(3), 339–342. doi:10.1093/bja/aev154 PMID:26034021

Gulamhussen, A., Hirt, R., Ruckebier, M., Orban de Xivry, J., Marcerou, G., & Melis, J. (2013, March). Big data in healthcare: What options are there to put patients in control of their data. In *Proceedings of the EIT Foundation Annual Innovation Forum* (*Vol. 26*). Academic Press.

Hansen, M. M., Miron-Shatz, T., Lau, A. Y. S., & Paton, C. (2014). Big data in science and healthcare: A review of recent literature and perspectives. *Yearbook of Medical Informatics, 23*(01), 21–26. doi:10.15265/IY-2014-0004 PMID:25123717

Heeks, R., & Stanforth, C. (2007). Understanding e-Government project trajectories from an actor-network perspective. *European Journal of Information Systems, 16*(2), 165–177. doi:10.1057/palgrave.ejis.3000676

Iyamu, T. (2018). A multilevel approach to big data analysis using analytic tools and actor network theory. *South African Journal of Information Management, 20*(1), 1–9. doi:10.4102ajim.v20i1.914

Iyamu, T., & Roode, D. (2012). The use of structuration theory and actor network theory for analysis: a Case study of a financial institution in South Africa. In *Social Influences on Information and Communication Technology Innovations* (pp. 1–19). IGI Global. doi:10.4018/978-1-4666-1559-5.ch001

Jagadish, H. V., Gehrke, J., Labrinidis, A., Papakonstantinou, Y., Patel, J. M., Ramakrishnan, R., & Shahabi, C. (2014). Big data and its technical challenges. *Communications of the ACM, 57*(7), 86–94. doi:10.1145/2611567

Kambatla, K., Kollias, G., Kumar, V., & Grama, A. (2014). Trends in big data analytics. *Journal of Parallel and Distributed Computing, 74*(7), 2561–2573. doi:10.1016/j.jpdc.2014.01.003

Kankanhalli, A., Hahn, J., Tan, S., & Gao, G. (2016). Big data and analytics in healthcare: Introduction to the special section. *Information Systems Frontiers, 18*(2), 233–235. doi:10.100710796-016-9641-2

Kuo, M. H., Chrimes, D., Moa, B., & Hu, W. (2015). Design and construction of a big data analytics framework for health applications. In *Smart City/SocialCom/SustainCom (SmartCity), IEEE International Conference on* (pp. 631-636). IEEE. 10.1109/SmartCity.2015.140

Latour, B. (2005). *Reassembling the social: An introduction to actor-network-theory*. Oxford University press.

Law, J. (1992). Notes on the theory of the actor-network: Ordering, strategy, and heterogeneity. *Systems Practice, 5*(4), 379–393. doi:10.1007/BF01059830

Leon, N., Schneider, H., & Daviaud, E. (2012). Applying a framework for assessing the health system challenges to scaling up mHealth in South Africa. *BMC Medical Informatics and Decision Making, 12*(1), 123–135. doi:10.1186/1472-6947-12-123 PMID:23126370

Lewandowski, L. B., Watt, M. H., Schanberg, L. E., Thielman, N. M., & Scott, C. (2017). Missed opportunities for timely diagnosis of pediatric lupus in South Africa: A qualitative study. *Pediatric Rheumatology, 15*(1), 14–23. doi:10.118612969-017-0144-6 PMID:28231857

Mancini, M. (2014). Exploiting big data for improving healthcare services. *Journal of e-Learning and Knowledge Society, 10*(2), 23-33.

Mauthe, B., & Webb, T. E. 2013. In the Multiverse What Is Real? Luhmann, Complexity and ANT. In *Luhmann Observed*. London: Palgrave Macmillan UK.

Mayosi, B. M., Lawn, J. E., Van Niekerk, A., Bradshaw, D., Karim, S. S. A., & Coovadia, H. M. (2012). Health in South Africa: Changes and challenges since 2009. *Lancet*, *380*(9858), 2029–2043. doi:10.1016/ S0140-6736(12)61814-5 PMID:23201214

Mgudlwa, S., & Iyamu, T. (2018). Integration of social media with healthcare big data for improved service delivery. *South African Journal of Information Management*, *20*(1), 1–8. doi:10.4102ajim.v20i1.894

Moore, K. D., Evestone, K., & Coddington, D. C. (2013). the big deal about big data. *Healthcare Financial Management*, *67*(8), 60–68. PMID:23957187

Nativi, S., Mazzetti, P., Santoro, M., Papeschi, F., Craglia, M., & Ochiai, O. (2015). Big data challenges in building the global earth observation system of systems. *Environmental Modelling & Software*, *68*, 1–26. doi:10.1016/j.envsoft.2015.01.017

Nepal, S., Ranjan, R., & Choo, K. K. R. (2015). Trustworthy processing of healthcare big data in hybrid clouds. *IEEE Cloud Computing*, *2*(2), 78–84. doi:10.1109/MCC.2015.36

Ojha, M., & Mathur, K. (2016). Proposed application of big data analytics in healthcare at Maharaja Yeshwantrao Hospital. In *Big Data and Smart City (ICBDSC), 2016 3rd MEC International Conference on* (pp. 1-7). Muscat, Oman: IEEE. 10.1109/ICBDSC.2016.7460340

Panahiazar, M., Taslimitehrani, V., Jadhav, A., & Pathak, J. (2014). Empowering personalized medicine with big data and semantic web technology: promises, challenges, and use cases. In *Big Data (Big Data), 2014 IEEE International Conference on* (pp. 790-795) IEEE. 10.1109/BigData.2014.7004307

Peisker, A., & Dalai, S. (2015). Data analytics for rural development. *Indian Journal of Science and Technology*, *8*(S4), 50–60. doi:10.17485/ijst/2015/v8iS4/61494

Priyanka, K., & Kulennavar, N. (2014). A survey on big data analytics in health care. *International Journal of Computer Science and Information Technologies*, *5*(4), 5865–5868.

Raghupathi, W., & Raghupathi, V. (2014). Big data analytics in healthcare: Promise and potential. *Health Information Science and Systems*, *2*(1), 1–10. doi:10.1186/2047-2501-2-3 PMID:25825667

Ruxwana, N. L., Herselman, M. E., & Conradie, D. P. (2010). ICT applications as e-health solutions in rural healthcare in the Eastern Cape Province of South Africa. *The HIM Journal*, *39*(1), 17–29. doi:10.1177/183335831003900104 PMID:20335646

Sacristán, J. A., & Dilla, T. (2015). No big data without small data: Learning health care systems begin and end with the individual patient. *Journal of Evaluation in Clinical Practice*, *21*(6), 1014–1017. doi:10.1111/jep.12350 PMID:25832820

Sathiyavathi, R. (2015). A survey: Big data analytics on healthcare system. *Contemporary Engineering Sciences*, *8*(3), 121–125. doi:10.12988/ces.2015.412255

Scotland, J. (2012). Exploring the philosophical underpinnings of research: Relating ontology and epistemology to the methodology and methods of the scientific, interpretive, and critical research paradigms. *English Language Teaching*, *5*(9), 9–16. doi:10.5539/elt.v5n9p9

Shah, T., Rabhi, F., & Ray, P. (2015). Investigating an ontology-based approach for Big Data analysis of inter-dependent medical and oral health conditions. *Cluster Computing*, *18*(1), 351–367. doi:10.100710586-014-0406-8

Tresp, V., Overhage, J. M., Bundschus, M., Rabizadeh, S., Fasching, P. A., & Yu, S. (2016). Going digital: A survey on digitalization and large-scale data analytics in healthcare. *Proceedings of the IEEE*, *104*(11), 2180–2206. doi:10.1109/JPROC.2016.2615052

Tsang, E. W. (2014). Case studies and generalization in information systems research: A critical realist perspective. *The Journal of Strategic Information Systems*, *23*(2), 174–186. doi:10.1016/j.jsis.2013.09.002

Ularu, E. G., Puican, F. C., Apostu, A., & Velicanu, M. (2012). Perspectives on big data and big data analytics. *Database Systems Journal*, *3*(4), 3–14.

Wang, W., & Krishnan, E. (2014). Big data and clinicians: A review on the state of the science. *JMIR Medical Informatics*, *2*(1), e1. doi:10.2196/medinform.2913 PMID:25600256

Yin, R. K. (2017). *Case study research and applications: Design and methods*. Sage publications.

Chapter 52

Applications of Big Data and Green IoT–Enabling Technologies for Smart Cities

Onur Dogan

https://orcid.org/0000-0003-3543-4012

Istanbul Technical University, Turkey

Omer Faruk Gurcan

Istanbul Technical University, Turkey

ABSTRACT

In recent years, enormous amounts of digital data have been generated. In parallel, data collection, storage, and analysis technologies have developed. Recently, there has been an increasing trend of people moving towards urban areas. By 2030 more than 60% of the world's population will live in an urban environment. Urban areas are big data resource because they include millions of citizens, technological devices, and vehicles which generate data continuously. Besides, rapid urbanization brings many challenges, such as environmental pollution, traffic congestion, health problems, energy management, etc. Some policies for countries are required to cope with urbanization problems. One of these policies is to build smart cities. Smart cities integrate information and communication technology and various physical devices connected to the network (the internet of things or IoT) to both improve the quality of government services and citizen welfare. This chapter presents a literature review of big data, smart cities, IoT, green-IoT concepts, using technology and methods, and applications worldwide.

INTRODUCTION

Data increases at exponential growth rate year after year. Advances in several technologies such as communications, sensors and mobile devices have enabled data collection (Yakoob et al., 2016). In the 2012 World Economic Forum, it is reported that big data has become an economic resource, which has a significance to gold and currency (Alharthi et al., 2017). Jeanne Ross from MIT (cited in Akoka et al.,

DOI: 10.4018/978-1-6684-3662-2.ch052

2017) suggests the SMACIT factors (Social media, Mobile systems, Analytics, Cloud and Internet of Things) that have critical parts of digital transformation. This classification has the goal of focusing on the link of SMACIT and Big Data (Akoka et al., 2017). With advances in IoT technology, interconnection of different networked embedded tools, such as sensors, cameras and home appliances associated with Internet (Jaradat et al., 2015; Zanella et al., 2014). Internet of Things (IoT) provides new services and facilitates human life considerably in different areas of life such as healthcare, transportation and emergency (Zanella et al., 2014; Rathore et al., 2016).

More than 53.86% of the population in the world was living in cities as of 2015. On the other hand, Turkey has an urban population of 73.40%. Cities go on to grow and a prediction declares that 70% of the people will live in urban areas by 2050 (URL 11). The growth increases management and complexity problems for authorities in many areas such as waste management, supply of energy, traffic management, healthcare environment, education and safety. With the increasing population, tremendous devices contact with each other. Significant increase in device variety, volume of data and sensor technologies have offered opportunities to build smart cities for countries (Rathore et al., 2016; Holler et al., 2014; Joshi et al., 2016; Souza et al., 2016). According to Doran et al. (2013) sensors are useful to determine what is happening, on the other hand, they are not successful to occur information about why and how. Cities have been equipped with many strategies to become smart and easy-to-manage.

The Smart City was a concept firstly introduced in the "Strategic Energy Technology Plan" (URL 12). In the plan smart city is defined as "...a city that makes a conscious effort to innovatively employ information and communication technologies (ICT) to support a more inclusive, diverse and sustainable urban environment..." (Rosati & Conti, 2016). According to Pike Research on Smart Cities, the smart city market is estimated at hundreds of billion dollars by 2020 (URL 13). The basic goal of the smart cities is solving common public problems for people (Consoli et al., 2017). Urban big data is a significant resource for smart city development projects. It is a huge amount of data collected from the subjects and objects including people, companies and other urban facilities (Pan et al., 2016). Smart city applications can be made on transportation systems, education, healthcare, energy management etc. with private companies and urban administration cooperation. Smart city applications offer both improved delivery of services to citizens and reduced environmental impact (Holler et al., 2014).

SMART CITY

Urban area has higher population than the rural area in the worldwide since 2008 and it is predicted that increase in population will not only go on but also be strengthened (United Nations, 2012). The fact means that there will be many difficulties for economies in cities with respect to efficiently use of resources and sustainability in the near future (Angelidou, 2015). High ratio of urbanization brings some problems related to health, traffic management, education, energy management, pollution and waste management. Table 1 presents implementation areas related to mentioned problems. These problems require to develop new strategies about the environment design. The digital developments have made easy cities and policy makers to recognize the relationship between technology benefits and urbanization. As a response, various conceptualizations have been introduced such as digital cities, wired cities, cyber cities, real-time city, techno cities, WIKI cities and networked cities. Although there are variety of city descriptions, the smart city concept has become most recognized among practitioners and urban researchers (Steenbruggen et al., 2015).

Table 1. Studies related to urbanization problems

Implementation	The study presents ...	Study
Health	an IoT hybrid monitoring system for health industry by combining RFID and WSN technologies.	Adame et al., 2018
	a novel term as smart health. Smart health uses mobile phones including context-aware complement in smart cities.	Solanas et al. 2014
	remote monitoring system based on daily living activity by supporting elderly people.	Maki et al, 2011
Traffic Management	a pilot system for public safety integrated in a campus microgrid. In addition, the system uncovers cyber security problems.	Jin et al, 2016
	An evaluation of passenger and commercial vehicles performance.	Melo et al. 2017
	a monitoring system based on mobility and some implementations related to traffic flows, security improvement and inside building energy.	Fernández-Ares et al., 2017
	an evaluation dynamic traffic network of a hotel service centers.	Yang et al., (in press)
Education	a study on integration of whole population and social inclusion in schools.	Aguaded-Ramírez, 2017
	a smart classroom environment for engineering education to develop co-learning.	Alelaiwi et al., 2015
	a smart class environment. It has a goal to generalize the Ambient Intelligence (AmI) vision in schools.	Santana-Mancilla et al. 2013
Energy Management	planning and operation models in the smart city based on energy.	Calvillo et al. 2016
	a load profile in buildings by analyzing the consumption of energy in a cooling/heating mechanical room	Capozzoli et al. 2017
	new method for operational management and mobile power infrastructure planning in smart cities.	Meenaa et al. 2017
	smart mobility solutions to manage energy savings with four main steps.	Chen et al. 2017
Pollution Monitoring	a study related to coastal and water areas, that is, pollution load in the coastal and modelling of dynamics in water.	Rahmat et al. 2016
Waste Management	different collection and transportation methods for solid waste.	Lella et al. 2017

Smart city is a term introduced in 1994. EU has supported smart city projects since 2010. It has become a popular topic in academia and industry. Some big companies such as Microsoft, IBM and Oracle have adopted smart city term to their visions since 2005 (Sta, 2016). Smart cities provide a smart economy, smart environment, smart living and smart governance by integration of technology, government and people. (Ahvenniemi et al., 2017). Townsend (2013) defines smart cities as "...places where information technology is combined with infrastructure, architecture, everyday objects, and even our bodies to address social, economic, and environmental problems..."

Smart city implementations aim to get the right information at the right place and on the right device to make a city-based decision with ease and to aid citizens more quickly (Rathore et al., 2016). The smart cities include millions of data sources. Sta (2016) expected that 50 billion devices would connect by IoT devices in 2020. A smart city monitors streets, people and objects continuously and gathers, analyses and uses data from different sources such as websites, smart phones and weblogs (Van de Pas et al., 2015). Smart cities have successful implementations in several areas such as smart mobility, smart living, smart environment, smart governance and smart economy (Del Chiappa & Baggio, 2015). Figure 1 presents a smart city concept with respect to big data sources and implementation areas.

Figure 1. Smart city concept

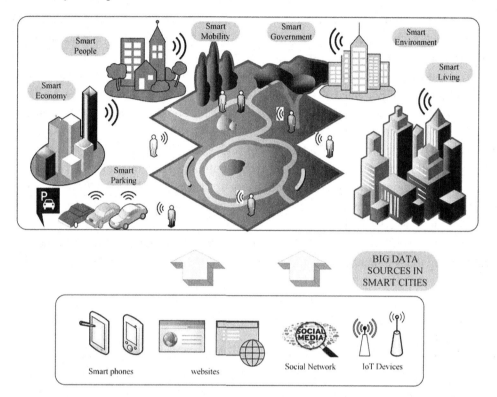

Smart Cities supported by Big Data and IoT help provide sustainable environment. They provide optimizing infrastructures, network security, convenience of the public services, better life environment, efficiency in city management and services, industry that is more modern and a dynamic and innovative economy (Susanti et al., 2016). Smart cities have also some economic outcomes such as workforce development and business or job creation (Joshi et al., 2016). At the same time, smart city initiatives with urban big data can increase people awareness and motivate the citizens to participate actively in public administration (Zanella et al., 2014).

BIG DATA

The volume of data has dramatically increased over the last decades with the use of several digital devices because of continuously huge amount of data generation. The generated data are generally heterogeneous, structured or unstructured data. Traditional database systems are inefficient with respect to storage, processing and analysis for big data. As an example of big data generation, Walmart tackles over 1 million transactions data and this value contains over 2.5 petabyte of data each hour (Yakoob et al., 2016).

Big data is a well-known concept arising from the requirement of big companies such as Google and Facebook that aim to analyze huge amount of data. Huge amounts of generated data are often called as big data. Various dimensions have been used to define big data. In 2001, Laney (2001) proposed the three dimensions of big data: volume, variety and velocity. Then the 3Vs have been accepted as a widespread big data concept (Chen et al., 2012; Kwon et al., 2014; Furht & Villanustre, 2016; Lee, 2017).

Volume is related to the collected and/or generated data. Sensors, social media, organizations and individuals generate large amount of unstructured data such as text, audio, images, and video (Anshari & Alas, 2015). John Gantz and David Reinsel (2011) put forward that the generated data volume in the world was 1.8 zettabytes (ZB), that 1 ZB equals to 1 trillion gigabytes, and it will be 35 ZB in 2020.

Velocity indicates the speed of created and processed data. The data velocity accelerates day by day. At the beginning, while companies analyzed their data with batch processing systems, today real time data processing has become well-advised because of high speed of data generating and processing. For instance, over one billion users open Youtube in each month and 100 hours of new videos of every few minutes. As another example to Big Data speed, users upload over 100 terabytes of data to Facebook in each day. Gartner (2015), a research and advisory company, forecasted that by 2020, the number of contacted devices will be 20.8 billion.

Variety indicates types of data. Big data are produced in various formats such as image, audio, text or clickstream using today's technologies (Yakoob et al., 2016). The generated data sets include several types of data such as complete or incomplete, structured, semi-structured or unstructured data and private or public (Oussous et al., 2017). According to the data type, analysis difficulty changes. For example, while structured data meet certain structural needs of applications, on the other hand, some extra transactions are applied to unstructured data.

In addition to the basic 3Vs, a number of new dimensions have introduced day by day, which help to understand big data. IBM put the fourth dimension as veracity, which presents the uncertainty because to data ambiguities, incompleteness and inconsistency. SAS introduced two additional concepts as variability and complexity. Variability means to the variation in data flow rates that may change due to unpredictable peaks and troughs. Complexity represents the number of data sources. Since big data are obtained from various sources, data formats and types make harder to analyze. Oracle added value as another dimension of big data. Value indicates worth of hidden insights in big data. Understanding the importance of using big is possible to uncover hidden information in collected data. Lee (2017) proposed decay that indicates the decreasing value of data in time. Because analyzing is a time-critical step of big data in different areas such as patient surveillance and environmental safety, decay of data is a significant element with respect to big data. Figure 2 shows the mentioned big data dimensions.

Multimedia data are created in different type such as video, audio, images, text and clickstream from several data sources such as organizations and individuals. For example, each individual generates data by connecting to the Internet at any moment. Facebook, Twitter, LinkedIn, YouTube and so on as social media platforms collect the generated huge amount of data (Bello-Orgaz et al., 2016). At the same time millions of people lives in urban areas which are big data resources. City data is obtained from individual citizens and visitors, private and public stakeholders and various governmental departments (van Zoonen, 2016). Notice that hidden patterns, correlations or other insight from city data can offer city planners to make successful urban policies and it can increase life quality of citizens.

Collected data from various sources as big data is used in many studies that provide collecting, observing, managing and analyzing for data-based decision making and various application goals (Işik et al., 2013; Jia et al., 2015; Jiang and Gallupe, 2015; Kung et al., 2015). In addition to the literature, organizations capitalize on big data by taking care of data flows (Akoka, 2017). Big data has an important effect for companies in generating new businesses, creating new services and products and developing business processes (Lee, 2017). Daimler produces about 10,000 cylinder heads used in car engine manufacturing.

Figure 2. Big data dimensions

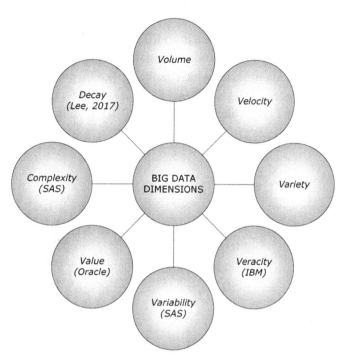

During the production process, Daimler gathers over 500 different data belonging to the product. The company analyzes the data, predicts errors and verifies variances before the production defects occur. Daimler cylinder manufacturing increased by approximately 25% after two years (Alharthi et al., 2017). Companies using data analytics in the processes have more effective and quick responses time to supply chain management. Southwest Airlines uses social media analytics to better meeting of customer requirements and representing better service. Tesco analyzes refrigerator data to decrease energy cost and achieved the saving near to $25 million in a year. Sears analyzes big data related to local weather conditions, prices at other retailers and product availability in the stores to determine prices dynamically. Innovative firms have applied social media to evaluate the credit risk and financing requirements of potential customers. They enable new types of financial items (Lee, 2017). Big data may enhance the potential value of the medical sector in US estimated at 300 billion $. When retailers exactly benefit from Big Data, they can raise the profit over 60% (Akoka, 2017).

Today, most of the people may be used as agents to gather data for real-time spatial observations (Steenbruggen et al., 2015). The applications are the basic data sources of generating big data (Yakoob et al., 2016). Social media can give information about the situation of traffic, environmental conditions, public transport and safety (Souza et al., 2016). Smart-phones, sensors, personal computers, cameras, intelligent/smart cars, Personal Digital Assistants (PDAs), social networking sites are possible data sources which generates big data (Hashem et al., 2016). Especially developed mobile operating systems have caused the smartphone as a necessary device in human life. One of the most critical characteristic of smartphones is the internet connectivity which provides to access internet at any moment (Anshari & Alas, 2017).

The Role of Data Analytics in IoT Applications

Big data analytics allow to store and process data in an IoT, rather than offering better decisions for business. IoT applications are one of the critical tools of big data. This subsection clarifies the role of big data and analytics in various IoT applications which include e-health, public utilities, transportation and logistics and smart inventory systems (Hashem et al., 2016; Al Nuaimi et al., 2015). Figure 3 presents a common framework for big data flow, which begins from IoT sources and results in useful information using various big data analytics.

Figure 3. Big data flow

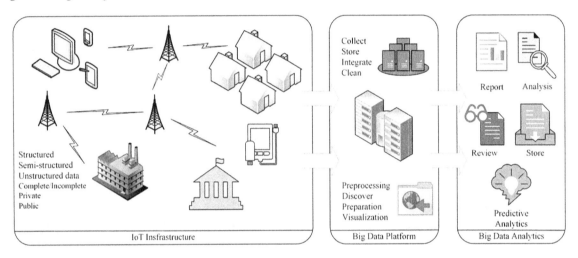

Smart grid case: Smart grids generate rapidly data from different data sources such as (Hashem et al., 2016). Monitoring smart grids operations and managing electronic power consumption and in real time are critical. This is achieved by connecting multiple IoT elements such as sensors, smart meters and control centers (Ahmed et al., 2017). Proper big data analytics helps to make correct decisions by detecting abnormal behaviors of the connected devices and identifying risk level of transformers. A real time analysis can simulate a model for incident scenarios. Energy consumption analytics can guide for management of power demand load (Stimmel, 2014).

- **Transportation:** Many transportation companies use RFID (Radio Frequency Identification) and GPS (Global Positioning System) systems to track and monitor vehicles (Rajaraman, 2016). These tracking systems can provide interesting information about passengers, routes and accidents after analysis of collected data. For example, mining big data can recommend different routes or frequency of trips for buses according to traffic jam or accident in the city. Passengers can obtain useful information about alternative ways to go to the desired destination. Big data analytics uses trips history of passengers to predict alternatives. Using real time systems provides valuable information for both passengers and bus routes. Passengers can get information on expected arrival time of buses and city planners have opportunity to change daily bus routes if needed. Collected data can be used to predict accident circumstances. It can define parameters causing an accident from previous accident. Therefore, number of road accidents can be minimized.

- **E-Health:** The basic idea on a big data application for healthcare is to personalize. To individualize health services, different health platforms are connected (Nambiar et al.,2013). As a result, large amount of data has been created in the healthcare sector over the last few years (Ahmed et al., 2017). Unless e-health analytics analyzes collected big data, personalization of healthcare is impossible. E-health analytics helps to analyze patients' data, created from several sources such as hospitals operations and clinical results data to learn their disease history. It is also used to optimize healthcare operations. In addition, insurance companies can benefit from big data e-health analytics to prepare policies.
- **Public Utilities:** Water supply and natural gas companies as an example of utilities use sensors in pipelines to observe and check flow of water/gas. A real-time tracking system to catch leakages and then control valves remotely to enable equitable supply of water/gas to different areas in the city (Oussous et al., in press). Big data public utilities analytics helps to decrease the number of operators accordingly reduce labor cost. In addition, it reduces time to identify and fix pipelines.
- **Smart Inventories:** It is used to monitor the flow of products in a company, create purchase orders, invoices and receipts etc. and control accounting related to inventory. The big data inventory analytics extract information on market trends, product recommendations and fraud detection from big data of inventory systems (Ahmed et al., 2017).

IoT and Green IoT

The term IoT first emerged in 1999. The data collection with various RFID tags and sensor technologies with the developments on Artificial Intelligence, Machine to Machine architectures, Wireless Sensor Networks and semantic technologies increased the applications of IoT (Hui et al., 2017).

IoT connectivity involves people, machines, tools and places such as mobile phones, watches, computers, cars, appliances using sensors, actuators, RFID, laser scanners, GPS etc. with unique addresses and enable these objects to interact with each other. Daily life devices such as fridge, air conditioning, switch, washing-machine can be easily communicated and managed with various Internet-based protocols. Many of these devices without IP support are resource constrained devices (Zhu et al., 2015; Kaur & Maheshwari, 2016; Bibri, 2018).

According to Zhu et al. (2015), IoT has six elements. These are identification, sensing, communication technologies, computation, services and semantic. Identification helps in naming and matching services with their demand. Electronic product codes are examples of identification methods used for the IoT. Sensing enables collecting data mostly from sensors and sending it to a database, data center, data warehouse etc. Communication technologies connect heterogeneous objects. Some protocols for the IoT are used such as Bluetooth, Wi-Fi, ultra-wide bandwidth etc. Computation is fulfilled by the hardware processing units and software applications. Cloud computing is essential in computation part of IoT. The services in IoT include identity-related services, information aggregation services, collaborative-aware services and ubiquitous services. Semantic aims to extract knowledge intelligently. The most frequently used semantic technologies are web ontology language (OWL), efficient XML interchange (EXI), etc. IoT has interconnection with Big Data and Cloud Computing to offer intelligent applications. The data is collected from various resources in a Smart City can be integrated with Cloud Computing (Albreem et al., 2017).

Green IoT aims a sustainable smart world, by decreasing the energy consumption of IoT (Zhu et al., 2015). The connected devices' number will be about 50 billion by 2020. Energy prices and carbon emissions increase correspondingly. Taking care of environmental issues through reducing the carbon dioxide emissions and greenhouse effects of devices, sensors, services etc. is crucial to acquire a green IoT reliability and smart city applications. Green RFID tags (such as reducing size of tags, producing printable and energy efficient tags), green sensing network (such as using renewable energy for charging, using energy saving optimization techniques, using context and data awareness algorithms to decrease data size) and green cloud computing networks (these networks have hardware that consumes less energy without losing performance and software that consumes less energy with minimum resource use) are some green IoT systems (Albreem et al., 2017).

BIG DATA AND IoT APPLICATIONS FOR SMART CITIES

Modern cities are getting smarter because technology grows rapidly. Problems can be prevented or their effects can be mitigated by analyzing huge data from variety of resources. This is where Big Data arises (Joshi et al., 2016). The need for smart cities has been emerging because of the increasing urbanization accompanies many problems. The processing power and storage capacity of computer technology increased with mobile broadband. Generated data from technological devices provides some of the solutions to urbanization problems by reducing environmental impact, creating new jobs, innovations, economic growth also helping traffic congestion, energy consumption, and behavioral change (Holler et al., 2014). According to van Zoonen (2016) data can be categorized as personal and impersonal that can be used service to citizens or surveillance of citizens in smart city applications.

Mobile phone data is one of the resources for smart city applications. Most of the people spend their time at a few places. To know these location points and routes can be used in effective network management and city management. Mobile phone data helps to find temporal and spatial level patterns. Then after analyzed properly, this data offers many benefits to city officers such as knowing where workers live and work can help manage public transportation traffic flows and plan services. As another example, knowing where and what times people come together for social activities, cultural or business institutions can target and price better their outdoor advertising as well as increase opening times and schedule of events. In city government point of view, mobile phone data can be used in crowd modeling. The smart city applications can appear in critical issues such as preventing dangerous situations, crime or planning an emergency evacuation (Steenbruggen, 2015).

The expansion of the IoT parallel to big data analytics is increasingly stimulating smart city applications. The amount of digital urban data which is enabled by the IoT increase exponentially (Bibri, 2018). These big data have many application areas for cities.

With the use of IoT, all citizen's cyber, physical, social and mental condition will be interconnected and intelligent. Citizens can obtain knowledge about their surroundings. For example, an audio sensor of a citizen's mobile phone will be able to detect any abnormality in citizen's voice to determine whether the person is ill or not (Zhu et al., 2015).

Big data is collected from different sources, such as energy utilization habits or energy consumption of citizen data which are measured by smart meters. When big data is analyzed, future need of power supply can be predicted, specific pricing plans can be made. Smart grids aim to manage the power supply of cities effectively. Information flow is very important subject in smart grid. Information flow and energy flow are integrated and large amounts of and various types of data are collected in smart grids. Such as device status, customer interaction data. Big data analysis enables accurate electricity demand prediction so firms can optimize power generation, firms can develop dynamic pricing using customers' electricity consumption patterns. Smart healthcare applications are related such as remote monitoring systems, management of electronic records or hospital asset management. When big healthcare data analyzed properly, epidemics, cures, and diseases can be predicted. Personalized medicine can be improved. Large amounts of traffic data can be used in traffic congestion problem by offering alternative routes, transport data can be used to optimize shipping movements or some solutions for parking, public transport can be developed. Smart education includes eLearning, massive open online courses (MOOCs). Smart buildings have smart meters, various sensors, heating, light or water and waste management systems (Hashem et al., 2016; Holler et al., 2016; Jaradat et al., 2015; Zhou et al., 2016).

When smart energy management is succeeded, energy big data has potential benefits in terms of operational efficiency and cost control, system stability and reliability, energy efficiency and environmental issues, customer engagement and service satisfaction improvement, renewable energy management (Zhou et al., 2016). City administrators or firms can increase comfort level of citizens besides decreasing heating/cooling costs by monitoring temperature and the salubrity of the environment in public buildings such as administration offices with different types of sensors (Zanella et al., 2014). Smart parking helps citizens using sensor and monitor technologies and tracks cars and empty places in parking areas. Drivers can use some applications and they can obtain free parking areas in nearest area or more suitable places to them (Rathore et al., 2016).

Smart governance is related to citizen participation and private/public partnerships. Smart governance enables service integration, collaboration, communication and data exchange (Joshi et al., 2016). Smart technologies can be used in waste management of cities to reduce cost and enhance efficiency. Predictive policing can be made collecting individual and aggregate data. Such as crime patterns can be analyzed and then police departments' performance is increased (van Zoonen, 2016).

Security is one of the most critical smart city subject for the citizens. Smart public safety initiatives by feeding real-time information such as continuous video monitoring to fire and police departments enables safety personnel to arrive quickly to emergency situation area. Another example is face recognition systems that can be helpful in criminal cases (Rathore et al., 2016; Washburn et al. 2009). The effects of light earthquakes on buildings can be observed with sensor data such as vibration and deformation sensors, and then building stress can be monitored (Zanella et al., 2014). The smart tourism destination concept is also a smart city application (Del Chiappa & Baggio, 2015).

Urban Big Data Lab project is developed by some universities and local government of Rotterdam. It aims to understand and use big and open data for smart applications and city planning (van Zoonen, 2016). Some sensors are placed on bins where how full the bins are measured. When a bin collects a certain level of waste, a dustcart will be warned to collect the waste. This application can save about 50% of waste logistics costs (van Zoonen, 2016). Dubai Roads and Transport Authority has smart city projects. Smart Parking collects sensors data from parking spots, and finds free parking spaces for citizens (Kaur & Maheshwari, 2016). In Padova Smart City project, environmental data such as air temperature and humidity, CO level, noise, vibrations are collected with different kind of sensors which are settled on street lights (Avijit & Chinnaiyan, 2018).

There are many smart cities in the world applying mentioned big data and IoT applications. Seoul is one of the leading cities using smart technology in mobility and transportation. Especially in healthcare facilities for disabled and elderly using mobile devices to assure they received timely medical attention.

Rio de Janeiro, hosting the 2014 World Cup and the 2016 Olympics, had a partnership with IBM to be a smart city with offering advanced emergency and traffic services to visitors and citizens (Angelidou, 2015). Istanbul has worked on IoT since 2009 for smart transportation. Collecting sensor information from 6000 buses and 1050 bus stops, passengers are informed with an application where the bus is, how many minutes later it will arrive etc. There is also a black box project. In this project scope, more than 80 varied data (Indoor temperature, fuel saving, breaking number, engine temperature, breakdown information, idle running time etc.) are collected with communication technology infrastructure in buses. It offers to increase passenger satisfaction level. New York City decreased crime rate by 27% with gathering data in a central location and delivering real time information to officers instantly. Police department has real-time dashboards which shows a single view of emergency needs and its resources. The department can access event notifications using a web portal, email and handheld devices (Washburn et al., 2009). The Virtual Power Operating Center (Vi-POC) project is developed to support renewable energy providers in Italy. Data is collected from heterogeneous energy production plants (such as geothermal, wind etc.) using sensors in a wide territory. Weather information is also collected from related institutions. Combining these data sources, real-time energy production of power plants is predicted (Bergamaschi et al., 2016). National New Urbanization Planning of China has smart city initiatives such as informationized planning and management, modernized industrial development and elaborate social governance, broadband access of network, smart infrastructures, convenient provision of public service (Wu et al., 2018). Stockholm uses laser scanning, radio frequency identification and automatic photographing sensors in urban roads. These sensors monitor traffic in downtown area. Based on collected data, special taxes can be collected from drivers to help traffic jam and decrease greenhouse gas emission (Wu et al., 2018).

According to the study of Vidiasova et al. (2017), smart transportation is very popular for Hague (URL 1), Chicago (Buntz, 2016), New York (Ratnikova, 2015), Toronto (Marshalls, 2016), Bangkok (Oko, 2016), Dubai (URL 2), Hong Kong (URL 3) and Moscow (URL 4). Smart living applications, which refer quality of life for citizens, has an important interest in Berlin (URL 5), Canberra (URL 6) and Melbourne (URL 7). Smart environmental projects have been implemented in Buenos Aires (Donato, 2016), Delft (URL 8), Bodo (URL 9), Helsinki (URL 10) and Malmo (Graham, 2016). While Buenos Aires and Delft have are interested for a smart response to the flooding, on the other hand, Scandinavian cities such as Bodo, Helsinki and Malmo have detected project related to sustainable environment and ecology.

TECHNIQUES AND METHODS

Data Analytics

There are three types of analytics. These are descriptive, predictive and prescriptive. Descriptive analytics summarize the data and show what happened before such as Twitter posts. Predictive one analyzes statistical data to predict the future and, the prescriptive analysis helps to make suggestion to take action or can also be used to identify necessary solutions (Anshari & Alas, 2015).

The entire data processing can be summarized as follows: Firstly, data is acquired and stored, and according to requirements of user pattern extraction and filtering is done from data stores. Then cleaning and preprocessing such as data filling, data merging, data optimization, data consistency check, data normalization is done. So, data is prepared to be processed by establishing the dataset. Next step is processing and analyzing prepared data set. This kind of processing includes such as linear or nonlinear analysis, sequential analysis, factor analysis, regression, bivariate statistics. Data is categorized and the inter data and inter category relationships are analyzed with algorithms such as support vector machine, random forest, logistic regression, naive bayes. Next among the categorized data, inherent relationships are observed and further patterns or rules are uncovered using algorithms such as neural network, genetic algorithm, cross media algorithm. Lastly relationships among the variables are explained interactively and visually to present deeper understanding of obtained results (Pan et al., 2016).

Big Data Analytics

Although the information and communication technologies' important role in collecting, transmitting, and storing the big data, smart city development and maintaining depends on mining the useful information existed in data storages (Wu et al., 2018). Most of the big data is unstructured data which is about 95%, so new analytic tools, methods or techniques specific to such data sets are needed (Miah et al., 2017).

Big data analytics have similarities with business intelligence (BI). Both concepts use data management technologies and computer-based analytical tools to discover actionable knowledge and to facilitate decision making. BI is often used on organizational data architecture which relies on finite set of highly structured and offline mode data sources. On the other hand, big data aims to develop data management technologies and analytical tools that can overcome an infinite number of data sets, highly complex and dispersed data in real-time formats (Alharthi et al., 2017). Big data analytics capabilities consist of descriptive, exploratory, inferential, predictive, causal and mechanistic techniques (Janssen et al., 2017).

Some techniques analyze considerable amounts of data in a certain time. Data mining, social network analysis, web mining, machine learning, deep learning, visualization approaches, computer vision and optimization methods are helpful big data analytic techniques. Data mining includes classification, regression, cluster analysis and association rule of learning; and uses statistical methods and machine learning algorithms extracting meaningful information from data. Web mining is used to obtain a pattern from large web repositories. It includes web content and web structure mining. Visualization approaches generate tables, figures or diagrams to understand the data. Visualization enables to identify patterns and relationships. Quantifiable problems can be solved with optimization methods. Some strategies to solve the problem quickly and find a solution near to optimum are quantum annealing, simulated annealing, swarm optimization, and genetic algorithms. Computer vision helps to gain high level of understandings from digital data. Lastly, social network analysis is applied to view social relationships in social network theory (Yakoob et al., 2016).

Machine learning and text mining are the main techniques for location and mobility mining. The core techniques used in literature are: k-Means, Self-organizing map, Density-based clustering, Spectral clustering and Mean-shift (Sacco et al., 2013).

Constraint programming, fuzzy possibilistic model, dynamic programming, Particle swarm optimization based method, Biogeography-based optimization algorithm, Time series models, autoregressive models, artificial neural network, Bayesian networks, support vector machine, quantile regression, artificial neural network, Sequential Monte Carlo simulation, Ant colony optimization, K-means clustering, Hierarchical clustering, Self-organized Mapping, fault tree analysis, autoregressive models are big data driven smart grid management methods (Zhou et al., 2016).

City data as a big data has various kinds of imperfection. These are imprecision, uncertainty, ambiguity. Several theories are applied to model these imperfections such as fuzzy set logic to model ambiguity and imprecise data, probability theory to model incomplete data, and possibility theory to model imprecise data. The bipolar logic and the set approximate (Rough Sets) and the Dempster, Shafer, theory are also used (Sta, 2017).

Architecture of Smart City and Big data is presented in Table 2. It is a 4-tier model and includes data resources, human resources, technologies, and tools. Developed smart city applications should be environment friend. Examples for each tier is given in Table 2.

Table 2. Architecture of smart city and big data

Data Resource	Human Resource	Technology	Tools
Machine data captured by sensors, meters etc.	Citizens	Mobile Phone	Data mining
Data from mobile phones	Data scientists	Network (4G LTE, LTE-A, and 5G)	Hadoop and its companion tools
Internet data	Predictive modellers	Smart meters	Predictive analytics
Web server logs	Statisticians	Sensors, screens	Machine learning
Social media	Other analytics professionals	Vehicle technology	Deep learning
GPS	Government officials	RFID	Cloud computing
Various records such as hospital data	Industry managers	PCs	Text mining
Other mobile phone data	Municipal authority	Wi-Fi, Ultra-wideband, ZigBee, and Bluetooth	Statistical analysis
Weather data		Camera	Data visualization tools
Vehicles		Wearable devices	Web mining
Applications			

CONCLUSION

Big Data is a new resource to maintain the high growth of the information industry. Today, firms' competitiveness is highly dependent on their skills to leverage the technologies related to Big Data (Akoka, Comyn-Wattiau, & Laoufi, 2017).

People produces digital signs increasingly interacting with devices, social media and other technological systems. This data gives many opportunities to support policies and planners in satisfying citizens' needs (Bergamaschi et al., 2016). Uncovering hidden patterns, correlations, and some other insights from big data offer organizations to improve their businesses and satisfy their customers (Hashem et al., 2016).

Rapid urbanization and growth of urban populations require some policies for countries. One of these policies is to build smart environments. Smart City applications are oriented on the strategic use of new technology and innovativeness to increase the efficiencies and the competitiveness of cities (Sta, 2016). Smart homes, smart transportation, smart grids and smart health cares have been introduced recently. Big data has the potential for especially for metropolis to get valuable insights from huge amount of data which is collected with variety of sources (Hashem et al., 2016). Big data can be shared, integrated, analyzed and mined to enable users a better understanding of urban operations. More informed decisions about urban administration can be taken with more scientific approaches (Pan, Tian, Liu, Gu, & Hua, 2016).

Smart cities have challenges about some regulatory issues, legal compliances and environmental issues. Both political and legal components are important to develop a smart city (Joshi, Saxena, Godbole, & Shreya, 2016). Becoming a smart city has technical, organizational or educational challenges (Holler et al., 2014). Another challenge in building smart cities is the extraction of relevant information from the information communication technology infrastructure of cities (Souza, Figueredo, Cacho, Araújo, & Prolo, 2016). A well-planned infrastructure should be set up and developed. The use of a variety of sensors have some challenges that are related to restricted physical capabilities (as energy, processing, and memory) (Souza, Figueredo, Cacho, Araújo, & Prolo, 2016).

While some argue that proper usage of big data makes cities cleaner, richer and more efficient, contrary to this, some argue that cities will turn into robotic places which are data driven. So creativity of these cities disappears (van Zoonen, 2016). Data is collected from various sources and has various kinds of imperfection: imprecision, uncertainty, ambiguity (Sta, 2016). Lack of data science skills in organizations, organizational cultures that are not leading to data driven operations or data driven decision making are another barrier (Alharthi et al., 2017).

REFERENCES

Adame, T., Bel, A., Carreras, A., Melià-Seguí, J., Oliver, M., & Pous, R. (2018). CUIDATS: An RFID–WSN hybrid monitoring system for smart health care environments. *Future Generation Computer Systems*, *78*(2), 602–615. doi:10.1016/j.future.2016.12.023

Aguaded-Ramírez, E. (2017). Smart city and Intercultural Education. *Procedia: Social and Behavioral Sciences*, *237*, 326–333. doi:10.1016/j.sbspro.2017.02.010

Ahmed, E., Yaqoob, I., Hashem, I. A. T., Khan, I., Ahmed, A. I. A., Imran, M., & Vasilakos, A. V. (2017). The role of big data analytics in Internet of Things. *Computer Networks*, *129*, 459–471. doi:10.1016/j.comnet.2017.06.013

Ahvenniemi, H., Huovila, A., Pinto-Seppä, I., & Airaksinen, M. (2017). What are the differences between sustainable and smart cities? *Cities (London, England)*, *60*, 234–245. doi:10.1016/j.cities.2016.09.009

Akoka, J., Comyn-Wattiau, I., & Laoufi, N. (2017). Research on Big Data–A systematic mapping study. *Computer Standards & Interfaces*, *54*, 105–115. doi:10.1016/j.csi.2017.01.004

Al Nuaimi, E., Al Neyadi, H., Mohamed, N., & Al-Jaroodi, J. (2015). Applications of big data to smart cities. *Journal of Internet Services and Applications*, *6*(1), 25–40. doi:10.118613174-015-0041-5

Albreem, M. A., El-Saleh, A. A., Isa, M., Salah, W., Jusoh, M., Azizan, M. M., & Ali, A. (2017). Green internet of things (IoT): An overview. In: Smart Instrumentation, Measurement and Application (IC-SIMA), 2017 IEEE 4th International Conference on. IEEE, 2017. p. 1-6.

Alelaiwi, A., Alghamdi, A. Shorfuzzaman, M., Rawashdeh, M., Hossain, M.S. & Muhammad, G. (2015). Enhanced engineering education using smart class environment. *Computers in Human Behavior, 51(Part B)*, 852-856.

Alharthi, A., Krotov, V., & Bowman, M. (2017). Addressing barriers to big data. *Business Horizons*, *60*(3), 285–292. doi:10.1016/j.bushor.2017.01.002

Angelidou, M. (2015). Smart cities: A conjuncture of four forces. *Cities (London, England)*, *47*, 95–106. doi:10.1016/j.cities.2015.05.004

Anshari, M., & Alas, Y. (2015). Smartphones habits, necessities, and big data challenges. *The Journal of High Technology Management Research*, *26*(2), 177–185. doi:10.1016/j.hitech.2015.09.005

Avijit, K., & Chinnaiyan, R. (2018). IOT for Smart Cities. International Journal of Scientific Research in Computer Science. *Engineering and Information Technology*, *3*(4), 1126–1139.

Bello-Orgaz, G., Jung, J. J., & Camacho, D. (2016). Social big data: Recent achievements and new challenges. *Information Fusion*, *28*, 45–59. doi:10.1016/j.inffus.2015.08.005

Bergamaschi, S., Carlini, E., Ceci, M., Furletti, B., Giannotti, F., Malerba, D., ... Perego, R. (2016). Big Data Research in Italy: A Perspective. *Engineering*, *2*(2), 163–170. doi:10.1016/J.ENG.2016.02.011

Bibri, S. E. (2018). The IoT for Smart Sustainable Cities of the Future: An Analytical Framework for Sensor-Based Big Data Applications for Environmental Sustainability. *Sustainable Cities and Society*, *38*, 230–253. doi:10.1016/j.scs.2017.12.034

Buntz, B. (2016). *Why Chicago is a Smart City King*. Retrieved 08 January, 2018 from http://www.ioti.com/smart-cities/why-chicago-smart-city-king

Calvillo, C. F., Sánchez-Miralles, A., & Villar, J. (2016). Energy management and planning in smart cities. *Renewable & Sustainable Energy Reviews*, *55*, 273–287. doi:10.1016/j.rser.2015.10.133

Capozzoli, A., Piscitelli, M. S., & Brandi, S. (2017). Mining typical load profiles in buildings to support energy management in the smart city context. *Energy Procedia*, *134*, 865–874. doi:10.1016/j.egypro.2017.09.545

Chen, H., Chiang, R. H. L., & Storey, V. C. (2012). Business intelligence and analytics: From big data to big impact. *Management Information Systems Quarterly*, *36*(4), 1165–1188. doi:10.2307/41703503

Chen, Y., Ardila-Gomez, A., & Frame, G. (2017). Achieving energy savings by intelligent transportation systems investments in the context of smart cities. *Transportation Research Part D, Transport and Environment*, *54*, 381–396. doi:10.1016/j.trd.2017.06.008

Cities Digest. (2017). *Smart City Moscow*. CitiesDigest. Retrieved from https://www.citiesdigest.com/2017/07/03/smart-city-moscow

CMD. (2014). *Digital Canberra: Action Plan 2014-2018*. Retrieved from http://www.cmd.act.gov.au/__data/assets/pdf_file/0006/565566/digcbractionplan_print.pdf

Consoli, S., Presutti, V., Recupero, D. R., Nuzzolese, A. G., Peroni, S., & Gangemi, A. (2017). Producing linked data for smart cities: The case of Catania. *Big Data Research*, *7*, 1–15. doi:10.1016/j.bdr.2016.10.001

Cumgeek. (2017). *Hong Kong becomes a Smart City*. (in Russian) Retrieved from https://cumgeek.com/articles/gonkong-skoro-stanet-umnym-gorodom

Del Chiappa, G., & Baggio, R. (2015). Knowledge transfer in smart tourism destinations: Analyzing the effects of a network structure. *Journal of Destination Marketing & Management, 4*(3), 145–150. doi:10.1016/j.jdmm.2015.02.001

Delft, The Netherlands. (2015). *Delft Smart City.* Retrieved from https://www.delft.nl/Bedrijven/ Stad_van_innovatie/Delft_Smart_City

Donato, C. (2016). Buenos Aires Preserves Old Charm by Becoming a Smart City. *SAP News Center.* Retrieved from http://news.sap.com/buenos-aires-preserves-old-charm-by-becoming-a-smart-city/

Doran, D., Gokhale, S., & Dagnino, A. (2013). Human sensing for smart cities. In *Proceedings of the 2013 IEEE/ACM International Conference on Advances in Social Networks Analysis and Mining* (pp. 1323-1330). ACM.

Economist. (2016). *The world`s most livable cities.* Retrieved from https://www.economist.com/blogs/ graphicdetail/2016/08/daily-chart-14

EU Smartcities. (2017). *The Hague- Smart communities market place.* Retrieved from https://eu-smartcities.eu/place/hague

European Commission. (n.d.). Strategic Energy Technology Plan. Retrieved from https://ec.europa.eu/ energy/en/topics/technology-and-innovation/strategic-energy-technology-plan

Fernández-Ares, A., Mora, A. M., Arenas, M. G., García-Sanchez, P., Romero, G., Rivas, V., ... Merelo, J. J. (2017). Studying real traffic and mobility scenarios for a Smart City using a new monitoring and tracking system. *Future Generation Computer Systems, 76*, 163–179. doi:10.1016/j.future.2016.11.021

Furht, B., & Villanustre, F. (2016). Introduction to big data. In B. Furht & F. Villanustre (Eds.), *Big Data Technology and Application* (pp. 3–11). Cham: Springer International Publishing. doi:10.1007/978-3-319-44550-2_1

Gantz, J. & Reinsel, D. (2011). Extracting value from chaos. *IDC iView Report.*

Gartner. (2015). Gartner says 6.4 billion connected things will be in use in 2016, up 30 percent from. Retrieved from https://www.gartner.com/newsroom/id/3165317

Graham, T. (2016). Smart city Malmo. *EIB.* Retrieved from http://www.eib.org/attachments/documents/ smart_city_initiatives_and_projects_in_malmo_sweden_en.pdf

Hashem, I. A. T., Chang, V., Anuar, N. B., Adewole, K., Yaqoob, I., Gani, A., ... Chiroma, H. (2016). The role of big data in smart city. *International Journal of Information Management, 36*(5), 748–758. doi:10.1016/j.ijinfomgt.2016.05.002

Helsinki Smart Region. (2016). Retrieved from https://www.helsinkismart.fi

Holler, J., Tsiatsis, V., Mulligan, C., Avesand, S., Karnouskos, S., & Boyle, D. (2014). *From Machine-to-machine to the Internet of Things: Introduction to a New Age of Intelligence.* Cambridge: Academic Press.

Hui, T. K., Sherratt, R. S., & Sánchez, D. D. (2017). Major requirements for building Smart Homes in Smart Cities based on Internet of Things technologies. *Future Generation Computer Systems, 76*, 358–369. doi:10.1016/j.future.2016.10.026

Işık, Ö., Jones, M. C., & Sidorova, A. (2013). Business intelligence success: The roles of BI capabilities and decision. *Information & Management, 50*(1), 13–23. doi:10.1016/j.im.2012.12.001

Janssen, M., van der Voort, H., & Wahyudi, A. (2017). Factors influencing big data decision-making quality. *Journal of Business Research, 70,* 338–345. doi:10.1016/j.jbusres.2016.08.007

Jaradat, M., Jarrah, M., Bousselham, A., Jararweh, Y., & Al-Ayyoub, M. (2015). The internet of energy: Smart sensor networks and big data management for smart grid. *Procedia Computer Science, 56*(6), 592–597. doi:10.1016/j.procs.2015.07.250

Jia, L., Hall, D., & Song, J. (2015). The conceptualization of data-driven decision making capability. In *Proceedings of the Twenty-First Americas Conference on Information Systems,* Puerto Rico, August 13–15.

Jiang, J., & Gallupe, R. B. (2015). Environmental scanning and business insight capability: the role of business analytics and knowledge integration. In *Proceedings of the Twenty-First Americas Conference on Information Systems,* Puerto Rico, August 13–15.

Jin, D., Hannon, C., Li, Z., Cortes, P., Ramaraju, S., Burgess, P., ... Shahidehpour, M. (2016). Smart street lighting system: A platform for innovative smart city applications and a new frontier for cyber-security. *The Electricity Journal, 29*(10), 28–35. doi:10.1016/j.tej.2016.11.011

Joshi, S., Saxena, S., Godbole, T., & Shreya. (2015). Developing Smart Cities: An Integrated Framework. *Procedia Computer Science, 93,* 902–909. doi:10.1016/j.procs.2016.07.258

Kaur, M. J., & Maheshwari, P. (2016, March). Building smart cities applications using IoT and cloud-based architectures. In *2016 International Conference on Industrial Informatics and Computer Systems (CIICS)* (pp. 1-5). IEEE. 10.1109/ICCSII.2016.7462433

Kim, T. H., Ramos, C., & Mohammed, S. (2017). Smart city and IoT.

Kung, L., Kung, H., Jones-Framer, A., & Wang, Y. (2015). Managing big data for firm performance: a configurational approach. In *Proceedings of the Twenty-First Americas Conference on Information Systems,* Puerto Rico, August 13–15.

Kwon, O., Lee, N., & Shin, B. (2014). Data quality management, data usage experience, and acquisition intention of big data analytics. *International Journal of Information Management, 34*(3), 387–394. doi:10.1016/j.ijinfomgt.2014.02.002

Laney, D. (2001). 3D data management: Controlling data volume, velocity, and variety. *Gartner.* Retrieved from http://blogs.gartner.com/doug-laney/files/2012/01/ad949-3D-Data-Management-Controlling-Data-Volume-Velocity-and-Variety.pdf

Lee, I. (2017). Big data: Dimensions, evolution, impacts, and challenges. *Business Horizons, 60*(3), 293–303. doi:10.1016/j.bushor.2017.01.004

Lella, J., Mandla, V. R., & Zhu, X. (2017). Solid waste collection/transport optimization and vegetation land cover estimation using Geographic Information System (GIS): A case study of a proposed smart-city. *Sustainable Cities and Society, 35,* 336–349. doi:10.1016/j.scs.2017.08.023

Maki, H., Ogawa, H., Matsuoka, S., Yonezawa, Y., & Caldwell, W. M. (2011). A daily living activity remote monitoring system for solitary elderly people. In *Proceedings of 2011 annual international conference of the IEEE engineering in medicine and biology society* (pp. 5608–5611). 10.1109/IEMBS.2011.6091357

Marshalls, A. (2016). How Toronto is becoming a smarter city. *Torontoist*. Retrieved from http://torontoist.com/2016/06/how-toronto-is-becoming-a-smarter-city

Meena, N. K., Parashar, S., Swarnkar, A., Gupta, N., Niazi, K. R., & Bansal, R. C. (2017). Mobile Power Infrastructure Planning and Operational Management for Smart City Applications. *Energy Procedia*, *142*, 2202–2207. doi:10.1016/j.egypro.2017.12.589

Melo, S., Macedo, J., & Baptista, P. (2017). Guiding cities to pursue a smart mobility paradigm: An example from vehicle routing guidance and its traffic and operational effects. *Research in Transportation Economics*, *65*, 24–33. doi:10.1016/j.retrec.2017.09.007

Miah, S. J., Vu, H. Q., Gammack, J., & McGrath, M. (2017). A big data analytics method for tourist behaviour analysis. *Information & Management*, *54*(6), 771–785. doi:10.1016/j.im.2016.11.011

Nambiar, R., Bhardwaj, R., Sethi, A., & Vargheese, R. (2013). A look at challenges and opportunities of Big Data analytics in healthcare. In *IEEE International Conference on Big Data*, Santa Clara, October 6-9. 10.1109/BigData.2013.6691753

Oko, Y. (2016). Bangkok strives to be 'smart city' to ease traffic. *Asian Review*. Retrieved from http://asia.nikkei.com/Business/Trends/Bangkok-strives-to-be-smart-city-to-ease-traffic

Oussous, A., Benjelloun, F.Z., Lahcen, A.A. & Belfkih, S. (in press). Big Data technologies: A survey. *Journal of King Saud University – Computer and Information Sciences*.

Pan, Y., Tian, Y., Liu, X., Gu, D., & Hua, G. (2016). Urban big data and the development of city intelligence. *Engineering*, *2*(2), 171–178. doi:10.1016/J.ENG.2016.02.003

Rahmat, A., Syadiah, N., & Subur, B. (2016). Smart Coastal City: Sea Pollution Awareness for People in Surabaya Waterfront City. *Procedia: Social and Behavioral Sciences*, *227*, 770–777. doi:10.1016/j.sbspro.2016.06.144

Rajaraman, V. (2016). Big Data Analytics. *Resonance*, *21*(8), 695–716. doi:10.100712045-016-0376-7

Rathore, M. M., Ahmad, A., Paul, A., & Rho, S. (2016). Urban planning and building smart cities based on the Internet of Things using Big Data analytics. *Computer Networks*, *101*(3), 63–80. doi:10.1016/j.comnet.2015.12.023

Ratnikova, L. (2015). 11 Ecological initiatives in megapolicies. *Recyclemag*. Retrieved from http://recyclemag.ru/article/11-ekologicheskih-initsiativ-mirovyh-megapolisov

Rosati, U., & Conti, S. (2016). What is a smart city project? An urban model or a corporate business plan? *Procedia: Social and Behavioral Sciences*, *223*, 968–973. doi:10.1016/j.sbspro.2016.05.332

Sacco, D., Motta, G., You, L., Bertolazzo, N., Chen, C., Pavia, U., & Pv, P. (2013). *Smart cities, urban sensing and big data: mining geo-location in social networks*. Salerno, Italy: AICA.

Santana-Mancilla, P. C., Echeverría, M. A. M., Santos, J. C. R., Castellanos, J. A. N. C., & Díaz, A. P. S. (2013). Towards Smart Education: Ambient Intelligence in the Mexican Classrooms. *Procedia: Social and Behavioral Sciences, 106*, 3141–3148. doi:10.1016/j.sbspro.2013.12.363

Smart Cities Council. (n.d.). Pike research. Retrieved from http://smartcitiescouncil.com/tags/pike-research

Smart Dubai. (2016). *Smart Dubai*. Retrieved from http://www.smartdubai.ae

Solanas, A., Patsakis, C., Conti, M., Vlachos, I. S., Ramos, V., Falcone, F., ... Martinez-Balleste, A. (2014). Smart health: A context-aware health paradigm within smart cities. *IEEE Communications Magazine, 52*(8), 74–81. doi:10.1109/MCOM.2014.6871673

Souza, A., Figueredo, M., Cacho, N., Araújo, D., & Prolo, C. A. (2016). Using Big Data and Real-Time Analytics to Support Smart City Initiatives. *IFAC-PapersOnLine, 49*(30), 257–262. doi:10.1016/j.ifacol.2016.11.121

Sta, H. B. (2016). Quality and the efficiency of data in "Smart-Cities". *Future Generation Computer Systems, 74*, 409–416. doi:10.1016/j.future.2016.12.021

Stadtentwicklung. (2015). *Smart City Strategy Berlin. State Department for Urban Development and the Environment*. Retrieved from http://www.stadtentwicklung.berlin.de/planen/foren_initiativen/smart-city/download/Strategie_Smart_City_Berlin_en.pdf

Steenbruggen, J., Tranos, E., & Nijkamp, P. (2015). Data from mobile phone operators: A tool for smarter cities? *Telecommunications Policy, 39*(3), 335–346. doi:10.1016/j.telpol.2014.04.001

Stimmel, C. L. (2014). *Big Data Analytics Strategies for the Smart Grid*. CRC Press. doi:10.1201/b17228

Susanti, R., Soetomo, S., Buchori, I., & Brotosunaryo, P. M. (2016). Smart Growth, Smart City and Density: In Search of The Appropriate Indicator for Residential Density in Indonesia. *Procedia: Social and Behavioral Sciences, 227*, 194–201. doi:10.1016/j.sbspro.2016.06.062

Townsend, A. M. (2013). *Smart cities: Big data, civic hackers, and the quest for a new utopia*. New York: WW Norton & Company.

United Nations. (2012). *World urbanization prospects; the 2011 revision*. New York: Department of Economic and Social Affairs.

van de Pas, J., van Bussel, G. J., Veenstra, M., & Jorna, F. (2015). Digital data and the city: An exploration of the building blocks of a smart city architecture. In D. Baker & W. Evans (Eds.), *Digital Information Strategies: From Applications and Content to Libraries* (pp. 185–198). Chandos Publishing.

van Zoonen, L. (2016). Privacy concerns in smart cities. *Government Information Quarterly, 33*(3), 471–480. doi:10.1016/j.giq.2016.06.004

Vegvesen. (2015). *Smart Bodo*. Retrieved from https://www.vegvesen.no/_attachment/1103917/binary/1076326?fast_title=Visjonen+om+verdens+smarteste+by+%E2%80%93+SMART+Bod%C3%B8+-+Asgeir+Jordbru.pdf

Vidiasova, L., Kachurina, P., & Cronemberger, P. (2017). Smart Cities Prospects from the Results of the World Practice Expert Benchmarking. *Procedia Computer Science, 119*, 269–277. doi:10.1016/j. procs.2017.11.185

Washburn, D., Sindhu, U., Balaouras, S., Dines, R. A., Hayes, N., & Nelson, L. E. (2009). *Helping CIOs understand "smart city" initiatives*. Cambridge: Forrester.

World Bank. (n.d.). Retrieved from data.worldbank.org/indicator/SP.URB.TOTL.IN.ZS?end=2015&start=1960&view=chart

Wu, Y., Zhang, W., Shen, J., Mo, Z., & Peng, Y. (2018). Smart City with Chinese Characteristics against the Background of Big Data: Idea, Action and Risk. *Journal of Cleaner Production, 173*, 60–66. doi:10.1016/j.jclepro.2017.01.047

Yang, J., Han, Y., Wang, Y., Jiang, B., Lv, Z., & Song, H. (in press). Optimization of real-time traffic network assignment based on IoT data using DBN and clustering model in smart city. *Future Generation Computer Systems*.

Yaqoob, I., Hashem, I. A. T., Gani, A., Mokhtar, S., Ahmed, E., Anuar, N. B., & Vasilakos, A. V. (2016). Big data: From beginning to future. *International Journal of Information Management, 36*(6), 1231–1247. doi:10.1016/j.ijinfomgt.2016.07.009

Zanella, A., Bui, N., Castellani, A., Vangelista, L., & Zorzi, M. (2014). Internet of things for smart cities. *IEEE Internet of Things Journal, 1*(1), 22–32. doi:10.1109/JIOT.2014.2306328

Zhou, K., Fu, C., & Yang, S. (2016). Big data driven smart energy management: From big data to big insights. *Renewable & Sustainable Energy Reviews, 56*, 215–225. doi:10.1016/j.rser.2015.11.050

Zhu, C., Leung, V. C., Shu, L., & Ngai, E. C. H. (2015). Green internet of things for smart world. *IEEE Access: Practical Innovations, Open Solutions, 3*, 2151–2162. doi:10.1109/ACCESS.2015.2497312

This research was previously published in the Handbook of Research on Big Data and the IoT; pages 22-41, copyright year 2019 by Engineering Science Reference (an imprint of IGI Global).

Chapter 53
Big Data for Satellite Image Processing:
Analytics, Tools, Modeling, and Challenges

Remya S.
VIT University, India

Ramasubbareddy Somula
VIT University, India

Sravani Nalluri
VIT University, India

Vaishali R.
VIT University, India

Sasikala R.
VIT University, India

ABSTRACT

This chapter presents an introduction to the basics in big data including architecture, modeling, and the tools used. Big data is a term that is used for serving the high volume of data that can be used as an alternative to RDBMS and the other analytical technologies such as OLAP. For every application there exist databases that contain the essential information. But the sizes of the databases vary in different applications and we need to store, extract, and modify these databases. In order to make it useful, we have to deal with it efficiently. This is the place that big data plays an important role. Big data exceeds the processing and the overall capacity of other traditional databases. In this chapter, the basic architecture, tools, modeling, and challenges are presented in each section.

DOI: 10.4018/978-1-6684-3662-2.ch053

1. INTRODUCTION

Day by day, we see the data is rapidly increasing in many forms. We have some traditional data processing software to process small quantity of data. But as trillions of bytes of information is being processed per second, the traditional software techniques fail in processing this data. We need to re-think of a solution which can process this data. Now Big Data gives us a solution. Big Data is a term used for creating, capturing, communicating, aggregating, storing and analyzing large amounts of data. Many attempts encountered to quantify the growth rate in the volume of data is called as Information Explosion.

Major milestones took place in the history of sizing data volumes plus the evolution of the term Big Data. The following are some of them:

- In 1971, Arthur Miller stated in "The Assault on Privacy" that:

Too many information handlers seem to measure a man by the number of bits of storage capacity his dossier will occupy.

- In April 1980, I.A.Tjomsland gave a talk titled "Where Do We Go From Here?" at "Fourth IEEE Symposium on Mass Storage Systems" in which he says:

Data expands to fill the space available, I believe that large amounts of data are being retained because users have no way of identifying obsolete data, the penalties for storing obsolete data are less apparent than are the penalties for discarding potentially useful data.

- In 1997, Michael Lesk publishes "How much information is there in this world?" in which he concludes that:

There may be a few thousand petabytes of information all told, and the production of tape and disk will reach that level by the year 2000. So in only a few years, (a) we will be able to save everything- no information will have to be thrown out, and (b) the typical piece of information will never be looked at by a human being. (https://www.forbes.com/sites/gilpress/2013/05/09/a-very-short-history-of-big-data/2/#1c3097c24343).

The term Big Data was coined in 1998 by Mr. John Mashey, Chief Scientist at SGI. Even though Michael Cox and David Ellsworth seem to have used the term 'Big Data' in print, Mr. Mashey supposedly used the term in his various speeches and that's why he is crediting from coming up with Big Data. But some various sources say that the first use of the term Big Data was done in an academic paper- Visually Exploring Gigabyte Datasets in Realtime(ACM) (OECD, 2015; Mark A. Beyer & Douglas Laney, 2012).

The following are the differentiators of Big Data over Traditional Business Intelligence solutions:

- Data is retained in a distributed file system instead of on a central server.
- The processing functions are taken to the data rather than data being taken to the functions.
- Data is of different formats, both structured as well as unstructured.
- Data is both real-time as well as offline data.
- Technology relies on massively parallel processing(MPP) concepts.

The Big Data challenges include capturing data, data storage, data analysis, search, sharing, transfer, visualization, querying, updating and information policy. Organizations have to compromise and balance against the confidentiality requirements of the data. Organizations must determine how long the data has to be retained. With the advent of new tools and technologies to build big data solutions, availability of skills is a big challenge for CIO's. A higher level of proficiency in the data science is required to implement big data solutions today because the tools are not user-friendly yet. (Bill Franks, 2012).

Analogous to the Cloud Computing architecture, the Big Data landscape can be divided into four layers.

- **Infrastructure as a Service (IaaS):** This includes the storage servers, and network as the base, inexpensive commodities of the big data stack.
- **Platform as a Service (PaaS):** The unstructured data stores and distributed caches that can be logically queried using query languages serves the platform layer of Big Data.
- **Data as a Service (DaaS):** The tools required to integrate the PaaS layer using search engines, integration adapters, batch programs and so on is housed in this layer.
- **Big Data Business Functions as a Service (BFaaS):** Industries like health, retail, e-commerce, energy and banking build applications that serve a specific purpose and hold the DaaS layer for cross-cutting data functions.

Recent Gartner's "Hype Cycle for Emerging Technologies", visualizes the absence of Big Data. Big Data got a permanent place in the Gartner Cycle for the past 5 years in the emerging technologies, but shockingly it was removed in July 2016. The reason was given by Burton, Gartner Analyst that *I would not consider big data to be an emerging technology. This hype curve is very much focused. I look at emerging trends.* (http://www.gartner.com/technology/research/hype-cycles/).

Here are some of the big data providers that are offering solutions in the specific industries:

- The Securities Exchange Commission (SEC) is using big data to monitor financial market activity. They are currently using network analytics and NLP to catch illegal trade activity in financial markets.
- In Communications, Media and Entertainment, industry simultaneously analyze customer data along with behavioral data to create detailed customer profiles.
- Some hospitals are using Big Data techniques to use evidence-based medicine as opposed to administering several medical/lab tests to all patients who go to the hospital.
- Big Data has also been used in solving today's manufacturing challenges and to gain competitive advantage among other benefits.
- In public services, Big Data has a very wide range of applications including energy exploitation, financial market analysis, fraud detection, health related search and environmental protection.
- In the field of Insurance, Big Data is used to provide customer insights for transparent and simpler products, by analyzing and predicting customer behavior through data derived from social media, GPS- enabled devices and CCTV footage.
- Smart meter readers allow data to be collected almost every 15 minutes as opposed to once a day with the old meter readers. This granular data is being used to analyze consumption of utilities better which allows for improved customer feedback and better control of utilities use (David R. Hardoon & Galit Shmueli, 2013).

We have 4 V's of Big Data:

- **Velocity:** The data is increasing at a very fast rate. It is estimated that the volume of data doubles every year.
- **Variety:** Now a days data is not stored in rows and columns i.e., structured format. We see data is being stored in the form of log files i.e. unstructured.
- **Volume:** The amount of data which we deal with is of very large size of peta bytes.
- **Veracity:** Explains the reliability of data (Foster Provost & Tom Fawcett, 2013).

2. BIGDATA MODELING (4 V'S)

Bigdata can be defined as a collection of large amount of data sets. Using traditional tools it is very difficult to handle such a vast amount of datasets. This is the reason that bigdata become important in storing and analyzing large amount of data. These data can be mined by using data mining tools or DBMS tools. Based on this the main components of big data can be termed as set of 4 V's (P. Hitzler & K. Janowicz, 2013).

Figure 1. Modeling of Bigdata

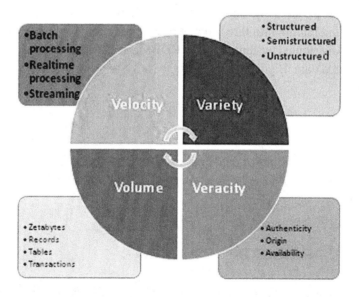

2.1 Volume, Velocity, Variety, Veracity

- Volume refers to the amount of data
- Velocity refers to the rate at which data can be generated and transmitted
- Variety refers to the different types of data such as structured, semi structured and unstructured
- Veracity refers to the integrity of the data

The bigdata differentiates from the traditional data based on these 4 components:

2.1.1 Volume

We live in the data age and in 2013 it was analyzed that the total volume of data storage is 4.4 zeta bytes and in 2020 it will become 44 zeta bytes (1 zeta byte is 10^{21} Bytes. These very much amount of data can need to be stored and analyzed. These data are from different sources and also need to be combined for better results.

2.1.2. Velocity

The data is from multiple sources and these sources are to be run parallel. Hence the important next issue is how to run these sources parallel with very high speed for data generation and transmission. For example consider a weather sensor which collects the weather data from multiple sources in each and every hour. These data is need to be move on to a particular storage and this data log is very high. Traditional systems are not capable of doing this storage and frequent movements.

2.1.3. Variety

The data sources can be of different types which can be collected from weather sensors, social networks, stock exchange and smart phones. The data includes text, images, audio, video or any other data logs. The data can be classified mainly into three such as structured data, semi structured data and unstructured data. Traditional distributed systems such as RDBMS, volunteer computing and grid computing can handle only structured data. Bigdata differs from these systems by it can handle semi structured and unstructured data also.

2.1.4. Veracity

The bigdata can handle huge amount of data and this data need to be correct also. Hence the Veracity refers to how we can clean the data for data preprocessing stage. The data need to be relevant and valuable (X. L. Dong & D. Srivastava, 2013).

3. ARCHITECTURE OF BIGDATA

Bigdata is treated as set of tools for developing and analyzing scalable, reliable and portable data. It serves as key for design infrastructure and solutions. It interconnects the existing and organizing the resources and consist different layers such as:

- **Bigdata Sources:** The location which produces the data.
- **Messaging and Storage:** The facilities where the data is stored.
- **Bigdata Analysis:** The different tools for analyzing the different types of data.

A bigdata architecture is designed so that it can handle processing, storage and analysis of complex large data .Bigdata can handle processing of big data sources, real time processing of data, predictive analytics using machine learning approaches and exploration of interactive data (K.Bakshi, 2012).

The architecture includes the following components:

- **Data Sources:** Real time data sources, application of data sources such as relational databases. Static files produced by webservers and other applications.
- **Data Storage:** Bigdata is not the first distributed processing systems. But it can store high volumes of data known as Data Lake, than other traditional systems. Bigdata can prepare the data for analysis and then these analytical data store can be used to serve different types of queries. The analytical data store can also provide metadata abstraction and low latency NoSQL technologies.
- **Processing of Data:** Bigdata provides interactive and batch processing including real time applications. Bigdata solutions process the data files using batch systems to filter and aggregate. If the solutions include real time sources, the bigdata architect can include stream processing also. The processed stream data is then written into an output sink (B. Ramesh, 2015).
- **Service Orchestration:** Most of the bigdata solutions consists of repeated data processing operations, then transform the encapsulated source data. The movement of data between multiple sources and destination and load the processing data in to an analytical store is an important issue in traditional systems. This can be automated by using service orchestration in bigdata by using the tools such as sqoop and Oozie.

Figure 2. Architecture of Bigdata

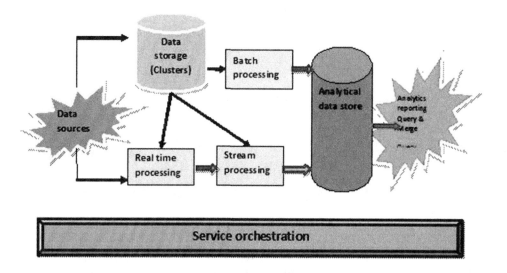

4. TOOLS USED IN BIGDATA ANALYTICS

4.1 Big Data Analytics with GIS Datasets

A number of open source tools, frameworks and query languages have been introduced to analyse big data. MongoDB is a famous NoSQL based data analytics tool that provides option to visualize, analyse and explore datasets. In this section let us explore a GIS dataset in Mongo Compass.

Here is the step by step implementation of the work:

Step 1: Install MongoDB Compass from mongodb.com as per the instructions provided in the website.
Step 2: Configure the MongoDB compass with the following details to get connected to the host.

Figure 3. Configuration screen of the mongoDB Compass

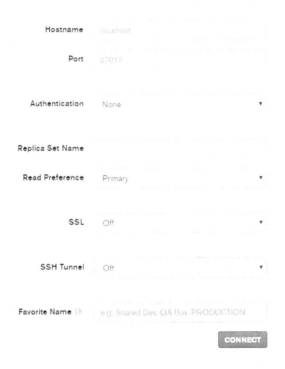

Step 3: Add the 100YWeather dataset to the MongoDB Compass. The dataset appears on the right side of the screen. Expand the title to see the data collection. Click on the data collection to view the records inside.

Figure 4. MongoDB Compass

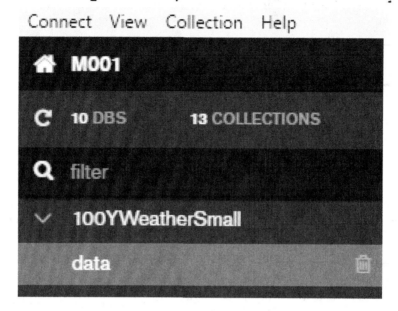

Step 4: Document View. In mongoDB records are named as json documents. The screen lists a huge collection of weather data in 250,000 json documents, with 5 Indexes and size of 403MB.

Figure 5. Document View

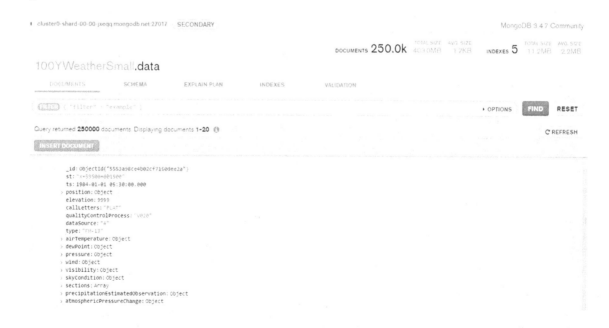

Schema View

Schema view lists the attributes information and visualizes the data with data types.

Figure 6. Schema View

To get the view of the Schema click on the Schema Tab at and top and then click on the green 'Analyse' button.

As shown in Figure 6, the query made to analyse the 100Y weather dataset has returned 250,000 json documents

The different tools in bigdata are summarized in Table 1.

Table 1. Tools in Bigdata

Name of the tool	Type	Developed by	Functionalities	Task
Microsoft Azure	Paid	Microsoft	Big data analytics, cloud computing, machine learning, HD Insight	Platform
Amazon Web Services	Pay for service	Amazon	Big data analytics, cloud computing, machine learning, hosting	Platform
Hadoop	Open source	Apache	Distributed data processing, HDFS, YARN and Map Reduce	Framework
HBase	Open Source	Apache	Large scalable online data storage	Storage
Ambari	Web based	Apache	Hadoop Cluster Manager	Dashboard
Avro	Open source	Apache	Rich data types, RPC, Binary data format, dynamic code integration	Data serialization
Cassandra	Open source	Apache	Robust storage with Scalability, reliability, fault tolerance, decentralization	Storage
Pentaho	Pay for Service	Hitachi	ETL tools, No Sql, integration with Hadoop, mongodb and other services	Platform
Cloudera	Enterprise service	Cloudera	Enterprise level Hadoop services	Platform
Mongodb	Open source	Mongo dB	Json storage, realtime customization with sandbox, atlas and compass, data management, visualization, scalable, NoSQL query processing, Visualization, data wrangling, security	Real-time Data management
Talend	Open Source	Talend	Data integration, Data management and sandbox, scalability, agility, business integration	Data integration and management

continues on following page

Table 1. Continued

Name of the tool	Type	Developed by	Functionalities	Task
Karmasphere Analyst and Studio	Pay for service	Karmasphere	Enterprise solution on clustered and unstructured Hadoop clusters, SQL, Map Reduce, Algorithm customization	Analytics
Skytree	Pay for sevice	Skytree	Highly accurate big data machine learning models, scalability, robust, automation, visualization	Advanced analytics and machine learning
Openrefine	Open source	Openrefine	Data pre-processing, scalable, works with messy data, Exploratory data analysis, ETL tools	Pre-Processing
Splunk	Pay for service	Splunk	User Behaviour analysis, Security, Machine data architecture, data integration and transformation	Analytics
Datacleaner 5.2	Pay for service	Neopost	Data pre-processing, anomaly detection, data cleaning, data health monitoring system, visualization, Standardization and profiling	Pre-Processing
RapidMiner	Pay for service	Rapidminer	GUI, Machine learning, data pre-processing, predictive analysis	Machine learning
Weka	Opensource	University of Waikato	GUI, Machine learning, data pre-processing, Jython, feature selection, classification, clustering, association rule mining, data visualization, integration with spark, python, big data analytics	Machine learning and visualization
IBM SPSS Modeler	Pay for service	IBM	Text analytics, statistical analysis, decision making, data management	Data management and analytics
Oracle cloud	Pay for service	Oracle	Big data storage, Big data preparation, Compute, development, analytics, golden gates, processing, MySQL, Java support, Internet of things integration.	Platform
Apache pig	Open Source	Apache	Parallel data analysis, map reduce, scalability, optimization	Platform
Teradata	Pay for service	Teradata	Unified big data architecture for enterprises, business insights, analytics	Analytics
Datawrapper	Pay for service	Datawrapper	Line plots, bar diagrams, donuts, stacked bar, geographical data mapping, tables	Visualization
Blockspring	Pay for service	Blockspring	Data warehousing, data synchronization with apps	Data integration
Magento	Pay for service	RJ Metrics	Business intelligence, data visualization and exploration	Analytics
Ideata analytics	Pay for service	Ideata	Business intelligence, data preparation, knowledge discovery, self-service analytics, big data analytics and visualization	Analytics
Thingspeak cloud	opensource	Thingspeak	Data storage, sensor integration, real time analytics, visualization of graphs, integration of api with social media, apps	Analytics and visualization

5. CHALLENGES IN BIGDATA

The term 'Bigdata' implies that it is a big volume of Data. As many industries are generating data volumes from terabytes to petabytes, there developed a need to process the raw data in to useful information. In order to provide benefits to business and Information technology, the concern for the enhancement of big data storage and processing architectures has increased. Potentially Bigdata undergoes a lot of challenges with the characteristics, data analytics and processing capabilities of the system. In this section, we mainly discuss about the challenges in major research areas (X. Yi, F. Liu, J. Liu, & H. Jin, 2014).

5.1 Data Complexity

The Bigdata collects a large scale data from different sources and solve the computational problems. The most significant characteristics of big data are types of data patterns, different structures and complicated communication between data samples. Big data refers to the data (or) Information which can always be processed with advance technology like analytics, visualization methods and can also find hidden pattern in order to make an accurate decision rather than using additional compute system ("Global Data Center Traffic"). Many Business organizations have large amount of data but that whole data is used properly due to the lack of efficient systems so that the percentage of data utilization is keep on decreasing (*Oracle Big Data Strategy Guide*). Now the technology is growing day by day, the mobile devices and sensors playing an important role for generating data and then stored. For example, people can monitor working people away from office because the office people staying far away from office (*Cloudera's 100% Open Source Distribution of Hadoop*). For instance, railway companies decided to install sensors for every few feet in order to monitor internal and external event which causes train to meet accidents. By monitoring every event, railway people comes to know that which part is required to replace and which one is repaired (James Manyika, Michael Chui, Brad Brown, Jacques Bughin, Richard Dobbs, Charles Roxburgh, & Angela Hung Byers, 2011). The roads are equipped with sensors to read the information for reducing the chances of occurring natural disaster by analyzing and predicting generated data ("Big Data, Big Impact: New Possibilities for International Development"). Everyday few terabytes of data is generated from every business organization, to deal with the traditional methods such as information retrieval, discovery, analysis, sentimental analysis, but they are not fit for huge data. Currently, we don't have good knowledge on data distribution law and association relation of big data. Also lack of deep understanding association between data complexity and computational complexity arises. The lack of the processing methods in big data and all the other aspects confine our ability to implement new method and models to solve all these problems in big data. The basic problem is to understand essential characteristics of complexity of big data. Basic study on complexity theory will give clear view on complexity and how they are formed, how they are associated with other pattern. By getting clear understanding on complex theory, we can design and implement novel models to resolve problems of big data complexity.

5.2 Computational Complexity

Big data includes three main features such as fast-changing, multiple sources, huge volume . These features become difficult for traditional processing methods such as machine learning, data retrieval, data analysis. New big data computing tools are needed to overcome problems coming from independent and identical distribution of data for generating accurate statistics. For addressing the problems of big data, we require examining computational complexity and used algorithms. The storage available for generating data through social websites is not enough, because of the popularity of big data on storage and network. Server's offloading the resource intensive data into cloud and sending more data into cloud for processing. Offloading data into cloud does not solve the problem. But big data require getting all the data collected and retrieving from terabytes to petabytes. Offloading the entire data into cloud will take large time and also data is changing in every second which will make the data hard to be updated in real time. Offloading data from the storage location to processing location can be avoided by two ways: one is to process the storage location and second one is offload only required data which will take more time to process. Building indexes for storing data which will make easy the retrieving process and moreover reducing processing time. In order to address computing complexity in big data we need to understand about life cycle application of big data to study of centralized processing mechanisms which depends upon the behavior of big data. We need to get way from tradition approach of computing-centric to distributed computing paradigms. We need to focus on new methods and data analysis mechanisms for distributed streaming mechanisms. We are also required to focus more on boot strapping and local computation, new algorithms for handling large amount of data.

5.3 System Complexity

Big data can process high-volume of heterogonous data types and applications to support research on big data. As big data processing are not enough to handle generating high volume of data and real time requirements, these constraints pose to establish new system architecture, processing system and energy optimization model. Addressing the complexity problems will lead to designing novel hardware and software frameworks for optimizing energy-consumption on big data. Systems can process data that are all similar in size and structure, but make difficult to process when data is presented in different patterns and sizes. We need to conduct small scale research on all big data tools, different work load conditions, different data types, various data pattern, and performance evaluation in distributed environment, centralized environment, machine learning algorithm for performance prediction, energy optimized algorithms, energy consumption per unit and recursive work. We should focus on novel data processing systems which is able to process all kinds of data in different situations.

6. APPLICATIONS OF BIGDATA

- **Big Data Analytics(BDA):** This kind of application analyzes massive data using parallel processing framework. BDA applications use sample data in pseudo-cloud environment. After that they build in real cloud environment with more processing power and large input data. These applications utilize large data, which is unable to fit in hard drive. The data is generated from different sources like traffic, social websites, the online game information, and stock market and during international games.
- **Clustering:** User can easily identify group of people by using algorithms such as k-means algorithms through points and click dialog and based on specific data dimension. Clustering plays an important role in big data in order to address group of people by considering customer type patient documents, purchasing pattern, behavior products.
- **Data Mining:** The decision tree will help user to understand outcome and relation between attributes in expected outcome. This decision tree reflects the structure of that probability hidden in your data. Decision tree helps us to predict fraud risk, online registrations, online shopping, and disease risk.

- **Banking:** In banking sector, the use of sensitive data leads to privacy issues. Research shows that more than 62% of bank employees are cautious about their bank customer's information to privacy issues. Distribution of customer's data to different branches also leads to security issues. The investigation happened on banks data containing user's sensitive information such as earnings, savings, and insurance policies ended up in the wrong hands. This discourages the customers in sharing personal details in bank transactions.
- **Stock:** Data analytics can be used to detect fraud by establishing a comprehensive system in data base during private stock exchange.
- **Credit Cards:** Credit card companies depend on in-data base analytics to identify fraud transactions with accuracy and speed. This fraud transaction deletion will follow up users sensitive data such as amount, location and follow up before authenticate suspicious activity.

Enterprise

It will help the industry people exist around the world. Data doesn't have to move to work and back. It provides insight to business people to make accurate decision for less expensive than traditional tools.

- **Customer Goods:** A manufacturer of customer products gather data related to customer preferences and purchasing data of surveys, web tags, customer call centers, the text taken up from online web sites, everything that being said about product extract. By following this kind of analysis business people will come to know that which product is to be succeeded and others are to be failed. Finally, they can spot feature trends the products in the marketing media.
- **Agriculture:** Using sensors, agriculture firm collect the data of efficiency of crops. Initially, experts of agriculture field plant crops and run simulation to find how crops react in different conditions. Research on agriculture will collect data including various attributes, temperature, growth level, soil composition, in order to find optimized environment for specific gene types.
- **Finance:** The popular financial companies are focusing more on credit scoring using third-party. Today financial institutions using their own analysis for generating credit score for existing users using wide range of information such as credit card, investments, transactions, savings.
- **Economy:** Hadoop can assist organization to perform low cost transactions.
- **Telecom:** People carry face reorganization technology in their pocket. Android users use remember app to recognize (or) collect data related to that snapped image from data base, while "I phone" users unblock their devices with recognize me, this app developed widely to save nearly $2.5 million per year for solving forgotten –passwords.
- **Health Care:** Traditional health care industries has lagged behind than the other industries in big data, every stack holder of hospital taking decision independently rather than depending upon big data tools (James Manyika, Michael Chui, Brad Brown, Jacques Bughin, Richard Dobbs, Charles Roxburgh, & Angela Hung Byers, 2011).

Most health care stakeholders invested in information technology because of accurate results. The traditional systems have limited ability to cause data become more certain. The healthcare industries itself create issues. It becomes difficult to share data among department even within hospital. The important information of payee, pharmaceutical company will be available within single department because organizations lack of knowledge on integrating data and result obtained. Big data advances healthcare ability to work with enormous data even though data is presented in different formats.

7. CONCLUSION

Bigdata is an important technology in our data era which can handle structured, semi structured and unstructured data. It provides a viable solution for large and complex data and become a challenge in nowadays. Each bigdata system provides a massive power and for providing this different tools are used. This paper presented the important aspects of big data, architecture and its applications. However the challenges are also presented in this paper. It is clear that now we are starting in the bigdata era and we have to discover many things about big data for competing this data world.

REFERENCES

Bakshi, K. (2012). Considerations for big data: Architecture and approach. *Aerospace Conference*, 1–7. 10.1109/AERO.2012.6187357

Big Data, Big Impact: New Possibilities for International Development. (n.d.). World Economic Forum.

Bill Franks. (2012). *Taming the big data tidal wave*. Wiley.

Cloudera's 100% Open Source Distribution of Hadoop. (n.d.). Retrieved from http://www.cloudera.com/content/clou dera/en/products/cdh.html

David, R. (2013). *Getting started with business analytics – insightful decision making*. Talor & Francis Group.

Dong, X. L., & Srivastava, D. (2013). Big data integration. In *Data Engineering (ICDE), 2013 IEEE 29th International Conference on*, 1245–1248. 10.1109/ICDE.2013.6544914

Global data center traffic – Cisco Forecast Overview. (n.d.). Retrieved from http://www.cisco.com/en/US/solutions/ collateral/ns341/ns525/ns537/ns705/ns 1175/Cloud_Index_White_Paper.html

Hitzler, P., & Janowicz, K. (2013). Linked Data, Big Data, and the 4th Paradigm. *Semantic Web, 4*(3), 233–235.

Manyika, Chui, Brown, Bughin, Dobbs, Roxburgh, & Byers. (2011). *Big data: The next frontier for innovation, competition, and productivity*. McKinsey Global Institute.

Mark, A. (2012). *Beyer and Douglas Laney. "The Importance of 'Big Data': A Definition*. Gartner.

OECD. (2015). *Data-driven innovation: big data for growth and well-being*. Paris, France: OECD Publishing.

Oracle Big Data strategy guide. (n.d.). Retrieved from http://www.oracle.com/us/technologies /big-data/big-data-strategy-guide- 1536569.pdf

Provost & Fawcett. (2013). *Data science for business.* O'Reilly.

Ramesh, B. (2015). Big data architecture. In *Big Data* (pp. 29–59). Springer. doi:10.1007/978-81-322-2494-5_2

Yi, X., Liu, F., Liu, J., & Jin, H. (2014). Building a network highway for big data: Architecture and challenges. *IEEE Network*, *28*(4), 5–13. doi:10.1109/MNET.2014.6863125

Section 4
Utilization and Applications

Chapter 54
An Analysis of Big Data Analytics

Vijander Singh
Manipal University Jaipur, India

Amit Kumar Bairwa
Manipal University Jaipur, India

Deepak Sinwar
(iD) https://orcid.org/0000-0001-9597-6206
Manipal University Jaipur, India

ABSTRACT

In the development of the advanced world, information has been created each second in numerous regions like astronomy, social locales, medical fields, transportation, web-based business, logical research, horticulture, video, and sound download. As per an overview, in 60 seconds, 600+ new clients on YouTube and 7 billion queries are executed on Google. In this way, we can say that the immense measure of organized, unstructured, and semi-organized information are produced each second around the cyber world, which should be managed efficiently. Big data conveys properties such as unpredictability, 'V' factor, multivariable information, and it must be put away, recovered, and dispersed. Logical arranged data may work as information in the field of digital world. In the past century, the sources of data as to size were very limited and could be managed using pen and paper. The next generation of data generation tools include Microsoft Excel, Access, and database tools like SQL, MySQL, and DB2.

1. INTRODUCTION

In the development of advanced world, information has been creating each second in numerous regions like Astronomy, Social locales, Medical fields, transportation, web based business, logical research, horticulture, video and sound download. As per an overview, in 60 second, 600+ new client on YouTube and 7 billions of queries are executed on Google. In this way, we can say that the immense measure of

DOI: 10.4018/978-1-6684-3662-2.ch054

organized, unstructured and semi organized information are produced each second around the cyber world which should be managed efficiently. Big Data conveys properties such as unpredictability, 'V' factor, multivariable information and it must be put away, recovered and dispersed the data.

Logical arranged data may works as information in the field of digital world. In past century the source of data so as to size are very limited which could be managed using pen paper. The next generation of data generation tools includes Microsoft Excel, Access and database tools like SQL, MySQL, and DB2 etc.

Now a day's, Advancement in Telecommunication and computation Technology are led on exponential growth and availability of data. When the data are increasing exponentially, parallel to it emerges many relative issues e.g. security, management, timeliness, incompleteness, Human collaboration, data Analysis skill.

2. LITERATURE REVIEWS

2.1 Need of Literature Review

The need of literature review is to overview the concepts, relations, cases and understanding the subjects to micro and macro level. Our chapter has been allowed to explore and review more literature part by part. Literature has been divided into different domains as (i) Big Data Analytics, (ii) Smart City, (iii) Water Management and (iv) Combinations of domains.

2.2 Literature Review

2.2.1 Big Data and Applications

Manish Kumar Kakhani, Sweetie Kakhani (2013) spoke about the basic concept of big data. The number of data is increasing continually in what percentage and area. What's the current & future research area expected in big data. They also spoke about big data in other fields of analytics. They're also mentioned about the tools and techniques the big data industry uses. The diverse possibilities of big data applications and how to manage, store, process and analyze big data were also discussed .

GuJifa, Zhang Lingling(2014) explained about the DATA, DIKW, Big Data, and Data Science relationship. The authors explained how information can be derived from small / big data, and it can be translated into knowledge and used with wisdom. It has gathered various meanings of big data and data science identified by different users.

Sampada Lovalekar (2014) defined Big Data definition, and how it varies from conventional data. They highlighted the problems and opportunities associated with big data. How various tools such as NOSQL, HADOOB and other HADOOB based projects are useful in big data research and management.

Amir Gangoti, Murtaza Haider (2015) identified academics and practitioners ' concepts & characteristics of big data. The paper also commented on analytical techniques (text, audio, video, social media & predictive analytics), statistical methods used for structured and unstructured data and characteristics, i.e. quantity, velocity and variety etc. The real-world data processing is not feasible for big data on a wide scale.

Justin Grimmer (2015) has clarified how machine learning and Big Data techniques operate on social media data. They defined data-generated behaviour, parameters by commenting on social media by users, watching, status, like, and these huge information can be used by Big Data and Machine Learning Technique, and useful information derived from it .

Cheikh Kacfah Emani, Nadine Cullot, Christophe Nicolle (2015) highlighted the concept of big data, tools and techniques such as Hadoop, Map reduces their problems and challenges in many fields such as business management, IT sector etc. 5 Vs of big data is defined in Hadoop feature and other tools handle high volume & data variety and produce useful information. Big Data tackled every aspect of its management to allow major changes.

2.2.2 Healthcare

Mentioned by Aisling O'Driscoll, Jurate Daugelaite etc (2013), there was a lot of difficulty in analyzing and processing Geomantic Data in large quantities. As in the beginning, it was very difficult to store and process significant quantities of signal (Peta Byte) and digital data in one place. They also identified cloud computing and big data technology, such as Infrastructure as a Service (IaaS), Software as a Service (SaaS), and Platform as a Service (PaaS) technologies.

J.Archenaa, E.A.Mary Anita (2015) talked about how healthcare & govt sector impacts on BDA, and how healthcare treatment improvements. In the government sector, big data often need to show consumer quality education. They also proposed DFS architecture for stable BDA enabling Linux environment where the device itself provided access control.

Rashid Mehmood, Gary Graham (2015) discussed Big Data approach to the issue of care in the medical industry. They suggested a model that could have data load balancing capability that could solve the question of demand and supply in smart city. They worked on the technique of network planning and time shearing control, using Markov process, operational management technique to share Smart City's Ambulance-related problem. They also discussed the potential reach of the same model in the sector of Bike Shearing, Manufacturing Industry and Waste management.

2.2.3 Information Security

Nir Kshetri (2015) described the use of big data as having an impact on the business associated costs, benefits and externalities. Author explained the characteristics of big data and business welfare and data collection, storage, sharing and accessibility relationships. It should have made it possible for consumers to be known about the concept of providing merchant with their information than it might be misused. Yet most organizations have not developed a good practice to safeguard consumer data privacy. It is also described in social & economic prediction about the cost of benefits and the external side of big data.

Gang Chen, Sai Wu, Yuan Wang Explained about the Netease system for information security. Developed a real-time analytical system to support spam detection, game log analysis and Netease social mining. Initially, it explained about offline Hadoop system that was useful when the burst of complaints arrived from the customer in a specific time and secondary, online streaming system for Netease is described. They highlighted the number of big data issues such as increasing data size, more complex user requirements to handle, new hardware requirements, performance issues, failure recovery issues, etc., so that new processing system for big data management is required and analyzed with security.

B.Saraladevi, N.Pazhaniraja etc. (2016) described the problems of big data and security. They suggested some security and algorithm-related approach that could enhance Big Data security. On Hadoop's distributed file system, security approaches were applied, first user was able to access the correct data block, secondary blue eye algorithm providing node-to-node security and checking team attack. Name node approach reduced coaches for future references on the server. They cherished resolving certain issues in HDFS on the name node and data node.

By using QC, GA and pair hand protocol, Vijey Thayananthan, Aiiad Albeshri(2014) proposed a method & security technique and key management in mobile data centers. This paper also described how data center & users are transmitting mobile data. It is also proposed that symmetric key and cipher should be used to secure and protect privacy. They explained the quantity cryptography used in the proposed model for big data security, authentication handover and pair hand authentication protocol. The overall paper description was to achieve security & privacy and deal with data traffic in mobile data centers with the help of QA, GA and pair hand authentication.

Raissa Uskenbayeva, Abu Kuandykov (2015) illustrated data integration model using new technology that supports data storage, data integrity, query executing operation, machine data from different sources. These new tools & techniques are more potential and account for timely statistics compared with traditional ones. The author combined' R' with steaming system, Rhive and RHadoop for data set processing. For best results such as ROBDC, RJBDC and Rhive, it has suggested combining other data analytics techniques & Hadoop Project.

A, Vinay s. Shekhar (2015) described different fields of Face Recognition. The methodology proposed was based on techniques from the cloud and ANN. Method used network traffic between user interface and cloud over multi-level security solutions. By applying highly patented extreme learning machine technology, the FR Framework was designed for the task of Face tapering in social networking system like Facebook. This technology could also relatively easily give Face chrome authentication and access control.

2.2.4 Social Media

Gemma bello Orgaz, Jason jung (2016) has described big data's challenging role in social media. They talked with Big Data.sa author about uses of Hadoop, Mahout, and other tools, and proposed a method that helps to store, access, and retrieve information from real-data .

Peter O'Donovan, Kevin Leahy, Ken Bruton (2016) explained the use of Big Data Technology in smart technology in manufacturing. They also used Internet of Things (IOT), machine learning techniques to build new smart production without wasting extra time and money. This paper also contained some questioner that could solve some of the problems that occurred in the manufacturing industry during research.

Azza abouzeid, described by Kamil bajda (2015), Hadoop DB, whose parallel database system was capable of achieving similar sources of fault tolerance and the ability to operate in a heterogeneous setting. Author explored both parallel database and map technology to reduce system for fault tolerance & parallel database and performance & efficiency.

2.2.5 Smart City

M.Mazhar Rathore, Anand Paul, Awais Ahmad, Suengmin Rho (2015) used IoT-based system and Big Data Analytics to illustrate the scope of smart city development. A complete system, consisting of various sensors and systems such as smart home, vehicle networking, weather & water sensors, etc. as an object, is proposed and a4-tier architecture in which each tier performs a specific task is proposed. Tier 1 was responsible for data generation and collection, Tier 2 was responsible for communication between sensors and base station, Tier 3 was responsible for data management and processing using Hadoop & shark and last Tier 4 was responsible for data analytics and this type of system generation is more useful for future enhancement of smart city decision making and development .

Rob Kichen(2013) illustrated how cities, using digital devices and infrastructure, would become smart cities by generating huge amounts of big data. These data allow to analyze city life in real time, new phase of governance etc. This paper was on the implications of big data on smart urbanization help in city planning .

A. Merchanta, and M.S. Kumarb Mohan, P.N. Ravindrac, and P. Vyasa, and U. Manohard (2013) used analytical approach to attempt and things real time case study of Bangalore city water problem. To solve the problem they used SCADA, GSM, Flow Meter, Pressure Meter and SQL Database Software. This was a theoretical approach in which ultrasonic flow meters were established at every critical point in the city and at the time measured water flow rate, and showed differentiation between present reading and previous reading. GSM Modem transmitted this data and it was stored on SCADA system in SQL Database. The current reading will be sent to the applicant after analysis and calculation, and will also be stored on server for future use. For this architecture security is identified as a major problem, without proper security data being misused .

A. Candelli1 & F. Archetti (2014) proposed an approach based on the analysis of urban water data in time series and implemented support vector machine for urban water demand forecast. The author had identified typical day-to-day urban water demand, seasonal demand and area-wise urban demand that helped to forecast urban water demand. They collected individual customer smart meter data and tackled big data analytics techniques on them. In smart city this approach may have helped save water and costs. The proposed approach was runnable in a distributed and parallel system .

Jason Shueh (2014) illustrated the impact of Big Data on government sectors with different authors ' approaches in the article. Author describes that Big Data Analytics is a technique that is very useful in future citizen demand prediction and other things .

Steve French, Camille Barchers and Wenwen Zhang (2015) outlined how big data might be used in urban planning and decision-making. This paper discussed the suitability of big data for short-term management applications and identified the factors whose use for longer-range planning had been limited. Data Visualization, Data Analysis techniques were described to represent a graph, table, map showing a better solution to the problem of urban utility requirements .

Mark Leinmiller and Melissa O'Mara (2016) spoke about smart water needs in smart cities. The big problem that smart city has faced was demand, and supply is not equal. Smart meter and other sources generated data are not properly stored and maintained for future use. Incorporating smart water technologies enabled water suppliers to minimize Non-Revenue Water (NRW) by quickly and even predicatively finding leaks using real-time SCADA data and comparing that to model network simulations.so, the main aim of this article was to reduce energy load by shaving, maintaining machines and other things in smart cities .

2.2.6 Water Management

This article discussed the scope of big data which can solve problems related to water. Smart water meters generate huge amount of data. High resolution, domestic water consumption data, could help predict daily user water demand in different household sections such as shower, toilet, kitchen etc and predict or predict water wastage, leakage and other things in artificial intelligence system . Piyushimita Thakur, Nebiyou Y. Tilahun etc. (2016) presented a survey on large data applications in urban system fields.it is an urban problem generated by poor data management for rich data management and attempts to solve problems. Commenting on challenges that are likely to arise in varying degrees when using Big Data for Urban Informatics in technological, methodological, theoretical and emerging political economy, the paper concludes .

2.2.7 Demand Prediction

R. J. Sousa, A. Gomes. (2013) addressed how District Metered Areas (DMA) influences nodal demand in different daily water demand patterns, and how it benefits pressure management. Their aim was to relate total cost investment to the given nodal demand and maximum benefits from leakage reductions. They identified demand and total cost of the condition of DMA design pressure, by managing pressure for two phases like before pressure reduction and then after pressure reduction. The author discussed a real case study and used the pressure simulation model to predict hydraulic behavior with different scenarios for the next 10 years and identified variation in total daily water production and reduction using DMA .

K. Thompsona, and R. Kadiyalab (2014) explained the application of M2M technology, Sensor and BDA are in government and private sector. They have described M2M technology such as sensors, smart meters etc. and how they collect and evaluate them to provide better problem solving . Tomasz Jacha, Ewa Magieraa etc. (2015) illustrated a comparative study assessing the performance of the Water Database Hadoop and MySQL. A real-time prototype project was used by the author to optimize water management system and reduce urban water usage. They collected various types of water related data such as user I d, type of record, average daytime temperature etc. They compared Hadoop and MySQL at various levels, such as maximum flow value in the entire data set, maximum pressure in a day, etc., and identified that Hadoop will deliver the best performance in water-related data set and also worked on distributed environment .

Cy Cheung en Martijn Nuijten (2015) showed that Big Data could potentially change the future of the water management system. It showed that not only could big data short analyze water management, it could also have implemented problems in real time. SCADA collects big data, predicting future demands and correcting man-made problems. Results showed that big data in the water industry could be archiving a great future and encouraging lower overall water levels .

John Quality (2015) suggested that the urban water demand (UWD) system requires a task to manage demand and response fluctuations properly at dynamic scale & time, ensuring rational, strategic water system management. A multi-scale approach is proposed-Boot Stack-Extreme Learning Machine (MBELM) approach which addresses issues related to supply system and water resource management. This model was Wavelet refinement-Bootstrap-Artificial Neural Network (WBANN) refinement. They used historical recording of urban water demand and split into temporal scale using DWT, then predicted using ELM technique, and also used bootstrap technique for assessing uncertainty. After forecasting results & intervals for the plot. It showed weekly and monthly quarterly forecasts of water reveling in a London .

DHI Solution (2016) presented Regional Water Distribution System (WDS) functioning. WDS has outdated or static water data information on assets: the biggest problems were slow and wrong emergency response and system maintenance. An online water distribution model with EPANET online water software is adopted, SCADA on monitoring system. Online system, based on data and information, could forecast system-user behavior .

2.2.8 Leakage Management

Archetti, Candelieri & E. Messina (2013) explained innovation approach to improve the process of leakage management through the technique of data analytics and the software for hydraulic simulation. The paper's aim was to reduce the time and costs of managing and intervening assets. They use tools such as SCADA, Customer Information System (CIS), Geographic Information System (GIS) and Hydraulic Simulation tools for an appropriate solution based on the web. The author has worked on case study of Brazil and has demonstrated that the sectoral water distribution system improves the management of leakage in the urban water industry .

Candelieri, D. Conti, F. Archetti (2013) discussed the need for water and the management of infrastructural assets through clustering. They collected data point sets of transformation and consisted of a scenario of leakage and represented them on graph to identify location of leakage on network. Open source R Software is used for algorithm clustering and partition algorithm used in it to identify network leakage. This approach to spectrum was very effective and gave better performance in analyzing the network of leakage localisation. It cuts down on system time and cost .

In. J. Habib, P. N. Marimuthu, S. Kim, Y. Pan (2013) presented Kuwait City's case study for solving water pipeline and management problems. Author worked on 3 different section & where they did statistical analysis of water production, water consumption and water distribution network status in town. They describe discovery of WPN computer network and original WPN network. They were using a smart device such as mobile robots to determine and authorize WPN layout. This integrated proposal has been discovered to help with manual inspection economically, long-term organization and scheduling assistances .

3. BIG DATA

3.1 Data, Information and Big Data

Data is a value & variable those are defining in one sense and uses for other purpose. Data after collection and analysis is known as Information which is used for making a decision.

Figure 1. Data to Conclusion Conversion

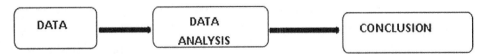

Need of database are to provide a rich set of information to manage, access and update of all available data and it is gradually increasing wrt to data. Now days, organization have released the importance of data for supporting business and decision making, so they keep maintaining data via different sources. Data hierarchy helps us to identify the problem, understand who, what, how and why should do use data for condition.

Figure 2. Journey of Data Hierarchy

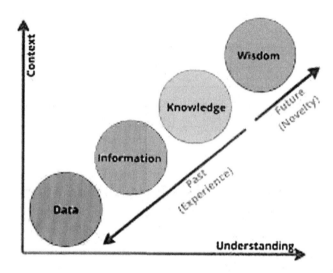

In the era of digital technology, every second, many users have been uploading photos on social sites, lots of people search videos on YouTube and many queries run on Google.as data size are increasing like GB to ZB, information retrieving may become comparatively challenging. This void opens the opportunities for new technologies. 'Big Data' is one of the technology among them. It is now a focus point for researcher and all service manufacturing industries. It needs tools and technique to efficiently process large volume of data within limited run times.

Figure 3. Supply chain of Data

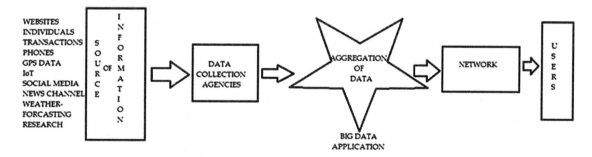

It may divide big data generated sources in to two categories Internal Source and External Source. Internal sources are some activity those are in under control of business like transaction, log data and email etc. These are stored on company own computer and use to managed organizations. External data may currently have owned by organization and generated publicly, and it may have in unstructured and semi structured format. Social media, audio, photo and video are examples of external data sources. According IBM Survey Report Source of Data has been divided in Internal and External Sources. They are following.

Table 1. Data sources

Internal		External	
1.	Search Engine (88%)	1.	Social Browsing (43%)
2.	Log File (73%)	2.	Audio (33%)
3.	Mails (57%)	3.	Multimedia (34%)

Internal data is used in own decision making of organization and it does not mean that is it only generated in organization, but it may be generated by outsiders also. External data are very useful in decision making and forecasting of organization to predict customer behavior, demand and other things. So we can say that both data should play an important role in a organization.

3.2 Properties and Characteristics of Big Data

3.2.1 'V' Factor

Big data is represented by several 'V', whose have been increasing day by day. In 2001, 'Doug lance' present a paper on data management, introduce 3 V's in data, after that according to Nir Kshetri, Mark Lei miller and Melissa O'Mara, Piyushimita, Nebiyou, R. Gomes, J. Sousa, A.sa.Marques, Cy Cheungen (2014) there are many new **'V'** added i.e. 5 V's,6 V's, 8 V's,10 V's, 42 V's and now 100 V's also have introduced in data sets that describe Big data qualities.

1. **Volume:** Volume deals with size or vast amount of data. It can refer as data in rest or Magnitude. The term volume refers to the size. When the data size increases, every time, there are problem from the traditional data base because the size of data is become double in every 2 sec. So, the big data pool has high volume of data.
2. **Variety:** It refers designed hierarchy of data sets. Data can be in any form i.e. structured, semi structured and unstructured. Variety refers that how many different forms of data is in structure, semi structure and in un-structure format.
3. **Velocity:** It deals with speed of data, the rate at which data are generated, analyzed and action taken on them. The term velocity means the rate at which big data is generated and the speed at which it is manipulated. The term velocity describes the customer last purchase rate, market condition, the customer behavior etc.

4. **Veracity:** Uncertainty in data due to incompleteness and inconsistency, introduce veracity in data. It refers data in drought. Veracity refers to accuracy of data that means, it represents uncertainty of data. For example, an organization needs to ensure that the data is correct as well as the analysis performed on data are also correct.

5. **Variability:** It refers variation in data flow rates.

6. **Value:** It refers to worth of data being extracted. There is huge amount of data, extract valuable information from data based on conditions. The sixth V of Big Data is value, that is all about quality of data and stored them and use in future perspective. For example, a large quantity of data has stored in telecommunication system, so that useful information can extract from all this information.

7. **Visualization:** present data in graphical view which help developer to understand data.

8. **Viscosity:** It is related to velocity that measures resistance to flow in the volume of data.

9. **Virality:** It refers how quickly data spreads in between node to node or people to people network.

10. **Vulnerability:** When size of people personal data increase, they have started feeling that it is being used to pry into their behavior to sell them things by different commercial websites.

3.2.2 Data Classification

There are three types of data in big data technologies.

1. **Structured data:** Structure data are most traditionally data sources. To manage the structure data, we use relational data. It represents only 5 to 10% of all informatics data. E.g. text data excel file etc. Structure data are most traditionally data sources. To manage the structure data, we use relational data. In RDBMS table to manage the generated data.

2. **Unstructured Data:** Now, the data are in different formats like audio, video, text PDF etc. All those data are considered as unstructured because it doesn't reside in a traditional database or not in tabular or delimiter format. It represents around 80% of data. e.g. satellite image, scientific data, social media data etc.

3. **Semi Structured:** data whose doesn't reside in a relational database but have some organizational properties that make it easier to analyze is known as semi structured data. e.g. XML and JSON are semi structure data. The file is in XML format is considered in semi structure data. big data carries many sources of semi structure data.

3.2.3 Inherent Features

1. **Heterogeneity:** Big data are heterogeneous in nature because it is obtained from different sources and represent information from different sub populations. It requires sophisticated statistical techniques for model creation.

2. **Noise accumulation:** Noise in variables have true effects within the model. Noise for dissimilar parameters could control magnitudes of variables that have true properties in model.

3. **Spurious correlation:** Unrelated variables being found falsely, due to correlation in massive datasets, it generates result of high dimensionality.

4. **Incidental endogeneity:** Independent variables and statistical method used in regression analysis depends on assumptions. It is present in big data.

Table 2. Inherent properties of big data

Features	Big Data	Required Methods
Heterogeneity	Highly Present	Sophisticated statistical methods
Noise accumulation	Some Variable present	Estimating Predictive model
Spurious correlation	Some unrelated independent variable	Simulation
Incidental endogeneity	Highly Present	Regression Analysis

3.3 Difference Between Traditional Data and Big Data

Big Data has become a Big Game Changer in Today's world. The major difference between Traditional data and Big Data are discussed in table 3.

Table 3. Difference between traditional data and big data

Parameter	Big Data	Traditional Data
Queries	Largely SQL	Traditional SQL
Data Type	Structured, Semi-Structured, Unstructured	Structured
Architecture	Distributed	Centralized
Data Modal	Distributed	Fixed Scheme
Data Traffic	More	Less
Data Volume	Petabyte	Terabyte
Data Relation	Unknown	Known relation
Data Integrity	Low	High

3.4 Big Data, Big Data Management and Big Data Analytics

3.4.1 Big Data

"Big Data is a term that describe large volume, complex and multivariable data that requires advanced techniques and technology to store, retrieve, analysis and distribute the information". According to Wikipedia "Big data is a collection of large and complex data sets that become difficult to process using on hand database management tools."

3.4.2 Big Data Management

According to Gu-jifa,zhang lingline in 2014 big data management involves people, policies and technologies in a place to ensure the accuracy, quality, security, maintenance and reliability of huge amount of data sets. It servers data for Analytics and reporting, by applying processes on data i.e. data cleaning, migration, integration and so on. It is a responsibly of Data Chief Officer, Data Manager, Data Administrator, Data Scientist, Developer and so on, to identify policy and approaches in organization to decide which and where information should be stored and placed in organization. Big data management can have categorized in 4 A's i.e. Acquisition, Assembly, Analyze, Action which shown in table 1.4.

Table 4. 4 A'S in big data management

S.No	A	Process	Output
1.	Acquisition	Filtering Data	Store useful data and raw data
2.	Assembly (organization)	Cleaning Data	Extract actual information from useful data
3.	Analyze	Running Queried Building Algorithm (Data ware house)	Find new insights, improve quality of data, understand semantics
4.	Action (decision)	Efficiently Interpret result from analysis	Given valuable decision to user

3.4.3 Big Data Analytics (BDA)

Big data analytics is a holistic approach that allows to improve data driven decision making. It manages, process and analyze dimension of big data. Gang Chen, Sai Wu, Yuan Wang in 2015 BDA uncover hidden patterns, unknown correlations, trends and other useful information with the help of programing skills, Statistics and machine learning approaches. David Gorbet explains, "Increases in data introduce complexity as biggest challenge, Business across industries have to not only store data but also be able to influence it quickly and effectively to grow business value". It helps organization to harness their data and used it to identify new opportunities. BDA is applicable in every field of life i.e. web & e-trading, telecommunication, government, healthcare, financial and banking and retails.

3.4.4 Big Data Analytics (BDA) Steps

BDA follows basically six steps in decision making. It starts with Problem Identification, identify problem which we want to solve then Designing Data Requirement, why and which type data is useful for problem, followed by Preprocessing Data, it includes data cleaning (remove unwanted data) techniques, then Performing Analytics Over Data, apply machine learning and statistics on data and last Visualizing Data, visualization can be done by any software like R, Tableau etc.

3.4.5 Considerations for Big Data Analytics

Scale, scope and nature provide interesting insight into design and architecture whose impact on hardware and software system.

1. **Hardware Considerations:** According to Raissausken bayeva, Abukuandykov, Young Imcho in 2015big data analytics is performed on huge amount, specifically called as 'hot data' (initially measured or collected), 'cold data' (archival data), 'periodical data' (season, celebrity headlines), 'single file with different versions' (language, format) data. These data access patterns (frequency of how data accessed) can process future memory hierarchy optimizations. Hardware platform con-

sider compatible storage, process, networking and energy as shown in table 4 for big data analytics applications.

2. **Software Stack:** software system in big data technology are used to optimized (a) scale and accommodate large data set (b) efficiently leverage the hardware platform and (c) Bridge the increasing gap between the growth of the data and computing power. Distributed software system should have the tolerance to become robust after sudden hardware failure. There is problem occur with existing software are consistency, availability and partition tolerance on huge data. To reduce these problems, there are some parameters which help advanced hardware and software solutions in distributed environments.

3. **Big Data Platform:** big data platform is a solution that combines features and capabilities of several big data application and functions within a single result. It contains storage, servers, database, management and other big data management functions.it should be able to accommodate new platforms and tool based on business condition. It should support linear scale-out. table 1.6 shows number of hardware platform that support big data applications.

4. **Data base:** Harsh, R., Acharya, G., & Chaudhary, S. in 2018 Databases whose used in Big Data Applications, depend upon operation and output of data analysis. Database supported by big data are MongoDB, Hive, oracle NoSQL, Apache HBase etc.

5. **Programming Language** J.Archenaa and E.A maryanita in 2015 provides a way to user to connect with software. Sometimes high-level data science platform is not sufficient for a specific analytics task, then need of lower level programming language emerged. table 1.7 shows most popular programming language in big data.

3.4.6 Applications of Big Data in Different Domain

Big Data is used in every field of life. It solves real world problems through many different software like Hadoop, map reduce and other tools. Internet-use and M2M connections are main reasons for data growth. Big data technologies are applicable on various areas as below.

1. **Health care:** In health care, the big data uses patient experience and overall population health record for reducing cost and improve services. It may detect diseases at earlier stages when they can have treated more easily and effectively. It accesses patient information and define type of cause in it and solve problem online. Rashid Mehmood, Gary grahamin in 2015 reduce the Ambulance Transportation problem. Massive amount of data are collected using many sources which help to improving medical facilities.

2. **Market and Business:** Big Data is the biggest game changing opportunities for the marketing and business. The growth of internet can improve market and business of an organization. People can buy and sale the products anywhere and everywhere in the world. It can also define the customer behavior, their choices those are helpful for marketing growth. Many companies are become on top through online sailing. According to a survey, in last 20 years the growth of market is develop 25% extra through online marketing. They collect data, manipulate them and use their information for future purpose like a person purchase a product from online site then their whole information is captured by merchant.

3. **Education System:** Big Data gives a remarkable result in education system. It provides lots of facilities to students for their studies. Suppose a student can't understand a topic in a classroom

than will check the topic on internet and clear his queries. Students can also attend online classes for their study. It will provide accuracy of answer. The analysis of data can also clarify about which type of data i.e. text, audio, video a student wants to use. As the result Instructor can guide choosing the future path efficiently.

4. **Sports:** In sports, data is collecting via Fan experience, data from wearable technologies (google glass, GPS tracker, fitness tracker etc.). it may have pulled out difference in scoring touchdowns, signing contracts or preventing injuries. It improves efficiency, accuracy and profitability in sports.

5. **Telecommunication:** Telecommunication plays a big role in today's digital life. In telecom industry, many different varieties of data are generating. Big data Technology creates scope for crowd-based antenna optimization, optimizing services with equipment monitoring, capacity planning and preventative maintenance (Dropped calls, Lack of network coverage, resulting in poor customer experience, Bandwidth issues, Poor download times, Inordinate service wait times, Switching, frequency utilization, capacity use etc.)

6. **Agriculture:** In the agriculture big data is play import role for check soil composition, water level, growth, output generation sequence of the plant. It can also helpful for future prediction of plant, growth of plant through the desire input.

7. **Smart Phone:** Smart Phones are current trends in 20th century. In Smart Phone there are lots of apps, finger print, facial reorganization patters etc, all are generating huge amount of data. those data identified the behavior of the person. A picture can define likes and dislikes of person and emotions at a time.

8. **Social Media:** face detection in social site with help of big data analytics and ANN Techniques are helpful in social media applications.45% of big data are generate through social media. People shares through information, chatting with each other, posted on Facebook, twitter, exchange picture share their emotion etc. All these data are helpful in business and marketing.

9. **Scientific Research:** The role of big data for scientific research is becoming increasingly apparent, the massive data processing has become valuable for scientific research. Big data has contribution in many scientific discoveries like Digital earth and Global change etc. Huge dataset will serve as important input for current scientific problem thus leading for a new finding. The massive amount of data provides an endless source of new knowledge without modeling the scientific phenomena. There is no dough that Big Data will extensively change the way of scientific Research.

10. **Economic Survey:** Big data is transforming how business leaders make decisions. Vast amount of data helps to researcher for manage and recognize the economic and statistical challenges of our time e.g. Population study, literacy, food security and related policy making, statistical study for policy and decision making.

11. **Water Management:** In Government all sectors like Electricity, Transportation, Water management, Food Industry are generating a huge quantity of data. This stored huge data helps for user demand prediction. In water industry it helps to improve Leakage Deduction, Non-Revenue Water (NRW) identification, Proper Water Utilities and help in Management between Man- Machine work etc. Big Data Analysis can also predict future water demand of user by their previous data record. It is also very useful in water management to forecast an equal ration between demand and supply of water.

Big data have application in many others field like Banking, Data Mining, Fraud Detection, Call Center analysis, IT Log Analytics, Airlines, Tourism, in Human Resource Management, Product Development and Manufacturing and Smart Grid etc.

3.5 Challenges of Big Data

Opportunities never comes alone, it always followed by challenges. The biggest challenges for big data is the protection and security of personal identification Information. Data and their aim is to centralize storage and analysis them for whole system design. Challenges for big data is the protection of end user's privacy such as system frequently contain a team orders amount of personal identification information.

1. **Data Capture:** Capturing of Data is biggest challenge in big data. Big Data Captures Web Based Content and Transforming it into Search application.
2. **Data Storage:** Big Data has a storage infrastructure that can store, retrieve and manage massive amount of data. It enables the storage and Sorting of data in a way that can easily accessed, used and processed by Application.
3. **Data Searching:** There is a huge amount of data is stored in big data tool. To identify correct data search is biggest challenge in Big Data.
4. **Data Shearing:** Data shearing is a process in which your original data is in controlled way. Only authorized person in organization can only see part of the whole data. Data shearing is a growing challenge for many organizations.
5. **Data Analysis and Visualization**: Data analysis is a process in which identified and examine a valid data, uncover hidden pattern and other useful information that is more helpful in organization to take more decision.

Figure 4. Possibility Places of Challenges in Big Data

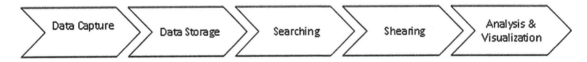

3.6 Big Data Issues

More data often means more issues. So, Big Data have many issues arising during its Management, Storage etc. Each issue has its own task as following below-

1. **Management Issue:** Manage a Huge Quantity of data is Biggest issue for Big data Engineers. The source of data is different by Size, Format of collection, Different Documents, Drawing, Pictures etc. There is not yet proper solution for them.
2. **Storage Issue:** The volume of user generated data has increases continuously. It is very hard to manage. User uploaded every second photos, video, text on social site that increased amount of

data continuously. So, we required a parallel and Distributed architecture to store those huge data and process them.

3. **Processing Issue:** How to process petabyte, Zeta byte (ZB) form of data is an issue in Big Data. for effective processing of ZB of data will require broad parallel processing and new analytics algorithms to provide timely and illegal information.

4. **Security Issue:** Security is a biggest issue for huge amount of data. From security point of view the protection of user's privacy is one of big challenge. Big data have contained huge amounts of personal information and therefore privacy of users is a huge concern. So, to solve this issue first understand what the weaknesses is are, then you have taken proper precautions to protect those weaknesses.

3.7 Big Data Analytics Tools and Techniques

With the help of data analysis, we uncover hidden pattern and correlation between data and pattern. As per growth of data it is not easy to identify correlation between huge amounts of data so that we use Big Data Analytics tools.

3.7.1 HADOOP

When it is used:

1. Data Size & Data Diversity
2. Life time data availability because it is scalable
3. For parallel data processing with Map reduce

Why it is used:

1. It is integrated with multiple frameworks (Mahout, R, spark, Mongo DB)

How it is used:
   Core components

1. HDFS
2. Hadoop Map reduce
3. Hadoop yarn

Where it is used

1. In Genomics for Parallelized and distributed data processing & Analysis with bioinformatics community
2. Information security application (Hadoop based system)
3. In Healthcare (Real time Analysis & Store huge data & Predictive Analysis)
4. Social Big Data visualization and analysis
5. Real time retrieval of image in distributed memory system

6.   Future prediction in water management

(Linux, window supported)

3.7.2 Map Reduce

When is used

1.   To solve web-based search index creating problems
2.   Presence of semi structured and unstructured data format

Why is used

1.   It creates cluster of large number of data & manage thousands of Hadoop cluster
2.   Reduce Network traffic

How is used

1.   Map job
2.   Reduce Job

Where is used

1.   Geospatial query processing (google map)
2.   Gap identification
3.   URL Access frequency count
4.   Reverse web link graph
5.   Clinical big data applications

OS Support: Linux (Red Hat Enterprise Linux),Cent OS,SLES, Ubuntu/Debian

3.7.3 STORM

When it is used

1.   Real time computing system,
2.   It analyses, clean & resolve large amount of non-unique data point.

Why it is used

1.   It processes vast amount of data in fault tolerance& distributed
2.   It works on stream processing data
3.   If super visor dies & we restart it, it will work from last point, no data loss

How it is used
  Zookeeper

1. It works on cluster
2. State less system

Where it is used

1. Weather channel
2. Yahoo & twitter use it
3. Meta Market

Linux & Unix must have Ambari

3.7.4 HPCC

When it is used

1. Deep data analytics
2. Parallel batch processing support & also work on online query processing by indexed data file.

Why it is used

1. While working on Web service protocol

How it is used

1. Cluster processing using commodity hardware & high- speed networking
2. It have Throe & Roxie

Where it is used

1. Web service application,
2. HTTP,REST & JSO N, XML data
3. Infosys (360°customer view) Supported by Linux OS

3.8 Big Data Analytics Programming Languages

3.8.1 Apache Pig (Pig Latin)

Supported Operating System

• Window, OSX, Linux

Work For

1. Data Analytics
2. Data Manipulation with Hadoop

Features

1. It handle very large data set with Hadoop
2. Ease of Program
3. Optimization opportunities
4. User create their own function according requirement

When

1. It is generally used with Hadoop
2. To perform map reduce task without Java code
3. It is fit in pipeline paradigm
4. It handles structured, unstructured & semi structured data.

Developed by

- Yahoo

3.8.2 R

Supported Operating System

- Windows, Linux, Mac

Work For

1. Statistical Computing
2. Data Analytics
3. Scientific Research
4. Graphics representation
5. GNU is very easy for new user

Features

1. R code have cross platform inter operativity
2. It is freely available with GNU license
3. Data handling & storage facility
4. Simple & effective programming includes array, loop, vector & list

When

1. It is used for retrieve, clean, analyze, visualization the data.
2. For business, market & other Research work data analytics & scientist used it.
3. It work on time series analysis & classification & clustering

Developed by

- Ross lhaka at University of Auckland, New Zealand (1993)

3.8.3 ECL (Enterprise Control Language)

Supported Operating System

- Linux

Work For

1. it is Query Language
2. Optimization Features

Features

1. It has high level Primitives such as join, transform, Short, Project etc.
2. It Perform Loading, Extraction of data.
3. Backup and Recovery of Production

When

1. when we required more Security of Data because it has security, recovery, audit and compliance layer.
2. Entrepreneur data and government data.

Developed by

- HPCC System

4. CONCLUSION

Variety of literature has been surveyed to explaine the big data. Based on data collection, data had segregated to fulfill the properties of Big Data and segregated into their various defined 'V's for confirmation of Big Data existence. There have been attempted a sample data study (due to limitation) to complement

Big Data Analytics. Water demand prediction has been taken as a sample problem and solved by steps of Big Data Analytics using Linear Regression and ANN model.

REFERENCES

Abouzeld & Bajda-Pawlikowsk. (2009). Hadoop DB: An Architectural hybrid of mapreduce and DBMS Technologies for analytics workloads. *VLDB Endowment, 9*, 24-28.

Archenaa & Maryanita. (2015). A survey of Big Data analytics in healthcare and government. *Procedia Computer Science, 50*, 408-413.

Bayeva, Abukuandykov, & Imcho. (2015). Integration of data using the Hadoop and R. *Procedia Computer Science, 56*, 145-149.

Borkar & Michallj. (2012). *Inside Big Data Management: Ogres, onions or partitas?* EDBT/ICDT, Joint Conference, Berlin, Germany.

Candelieri, A., & Archetti, F. (2014). Smart Water in Urban Distribution Networks: Limited Financial Capacity and big data analytics. WIT Transaction on Built Environment, 139, 63-73.

Candelieri, A., Archetti, F., & Messina, E. (2013). Improving leakage Management in Urban Water Distribution Network through Data Analytics and Hydraulic Simulation. WIT Transactions on Ecology & the Environment, 171, 107-117. doi:10.2495/WRM130101

Candelieri, Conti, & Archetti. (2014). Improving Analytics in Urban Water Management: A Spectral clustering based approach for leakage localization. *Procedia Science and Behavioral Science, 108*, 235-248.

Chen, G., Wu, S., & Wang, Y. (2015). The Evolvement of Big Data System: From Perspective of an information security Application. Big Data Research, 1-5.

Cheungen, C. (2014). Big Data and Future of Water Management. Academic Press.

Driscoil & Daugelaite. (2013). Big Data Hadoop and cloud computing in genomics. *Journal of Biomedical Informatics, 46*, 774-781.

French. (2015). *Moving beyond operations leveraging Big Data for Urban Planning decision.* CUPUM.

Gandomi & Haider. (2015). Beyond the hype: Big data concept, methods and analytics. *International Journal of Information Management, 35*, 137-144.

Gomes, R., & Sousa, J. (2014). Influence of Future Water Demand patterns on the District Metered areas design and benefits yields by pressure management. Procedia Engineering, 70, 744-752.

Grimmer. (2015). We all are social scientist now: how big data, machine learning and causal inference work together. *American Political Science Association*, 1-3.

Gu-Jifa. (2014). Data, DIKW, Big Data and Data Science. *Procedia Computer Science, 31,* 814-821.

Harsh, Acharya, & Chaudhary. (2018). Scope of Big Data Analytics in Bikaner Urban Water Management. *International Journal of Computational Intelligence & IoT, 2*(3).

Harsh, R., Acharya, G., & Chaudhary, S. (2018, July). Epistemological View: Data Ethics, Privacy & Trust on Digital Platform. In *2018 IEEE International Conference on System, Computation, Automation and Networking (ICSCA)* (pp. 1-6). IEEE. 10.1109/ICSCAN.2018.8541166

Harsh, R., Acharya, G., & Chaudhary, S. (2018). Scope of Big Data Analytics in Bikaner Urban Water Management. *International Journal of Computational Intelligence & IoT, 2*(3).

Jach. (2015). Application of Hadoop to store and big data gathered from urban water distribution system. *Procedia Engineering, 119*, 1375-1380.

Kacfahemani, C. (2015). Understandable Big data: A survey. *Computer Science Review*, 1–10.

Kakhani & Kakhani. (2015). Research issues in Big data analytics. *IJAIEM, 2*, 1-5.

Kitchin. (2014). The real time city? Big data and smart urbanization. Geo Journal, 1-14.

Kshetri, N. (2014). *Big data Impact on privacy, security and consumer Welfare. Telecommunication Policy.*

Lovalekar. (2014). Big Data: An Emerging trend in future. *IJCSIT, 5*, 538-541.

Mehmood & Graham. (2015). Big data logistics: a healthcare transport capacity sharing model. *Procedia Computer Science, 64*, 1107-1114.

Merchant & Kumar. (2014). Analytics driven Water management System for Bangalore city. *Procedia Engineering.*

Miller & O'Mara. (n.d.). Smart Water: A Key Building Blocks of The Smart City of The Future. *Hydro informatics-Big Data Solution for Water Savings.*

O'Donovan & Kevinleahy. (2015). Big data in manufacturing: a systematic mapping study. *Journal of Big Data*, 2-20.

Orgaz. (2015). Social Big Data: Recent achievements and new challenges. *Information Fusion.*

Piyushimita. (2015). *Big Data and Urban Informatics: Innovation and Challenges to urban planning and Knowledge Discovery.* Academic Press.

Quality. (2015). *Solving uncertainty: using big data to predict urban water demand.* Academic Press.

Saraladevi, Raja, & Victerpaul. (2015). Big data and Hadoop-A study in security perspective. *Procedia Computer Science, 50*, 596-601.

Shueh. (2014). *Big Data Could Bring Government Big Benefits.* Academic Press.

Thayananthan, V., & Albeshri, A. (2015). Big Data Security issues based on Quantum cryptography and privacy with authentication for mobile data center. Procedia Computer Science, 50, 149-156. doi:10.1016/j.procs.2015.04.077

Thompson & Kadiyala. (2014). Making Water System Smarter using M2M Technology. *Science Direct 16th conference on water distribution system Analysis, 89*, 437-443.

Zarli, A. (2014). *Water Analytics and Intelligent sensing for demand optimized management: The Wisdom Vision and approach. 16*th *Conference on Water Distribution System Analytics WDSA*. https://images. app.goo.gl/LjAxWcvqDTavG4mE8

Chapter 55
Insight Into Big Data Analytics:
Challenges, Recent Trends, and Future Prospects

Mohd Vasim Ahamad
Aligarh Muslim University, India

Misbahul Haque
Aligarh Muslim University, India

Mohd Imran
Aligarh Muslim University, India

ABSTRACT

In the present digital era, more data are generated and collected than ever before. But, this huge amount of data is of no use until it is converted into some useful information. This huge amount of data, coming from a number of sources in various data formats and having more complexity, is called big data. To convert the big data into meaningful information, the authors use different analytical approaches. Information extracted, after applying big data analytics methods over big data, can be used in business decision making, fraud detection, healthcare services, education sector, machine learning, extreme personalization, etc. This chapter presents the basics of big data and big data analytics. Big data analysts face many challenges in storing, managing, and analyzing big data. This chapter provides details of challenges in all mentioned dimensions. Furthermore, recent trends of big data analytics and future directions for big data researchers are also described.

INTRODUCTION

Big data analytics is the process of extracting hidden patterns and correlations, consumer behavior and preferences, market trends and decision making, by examining huge data sets coming from various sources such as web log files, social media, satellites and sensors, GPS data, IoT (Internet of Things) enabled devices, etc. When we click on a website, a large data is saved in the form of web log files. Which can

DOI: 10.4018/978-1-6684-3662-2.ch055

be used in recommender services in future transactions. Facebook, Tweeter, Instagram and various other social media are generating very huge data every day in terms of contents, tweets, photos etc. They must be saved for further processing. Sensor can be embedded in machines that senses the inputs from the outer world and provide it to the machine for further analysis. Hence, sensors can generate a large volume of data. There many handheld and IoT enabled devices which generated huge data. To extract meaningful pattern from big data, we need to apply application specific analytical methods. As, enormous data are coming from thousands of sources in structured, unstructured and semi-structured formats, it's a very challenging task to analyze it.

There are following challenges with respect to data storage, data management, analyzing and processing the big data, scalability, privacy and security. Huge data are coming from thousands of sources in different formats, it is a big challenge to store them in an efficient, unambiguous and scalable form. Big data is in the scale of Exabyte. Big data requires special kind of techniques to handle the data. It is not possible for the traditional tools to process the big data. To process them, we need a cluster of machines that can process the data in parallel. So, we use some big data analytics technologies such as Hadoop, Spark, Pig, Hive, etc., to manage and process the big data.

In big data analytics, we deal with huge amount of data with different format, inconsistent, noisy and incomplete data, which generates following challenges. Do all the data need to be analyzed? Do the stored data suitable for analysis? How to find interesting patterns from such a huge, multi-formed, inconsistent, incomplete, uncertain and noisy data? etc. It is much possible that the approach used for big data analytics provides good results on "small" big data but performance degrades rapidly for comparatively larger datasets. It's a challenging task to produce high quality of information from huge datasets with minimum time, resources and cost.

In recent years, large numbers of techniques and tools & technologies have been developed to analyze the big data. The techniques used for big data are clustering, classification, machine learning, neural networks, topic modelling, etc. To incorporate these techniques to analyze the big data, we have technologies such as Hadoop, Spark, Cassandra, Pig, Hive, NoSQL, HBase, MapReduce, etc. In future, advanced analytics and visualization techniques will be applied on real time business intelligence. To get high performance, in-memory datasets usage will be accelerated.

BACKGROUND

Big Data

Before the evolution of Big Data, data around the world was not so huge with limited types. Analytics methods were developed to deal with the less amount of data, some defined sources and limited types of data. Now, data is in the scale of Petabytes and Exabytes (Akhtar *et al*, 2015).

The big data is different from the traditional types of data in many dimensions. These dimensions are the foundation for defining the term Big Data. Doug Laney defined the term big data with three Vs: Volume, Velocity and Variety (Doug Laney, 2001). Some literatures also supports two other dimensions that characterizes the big data namely Variability and Value (A. Katal *et al*, 2013).

Figure 1. Five V's of Big Data

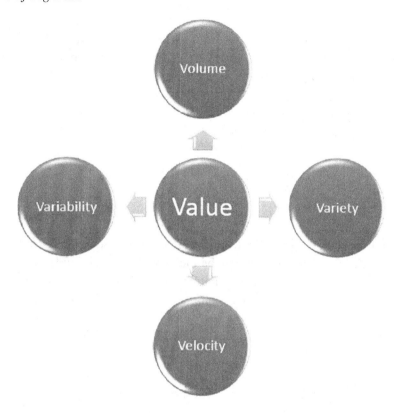

Volume

Volume characterizes the size of the data. It describes the capacity of stored as well as generating large amount of data everywhere. Nowadays, huge amount of data is generated by computers, satellites, PDAs, scientific simulators, sensors and user interaction with social media. The size of data has hugely increased than ever before and chasing the level of Exabytes and Zettabytes (N. Akhtar *et al,* 2015; Yojna Arora, Dinesh Goyal, 2016).

Variety

Variety characterizes the various sources from which data are coming. The data can be of structured, unstructured or semi-structured format. Structured data are stored in relational tables having rows and columns, where columns define the attributes of entity whose data are being stored and rows define records for each attribute. Researchers found that structured data are in very small amount, around 5-10% of all data available (Yojna Arora, Dinesh Goyal, 2016).

Most of the data available all around the world are unstructured in nature. Unstructured data can be in the form of audio, video, images, text, web log files, user search histories, scientific simulation results, satellite data, sensor data, etc. It is very difficult to store and use them effectively without any uncertainty, inconsistency and noise. Semi-structured data possesses the properties of both structured and unstructured data.

Velocity

Velocity describes the speed of data coming in from various sources and going out from the system. There are a large number of sources of data which are generating huge amount of data every moment. It can be analyzed using following statistics

- Facebook is capturing 100 TB data every day and has 40 PB of data
- Yahoo has 60 PB of data
- Twitter is generating 8 TB data per day
- EBay has 40 PB of data and capturing 50 TB data every day

Variability

Variability refers to the inconsistency in the data as well as speed with which data is coming. As most of the data is in the unstructured form, there can be inconsistency, uncertainty and noise in data being stores coming from number of sources. Before applying the big data analytics method, data need to be preprocessed to remove all anomalies, errors and noises. Variability also refers to the inconsistent velocity of data generation.

Value

Value refers to the meaningfulness of extracted data from the huge amount of variety of data coming from various resources. If analysis process doesn't provide quality results, it is of no value. This characteristics is very crucial to big data because quality results can be used in extreme personalization, target marketing, fraud detection, optimization problems, etc.

Figure 2. Sources of Big Data

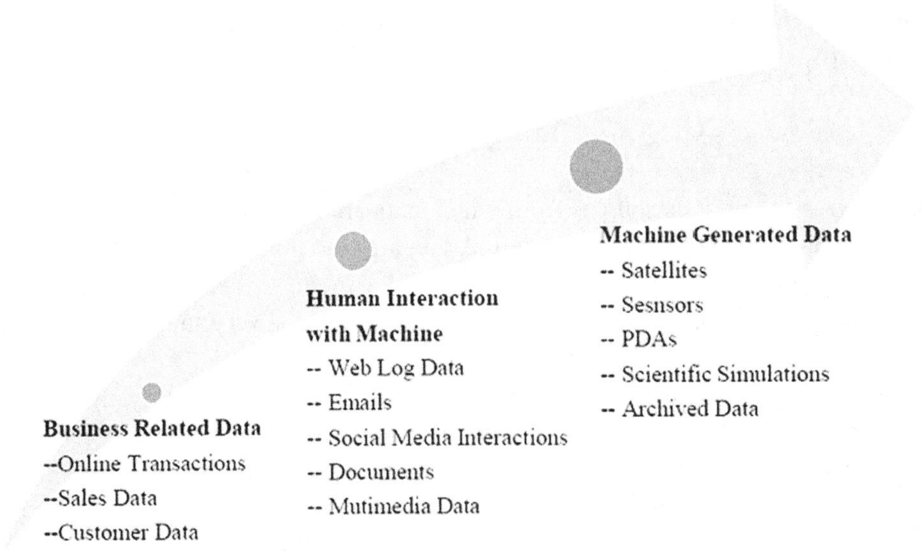

Machine Generated Data
-- Satellites
-- Sesnsors
-- PDAs
-- Scientific Simulations
-- Archived Data

Human Interaction with Machine
-- Web Log Data
-- Emails
-- Social Media Interactions
-- Documents
-- Mutimedia Data

Business Related Data
--Online Transactions
--Sales Data
--Customer Data

Sources of Big Data

Nowadays, very huge amount of data are generated and collected from a number of sources such as web log files, stored or archived data, social media, satellites and sensors, GPS data, IoT (Internet of Things) enabled devices, etc.

Web Data

World Wide Web is considered as one of the largest data sources. When a user visits a website, a large data is saved in the form of web log files which includes user's search pattern, personalization of web pages information, etc. This information can be used to provide better services and recommendation to the user for future visits.

Archived Data

Business entities are maintaining data centers to store the data for further analysis. These data centers stores data like customer and employee's related data, sales related data, daily transactions, and customer feedbacks. Big Data Analytics tools are used to get insight into these data which can be used in decision making in business.

Social Media

Nowadays, social media networks are heavily used interaction medium among people over the web. People are using social networks for news feeds, trending topics information, collecting opinion, connecting to a community, etc (Akhtar, Ahamad, 2017).

Social media platforms like Facebook, Tweeter, and Instagram, etc are generating very huge data every day in terms of contents, tweets, photos etc.

Sensor and Satellite Data

Sensor senses the inputs from the outside world and send it to the machine, in which it is embedded, for further analysis. Sensors embedded in scientific instruments, smart vehicles, flight simulators, etc are generating huge volume of data. Satellites are also primary source of huge amount of data. Weather forecasting systems, GPS tracking systems etc are the main example of this source.

Characteristics of Big Data

There are following characteristics of big data (Inukollu *et al*, 2014).

- Big Data integrates the structured, semi-structured and unstructured data.
- Big Data deals with speed and scalability of data coming from various data sources.
- The information extraction time and value of information is crucial.

Big Data Analytics

Nowadays, data are generated and collected more and more than ever before. But, this huge amount of data is of no use until it is converted into some useful information. Data mining techniques can be to the data stored in data warehouses to extract meaningful information using ETL (Extract, Transform and Load) process (Han, Kamber, 2000). Using these techniques, useful information are collected from data which are mostly structured. This kind of information retrieval is time taking process because ETL process is a batch oriented task.

Big data analytics is the process of extracting useful patterns and correlations from huge data coming from various sources and in various formats. Because very huge amount of data are coming from thousands of sources in structured, unstructured and semi-structured formats, it's a very challenging task to analyze it (Tiwari and Thakur, 2016). As, incoming data may be inconsistent, noisy or uncertain, it is preprocessed before applying analytics method. This makes it more complex and challenging task to get insight into the huge amount of data (Lovalekar, 2014). Traditional analytics methods forms a cluster of expensive hardware like state of the art processors to process the huge data in parallel. Big data analytics tools like HADOOP uses commodity hardware and programming models to process massive data in parallel.

To extract meaningful hidden patterns and high valued information from huge amount of structured, semi-structured and unstructured data coming from various sources, big data analytics uses advanced analytics tools and technologies. To enable such kind of analytical ability, these tools provides number of algorithms which discover meaningful hidden patterns, market trends, recommendations and correlations in the data. These big data analytics tools not only analyses the data, but also visualize and present in the form of graphs, tables, charts, statistics, etc. These results can be used in efficient decision making and optimization (Marjani *et al*, 2017).

Key Challenges of Big Data Analytics

Big data analytics deals with Exabytes, or even more, structured, semi-structured and mostly unstructured data, which may incomplete, inconsistent or noisy at times. To extract informative and business centric pattern, big data analytics tools faces following challenges:

- We have such a huge amount of data, do all these data need to be analyzed?
- We have a composition of various formats of data, Does this composite data suitable for analysis? (Tiwari and Thakur., 2015).
- We have multi-formed, inconsistent, incomplete, uncertain and noisy data, how to find interesting patterns from such kind of data?
- How to ensure that performance of big data analytics tools doesn't degrade with the increase of size of data?
- How to produce high quality decision based results from huge datasets with minimum time, resources and cost? (Tiwari andThakur., 2015).

This list of challenges in big data analytics grows rapidly, if we consider finer granularities of data and algorithms to extract hidden patterns. However, in this chapter, challenges in storing, managing and analyzing the big data are discussed.

Data Storage Challenges

Data volume is increasing day by day in huge proportion. Data are coming from social media, e-commerce portals, online transactions, handheld devices, scientific simulations, web log files, satellites and sensors, GPS data, IoT (Internet of Things) enabled devices, etc. These sources generating the multi-formed data with high velocity, say terabytes per second. It is the biggest challenge to store the data coming from various sources, in various formats into a structure suitable for analytics.

Data Management Challenges

Data management is a key challenge in big data analytics. Individuals are generating data in various formats like images, audios, videos, text documents, etc without giving much information about the data they are generating. This creates issues while collecting them into unified schema, and validating them for analytics task. It is also very challenging task to differentiate relevant and irrelevant data for analytics, as all data we collect are not relevant for a particular scenario.

Data Processing Challenges

Nowadays, variety of data are generated and collected in huge amount. But, this huge amount of data is of no use until it is converted into some useful information. Using traditional information retrieval (IR) techniques, one can get hidden patterns from data. But, this kind of information retrieval is time taking process and mostly work with structured and relatively less amount of data. It's a very challenging task to analyze very huge amount of data are coming from thousands of sources in structured, unstructured and semi-structured formats. There are many big data analytics tools like HADOOP, Spark, Pig, Hive, etc. which process massive data in parallel.

Data Security and Privacy Challenges

Before setting environment for big data analytics, one should consider the following set of security and privacy challenges (Gahi *et al*, 2016).

1. **Transparency in Data Distribution:** To analyze huge amount of data with big data analytics tools, cluster of systems are used to process the data in distributed manner. The cluster of system is a set of computers all around the world in close communication. The huge amount of data is distributed to these systems in the cluster and then processed in parallel. The main problem with this cluster structure is that the exact location of storage of part of data and its processing location is transparent and hard to know. This can result in security problems and some regulation breaches.
2. **Privacy:** The privacy of data is dependent on the fact the how the sensitive data is being used and get the special attention that it should have. Currently, big data analytics is more concerned with getting more interesting results for decision purpose rather than providing security on the data. Due to this weakness, if unauthorized user gets access of any of the system in the cluster, she can have access, exploit, destroy, and alter the data.
3. **Integrity:** Before using the analytics results from big data analytics tools, it is necessary to check the validity and the trust level of data to avoid compromised and outlier records. The validation of

data is necessary because, data can be noisy, incomplete, and inconsistent. If they are not properly pre-processed before analysis, results may be inaccurate and must be validated.

4. **Secure Communication:** To analyze big data, it is divided into data chunks and stored on several computers in cluster. These data chunks are then processed in parallel on all systems and partial results of each system is communicated with others to get final results. Currently, these communications are done through ordinary public and private networks, which are vulnerable to security breach. To protect the communication among nodes of cluster, we need some secure communication protocols.

5. **Data Provenance:** Data provenance refers to the origin of data. That means, the location and time for generated data. Data are coming from number of sources, many of them may not be trustworthy (Lei Xu *et al*, 2014). If data generated from these malicious sources are taken into account, results may be faulty. It is a big challenge to detect the trustworthy and malicious sources of data.

6. **Access Control:** To protect the data from malicious data source and users, we need to deploy strong and effective access control mechanism. Only authorized users with administrative rights can participate to process the data, can be elementary access control mechanism. Applying more effective access control mechanism is still a big challenge to big data analytics.

Recent Trends of Big Data Analytics Tools

We are now in the era of Big Data. Business organizations are using big data analytics to generate decision making analytics which improves business processes (Jagadish et al, 2014). In 2017, the following trending tools and technologies are used by researchers and industries:

Hadoop

The Apache Hadoop is an open source, Java based framework developed for the distributed processing of huge amount of data in parallel with the help of clusters of computer systems. Hadoop framework is developed to scale up from single system (node) to a clusters of multiple computer systems having their own computation and storage capabilities. To provide high availability of information, it is designed to detect and handle failures automatically (N. Akhtar et al, 2015). The Apache Hadoop frameworks consists of following components:

1. **Hadoop Common:** Hadoop Common is the collection of common utilities and libraries to support its other modules.

2. **Hadoop Distributed File System (HDFS):** HDFS is the distributed file system responsible for storage, management and high throughput access of application data. HDFS splits the input dataset into manageable data chunks and stores them to different machines on Hadoop cluster. The default size of these data chunks is 64 MB for Hadoop 1.x and 128 MB for Hadoop 2.x. HDFS manages these files across number of machines on cluster and process them in distributed manner. Reliability is one of the most important feature of a distributed system. To achieve high reliability, HDFS stores data on multiple nodes by replicating them.

3. **Hadoop YARN:** It is a sub-project of Apache Foundation which provides a framework for job scheduling and cluster management.

4. **Hadoop MapReduce:** It is a YARN based programming model for distributed processing of large data. It is designed to write applications to process large datasets in parallel on large number of machines in a cluster. Hadoop MapReduce programming model process the data as a set of key-value pairs, and generates result in a set of key-value pairs.

Spark

The Apache Spark is an open source, fast, in-memory data processing framework designed to process read-only multi-set of data items called as resilient distributed dataset (RDD), distributed over a cluster of systems. The support for in-memory datasets makes it much faster than Hadoop. To process big data, Apache Spark needs a cluster manager and a system for distributed storage. Hadoop YARN can be used as a cluster manager and HDFS can be used for managing distributed storage. The Apache Spark consists of the Spark Core, Spark SQL, Spark SQL, Spark Streaming and MLlib (Machine Learning Library).

NoSQL

NoSQL is a database which is centered on the distributed databases. Using NoSQL, unstructured data can be stored on multiple nodes in distributed manner. This distributed architecture allows NoSQL databases to add up more system to deal with increasing data to support scalability and performance.

Pig

Pig is a high level scripting language as well as a platform to write codes that runs on Apache Hadoop. Pig enables data workers to write complex data transformations without knowing Java. Using Pig all required data manipulations can be done in Apache Hadoop. Pig can invoke codes of languages using user defined functions, also it can be embedded in codes of other programming languages. Pig processes structured, semi-structured and unstructured data, and then stores the results into the Hadoop Data File System.

Apache Hive

Apache Hive is a distributed data management software developed which runs on top of Apache Hadoop for providing data summarization, querying data, and data analysis. Apache Hive supports SQL-like queries to manage the distributed data.

Data Lake

A data lake can be defined as a method of storing data in a repository without changing its natural format. The idea behind the Data Lake is to create a single repository of all data. This data ranges from raw data coming from various sources to transformed data to be used for analytics purpose such as reporting, visualization, analytics and machine learning. The data lake creates a centralized data store by combining structured data coming from relational databases in the form of tables, semi-structured data such as CSV, log files, XML data, JSON data, and unstructured data like emails, documents, tweets, images, audio and video (Campbell Chris, 2017).

FUTURE PROSPECTS

In coming years, there will be a continued growth of analytics tools that support structured, semi-structured and unstructured forms of huge volume of data. These tools and technologies will evolve and optimize to provide much better and accurate business centric and decision based results. There are following areas where evolution and advancements will be done in coming years.

Ubiquitous Machine Learning

The importance of applying machine learning to massive amount of data is increasing day by day. It can be defined as the knowledge discovery and learning inside dynamic, distributed massive amount of data. For consumers, some sort of machine learning is already implemented in their everyday online lives, from target marketing over online shopping to extreme personalization of searched results. In future, we can expect a huge increase in the availability and capabilities of machine learning in big data analytics for end users and business organizations as well.

Big Data and the Cloud

Due to privacy issues, regulations and authorization, it's not always possible to move big data to an external data center. Sometimes, moving cost of this huge amount of data may surpass its overall benefit. To deal with such scenario, move the data to cloud. Currently, Amazon EMR, Cloudera, MapR, and Hortonworks, etc are using cloud to provide services to its users. Trends shows that, in the future, many other organizations will use cloud technologies for handling big data in multiple locations.

Big Data and the Internet of Things

The Internet of Things is a network of things (handheld/household devices). Using IoT and machine learning, analytics can be done on big data to provide healthcare services, target marketing, extreme personalization and other services through mobile applications. In future, this application can be extended to meet the requirements of business organizations and smart cities.

Big Data and the Deep Learning

Deep learning is a hierarchical approach of learning which uses multi-layer artificial neural networks to extract high-level, complex abstractions as data representations. Deep Learning is considered as the analysis and learning of huge amount of unsupervised data. This property makes deep learning a valuable approach for analyzing unlabeled and un-categorized data (Maryam M Najafabadi *et al*, 2015). As discussed earlier, most of the big data is un-categorized or unstructured, deep learning will play an evolutionary role in big data analytics.

CONCLUSION

Big data can be defined as the huge amount of data coming from various sources in various formats. Before the advent of Big Data, digital data around the world was not so big and unstructured. To gain insight to such a massive amount of data, big data analytics tools and technologies are used. Big data analytics is the process of extracting useful patterns and correlations from huge data coming from various sources and in various formats. As, enormous data are coming from thousands of sources in structured, unstructured and semi-structured formats, it's a very challenging task to analyze it.

The big data analytics challenges raise the following questions: Do all these data need to be analyzed? Does this composite data suitable for analysis? We have multi-formed, inconsistent, incomplete, uncertain and noisy data, how to find interesting patterns from such kind of data? How to ensure that performance of big data analytics tools doesn't degrade with the increase of size of data? How to produce high quality decision based results from huge datasets with minimum time, resources and cost?

To answer the above questions, business organizations are currently using big data analytics tools and technologies such as Hadoop, MapReduce, Spark, Pig, Hive, NoSQL, etc. These tools distribute the huge amount of data over distributed nodes in cluster. Each data chunk is processed in parallel on each node and finally clubbed together to provide analytics results in the form of graphs, charts, documents, etc. In future, big data analytics can be merged with cutting edge technologies like cloud computing, Internet of Things, Deep Learning, etc, to provide more accurate, secure, scalable and cost effective analytics.

REFERENCES

Akhtar, Ahamad, & Khan. (2015). Clustering on Big Data Using Hadoop MapReduce. *Proceedings of International Conference on Computational Intelligence and Communication Networks.*

Akhtar, N., & Ahamad, M. V. (2017). Graph Tools for Social Network Analysis. In Graph Theoretic Approaches for Analyzing Large-Scale Social Networks. IGI Global. Doi:10.4018/978-1-5225-2814-2.ch002

Akthar, N., Ahamad, M. V., & Khan, S. (2015). MapReduce Model of Improved K-Means Clustering Algorithm Using Hadoop MapReduce. *Proceedings of 2016 Second International Conference on Computational Intelligence & Communication Technology.*

Bansal, P., & Ahmad, T. (2016, August). Methods and Techniques of Intrusion Detection: A Review. In *International Conference on Smart Trends for Information Technology and Computer Communications* (pp. 518-529). Springer.

Campbell, C. (n.d.). *Top Five Differences between DataWarehouses and Data Lakes.* Blue-Granite.com.

Chawda & Thakur. (2016). Big Data and Advanced Analytics Tools. *2016 Symposium on Colossal Data Analysis and Networking (CDAN).*

Choudhury, T., Chhabra, A. S., Kumar, P., & Sharma, S. (2016). A Recent Trends on Big Data Analytics. *Proceedings of the SMART -2016, 5th International Conference on System Modeling & Advancement in Research Trends.*

Najafabadi, Villanustre, Khoshgoftaar, Seliya, Wald, & Muharemagic. (2015). Deep learning applications and challenges in big data analytics. *Journal of Big Data, 2015*. doi:10.118640537-014-0007-7

Gahi, Y., Guennoun, M., & Mouftah, H. T. (2016). Big Data Analytics: Security and Privacy Challenges. *Proceedings of 2016 IEEE Symposium on Computers and Communication (ISCC)*.

Han, J., & Kamber, M. (2000). Data Mining: Concepts and Techniques. Morgan Kaufmann.

Inukollu, Arsi, & Ravuri. (2014). Security Issues Associated With Big Data In Cloud Computing. *International Journal of Network Security & Its Applications, 6*(3).

Jagadish, H., Gehrke, J., Labrinidis, A., Papakonstantinou, Y., Patel, J., Ramakrishnan, R., & Shahabi, C. (2014). Big data and its technical challenges. *Communications of the ACM, 57*(7), 86–94. doi:10.1145/2611567

Katal, A., Wazid, M., & Goudar, R. H. (2013). Big data: Issues, challenges, tools and Good practices. Academic Press.

Laney. (2001). 3d Data management: Controlling data volume, velocity and variety. *Appl. Delivery Strategies Meta Group, 949*.

Lovalekar, S. (2014). Big Data: An Emerging Trend In Future. *International Journal of Computer Science and Information Technologies, 5*(1), 538–541.

Marjani, Nasaruddin, Gani, Karim, Hashem, Siddiqa, & Yaqoob. (n.f.). *Big IoT Data Analytics: Architecture, Opportunities, and Open Research Challenges*. IEEE, DOI doi:10.1109/ACCESS.2017.2689040

Mashkoor & Ahamad. (2017). Visualization, Security and Privacy Challenges of Big Data. *International Journal of Advanced Technology in Engineering and Science, 5*(6), 394 - 400.

Mishra, A. D., & Singh, Y. B. (2016). Big Data Analytics for Security and Privacy Challenges. *Proceedings of International Conference on Computing, Communication and Automation (ICCCA2016)*. 10.1109/CCAA.2016.7813688

Tiwari, V., & Thakur, R.S. (2015). P2MS- A Phase-Wise Pattern Management System for Pattern Warehouse. *Int. J. of Data Mining, Modeling and Management, 7*(4), 331-350.

Tiwari, V., & Thakur, R. S. (2016). Pattern Warehouse: Context Based Modeling and Quality Issues, National Academy of Sciences, India Section A: Physical Sciences, 85(3), 1-15.

Xu, Jiang, Wang, Yuan, & Ren. (2014). *Information Security in Big Data: Privacy and Data Mining*. IEEE. DOI doi:10.1109/Access.2014.2362522

Zaharia, M., Chowdhury, M., Franklin, M. J., Shenker, S., & Stoica, I. (n.d.). Spark: Cluster Computing with Working Sets (PDF). *USENIX Workshop on Hot Topics in Cloud Computing (HotCloud)*.

KEY TERMS AND DEFINITIONS

Big Data Analytics: Big data analytics is the process of extracting useful patterns and correlations from huge data coming from various sources and in various formats.

Big Data: Big data is a term that is used to describe data that is high volume, high velocity, and/or high variety; requires new technologies and techniques to capture, store, and analyse it; and is used to enhance decision making, provide insight and discovery, and support and optimize processes.

Data: It is a collection of raw facts about something.

HDFS (Hadoop Distributed File System): HDFS is the distributed file system responsible for storage, management and high throughput access of application data. HDFS splits the input dataset into manageable data chunks and stores them to different machines on Hadoop cluster.

Information Retrieval: The extraction of hidden information from stored data.

Pattern: It is a summarized and information rich semantic representation of raw data.

Resilient Distributed Datasets (RDD): It is an immutable distributed collection of objects. Each dataset in RDD is divided into logical partitions, which may be computed on different nodes of the cluster.

This research was previously published in the Handbook of Research on Pattern Engineering System Development for Big Data Analytics; pages 67-79, copyright year 2018 by Engineering Science Reference (an imprint of IGI Global).

Chapter 56
A Study of Big Data Processing for Sentiments Analysis

Dinesh Chander
Panipat Institute of Engineering and Technology, India

Hari Singh
Jaypee University of Information Technology, India

Abhinav Kirti Gupta
Jaypee University of Information Technology, India

ABSTRACT

Data processing has become an important field in today's big data-dominated world. The data has been generating at a tremendous pace from different sources. There has been a change in the nature of data from batch-data to streaming-data, and consequently, data processing methodologies have also changed. Traditional SQL is no longer capable of dealing with this big data. This chapter describes the nature of data and various tools, techniques, and technologies to handle this big data. The chapter also describes the need of shifting big data on to cloud and the challenges in big data processing in the cloud, the migration from data processing to data analytics, tools used in data analytics, and the issues and challenges in data processing and analytics. Then the chapter touches an important application area of streaming data, sentiment analysis, and tries to explore it through some test case demonstrations and results.

DATA PROCESSING

Since last decade, rapid development of Internet enabled services such as social media, Internet of Things, and cloud based services have led to tremendous growth of data termed as big data. This data has become very difficult to be handled and managed for further processing (Jin et al., 2015). It has been estimated that around 2.5 quintillion bytes of new data is generated per day and expected to be more in near future as the number of internet users are growing unprecedentedly. This exponential growth of data has posed many challenges in front of researchers, academia and Industry across the globe. Moreover,

DOI: 10.4018/978-1-6684-3662-2.ch056

the big data is unstructured: it varies in volume, velocity, veracity and variety makes (4Vs) it more challenging to manage and process (Mishra, R. K., & Mishra, R. K., 2018). This sudden explosion of data in terabytes, petabytes and exabytes could not be handled by the traditional database such as SQL led to the emergence of new tools and techniques to process the big data (Storey, V. C., & Song, I. Y., 2017).

Figure 1. Big data chain

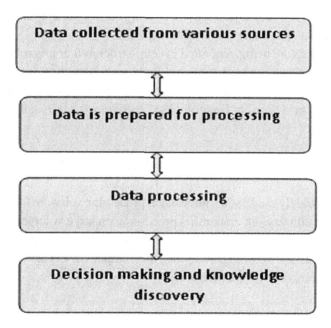

Big data processing and analysis have become very crucial for better decision making, knowledge discovery, business intelligence and actionable insights. The Fig-1 represents the big data chain i.e. from data collection to decision making (Janssen, M., van der Voort, H., & Wahyudi, A., 2017). Big data is collected in raw form from various sources of interest which need to be prepared for processing. Next the quality data sets are prepared for further processing using data cleansing and standardization. After that, data processing takes place which includes transformation, aggregation and pattern generation. Once the data processing is completed, various reports are generated and analyzed for better decision making, knowledge discovery and insight or trends. Analysis of data could be classified as descriptive, diagnostic, predictive and prescriptive (Perwej, Y., 2017).

This book chapter proposes to show various tools, techniques, and technologies of data processing and analytics. Later, the use streaming data for sentiment analysis through executable test cases is presented. Sentiment analysis is performed on run-time tweets with Python using twitter API "tweepy" and obtained results are presented through plots.

A survey on various sentiment analysis methods used by researchers is also presented. This would also help in identifying the best one and possibly may be in predicting a newer one.

FAILURE OF TRADITIONALSQL IN HANDLING BIG DATA

The volume of data is expected to grow 50% per year, and data production by 2020 will be 50 times larger than what it was in 2009. This rapid increase in volume requires powerful tools and techniques to process big data (Yaqoob, I., Hashem, I. A. T., Gani, A., Mokhtar, S., Ahmed, E., Anuar, N. B., & Vasilakos, A. V., 2016). The conventional tools such as SQL are unable to process it due to high volume, velocity and veracity of data. With such a diversification of data, ACID properties (Atomicity, Consistency, Integrity, and Durability) of databases are very difficult to meet using conventional tools; also desired outcome is difficult to produce within a reasonable frame of time period.

Secondly, most of the data are being generated in semi-structured or unstructured format in the form of images, text, audio, video and mails. Traditional tools are mainly designed to deal with structured data only. Therefore, new and advanced technologies have been devised to cope up the processing of big data in batches. In the next section, Hadoop based technologies to handle this increasing amount data has been discussed.

Database Technologies for Big Data Based on Hadoop

Apache Hadoop is one of widely used open source batch processing software for big data. Hadoop serves the basis for software that aim to work on parallel processing on large volume of data (Mishra, A.D., & Singh, Y.B., 2017). Hadoop works in two main phase i.e. storage and computation. Hadoop is assisted by two main components as shown in Figure 2, the first component is Hadoop distributed file system (HDFS) and the second component is MapReduce.

Figure 2. Hadoop component

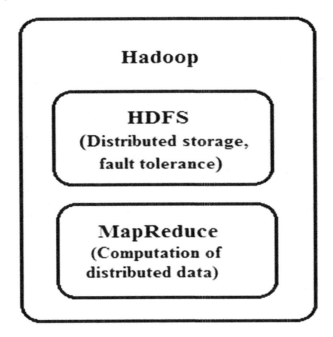

HDFS allows a network of computers to form a cluster for data storage and processing. The MapReduce performs computation on stored data (Huang, W., Wang, H., Zhang, Y., & Zhang, S., 2017). The HDFS follows a master slave model to process data. The main issue with MapReduce is that it is unable to process iterative algorithms up to an optimum level. This section discusses some advanced technologies (Hadoop eco system) which have contributed in improving performance in batch processing of big data.

1. **Apache Spark:** Apache Spark is also a general purpose, distributed open source project that extends the capabilities of MapReduce by supporting processing of multiple data types such as SQL-like queries, streaming, machine learning, graph and data flow processing (Mavridis, I., & Karatza, H., 2017). Spark is considered to be very good for iterative as well as batch processing algorithms which processes data in memory. It reduces usages of disk by keeping data in memory during map and reduce phases. Spark has many higher level specialized library items to process specific kind of data as shown in Figure 3. Many programming tools such as Java, Python, R and Scala can be used for implementation of algorithms.

Figure 3. Spark with specialized library to process the data

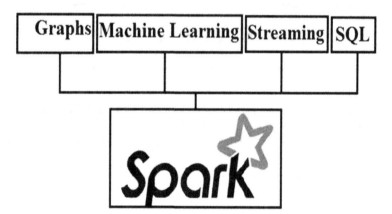

2. **Apache PIG:** Apache Pig is a scripting platform to process and analyze the large volume of data set present in Hadoop cluster (Kaur, R., Chauhan, V., & Mittal, U., 2018). The language used for scripting is known as PIG Latin. PIG runs the programs, convert it into the map reduce tasks, and finally executes the tasks. PIG is best suitable for the programming of the data in semi structured form.

3. **Apache Hive:** Hive is a Haddop eco-system tool which acts as an interface for the data warehouse for MapReduce programming. Hive has its own SQL, known as Hive query language (HQL). HQL is used to query data from the HDFS, generate MapReduce code and finally execute on Hadoop cluster as shown in Figure 4. Hive is not compatible with only HDFS, but also with Spark and other big data frameworks. Hive is fast, extensible and scalable, mainly developed for the OLAP (Mahmood, Z., 2016).

4. **HBase:** HBase is an open source, column-oriented, distributed, and non-relational database management system that runs on top of HDFS. HBase belong to the family of NoSQL database with the capability to handle massive amounts of data from terabytes to petabytes. Tables in Hbase are stored logically in the form of rows and columns. The benefit of such table storage is that they can process a million of rows and columns (Oussous, A., Benjelloun, F. Z., Ait Lahcen, A., & Belfkih, S., 2018). It provides many features at low latency such as, natural language processing, real-time queries, linear and modular scalability, and consistent access to Big Data from various sources. However, HBase has the limitation of not supporting a structured query language like SQL.

Figure 4. Hive code execution

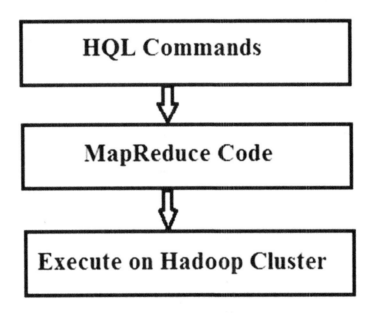

5. **Apache Kafka:** Apache Kafka is an open-source stream-processing software platform written in Scala and Java with an aim to provide low-latency platform for handling real-time data feeds with high throughput. The main components of Kafka architecture are Producer, Consumer, Broker and Topic (Vohra, D., 2016). In Kafka, a message is termed as the smallest unit of data that can flow from a producer to a consumer through a Kafka server (Broker) as shown in Figure 5. The message can persist on the server to be processed at a later time and feeds in topics. A topic, in Kafka, is a stream of messages of a similar category. In comparison to other messaging systems, Kafka has better built-in partitioning, replication, inherent fault-tolerance and throughput which make it one of best suitable platform for large-scale message processing applications.

All the above mentioned Hadoop based technologies are a very popular data analytics framework for the distributed batch-data processing to produce patterns, knowledge and actionable insights. However, shortcomings are found in the Hadoop framework in processing and analyzing the streaming data.

Figure 5. Message flow in Apache Kafka

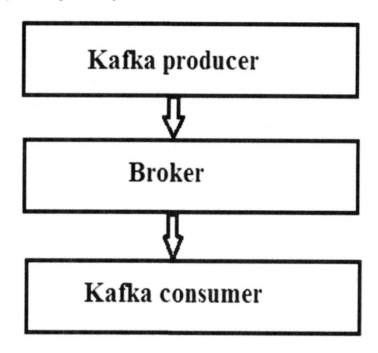

NATURE OF DATA PRESENT AT PRESENT

As discussed in previous sections that data are generated from various resources such as social networks, web logs, e-commerce transactions, sensors and emails, could be batch-processed using the Hadoop framework with long period of latency. Data-stream processing and batch processing are considered as two different types of applications (Carbone, P., Katsifodimos, A., Kth, †, Sweden, S., Ewen, S., Markl, V., Haridi, S., & Tzoumas, K., 2015). A batch processing frameworks works on MapReduce component and is generally focus on the size and complexity of tasks than latency period of computation (Vakilinia, S., Zhang, X., & Qiu, D., 2016). There are many research works that improved efficiency of data processing in MapReduce. One such indexing in Hadoop is presented (Mittal, M., Singh, H., Paliwal, K., & Goyal, L. M., 2017). Similarly, MapReduce has been exploited for spatial data processing (Singh, H., & Bawa, S., 2012) and (Singh, H., & Bawa, S., 2016).

Now a day, big data applications are rapidly moving from batch oriented processing to stream oriented processing. The exponential growth of stream data, real-time stream processing becomes a major concern for research community and industry. Processing and analysis of stream data have become necessary in today's world to support a variety of applications such as IOT, medical, transportation, e-commerce, finance, and gaming. The major concern of data stream processing is real-time processing, high throughput, low latency period, and highly scalable to adjust large number of producers. The processing of data streaming heavily relies on immediate data partitioning of data generated by producers (Marcu, O., Costan, A., Antoniu, G., & P, S., 2018). A typical stream data processing pipeline is shown in Figure 6. Data producer refers all sources that generate continue data streams. Secondly, the data partition phase, acquires the stream for partition and preprocessing, to facilitate the consumption. At last, the processing engine consumes data stream for analysis.

Figure 6. Data streaming pipeline

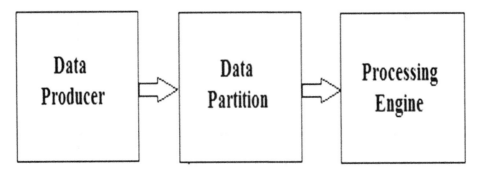

DATA STREAM PROCESSING TOOLS

Unlike batch processing where data is defined by a start and an end in a job and a job finishes after processing that finite data, streaming refers to processing unbounded data coming in real-time continuously on a regular basis. Stream processing is harder to achieve as many characteristics such as fault tolerance, guaranteed delivery, low latency and throughput are the essential QoS parameters to be adhered by the applications. In this section few widely used stream processing tools have been discussed:

1. **Apache Flink:** Apache Flink is distributed open source framework for stream data processing. It is capable to handle huge amount of data for real time processing with low latency and high fault tolerance (García-gil, D., Ramírez-gallego, S., García, S., & Herrera, F., 2017). It support two main API i.e. data stream and data set for stream and batch processing respectively. Flink supports following four libraries to support stream processing:
   a. Flink ML: This library is concerned with ML algorithms to deal with supervised and unsupervised learning.
   b. Gelly: It contains the methods and utilities to support graphical processing and analysis in Flink.
   c. Flink CEP: This library is helpful in the processing of complex events and to generate the complex event patterns.
   d. Table API and SQL: It supports the execution of SQL like statements for the relational data stream.
2. **Apache Storm**: It is distributed, real time, and fault tolerant computation system; written in Java and Clojure to process the large amount of streaming data (Lopez, M. A., Lobato, A. G. P., & Duarte, O. C. M. B., 2016). The working of storm cluster is similar to Hadoop cluster. The clusters on storm can use different topologies for different storm tasks. A topology is similar to a MapRedude Job in Hadoop, but it operates under the control of user. A storm cluster has two types of nodes i.e. master node and worker node. The master node assigns the job to worker node and monitors the whole system. Whereas, worker nodes process assigned tasks for analysis (Achariya, D., & Kauser, A., 2016).

3. **Apache Spark streaming:** Spark is distributed platform stream processing is written in Java and Sacala. Spark has special libraries called Spark Streaming to support the stream processing with short latency. An Apache Storm topology consumes streams of data; repartition the streams between each stage of the computation for real time processing. It is primarily based on micro-batch processing mode where events are processed together based on specified time intervals. Spark has three main components; the driver program responsible for the proper scheduling the task and creating spark context; cluster mangers are responsible for the resource allocation between applications; task managers responsible for computation and storage. The processing rate of Spark is lower as compared to Strom and Flink due to formation of micro-batch before processing (Hesse, G., & Lorenz, M., 2016).

CLOUD COMPUTING IN DATA PROCESSING

As discussed, 4Vs has posed many challenges in efficient processing of big data. Now, need of the hour is transformation of 4Vs in to 5Vs. Value is big issue for the processing capacity (Yang, C., Yu, M., Hu, F., Jiang, Y., & Li, Y., 2017). Cloud computing has become an amazing computation utility to address issues associated with big data with on demand service, ubiquitous network access, location independent resource pooling, rapid expansion and metered services (Verma, D.C., Mohapatra, A.K., & Usmani, K., 2012).

The rapid development in virtualization has made computation more economical sharable and accessible. Cloud computing eliminate the need of expensive resources such as processor, storage, operating system and memory for the large scale processing and complex computation. Large amount of data from the web and cloud are kept in a fault-tolerant distributed database and processed by a programming model for large volume of dataset with the help of parallel distributed algorithm in a cluster (Hashem, I. A. T., Yaqoob, I., Anuar, N. B., Mokhtar, S., Gani, A., & Ullah Khan, S., 2015).

After processing of a large dataset, data visualization is used to present results in different graphs for decision making. The Figure 7 depicts the use of cloud computing for big data processing and analysis. Data sources in Figure 7 represent main contributor of data such as web, IOT, sensors and cloud. The main components of cloud data processing are: fault tolerant databases to store captured data, programming data model to process the clustered data through parallel computing and the query engine to execute queries.

There are many cloud service model that offers the storage and computing facilities for big data, such as Amazon, Google, Microsoft, and Cloudera with different tools and techniques. Therefore, cloud computing technologies are the platform used to process and analyze big data without any major investment on resources such as tools, storage, and processors. But there are certain issues that must be adhered of while dealing with big data processing with a cloud service model.

Challenges in Big Data Processing in the Cloud

Though cloud computing is seen as an emerging technology for users and enterprises to process big data without any major investment. But, it poses few challenging and issues in front of industry, academia, and researchers that need be addressed to make it sustainable technology for big data processing (Stergiou, C., Psannis, K. E., Gupta, B. B., & Ishibashi, Y., 2018).

Figure 7. Cloud computing for big data processing and analysis

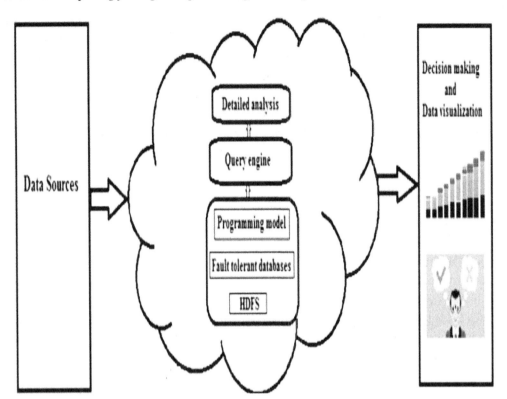

1. **Data security:** Data is considered as an asset for the users and the enterprises. In cloud, data located at some third-party data center for the processing. Although, most of the cloud service providers use encryption techniques to ensure the security issues of the user's data, still some security breach makes the users reluctant to use the cloud computing services (Moreno, J., Serrano, M. A., & Fernández-Medina, E., 2016).
2. **Privacy:** Big data processing in cloud also leads to privacy issues. For example, social media and medical records contains personal information may be misused by the third party or by the attackers raises serious concerns while dealing in cloud computation.
3. **Performance:** Encryption techniques used to secure the data at third party is directly related to the performance issues of the cloud service providers. The consequences of the complex encryption techniques may lead to degraded performance in terms of computation and data decryption. Therefore, a light-weight and secure encryption technique is required for the optimized performance.
4. **QoS:** It is very difficult to meet all the QoS parameters while processing the big data in the cloud. QoS parameters such as throughput, efficiency, time to upload and download the data from the cloud are few essential parameters to achieve.
5. **Reliability:** Data processing with cloud computing also raises the question mark on the reliability and the accessibility of the infrastructure.
6. **Heterogeneity and compatibility:** One of the major challenge need to be adhered of with cloud computing are the heterogeneity and compatibility of the devices, platforms, operating systems, infrastructure and services.

7. **Network bandwidth:** Big data processing is directly affected by the available network bandwidth (Yang, C., Huang, Q., Li, Z., Liu, K., & Hu, F., 2017).

8. **Data integration:** The 5th V (value) of the big data is very critical to achieve through the cross-domain processing and analysis is also a major concern of cloud computing.

All the above mentioned challenges are very critical to achieve while processing the big data through the cloud computing and most of the issues are open for the further research work.

MIGRATION FROM DATA PROCESSING TO DATA ANALYTICS

The data generated from various sources such as social networks, sensor networks, IOT, web logs, e-commerce transactions and email are of no use if they are not processed and analyzed for better decision making, knowledge discovery and meaningful pattern search (Acito, F., & Khatri, V., 2014). Big data analytics refers the quantitative and qualitative techniques and processes used to enhance the decision making capability for business gain.

Data analytics involve applying an algorithmic or mechanical process systematically to derive meaningful patterns and correlations between the data sets. Today's almost every organization has maintained data warehouse to collect data related to their customers, markets and business process for data processing. This data is then stored, categorized, and analyzed to transform the 4Vs into 5th V i.e. value or sense of it to derive meaningful insights from it. In next section various types of data analytics that is used to infer some logical conclusion from the data set will be discussed.

Challenges in Big Data Processing in the Cloud

In the literature various types of data analytics methodology are found to infer meaningful and logical information for the processed data set, few of them are discussed here (Chakraborty, K., & Bhattacharyya, S., 2018) as shown in Figure 8.

1. **Predictive analytics**: It refers the process of prediction of the events in advance based on the use of big data can (Akter, S., & Wamba, S. F., 2016). The quality of the prediction depends on the availability of the robust data set and it's mining. Therefore, predictive analytics helps the organizations to prepare more precise budgets and optimized processes. The preparation of these budgets helps e-commerce firms predict future sales trend, inventory management, and customer behavior from past data. The major concern that must be adhered of with predictive analysis is faster data access and mining methods for structured and unstructured for the improved prediction (Marjani, M., Nasaruddin, F., Gani, A., Karim, A., Hashem, I. A. T., Siddiqa, A., & Yaqoob, I., 2017). Predictive analytics helps in answering to the questions 'What will happen?'

2. **Prescriptive analytics**: touches various aspects of business processes to provide insights on what is required to do in terms of data analytics. Predictive analytics talks about an analysis based on a defined set of rules and recommendations in order to prescribe a certain analytical path for the organization. A firm can deploy prescriptive analytics regardless of the industry vertical based on the same rules and regulations. Prescriptive analytics helps in finding the answers to the question 'How can we make it happen?'

Figure 8. Types of Data Analytics

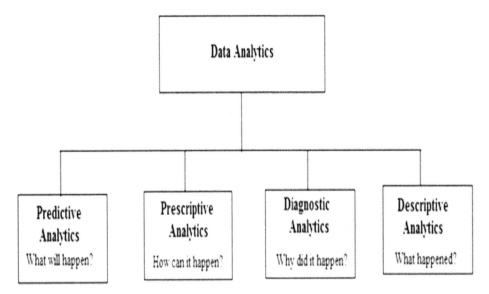

3. **Diagnostic analytics**: is used for the specific purpose, such as discovering or determining why a certain course of action took place in the past. For example, this analytics are very useful to review a certain social media campaign and its outcome based on the number of followers, page views, reviews, fans, and such other metrics to diagnose why a certain thing happened. Diagnostic analytics are used answers to the questions 'Why did an event happen?' (Coraddu, A., Oneto, L., Baldi, F., & Anguita, D., 2017).

4. **Descriptive analytics:** used to explain what is happens in a given situation and uncovering patterns that can add value to an organization (Amirian, P., Loggerenberg, F. van, Lang, T., Thomas, A., Peeling, R., Basiri, A., & Goodman, S. N., 2017). Descriptive analytics basically answers to the question 'What happened to system?'. For example, the credit risks assessment of a customer. It takes into consideration various aspects such as the previous financial performance of the customer, inputs from past financial institutions, and CIBIL report and other online information available on web-based solutions.

Since no organization in this competitive era can survive with business gain without using proper data processing and data analytics, so data analytics is an indispensable part of the data life cycle in an organization. In the next section we discuss few widely used data analytics tools and techniques for better decision making and knowledge discovery.

Tools Used in Data Analytics

Data analytics tools are required in almost every organization to analyze the large, diverse and complex dataset to extract meaningful insights for business gains and to overtake the competitors. There are many platforms available nowadays for the efficient data analytics; few of them are briefly discussed here (Chawda, R. K., & Thakur, G., 2016).

1. **Apache Spark:** Spark is very powerful open source framework used for real-time Data analytics. As discussed in section 2.1, Spark is a component of the Hadoop ecosystem and used to store, process and analyze the stream at low very low latency.

2. **IBM InfoSphere BigInsights:** InfoSphere is a big data analytics platform developed by IBM. InfoSphere build on the top of Hadoop for the big data analytics through interactive user interface. It is used for analytics of social media data, sensor data, GPS data and textual data. The main components of InfoSphere are BigSQL (SQL interface), Jqal (Declarative query language) and Bigsheets (spreadsheet interface) modules which are used in data analytics.

3. **Cloud based analytics:** There are many cloud based data analytics tools to deal with huge volume of data. Amazon EC2, Microsoft Azure, and Google AppEngine are few popular cloud platforms are used by the organizations to draw meaningful insights. With ample of advantages of cloud based analytics, data security and privacy are major concern for the research community.

4. **Python:** Python is open and free to use data analytics tool with rich set of libraries, package, and dictionary to achieve the outcome in a well organized way (Siddiqui, T., Alkadri, M., & Khan, N. A., 2017). This is one of the most versatile programming languages that are rapidly being deployed for various applications including Machine Learning. Python ecosystem includes packages like Numpy, Pandas, SciPy, Matplotlib and PySide for the efficient data analytics.

5. **SAP HANA:** SAP's Event Stream Processor (ESP) has made the SAP HANA a standalone, in-memory analytics platform used for stream analysis. SAP HANA is a combination of software and hardware, which integrates different components like SAP HANA Database, SAP SLT (System Landscape Transformation) Replication server, SAP HANA Direct Extractor connection and Sybase replication technology. SAP HANA can be deployed on premises or in cloud to provide real-time reporting at very high speed. The main limitation of SAP HANA is difficult maintenance of HANA database.

6. **SAS:** SAS is an advanced analytical tool for accessing, transformation and reporting data through its extensible, flexible and web based interface. The SAS platform comes with many applications such as SAS Text Miner, SAS Model Manager, and SAS Forecast Server for working with huge volumes of data and deriving valuable insights from it.

7. **Tableau:** This is one of the most popular Business Intelligence tools that is deployed for the purpose of business analytics and data visualization in the best presentable way. Tableau is the best tool among its competitor product such as Qlikview and Spotfire. The main advantages of the Tableau are amazing data visualization, excellent mobile support and low-cost solutions to upgrade (Yaqoob, I., Hashem, I. A. T., Gani, A., Mokhtar, S., Ahmed, E., Anuar, N. B., & Vasilakos, A. V., 2016). Whereas, the major limitation of Tableau is lack of predictive capabilities.

8. **Splunk:** Splunk is scalable and fault tolerant tool of choice for parsing the machine-generated data and extracting valuable business insights out of it. Splunk used for the real time data analytics tool for generating reports, alerts and data visualization from the stream.

9. **R Programming:** R is created by a group of colleagues at the University of Auckland in New Zeaklan in 1993. R is free and open source software and most widely used analytics tool used by data Scientists. R enables to perform the statistical computation and graphical presentation on dataset for better analysis as compared to other analytics tools (Ozgur, C., Colliau, T., Rogers, G., Hughes, Z., & Myer-Tyson, E. B., 2017).

DATA PROCESSING AND ANALYTICS: ISSUES AND CHALLENGES

This section discusses few important issues that are being faced by the industry in data processing and open for future research.

1. **Understanding of data:** It is very crucial to understand and select the right dataset out of the huge lump of data. It is just like finding the signal in the noise. Right dataset may lead towards the leap and bound business gain, whereas wrong dataset and correlation may lead to drastic loss.

2. **Scalability:** It refers the capability to accommodate the increasing amount of data. Data are generated at very rapid and unpredictable manner, which very difficult to store and process. Traditional databases are not suitable to handle this uneven data generation leads to the popularity of NoSQL (Hashem, I. A. T., Yaqoob, I., Anuar, N. B., Mokhtar, S., Gani, A., & Khan, S.U., 2015). Although, the scalability issue has been addressed by many advance tools and techniques, but still lot many issues are open and need to be further researched.

3. **Data quality:** The heterogeneity of data creates lot many issues during processing and analysis. Therefore, obtain the highest quality data from the various sources is an open challenge for the research community.

4. **Privacy:** Encryption techniques are used to maintain the privacy of the data, but somewhere encryption and decryption of data consume significant amount processing time, which need to be optimized.

5. **Security:** Security threats to data have always been a major issue for the research community. This issue magnified in the case of big data due to volume, velocity, and veracity of the data and need to be talked wisely.

6. **Computation complexity:** The design of energy efficient, high performance computing frameworks with low latency is one of the biggest and open challenge for the Industry and researchers (Jin, X., Wah, B. W., Cheng, X., & Wang, Y., 2015).

7. **Communication between systems:** Most of the computation involved in big data are of distributed in nature and based on parallel computation (Tsai, C. W., Lai, C. F., Chao, H. C., & Vasilakos, A. V., 2015). This kind of the framework needs stringent coordination and communication among the constituent systems for efficient processing, failing which results in high cost and degraded performance.

8. **Data integrity:** Integrity refers that only authorized users can access the data. It is utmost important to prevent the misuse of data and frauds. Data with the third party need a mechanism to ensure the integrity of the data. Therefore, a strong and robust authorization scheme mechanism to maintain the data correctness.

9. **Data transformation:** Data must be pre-processed before the storage in the database and further analysis. Improper transformation leads to wrong knowledge discovery and correlations of the datasets, results in huge business loss.

SENTIMENTS ANALYSIS AND REVIEWS

The opinion mining and sentiment analysis deals with computational treatment of opinion, sentiment, and subjectivity in text. A deep survey on the opinion oriented information seeking system along with challenges faced in the sentiment aware application as compared to the fact-based system is presented (Pang, B., & Lee, L., 2008). The following section presents a survey of various existing techniques of sentiment analysis.

A domain-specific sentiment analysis using contextual feature generation uses clue set (Choi, Y., Kim, Y., & Myaeng, S.-H., 2009). The clue set contains most likely feature words for the word that is to be checked. This method has a four step algorithm for generating the new clue set of sentiment words. Initially, this is consisting of sentence as well as polarity (training) example, then generates corresponding clues. Second step involves the identification of sentiment topics from training (sample) example. Then the sentiment clues which gets identified to sentiment topics are put to its current clue set. This updated classifier is then used for identifying other domains under sentiment clues from the sample data set. Recently, automatic opinion analysis in many domains has become very popular.

In another approach, exploiting new sentiment-based meta-level features for effective sentiment analysis is presented (Canuto, S., Gonçalves, M. A., & Benevenuto, F., 2016). This method contains large set of pre-classified words/sentence. For a new word that has to be checked the features (which discuss issues for the work) are checked for similarities with the pre classified data set. The one with the most resembling contents matched is considered as the true sentiment word for the given content. Thus the given contents' sentiment is taken as the sentiment of the pre-classified sentence with whom the maximum feature similarities are got.

The measure of sentiment of user towards each political party is checked using sentiment index which takes the log of ratio of total words raised to the power positive and negative added to unity (Sandoval-Almazan, R., & Valle-Cruz, D., 2018).

$$Sentiment\ Index = ln\left[\frac{1 + Total^{Positive}}{1 + Total^{Negative}}\right].$$

The study indicated that the emotions of voters can be found but not their intention to vote. It was found that the political party that won had a bad perception on social media while the one having well was unable to win the Mexican election.

Another approach allowed a multi level representation of three categories: Target, Modifier, and Appraisal group (Bari, M. D., Shroff, S., & Thomas, M., 2013). Target is the expression that the sentiment refers to. Modifier is the expression conveying the sentiment and appraisal group includes the set of targets and modifiers. The meaning of a sentence gets reversed when certain words were present which are k/a modifiers.

In another approach, evaluation of features on sentimental analysis is presented (Shahana, P., & Omman, B., 2015). This involves four step procedures. Firstly data is preprocessed, in it initially all text are converted into lowercase words for simplicity of feature extraction. Then the words ending with apostrophizes are converted back to original form like don't -> do not, any non ASCII character is removed. This is followed by removal of stop words (e.g. aan the) as they do not convey any feature so removal of stop words is preferred. Second setup involves partitioning data into training and test data. For training data after performing stemming (removing suffixes like ing eg.: computing->compute) feature selection is to be performed in which various statistical methods are applied to check whether sentiment of review can be extracted from the count of words in each sample.

Review of sentimental analysis methods using lexicon based approach is presented (Rajput, R., & Solanki, A. K., 2016). This approach includes the calculation for the inclination of sentiments in words by checking their semantic alignment of words in the document .Phrases can also be used. Lexicon-based approach dictionaries can be created automatically as well as manually; with the help of seed words we can expand the list of words. This research was focused mainly on using adjectives as predictors of the semantic alignment of text. It starts with compilation of adjectives and their (SO) Sentiment Orientation into a dictionary and from there patterns are matched for sentimental calculation.

Sentimental analysis of twitter data using text mining and hybrid classification approach is presented (Goyal, S., 2016). This begins with the extraction of tweets which is then pre-processed followed by application of classifier algorithm. It involves five step mechanisms. Firstly a structured data is formed, and then common grammar words like verbs, preposition articles (c/a stop words) are removed. This is followed by the step where words ending with "ing","ize","ed" are reduced to their root word. This is known as steaming. The term frequency – inverse term frequency score is calculated for each term and a 2D matrix is created in which rows represent documents and columns represent the word extracted from document after the above preprocessing which is filled with the TF-IDE score.

Sentimental analysis of Flipkart reviews using Naïve Bayes and Decision Tree algorithm is presented (0Kaur, G., & Singla, A., 2016). Naïve Bayes approach for classifying is based on probabilistic classifying where Bayes Theorem is used and theory of total probability is used. The paper claims it's suitability for large datasets. Just like text mining it starts with tokenization then removal of stop words followed by text transformation. Then features are selected for the parts of document that contribute for positive and negative words. These parts are joined in such a way such that the probability is maximum of the resulting sentence existing in either of the two positive or negative terms.

Sentiment analysis using Neuro-Fuzzy and Hidden Markov Models of text is presented (Rustamov, S., Mustafayev, E., & Clements, M. A., 2013). The data were taken from different files c/a data set which was combined into a one source file called "corpus". Once combined, the text was converted into array of words and further step was to sort this array of collection. Like other works stemming was skipped so that the words like remind and reminded make different sense to the text in consideration. Now a final part of calculation of membership degree of each term is calculated by an analytical formula before being processed by the neural network.

Rating prediction based on social sentiment from textual reviews is presented (Lei, X., Qian, X., & Zhao, G., 2016). Here two type of list is discussed: Word List: Contains both positive polarity and negative polarity words. Topic list: Contains list of topics that will be depicted as the root sentiment. The model involves the following steps: Firstly pre-processing tasks such as stop word removal, noise word removal are performed and then remaining product features are extracted using Latent Dirichlet Allocation (which computes the relationship of reviews and topics with words). The generative process is followed that matches user words to a set of its most probable topic list. Secondly sentiment degree is matched by the SDD(sentiment degree dictionary).From the combined word list(sentiment dictionary) from where a review is matched before the product feature and assigned a score +1.0,-1.0for positive and negative respectively.

Finally the words with prefix words as negative from ND (negation dictionary) are checked and a default value coefficient of +1.0 c/a negation check coefficient is added the sentiment polarity is reversed, and the coefficient is set to −1.0 if the sentiment word is preceded by an odd number of negative prefix words and hence therefore the normalized score is generated.

In another approach, a Hidden Marker Model (HMM) is used that assumes data to be in unobserved states (Jurafsky, D., & Martin, J. H., 2019). According to it, the results are a probabilistic function of the classes to which the classification is to be performed. The data set are pre classified as objective or subjective using Naïve-Bayes model. The Sequence recognition feature includes probabilistic distribution of subjectivity degree. The HMM parameters were calculated from them using specific equations and results stored.

A pattern based approach uses binary to multi-class classification (Bouazizi, M., & Ohtsuki, T., 2016). Binary Classification refers to classifying the work in either of two polarities i.e. positive or negative. The model works on a pattern based approach and had accuracy of 87.5% in binary classification .The author defined seven classes for which tweets were matched namely happy, sad, anger, love, hate, sarcasm and neutral. Emotional scores for words are calculated using Senti-Strength that assigns a score ranging from -1 to -5 and +1 to +5 based on the severity of the sentences. This is followed by getting a total of four parameters

i)   Net score for PW (+ve words)
ii)   Net score for NW(-ve words)

Using it ratio of emotional words is calculated as:

$$\rho(t) = \frac{PW(t) - NW(t)}{PW(t) + NW(t)}$$

In another research work, the most frequent words are to be generated as output in the form of a word cloud and its size will depends upon the extent of the frequency of occurrence of words collected (Bouazizi, M., & Ohtsuki, T., 2015). This implements the sentimental analysis algorithm for searching the most used words in Smartphone industry. The data set is taken from CSV (common separated value) file. The category to which these words used for is also checked. Each frequency is noted for the term. These words are displayed in a clustered manner and its size depends upon the frequency meaning large frequency words are having size that is large in number.

SENTIMENT ANALYSIS: CASE STUDIES

The work presented in this section is implemented on Intel Core i5 processor with 64 bit Windows 10 operating system with Python 3.7. It is highly recommended to use i5 or higher processor. A total of five test cases are presented here; three test cases are taken from the variable search space and two from the continuous search space. The section starts with describing the processing model used, libraries used, processing model's code, results and performance analysis, and lastly ends with a conclusion.

Processing Model

The functioning of the processing models is described in four stages: Input, Processing, Fetch and Store, and Data Visualization as also shown pictorially in Figure 9.

1. **Input:** The tweets are take these can include the live streams also or tweets generated in a particular date.
2. **Processing:** The textblob library is an open source library that is maintained in github and includes functions specifically for natural language processing tasks. Through it the characterization is either positive, negative or neutral is performed
3. **Fetch and Store:** On run time when the results are calculated then the need to be stored in file to be viewed at a later stage. Thus those results are stored in csv format and the file name is the search-term itself.
4. **Data Visualization:** The matplotlib is used to extract data from the saved files to show the variation in positive and negative with respect to their creation dates.

Figure 9. Processing model

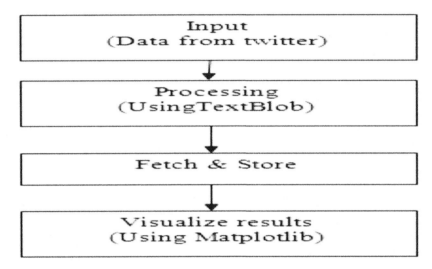

Libraries Used

Three main libraries have been used: tweepy, textblob, and matplotlib.

1. **tweepy:** Tweepy is the official Programming interface for dealing with twitter related works. It was utilized for getting tweets. This Programming interface has techniques for doing retweets, refresh status, seek terms, get client data, getting devotees and so forth. The following classes are used.
    a. API: This class has methods to confirm an application to interact with twitter.
    b. OAuthHandler: It takes customer key and buyer mystery as parameters that are novel for every application.
    c. Cursor: This class can play out all the page association related works. This was utilized in getting tweets from a few courses of events.

    The following methods are used.

    d.   set_access_token: It takes get to token and access token mystery as parameters and is utilized in verifying that the 4 parameters relate to a substantial application.

    e.   Cursor: The programming interface protest was passed as first contention and the term to be sought as second.

    f.   items(): This was utilized to process result per page for the tweets.

2.   **textblob:** It is that library that has vast methods for the purpose of data processing. The Sentiment class is used that examines techniques that can be utilized in getting conclusion from words or some other dialect handling. The Polarity method distinguishes extremity from a content that is inputted in its bracket.

3.   **Matplotlib:** Matplotlib is accounts for the graphical visualization of data for 2D plotting. It uses pyplot class that incorporates capacities to give a pictorial perception of the inputted information. It was utilized in producing the pie outline. The following methods are used.

    a.   pie: Produces pie outline for first contention with hues in second contention.

    b.   legend(): Creates legend that contains depiction identified with shading.

    c.   title():Assign title to outline for better comprehension of pie chart.

    d.   axis():sets hub information limit for the sort of diagram being utilized.

    e.   light_layout(): Naturally change subplot parameters to give cushioning.

    f.   appear():It shows the pie outline with title, legend as provided.

Processing Model's Code

```
import tweepy
from tweepy import OAuthHandler
from textblob import TextBlob
from matplotlib.pyplot import plt
class twitter_sent(object):
consumer_key = 'XXXXXXXXXXXXXXXXXXXXXXX'
consumer_secret = 'XXXXXXXXXXXXXXXXXXXXXXXXXXXX'
access_token = 'XXXXXXXXXXXXXXXXXXXXXXXXXXX'
access_token_secret = 'XXXXXXXXXXXXXXXXXXXXXXXXX'
try:
# create OAuthHandler object
auth = OAuthHandler(consumer_key, consumer_secret)
# set access token and secret
auth.set_access_token(access_token, access_token_secret)
# create tweepy API object to fetch tweets
api = tweepy.API(self.auth)
except:
print("Error: Authentication Failed")
pos=[]
neg=[]
dy=[]
def process():
query=input('Enter the search term')
```

```
count=int(input('Please provide the number of search terms'))
start_date= input('Please enter the start date')
end_date = input('Please enter the end date')
mth = input('Please enter the month')
tweets = []
try:
# call twitter api to fetch tweets
For d in range(start_date,end_date+1):
dd=str(d)+'-'+str(mth)+'-2019'
d2=str(d+1)+'-'+str(mth)+'-2019'
fetched_tweets = self.api.search(q = query, count = count, from= dd,to=d2)
# parsing tweets one by one
posc=0
negc=0
for tweet in fetched_tweets:
# empty dictionary to store required params of a tweet
parsed_tweet = {}
# saving text of tweet
parsed_tweet['text'] = tweet.text
# saving sentiment of tweet
analysis = TextBlob(tweet)
# set sentiment
if analysis.sentiment.polarity > 0:
sent='positive'
posc=posc+1
elif analysis.sentiment.polarity == 0:
sent='neutral'
else:
sent= 'negative'
negc=negc+1
pos.append(posc)
neg.append(negc)
dy.append(d)
parsed_tweet['sentiment'] = sent
# appending parsed tweet to tweets list
if tweet.retweet_count > 0:
# if tweet has retweets, ensure that it is appended only once
if parsed_tweet not in tweets:
tweets.append(parsed_tweet)
else:
tweets.append(parsed_tweet)
# return parsed tweets
#return tweets
except tweepy.TweepError as e:
```

```
# print error (if any)
print("Error: " + str(e))
for twt in tweets:
print(twt)
def draw():
plt.plot(pos,dy,label='Positive')
plt.plot(neg,dy,label='Negative')
plt.show()
obj=twitter_sent()
obj.process()
obj.draw()
```

Results and Performance Analysis

This section presents the search set tested on twitter stream, result classification on various test cases, and the conclusion in the end.

Search Set Used

Several test plans are conducted over the following search set on the twitter stream.

1. **New set:** Here both the keyword variable and the number of tweet variable are reset and manually stored.
2. **Same keywords but on different number of tweets:** Keeping the keyword/hashtag same, user is asked to input a fixed number of tweets upon which the keyword is to be matched after execution the new set.
3. **Different keywords but same number of tweets**: Keeping the number of matching words/hashtags same the value of number of tweets is to be re entered that will be used in getting the sentiments reflected over, after executing either the first or second search set.

Result Classification

Results are classified over variable search set and continuous search set categories.

1. **Variable Search Set:** Values of trending words are matched to the number of tweets and the results are plotted. The ratio of positive, negative and neutral are combined to form the whole set. A pie chart is presented to depict their corresponding shares in respective categories; and is presented in Figure 10, Figure 11, and Figure 12.

    Test Case#1: This shows the result of search set 1. Here the search term and number of search terms both are inputted initially to start the working of the software.
    Test Case#2: This is search set 2, where we keep the search term same <modi>, only the <no of search terms> are changed from 15 to 150.

Test Case #3: This is search set 3, the search term is kept as #Congress and the number of Search Terms <150> is remained same.

Figure 10. (Test Case #1)

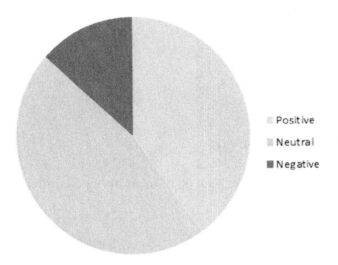

Figure 11. (Test Case #2)

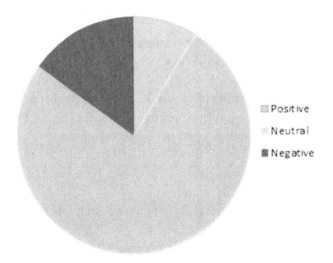

2. **Continuous Search Set:** The following domains are collected from twitter by setting the tweet limit to hundred and the results are plotted for the starting week of May for the domains underlined.

Test Case #4: Cricket: In this category, the results of Champions League Final, Kings XI Punjab, and IPL 2019 are plotted in Figure 13, Figure 14, and Figure 15. The tabular analysis for the same is presented in Table 1 and Table 2.

Figure 12. (Test Case #3)

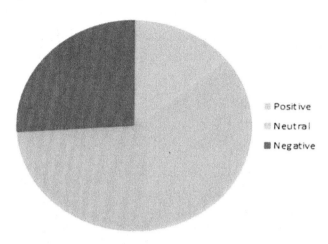

Table 1. Recorded positive and negative sentiments on test case #4 (Cricket) for the first week of May

	Champions League Final		Kings XI Punjab		IPL 2019	
Day	Positive	Negative	Positive	Negative	Positive	Negative
1	0	4.67	28.64	14.13	49	6
2	0	0	30.08	11.50	42	3
3	20	0	32.84	4.07	38	3
4	20	0	39.01	10.28	34	6
6	33.33	0	42.81	8.23	33	2
7	42	11	38.18	18.78	42	3

Table 2. Statistical analysis on test case #4 for the first week of May

Statistical analysis	Champions League Final		Kings XI Punjab		IPL 2019	
	Positive	Negative	Positive	Negative	Positive	Negative
Mean	19.22	2.94	33.79	14.14	38.71	3.71
Standard deviation	14.58	4.35	4.93	10.30	4.54	1.48

From the Figure 14, it is shown that there has been an increase in tweets for opposition for this team which reached a maximum of 38% from 8.2% in just an interval of two days only, moreover the support reduced from 42% to just 25% that was a decline in around 20% of popularity while parallel the increase in opposition had around 30%.

As per the Figure 15, the overall craze for IPL as reflected from tweets had been in its favor, the tweets in opposition could hardly had an average of less than 4%. On the other hand the maximum supporting tweets were close to 50% on the start of the month while the minimum being at a fraction of 33% in support and 2% for non favorable tweets. As of May7, we conclude that the sentiments (average) for the search term: "IPL 2019" was the highest amongst the 3 terms takes. On the other hand the maximum positive sentiments recorded were for IPL 2019.

Figure 13. Variation of tweets in percentage (y-axis) on Champions League Final for the first week of May (x-axis)

Figure 14. Variation of tweets in percentage (y-axis) on Kings XI Punjab for the first week of May (x-axis)

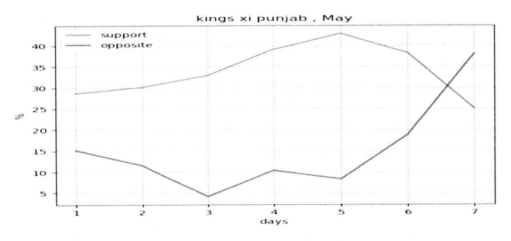

Figure 15. Variation of tweets in percentage (y-axis) on IPL 2019 for the first week of May (x-axis)

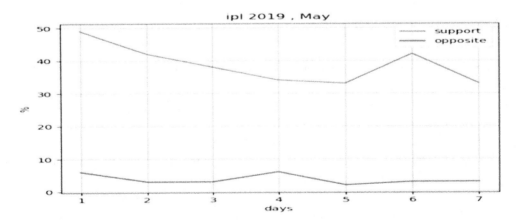

Test Case #5: Technology

In this category, the results of Fog Computing, 5G, OnePlus7Pro, and Cryptocurrency are plotted in Figure 16, Figure 17, Figure 18, and Figure 19. The tabular analysis for the same is presented in Table 3 and Table 4.

Table 3. Positive and negative sentiments on test case #5 (Technology) for the first week of May

Day	Fog Computing		5G		OnePlus7Pro		Cryptocurrency	
	Positive	Negative	Positive	Negative	Positive	Negative	Positive	Negative
1	3.33	13.33	17	7	15	3	60	4
2	40.90	0	23	15	52	1	34	6
3	37.5	8.33	14	10	55	2	39	5
4	81.81	9.09	10	9	27	7	35	8
6	47.36	4.26	18	10	60	5	35	17
7	17.94	10.25	20	8	36	0	43	16

Table 4. Statistical analysis on test case #5 for the first week of May

Statistical analysis	Fog Computing		5G		OnePlus7Pro		Cryptocurrency	
	Positive	Negative	Positive	Positive	Positive	Negative	Positive	Negative
Mean	37.33	8.39	17.57	9.57	44.28	2.57	40.14	9.85
Standard deviation	22.82	4.23	4.10	2.44	18.54	2.44	8.62	4.99

As shown in Figure 16, Fog computing is the emerging art of technology that has the potential in replacing cloud computing sooner or later. From, the data collected it was revealed that the maximum popularity reflected was 83% a standard deviation of 22% is sufficient in revealing that there had been an high variation for its support since the minima was 3.3% recorded i.e. a very high difference of 80%.

In the Figure 17, on each interval taken, the tweets counted in opposition were not more than the tweets considered in its support. Maximum recorded tweets covered an altitude of 15% in opposition while the one in support were 23% as recorded. Taking the minimum value in account the number was 7% and 10% in opposition and support respectively.

It appears from Figure 18 that this handheld device will be one of the next most successes in device technology. Making place in top 10 trending hashtags with good support of average 45% tweets in support against 2.5% in opposition and the maximum support of 72% when no tweets were recorded in opposition reveals the fact of it's becoming a grand success for technological goods.

Figure 16. Variation of tweets in percentage (y-axis) on Fog Computing for the first week of May (x-axis)

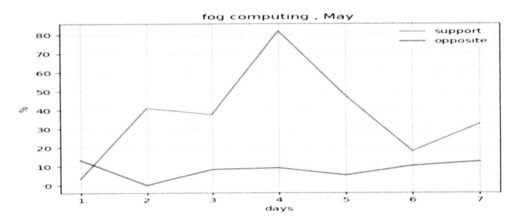

Figure 17. Variation of tweets in percentage (y-axis) on 5G for the first week of May (x-axis)

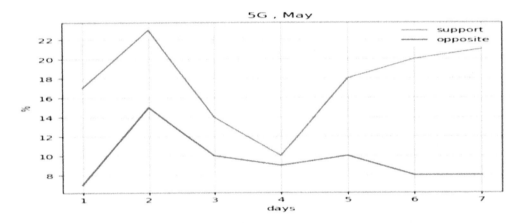

Figure 18. Variation of tweets in percentage (y-axis) on OnePlus7Pro for the first week of May (x-axis)

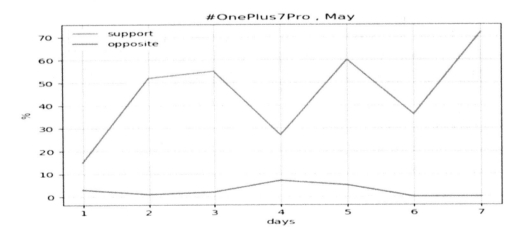

The Figure 19 shows that cryptocurrency on each sample interval has a net positive support of 34% while the opposition is just 17% as recorded. Cryptocurrency could help in contributing in saving the global warming scenario also since using this technology could replace the current use of paper-based currency for which to manufacture a lot of damage had been caused to the ecosystem. Thus the support reflected form the platform of colleting tweets is true. From the weekly analysis we conclude that fog computing got the maximum positive tweets on Saturday i.e. May 4 while the average analysis showed that OnePlus&Prohad the most highlighted positive with maximum reaching to 72% on May 7. It is shown that 5G had the minimum standard deviation and the maximum of opposite were close to the average in positive.

Figure 19. Variation of tweets in percentage (y-axis) on Cryptocurrency for the first week of May (x-axis)

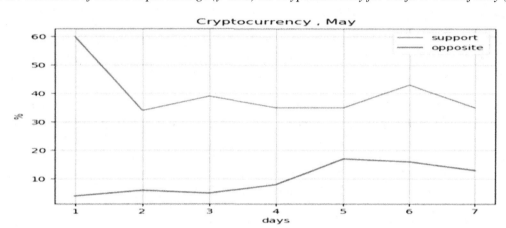

CONCLUSION

The section present a different way of analysis for prediction for topics like product launch success, political campaigns etc. In general the opinions were collected through polling each individual from regions to know the status of their taste. This method consumed a lot of human work and was tedious too. In contrast to that if the required work is carried from the largest social network then it could be efficiently done also, we can analyze the trend in the same as collection of tweets from previous posts is still feasible. It has seen that there occurs a vast variation of polarity and sentiments collected over time that helps in governing the mood of global people across different geographical locations. Moreover some words like study showed zero negative ratios.

REFERENCES

Achariya, D., & Kauser, A. (2016). Survey on Big Data Analytics: Challenges, Open Research Issues and Tools. *International Journal of Advanced Computer Science and Applications*, *7*(2), 511–518.

Acito, F., & Khatri, V. (2014). Business analytics: Why now and what next? *Business Horizons*, *57*(5), 565–570. doi:10.1016/j.bushor.2014.06.001

Akter, S., & Wamba, S. F. (2016). Big data analytics in E-commerce: A systematic review and agenda for future research. *Electronic Markets*, *26*(2), 173–194. doi:10.100712525-016-0219-0

Amirian, P., van Loggerenberg, F., Lang, T., Thomas, A., Peeling, R., Basiri, A., & Goodman, S. N. (2017). Using big data analytics to extract disease surveillance information from point of care diagnostic machines. *Pervasive and Mobile Computing*, *42*, 470–486. doi:10.1016/j.pmcj.2017.06.013

Bari, M. D., Shroff, S., & Thomas, M. (2013). SentiML: functional annotation for multilingual sentiment analysis. *Proceedings of the 1st International Workshop on Collaborative Annotations in Shared Environment: Metadata, Vocabularies and Techniques in the Digital Humanities*. 10.1145/2517978.2517994

Bouazizi, M., & Ohtsuki, T. (2015). Opinion mining in twitter: how to make use of sarcasm to enhance sentiment analysis. *2015 IEEE/ACM International Conference on Advances in Social Networks Analysis and Mining*, 1594–1597. 10.1145/2808797.2809350

Bouazizi, M., & Ohtsuki, T. (2016). Sentiment analysis: From binary to multi-class classification: A pattern-based approach for multi-class sentiment analysis in Twitter. *2016 IEEE International Conference on Communications, ICC 2016*, 1–6. 10.1109/ICC.2016.7511392

Canuto, S., Gonçalves, M. A., & Benevenuto, F. (2016). Exploiting new sentiment-based meta-level features for effective sentiment analysis. *WSDM 2016 - Proceedings of the 9th ACM International Conference on Web Search and Data Mining*, 53–62. 10.1145/2835776.2835821

Carbone, P., Katsifodimos, A., Sweden, S., Ewen, S., Markl, V., Haridi, S., & Tzoumas, K. (2015). *Apache Flink™: Stream and Batch Processing in a Single Engine*. Academic Press.

Chakraborty, K., & Bhattacharyya, S. (2018). *Comparative Sentiment Analysis on a Set of Movie*. doi:10.1007/978-3-319-74690-6

Chawda, R. K., & Thakur, G. (2016). Big data and advanced analytics tools. *2016 Symposium on Colossal Data Analysis and Networking, CDAN 2016*. 10.1109/CDAN.2016.7570890

Choi, Y., Kim, Y., & Myaeng, S.-H. (2009). Domain-specific sentiment analysis using contextual feature generation. *Proceedings of the 1st International CIKM Workshop on Topic Sentiment Analysis for Mass Opinion*, 37–44. 10.1145/1651461.1651469

Coraddu, A., Oneto, L., Baldi, F., & Anguita, D. (2017). Vessels fuel consumption forecast and trim optimisation: A data analytics perspective. *Ocean Engineering*, *130*(September), 351–370. doi:10.1016/j.oceaneng.2016.11.058

Dev Mishra, A., & Beer Singh, Y. (2017). Big data analytics for security and privacy challenges. *Proceeding - IEEE International Conference on Computing, Communication and Automation, ICCCA 2016*, 50–53. 10.1109/CCAA.2016.7813688

García-gil, D., Ramírez-gallego, S., García, S., & Herrera, F. (2017). Open Access A comparison on scalability for batch big data processing on Apache Spark and Apache Flink. *Big Data Analytics*, 1–11. doi:10.1186/s41044-016-0020-2

Goyal, S. (2016). Sentimental analysis of twitter data using text mining and hybrid classification approach. *International Journal of Advance Research Ideas and Innovations in Technology*, *2*(5), 1–9.

Hashem, I. A. T., Yaqoob, I., Anuar, N. B., Mokhtar, S., Gani, A., & Ullah Khan, S. (2015). The rise of "big data" on cloud computing: Review and open research issues. *Information Systems, 47*, 98–115. doi:10.1016/j.is.2014.07.006

Hesse, G., & Lorenz, M. (2016). Conceptual survey on data stream processing systems. *Proceedings of the International Conference on Parallel and Distributed Systems - ICPADS,* 797–802. 10.1109/ICPADS.2015.106

Huang, W., Wang, H., Zhang, Y., & Zhang, S. (2017). A novel cluster computing technique based on signal clustering and analytic hierarchy model using hadoop. *Cluster Computing*, 1–8. doi:10.100710586-017-1205-9

Janssen, M., van der Voort, H., & Wahyudi, A. (2017). Factors influencing big data decision-making quality. *Journal of Business Research, 70*, 338–345. doi:10.1016/j.jbusres.2016.08.007

Jin, X., Wah, B. W., Cheng, X., & Wang, Y. (2015). Significance and Challenges of Big Data Research. *Big Data Research, 2*(2), 59–64. doi:10.1016/j.bdr.2015.01.006

Jurafsky, D., & Martin, J. H. (2019). Part-of-Speech Tagging. Speech and Language Processing.

Kaur, G., & Singla, A. (2016). Sentiment analysis of flipkart reviews using naive bayes and decision tree algorithm. *International Journal of Advanced Research in Computer Engineering & Technology, 5*(1), 148–153.

Kaur, R., Chauhan, V., & Mittal, U. (2018). Metamorphosis of data (small to big) and the comparative study of techniques (HADOOP, HIVE and PIG) to handle big data. *International Journal of Engineering & Technology, 7*(2.27), 1. doi:10.14419/ijet.v7i2.27.11206

Lei, X., Qian, X., & Zhao, G. (2016). Rating Prediction Based on Social Sentiment from Textual Reviews. *IEEE Transactions on Multimedia, 18*(9), 1910–1921. doi:10.1109/TMM.2016.2575738

Lopez, M. A., Lobato, A. G. P., & Duarte, O. C. M. B. (2016). A performance comparison of open-source stream processing platforms. *2016 IEEE Global Communications Conference, GLOBECOM 2016 - Proceedings*. 10.1109/GLOCOM.2016.7841533

Mahmood, Z. (2016). Data science and big data computing: Frameworks and methodologies. *Data Science and Big Data Computing: Frameworks and Methodologies*. doi:10.1007/978-3-319-31861-5

Marcu, O., Costan, A., Antoniu, G., & P, S. (2018). *KerA: Scalable Data Ingestion for Stream Processing*. doi:10.1109/ICDCS.2018.00152

Marjani, M., Nasaruddin, F., Gani, A., Karim, A., Hashem, I. A. T., Siddiqa, A., & Yaqoob, I. (2017). Big IoT Data Analytics: Architecture, Opportunities, and Open Research Challenges. *IEEE Access: Practical Innovations, Open Solutions, 5*(c), 5247–5261. doi:10.1109/ACCESS.2017.2689040

Mavridis, I., & Karatza, H. (2017). Performance evaluation of cloud-based log file analysis with Apache Hadoop and Apache Spark. *Journal of Systems and Software, 125*, 133–151. doi:10.1016/j.jss.2016.11.037

Mishra, R. K., & Mishra, R. K. (2018). The Era of Big Data, Hadoop, and Other Big Data Processing Frameworks. *PySpark Recipes*, 1–14. doi:10.1007/978-1-4842-3141-8_1

Mittal, M., Singh, H., Paliwal, K., & Goyal, L. M. (2017). Efficient Random Data Accessing in MapReduce. *International Conference on Infocom Technologies and Unmanned Systems (Trends and Future Directions)*, 552–556.

Moreno, J., Serrano, M. A., & Fernández-Medina, E. (2016). Main issues in Big Data security. *Future Internet, 8*(3), 44. Advance online publication. doi:10.3390/fi8030044

Oussous, A., Benjelloun, F. Z., Ait Lahcen, A., & Belfkih, S. (2018). Big Data technologies: A survey. *Journal of King Saud University - Computer and Information Sciences, 30*(4), 431–448. doi:10.1016/j.jksuci.2017.06.001

Ozgur, C., Colliau, T., Rogers, G., Hughes, Z., & Myer-Tyson, E. B. (2017). MatLab vs. Python vs. R. *Journal of Data Science: JDS, 15*(3), 355–372.

Pang, B., & Lee, L. (2008). Opinion mining and sentiment analysis. In *Foundations and trends in information retrieval* (Vol. 2, pp. 1–2). Issues.

Perwej, Y. (2017). An Experiential Study of the Big Data. *Science and Education, 4*(1), 14–25. doi:10.12691/iteces-4-1-3

Rajput, R., & Solanki, A. K. (2016). Review of sentimental analysis methods using lexicon based approach. *International Journal of Computer Science and Mobile Computing, 5*(2), 159–166.

Rustamov, S., Mustafayev, E., & Clements, M. A. (2013). Sentiment analysis using Neuro-Fuzzy and hidden markov models of text. *Proceedings of IEEE Southeastcon*.

Sandoval-Almazan, R., & Valle-Cruz, D. (2018). Facebook impact and sentiment analysis on political campaigns. *ACM International Conference Proceeding Series*. 10.1145/3209281.3209328

Shahana, P., & Omman, B. (2015). Evaluation of features on sentimental analysis. *Procedia Computer Science, 46*, 1585–1592. doi:10.1016/j.procs.2015.02.088

Siddiqui, T., Alkadri, M., & Khan, N. A. (2017). Review of Programming Languages and Tools for Big Data Analytics. *International Journal of Advanced Research in Computer Science, 8*(5), 1112–1118.

Singh, H., & Bawa, S. (2012). Evolution of Grid-GIS Systems. *International Journal of Computer Science and Telecommunications, 3*(3), 36–40.

Singh, H., & Bawa, S. (2016). Spatial Data Analysis with ArcGIS and MapReduce. *Proceedings of International Conference on Conference Computing, Communication and Automation*. 10.1109/CCAA.2016.7813687

Stergiou, C., Psannis, K. E., Gupta, B. B., & Ishibashi, Y. (2018). Security, privacy & efficiency of sustainable Cloud Computing for Big Data & IoT. *Sustainable Computing: Informatics and Systems, 19*, 174–184. doi:10.1016/j.suscom.2018.06.003

Storey, V. C., & Song, I. Y. (2017). Big data technologies and Management: What conceptual modeling can do. *Data & Knowledge Engineering, 108*(February), 50–67. doi:10.1016/j.datak.2017.01.001

Tsai, C. W., Lai, C. F., Chao, H. C., & Vasilakos, A. V. (2015). Big data analytics: A survey. *Journal of Big Data, 2*(1), 1–32. doi:10.118640537-015-0030-3 PMID:26191487

Vakilinia, S., Zhang, X., & Qiu, D. (2016). Analysis and optimization of big-data stream processing. *2016 IEEE Global Communications Conference, GLOBECOM 2016 - Proceedings*, 9–14. 10.1109/GLOCOM.2016.7841598

Verma, D., Mohapatra, A., & Usmani, K. (2012). Light Weight Encryption Technique for Group Communication in Cloud Computing Environment. *International Journal of Computers and Applications*, *49*(8), 35–41. doi:10.5120/7649-0743

Vohra, D. (2016). Practical Hadoop Ecosystem. *Practical Hadoop Ecosystem*, 339–347. doi:10.1007/978-1-4842-2199-0

Yang, C., Huang, Q., Li, Z., Liu, K., & Hu, F. (2017). Big Data and cloud computing: Innovation opportunities and challenges. *International Journal of Digital Earth*, *10*(1), 13–53. doi:10.1080/17538947.2016.1239771

Yang, C., Yu, M., Hu, F., Jiang, Y., & Li, Y. (2017). Utilizing Cloud Computing to address big geospatial data challenges. *Computers, Environment and Urban Systems*, *61*, 120–128. doi:10.1016/j.compenvurbsys.2016.10.010

Yaqoob, I., Hashem, I. A. T., Gani, A., Mokhtar, S., Ahmed, E., Anuar, N. B., & Vasilakos, A. V. (2016). Big data: From beginning to future. *International Journal of Information Management*, *36*(6), 1231–1247. doi:10.1016/j.ijinfomgt.2016.07.009

This research was previously published in Large-Scale Data Streaming, Processing, and Blockchain Security; pages 1-38, copyright year 2021 by Information Science Reference (an imprint of IGI Global).

Chapter 57
Big Data for Prediction:
Patent Analysis – Patenting Big Data for Prediction Analysis

Mirjana Pejic-Bach

 https://orcid.org/0000-0003-3899-6707
University of Zagreb, Croatia

Jasmina Pivar
University of Zagreb, Croatia

Živko Krstić
Atomic Intelligence, Croatia

ABSTRACT

Technical field of big data for prediction lures the attention of different stakeholders. The reasons are related to the potentials of the big data, which allows for learning from past behavior, discovering patterns and values, and optimizing business processes based on new insights from large databases. However, in order to fully utilize the potentials of big data, its stakeholders need to understand the scope and volume of patenting related to big data usage for prediction. Therefore, this chapter aims to perform an analysis of patenting activities related to big data usage for prediction. This is done by (1) exploring the timeline and geographic distribution of patenting activities, (2) exploring the most active assignees of technical content of interest, (3) detecting the type of the protected technical according to the international patent classification system, and (4) performing text-mining analysis to discover the topics emerging most often in patents' abstracts.

INTRODUCTION

Patent databases are an abundant and important source of information about the particular technical field, and patent analysis has been proven as effective tool for decision makers who seek for a comprehensive overview of different technologies' topics, such as big data technologies (Madani & Weber, 2016). De-

DOI: 10.4018/978-1-6684-3662-2.ch057

cision makers may want to understand relevant trends, to spot new technologies in particular area or to estimate the importance of the emerging new technologies. Moreover, patent information is a relevant source for those who want to get familiar with key players of a particular technology, or to learn about their productivity and patenting behavior.

Big data technologies have attracted lots of attention due to their ability to analyze large amounts of various data sources, and extract useful information from them. Recently, big data technologies have become not only a methodology for analyzing the current situation, but are also used as tools for prediction in various fields, such as retailing, marketing and social media (e.g. Bradlow et al., 2017; Miah, Vu, Gammack & McGrath, 2017; Shirdastian et al., 2017).

Goal of this chapter is to analyze and help to understand patents related to big data for prediction. The paper will provide answers to the following questions that are of interest to big data inventors and investors: (1) What is the timeline of patents of big data solutions for prediction?; (2) Who are assignees of patents of big data solutions for prediction, and what is their geographic origin?; (3) What are the most frequent IPC patent areas of patents of big data solutions for prediction?, (4) What are the most often topics of patents of big data solutions for prediction? Answers to these questions will provide useful guidance related to competitiveness and new trends that emerge in the usage of big data technologies for prediction. Additional goal of this paper is to assess the usability of several data mining and text mining methods for the purpose of patent analysis, specifically association analysis of IPC patent areas, key-terms extraction and clustering. For this purpose, Statistica Text Miner 13.0, and Provalis Wordstat 8.0 has been used.

The chapter consists of the following sections. After the introduction, the second section presents the background of the research, encompassing the notion of big data, usage of big data for prediction, and usage of patent analysis. The third section describes the methodology used. The results of the analysis are presented in the fourth section. Finally, the last section is used to synthesise findings, present limitations, and future research directions of the chapter.

BACKGROUND

Big Data and Predictive Analytics

Big data has become an exciting field of study for practitioners and researchers, due to the need to adapt to the emergence of huge databases (Parr Rud, 2011). Each of them has different focus and concerns in this area, which yielded various definitions and descriptions of big data. Practitioners, such as consulting companies and multinational corporations, define big data by mainly focusing on the technology necessary to handle such data. For example, the National Institute of Standards and Technology describes it as data that exceed capacity or capability of conventional systems and "require a scalable architecture for efficient storage, manipulation and analysis" (NIST, 2017, p. 8). On the other hand, scientists describe big data as the phenomenon related to various characteristics of data generated by different actions, e.g. social media and business transactions. Boyd and Crawford (2012, p. 662) define big data as "cultural, technological, and scholarly phenomenon that rests on the interplay of technology, analysis and mythology". Furthermore, scientists often use following three characteristics in order to describe big data: Volume, Variety and Velocity. Volume describes the large amount of data that depends on the type of data, time and industry, which "make it impractical to define a specific threshold for big data volumes" (Gandomi

& Haider, 2014, p. 137). Variety refers to the various types of data including structured, semi-structured and unstructured data (Chen et al., 2014), while velocity relates to the rapid and timely conducted data collection and data analysis (Chen et al., 2014; Dmitriyev et al., 2015; Vera-Baquero et al., 2015).

Harnessing big data is believed to result in more efficient and effective operations (Günther et al., 2017). Moreover, big data is being perceived as support for decision-making (Sharma & Kankanhalli, 2014) or as a source of business opportunities (McAfee & Brynjolfsson, 2012; Gandomi & Haider, 2014). Günther et al. (2017) stress out that continuous interaction between work practices, organizational models and stakeholder interests are the prerequisites for the successful usage of big data. Big data analytics is the main source of value generated by big data technologies, since it allows generation of the new knowledge from huge databases, which only recently emerged as a possibility. Big data analytics refers to exploitation of algorithms that can process a large volume of various types of data at increasing speeds, which can be classified into following groups: text analytics or text mining, multimedia analytics, social media analytics and predictive analytics:

- Text analytics denotes techniques for extraction of useful information and knowledge from unstructured textual data (e.g. business documents, emails, social media). Text mining is primarily based on natural language processing (NLP) which enables computational text analysis, interpretation and generation (Chen, Chiang & Storey, 2012; Chen et al., 2014; Gandomi & Haider, 2015). Examples of common NLP-based techniques used in text analytics are text summarization techniques, opinion mining, clustering, and so on.
- Multimedia data analytics refers to information extraction from unstructured audio, images and video streams data. The transcript-based approach and phonetic-based approach are two common technological approaches to audio analytics (Gandomi & Haider, 2015). Video analytics or video content analysis refers to various techniques for analyzing and extracting information from video data.
- Social media analytics encompasses techniques for analyzing both structured and unstructured data generated by social media (Chen et al., 2012; Gandomi & Haider, 2015). Social media analytics is classified into content-based analytics and link-based analytics. Content-based analytics refers to usage of text; video and audio analytics for analyzing data generated by users of social media, such as images, reviews and so on. Link-based analytics is focused at structure of social networks and relationships among entities that participate in networks. For example, community detection techniques can be used to uncover behavioral patterns and predict properties of certain network. Additionally, participants' influence or strength of connections in networks can be evaluated by using so-called social influence analysis. Similarly, link prediction strives to predict future linkages between entities in a network.
- Predictive analytics use both quantitative and qualitative approaches to learn from past behavior, uncover patterns in data and to optimize business processes based on new insights. It usually refers to the application of statistical techniques, data mining and machine learning algorithms to extract information and knowledge from structured data. Common goals of various predictive analytics approaches are to found patterns in data and to explore relationships in data.

Business application domains that current focus for big data and predictive analytics are retail, marketing, and social media. Bradlow et al. (2017) examine the opportunities of using data about customers, products, time, location and channel for the purpose of decision making in retailing, using Bayesian techniques on large dataset. Miah et al. (2017) propose the method for analysing unstructured data, geo-tagged photos uploaded by tourists to social media, to support strategic decision-making in tourism destination management. Salehan and Kim (2016, p. 31) suggest an approach for development of "scalable, automated systems for sorting and classification of big online consumer reviews data, which will benefit both vendors and consumers". Yi and Wang (2017, p. 188) presented "a big data analytics based fault prediction approach for shop floor scheduling". Latent semantic analysis and the support vector machine were used to examine the sentiments toward a brand to identify the reasons for positive or negative sentiments on social media (Shirdastian et al., 2017).

Some authors discussed application areas that predictive analytics using big data will greatly influence in future. Akter and Wamba (2016) review usage of big data analytics in e-commerce. They concluded that main application areas of big data analytics in e-commerce are personalization, dynamic pricing, customer service, supply chain visibility, security and fraud detection, as well as predicting individual customer's theoretical values to company, to predict sales patterns, to forecast and determine inventory requirements and to predict consumer preferences and behavior. Big data analytics attracted attention in various areas such as logistics and supply chain management (Waller and Fawcett, 2013), cyber-physical systems (Lee et al., 2015), auditing (Geep et al., 2018), cognitive computing (Garret, 2014) helath care services (Wu et al., 2016), cybersecurity (Rassam et al., 2017).

Patent Analysis for Decision Making

Decision makers who seek for a comprehensive overview of different technology topics in a technical field of interest may rely on patent analyzes, which often utilizes text mining (Pejić Bach et al., 2017). Madani and Weber (2016) analyze the evolution of patent analysis, focusing to text mining. Brügmann et al. (2014) present workbench for intelligent patent document analysis, which includes modules for summarization, entity recognition, segmentation, lexical chain identification and claim-description alignment. For example, Kim et al. (2016) use the semantic patent topic analysis-based bibliometric method to generate patent development maps related to 3D printing technologies. Altunas et al. (2014) analyzed patent documents by using weighted association rules that recognise the different importance of protected technical content based on following criterion: commercial significance and technological impact. Patent lanes developed regard semantic similarities, which can be seen as the deployment of patent clusters, were suggested by Niemann et al. (2017) in order to describe the development of a technological field in the course of time. Han et al. (2017) presented usage of natural language processing technologies to extract concepts and patent similarity assessments, and to support content-oriented visualisation.

Valuable insights lie in patent citations which analysis can reveal patterns of knowledge spillover and diffusion of information between different stakeholders such as countries, universities and companies. Patent citation analysis reveals its applicability across different technical fields that serve the creation of technology (Sharma & Tripathi, 2017). Kyebambe et al. (2017) used supervised learning methods to forecast emerging technologies. Furhermore, Kim and Bae (2017) suggested a three-step methodology for technology forecasting. The first step is to cluster patent documents based on cooperative patent classification. The second step is to examine the combination of cooperative patent classification of each derived clusters. The final step is to determine which clusters are promising based on analysis of patent indicators such as citations, triadic patent families as well as independent patent claims. Song et al. (2018) used a bibliographic coupling to patents to produce a list of outlier patents, developed the technological and market measures to evaluate them and determined promising technologies based on the developed measures.

Patents can be searched and analyzed by using numerous patent databases or platforms. Patent databases can be divided into national databases and world databases. Examples of national databases are United States Patent and Trademark Office (USPTO) patent database, Canadian Intellectual Property Office patent database, Australian patent database - AutPat or DEPATISnet, which contains patents from the German Patent and Trade Mark Office. Patent databases that contain patent documents from around the world are Espacenet, Google Patents, The Lens, Patentscope, which provides access to international Patent Cooperation Treaty (PCT) applications, and OECD Patent Database that contains data on patent applications to the European Patent Office - EPO and USPTO. Commercial patent platforms allow advanced patent search and analysis such as patent network analysis or citation analysis. Examples of commercial patent platforms are PatSeer, Clearstone Elements, PatentCloud, LifeQuest, Derwent Innovation by ClarivateAnalytics, Total Patent One by Lexis Nexis and Octimine.

METHODOLOGY

Patents from the PatSeer database related to big data usage for prediction analytics from 2013 to 13 October 2017 are analyzed, using the longitudinal approach in combination with text mining techniques. The patent analysis consists four phases related to (i) the patent search and selection, (ii) timeline, geographic origin and patents assignees analysis, (iii) patents analysis according to IPC system patent area, and (iv) text mining.

Phase One: Patent Search and Selection

A patent, in general, is an exclusive right granted for an invention to exclude others from making, using, or vending the patented invention without the patent owner's permission. Each patent's information or so-called meta-data of patents are provided in the form of highly structured documents. Patent documents usually contain following patent's data: title, abstract or description, publication or issue year, filing/application year, priority country, assignee country, The International Patent Classification codes, The Cooperative Patent Classification CPC codes, File Index codes, backward/forward citations and so on. Analysis of patents' documents containing all of these data sheds light on a technical area of interest and can serve to stakeholders in their decision-making. Patent databases should provide accurate data in comprehensible format and deliver data promptly (Madani & Weber, 2016) in order to be relevant and valuable for decision makers.

PatSeer is an online patent database storing the patents in the forms of simple patent families. PatSeer is available in several editions: Lite, Standard, Premier, Pro, Explorer and Projects Edition. Authors used Lite Edition to conduct a preliminary search of the simple patent families to detect the patents related to big data for prediction. In general, Lite Edition is used to search the worldwide patent database and allows users to manage and save search strings, to narrow down search results by using filters, as well as to extract data in excel format. Therefore, authors used PatSeer solution for searching and extracting patent data only. Other PatSeer's Editions offer more capabilities in comparison to Lite Edition. For example, PatSeer Pro allows advanced patent analysis such as patent network analysis with semantic spatial-mapping, to conduct citation analysis, text clustering and more.

The PatSeer database was searched on 13 October 2017 by using the search string search string (TA: (data AND (predict OR prediction OR forecasting OR forecast OR prognosis OR prognosticate OR foresight OR foresee))), with an option for searching simple patent families. Authors found 316 of records for simple family families in total. Among these records, 296 simple patent families had status "active" at the time of the search. Therefore, a patent analysis of the 296 simple patent families related to big data for prediction was conducted to achieve the goal of this research.

Phase Two: Timeline, Geographic Origin and Patents Assignees Analysis

Authors performed an extensive analysis of timeline, geographic origin and current assignees in order to detect which of them were most active in patenting technical content related to big data for prediction. A current assignee is an entity, organization or individual, inventor, that has the property right to the patent (Sinha and Pandurangi, 2015).

Phase Three: Patents According to IPC System Patent Area

Authors analyzed the protected technical content of big data for prediction simple patent families, using International Patent Classification (IPC) system established in 1971 by the Strasbourg Agreement, used in more than 100 countries worldwide. The IPC describes technical knowledge by using the systematic and hierarchical classification, which includes section, class, subclass, group and subgroup (WIPO, 2017). In this research, the analysis of the active simple patent families related to big data usage for prediction according to the sections, subclasses and groups will be conducted. In order to determine whether the technical content of the selected simple patent families is heterogeneous or homogeneous, authors use association rules.

Phase Four: Text Mining Patent Analysis

Text mining approach was utilised in order to detect the topics emerging most often in abstracts of simple patent families related to big data solutions for predictive analytics. Software WordStat Provalis was used for text mining. First, phrases of maximum five words, which occur in more than five simple patent abstracts, are extracted. Second, extracted phrases were used to conduct cluster analysis in order to detect which topics occur together. Cluster analysis of phrases was conducted using of average-linkage hierarchical clustering algorithm, which creates clusters from a similarity matrix (Everitt et al., 2011). The distance between two clusters is the average distance between each observation in one cluster to every observation in the other. This method is also called Unweighted Pair Group Mean Averaging. For example, distance between clusters "A" and "B" refers to average length of each arrow connecting observations within the clusters (Figure 1) as expressed in Formula 1.

Equation 1. Distance Between Clusters – Average Linkage Method

$$d_{ab} = \frac{1}{kl} \sum_{i=1}^{k} \sum_{j=1}^{l} d\left(A_i, B_j\right) \tag{1}$$

Figure 1. Average linkage method
Source: (Authors)

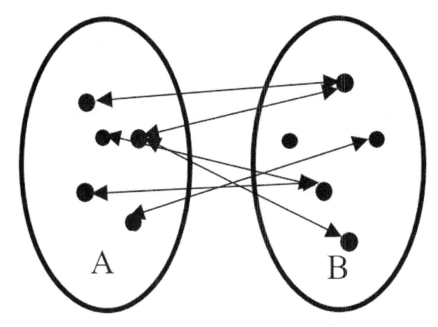

Notation:

$A_1, A_2,..., A_k$ = Observations from cluster A
$B_1, B_2,..., B_l$ = Observations from cluster B
d (a,b) = Distance between a cluster with observation vector a and a cluster with observation vector
        b

The cluster analysis was conducted by using Jaccard's coefficient as a similarity measure. Jaccard's coefficient determined the association between two phrases that occur together in simple patent abstract. The result is represented by the dendogram. Single-word clusters were hidden from the dendrogram to simplify the use of the dendrogram and being able to focus only on the strongest associations of meaningful phrases. Since a dendrogram determines only the temporal order of the branching sequence, the sequence of phrases cannot be seen as a linear representation of those distances. That means that any cluster can be rotated around branches on the dendrogram without affecting its meaning. For that reason, authors used proximity plots generated in WordStat Provalis software in order to represent the distance between most frequent phrases to all other phrases. In proximity plot, phrases that often tend to appear near selected phrase are shown on the top of the plot. In addition, network graphs were used in order to represent the relationships between phrases by lines connecting those phrasest.

RESULTS

In this part of the chapter, patent analysis results are presented as following: timeline, geographic origin and patents assignees of related to big data for prediction, the result of patents analysis according to IPC system patent area and results of the text mining patent analysis.

Timeline, Geographic and Assignee Patent Analysis

In order to provide answers to when, where and who pursues protection of big data analytics solutions for predictive analysis, the timeline, geographic and assignee analysis was conducted.

Table 1 represents the timeline for the period between 2013 and October 2017, and geographic origin of simple patent families.

Table 1. Number of big data for prediction simple patent families per publication/issue year and priority country (from 2013 to 13th October 2017)

Publication / Issue Year	No. of Simple Patent Families	% of Total No. of Simple Patent Families
Timeline		
2013	1	0%
2014	16	5%
2015	50	17%
2016	122	41%
October 2017	107	36%
Total	296	100.00%
Country of Origin		
Priority Country	No. of Simple Patent Families	% of Total No. of Simple Patent Families
China (CH)	233	79%
South Korea (KR)	35	12%
United States of America (USA)	17	6%
India (IN)	4	1%
Taiwan (TW)	3	1%
Japan (JP)	1	0%
None	3	1%
Total	296	100.00%

Source: (Authors, PatSeer, 13th October 2017)

Most of the most of the assignees related to big data for prediction are spread across China and South Korea. Figure 2 provides details on the timeline and geographic origin of simple patent families according to priority countries for the period between 2013 and October 2017.

Figure 2. Number of big data for prediction simple patent families per priority country (from 2013 to 13th October 2017)
Source: (Authors, PatSeer, 13th October 2017)

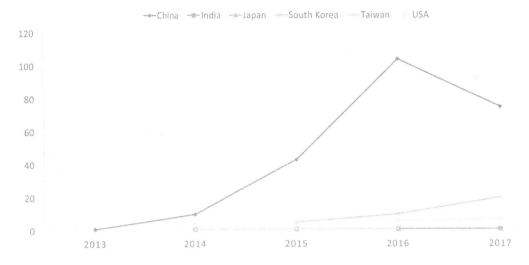

Table 2 provides details on the number of simple patent families related to big data for prediction according to current assignees and countries, which indicates that all organizations with more than 5 patents come from China.

Table 2. Number of big data for prediction simple patent families according to current assignee and country (from 2013 to 13th October 2017)

Current Assignee	Country	No. of Simple Patent Families	% of Total No. of Simple Patent Families
State Grid Corporation	China	22	7.4%
Inspur Group	China	7	2.4%
Nanjing University	China	7	2.4%
Business Big Data	China	5	1.7%
Hohai University	China	5	1.7%
Other	-	250	84.5%
Total		296	100.00%

Source: (Authors, PatSeer, 13th October 2017)

Patents According to IPC System Patent Area

Majority of the simple patent families were assigned to more than one IPC's main groups or sub-groups. A simple patent family is usually registered under multiple ICR codes, so the total number of ICR codes (561 codes) is larger than the number of simple patent families examined (296 simple patent families), which indicates that one simple patent family is registered to approximately two IPC's main groups or sub-groups on average. Observed simple patent families were registered under following seven five IPC sections: A Human Necessities; B Performing Operations; Transporting; C Chemistry, Metallurgy; E Fixed Constructions, F Mechanical Engineering; Lighting; Heating; Weapons; Blasting Engines or Pumps, G Physics and H Electricity.

Table 3 presents the number of big data for prediction simple patent families according to the IPC system – Sub-class level, that occur in more than 10 simple patent families. Among classes assigned to 296 simple patent families are computing, calculating or counting instruments such as G06Q - Analogue computers (228 times), G06F - Electrical digital data processing (132 times) and G06N - Computer systems based on specific computational models. Additionally, simple patent families that were registered as an electric communication technique were mostly related to the sub-class H04L - Transmission of digital information.

Table 3. Number of big data for prediction simple patent families according to the IPC system – Subclass level (>10 simple patent families)

Subclass	Description	No. of Simple Patent Families
A Human Necessities		
A61B	Medical diagnosis, surgery and identification	12
G Physics		
G06Q	Analogue computers	228
G06F	Electrical digital data processing	132
G06N	Computer systems based on specific computational models	26
G08G	Traffic control systems	16
G06K	Instruments for recognition and presentation of data	14
G08B	Signaling or calling systems - order telegraphs, alarm systems	13
G05B	Monitoring or testing arrangements/elements for control systems	12
H Electricity		
H04L	Transmission of digital information	27
Other		76
Total		561

Source: (Authors, PatSeer, 13th October 2017)

Table 4 presents simple patent families according to IPC main group and sub-group level. Data processing systems or methods adapted forecasting or optimization was the most frequent IPC's group. A substantial number were related to administrative, financial, managerial or supervisory purposes – IPC's group G06F17/30 (62 simple patent families). Additionally, 40 of 228 simple patent families that were registered for electricity, gas or water supply purposes.

Table 4. Number of simple patent families related to big data for prediction according to the IPC system – Main group/Sub-group level (>10 simple patent families)

Main/Sub Group	Description	No. of Simple Patent Families
G06 Physics - Computing, Calculating and Counting Instruments		
G06F Digital Computing or Data Processing Equipment or Methods for:		
G06F17/30	Administrativec, financial, managerial, supervisory purposes	62
G06F19/00	Specific applications	28
G06Q Data Processing Systems or Methods Specially Adapter for:		
G06Q10/04	Forecasting or optimization	64
G06Q50/06	Electricity, gas or water supply	40
G06Q10/06	Resources, enterprise planning, organizational model	22
G06Q30/02	Marketing, e.g. Buyer profiling, price estimation	19
G06Q50/26	Government or public services	12
G06Q50/10	Services	11
H04 – Electricity - Electric Communication Technique		
H04L Transmission of Digital Information		
H04L29/08	Control procedure, e.g. Data link level control procedure	12
Other		291
Total		561

Source: (Authors, PatSeer, 13th October 2017)

Co-Occurrence of IPC Areas

In order to detect relationships between IPC codes, association rule analysis was conducted. IPC's main group or sub-group code is considered as an item, and each record of a simple patent family is considered as a transaction. Due to the heterogeneity of IPC codes, task for finding association rules was non-trivial and association rules between different IPCs' main groups or sub-groups level codes were challenging to detect. Therefore, minimal support and confidence at 1% level was set, which resulted in 39 association rules. Table 5 shows only rules with the minimal support of 2% and minimal correlation of 10%, which reveals that the simple patent families registered as data processing systems or methods for forecasting or optimization were specially adapted for electricity, gas or water supply purposes in 10.47% of the total number of simple patent families (Rule G06Q10/04 → G06Q50/06). Data processing systems or methods for resources management were specially adapted for electricity, gas or water supply purposes in 2.70% of the total number of simple patent families (Rule G06Q10/06 → G06Q50/06).

Patent Topics

In order to detect most frequent topics of the simple patent families' abstracts, authors used the phrase extraction process combined with the cluster analysis conducted by Wordstat Provalis software. Authors detected following most frequent phrases: real-time, data mining, early warning and neural networks.

Table 5. Summary of association rules - Min. support = >2%, Min. confidence = >2%, Min. correlation = 10%

Body – Description (Application Area or Method)	Head – Description (Application Area or Method)	Support/ Confidence	
G06Q10/04 - forecasting method	G06Q50/06 - energy supply	10%	48%
G06Q50/06 - energy supply	G06Q10/04 - forecasting method	10%	78%
G06Q10/06 - enterprise resources planning	G06Q50/06 - energy supply	3%	36%
G06Q50/06 - energy supply	G06Q10/06 - enterprise resources planning	3%	20%
G06F17/30 - finance/management	G06Q10/04 - forecasting method	2%	11%
G06Q10/04 - forecasting method	G06F17/30 - finance/management	2%	11%
G06Q10/04 - forecasting method	G06Q50/26 - government/public services	2%	9%
G06Q10/04 - forecasting method	G06Q50/26 - government/public services	2%	9%
G06Q10/06 - enterprise resources planning	G06Q10/04 - forecasting method	2%	27%
G06Q50/26 - government/public services area	G06Q10/04 - forecasting method	2%	50%

Source: (Authors, PatSeer, 13th October 2017; Statistica Text Miner)

Table 6 shows most frequent phrases in patent applications with the frequency of occurrence ≥ 5. Column TF*IDF of Table 7 contains values of metrics for a phrase's importance. The Term Frequency-Inverse Document Frequency (TF-IDF) is a metric that helps to estimate how important is a phrase in a whole collection of documents (e.g. abstracts of all analyzed patents in a certain area) and not only in a particular document (e.g. abstract of only one patent). Therefore, for this chapter, TF-IDF is a metric that helps authors to estimate how important is a phrase in a whole collection of analyzed patents. Specifically, for this research, the collection of patents refers to patents' abstracts.

Table 6. Most frequent phrases in patent applications (>5% of Cases)

Phrase	Frequency	No. of Cases	% Cases	TF - IDF
real time	109	55	18.58%	79.7
data mining	52	34	11.49%	48.9
early warning	58	29	9.80%	58.5
neural network	57	23	7.77%	63.2
management system	30	18	6.08%	36.5
machine learning	29	16	5.41%	36.7
historical data	17	15	5.07%	22.0
data platform	25	15	5.07%	32.4

Source: (Authors by using WordStat Provalis software)

Reason for using TF-IDF metric is that common words usually appear several times in a document (an abstract of certain patent), but they are not important as key-phrases to be searched or indexed. Term Frequency measures how frequently a phrase occurs in an abstract of patent. The Term Frequency value for the certain phrase "p" in the certain patent's abstract is defined as the ratio between the frequency of phrase "p" in the patent's abstract, and the total number of phrases in the same patent's abstract. Furthermore, Inverse Document Frequency measures how important is a certain phrase "p" concerning the whole collection of patents' abstracts. The IDF for a given keyword "p" in the collection of patents is calculated as the logarithm of the ratio between the total number of patents' abstracts in a collection and is the number of abstracts in which the phrase "p" appears. Finally, the product of TF and IDF value gives its TF-IDF value for a certain phrase "p". Therefore, a phrase that has higher TF-IDF values is of higher importance. Phrases that are most important in the whole collection of patents related to big data for prediction, indicated by their TF-IDF values, are real-time (TF-IDF value 79.7), data mining (48.9), early warning (58.5) and neural networks (63.2).

Figure 3 presents the results of the cluster analysis that identified six groups of topics regard simple patent families related to big data for prediction.

- Cluster 1 includes 28 simple families patents' abstracts, with the co-occuring phrases: real-time systems used for weather forecasting to provide weather information to a client-side; early warning management system based on monitoring data for managing power supply.
- Cluster 2 includes 10 simple families patents' abstracts with the co-occuring phrases: data analysis supported by efficient database technologies such as managing power grid based on power load forecasting method or preprocessing of big traffic data.
- Cluster 3 includes 6 simple families patents' abstracts with the co-occuring phrases: environment information and prediction data supported by wireless communication; storage systems and wireless communication supported by cloud computing and wireless networks.
- Cluster 4 includes 11 simple families patents' abstracts with the co-occuring phrases: predicting and monitoring public opinion, and analyzing behavior data by using feature extraction and neural networks.
- Cluster 5 includes from 12 simple families patents' abstracts with the co-occuring phrases: using support vector machine to increase prediction accuracy.
- Cluster 6 includes 12 simple families patents' abstracts with the co-occuring phrases: information extraction based on data mining and machine learning to analyze historical data; information extraction based on deep learning for control systems and risk assessment, as well as a medical diagnosis based on natural language processing.

In a dendrogram, the phrases (keywords) that co-occur tend to appear near each other but dendrogram determines only the temporal order of the branching sequence. For that reason, reading dendrograms is not intuitive or very easy. Therefore, authors used proximity plots generated to detect phrases that often tend to appear near selected phrase (Figure 4). Such phrases are shown on the top of the plot.

Figure 4 presents four proximity plots indicating which phrases occur the most often with the most frequent and most important phrases: real-time, data-mining, early warning and neural network. Authors found following:

- The phrases that occur the most often with the phrase *real-time* are mostly related to *data analysis* such as historical data, management systems, real-time performance and monitoring data; methods and techniques for data analysis such as statistical analysis, neural networks, machine learning or data visualization, as well as specific purposes such as traffic big data, power supply, risk assessment, social networks or behavior analysis.

- The phrases that occur the most often with the phrase *data mining* are mostly related to the phrase historical data, methods and techniques of data analysis such as machine learning, natural language or deep learning, and applications such as medical diagnosis, risk assessment or control systems.

Figure 3. Cluster dendrogram of phrases that occur in most frequent phrases
Source: (Authors by using WordStat Provalis software)

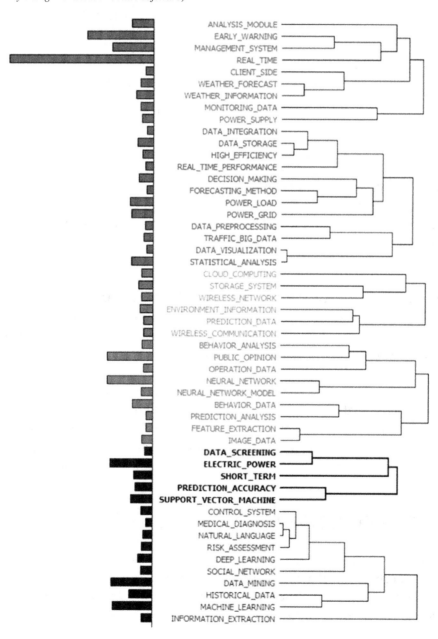

Figure 4. Proximity plots of phrases that occur in more than 20 patent applications
Source: (Authors by using WordStat Provalis softwareFigure 5. Network graphs of phrases that occur most frequent

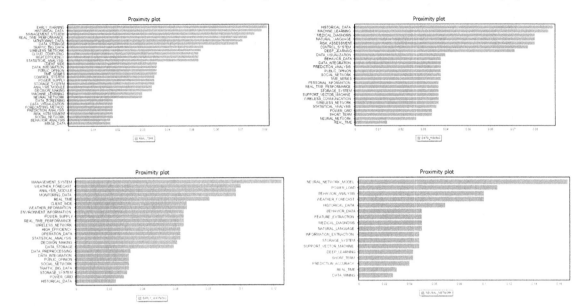

- The phrases that occur the most often with the phrase *early-warning* indicate general technical parts of early warning systems such as management system, an analysis module, real-time and client side, as well as particular purposes of early-warning systems such as weather forecasting and power supply management. The phrase is also related to phrases indicating source or type of data used or generated by early-warning systems such as monitoring data, weather information, environment information.
- The phrase *neural network* occurs the most often with the phrase neural network model. Other phrases that occur with the phrase neural network indicate its's specific application areas such as power load, behavior analysis, weather forecast, feature extraction or medical diagnosis. Additionally, types of data analyzed by neural networks are indicated by phrases historical data and behavior data.

Furthermore, the connections between keywords – phrases are visualized by using a network graph that allows us to explore relationships, to detect underlying patterns and structures of co-occurrences. Network graph was generated for each of the six clusters in the dendrogram. Elements are represented as a node while their relationships are represented as lines connecting those nodes. Figure 5 presents six network graphs indicating which phrases co-occurred most often within each of the cluster.

FUTURE RESEARCH DIRECTIONS

This chapter provides an outlook to the possible questions that can be answered for the investors and inventors interested in big data solutions for predictive analytics. Patent analysis can provide answer to the most basic questions, relating to when and where most of the patenting was conducted, by whom and in which areas. Therefore, future research directions are provided as the answers to these questions.

Figure 5.
Source: (Authors by using WordStat Provalis software)

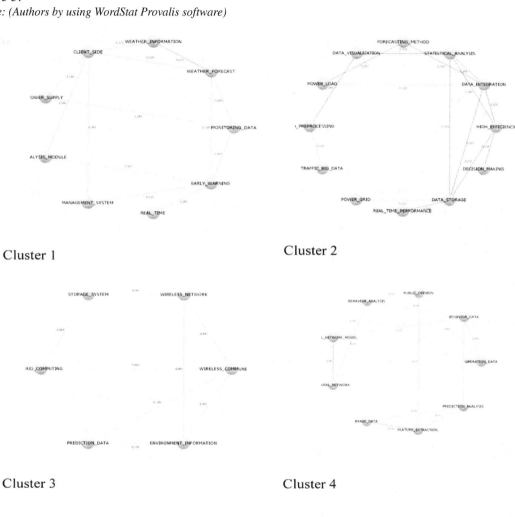

Cluster 1

Cluster 2

Cluster 3

Cluster 4

Cluster 5

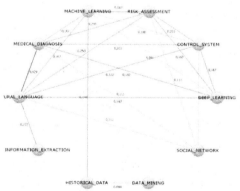

Cluster 6

When?

Analysis indicate that area of big data usage for predictive analytics emerged recently. Only one simple patent family related to big data for prediction was registered in 2013. After that period, the number of simple patent families increases rapidly, with 122 simple patent families registered in 2016 and 107 simple patent families registered in 2017, until October. The emerging trend is expected to continue in the period of at least several years.

Where?

China is the leading country in patenting activities related to big data for prediction. Chinese organizations began publishing patents related to this technical area in 2013. South Korea began publishing big data for prediction patents two years later, in 2015. Among other countries, only India, Japan and Taiwan published big data for prediction patents.

Who?

The organization that registered the most substantial number of simple patent families related to big data for prediction in the observed period is State Grid Corporation registered in China (227 simple patent families). Inspur Group (7 simple patent families) and Nanjing University (7 simple patent families) were active assignees from China as well. Kim Seung Chan, the inventor, registered three simple patent families, which makes him being the only individual on a list of first ten assignees of the area of interest. Other organizations that registered a more substantial number of simple patent families are companies such as Business Big Data, NAT Computer Network Information Security, Shanghai Fuli Information Technology and academic institutions such as Hohai University, Beijing Jiaotong University and the University of South China.

Patenting applications related to big data and prediction have been followed trends that are present in patent activities worldwide generally. According to patenting indicators for 2016, published by World Intellectual Property Organization (2017), China is the largest contributor in number of filing. The State Intellectual Property Office of The People's Republic of China (SIPO) received more than 1.3 million patent applications in 2016, which was more than the European Patent Office, the United States Patent and Trademark Office, the Japan Patent Office and the Korean Intellectual Property Office received together. Many of patents are related to new technological content in computing, medical technology, semiconductors, and so on. Reasons, why patenting activities in China have been growing, are following. In 2012, China's government set the goal regard growth of all type of patenting activities. Since then, they supported patenting activities with various incentives, and by setting new, more patenting friendly, regulations regarding the examination of patent applications. Moreover, China's high-tech companies and telecoms have become significant global players, not only conducting patenting activities but also buying patent rights. State Grid Corporation of China, which is in top 100 patent applicants worldwide, leads in patenting activities regard big data and prediction. Specifically, State Grid Corporation took ninth place when it comes to the application of patent families for the period between 2011 and 2014, especially for the following technological fields: electrical machinery, apparatus and energy, as well as technical content related to measurement.

Stakeholders who are interested in harnessing big data analytics solutions can choose between numerous vendors. However, vendors often acquire patents' rights, so they do not have to be patent assignees or inventors. Instead, they make strategic investments in patents, acquire patents and manage patent portfolios, which allows them to focus on their core activities and provide innovative solutions to clients. For example, in 2015, Avigilon Corporation, a global provider of surveillance solutions, including video analytics, acquired 126 USA and international patents from VideoMining Corporation, FaceDouble Incorporated, Behavioral Recognition Systems and ITS7 Pty. The total value of patents was US$135,375,000, covering technical content: different video analytics capabilities such as behavioral analysis, in-store object tracking, video segmentation, anomaly detection, image classification, as well as patents related to programming of remote security camera and network camera system.

What?

Search revealed the most frequent patent topics are related to technological solutions (G06Q - Analogue computers), data processing (G06F - Electrical digital data processing), and specific areas (G06N - Computer systems based on specific computational models). This finding is in line with the specific challenges related to big data identified by Sivarajah et al. (2017): (i) data challenges that are related to the characteristics of big data, (ii) process challenges, including challenges related to big data analysis and modelling, and (iii) management challenges that cover privacy, security, data governance, data and information sharing, cost and operational expenditure and data ownership challenges.

Number of patent families focus to technological solutions and data processing solutions, which try to solve specific challenges related to big data analytics. Techniques of predictive analytics can be divided into two group (Gandomi and Haider, 2015): (i) techniques for discovering historical patterns and extrapolating an outcome variable(s), and (ii) techniques for exploring the interdependencies between outcome and explanatory variables. Predictive analytics mostly relies on statistical techniques. However, while the conventional statistical methods rely on statistical significance to examine a significance of the specific relationship, big data analysis is often conducted on majority or entire population, so statistical significance is not that important for big data as compared to small samples of a population. Furthermore, when it comes to computational challenges, many conventional methods for small samples do not scale up to big data. For that reason, existing methods are extended and modified for parallel and distributed tasks. Additionally, big data unique characteristics cause some problems when it comes to estimating predictive models for big data (Gandomi & Haider, 2015): noise accumulation, spurious correlation and incidental endogeneity. Noise accumulation or accumulated estimation error sometimes results in overlooking some significant variables. Spurious correlation appears when some variables appear to be correlated because of high dimensionality of big data. In addition, incidental endogeneity, the dependence of the error term and variables, is common in big data. Extreme machine learning techniques have been extended for tasks such as clustering and adapted for parallel computation, which makes them feasible for big data analytics (Huang et al., 2014). Zhang et al. (2018) discussed the role and future of deep learning techniques in big data analytics that are used for image, audio and text analytics. Another issue of big data analytics is related to big data proneness to noise, outliers, inconsistencies and incompleteness (Wu, X., Zhu, Wu, G.-Q. & Ding, 2014). Additionally, re-utilization of existing big data should be taken into account. Most of the big data analytics algorithms will be designed to support parallel and distributed computing. This raise problem regard bottlenecks of algorithms that may occur because of synchronization and information exchange issues (Tsai et al., 2015; Wu et al., 2014). Additionally, big data technology needs improvements regard efficiency of format conversion of heterogeneous data, big data transfer and performance of real-time processing of big data.

Identified association rules indicate some specific domains of their usage such as market research, buyer profiling, price estimation or determination, computer-aided design and so on. Text mining revealed that following topics occur together: (i) real-time systems focusing to e.g. weather forecasting, (ii) database technologies related to preprocessing of specific data, such as big traffic data, (iii) technical challenges, such as cloud computing, (iv) specific topics, such as monitoring public opinion, and analyzing behavior data, (v) methodological challenges, such as usage of support vector machine to increase prediction accuracy, and (vi) specific topics related to information extraction from historical data, e.g. risk assessment.

Some of these topics indicate patenting activities for challenges related to data management and data integration. Safety and privacy are always key challenges and concerns when it comes to information and communication technology, as well as data. Security-related big data challenges are big data privacy, safety and big data application in information security (Chen et al., 2014). Big data privacy includes protection of personal privacy during data handling. Nowadays, usage of information and communication technology potentiate easy and simple generation and acquisition of large amounts of users' data. Hence, it is highly important for users to raise their awareness on which of their personal data third parties collect and how it is used. Big data safety mechanisms, such as efficient cryptography of big data and schemes for safety management, are under development. Efficiency of big data mechanisms is assured only if data availability, completeness, controllability, traceability and confidentiality are enabled (Chen et al., 2014).

CONCLUSION

Big data will influence society, economy and it will drive the progress of technologies in the near future. It causes fusion of different disciplines, which is particularly visible when it comes to big data analytics. Big data influence operations and decision making in various application fields. On the other hand, society promotes the progress of technologies, including widespread usage and development of big data. Additionally, big data encouraged fusion of different technologies, such as the Internet of Things, cloud computing and so on, and forces exploration of new and innovative technologies for handling big data. People are participants of big data, both users and generators of big data. Generation of real-time and streaming data, online network data, Internet of Things and mobile data, geography data (e.g. geo-tag or location-based real-time geographic data), spacial-temporal data, and visual data represent trends in big data area (Lv et al., 2017; Brown et al., 2011). Shortly, it is expected that the volume of such data will grow to a large degree due to technological advances and development in related areas, such as geo-databases or wireless sensor networks. Furthermore, demands from a wide range of application areas, along with new database and processing technologies, drive the modification of existing techniques and development of new techniques for big data analytics.

The chapter presents a patent analysis technical area of big data for prediction based on data searched and gathered from PatSeer patent database. Authors analyzed 296 active simple patent families related to big data for prediction assigned from 2013 to October 2017. The patent analysis was conducted in four stages related to (i) the patent search and selection, (ii) timeline, geographic origin and patents assignees analysis, (iii) patents according to IPC system patent area, and (iv) text mining patent analysis.

An analysis of the 296 simple patent families related to big data for prediction was conducted to achieve the goal of this research.

The analysis provided insights into the technical area of big data for prediction. The increasing trend is in patenting the technical content of big data for prediction is present from 2013, with 122 simple patent families registered in 2016 and 107 simple patent families registered in 2017, until October. This is due to an increasing interest in big data and new opportunities big data brings. Authors revealed that the patenting activities related to big data for prediction are spread across China and South Korea which organizations assigned the majority of patents related to the technology of interest. The organization that registered the largest number of simple patent families related to big data for prediction in the observed period is State Grid Corporation registered in China (227 simple patent families or 7.43%). Other organizations that registered a larger number of simple patent families are companies such as Business Big Data, NA Computer Network Information Security MAN, Shanghai Fuli Information Technology and academic institutions such as Hohai University, Beijing Jiaotong University, University of South China and so on.

Next, the protected technical content of big data for prediction simple patent families was analyzed by using the International Patent Classification system at the section, class, sub-class, main group or sub-group level. The simple patent families were mostly registered under the section G codes (474 times) with the following classes most frequently assigned: G06 - Computing; calculating; counting instruments (407 times), G08 – Signaling instruments (29 times) and G01 – Measuring; testing instruments (24 times). Therefore, computing instruments have been the major focus of assignees-inventors. Specifically, a significant number of simple patent families were information retrieval, database structures or file system as a part of data processing systems specially adapted for administrative, commercial, financial managerial, supervisory or forecasting purposes.

Furthermore, association rules analysis revealed rules that are trivial due to dataset limitations. For better results, weighted association rules should be applied in future research with additional patent data such as backward citations and the number of IPC codes. Therefore, authors conclude that the technical content of the observed simple patent families is not heterogeneous, but association rules indicate some specific domains.

Finally, authors used the phrase extraction process combined with the cluster analysis to detect most common topics appearing in big data for prediction simple patent families' abstracts. Most frequent phrases occurring in big data for prediction simple patent families' abstracts were real time, data mining, early warning and neural networks. The phrases that occur the most often with the phrase real-time are mostly related to data analysis such as historical data, management systems, real-time performance and monitoring data (Belfo et al., 2015). The phrases that occur the most often with the phrase data mining are mostly related to the phrase historical data, and methods and techniques of data analysis such as machine learning, natural language or deep learning. The phrases that occur the most often with the phrase early-warning indicate specific purposes of the weather forecast and power supply domain, and source of data analyzed by early-warning systems such as monitoring data, weather information, environment information. The phrase neural network occurs with phrases that indicate its specific applications areas such as power load, behavior analysis, weather forecast, feature extraction or medical diagnosis. Cluster analysis identified 6 groups of topics regard big data for prediction patents and the connections between keywords – phrases are visualized by using a network graph to explore relationships, to detect underlying patterns and structures of co-occurrences.

REFERENCES

Akter, S., & Wamba, S. F. (2016). Big data analytics in E-commerce: A systematic review and agenda for future research. *Electronic Markets*, *26*(2), 173–194. doi:10.100712525-016-0219-0

Altunas, S., Dereli, T., & Kusiak, A. (2015). Analysis of patent documents with weighted association rules. *Technological Forecasting and Social Change*, *92*, 249–262. doi:10.1016/j.techfore.2014.09.012

Belfo, F., Trigo, A., & Estébanez, R. P. (2015). Impact of ICT Innovative Momentum on Real-Time Accounting. *Business Systems Research Journal*, *6*(2), 1–17. doi:10.1515/bsrj-2015-0007

Boyd, D., & Crawford, K. (2012). Critical questions for big data. *Communicatio Socialis*, *15*(5), 662–679.

Bradlow, E. T., Gangwar, M., Kopalle, P., & Voleti, S. (2017). The Role of Big Data and Predictive Analytics in Retailing. *Journal of Retailing*, *93*(1), 79–95. doi:10.1016/j.jretai.2016.12.004

Brown, R. A., & Sankaranarayanan, S. (2011). Intelligent store agent for mobile shopping. *International Journal of E-Services and Mobile Applications*, *3*(1), 57–72. doi:10.4018/jesma.2011010104

Brügmann, S., Bouayad-Agha, N., Burga, A., Carrascosa, S., Ciaramella, A., Ciaramella, M., ... Wanner, L. (2015). Towards content-oriented patent document processing: Intelligent patent analysis and summarization. *World Patent Information*, *40*, 30–42. doi:10.1016/j.wpi.2014.10.003

Chen, H., Chiang, R. H. L., & Storey, V. C. (2012). Business Intelligence and Analytics: From Big Data to Big Impact. *Management Information Systems Quarterly*, *36*(4), 1165–1188.

Chen, M., Mao, S., & Liu, Y. (2014). Big Data: A Survey. *Mobile Networks and Applications*, *19*(2), 171–209. doi:10.100711036-013-0489-0

Dmitriyev, V., Mahmoud, T., & Marín-Ortega, P. M. (2015). SOA enabled ELTA: Approach in designing business intelligence solutions in Era of Big Data. *International Journal of Information Systems and Project Management*, *3*(3), 49–63.

Everitt, B. S., Landau, S., Leese, M., & Stahl, D. (2011). Hierarchical clustering. In Cluster Analysis (5th ed.). John Wiley and Sons, Ltd. doi:10.1002/9780470977811.ch4

Gandomi, A., & Haider, M. (2014). Beyond the hype: Big data concepts, methods, and analytics. *International Journal of Information Management*, *35*, 137 – 144.

Garret, M. A. (2014). Big Data analytics and cognitive computing – future opportunities for astronomical research. *IOP Conference Series. Materials Science and Engineering*, *67*, 012017. doi:10.1088/1757-899X/67/1/012017

Gepp, A., Linnenluecke, M.K., O'Neill, T.J., & Smith, T. (2018). Big data techniques in auditing research and practice: Current trends and future opportunities. *Journal of Accounting Literature, 40*, 102-115.

Günther, A. W., Rezazade, M. H., Huysman, M., & Feldberg, F. (2017). Debating big data: A literature review on realizing value from big data. *The Journal of Strategic Information Systems*, *26*(3), 191–209. doi:10.1016/j.jsis.2017.07.003

Han, Q., Heimerl, F., Codina-Filba, J., Lohmann, S., Wanner, L., & Ertl, T. (2017). Visual patent trend analysis for informed decision making in technology management. *World Patent Information*, *49*, 34–42. doi:10.1016/j.wpi.2017.04.003

Huang, G., Huang, G.-B., Song, S., & You, K. (2014). Trends in extreme machine learning: A review. *Neural Networks, 61*, 32-48.

Ji, W., & Wang, L. (2017). Big data analytics based fault prediction for shop floor scheduling. *Journal of Manufacturing Systems*, *43*(1), 187–194. doi:10.1016/j.jmsy.2017.03.008

Kim, G., & Bae, J. (2017). A novel approach to forecast promising technology through patent analysis. *Technological Forecasting and Social Change*, *117*, 228–237. doi:10.1016/j.techfore.2016.11.023

Kim, M., Park, Y., & Yoon, J. (2016). Generating patent development maps for technology monitoring using semantic patent-topic analysis. *Computers & Industrial Engineering*, *98*, 289–299. doi:10.1016/j.cie.2016.06.006

Kyebambe, M., Cheng, G., Huang, Y., He, C., & Zhang, Z. (2017). Forecasting emerging technologies: A supervised learning approach through patent analysis. *Technological Forecasting and Social Change*, *125*, 236–244. doi:10.1016/j.techfore.2017.08.002

Lee, J., & Ardakani, H. D. (2015). Industrial Big Data Analytics and Cyber-ph. Academic Press.

Lv, Z., Song, H., Basanta-Val, P., Steed, A., & Jo, M. (2017). Next-Generation Big Data Analytics: State of the Art, Challenges, and Future Research Topics. *IEEE Transactions on Industrial Informatics*, *13*(4), 1891–1899. doi:10.1109/TII.2017.2650204

Madani, F., & Weber, C. (2016). The evolution of patent mining: Applying bibliometrics analysis and keyword network analysis. *World Patent Information*, *46*, 32–48. doi:10.1016/j.wpi.2016.05.008

McAfee, A., & Brynjolfsson, E. (2012). Big data: The management revolution. *Harvard Business Review*, *90*(10), 60–68. PMID:23074865

Miah, S. J., Vu, Q. H., Gammack, J., & McGrath, M. (2017). A Big Data Analytics Method for Tourist Behavior Analysis. *Information & Management*, *54*(6), 771–785. doi:10.1016/j.im.2016.11.011

Niemann, H., Moehrle, M. G., & Frischkorn, J. (2017). Use of a new patent text mining and visualization method for identifying patenting patterns over time: Concept, method and test application. *Technological Forecasting and Social Change*, *115*, 210–220. doi:10.1016/j.techfore.2016.10.004

NIST Big Data Public Working Group. (2017). *Big Data Interoperability Framework: Volume 1, Definitions*. Accessed at: http://bigdatawg.nist.gov/home.php

Parr Rud, O. (2011). Invited article: Adaptability. *Business Systems Research Journal: International Journal of the Society for Advancing Business & Information Technology, 2*(2), 4-12.

PatSeer. (2017). Retrieved from http://patseer.com/

Pejić Bach, M., Pivar, J., & Dumičić, K. (2017). Data anonymization patent landscape. *Croatian Operational Research Review, 8*(1), 265–281. doi:10.17535/crorr.2017.0017

Rassam, M. A., Maarof, M. A., & Zainal, A. (2017). Big Data Analytics Adoption for Cyber-Security: A Review of Current Solutions, Requirements, Challenges and Trends. *Journal of Information Assurance and Security, 12*(4), 124–145.

Salehan, M., & Kim, D. J. (2016, January). Predicting the performance of online consumer reviews: A sentiment mining approach to big data analytics. *Decision Support Systems, 81*, 30–40. doi:10.1016/j.dss.2015.10.006

Sharma, P., & Tripathi, R. C. (2017). Patent citation: A technique for measuring the knowledge flow of information and innovation. *World Patent Information, 51*, 31–42. doi:10.1016/j.wpi.2017.11.002

Sharma, R., & Kankanhalli, A. (2014). Transforming decision-making processes: A research agenda for understanding the impact of business analytics on organizations. *European Journal of Information Systems, 23*(4), 433–441. doi:10.1057/ejis.2014.17

Shirdastian, H., Laroche, M., & Richard, M. O. (2017). Using big data analytics to study brand authenticity sentiments: The case of Starbucks on Twitter. *International Journal of Information Management*. doi:10.1016/j.ijinfomgt.2017.09.007

Sinha, M., & Pandurangi, A. (2015). *Guide to Practical Patent Searching And How To Use Patseer For Patent Search And Analysis*. Pune: Gridlogics Technologies.

Sivarajah, U., Kamal, M. M., Irani, Z., & Weerakkody, V. (2017). Critical analysis of Big Data challenges and analytical methods. *Journal of Business Research, 70*, 263–286. doi:10.1016/j.jbusres.2016.08.001

Song, K., Kim, K., & Lee, S. (2018). Identifying promising technologies using patents: A retrospective feature analysis and a prospective needs analysis on outlier patents. *Technological Forecasting and Social Change, 128*, 118–132. doi:10.1016/j.techfore.2017.11.008

Tsai, C. W., Lai, C. F., Chao, H. C., & Vasilakos, A. V. (2015). Big data analytics: A survey. *Journal of Big Data, 2*(1), 21. doi:10.118640537-015-0030-3 PMID:26191487

Vera-Baquero, A., Colomo-Palacios, R., Molloy, O., & Elbattah, M. (2015). Business process improvement by means of Big Data based Decision Support Systems: A case study on Call Centers. *International Journal of Information Systems and Project Management, 3*(1), 5–26.

Waller, M. A., & Fawcett, S. E. (2013). Data Science, Predictive Analytics, and Big Data: A Revolution that Will Transform Supply Chain Design and Management. *Journal of Business Logistics, 34*(2), 77–84. doi:10.1111/jbl.12010

World Intellectual Property Organization, Economics and Statistics Division. (2016). *World Intellectual Property Indicators 2016*. Accessed at: http://www.wipo.int/edocs/pubdocs/en/wipo_pub_941_2016.pdf

World Intellectual Property Organization (WIPO). (2017). *Guide to the International Patent Classification.* Accessed at: http://www.wipo.int/export/sites/www/classifications/ipc/en/guide/guide_ipc.pdf

Wu, X., Zhu, X., Wu, G.-Q., & Ding, W. (2014). Data Mining with Big Data. *IEEE Transactions on Knowledge and Data Engineering*, 26(1), 97–107. doi:10.1109/TKDE.2013.109

Zhang, Q., Yang, L. T., Chen, Z., & Li, P. (2018). A survey on deep learning for big data. *Information Fusion*, 42, 146–157. doi:10.1016/j.inffus.2017.10.006

Chapter 58
The Impact of Big Data Analytics and Challenges to Cyber Security

Anandakumar Haldorai

Akshaya College of Engineering and Technology, India

Arulmurugan Ramu

Bannari Amman Institute of Technology, India

ABSTRACT.

In order to scrutinize or evaluate an extremely high quantity of an ever-present and diversified nature of data, new technologies are developed. With the application of these technologies, called big data technologies, to the constantly developing various internal as well as external sources of data, concealed correlations between data can be identified, and promising strategies can be developed, which is necessary for economic growth and new innovations. This chapter deals with the analysis of the real-time uses of big data to both individual persons and the society too, while concentrating on seven important areas of key usage: big data for business optimization and customer analytics, big data and healthcare, big data and science, big data and finance, big data as enablers of openness and efficiency in government, big data and the emerging energy distribution systems, and big data security.

INTRODUCTION

Big data analysis has not been entirely new to the world as it has been around the corner and discussed by a lot of analytics. Though it is been viewed or thought to be a highly sensitive buzzword, big data analytics is just a means to bird's view of extremely large data to identify concealed patterns, new correlations, preference of the customers, marketing trends or priority, and other business-related information. Various business corporate structures are bound to take a leap in their decisions to maintain their stand in the highly competitive business world and they have to definitely control their data to develop strategies that can be put into actions (Xia, Liu, Lee, & Cao, 2016). The last few years have seen a major

DOI: 10.4018/978-1-6684-3662-2.ch058

explosion in the quantity of data and the variety of it generated by individuals and about them. Such a huge data is easily copied at a very low price and is conveniently stored in public databases where they are easily accessed through the Internet.

As per the IBM estimation which is released recently, an awesome amount of 2.5 billion Gigabytes (GB) of data are produced every day all of the world and this volume are ever growing every minute. And what more to add to this along with the Web 2.0 applications, the literally baseline cost of computational storage, the fast-evolving of entirely new range of computing prototypes like cloud computing, the field of artificial intelligence and data mining which is in the process of major breakthrough innovations (Li, Tang, & Xu, 2016), all of which join hands with an extremely wide range of sensor endowed and Internet-friendly mobile instruments helps greatly in enabling the big data phenomenon on itself. The term big data by itself still do not have a strict definition but is widely used to explain the magnanimous development and feasibility and the varied nature of data and the rate of momentum at which these data (different nature, format, and origin) are created and transported.

The NIST (National Institute of Standards and Technology) promoted a feasible definition for big data in cooperate with major areas like Velocity (data speed), Volume (data volume), and the Variety (data source). Big data is entirely different than conventional data warehousing and the other areas of analysis (Jiang & Wang, 2016) of business intelligence which has been in the scenario for quite some time. An unsurpassable amount of big data is quite unstructured and they comprise of literally raw data which is created with an increasing speed unlike anything earlier.

Today's real-time analysts are continuously able to wring out highly difficult patterns, identify correlations and pull out information that is valuable from collections of real-time data which are the cross-domain in nature. This is done with the use of technologies that are high in performance, storage infrastructures that are nominal in pricing, statistical correlation algorithms and strong techniques in data mining (Bhatt, Dey, & Ashour, 2017). The examples of big data sources are quite rich and varied in nature. They range from big corporate companies' Intranets, government directories which are online, the enormous search data, mobile communication finds, the users' data of their live interactions on social communication platforms, as well as the cyber physical systems like the ITS or intelligent transport system, smart energy distribution, smart cars, ultra modern home equipments which merge into the various home entertainment needs as well as domestic appliances to house security devices which have applications that use face, emotion recognition and motion detectors (Shrivastava et al., 2011).

This is a fast-growing trend which is highly used in various services which affect our day to day life and has a great impact on the socio-economic scenario. The big data analysts are derive and relate algorithms and make use of the artificial intelligence which uncovers concealed insights from a large amount of collected data for different areas of life. They range from decision optimization from the given data which can be utilized in the police force by the practical strategic assessment which helps to decrease the public crimes, and in the medical environment, patient's hazard to certain diseases are calculated along with the spreading of contagious diseases. It also helps to understand the nature of human reactions and consequences in typical socio-technical situations. These days the acquiescence of data is a form of currency and is a rich and rare commodity. The holding of such big data reduces to face new privacy challenges of individuals and society in whole as these accumulated data are linked to other databases as well. Based on this big data, its storage, analytics, and decisions which are automated through computational algorithms make a heavy impact on individuals and society and it also poses a great threat to the basic rights on various platforms like unfair discrimination, prejudicial outcomes, and many personal issues.

RELATED REVIEWS

Today's world of business and institution is certainly data driven. By and through, the usage of big data technology and its extensive reach makes a significant impact on productivity, innovation and economic growth. This enables both the society and businesses to benefit extensively.

Big Data for Business Optimization

Using big data is the iconic cornerstone and the key to a new business era, as this means personalized service in delivery of business and the same could do wonders for the marketers and the business pioneers (Shamoto, Shirahata, Drozd, Sato, & Matsuoka, 2016). The hidden patterns can be isolated and viewed by the business analysts and highly in-depth knowledge from the different sources both internal and external data is extracted from the assimilation of both the advanced analysis of big data and the modern warehouse data platforms. The big data knowledge thus acts as leverage to the business leaders as they continuously add more intelligence to their processes, their operational efficacy is greatly improved, and the end results in gaining the advantage in their business competition. The interlinking of the large volume of data which is heterogeneous and extremely complex along with the externally available growing amount of big data leads the business pioneers and their analysts to shortlist and zoom down to optimize the various strategic plans in advertisements as well as marketing (Wu, Zhu, Wu, & Ding, 2014). They also help in knowing the exact needs of the customers, their usage, buying trend and also the new developing patterns can be identified at the very early onset itself.

Most of the online, as well as other company retailers, are relying greatly on these big data technology to sort out their clients and customers' history of purchase, other transactions and inventory to their databases in order to

1. Gather a higher knowledge about their clients,
2. Deliver personalized goods, service and commendable guidance to their existing and potential clients,
3. Identification of changes in client-based needs.

With the help of the growing amount of data of the customers who rely on their mobile devices or smart devices for all their purchase, transactions and usage of electronic cards, and making use of the OSN or social networks where they register their views and share their intimate and personal ideas and whereabouts, allow the marketing personnel of most of the companies to gain leverage with simple analytic technology to reach out to the client with the exact need during the exact time and phase of life. This could be seen very well in the near future as its course has already been set into motion. This means a healthy situation in competitive business intelligence and the continuance of a business is kept stable for a reasonable future keeping in mind the changes in technology and persistent market needs.

Big Data and Big Science

Science could be influenced to change with the help of highly potential big data. The future of the data-intensive science is molded greatly with the developments that are seen in conventional decade. The major areas of computer model along with difficult and practical analytics coupled with the persistent growth in quantity and variety of data derived from different databases like health and medical data, internet browsing and searching pattern data, security and surveillance video data, genomic data, observatories which provide data of the images of the earth, sensor networks, wire free networks, as well as mobile devices help in the growth of the big data as well as its importance in the field of science (Suganya & Anandakumar, 2013).

Virtually a new idea to tackle the challenges of exploration and invention in the field of science looms intensively with the future of data-intensive science in use. The ubiquitous volume of data researched allows a good amount of leverage and needs new simulations, computations, tools, and technology for data management. This approach of data-intensive science allows a new lease of promise in the integration of various features of life in physical and social sciences. This also covers areas of application right from earth computations, genomics, nature and environmental studies, to the ends of computed social research studies. All this is done with the pure aim and hope that mankind will be better enabled and usage of data-intensive study or science will meet out at least a few of the challenges that pose globally like global warming, pandemics, efficacy in delivering and usage of better energy resources, as well as monitoring of global health amongst various other matters.

Big Data in Medicine and Health Care

The healthcare industry, on the whole, has started its reliance in all wakes of the healthcare department like that of monitoring of the public healthcare, delivery, and research of the healthcare industry towards big data. The growing dependence on information technology, the industry's stakeholders and its financial data to be collected, develop and inter distribute numerous data through the systems which adds up to the biological sample data of the person, medical imaging data, patient insurance and claims, medical prescriptions, health notes and other medical related statistics (Anandakumar, & Umamaheswari, 2017a). In the healthcare industry, keeping record of all the above said data has been done through the age, but what is new is the a) the ability to interlink both the internal and external health details when putting on whole allows to develop a pattern in the geographic, behavior and health fitness over a higher quantity of human health data allows to form a pattern and for better understanding of the healthcare industry of a particular geographical location and its people. b) This will help in aiding better understanding of research, exploration new medicinal values and controlled observation of concealed health trends in a particular society and will definitely allow better medical products and service to them.

Big Data in Marketing Economic Services

Big data related technology plays an exorbitant role in financial institutions and its market which has the fastest growth in IT department. The technology is used mainly in the compilation and analyzing high volume of financial data of both personal and economic in nature from live streams of finance like that of both the stock and share markets. This helps to have a clear idea of the risks and challenges faced by the complex system of finance and its possibility of newer investments (Kaseb, Mohan, Koh, & Lu, 2017). These last years, the insurance and credit companies are capitalizing on the IT field and its developments to gain fast access to analyze through social network data. They can go back and find out the complex designs which help to identify fraudulent activities (Yang, Wang, Song, Yang, & Patnaik, 2018).

This financial big data implementation helps in making otherwise hard decisions in newer market areas. Their source data are analyzed, viable and profitable patterns which may not be able to track will be revealed and they would allow valuable knowledge to foresee changes in stock markets and take revolutionary decisions which would have a greater impact in the financial market and institutions.

Big Data in Energy Distribution Environment

Emergence of smart grids in the Energy Distribution Systems is another new field in which the big data analysis remains to gather momentum in its usage. The data-driven techniques and its analytical devices use the smart meters, secure field devices, IT components which latest energy configurations which help in the compilation of newer data. The practical and real-life compilation and scrutinizing big data help the energy sector to come to a conclusion to develop better means in generating power, its supply, distribution, and transmission.

Big Data in Government Sector

The monumental decision of the government sector to display big/open data in the past decade had seen a great impact all over. A great volume of public details like the population census, crime details, real-life traffic status, healthcare data, meteorological statistics has been all over the Internet for public viewing. This is rather done to keep open end accountability and transparency of data which would improve the government respect among the public. The government hopes that by allowing this easy access and use will create a formidable economic growth and create new innovations by the private parties and commercial agencies (Lecuyer, Spahn, Geambasu, Huang, & Sen, 2017). This data provided freely by the government proves to a rich source of monumental data mine. As the British government foresees, this data can be exploited both by the government organizations and individual to unimaginable heights. This ubiquitous amount of poorly used government data will allow the private and other agencies to make use of latest techniques in data processing and analysis and they will be cross-linked to help improve governments' operational efficacy and cost reduction. A $100 billion dollars per annum is saved from the European public sector by disabling the potentiality of big data in its efficacy in operation. The same is expected in other areas as well. In private sectors, for example, the real estate scenario will be changing greatly with its knowledge of the available property, its location and value along with its criminal data. They will be better equipped to advise their customers about where to invest and where not to (Kimbahune, Deshpande, & Mahalle, 2017).

Detecting Cyber Crime With Big Data

Cybercrime is one of the latest criminal scenarios which affect both the public, private and personal area of oneself. Taking up against this crime needs a lot of analysis and a sure knowledge of all the possible evidential tools, making the exact and detailed prediction about the activities of the criminals. The criminals' behavior and their flexible adapting ability to changing and challenging measures should be taken into account. The cyber security personnel or information officers take a great amount of exercise to constantly oversee and secure their corporate companies against these high techno-savvy cybercriminals who evolve constantly in their criminal activities and threats (Park, Chung, Khan, & Park, 2017). Due to this growth rate of cyber crime the private companies tend to move slowly and surely to use big data analytical devices and technology to safeguard themselves. The changing trends of malicious attacks by these cyber criminals and their activities which are deeply hidden are identified. Their pattern of activity, motivation, and intentions are detected and continual supports of insight into security details are thus provided. Also, these type of data is inter-shared among other corporate companies as well as cross-border interstate and inter-country knowledge is shared to identify and reduce the cybercrime rate. This also helps to identify any network activities of similar types across various state and country jurisdictions. This compilation of big data and its analysis of security and information satisfy the craving of the law makers and its enforcement agencies for new information from different sources such as the Internet usage, mobile compatible wireless networks, financial data, travelers' data, and many other means like surveillance videos, satellite images and the like of them. When all these data are cleverly compiled and put together for the analytical purpose, the security personnel are able to detect the criminals' behavioral patterns, their identities, and much more insight (Chowdhuri, Dey, Chakraborty, & Baneerjee, 2015).

REAL-TIME PROBLEMS AND CHALLENGES OF BIG DATA

There is no doubt that the individual personalities, companies, societies, organizations, government and non-government sectors receive a great deal of positive opportunities with the use of big data techniques and its various tools but on the other hand, there is also a query on much more important issues of privacy and ethics. The big data's analytical devices or mechanisms and configurations will have a greater effect which may be negative to the privacy aspect, both legally and morally (Zhang, Shang, Lin, Li, & Tan, 2017). This will be a definite hurdle to the potentiality of the big data theory which has to be foreseen at this juncture.

Challenges in Big Data Security and Privacy

Usage of big data analytical tools on various grounds such as financial, economic, social, and other transactional definitely paves the way to the loss of civil rights as there is the complete deprivation of individual autonomy and privacy. From this aspect, they lose the liberty to maintain control or monitor their private data and prevent any misuse and/or abuse by cybercriminals, data analysts though the utility, growth, and innovation depends on big data preservation and use. The given below areas pose a few relative threat to the concept of big data's privacy and security.

Increased Prospective of Sensitive Data

While the increased amount of data is stored, accessed and shared online through internet by the third parties, the chance of the breach of data is also increased. So there arises an immeasurable list of queries regarding personal data's access, storage, and usage which is of paramount importance.

There are Two Different Opponent Components in Unauthorized Access as Follows

The initial adversary likes to enter into the database of raw data with a plan to compromise the process of interpretation or analysis. This is done by processing wrong data into the database or takes over the immense volume of identity or financial data which are highly sensitive. The other adverse act is to act upon already analyzed databases and steal the actions and intelligence of the legal analysts of the big data (Schmidt, Chen, Matheson, & Ostrouchov, 2017). To perform this breach of privacy in data, both the software and the hardware of these data platforms are scrutinized and their flaws are used.

Therefore the large data infrastructures like the cloud platforms and the data centers which are open to attack are largely protected from security breach and malware attacks. These are the places where all the original information and knowledge are stored highly sensitive data. An individual may suffer from identity exposure, confidential data like credit, debit card details, financial transactions while a company's breach would lead to grave damage to its brand image, loyalty of the partners and its consumers, loss of share market value, intelligence data, and penalties legal in nature due to non compliance of privacy regulations.

Loss of Personal Data in Individual Control

The process of big data technology is ever growing in nature and so the collection of data, its sharing and processing have become very difficult to control the privacy of an individual's personal data. The real reason at the back of this issue is as follows:

1. In the large scenario of big data sets, the information technology infrastructure processes multiple individuals' data by collecting and storing to make an inference. This is not in the hands of the individual.
2. The concept of big data's need to store all data in large measures and the basic privacy regulation needs of individuals and organizations are at war here. The minimization of data and principles of purpose binding are fundamental needs which pose to be highly contradictory and ridiculous to achieve simultaneously with the principles of big data performance.
3. There still remains a controversy over the ownership of data and intelligence derived from the big data analysis like that of the other online platforms of social media and e-commerce.

All the above-cited problems not only raise queries over the individual's right to monitor and control their personal data both implicitly and explicitly but also whether disclosure at proper juncture can be maintained. Also, it is difficult to know if the monitoring and control of private data can be achieved all through the lifetime of the data (Yusuf, Thomas, Spichkova, & Schmidt, 2017). Above all these, there is the major issue of the freedom to access data of individuals as per the norms of European Data Protection Directive which is closely connected to the individual privacy and control of their personal data.

Availability of Sensitive Datasets in Long-Term

The storage prices paired with developing needs to get back all the big data which is perennially legal and business oriented, permits the entire community of government, private organizations and individual researchers to assemble their large data platforms. In this database, only the identity attributes vary rarely, and the rest of the data regarding behavioral styles, lifestyle, personal view, and emotional feeling of an individual is recorded. All these data of an individual is possible (Zong, Ge, & Gu, 2017) to change many times in a person's lifetime. The social digitalization has definitely changed the meaning and discussion in connection with personal digital info. All these information are easy to duplicate and made available in cross-linked data platforms which are easily accessible online and the deletion of this data is not practically expected of. Big database of analytical intelligence that is inferred keeps on record permanently along with all the disclosures and silly blunders have done by the individual person online (Arulmurugan, Sabarmathi, & Anandakumar, 2017). These would rather not be remembered by anyone even after long period of time about the data subject.

Data Integrity and Provenance Issues

All the applications that are enabled by big data are rich in information and sensitive in context. This frequently needs a clear wisdom of the data subjects' genealogy and history, also keeping in view the issues regarding data quality, provenance, and integrity in connection to the proximity of raw and unreliable databases which poses a serious challenge to the analytics of big data. These data analysts do not have the means or method to have a stable integrity as well as quality data and also do not have clear idea to collect or recognize the pedigree nature of the big data and its context (Anandakumar, & Umamaheswari, 2017b). This leads to a difficult condition to derive optimization in businesses, to administer the monumental level of data received and also to run through any important operation or process which is data driven. The quality of the data, its provenance and also the integrity part of it determines the activity part of the analytics on how these data should be interpreted along with their results. Special accordance should be given to sensitive contexts like analysis of data dependency, decision optimization of both tactical and strategic in nature within the constraints of an organization, and as well as detection of criminal and malicious behavior by the law enforcement sector (Matallah, Belalem, & Bouamrane, 2017).

Data Inferences and Correlation

The entire accumulated personal data of individuals which are accessed from multiple sources helps in identifying concealed designs of big data. The big data already has the needed potency to increase the privacy implications of all the database correlations. In almost all the big data platforms or database, compilation and correlation of data from diverse nature is a strenuous operation which also adds up to the challenge of re-identification.

Lack of Transparency and Management

The major two key needs of legal procedures which are needed from the individuals or both the private/public organizations which help in collecting, processing and sharing PII or Personal Identifiable Information are the electric consent and the notion of Notice. All over the world, both these methods have an integral position in the legislation regulations of privacy and protection of data. Although this is common procedure, different countries and different jurisdictions may have multiple definitions to the notion of consent and notice as to the needs and interpretations of its subjects like their advocates, citizens, legislators and legal authorities.

Implementation of all these regulations is a risky task in the big data sets as there is a constant change from the individuals when data is collected where they have an option to check in/out of the privacy notice, to the exact point of time when the decision of consent made is already informed to them. In spite of all this clarity processed to the individual, the recent practice of the individuals seems to have lack of understanding and limited attention is paid to these consent notices during the installation of digital services (Matallah, Belalem, & Bouamrane, 2017). At a later point in time, the consequence of this particular action implies differently and the situation is further aggravated by the entire nature of big data processing. Also, all the details or information gathered at the point of data collection do not have the complete context inference and no prediction can be done based on this data as individuals do not and will not be aptly able to give consent beforehand itself. In addition to this, the different data and information gathered with the use of big data analytics, the numerous reasons, and contexts used by the persons in connection to their private data are far exceeding in nature and have nature to persistently undergo changes. Based on this pattern, it is highly difficult for the users to assess their needs beforehand and make a potential assessment when it is in connection with the analysis of cost-benefit and there is a slight tremor to allow consent to make use of their private details, comprise and reveal all of it for any other different purpose (Mukherjee, Dey, Kausar, Ashour, Taiar, & Hassanien, 2016).

In truth, the individuals are completely unaware of the process of the big data working techniques, their infrastructures, and the functioning of their algorithms. All this is done without the exact knowledge of the data subject. They do not know the context and concept of notice and management of the consent given by them and how it is made use of in the large-scale big data compilation and how it helps in making decisions. So a need for transparency and empowering knowledge to the subject should be done by data controllers of the big data scheme.

These constraints or restrictions in the big data collection of consent calls out for a change in policy with regard to give more clear support in consent specifics and clarification (i.e. signaling of consent decision), transparency in consent management, refining the process of consent or notice management, enforcing or implementation as well as the revoking the data-driven business models of the emerging big data technology (Goswami, Roy, Dey, & Chakraborty, 2017).

Big Accountability

The accountability of the big data algorithms also poses another major challenge along with that of transparency. Although the big data algorithms help to achieve beneficial outputs to the society, on the whole, do have disapproving or harmful effects to the individuals in par with the mounting profiles, surveillance was done and many more discriminatory methods. To react to these problems and finding redressal to all the issues makes it important to change the path from the current approach to algorithmic accountability. There should sufficient leniency and accessibility allowed to the data subjects so that they can personally counter check the information fed into the system for computation is accurate and as per their individual preference for privacy and conceding to the current norms that exist.

ETHICAL ISSUES AND SOCIAL CHALLENGES

Apart from the technological queries and legal challenges which have been discussed extensively in the above-mentioned sections, the moral and ethical implication of big data analytics is yet another huge hurdle that has to be completely addressed to. The following are a few of the issues listed (Yamin, & Sen, 2018).

Issue of Power and Information Asymmetry

Information asymmetry is nothing but the business environments wherein one of the parties have more information and information is nothing but power ready to be used. For example, in a retail business transaction, the buyer has relatively less and few experience compared to the retailer who stands in the business for quite a long time. This knowledge of the retailer about the exact details about the availability, quality and prevailing rates of the goods and the ability to assess market value through long experience is extremely more than that of the buyer. The buyer has to rely on his limited knowledge and peer lent feedback and accepts the retailer's demands. This asymmetry in information permits a selected few to withhold power against the majority of the common with the aid of big data. The larger public or individuals do not have the access to this type of knowledge and this develops into a situation wherein power is accumulated between the state or the respective big business centers and the people or the respective customers. When this amount of unprecedented data is accrued and the ability to manipulate information about citizens and clients is allowed or accessed by the larger organizations, this might lead to having private and selfish agenda, and when authoritarian government bodies or politicians who are intrusive might do away with unwarranted societal control, and unimaginable scale of negative impact is bound to the democracy of many countries there in igniting great harm on the whole.

Big Surveillance

Surveillance is another great field wherein big data technology has its playground. There is a great need for the continuous growing and system based surveillance both offline and online. These are not just used by the law governing bodies and intelligence sectors but also by individuals and business institutions on a commercial basis. The algorithms used by big data and its exceptional infrastructure are used online by many service providers commercially. They, in turn, compile and scrutinize the high volume of information about customer needs and preference much better and in turn help to improve their services for higher client-friendly services and helps in targeted commercial ads. This constant and continuous surveillance over the customers helps them to amass valuable knowledge on the customers' needs, bias, preference, spending habits, interests in social interactions and places visited, daily routines, browsing history, brand preference and continue in all walks of life in a person. Nothing is a secret anymore and all this collection turns out to be the digital treasure trove to the data controller and knowledge definitely turns out to be power. Making use of this digital dossier of individuals, spy sectors of both private and government intelligence derive sensitive knowledge about the selected personalities and help to keep a tab on them through the internet in reality.

Social Sorting and Social Control

Conventionally it is said that the powerless segments of the population and the minority sector needs to be kept in solidarity and they require protection. But with the big data analytics detailing, all these info is accessible to only a select few in power and so the security, privacy, fairness, and morality of all this becomes questionable. Big data permits untoward discriminatory activities aimed at particular individuals and this is made extremely easy with predictable accuracy. Though the positive nature of big data technology allows compilation and analysis of vast amount of data to help in improved efficacy in operations, decision making and provide services to the specific needs of the people, this type of knowledge tends to be used to discriminate the same public if allowed in wrong hands (Anandakumar & Umamaheswari, 2017c). At times when there is discrimination of pricing is there and few other aims like law enforcement, customer scoring, and personal and group behaviors are identified, they could be treated badly and completely stopped in public scenarios. Advanced mathematics models aid in understanding both the differences and similarities of individuals and groups and also help in categorizing them into various cadres. In case used negatively, these poor individuals may face the wrath of discrimination but are kept in dark against why they have been in such state and also do not possess any means to save themselves. In the fields of the healthcare community and insurance companies, they make use of the big data technology to perfection. They identify the entire patients' list of data, their sickness oriented internet browsing history, patients' online group discussions and all these may actually provide better insight and services to the individual. But it also allows them to discriminate certain persons due to their sex and gender biased orientation (Elhayatmy, Dey, & Ashour, 2017).

Moreover, in real estate field, data regarding property and crime statistics revealed by governmental bodies help them to plot the area and thereby discriminate poor people's livelihood and their residential area go down in value. This technique is majorly used by the sophisticated chain of hotels, airline companies for collection and analyzing the extensive volume of data with regard to rooms, seats that are available, their rates and demand in particular. These findings allow them to make variations in price and availability to increase their profits. These particular environments suggest the consumer's interest to spend towards a necessary service or computational skill. They also dispense with scores that are creditworthy which is definitely based on big data models who have all the necessary data about the person's age, sex, religion, income, race, medical conditions, geographical location and their habit of purchase. At this particular point itself, the consumer is discriminated for better or worse and neatly put under the specific category that is treated differently.

In connection with the law enforcement sector or agencies, big data analysis place and divide the community into various segments and without confirmed knowledge, many correlations and inferences are derived. Racial profiles are created thus to encourage the dark nature of preventive policing. They also raise concerns about civil rights and negative stereotypes are thus perpetuated.

CASE STUDY ANALYSIS

NTT DATA Telecommunication Company Case Study for Big Data Analytics

NTT DATA is a leading national service provider of wireless voice, messaging and data services capable of reaching over hundreds million users. NTT DATA engaged with the customer to upgrade their BI systems and revitalized their architecture to increase BI adoption and user acceptance. Currently supporting the application development for all their BI and Data warehouse systems across platforms

NTT DATA faced many business problems including Lack of Reporting in Finance, logistics and point of sales, Low customer service, Inability to track and capture e-commerce and telesales, Supply & Demand Variations, Outdated system versions, Redundant Data, Too many user security Roles, Lack of better data exchange and collaboration.

Big data Analytics can be improved with Upgrade to BW 7.0 & Revitalize, Migrate to Business Objects XI 3.1, Optimize Data models / Universes, Re-design of security, P.I used to connect POS Bwand 3rd party tools.

After upgrade their system to big data analytics and improved 35% reduction in data models, 70% reduction in user roles, Reduce data redundancy, Single version of truth, Optimized BI Security, BI Standardization, Increase in tele & E-commerce sales by 21% annually, Reduce the effort of online order system by 85%, Store/Article analytics, Event Analytics, Cashier analytics.

ZIONS Bancorporation

Big Data analytics used for security purposes n a recently published case study, Zions Bancorporation announced that it is using Hadoop clusters and business intelligence tools to parse data more quickly than with traditional SIEM tools. In their experience, the quantity of data and the frequency analysis of events are too much for traditional SIEMs to handle alone. In their traditional systems, searching among a month's load of data could take between 20 minutes and an hour. In their new Hadoop system running queries with Hive, they get the same results in about one minute (Mythili & Anandakumar, 2013).

The security data warehouse driving this implementation not only enables users to mine meaningful security information from sources such as firewalls and security devices but also from website traffic, business processes and other day-to-day transactions.

This incorporation of unstructured data and multiple disparate data sets into a single analytical framework is one of the main promises of Big Data.

HP Labs

Routinely Enterprises collect and process terabytes of security-relevant data like networking events, software applications, and action events of people for various reasons. This includes regulatory compliance requirements and post forensic analysis. But drastically, this volume of data becomes extremely overwhelming where these enterprises only store the data, rather do anything useful with this data. An estimate states that HP currently (in 2013) generates 1 trillion events per day or roughly 12 million events per second. This amount will grow as enterprises enable event logging via dynamic sources, hire huge employees, deploy more devices, and run parallel software. Prevailing analytical techniques do not work efficiently at this scale and typically produce so many false positives such that their capability is undermined. This problem becomes even worse as enterprises move towards cloud architectures and collect huge data. This results in deriving less actionable information as more data is being collected (Kamal, Ripon, Dey, Ashour, & Santhi, 2016).

An effort in recent research at HP Labs aims to move towards a scenario where more data leads to better analytics and more actionable information. Algorithms and systems are designed and implemented in order to identify actionable security information from large enterprise data sets and drive false positive rates down to a manageable level. The more the data that is to be collected, the more valuable information can be derived from that data. Despite, many challenges must be overcome to realize the actual capability of Big Data analysis. Among these challenges there prevail privacy, legacy and technical aspects regarding scalable data collection, transport, storage, analysis, and visualization. Despite the challenges, the group at HP Labs has successfully addressed various Big Data analytics for security challenges, some of which are highlighted in this section.

At first, a large-scale graph interpretation was undertaken to identify malware-infected hosts in an enterprise network and the malicious domains accessed each enterprise hosts. A host-domain access system was constructed graphically from large enterprise data sets by adding edges between every host in the enterprise and the domains visited by the host. The graph was then seeded with minimal ground truth information from a black list and a white list, and belief propagation was used to estimate the likelihood that a host or domain is malicious. Experiments over 2 billion HTTP request dataset was collected in this huge enterprise and a 1 billion DNS request data set was collected at an ISP and a 35 billion network intrusion detection system alert data set collected from over 900 enterprises worldwide indicates high true positive rates and low false positive rates can be achieved with minimum amount of truth information that is, having limited data labeled as normal events or attack events used to train anomaly detectors.

CONCLUSION

The imminent value of Big Data Analytics has been proved profoundly as global wide business opportunities have opened up ensuring new future and also thereby assuring a great deal of security too. The knowledge that has been revealed through big data has proven to easily convert into valuable business. Decisions that are highly effectual could be made with the available data analysis techniques and tactical data administration by the corporate organizations. As an emerging data analyst, one should be thoroughly equipped to make use of the three V's (volume, variety, and velocity) and should be updated with the latest and new technologies. Better understanding and implementation of this technology by the higher officials in administration aids in better and effective decision-making process. The future will see the rise of democracy in data analysis and big data will be widely used globally by the entire business organizations. To improve the effectiveness, it is necessary to construct strategies of big data, and paving way for futuristic and new databases. Kick starting powerful merging in the BDM organization, trained staff to follow clarity filled governing model, and to help in making business decisions in connection with the budget of the IT field. Though it is not an entirely new concept to compile, store and analyze the large volume of data, banking and finance industries tend to use algorithms that are complex in nature and many devices to deal with this nature of structured data and derive composite meaning from it. This has helped in the long run for many years so far. But the recent emergence of Big Data Analytics is seen to be replacing these old methods and puts on fresh face to the situation with more productive and effective results.

REFERENCES

Anandakumar, H., & Umamaheswari, K. (2017a). Supervised machine learning techniques in cognitive radio networks during cooperative spectrum handovers. *Cluster Computing*, *20*(2), 1505–1515. doi:10.100710586-017-0798-3

Anandakumar, H., & Umamaheswari, K. (2017b). An Efficient Optimized Handover in Cognitive Radio Networks using Cooperative Spectrum Sensing. *Intelligent Automation & Soft Computing*, 1–8. doi:10 .1080/10798587.2017.1364931

Anandakumar, H., & Umamaheswari, K. (2017c). A bio-inspired swarm intelligence technique for social aware cognitive radio handovers. *Computers & Electrical Engineering*. doi:10.1016/j.compeleceng.2017.09.016

Arulmurugan, R., Sabarmathi, K. R., & Anandakumar, H. (2017). Classification of sentence level sentiment analysis using cloud machine learning techniques. *Cluster Computing*. doi:10.100710586-017-1200-1

Bhatt, C., Dey, N., & Ashour, A. S. (2017). Internet of Things and Big Data Technologies for Next Generation Healthcare. In *Studies in Big Data*. Springer International Publishing.

Chowdhuri, S., Dey, N., Chakraborty, S., & Baneerjee, P. K. (2015). Analysis of Performance of MIMO Ad Hoc Network in Terms of Information Efficiency. In *Advances in Intelligent Systems and Computing* (pp. 43–50). Springer International Publishing; . doi:10.1007/978-3-319-13731-5_6

Elhayatmy, G., Dey, N., & Ashour, A. S. (2017). Internet of Things Based Wireless Body Area Network in Healthcare. In *Studies in Big Data* (pp. 3–20). Springer International Publishing; .

Goswami, S., Roy, P., Dey, N., & Chakraborty, S. (2017). Wireless Body Area Networks Combined with Mobile Cloud Computing in Healthcare. In *Classification and Clustering in Biomedical Signal Processing* (pp. 388–402). IGI Global.

Jiang, Y.-G., & Wang, J. (2016). Partial Copy Detection in Videos: A Benchmark and an Evaluation of Popular Methods. *IEEE Transactions on Big Data*, *2*(1), 32–42. doi:10.1109/TBDATA.2016.2530714

Kamal, S., Ripon, S. H., Dey, N., Ashour, A. S., & Santhi, V. (2016). A MapReduce approach to diminish imbalance parameters for big deoxyribonucleic acid dataset. *Computer Methods and Programs in Biomedicine*, *131*, 191–206. doi:10.1016/j.cmpb.2016.04.005 PMID:27265059

Kaseb, S. A., Mohan, A., Koh, Y., & Lu, Y.-H. (2017). Cloud Resource Management for Analyzing Big Real-Time Visual Data from Network Cameras. *IEEE Transactions on Cloud Computing*, 1–1. doi:10.1109/tcc.2017.2720665

Kimbahune, V. V., Deshpande, A. V., & Mahalle, P. N. (2017). Lightweight Key Management for Adaptive Addressing in Next Generation Internet. *International Journal of Ambient Computing and Intelligence*, *8*(1), 50–69. doi:10.4018/IJACI.2017010103

Lecuyer, M., Spahn, R., Geambasu, R., Huang, T.-K., & Sen, S. (2017). Pyramid: Enhancing Selectivity in Big Data Protection with Count Featurization. *2017 IEEE Symposium on Security and Privacy (SP)*. 10.1109/SP.2017.60

Li, T., Tang, J., & Xu, J. (2016). Performance Modeling and Predictive Scheduling for Distributed Stream Data Processing. *IEEE Transactions on Big Data*, *2*(4), 353–364. doi:10.1109/TBDATA.2016.2616148

Matallah, H., Belalem, G., & Bouamrane, K. (2017). Towards a New Model of Storage and Access to Data in Big Data and Cloud Computing. *International Journal of Ambient Computing and Intelligence*, *8*(4), 31–44. doi:10.4018/IJACI.2017100103

Mukherjee, A., Dey, N., Kausar, N., Ashour, A. S., Taiar, R., & Hassanien, A. E. (2016). A Disaster Management Specific Mobility Model for Flying Ad-hoc Network. *International Journal of Rough Sets and Data Analysis*, *3*(3), 72–103. doi:10.4018/IJRSDA.2016070106

Mythili, K., & Anandakumar, H. (2013). Trust management approach for secure and privacy data access in cloud computing. In *2013 International Conference on Green Computing, Communication and Conservation of Energy (ICGCE)*. IEEE.

Park, G., Chung, L., Khan, L., & Park, S. (2017). A modeling framework for business process reengineering using big data analytics and a goal-orientation. *2017 11th International Conference on Research Challenges in Information Science (RCIS)*. doi:10.1109/rcis.2017.7956514

Schmidt, D., Chen, W.-C., Matheson, M. A., & Ostrouchov, G. (2017). Programming with BIG Data in R: Scaling Analytics from One to Thousands of Nodes. *Big Data Research*, *8*, 1–11. doi:10.1016/j. bdr.2016.10.002

Shamoto, H., Shirahata, K., Drozd, A., Sato, H., & Matsuoka, S. (2016). GPU-Accelerated Large-Scale Distributed Sorting Coping with Device Memory Capacity. *IEEE Transactions on Big Data*, *2*(1), 57–69. doi:10.1109/TBDATA.2015.2511001

Shrivastava, G., & Bhatnagar, V. (2011). Secure Association Rule Mining for Distributed Level Hierarchy in Web. *International Journal on Computer Science and Engineering*, *3*(6), 2240–2244.

Suganya, M., & Anandakumar, H. (2013). Handover based spectrum allocation in cognitive radio networks. *2013 International Conference on Green Computing, Communication and Conservation of Energy (ICGCE)*. 10.1109/ICGCE.2013.6823431

Wu, X., Zhu, X., Wu, G., & Ding, W. (2014). Data mining with big data. *IEEE Transactions on Knowledge and Data Engineering*, *26*(1), 97–107. doi:10.1109/TKDE.2013.109

Xia, F., Liu, H., Lee, I., & Cao, L. (2016). Scientific Article Recommendation: Exploiting Common Author Relations and Historical Preferences. *IEEE Transactions on Big Data*, *2*(2), 101–112. doi:10.1109/ TBDATA.2016.2555318

Yamin, M., & Sen, A. A. A. (2018). Improving Privacy and Security of User Data in Location Based Services. *International Journal of Ambient Computing and Intelligence*, *9*(1), 19–42. doi:10.4018/ IJACI.2018010102

Yang, W., Wang, X., Song, X., Yang, Y., & Patnaik, S. (2018). Design of Intelligent Transportation System Supported by New Generation Wireless Communication Technology. *International Journal of Ambient Computing and Intelligence*, *9*(1), 78–94. doi:10.4018/IJACI.2018010105

Yusuf, I. I., Thomas, I. E., Spichkova, M., & Schmidt, H. W. (2017). Chiminey: Connecting Scientists to HPC, Cloud and Big Data. *Big Data Research*, *8*, 39–49. doi:10.1016/j.bdr.2017.01.004

Zhang, C., Shang, W., Lin, W., Li, Y., & Tan, R. (2017). Opportunities and challenges of TV media in the big data era. *2017 IEEE/ACIS 16th International Conference on Computer and Information Science (ICIS)*. doi:10.1109/icis.2017.7960053

Zong, Z., Ge, R., & Gu, Q. (2017). Marcher: A Heterogeneous System Supporting Energy-Aware High Performance Computing and Big Data Analytics. *Big Data Research*, *8*, 27–38. doi:10.1016/j. bdr.2017.01.003

Chapter 59
Big Data Analytics Adoption Factors in Improving Information Systems Security

Marouane Balmakhtar
Northern Virginia Community College, USA

Scott E. Mensch
Indiana University of Pennsylvania, USA

ABSTRACT

This research measured determinants that influence the willingness of IT/IA professionals to recommend Big Data analytics to improve information systems security in an organization. A review of the literature as well as the works of prior researchers provided the basis for formulation of research questions. Results of this study found that security effectiveness, organizational need, and reliability play a role in the decision to recommend big data analytics to improve information security. This research has implications for both consumers and providers of big data analytics services through the identification of factors that influence IT/IA professionals. These factors aim to improve information systems security, and therefore, which service offerings are likely to meet the needs of these professionals and their organizations.

INTRODUCTION

Organizations rely on information systems to excel in business and in their relevant industries. Hence, proposing strategies and investigating new information systems are not only beneficial for creating healthy business organizations, but also for their long-term existence as solid organizations in the face of evolving security threats. According to Yen et al. (2013), using Big Data analytics helps detect these attacks by aggregating large and diverse datasets from various data sources and by conducting long-term historical correlations to incorporate a posteriori information of an attack in the network's history. Big Data analytics, which is an alternative to other security tools and mechanisms that can be provided on and/off of an organizations' premises, helps information technology/information assurance (IT/IA) professionals

DOI: 10.4018/978-1-6684-3662-2.ch059

tackle many modern threats facing organizations such as ransomware and advanced persistent threats. IT/IA professionals must keep exploring novel means to alleviate and contain sophisticated attackers in the Big Data era which is transforming the landscape of security mechanisms in the perpetual arms race of attack and defense.

Since the 1990s, it has been quite remarkable how fast Big Data analytics has grown (Chen, Chiang & Storey, 2012; Oghuma, 2013; Ramamurthy et al., 2008). Organizations have tried to create a competitive edge through leveraging their source of data in decision making for strategic intelligence purposes (Barney, 1991; Grant, 1996; Halawi, Aronson, & McCarthy, 2005; Bell, 2013). Big Data analytics is used to process multiple data sources of various data sets for the intention of improving problem identification and persuading critical management decision needs (Giura & Wang, 2012). Simply put, as Brynjolfsson, Hitt, and Kim (2011) indicated, organizations that stress decision making based on Big Data analytics have greater overall organizational performance and productivity.

The recent paradigm shift of security attacks against the technology infrastructure requires a serious look at the best possible means of leveraging Big Data analytics for the purpose of enabling security. Security of information has become more of a Big Data analytics problem where huge amounts of data are used to correlate, analyze, and mine information to identify useful patterns for creating knowledge and protecting existing technologies (Gartner, 2012). The big data analytics leverages tools and mathematical models using large amounts of data to improve an organization's technological infrastructure (Raja & Rabbani, 2014).

Security attacks against the technology infrastructure may target any information system in the organization, and without formulating an end-to-end picture of the overall security health of the infrastructure, threats may go undetected over long periods of time (Hurst, Merabti, & Fergus, 2014; Munirathinam & Ramadoss, 2014). This causes a flaw, which results by having a suite of local tools that manage their own specific information systems and the absence of a common repository where data is stored (Al-hyasat & Al-Dalahmeh, 2013; Tankard, 2012). While Big Data analytics continues to gain ground in cyber defense inside many organizations (François et al., 2011; Giura & Wang, 2012; Microsoft, 2014; Ponemon, 2014; Yen et al., 2013), Big Data tools and data management techniques are evolving that can efficiently evaluate security threats while sustaining the volume and velocity of growing information systems data (Gupta & Jyoti; 2014). Big Data analytics is a tool that helps improve business intelligence, but prior research does not show how it can help improve security of an organization's information systems (Evers, 2014; Hawking & Sellitto, 2012; Yeoh & Koronios, 2010). In other words, Big Data analytics, as a source of knowledge to information security professionals, could help improve security of an organization's information systems. Previous research provides a series of examples where economic, modeling and empirical methods are combined to improve security decision making. These include studies of business intelligent decision making (Wieder & Ossimitz, 2013), decision support system for security investment (Beresnevichiene, Pym, & Shiu, 2010), predictive analytics in data mining (Lam, 2014), metadata and data quality perception (Shankaranarayanan, Even, & Watts, 2006), and human and technical factors (Beautement, 2013). But no study actually measures whether Big Data analytics can leverage its analysis to uncover insights from data sources that help discover security patterns and develop actionable insights to secure an organization's information system (Baldwin, Beres, Duggan, Cassa-Mont, Johnson, Middup, Shiu, 2011).

Chen et al. (2012) and Evers (2014) demonstrated that big data analytics is a tool that helps improve business intelligence, but no research exists to validate factors that enable the adoption of big data analytics to help improve an organization's security posture (Alspaugh et al., 2014; Chrun et al., 2008;

Cotroneo, Paudice, & Pecchia, 2016; Evers, 2014; Hawking, 2013; Miani et al., 2012; Yeoh & Koronios, 2010). Multiple other studies used economic modeling and empirical methods to improve the level of security, but none of these studies address the gap as it applies to adopting big data analytics to secure IS (Alaraifi et al., 2012; Da Silva, Chiky, & Hébrail, 2012; Krishnamurthy & Desouza, 2014). This research investigated the factors influencing the adoption of big data analytics to improve IS security.

THEORETICAL FRAMEWORK

An IT/IA professional's willingness to recommend a new technology such as big data analytics in an organization is influenced by a variety of factors. There is a wealth of knowledge documented in adoption theory, organizational decision-making theory, the specifics of big data analytics technology, as well as the role of the IT/IA professionals in influencing the adoption of new technologies.

Figure 1. Theoretical framework of the study

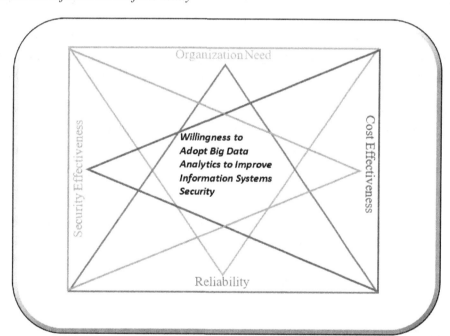

The theoretical framework presents a conceptualization of factors found to influence a willingness to recommend new technologies. This conceptualization uses overlapping triangles to show logical connections and to depict the layers of interconnectedness across the areas of theory as well as the roles of IT/IA professionals. At the center of Figure 1 is the dependent variable: willingness to recommend big data analytics. There are four independent variables: security effectiveness, organizational need, reliability, and cost effectiveness found to influence a willingness to adopt a new technology (Cole, 2008; Comings, 2008; Craig & Hamidi-Noori, 1985; Ettlie, 2000; Gerwin, 1982; Gunn, 1982; Lease, 2005;

Meredith & Hill, 1987; O'Neal, 2015; Putnam, 1987: Roberts & Pick, 2004; Stavinoha, 2013; Ting, 2008; Turek, 2011).

Adoption theory, big data analytics technology, and IT/IA professional role are elements that influence the willingness to recommend and are discussed in detail in the next section. Dynes, Brechbuhl, and Johnson (2005), Fichman (1992), and Johnson and Goetz (2007) suggested that the decision to adopt a technology, particularly IT, is a complex process and that people often rely on IT professionals for their expertise and recommendations when organizations consider adopting new technologies. In the case of big data analytics, it is even more critical to ensure the required expertise and skillset exist within the organization. Davenport et al. (2013) made the case that big data analytics requires creative IT skills.

Although data analysts are always needed in the organization, the required analytics skills are different with big data because these skills require analysts to have a high level of analytical capacities and the ability to bring structure to large quantities of data (Griffin, Scott, & Golden, 2014). Ting (2008) explained that practitioners should be aware that technology adoption is also dependent on the perceived benefit. Practitioners should be prepared to improve perceptions associated with adoption based on security function effectiveness, organizational need, reliability, and cost-effectiveness when introducing new technology. Issues such as lack of IT skillset, large amounts of complex data, and different data formats, increase the likelihood of problems with the level of proposed integration for big data analytics technology in the organization (Davenport et al., 2013; Labrinidis & Jagadish, 2012; Manyika et al., 2011; Ularu et al., 2012). This suggests that the level of integration of big data analytics tools could pose on-going problems, both internally and externally, if an organization has not fully vetted the proposed use of big data analytics in the organization.

This could be a key issue for successful implementation of big data analytics technologies within the organization. Organizational decision makers claim that IT/IA professionals are too focused on financial, organizational, and social consequences to embrace the organizational environment and ensure the mitigation of any foreseeable negative impact to the organization's customer base (Weiss & Anderson, 2003). Decision makers take this perspective because characteristics such as age, educational level, and job tenure of IT/IA professionals have proven to be consistent in the profession (Baase, 2008; Ozturk & Hancer, 2014). When considering the decision to adopt new technology tools or a new technology like big data analytics, Dynes, Brechbuhl, and Johnson (2005), Fichman (1992), and Johnson and Goetz (2007), suggested relying on the expertise and recommendations of IT/IA professionals because their expertise facilitates overall decision making.

EXPERIMENTS

Based on research by Dynes, Brechbuhl, and Johnson, (2005), Fichman (1992), Johnson and Goetz (2007), and prior willingness to adopt technology research by Cole (2008), Comings (2008), Lease (2005), O'Neal (2015), Stavinoha (2013), and Turek (2011), it was deemed relevant to solicit the perceptions of IT/IA professionals on their willingness to adopt Big Data analytics to improve information systems security in the organization. The four independent variables for this research—security effectiveness, organizational need, reliability, and cost effectiveness—were identified by a number of researchers as factors in the decision to adopt a technology (Cole, 2008; Comings, 2008; Craig & Hamidi-Noori, 1985; Lease, 2005, Meredith & Hill, 1987; Putnam, 1987; Roberts & Pick, 2004; Stavinoha, 2013; Ting, 2008; Turek, 2011) and yielded the four research questions posed in this study:

RQ1a: Is IT/IA professional's willingness to recommend Big Data analytics to improve information systems security in the organization dependent of his/her perception of its security effectiveness?

RQ1b: Is IT/IA professional's willingness to recommend Big Data analytics to improve information systems security in the organization dependent of his/her perception of its organizational need?

RQ1c: Is IT/IA professional's willingness to recommend Big Data analytics to improve information systems security in the organization dependent of his/her perception of its reliability?

RQ1d: Is IT/IA professional's willingness to recommend Big Data analytics to improve information systems security in the organization dependent of his/her perception of its cost effectiveness?

To measure the dependent variable – willingness to adopt Big Data analytics to improve information systems security – participants were asked "Would you recommend Big Data analytics to improve information systems security in your organization?" To measure security effectiveness, the participants were asked if they think the use of Big Data analytics to improve information systems security is an effective security solution. To measure organizational need, the participants were asked if they think that Big Data analytics provide a significant benefit to my organization. To measure reliability, the participants were asked if Big Data analytics technologies are more reliable than traditional security technologies. To measure cost-effectiveness, the participants were asked if they think that Big Data analytics technologies provide a good value or good return on investments.

A quantitative method was used to collect and analyze the data to address what factors influence the adoption of Big Data analytics to improve information systems security through a survey. The survey instrument used in this research was comprised 13 questions covering the four constructs of interest (security effectiveness, organizational need, reliability, and cost effectiveness). Relevant hypotheses were derived and tested to measure the Big Data analytics adoption to improve information systems security as a dependent variable. The sampling frame was comprised of 400 IT/IA professionals serving the US telecommunications firm. The questionnaire was structured to capture information about the IT/IA professionals work and experience profile and the factors that influence the adoption of Big Data analytics. Participation was fully voluntary, anonymous and confidential. Before launching the online survey, it was reviewed and pilot tested to guarantee the suitability of wording, style, format and structure. All study constructs were measured using 5-point Likert scale (strongly agree=1 to strongly disagree=5). All the survey instrument questions are listed in Table 1.

SIGNIFICANCE OF THE STUDY

The understanding of the factors that drive Big Data analytics adoption could reveal important information about data and its connection with improving an organization's security posture. This approach is significant because telecommunication organizations' business models are no longer sustainable due to many factors like fierce competition and market saturation. Organizational leaders must think of new and innovative ways to galvanize their existing systems to become smarter and more secure by leveraging technology solutions such as Big Data analytics which could serve to improve the security posture of information systems and create a disruptive innovation in the industry.

The findings also contribute to the growing body of literature in Big Data analytics. The vendors of Big Data analytics technologies may gain from the findings of the study by addressing the shortcomings arising from the use or non-use of the technology. The vendors of the technology may also be interested in the findings of this study as it could motivate them to continue to invest in Big Data analytics technologies to be high in security, quality, and performance.

Table 1. Survey instrument questions

Below are 13 statements about the use of Big Data analytics to improve information systems security. Please indicate if you agree or disagree with each statement by selecting the appropriate number on the scale of 1 (strongly agree) to 5 (strongly disagree) that most closely matches your perception of Big Data analytics to improve information systems security.						
Survey Question #		**Strongly Agree**	**Agree**	**Neutral**	**Disagree**	**Strongly Disagree**
5	Do you think the use of Big Data analytics to improve information systems security is an effective security solution?	1	2	3	4	5
6	Would you be concerned about technology used to improve information systems security (e.g., Hadoop)?	1	2	3	4	5
7	Do you think the use of Big Data analytics to improve information systems security is more effective than other traditional security tools?	1	2	3	4	5
8	Would you recommend Big Data analytics to improve information systems security in your organization?	1	2	3	4	5
9	Big Data analytics technologies are becoming more effective.	1	2	3	4	5
10	Do you think that your organization needs Big Data analytics to secure its Information System assets (e.g., physical and core infrastructure, data, messaging)?	1	2	3	4	5
11	Do you think that Big Data analytics provides a significant benefit to my organization?	1	2	3	4	5
12	Do you think that Big Data analytics to improve information systems security is a reliable solution?	1	2	3	4	5
13	Big Data analytics technologies are more reliable than traditional security technologies (e.g., security information and event management or SIEM, Splunk).	1	2	3	4	5
14	Do you think that Big Data analytics technologies provide a good value or good return on investments?	1	2	3	4	5
15	The Operational Expense (OpEx) is lower with Big Data analytics than the other methods (or tools) for improving information systems security.	1	2	3	4	5
16	Would you consider Big Data analytics technologies to have considerable cost savings over traditional information security tools?	1	2	3	4	5
18	Do you think that Big Data analytics to improve information system security uses a proven technology?	1	2	3	4	5

RESULTS

The overall goal of this research effort is to provide organizational decision makers with improved insight and knowledge for making often-complex security and technology adoption decisions and to understand any factors in allowing Big Data analytics into their organizations. This study examined four facets of an IT/IA professional's willingness to adopt Big Data analytics. It measured the IT/IA professionals' perceptions of the security effectiveness, organizational need, reliability, and cost effectiveness of Big Data analytics and tested four hypotheses.

Table 2 summarizes the descriptive statistics which include the item means and standard deviations. On a 5-point scale, where 1 = strongly agree to 5 = strongly disagree, the means ranged from 1.93 (Item 11, "Do you think that Big Data analytics provide a significant benefit to my organization?") to 2.52 (Item 15, "The Operational Expense (OpEx) is lower with Big Data analytics than the other methods (or tools) for improving information systems security"). Standard deviations ranged from .653 (Item 12, "Do you think that Big Data analytics to improve information systems security is a reliable solution?") to 0.922 (Item 6, "Would you be concerned about technology used to improve information systems security (e.g., Hadoop)?").

Table 2. Means and standard deviations

	S1	S2	S3	S4	D1	N1	N2	R1	R2	V1	V2	V3	R3
Mean	2.07	2.19	2.18	1.95	2.12	2.15	1.93	2.39	2.46	2.23	2.52	2.52	2.33
Standard Deviation	0.694	0.922	0.849	0.715	0.720	0.706	0.758	0.653	0.806	0.734	0.807	0.799	0.781

Table 3 illustrates the inter-item correlations matrix which is an essential component in performing an item analysis of the survey questions. Inter-item correlations evaluate the extent to which scores on one item are related to scores on all other items in a scale. The average inter-item correlation for a set of items should be between .20 and .40, indicating that the items contain satisfactorily unique variance, so they are not considered to be isomorphic with each other (Michalos, 2014). The mean of the inter-item correlations is .310 which adequately falls in the [.20 - .40] range.

Table 3. Inter-item correlation matrix

	S1	S2	S3	D1	S4	N1	N2	R1	R2	V1	V2	V3	R3
S1	1.000	.197	.283	.489	.182	.291	.302	.393	.368	.097	.182	.147	.374
S2	.197	1.000	.373	.256	-.067	.264	.154	.284	.409	.022	.063	.071	.356
S3	.283	.373	1.000	.521	.080	.457	.290	.522	.686	.339	.351	.402	.614
D1	.489	.256	.521	1.000	.231	.542	.346	.524	.512	.250	.341	.262	.498
S4	.182	-.067	.080	.231	1.000	.093	.424	.025	.084	.236	.088	.171	-.008
N1	.291	.264	.457	.542	.093	1.000	.344	.512	.431	.192	.300	.230	.468
N2	.302	.154	.290	.346	.424	.344	1.000	.193	.263	.318	.138	.251	.210
R1	.393	.284	.522	.524	.025	.512	.193	1.000	.578	.144	.323	.321	.634
R2	.368	.409	.686	.512	.084	.431	.263	.578	1.000	.223	.429	.397	.612
V1	.097	.022	.339	.250	.236	.192	.318	.144	.223	1.000	.382	.440	.202
V2	.182	.063	.351	.341	.088	.300	.138	.323	.429	.382	1.000	.643	.383
V3	.147	.071	.402	.262	.171	.230	.251	.321	.397	.440	.643	1.000	.276
R3	.374	.356	.614	.498	-.008	.468	.210	.634	.612	.202	.383	.276	1.000

Hypothesis testing using the One-way ANOVA and Chi-Square tests of independence was undertaken to evaluate the research questions. Both One-way ANOVA and Chi-Square testing rejected the null hypothesis in all four cases. Table 4 provides the results of hypothesis testing for this research and indicates H1, H2, H3, and H4 are dependent, with the null hypothesis rejected, with the support of the data collected ($n = 151$, $p \leq .05$). The data indicates that an IT/IA professional's decision to recommend Big Data analytics to improve information systems security is dependent on his/her perception of its security effectiveness, reliability, cost effectiveness, and organizational need.

Table 4. Hypothesis results

Hypothesis 1	Rejected	H01 NULL: There is no significant IT/IA professional's willingness to recommend Big Data analytics to improve information systems security in the organization is independent of his/her perception of its security effectiveness.
	Accepted	HA1 ALTERNATIVE: There is a significant IT/IA professional's willingness to recommend Big Data analytics to improve information systems security in the organization is dependent of his/her perception of its security effectiveness.
Hypothesis 2	Rejected	H02 NULL: There is no significant IT/IA professional's willingness to recommend Big Data analytics to improve information systems security in the organization is independent of his/her perception of its organizational need.
	Accepted	HA2 ALTERNATIVE: There is a significant IT/IA professional's willingness to recommend Big Data analytics to improve information systems security in the organization is dependent of his/her perception of its organizational need.
Hypothesis 3	Rejected	H03 NULL: There is no significant IT/IA professional's willingness to recommend Big Data analytics to improve information systems security in the organization is independent of his/her perception of its reliability.
	Accepted	HA3 ALTERNATIVE: There is a significant IT/IA professional's willingness to recommend Big Data analytics to improve information systems security in the organization is dependent of his/her perception of its reliability.
Hypothesis 4	Rejected	H04 NULL: There is no significant IT/IA professional's willingness to recommend Big Data analytics to improve information systems security in the organization is independent of his/her perception of its cost effectiveness.
	Accepted	HA4 ALTERNATIVE: There is a significant IT/IA professional's willingness to recommend Big Data analytics to improve information systems security in the organization is dependent of his/her perception of its cost effectiveness.

As shown in Table 5, Spearman's Rho was used to examine the strength of relationships between the independent and dependent variables. Spearman's Rho was selected because it is suitable for indicating the magnitude of a relationship between ordinal level variables. Pearson's Product Moment Correlation showed that the strongest relationships between dependent and independent variables were, ascending direction, cost effectiveness ($r=.355$), organizational need ($r=.368$), reliability ($r=.498$), and security effectiveness ($r=.525$). All of the relationships were statistically significant ($n = 151$, $p =.001$).

Regression analysis was used to test the relationship between the dimensions of security effectiveness, organizational need, reliability, and cost effectiveness on the adoption of Big Data analytics to improve information systems security. The regression model involved security effectiveness, organizational need, reliability, and cost effectiveness as independent variables and adoption of willingness to adopt Big Data analytics to improve information systems security as the dependent variable. From regression in Table 6, the coefficient of $R^2 = .407$ indicates that all the independent variables account for 40.7% of the variance in adoption of Big Data analytics to improve information systems security. The independent variables statistically significantly predicted willingness to adopt Big Data analytics to improve information systems security, $F(4, 146) = 25.024$, $p < .0005$, $R^2 = .407$. All four variables added statistically significantly to the prediction, $p < .05$.

Table 5. Dependent and independent variables correlations

			D1
Spearman's Rho	D1	Correlation Coefficient	1.000
		Sig. (2-tailed)	.
		N	151
	S3	Correlation Coefficient	.525*
		Sig. (2-tailed)	.000
		N	151
	N2	Correlation Coefficient	.368*
		Sig. (2-tailed)	.000
		N	151
	R1	Correlation Coefficient	.498*
		Sig. (2-tailed)	.000
		N	151
	V2	Correlation Coefficient	-.355*
		Sig. (2-tailed)	.000
		N	151

Table 6. Multiple regression analysis results

Model	R	R Square	Adjusted R Square	Std. Error of the Estimate	R Square Change	F Change	df1	df2	Sig.
1	.638[a]	.407	.390	.562	.407	25.024	4	146	.000

a. Predictors: (Constant), V2, N3, R1, S3
b. Dependent Variable: D1

Both hypothesis testing and regression analysis showed the willingness of IT/IA professionals to recommend Big Data analytics to improve information systems security is dependent on their perception of its security effectiveness, reliability, organization need, and cost effectiveness. The results in this study align with those of previous researchers and direction in the literature, as previously cited, in noting the influence of the four independent variables in the decision to adopt a technology to improve information systems security.

Additional supplemental analysis of management participants was performed. A total of 20 (14.1%) survey participants identified themselves as being in an IT/IA management role and additional analysis was performed on this subset of data. The mean of 2.00 was slightly lower than that for the entire sample (2.12) and the percentage of this segment who both strongly agreed and agreed with the dependent variable, "Would you recommend Big Data analytics to improve information systems security in my organization?" was higher at 80.0% than the percentage of the entire sample (70.2%) (see Figure 2). The management portion of the sample appeared marginally more committed to adopting Big Data analytics to improve information systems security in the organization than the sample as a whole.

Figure 2. Management vs. Non-management role, willingness to adopt big data analytic to improve information systems security

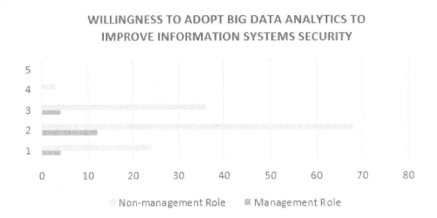

Due to the immaturity of this field of knowledge, three supplemental questions were included, in addition to the previously discussed questions, to explore aspects of Big Data analytics technologies that are thought to contribute to the adoption of technology innovation within traditional IT environments (see Table 7). One question "Would you consider using Big Data analytics to improve information systems security in your organization?" forms additional inquiry of IT/IA professionals based on a 5-point Likert scale of strongly agree, agree, neutral, disagree, and strongly disagree. This question revolved around trying to understand the importance of using Big Data analytics as a security solution in the organization. The other supplemental question "Is your organization a provider or user of any Big Data analytics products or services?" focused on the organization analytics background and its level of involvement related to Big Data analytics technologies. The last supplemental question "If Big Data analytics was not an option to improve information systems security, I would…" is presented to help IT/IA professionals identify an alternative security option to Big Data analytics.

Taking this opportunity to inquire with IT/IA Professionals more intimately about their personal knowledge and/or usage of Big Data analytics and information systems security, this research seeks to expand on thoughts gained from conducting the *a priori* research, as well as to extrapolate the current conditions within organizations. Concerning Big Data analytics, this research seeks to build further on the information assurance field of knowledge, as well as understand possible lags in official early adoption and/or gaps presently within organizations.

The supplemental questions (S5, O1, and P1) revolved around additional aspects of Big Data analytics. This section provides a detailed analysis of these supplemental questions and discusses their possible implications. S5 focused on the use of Big Data analytics in the organizations. P1 identified whether the organization is a user of Big Data analytics or not. O1 examined the different options to Big Data analytics.

Table 7. Supplemental questions

Question	Code	Answer	Numeric Value
Would you consider using Big Data analytics to improve information system security in your organization?	S5	Strongly Agree	1
		Agree	2
		Neutral	3
		Disagree	4
		Strongly Disagree	5
Is your organization a provider or user of any Big Data analytics products or services?	P1	Yes	1
		No	2
If Big Data analytics was not an option to improve information systems security, I would…	O1	Rely on using existing traditional security tools to improve information systems security.	1
		Rely on using existing traditional security tools to improve information systems security.	2
		Rely on the contract with the vendors to ensure they supply better security products.	3

Item 17 (S5) in the survey asked respondents the use of Big Data analytics to improve information systems security. Table 8 shows the One-Way ANOVA results associated with this question. The p-value was less than .05 which indicates significance and that there is a relationship between the dependent variable, "Would you recommend Big Data analytics to improve information systems security in my organization?" and the potential use (or familiarity level) of Big Data analytics as a potential independent variable. Therefore, the respondents' perception of the use of Big Data analytics is dependent upon their willingness to adopt Big Data analytics technologies in their organization.

Table 8. One way ANOVA for big data analytics use

ANOVA Table					
Source	*DF*	*SS*	*MS*	*F*	*p-value*
(S5) Would you consider using Big Data analytics to improve information system security in your organization?					
Factor	3	21.030	7.010	28.279	0.000
Error	138	34.209	.248		
Total	141	55.239			

Item 2 (P1) in the survey asked respondents whether their organization is a user or provider of Big Data analytics to gauge their initial familiarity with the concept of Big Data analytics. The vast majority of respondents (90.1%) indicated that they belong to an organization that either uses or provides some aspect of Big Data analytics. This further strengthens the relevance of the selected sample population which is paramount to gaining pertinent insights in the area of Big Data analytics. Only 9.9% of the respondents indicated they do not use or provide Big Data analytics within their organizations.

Item 19 (O1) in the survey asked respondents to select a course of action if Big Data analytics was not available as an option to improve information systems security in the organization. The majority of respondents (62.3%) indicated that they would implement more security tools to improve information systems security if Big Data analytics was not an option to secure information systems, while the next highest percentage of respondents (29.1%) replied that existing traditional security tools would be relied upon if Big Data analytics was not available. Only 8.6% of respondents felt that technology vendors must do better to ensure improved security products if Big Data analytics was not available. Figure 3 shows the details.

Figure 3. Big data analytics alternative options – item 19 survey results

In addition to analyzing each of the supplemental questions separately as discussed above, a collective analysis of these questions was also conducted. A similarity matrix that can be accounted for by computing the correlation between two vectors of values as a measure of similarity (i.e., high correlation coefficients indicate a high degree of similarity) was performed on the willingness to recommend Big Data analytics (D1) and the supplemental questions to determine if there was any correlation between use of Big Data analytics (S5), being a user or provider of Big Data analytics (P1), and the alternative selected (O1) if Big Data analytics was not an available option. As can be seen in Table 9, all measures of similarity values in the similarity matrix between the dependent variable (D1) and the two supplemental questions "Is your organization a provider or user of any Big Data analytics products or services?" and "If Big Data analytics was not an option to improve information systems security, I would…", were low which indicate a low degree of similarity between the willingness to recommend Big Data analytics to improve information systems security and being a user or provider of Big Data analytics, and between the willingness to recommend Big Data analytics to improve information systems security and regardless what Big Data analytics alternative option was selected. The only measure of similarity that was high

(.603) in the similarity matrix included the dependent variable and the supplemental question "Would you consider using Big Data analytics to improve information systems security in your organization?" which indicate a high degree of similarity between the willingness to recommend Big Data analytics to improve information systems security and the use of Big Data analytics.

Table 9. Similarity matrix for dependent variable and supplemental questions

	O1	P1	S5	D1
O1	1.000	0.03	-.277	-.339
P1	.003	1.000	.235	.253
S5	-.277	0.235	1.000	.571
D1	-.339	.253	.571	1.000

Patil and Seshadri (2014), Oltsik (2013), Srivastava and Venkatesh (2015) stated that organizations need to use Big Data analytics to a certain extent regardless of whether or not they adopt Big Data analytics within their organization. Now, while the use of Big Data analytics was not a specific focus of this research, in conducting the research the supplemental questions presented immediate interest. Thus, these questions were provided to the research sample in addition to the *a priori* questions at the core of this research. Supplemental questions, as presented previously in Table 7, provided an opportunity for IT/IA Professionals to expand on their perceptions, knowledge, and use of Big Data analytics.

While researchers have voiced opinions about the importance of using Big Data analytics within organizations, this research shows that organizations' staff is generally familiar with Big Data analytics. Dynes, Brechbuhl, and Johnson (2005), Fichman (1992), and Johnson and Goetz (2007) contended that IT/IA professionals are often relied upon for their expertise and recommendations when organizations consider adopting new technology solutions. In association with Big Data analytics use, this research has shown that IT/IA professionals are aware of its use (supplemental analysis). Although the use of Big Data analytics is important, IT/IA professionals may consider having appropriate processes in place to provide assistance with technology decision making based on Big Data analytics itself. This perception may stem from the aspects of organizational benefit that Big Data analytics brings to bear. For example, Big Data analytics can identify insights for instantaneous technology decisions which enable IT/IA professionals to have a competitive edge that they did not have before to improve their information systems security in the organization. This would potentially be biased based on the common notion of Big Data analytics hype. This is an area in need of research and brief discussion will take place within the recommendation for further research section.

CONCLUSION AND RECOMMENDATIONS

This research provides insight in the factors affecting the adoption process of Big Data analytics to improve information systems security in the organization. The perception of IT/IA professionals' willingness to recommend Big Data analytics to improve information systems security is dependent on security effectiveness, organizational need, reliability, and cost effectiveness. The information provided in this research is valuable to both those considering the use of Big Data analytics as well as those developing and/or providing Big Data analytics products and services. Big Data analytics is an often-recommended solution in which IT/IA professionals have years of experience and a large percentage of those professionals will implement more security tools if Big Data analytics is not an option to improve information systems security. This is why it is significant that the adoption of Big Data analytics is being researched; only awareness of both possibilities and current practices creates the ability to steer these technological expansions in a positive direction for improving the cyber security posture.

Big Data analytics can be incorporated into a holistic organization policy or framework for development and integration. Big Data analytics can shape the development of sustainable strategies by organizations in safeguarding information systems security which can further increase its adoption amongst IT/IA professionals. Furthermore, organizations are encouraged to make Big Data analytics an integral part of their security technology offerings to remain safe in the wake of complex security threats. IT/IA professionals are encouraged to maximize the use of Big Data analytics where and when it makes sense throughout the organization. In particular, Big Data analytics systems must be developed to integrate flawlessly with the existing IT systems to ensure end to end visibility of the IT infrastructure. The recommendations when Big Data analytics is leveraged can improve uptake tremendously and help fill in the security gaps in the organization.

REFERENCES

Alaraifi, A., Molla, A., & Deng, H. (2012). An exploration of data center information systems. *Journal of Systems and Information Technology*, *14*(4), 353–370. doi:10.1108/13287261211279080

Alhyasat, E. B., & Al-Dalahmeh, M. (2013). Data warehouse success and strategic oriented business intelligence: A theoretical framework. *Journal of Management Research*, *5*(3), 169–184. doi:10.5296/jmr.v5i3.3703

Baase, S. (2008). *A gift of fire: Social, legal, and ethical issues for computing and the internet* (3rd ed.). Upper Saddle River, NJ: Prentice Hall.

Baldwin, A., Beres, Y., Duggan, G. B., Mont, M. C., Johnson, H., Middup, C., & Shiu, S. (2013). Economic methods and decision making by security professionals. In *Economics of Information Security and Privacy III* (pp. 213–238). Springer.

Balmakhtar, M. (2017). *Determinants influencing the adoption of big data analytic to improve information systems security – A Quantitative Study*. Unpublished doctoral dissertation, University of Fairfax, Roanoke, VA.

Barney, J. (1991). Firm Resources and Sustained Competitive Advantage. *Journal of Management*, *17*(1), 99–120. doi:10.1177/014920639101700108

Beautement, A. (2013). *Optimising Information Security Decision Making* [Doctor of Philosophy dissertation]. University of London.

Bell, P. (2013). Creating competitive advantage using big data. *Ivey Business Journal*. Retrieved from http://iveybusinessjournal.com

Beresnevichiene, Y., Pym, D., & Shiu, S. (2010). Decision support for systems security investment. *Proceedings of the Network Operations and Management Symposium Workshops (NOMS Wksps) IEEE/IFIP* (pp. 118-125). Academic Press. 10.1109/NOMSW.2010.5486590

Brynjolfsson, E., Hitt, L., & Kim, H. (2011). Strength in numbers: How does data-driven decision making affect firm performance? doi:10.2139/ssrn.1819486

Chen, H., Chiang, R. H. L., & Storey, V. C. (2012). Business intelligence and analytics: From big data to big impact. *Management Information Systems Quarterly*, *36*(4), 1165–1188. doi:10.2307/41703503

Chrun, D., & Cukier, M., & Sneeringer. (2008). Finding corrupted computers using imperfect intrusion prevention system event data. *Proceedings of the 27th international conference on computer safety, reliability, and security* (pp. 221-234). Academic Press. 10.1007/978-3-540-87698-4_20

Cole, S. (2008). *Adopting biometrics: Factors that influence decision making managers.* Unpublished Doctoral dissertation, University of Fairfax, Vienna, Virginia.

Comings, D. (2008). *Factors influencing the development of COTS information security products that meet federal requirements for national security systems.* Unpublished Doctoral dissertation, University of Fairfax, Vienna, VA.

Cotroneo, D., Paudice, A., & Pecchia, A. (2016). Automated root cause identification of security alerts. *Journal Future Generation Computer Systems*, *56*(C), 375–387. doi:10.1016/j.future.2015.09.009

Craig, R., & Hamidi-Noori, A. (1985). Recognition and use of automation: A comparison of small and large organizations. *Journal of Small Business and Entrepreneurship*, *3*(1), 37–44. doi:10.1080/08276331.1985.10600221

Da Silva, A., Chiky, R., & Hébrail, G. (2012). A clustering approach for sampling data streams in sensor networks. *Knowledge and Information Systems*, *32*(1), 1–23. doi:10.100710115-011-0448-7

Davenport, T.H. (2013). Big data in big companies. SAS. Retrieved from http://www.sas.com/resources/asset/Big-Data-in-Big-Companies.pdf

Dynes, S., Brechbuhl, H., & Johnson, M. E. (2005). *Information security in the extended enterprise: Some initial results from a field study of an industrial firm.* Infosecon. Retrieved from http://infosecon.net/workshop/pdf/51.pdf

Ettlie, J. E. (2000). *Managing technological innovation.* New York, NY: John Wiley & Sons.

Evers, J. M. (2014). *Critical success factors of business intelligence and big data analysis: Utilizing hidden business value from big data for business intelligence* [Master thesis]. Tillburg University.

Fichman, R. (1992). Information technology diffusion: A review of empirical research. In J.I. DeGross, J.D. Becker, & J.J. Elam (Eds.), *ICIS '92 Proceedings of the Thirteenth International Conference on Information Systems* (pp. 195-206). Minneapolis, MN: University of Minnesota.

Francois, J., Wang, S., Bronzi, W., State, R., & Engel, T. (2011, November). Botcloud: Detecting botnets using mapreduce. *Proceedings of the 2011 IEEE International Workshop on Information Forensics and Security* (pp. 1-6). IEEE.

Gartner. (2012). Information security is becoming a big data analytic problem. Retrieved from https://www.gartner.com/doc/1960615

Gerwin, D. (1982). Do's and don'ts of computerized manufacturing. *Harvard Business Review, 60*(2), 107–116.

Giura, P., & Wang, W. (2012). Using large scale distributed computing to unveil advanced persistent threats. *Science Journal, 1*(3), 93–105.

Grant, R. M. (1996). Toward a Knowledge-Based Theory of the Firm. *Strategic Management Journal, 17*(Special Issue), 109–122. doi:10.1002mj.4250171110

Griffin, C. R., Scott, M., & Golden, W. (2014). Exploring factors that influence the knowledge worker in a business environment. Retrieved from https://dss20conference.files.wordpress.com/2014/05/phd_consortium_coleen.pdf

Gunn, T. G. (1982). The mechanization of design and manufacturing. *Scientific American, 247*(3), 114–130. doi:10.1038cientificamerican0982-114

Gupta, B., & Jyoti, K. (2014). Big Data analytics with Hadoop to analyze Targeted Attacks on Enterprise Data. *International Journal of Computer Science and Information Technologies, 5*(3), 3867–3870.

Halawi, L., Aronson, J., & McCarthy, R. (2005). Resource-Based View of Knowledge Management for Competitive Advantage. *Electronic Journal of Knowledge Management, 3*(2), 75–86.

Hawking, P. (2013). *Factors critical to the success of business intelligence systems* [Doctoral dissertation]. Victoria University.

Hawking, P., & Sellitto, C. (2010). Business Intelligence (BI) Critical Success Factors. *ACIS 2010 Proceedings*. Academic Press. Retrieved from http://aisle.aisnet.org/acis2010/4

Hurst, W., Merabti, M., & Fergus, P. (2014). Big data analysis techniques for cyber-threat detection in critical infrastructures. In *Advanced Information Networking and Applications Workshops (WAINA)* (pp. 916-921). Academic Press. doi:10.1109/WAINA.2014.141

Johnson, M. E., & Goetz, E. (2007). Embedding information security into the organization. *IEEE Security and Privacy, 5*(3), 16–24. doi:10.1109/MSP.2007.59

Krishnamurthy, R., & Desouza, K. C. (2014). Big data analytics: The case of the social security administration. *Information Polity: The International Journal of Government & Democracy in the Information Age, 19*(3/4), 165–178. doi:10.3233/IP-140337

Labrinidis, A., & Jagadish, H. V. (2012). Challenges and opportunities with big data. *Proceedings of the VLDB Endowment International Conference on Very Large Data Bases, 5*(12), 2032–2033. doi:10.14778/2367502.2367572

Lam, D. W. H. (2014). *A survey of predictive analytics in data mining with big data* [Masters thesis]. Athabasca University. Retrieved from http://library.athabascau.ca/ThesesDissertations.html

Lease, D. R. (2005). *Factors influencing the adoption of biometric security technologies by decision making information technology and security managers* [Doctoral dissertation]. Capella University.

Manyika, J., Chui, M., Brown, B., Bughin, J., Dobbs, R., Roxburgh, C., & Byres, A. H. (2011). *Big data: The next frontier for innovation, competition, and productivity*. Washington, DC: McKinsey Global Institute.

Meredith, J. R., & Hill, M. M. (1987). Justifying new manufacturing systems: A managerial approach. *Sloan Management Review, 28*(4), 49–61.

Miani, R. S., Cukier, M., Zarpelao, B. B., Breda, G. D., & Mendes, L. D. (2012). An empirical study of connections between measurements and information security. In *SECURWARE 2012: The Sixth International Conference on Emerging Security Information, Systems, and Technologies*. Academic Press. Retrieved from https://www.thinkmind.org/download.php?articleid=securware_2012_4_40_30118

Microsoft. (2014). Enhancing Cybersecurity with Big Data: Challenges & Opportunities. Ponemon Institute LLC. Retrieved from http://download.microsoft.com

Munirathinam, A., & Ramadoss, B. (2014). Big data predictive analytics for proactive semiconductor equipment maintenance. *Proceedings of the 2014 IEEE International Conference on Big Data* (pp. 893-902). IEEE Press. 10.1109/BigData.2014.7004320

O'Neal, A. (2015). *Critical factors affecting the adoption of "bring your own device" computing environments: A big data analytics adoption and implementation*. Unpublished doctoral dissertation, University of Fairfax, Vienna, VA.

Oghuma, P. (2013). Big data analytics adoption in telecommunications industry: The Korean telcos perspectives. *Proceedings of the 33rd Annual International Symposium on Forecasting*, KAIST College of Business Seoul, South Korea. Academic Press.

Oltsik, J. (2013). Defining big data security analytics. Network world. Retrieved from http://www.networkworld.com/article/2224394/cisco-subnet/defining-big-data-security-analytics.html

Ozturk, A. B., & Hancer, M. (2014). Hotel and IT decision-maker characteristics and information technology adoption relationship in the hotel industry. *Journal of Hospitality and Tourism Technology, 5*(2). doi:10.1108/JHTT-12-2013-0038

Patil, H. K., & Seshadri, R. (2014). Big data security and privacy issues in healthcare. *Proceedings of the 2014 IEEE International Congress on Data (Big Data Congress)* (pp. 762-765). IEEE Press. doi:10.1109/BigData.Congress.2014.112

Ponemon. (2014). Big data analytics in cyber defense. Retrieved from http://www.ponemon.org/local/upload/file/Big_Data_Analytics_in_Cyber_Defense_V12.pdf

Putnam, R. G. (1987). Selling modernization within your company. *Commline*, 13.

Ramamurthy, K. R., Sen, A., & Sinha, A. P. (2008). An Empirical Investigation of the Key Determinants of Data Warehouse Adoption. *Decision Support Systems, 44*(4), 817–841. doi:10.1016/j.dss.2007.10.006

Roberts, G., & Pick, J. (2004). Technology factors in corporate adoption of mobile cell phones: A case study analysis. *Proceedings of the 37th Annual Hawaii International Conference on System Sciences (HICSS'04)*. Academic Press. 10.1109/HICSS.2004.1265678

Shankaranarayanan, G., Even, A., & Watts, S. (2006). The Role of Process Metadata and Data Quality Perceptions in Decision Making: An Empirical Framework and Investigation. *Journal of Information Technology Management*. Retrieved from http://hadjarian.org/e_IT_Management/article19.pdf

Srivastava, A., & Venkatesh, K. (2015). Employing big data for cyber attacks analysis. *International Journal of Science and Research*, 1476-1478. Retrieved from http://www.ijsr.net/archive/v4i3/SUB152398.pdf

Stavinoha, K. E. (2013). Factors influencing adoption of encryption to secure data in the cloud. In *Human aspects of information security, privacy, and trust*. Berlin: Springer. doi:10.1007/978-3-642-39345-7_38

Tankard, C. (2012). Big data security. *Network Security, 2012*(7), 5–8. doi:10.1016/S1353-4858(12)70063-6

Ting, W. (2008). *Factors influencing the adoption of enterprise wide information security metrics by decision making managers*. Unpublished doctoral dissertation, University of Fairfax, Vienna, VA.

Turek, J. (2011). *Factors that influence security executives to recommend unified threat management*. Unpublished doctoral dissertation, University of Fairfax, Vienna, VA.

Ularu, E. G., Puican, F. C., Apostu, A., & Velicanu, M. (2012). Perspectives on big data and big data analytics. *Database Systems Journal, 3*, 3–14.

Weiss, J. W., & Anderson, D. (2003). CIOs and IT professionals as change agents, risk and stakeholder managers: A field study. *Proceedings of the 36th Annual Hawaii International Conference on System Sciences*. Academic Press. 10.1109/HICSS.2003.1174639

Wieder, B., & Ossimitz, M. (2013). Managing business intelligence for success: Factors and mechanisms. *Proceedings of the International Conference on Management and Information Systems*. Academic Press.

Yen, T.-F., Oprea, A., Onarlioglu, K., Leetham, T., Juels, A., Kirda, E., & Robertson, W. (2013). Beehive: Large-scale log analysis for detecting suspicious activity in enterprise networks. *Proceedings of the Annual Computer Security Applications Conference*. Academic Press. 10.1145/2523649.2523670

Yeoh, W., & Koronios, A. (2010). Critical Success factors for business intelligence systems. *Journal of Computer Information Systems, 50*(3), 23–32.

This research was previously published in the International Journal of Strategic Information Technology and Applications (IJSITA), 10(3); pages 1-21, copyright year 2019 by IGI Publishing (an imprint of IGI Global).

Chapter 60
Big Data and Global Software Engineering

Ramgopal Kashyap
https://orcid.org/0000-0002-5352-1286
Amity University, Raipur, India

ABSTRACT

A large vault of terabytes of information created every day from present-day data frameworks and digital innovations, for example, the internet of things and distributed computing. Investigation of this enormous information requires a ton of endeavors at different dimensions to separate learning for central leadership. An examination is an ebb-and-flow territory of innovative work. The fundamental goal of this paper is to investigate the potential effect of enormous information challenges, open research issues, and different instruments related to it. Subsequently, this article gives a stage to study big data at various stages. It opens another skyline for analysts to build up the arrangement in light of the difficulties, and open research issues. The article comprehended that each large information stage has its core interest. Some of this is intended for bunch handling while some are great at constant scientific. Each large information stage likewise has explicit usefulness. Unique procedures were utilized for the investigation.

INTRODUCTION

The world has changed into information society that very relies upon data. Since information structures make proportions of records every day, reliably, it shows up the world is accomplishing the dimension of data overweight. It is apparent now that remembering the real objective to process such volumes of data an enormous limit required in regards to amassing and figuring resources. Even though the improvement of limit confined by the headway of hardware and advances getting progressively specific, nowadays various affiliations have grasped and widely use information structures running on mechanical stages, various their inspiration has pushed toward acquiring to be subject to data. In the built-up affiliation's evidence explicitly impact the justification of business shapes; information has transformed into a focal point of their business or business end. Along these lines, the business asks for the data, other than

DOI: 10.4018/978-1-6684-3662-2.ch060

the availability of specific data specifically time. Progressively unusual likewise, unsafe fundamental administration process relies upon rightness and straightforwardness of data.

Motivation

Interesting driver related to this subject says that the advancement of data is limitless. What is the overall population going to do about the data overweight? The best strategy to manage and moreover to process all the data? It seems like we are having an enormous information issue. Another driver for this subject is recuperating the information not to collect all data for further examination. Among all of the data, how to recover the appropriate information and inside a required time? Which test should associate with data? What is the agreement between the expense of recuperation and estimation of that information? What are the costs of capacity to recuperate needed information? It seems like it is about the advantage, the trade-off between the opinion of the information, what's more, the expense to get it. Besides the two drivers, the test is to picture the information to such an extent that its regard is expansive and legitimate. The essential issue is the information overweight. Examination in the ordinary mode, to the area the enormous information, is anchoring data that might require for consideration. All need an original point of view, the other methodology, structure or system, accepting any. The unrivaled examination is one of them. Grasping new advancements requires processing, finding and separating these large instructive lists that can't be overseen using traditional databases and models were given the nonattendance of limit resources to the extent computation and limit. Tip top examination addresses one of the creative techniques that can associate with the extending volumes, speed, and collection of data.

Goals

Colossal information wonder, which is portrayed by brisk advancement of volume, combination, and speed of data information assets, thrives the adjustment in the context in logical data getting ready. Superior Analytics can be one of the philosophies. The purpose of the hypothesis is an investigation layout, request, and chats on issues and challenges on the initiating state of a forte of forefront examination utilizing different procedures HPA strategies that could raise and enhance the count execution of the test.

Outcome

The degree of the hypothesis resolved to research and procedures of extensive information and superior Analytics. Speculative bit of the theory is an aftereffect of finish examine that shortens a state of craftsmanship graph for this issue, describes the drivers and consequences of huge information marvel, and gives approaches for managing great information, in explicit methodology in perspective of High-Performance Analytics. Especially the aftereffect of the examination arranged on an audit of HPA, request, characteristics and central purposes of a specific procedure for HPA utilizing the distinctive blend of system resources. A useful bit of the proposition is an aftereffect of exploratory errand that joins illustrative getting ready of the large dataset using insightful stage from SAS Institute. The investigation displays sound taking care of for particular HPA systems that discussed in speculative part. One a player in the examination consolidates shaping different consistent circumstances on which the inclinations and settlement of HPA organize are delineated.

PROBLEM IDENTIFICATION AND SUMMARY

As said in the introduction a fundamental issue of this hypothesis is data, data getting ready, removing information and stuff around it. Let us initially start with the general methodology of matter.

Theoretical Problem

The data volume addresses a test everything considered, not just like that, should be put inside a set. The open data like customer data in their business setting that creates in all estimations are point by point in portions later, and the associated data with explanatory and execution limit (Kuner, Cate, Millard and Svantesson, 2012), outlined in Figure 1.

Figure 1. The information volume challenge

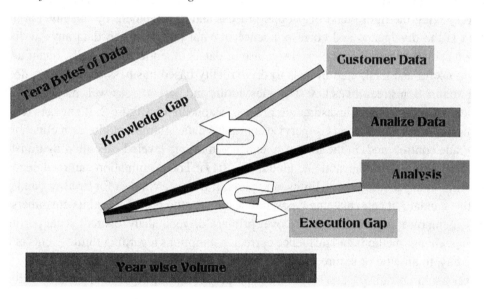

Pondering the authentic examples, when all of the lines are building up, the openness of data has overburdened ability to separate data examination, and what's more a capacity to use the investigation either to run inspection or store investigation enlisting and limit. A data opening conveys the weakness to separate data given the limited interpretive techniques may fuse data mining computations, trademark tongue taking care of, etc., e.g., pushed feeling examination of printed comments of online life (Hassani-Mahmooei, Berecki-Gisolf, and Collie, 2017). An execution opening imparts inability to utilize inspection as a result of the confined openness of advantages may fuse taking care of units, data reserves, etc. for the requested period, e.g., undertaking to process the throughout the step by step trade at a bank in the required design of the clearinghouse over one night.

Where Is the Issue?

While an execution limits the extent that gear is creating at a stable rate, data volumes are growing exponentially. Along these lines, the learning gap is getting progressively broad, and the domain of the lost information openings in a set of available data containing the information noteworthy as to the information needs. The fact of the matter is to support the course of action of essential data that possibly includes the gainful information. Henceforth, the volume and availability of data are not an issue rather than the getting ready and relationship of data.

Enormous Information and Examination

Colossal data poses the two openings and troubles for associations to remove regard from extensive data, it must be arranged and inspected advantageously, and the results require being available to have the ability to affect positive change or affect business decisions. The ampleness furthermore relies upon an affiliation having the right blend of people, process and development by unadulterated definition, examination is the divulgence and correspondence of vital precedents in data anyway for business, consideration should e viewed as the extensive use of data, authentic additionally, quantitative examination, using useful and farsighted models to drive reality-based business organization decisions and exercises. Examination streamlines key strategies, limits and parts it very well may be used to add up to both inside and external data investigation process is appeared in figure 2. It engages relationship to meet accomplice declaring demands, supervise enormous data volumes, publicize inclinations, regulate danger, upgrade controls and, in the long run, enhance multiple leveled execution by transforming information into learning (Ahmadvand and Goudarzi, 2017). The examination can recognize innovative open entryways in key methodology, limits, and parts. It makes a catalyst for headway and change and by testing the standard; it can create new possible results for the business and its customers. Propelled strategies can empower associations to discover primary drivers, analyze small-scale portions of their business areas, change methods and influence correct assumptions regarding future events or customers' tendency to buy, to unsettle or secure.

It is never again enough for associations to appreciate current process or errands with a view on upgrading what starting at now exists when there is by and by the capacity to address if a procedure is material to the business, or whether there is another strategy for handling a specific issue. The key driver for improvement inside affiliations is to test existing practices rather than dependably recognizing the equivalent ceaselessly. Most associations have many-sided and partitioned structure scenes that make the substantial similarity and dispersing of data troublesome. The critical objective of picture division is to fragment the data picture into critical non-covering districts areas for help examination or observation. There is an arrangement of philosophies keeping an eye on this endeavor, abusing different picture properties to achieve the given goal (Kashyap and Gautam, 2017a). They cross from low-level strategies using power limits, edge following or region creating, over outline based and quantifiable procedures, to demonstrate based computations additionally, other increasingly lifted sum systems. The blend based game plan has Tbeen introduced, where the last bundle is molded using a mix of eventual outcomes of a couple of division methods and like this quelling their insufficiencies (Kashyap, Gautam and Tiwari, 2018). Notwithstanding the dependable push to develop incredible division estimations, there has not been any comprehensive division strategy examined. Under these conditions, there is a situation which procedure to choose for given explicit educational accumulation and whether the blend of division results

Figure 2. Analytics process

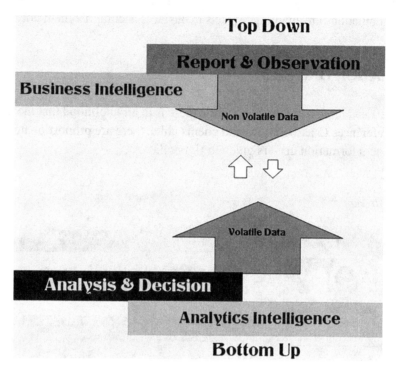

would be valuable (Kashyap, Gautam, 2017b). This undertakings to answer these request for portrayed grouping of picture taking care of data set of images of little photos the execution of a couple of division systems on pictures of moment models in three one of a kind modalities was penniless down. The course of action often quality records were used to achieve evaluation as objective gave the idea that there was no single division procedure which out and out beat the others in the straight set. The symbolic execution of the systems was by then surveyed with an end that Mean Shift computation played out the best and can en as the best division strategy all around (Kashyap, Anderson, 2018). New legitimate plans are having a fundamental influence in enabling a practical Intelligent Enterprise (IE) given in figure 2. An IE makes a single view over your relationship by utilizing a blend of standard itemizing and data observation (Rho and Vasilakos, 2017):

- Data from various source structures are washed, institutionalized and requested
- External feeds can amass from the latest research, best practice tenets, benchmarks, and other online vaults
- Use of updated recognition techniques, benchmarking documents and dashboards can enlighten organization and customers by methods for mobile phones, PCs, tablets, etc. in-house or on the other hand remotely.

All associations need to start contemplating gathering and using large tremendous data. Data-driven decisions can reduce inefficiency between the business, real and IT, advance existing information assets and address isolates between different components of an affiliation. Regardless, it is imperative that the best data and the most dynamic logical gadgets and frameworks add up to nothing if they not used by people who are asking the correct request. Gigantic data, rising accumulating advancement stages, and the latest indicative computations are enabling impacts to business accomplishment not an affirmation of it.

HUGE INFORMATION DRIVERS

The points of interest and threats of large data while there is in all likelihood that the massive data upset has made liberal preferences to associations and clients alike, there are proportionate perils that go with using large data huge information drivers given in figure 3.

Figure 3. Big data drivers

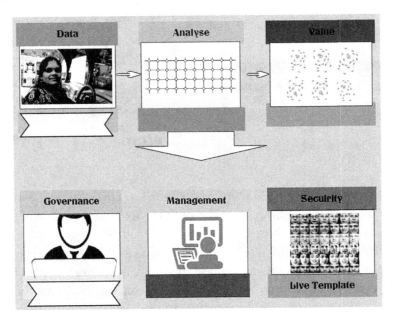

The need to stay sensitive data, to guarantee private information and to administer data quality, exists whether instructive accumulations are gigantic or little (Rey-del-Castillo and Cardeñosa, 2016). In any case, the specific properties of immense data volume, variety, speed, and integrity make new sorts of risks that require a full methodology to engage an association to utilize large data while avoiding the devices. It should be done in a sorted out way with the objective that associations can start to comprehend the upsides of significant data in the endeavor with managing the perils. The going with pages look at the possible results and risks related to extensive data and give instances of how large data is being used to comprehend a segment of the erratic issues associations stand up to today. We recognize regular and new risks and considerations for the seven key advances to advance: organization, organization, building, usage, quality, security and insurance (Waterman and Hendler, 2013). The idea of instructive accumulations and the conclusion drawn from such enlightening collections are continuously ending up progressively essential what's more; affiliations need to create quality and checking limits and parameters for significant data. For example, altering a data error can be extensively more over the top than getting the data right the first run through and getting the data wrong can be cataclysmic what's more, inherently increasingly costly to the affiliation if not cured. For quite a while the human administration's condition has gotten a handle on extensive data. With the ability to reach every patient touch point, the proportion of data inside the social protection natural framework has exploded. The advancement of new data sources and the knowledge to squash that data with existing data sources is progressing colossal information is making the probability of new positive patient outcomes.

A part of these new data sources consolidate the mix of disease libraries, tissue vaults, and genomic information, and a short time later altering them to imperative uses clinical models. It is portraying fundamental consideration treatment approaches in light of new inherited bits of learning and clinical tradition organizing estimations, and describing focused patient consideration treatment bits of information earlier inside the consideration movement process. The impetus from these new colossal data bits of information will be valuable for the patient. The nature of the data will in a like manner straightforwardly influence driving new key social protection bits of information in making brilliant outcomes while effectively administering expenses.

Analytics

The examination is another famous articulation in the development business and it "insinuates our ability to assemble and use data to deliver bits of learning that instruct assurance based fundamental administration." The data that was destitute down was generally used to anticipate what may happen later on and was wholly clutched by ventures, for instance, banks and insurance associations, yet not by relationship, for example, retailers. Tremendous information and examination go as the same unit in the current imaginative age. Gigantic information examination uses a thorough and prescriptive investigation and is changing the examination scene (Hussain and Roy, 2016). An accurate examination uses data from the past to envision what may occur, and its likelihood is happening later on. However, the customary inspection is taking data from the past, using it to pick what should be done close by achieving perfect results.

Methodologies

The issue has assorted settling approaches hypothetically; the data opening can be closed by compelling or reducing the advancement of data. The logical limit is settled and subject to investigate bleeding edge examination. Everything considered, having created a dimension of inquiry might be an OK approach except if the study is physically possible to continue running on exchange advancements and hardware. The execution opening It can close by growing use limit, for instance, dispersed or parallel getting ready confined by a dimension of the division of undertaking running with additional units for planning CPU, RAM and securing data. This methodology has a disadvantage in generally limited resources and won't handle the issue as a result of first extent supply: request of data. Beside limit, another perspective of enhancing may be input itself. Is all the data required? Imperative to separate or store? Given the requirements the dull or unimportant data that holds small, accepting any, information can be filtered through, with the peril of lost information opportunity in missing data yet we don't understand what we don't have the foggiest thought. By applying "beast compel" count on the whole dataset the issue is beginning once again from the earliest starting point.

Insights to Foresight

Advanced Analytics can be fitting for various business examination regarding explore customer designs lead, contention, deception acknowledgment, inefficiency in process Capacity Maturity Model (CMMI), grandstand carton examination conditions, causalities, relations in things' arrangements, etc. (Weber, Königsberger, Kassner, and Mitschang, 2017). All that truly matters is different examination usages can be orchestrated by the speed of data with time conditions ceaseless, aggregate planning, or to the collection of data sorted out, semi-organized, unstructured.

Specify that examination can recuperate helpful information from data that may address bits of learning. With encourage, the test can move into hunches — new creating district of the survey addressed by unstructured data content with broad use of online life (Lomotey and Deters, 2015). Content examination recognizes and isolates the vital information and deciphers mines and structures it to reveal precedents, ends, and associations inside and among records.

- The automated content request makes information looks far speedier and afterward some fruitful than manual or survey naming techniques.
- Ontology organization consolidates content storage facilities, approving data quality with unsurprising and purposely described associations.
- Sentiment examination usually finds and perceives presumption conveyed in online materials, for instance, individual to individual correspondence goals, comments, and sites on the Web, and from inside electronic documents.
- Text mining gives dangerous ways to deal with explore unstructured data gatherings and discover officially darken thoughts and models.

Business Intelligence

Business Intelligence (BI) and OLAP ordinarily invest critical energy in addressing, declaring, and separating chronicled data to grasp and balance happens with a date or for specific times beforehand. Affiliations can use BI and OLAP tallies to broaden a point of view of what the numbers say is likely going to happen later on (Kekwaletswe and Lesole, 2016). Regardless, the advanced examination can give an extensively progressively significant perception of why what more, a deductively based, the insightful viewpoint is without limits. The advanced examination enables customers to research various variables to refine understanding. Advanced investigation consistently needs to explore unrefined, bare essential data instead of tinier precedents and collections, which typically used for BI and OLAP.

BI frameworks offer client connections through dashboard interfaces that incorporate information get to what's more, representations, for example, diagrams and charts with cautions, pointers, and different changes trackers. Current BI frameworks can revive information in dashboards all the more much of the time, enabling clients to track measurements that can caution spikes, plunges, or different deviations from anticipated standards in something closer to constant. What BI frameworks need is both the more profound, more exploratory point of view that best in the class examination can give and the bits of knowledge driven by prescient and other systematic models. By connecting with dashboard gateways, BI clients can devour progressed investigation through representations, and utilize information disclosure capacities to pick up a "why" comprehension of what the BI execution measurements are appearing. Associations can go further and make progressed investigation tasks themselves the drivers, and execute

BI dashboards and measurements to give sees into the consequences of the logical tasks. Illustrations incorporate examination that gives understanding into consumer loyalty, an accomplishment in extortion anticipation (Arbel, 2015). A vital piece of huge information investigation capacities is access to enormous information. Business associations are ending up increasingly mindful of the estimation of information. Five information composes distinguished: open information, private information, information debilitate, network information, and self-evaluation information. The meanings of this information write they are particular source information, e.g., nonindividual information when they characterize the accompanying information composes (Tromp, Pechenizkiy & Gaber, 2017). Public information regularly free information gave by legislative establishments, private associations or people. Private information is association claimed information. Data deplete speaks to information with no, or little incentive in its unique situation yet may give valuable Intel when associated with other information. Community information is, for example, Facebook, Twitter, and other web-based social networking created information. Self-measurement information is information produced from wearable advancements like savvy watches, wellness groups and so forth (N. Smith, 2015). Information can come additionally into outside and personal information: Internal information is hierarchical information made by the authoritative procedures. Illustrations are stock updates, deals, exchanges or other inside procedures. External information is information from outside sources, open, private yet achievable through purchasing or exchanging, network information among others.

Huge Data Analytics

Enormous Data Analytics can be portrayed with the accompanying chain of activities with information to reveal groupings or connections and uncover useful perceptions (Figure 4).

Figure 4. Handling ventures of big data analytics

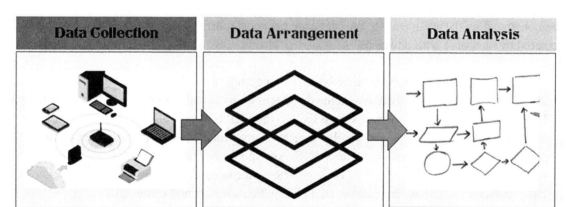

Huge data analytics offers an organization an understanding perspective inside its structure and acquires radiant data for present and future business arrangements. The objective for big data researchers is to pick up learning, got from the information preparing. Ongoing information alludes to floods of information that are conveyed specifically after information accumulation. So, there exists no deferral in the change from raw information accumulation to the data given from continuous information. Beside continuous information, organizations additionally confer assets to extricate an incentive from present and correct information. Over the top accentuation on constant information can lead bring about difficulties and disappointment of information-driven central leadership (Diesner, 2015)? The accessibility of present and correct information is important to position consistent information into the set of examples and patterns. Further, "right time information" and unique information should be given to help central leadership. Henceforth, applicable information should e assembled and incorporated for particular necessities or situations, types, and source of data is provided in Table 1.

Table 1. Sort of data and data sources

S.N.	Types of Data	
1.	Organized Data	Table and Records
2.	Unstructured Data	Human Language, Audio and Video
3.	Semi-Structured Data	XML and Similar Standards
4.	Occasion Data	Messages (typically in Real Time)
5.	Complex Data	Hierarchical or Legacy Sources
6.	Spatial Data	Long/Lat Coordinates and GPS Output
7.	Online networking Data	Blogs, Tweets and Social Networks
8.	Logical Data	Astronomy, Genomes, and Physics
9.	Machine Generated Data	Sensors, RFID and Devices
10.	Metadata	Data that depicts the substance of other information

The Principle of Work

As demonstrated by the arrangement, the exchange between enormous information and the association is depicted by the going with advances:

1. The creation data, delivered in the midst of the amassing of the Intelligent Engineering Products, is sent to the association's ERP where the data secured in the standard databases. Furthermore, the Case Company ensures customer's analysis into the ERP too.
2. Next, the ERP programming normally transmits unrefined data to the enormous information Analytics Tool that disperses it in the SQL Server and makes the examination to demonstrate the working adequacy of the vendor in various zones: mechanical assembly use, time use, execution rate, false coefficient, quality degree, etc (Tromp, Pechenizkiy and Gaber, 2017).
3. Finally, the Case Company can follow and streamline the work procedure, manage the business methods and finish new upgrades in the establishment strategy.

The examination result can be challenging to get with one original additional data examination works can be repeated for a couple of times by affirming the conclusion and choosing the estimation of the examination result. The methodology of tremendous data examination may yield in each examination strategy with the goal that the incredible outcome can be gotten just by repeated displays of various techniques.

Methodological ideal models and troubles of great information methodologically, large data empowers us to utilize both desire and causal examination. Best in class gigantic data research and practice draws on a collection of frameworks from machine learning, built up estimations, and econometrics, to plan of tests industry calls this A/B or multivariate testing to test existing hypotheses and hypotheses, making new theories, and making colossal scale business regard (Yu, Yurovsky and Xu, 2011). Researchers can layout and lead investigations and accumulate the data anticipated that would procure answers to a grouping of the request including:

(1) Effects of partner affect, (2) impacts of the impact of dynamic ties, (3) has implications of anonymity on online associations, (4) comes to fruition from elective assessing strategies for cutting-edge media, (5) the impact of meticulously created front line recommender systems, and (6) the changing tendency structures of Generation Y and Z customers. Separating these issues completely present methodological troubles, anyway, we see the challenges as open entryways for able investigators.

The colossal data strategies indicated above have in like manner raised disputes. Late revelations from two surely understood destinations, Facebook and OkCupid, the two of which investigated diverse roads in regards to their customers, have begun eagerness for the subject of what, assuming any, fitting applications exist for the use of the online social space as an examination place for advancing our perception of human direct (Davalos and Merchant, 2015). The critical inquiry is whether such experimentation by associations or conceivably by scholastics as a group with associations offers favorable circumstances to society all over the place, and, accepting this is the situation, what proper examination is legitimate and implementable? We battle that there is a strong case for such experimentation, not just to keep up a vital separation from costly terrible decisions, yet also for the journey for a better understanding of what drives human social correspondences. Dreadful decisions hurt all that genuinely matters of associations, and even they cost society since poor choices result in a misallocation of essential resources. As far back as that phlebotomy was a valuable therapeutic practice, correctly made experimentation has driven legitimate examination and learning revelation. Directly, with the openness of immense scale experimentation yielding large data, the potential for inspection, testing, and new learning enhancement are dazzling.

Past updated essential authority in business settings, we fight great societal favorable position from such experimentation. We by and by have remarkable digitization of conventional techniques (Soltani and Navimipour, 2016). The enormous proportion of little-scale level tremendous data about human interchanges offers openings never available in the physical world in light of expense or infeasibility of similar data gathering. We as of now have opportunities to deliver new causal encounters, to test the suitability of age-old reliable rules and norms that speak to social cooperation's. We can thoroughly test existing speculations and collect and test new theories. So, we can go where social scientists could merely dream of going previously. It passes on us to the need to exactly address the issue of paying little mind to whether such broad-scale field investigations would cause more societal insidiousness than extraordinary. This clear idea of preferred societal standpoint is irrefutable of essential excitement for our individual universities' ethics and human subjects warning gatherings generally called institutional review sheets. Associations need to remove a leaf from, or perhaps collaborate with, the insightful network and set up near ethics warning gatherings overseeing human subjects. In case, as an overall population, we place stock in enthusiasm about us as a creature assortments, by then we need to pick up from what testing them on the web social graph tells us. Of course, we require our establishments to compensate for lost time for development. Using large data and examination goes with a huge gathering of challenges, countless are ready ground for future research. Immense data is a larger number of brains boggling to regulate than standard corporate data. Already, associations generally administered very much organized data. Regardless, associations by and by the need to manage a great deal of internal and external data that in many cases will be unstructured or around sorted out. Counting appropriate what's increasing, innovative survey data from any of the about inescapable review decisions, firms presently can go up against a large display of inside, external, and diagram data.

Pervasive Informing

Today, individuals and associations record what they find interesting, store this information for themselves or others, also, share the data for individual and furthermore business purposes. For ease, we imply this wonder as ubiquitous lighting up since a specific target is to instruct someone about something reaching out from a beautiful dish, someone's pulse, the video gets, social cooperation's, vehicle assignments, and street observation in every practical sense any bit of information. General enlightening is possible in light of mechanical pushes in flexible enlisting, video spouting, social sorting out, astute vehicles, and the Internet of things. Information grabbing and exchanging are without a doubt basic; the test is to find a motivator in putting aside the chance to complete such assignments (Ding, Erickson, Kellogg and Patterson, 2011). The issue is whether one can use large data and data examination to get authentic regard. Can an association turn out to be increasingly familiar with its customers better? Can the association recognize its by and large critical clients and enhance benefits through giving these customers with more modified customer associations or better customer organizations? Will the association use information to build a more grounded publicize position? The troubles from inescapable prompting fuse are becoming much better large data building and examination to manage and utilize extensive data to pass on business regard.

Usage Environments

From an unadulterated amassing perspective, stack circumstances, for instance, Hadoop have been familiar with administer large data 3D shapes. Similarly, as with any new development, such making things should be moved nearer with clear vision and sound input. As noted (Nurika, Hassan and Za-karia, 2017), in any case, great the philosophy, one should now and again look at the results. Much of the time, stack circumstances remain overwhelmingly underutilized with the risk of showing one more costly legacy inconvenience and endangering future tremendous data-driven advancements. Progres-sively moderate in-memory setups could display an exciting choice in the movement towards the create gigantic data affiliation.

COORDINATION ISSUES

A key gigantic data challenge for any firm is to recognize and disentangle the interrelationships of the large data shape and draw out the regard recommendations by interfacing the distinctive data streams using appropriately described unique identifiers; it may wind up possible to get an increasingly add up to picture of customer lead (Mynarz, 2014). In a security setting, an arrangement of associated components, for instance, claims, candidates, policyholders, automobiles, locally available diagnostics contraptions, auto fix shops, charge cards, and small numbers might be worked to unveil an unusual perspective on complex interest practices or blackmail plans.

Esteem Assessment

The troublesome impact and creative uses of large data because certified challenges for the descriptive frameworks and models that will make. These models generally start from customary estimations, econometrics, machine learning, or artificial thinking. A key typical for these illustrative systems is that they fixate on enhancing a specific exactness worldview or experiences based target work, e.g., constraining a mean squared bungle or expanding likelihood. Commonly, execution is condensed using looking at official estimates that can be troublesome to understand for end customers or no specialists (Thompson, Varvel, Sasinowski and Burke, 2016). As analytic models gain and more effective in the critical decisions of a firm, it is essential to associate this correspondence opening to make critical trust. Specifically, to get trust in an insightful model, the two data scientists and boss should get a most generally utilized dialect in which the possibility of enormous worth accept an essential part. Different as unadulterated authentic execution e.g., assessed using misclassification rates, mean squared missteps, twists, top decile, certified regard based criteria transform into the shared segments. The reasonable standards are uncommonly poor upon the specific business setting.

Expository Models Ought to Be Justifiable to Chiefs

Unmistakably, this has an emotional part to it and depends upon both the depiction and precise multifaceted nature of the deliberate model and moreover the guidance or establishment of the end customer. Black box analytical models in light of extraordinarily complex logical formulas are likely not going to be trusted to reinforce key business systems, for instance, credit risk estimation, distortion ID, or even remedial finding. In any case, if a revelation procedure passes on exact therapeutic dissect, again and again, would the patient-driven expert select for less correct yet easily sensible decisions? Regard based execution premise concerns operational efficiency including model evaluation, indicate checking, and show reviving. The first of these implies the benefits that are relied upon to collect the critical data follow up on the obtained yield. Consistently original initiative settings, brisk model appraisal are a key essential. Consider the instance of charge card distortion area, where frequently a decision ought to be made in less than five seconds after the trade began. Recommender systems are another situation where any customer action or event, for example, recorded using zone-based organizations (Angelis and Kanavos, 2013). Despite model evaluation tries, operational capability in like manner includes the advantages anticipated that would screen, backtest, and, where relevant, extend test the logical models. Finally, the model must be stimulated or revived as new data creates or business conditions change. The association that can perceive changing conditions and quickly modify its models is the association that will succeed.

Overseeing Analytic Decisions

Drawing out decision arranged determinations from large data examination impacts and enhances the affiliation's first initiative. With examination, we will see more decisions being automated, as such influencing the decision systems and commitments all through the association. With decisions being motorized potentially in light of gigantic data examination, administering and exhibiting business decisions is a rising test. Alliances are sharply drawn in with enhancing their business frames and engaging quick and convincing reaction to new troubles, openings, or controls. By explicitly exhibiting decisions and the basis behind them, arrangements can be directed freely from the strategies, radically growing business spryness. It requires reasonable decision examination techniques for business (Ploskas, Stiakakis, and Fouliras, 2014) and what's more methodologies and measures to delineate, appear, additionally, direct business essential administration. The decision demonstrates what's more, documentation is such a standard for decision showing, gotten by the Object Management Group, to overcome any obstacle between business process blueprint and business decisions.

Quantifiable Profit and Trust

Finally, an asymptomatic model ought to incorporate economic motivating force by either delivering advantages or cutting costs or both. A benefit driven evaluation of an indicative model is crucial to make trust transversely over various dimensions and claim to fame units in any affiliation. Regulatory decisions are customarily in perspective of money related return, rather than a truthfully basic logical model. Besides, that is the place examination can deliver the question and subsequently miss the mark. It is our firm conviction this should be catalyzed by more research in no under two domains, To begin with, innovative systems should e made to accurately quantify the landing on endeavor of an analytical model thinking about the low expense of model proprietorship, including distorted and opportunity costs, and covering a satisfactorily long and fitting time horizon. As a next subject on the investigation plan, the consequent money related bits of learning and measures should e explicitly introduced into a deliberate model building process, instead of essentially used as ex-post appraisal measures (Batarseh, Yang and Deng, 2017). Specifically, legitimate models ought to never again aimlessly revolve around enhancing a likelihood work or constraining a misclassification rate, anyway go for including business regard where it is vital, thinking about all the recently referenced criteria. At precisely that point will the fundamental trust be gained over every decision level and claim to fame units in a firm?

METHODOLOGIES FOR ANALYZING BIG DATA: A NEW APPROACH

When you use SQL request to investigate cash related numbers or OLAP gadgets to make bargains gauges, you generally appreciate what kind of data you have and what it can tell you. Salary, geography and time all relate to one another in distinct ways. You don't generally fathom what the proper reactions are in any case you do know how the diverse segments of the instructive accumulation relate to one another. BI customers routinely run standard reports from sorted out databases that have been purposely shown to utilize these associations. Gigantic data examination incorporates making "sense" out of immense volumes of moving data that in its unrefined edge does not have a data model to portray what each segment infers concerning the others. There are a couple of new issues you should consider as you set out on this new kind of examination: Discovery in various cases you don't go by and large fathom what you have and how individual instructive files relate to one another. You should understand it through a methodology of examination and divulgence. Cycle because the real associations are not commonly known early, uncovering understanding is every now and again an iterative procedure as you find the appropriate reactions that you search. The possibility of accentuation is that it all overdrives you down a way that winds up being a halt. That is okay experimentation is a bit of the strategy. Various examiners and industry experts prescribe that you start with close to nothing, notably portrayed endeavors, gain from each cycle, and persistently continue forward to the accompanying idea or field of demand (Yang and Yecies, 2016). Adaptable Capacity due to the iterative thought of extensive data examination is set up to contribute more vitality and utilize more resources to deal with issues. Mining and anticipating huge data examination isn't very differentiating. You don't, for the most part, know how the distinctive data segments relate to one another. As you mine the data to discover models and associations, a thorough examination can yield the encounters that you search. Choice Management thinks about trade volume and speed. In case you are using gigantic data examination to drive various operational decisions, for instance, redoing a site or inciting call center masters about the affinities and activities of purchasers by then you need to consider how to motorize and enhance the execution of all of those exercises.

For example, you may do not understand paying little respect to whether social data uncovers knowledge into arrangements designs. The test accompanies comprehending which data segments relate to which other data parts, and in what limit. The strategy of exposure not directly incorporates examining the data to perceive how you can use it yet likewise choosing how it relates to your regular undertaking data. New sorts of demand include what occurred, and also why. For example, a critical measurement for a few, and associations are customer unsettle. Assessing blend is straightforward. However, for what reason does it occur? Customer support asks for, web-based life examination, and other customer info would all have the capacity to help clear up why customers blemish (Pan, Wang, and Han, 2016). Near strategies can be used with various sorts of data and in multiple conditions. For what reason did bargains fall in a given store? For what reason do certain patients endure longer than others? Attempt to find the right data, discover the covered associations, and analyze it precisely.

Huge Data Analysis Requirements

In the past fragment, Techniques for breaking down great information, we discussed some of the methodologies you can use to find which means and find covered associations in large data. Here are three immense necessities for coordinating this demand essentially:

1. Limit data improvement
2. Use existing aptitudes
3. Deal with data security

Restricting data improvement is tied in with directing figuring resources. In standard examination circumstances, data is passed on to the PC, dealt with, and after that sent to the accompanying objective. For example, creation data might be isolated from e-business systems, changed into social data compose, and stacked into an operational data store sorted out for enumerating. However, the volume of data builds up; this sort of ETL designing pushes toward winding up continuously less viable. There's essentially an unreasonable measure of data to move around. It looks good to store and process the data in a similar place. With new data and new data sources comes the need to acquire new capacities. The present scope of capabilities will make sense of where examination ought to and should be conceivable (Horton and Tambe, 2015). Right when the necessary capacities are insufficient concerning, a blend of getting ready, securing and new instruments will address the issue. Since most affiliations have more people who can analyze data using SQL than using MapReduce, it is necessary to have the ability to help the two sorts of taking care. Data security is fundamental for some corporate applications. Data appropriation focus customers are accustomed not solely to intentionally described estimations and estimations and properties, yet moreover to a regular course of action of association techniques and security controls. These exhaustive methodologies are consistently absent from unstructured data sources and open source examination instruments. Concentrate on the security and data organization necessities of each examination adventure and make without question that the gadgets you are using can oblige those requirements.

Database Processing With Oracle Advanced Analytics

Most Oracle customers are incredibly familiar with SQL as a vernacular for inquiry, declaring, and examination of sorted out data. It is the acknowledged standard for testing and the development that underlies most BI mechanical assemblies. R is a pervasive open source programming dialect for verifiable examination. Agents, data analysts, researchers, and scholastics by and considerable use R, provoking a creating pool of R programming engineers. At the point when data has stacked into Oracle Database, customers can benefit themselves of Oracle Advanced Analytics (OAA) to uncover covered associations in the data. Prophet Advanced Analytics, an option of Oracle Database Enterprise Release, offers a blend of extraordinary in database estimations and open source R figurings, accessible through SQL and R tongues. It joins first-class data mining limits with the open source R vernacular to engage thorough examination, data mining, content mining, quantifiable examination, advanced numerical counts and original plan all inside the database (Jin, Liu, and Qi, 2012). Prophet Advanced Analytics gives all middle logical limits and lingos on extraordinary in database designing. These illustrative limits fuse data mining figurings realized in the database, nearby SQL capacities with regards to fundamental critical techniques, and joining with open source R for quantifiable programming and access to a progressively broad plan of measurable strategies.

This serious analytic condition offers a large extent of abilities to Oracle Database customers dealing with large data stretches out by restricting data improvement and ensuring internal security, adaptability, and execution. It consolidates data mining devices that let you make complex models and pass on them on sweeping instructive accumulations. You can utilize the outcomes of these perceptive models inside BI applications. For example, you can use backslide models to predict customer age in perspective of acquiring behavior and measurement data. You can in like manner collect and apply insightful models that help you center around your best customers, make bare essential customer profiles, find and check distortion, and comprehend various other logical troubles.

Productive Data Mining

The data mining instruments in OAA enable data examiners to work explicitly with data inside the database, explore the data graphically, make and evaluate various data mining models, and send gauges and bits of information all through the endeavor. It consolidates data burrowing counts for portrayal, grouping, promotes compartment examination, deception ID, and substance mining that can be associated with settle a broad assortment of data-driven issues. It furthermore consolidates twelve figurings that you can use to manufacture and send insightful applications that like this mine star chart data to pass on consistent results and desires. Since the data, models, and results remain in the Prophet Database, data improvement is wiped out, information torpidity is restricted, and security is kept up. Using standard SQL charges you can get to tip top figurings in the database to mine tables, sees, star developments, and esteem based and unstructured data (Bacardit and Llorà, 2013). Any person who can get to dataset away in an Oracle Database can get to OAA occurs, desires, recommendations, and disclosures using standard reports and BI instruments.

Factual Analysis With R

Prophet Advanced Analytics has been expected to engage examiners to use R on huge instructive lists. Insightful models can be made in R. The related tables, and points of view in Oracle Database appear as R objects SQL declarations. Inspectors can create an R code to control the data in the database. By running R programs right in the database, there is no convincing motivation to move data around. This organized designing ensures unprecedented security and execution since you can apply huge, flexible gear advantages for complex issues. OAA supports existing R substance and pariah packages as well. All present R enhancement capacities, gadgets, and element can run clearly with OAA, and scale against dataset away in Oracle Database 11g. The powerful blend between R, Oracle Database, and Hadoop engages inspectors to stay in contact with R content that can continue running in three unmistakable conditions: a workstation running open source R, Hadoop running with Oracle enormous information connectors, and Oracle Database (Duque Barrachina and O'Driscoll, 2014). It is not hard to associate the outcomes of the examination to business examination gadgets, for instance, Prophet Business Intelligence and Oracle Analytics, as depicted in the going with the region.

Connecting Hadoop and Oracle Database

There are two distinct options for associating data and interim achieves Hadoop with your Oracle data dissemination focus. Dependent upon your use case, you may need to stack Hadoop data into the data stockroom, or forsake it set up and request it using SQL. Prophet Loader for Hadoop gives an essential technique to accumulate HDFS data into an Oracle data stockroom. MapReduce to make progressed enlightening accumulations that can capably e stacked into Oracle Database. Not in any way like other Hadoop loaders, has it made Oracle interior designs, enabling it to accumulate data speedier with fewer system resources. When stacked, the data can get to with ordinary SQL based Business Intelligence gadgets (Hossen, Moniruzzaman, and Hossain, 2015). Prophet SQL Connector for HDFS is a quick connector for getting to HDFS data clearly from Oracle Database, overcoming any prevention among HDFS and data conveyance focus conditions. The dataset away in HDFS can by then addressed by methods for SQL, joined with dataset away in Oracle Database, or stacked into Oracle Database.

Prophet's Big Data Platform

Prophet has three assembled structures that light up particular parts of the significant data issue. Each stage fuses all the first gear and programming critical for remarkable data dealing. All pieces are pre-composed what's increasing, readied to send and work. Prophet has done the tireless work of incorporating these constructed structures so you can remove an impetus from your data by methods for extensive advanced data arrange with the facilitated examination. This complete course of action fuses unique systems managing data acquirement, stacking, limit, organization, analysis, blend, and presentation so you can quickly expel a motivation from large data with the composed examination. Prophet enormous information Appliance consolidated a mix of open source programming and focused programming made by Oracle to address immense data essentials. It is expected to anchor and mastermind gigantic data capable, and to be the savviest stage to run Hadoop (AlMahmoud, Damiani, Otrok and Al-Hammadi, 2017). For extra information on the sufficiency of this methodology, see the white paper "Getting genuine about huge information: Build Versus Buy" from the Enterprise Strategy Group. Prophet Exadata Database Machine passes on phenomenal execution and flexibility for an extensive variety of database applications. It is the speediest stage open for running Oracle Database and the detailed examination discussed in this section.

Prophet examination is an assembled system that consolidates an undertaking BI organize, in memory examination writing computer programs, also, gear updated for the broad-scale survey. With mechanical assemblies for frontline data discernment and study, it enables customers to gain great comprehension from a great deal of data. Right, when Oracle Analytics used with Prophet Advanced Analytics, customers have an expansive stage that passes on understanding into important business subjects, for instance, beat figure, thing recommendations, end examination, and deception disturbing.

Analytics for the Enterprise

The relationship in every industry are trying to grasp the enormous storm of astronomical data, and furthermore to make demonstrative stages that can arrange customary sorted out data with semi-composed and unstructured wellsprings of information. Right when fittingly got and researched, extensive data can give interesting bits of learning into promote designs, outfit frustrations, obtaining practices, bolster cycles and various diverse business issues, cutting down costs, and engaging centered around business decisions. To get a motivating force from extensive data, you require a solid game plan of answers for getting, dealing with, and separating the data, from acquiring the data and finding new bits of information to settling on repeatable decisions and scaling the related information structures. Prophet progressed investigation is ideal for uncovering covered associations in large data sources. Notwithstanding whether you need to anticipate customer lead, imagine cross/up offer openings, upgrade displaying exertion response rates, check disturb, analyze "publicize holders" to discover affiliations, precedents and associations, use influencers in relational associations, decline deception, or predict future demand, Oracle Advanced Analytics can help (Ravada, 2015). Correctly when used as a piece of combination with open source instruments, for instance, Hadoop and MapReduce. This excellent orderly course of action passes on all that you need to get, deal with, separate and extend the estimation of large data inside the endeavor while fulfilling essential requirements for constraining data improvement, using existing scopes of capacities, and ensuring lifted measures of security.

- A unique data examination game plan includes organizations or estimations that experience both machine capacity data-driven organizations and human information cooperation driven organizations.
- To support and ensure the compromise of machine limit and human learning, joining driven organizations are required to enable customers to associate with the two data-driven organizations and joint exertion is driven organizations and offer instruments to fuse the delayed consequence of two sorts of organizations.
- All organizations or computations together help the large data change from an unrefined association to adapting thing (base up) or from hypothesis to resources (top-down) (Kuiler, 2014).

- Human learning should be related to the whole technique of data change, including planning data-driven organizations, interpreting the eventual outcome of data-driven organizations, cooperating with various authorities on deciphering and sharing the results.
- As showed up in the plan chart, there are three sorts of portions:
- Data-driven organizations, which misuse significant data taking care of advancement to look, separate and aggregate data from heterogeneous data sources. The commitment of the data-driven organizations is sorted out or possibly unstructured data from different data sources. The yield of data-driven organizations s looked, or private information discovered models or records, etc. The data-driven organizations hope to improve the systems of individual sense-making (Luo, Zhang, Zukerman, and Qiao, 2014).

The comments among individuals, so to support the total appreciation of the issues related to data examination. The commitment of the joint exertion driven organizations could be the yield of data-driven organizations, and moreover, the participation's comments, disputes and talks, etc. (Luo, Zhang, Zukerman, and Qiao, 2014) figure 5 demonstrated this idea for online networking. The adapting thing hypothesis, methods, etc. should be the aftereffect of their affiliation. The joint exertion driven organizations mean to help synergistic sense-making.

Coordination driven organizations are to ensure and support the steady coordination of the independent organizations made. Related limits consolidate UI, data storing and coordination segments, etc. (Dafferianto Trinugroho, 2014).

Figure 5. Conceptual Architecture for Big DataAnalytics in Social Media Monitoring

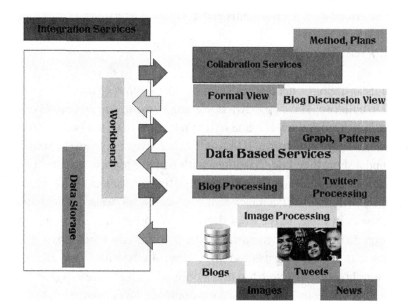

This methodology opens up an extra station to necessities showing and examination, which relies upon changing and separating speculative models from humanism and emotional science to an arrangement knick-knack. The investigation work reported in this area gives a depiction of how theoretical models were picked and associated with the examination and blueprint of the structure has appeared in figure 5. We believe this inconspicuous undertaking at bringing human science or mental science models into essential structuring will enhance the natural need showing process. Significantly more work is relied upon to refine to meet the practical necessities of essentials master.

Approaches to Deal With Big Data

Colossal information can be seen as an issue, of course as luck this zone contains systems of dealing with the large relative data from the perspective of plan, methods, establishment, and headways.

Approaches

The regular BI designing can start stage for structures with its procedure tallying masterminding an area, data conveyance focus, data stores, ETL, etc. One may find that it is most likely not going to store all data in central, adventure data dispersion focus and not all data are critical to being secured. There has been new structure approaches created: Hybrid Storage Architecture blend of reserves for various data makes and arranges, temporary data reserves, data stream taking care. Upstream Intelligence sensible and quantifiable limits are associated immediately in the process in the anchoring of data that consolidates specific Stream and occasion moreover getting ready based oversee based systems, plan to recognize evidence (Askitas, 2016). As results of this advancement, Post current BI Architecture addresses a complicated course of action that has procured, generally from ordinary Business Intelligence and incorporates the possibility of blend storing structure, upstream understanding, and stream an event getting ready. Postmodern BI Architecture includes circled data circulation focus, consolidated Metadata layer, made an organization out of data streams and composed exertion learning organization.

Post Current Bi Architecture

Due to an arranged assortment of necessities from business symmetrical BI models propelled: a Top Down and Bottom Up building. The Top Down designing stressed a report drove or a data-driven methodology where a data stockroom show is made first in perspective of the business/declaring necessities. Methods of this methodology start with an ETL routine to move data from the source system to the data conveyance focus, and a short time later continues with making reports and dashboards to address data in DW. This methodology generally satisfies accommodating customers with periodical uncovering and checking. Besides that, affiliation's advantages control customers to wear down extraordinarily delegated examination or endeavors in imaginative work division. With past methodology control customers are left aside to use uniquely designated spreadsheets, free/neighborhood database events, SQL and data mining workbenches with Top Down methodology control customers find BI instruments relentless and an information warehousing structure too much obliged for their stresses (Kekwaletswe and Lesole, 2016). Open entryway for Bottom-Up configuration approach has appeared.

The Bottom Up methodology suits better for business analysts and data scientists who require the off the cuff examination of any data source, both inside and outside corporate points of confinement, working personally with business executives to enhance existing strategies. Post present day BI configuration is an eventual outcome of improvement of data warehousing structures, data organization programs and adding advanced examination to alter the dynamic between best down and base up necessities. This compositional thought is generally called creamer building depicted. Colossal Data and HPA don't change data warehousing or BI structures. They fundamentally supplement them with new headways and show signs of improvement handcrafted to meet the information essentials. Crossbreed configuration can, on the other hand, contain the following correlative advancements like:

Hadoop clusters to help to amass for semi-sorted out data, used as a piece of orchestrating district or of course interpretive sandboxes. Streaming and Complex Event Processing Engines to encourage predictable understanding, used as brilliant sensors that can associate with streams. Analytical Sandbox to help examination dealing with, extraordinarily delegated inquiries, to satisfy transient examination needs, used as a section for other BI structures. A nonsocial database system to store unstructured or unrefined data, used as a piece of the descriptive sandbox, or masterminding locale •Data focus point to support unique systems and applications rather than to have uncovering or examination applications explicitly, data stockroom used as a middle (Shmueli, 2017).

Big Data Analytics Tools

BDA structures, passed on Cloud or in-house server farm, have to wind up essential to going up against the computational demand errands. In the going with, we show a survey of the most used BDA mechanical assemblies in composing.

Apache Hadoop

Apache Hadoop is an open source passed on preparing the structure for moving on the limit and gathering treatment of large educational accumulations on clusters worked from product gear using fundamental programming models, i.e., MapReduce. It is planned to scale up from single to a large number of servers, all of which offers both neighborhood count and limit. It grants getting huge ready data by using group dealing. Rather than rely upon hardware to pass on high openness, the library itself is planned to perceive, what's more, handle disillusionments at the application layer (Mavridis and Karatza, 2017). Hadoop focus sections offer organizations to work arranging, a passed on record system and data dealing with MapReduce, huge information investigation for clump examinations.

Apache Kafka

Apache Kafka is a snappy, flexible, dependable, and fault tolerant distribute in advising system. Kafka routinely used as a piece of the place of regular message vendors like JMS and AMQP because of its higher throughput, resolute quality and replication [Kafka] exhibiting the structure spilling examination. Apache Kafka can work in the mix with different systems for regular examination and the rendering of spouting data, for instance, Apache Storm, Apache HBase or Apache Spark. As a rule, it is used for two sorts of usage, developing consistent data work forms, exchanging messages between structures or applications reliably, and continuous spilling applications that change or react to the data stream (Shaheen, 2017). Kafka is a message delegate on a dimension plane versatile, and fault tolerant. In spite of the usage case, Kafka operator's enormous surges of messages for low dormancy examination in the Apache Hadoop natural framework.

DISCUSSION

Tremendous information wonder has delineated in this section with its causalities, definitions, effects, and impacts. Notice that the adjustment in context from data drove methodology towards information-driven methodology may be seen perilously on the conventional idea of central data stockroom and physically approved data decency and consistency. Rather than that, it makes required courses of action that satisfy necessities for versatility and adaptability supporting data examination. Information Driven Approach is a starting stage for Upstream Insight. Tremendous information adjusts building in that way that Post Modern BI Architecture made in mélange of Hybrid Storage Architecture Analytical Sandboxes, Hadoop, NoSQL, RDBMS, Upstream Intelligence mainly supported by Complex Event Processing and standard data warehousing (Omidi and Alipour, 2016). Another superb idea, following the Hybrid Storage Architecture, is Information Federation that inclinations to discover data on various mechanical assemblies in different structures what's more, plans. In any case, it supports examination and ensures giving of consistent access to data by methods for primarily united data get to having the BI configuration completely extended post current BI Architecture; there are anyway propels that twist for imaginative approaches to manage to handle Big Data. Area of high execution examination isn't broadly portrayed and mapped. The progression of HPA is generally dictated by business enthusiasm for having information delayed consequences of data taking care of immediately and by the availability of benefits structure figuring, free memory with facilitating.

Analytic phases of HPA move among the traders and principle speaking realized as prohibitive courses of action. Specialization of stages relies upon business requirements and business applications. Moreover extraordinary particular drivers impact the use of phase, which can be for instance a number of clients/supporters with respect to applications and customers, data volumes, sort of data, fit in the overall structure of BI plan, e.g. organizing domain, information distribution center, subordinate/self-sufficient data bazaars, off the cuff look into and prototyping office. Information storage facilities are moving towards pooled resources where data are independent as demonstrated by the data essentialness require planning; data orchestrate composed, semi-sorted out, unstructured. Establishment and plan of data examination and organization structure are moving from being execution tuned towards being specifically versatile in linkage with scattered parallel getting ready, arrange to figure, and in memory examination (Hamoud and Obaid, 2013). Flexibility goads another perspective that developments on premises association towards cream standard and devices arranged a game plan, where adaptability can be adaptable with private cloud.

CONCLUSION

Since the huge information has endlessly perceived for a long time, there is an important measure ask about done in composing, white papers, and online references. In this hypothesis, the critical information Phenomenon delineated in a survey including its causalities, definition, effect, and impacts. It addresses a starting stage and driver for High-Performance Analytics concerning rough material that contains covered information, precedents, and regard. Shutting from investigating, enormous information, with its dynamic estimations, should not be considered as an issue, instead of the situation to change it into a preferred standpoint. Analytics is comprehensively asked about in this proposition as a methodology towards dealing with great information as a result of this area. It is so far rising, being refined and formalized among vendors, investigate on HPA is taking a stab at remembering the ultimate objective to bring outline, the portrayal of HPA techniques and strategies database examination and parallel enrolling their traits, and appropriate usage. HPA is driven by the business world with broad necessities to figure to fruition as snappy as possible on the greatest dataset. The improvement HPA ends up imaginable with creative progression vast memory, 64bit location, Grid Computing and moderateness of gear costs, value: execution marker. Until further notice, HPA can see as an answer compared to the Business Intelligence, yet exceedingly on premises, the progression will continue further. The exploration could be extended to bounce into HPA game plans from different vendors differentiating distinctive prohibitive strategies in unobtrusive components. Test assignments as it has been laid out, show the execution of HPA approach on massive datasets. Unmistakable intellectual exercises and their blends have displayed the upsides of the consistent stage in light of In-Memory Analytics approach. In Memory Analytics building has found as supportive for the count different exercises association, inclined lines, checking, percentile, since all data are stacked in memory and can be explicitly tended. There are a couple of imperatives of preliminary assignments. For the future work, the analytical exercises can attempt on informative stages that realize other HPA approaches, n addition against common methodology in Business Intelligence, e.g., OLAP. Now and again, merchants offer the formative stage that would complete all discussed HPA approaches and in case, it is trying to perform them on a comparable system establishment. The examinations are satisfactory for taking a gander at the execution of analytical action among one another, to perceive central focuses and points of interest of picked precise stage.

REFERENCES

Ahmadvand, H., & Goudarzi, M. (2017). Using Data Variety for Efficient Progressive Big Data Processing in Warehouse-Scale Computers. *IEEE Computer Architecture Letters*, *16*(2), 166–169. doi:10.1109/LCA.2016.2636293

AlMahmoud, A., Damiani, E., Otrok, H., & Al-Hammadi, Y. (2017). Spamdoop: A privacy-preserving Big Data platform for collaborative spam detection. *IEEE Transactions On Big Data*, 1-1. doi:10.1109/tbdata.2017.2716409

Angelis, A., & Kanavos, P. (2013). A Multiple Criteria Decision Analysis Framework For Value-Based Assessment Of New Medical Technologies. *Value in Health*, *16*(3), A53. doi:10.1016/j.jval.2013.03.302

Arbel, L. (2015). Data loss prevention: The business case. *Computer Fraud & Security*, *2015*(5), 13–16. doi:10.1016/S1361-3723(15)30037-3

Askitas, N. (2016). Big Data is a big deal but how much data do we need?. *Asta Wirtschafts- Und Sozialstatistisches Archiv, 10*(2-3), 113-125. doi:10.1007/s11943-016-0191-3

Bacardit, J., & Llorà, X. (2013). Large-scale data mining using genetics-based machine learning. *Wiley Interdisciplinary Reviews. Data Mining and Knowledge Discovery*, *3*(1), 37–61. doi:10.1002/widm.1078

Batarseh, F., Yang, R., & Deng, L. (2017). A comprehensive model for management and validation of federal big data analytical systems. *Big Data Analytics*, *2*(1), 2. doi:10.118641044-016-0017-x

Dafferianto Trinugroho, Y. (2014). Information Integration Platform for Patient-Centric Healthcare Services: Design, Prototype, and Dependability Aspects. *Future Internet*, *6*(1), 126–154. doi:10.3390/fi6010126

Davalos, S., & Merchant, A. (2015). Using Big Data to Study Psychological Constructs: Nostalgia on Facebook. *Journal of Psychology & Psychotherapy*, *05*(06). doi:10.4172/2161-0487.1000221

Diesner, J. (2015). Small decisions with big impact on data analytics. *Big Data & Society*, *2*(2). doi:10.1177/2053951715617185

Ding, X., Erickson, T., Kellogg, W., & Patterson, D. (2011). Informing and performing: Investigating how mediated sociality becomes visible. *Personal and Ubiquitous Computing*, *16*(8), 1095–1117. doi:10.100700779-011-0443-8

Duque Barrachina, A., & O'Driscoll, A. (2014). A big data methodology for categorizing technical support requests using Hadoop and Mahout. *Journal Of Big Data*, *1*(1), 1. doi:10.1186/2196-1115-1-1

Hamoud, A., & Obaid, T. (2013). *Building Data Warehouse for Diseases Registry: First Step for Clinical Data Warehouse*. SSRN Electronic Journal. doi:10.2139srn.3061599

Hassani-Mahmooei, B., Berecki-Gisolf, J., & Collie, A. (2017). Using Bayesian Model Averaging to Analyse Hierarchical Health Data: Model implementation and application to linked health service use data. *International Journal For Population Data Science*, *1*(1). doi:10.23889/ijpds.v1i1.89

Horton, J., & Tambe, P. (2015). Labor Economists Get Their Microscope: Big Data and Labor Market Analysis. *Big Data*, *3*(3), 130–137. doi:10.1089/big.2015.0017 PMID:27442956

Hossen, A., Moniruzzaman, A., & Hossain, S. (2015). Performance Evaluation of Hadoop and Oracle Platform for Distributed Parallel Processing in Big Data Environments. *International Journal Of Database Theory And Application*, *8*(5), 15–26. doi:10.14257/ijdta.2015.8.5.02

Hussain, A., & Roy, A. (2016). The emerging era of Big Data Analytics. *Big Data Analytics*, *1*(1), 4. doi:10.118641044-016-0004-2

Jin, C., Liu, N., & Qi, L. (2012). Research and Application of Data Archiving based on Oracle Dual Database Structure. *Journal of Software*, *7*(4). doi:10.4304/jsw.7.4.844-848

Kekwaletswe, R., & Lesole, T. (2016). A Framework for Improving Business Intelligence through Master Data Management. *Journal of South African Business Research*, 1-12. doi:10.5171/2016.473749

Kuiler, E. (2014). From Big Data to Knowledge: An Ontological Approach to Big Data Analytics. *The Review of Policy Research*, *31*(4), 311–318. doi:10.1111/ropr.12077

Kuner, C., Cate, F., Millard, C., & Svantesson, D. (2012). The challenge of 'big data' for data protection. *International Data Privacy Law*, *2*(2), 47–49. doi:10.1093/idpl/ips003

Lomotey, R., & Deters, R. (2015). Unstructured data mining: Use case for CouchDB. *International Journal of Big Data Intelligence*, *2*(3), 168. doi:10.1504/IJBDI.2015.070597

Luo, H., Zhang, H., Zukerman, M., & Qiao, C. (2014). An incrementally deployable network architecture to support both data-centric and host-centric services. *IEEE Network*, *28*(4), 58–65. doi:10.1109/MNET.2014.6863133

Mavridis, I., & Karatza, H. (2017). Performance evaluation of cloud-based log file analysis with Apache Hadoop and Apache Spark. *Journal of Systems and Software*, *125*, 133–151. doi:10.1016/j.jss.2016.11.037

Mynarz, J. (2014). Integration of public procurement data using linked data. *Journal Of Systems Integration*, 19-31. doi:10.20470/jsi.v5i4.213

Nurika, O., Hassan, M., & Zakaria, N. (2017). Implementation of Network Cards Optimizations in Hadoop Cluster Data Transmissions. *ICST Transactions On Ubiquitous Environments*, *4*(12). doi:10.4108/eai.21-12-2017.153506

Omidi, M., & Alipour, M. (2016). Why NoSQL And The Necessity of Movement Toward The NoSQL Data Base. *IOSR Journal Of Computer Engineering*, *18*(05), 116–118. doi:10.9790/0661-180502116118

Pan, E., Wang, D., & Han, Z. (2016). Analyzing Big Smart Metering Data Towards Differentiated User Services: A Sublinear Approach. *IEEE Transactions On Big Data*, *2*(3), 249–261. doi:10.1109/TBDATA.2016.2599924

Ploskas, N., Stiakakis, E., & Fouliras, P. (2014). Assessing Computer Network Efficiency Using Data Envelopment Analysis and Multicriteria Decision Analysis Techniques. *Journal Of Multi-Criteria Decision Analysis*, *22*(5-6), 260–278. doi:10.1002/mcda.1533

Ravada, S. (2015). Big data spatial analytics for enterprise applications. *SIGSPATIAL Special*, *6*(2), 34–41. doi:10.1145/2744700.2744705

Rey-del-Castillo, P., & Cardeñosa, J. (2016). An Exercise in Exploring Big Data for Producing Reliable Statistical Information. *Big Data*, *4*(2), 120–128. doi:10.1089/big.2015.0045 PMID:27441716

Rho, S., & Vasilakos, A. (2017). Intelligent collaborative system and service in value network for enterprise computing. *Enterprise Information Systems*, *12*(1), 1–3. doi:10.1080/17517575.2016.1238962

Shaheen, J. (2017). Apache Kafka: Real Time Implementation with Kafka Architecture Review. *International Journal Of Advanced Science And Technology*, *109*, 35–42. doi:10.14257/ijast.2017.109.04

Shmueli, G. (2017). Research Dilemmas with Behavioral Big Data. *Big Data*, *5*(2), 98–119. doi:10.1089/big.2016.0043 PMID:28632441

Smith, N. (2015). Wearable Tech: Smart Watches. *Engineering & Technology*, *10*(4), 20–21. doi:10.1049/et.2015.0451

Soltani, Z., & Navimipour, N. (2016). Customer relationship management mechanisms: A systematic review of the state of the art literature and recommendations for future research. *Computers in Human Behavior*, *61*, 667–688. doi:10.1016/j.chb.2016.03.008

Thompson, S., Varvel, S., Sasinowski, M., & Burke, J. (2016). From Value Assessment to Value Co-creation: Informing Clinical Decision-Making with Medical Claims Data. *Big Data*, *4*(3), 141–147. doi:10.1089/big.2015.0030 PMID:27642718

Tromp, E., Pechenizkiy, M., & Gaber, M. (2017). Expressive modeling for trusted big data analytics: Techniques and applications in sentiment analysis. *Big Data Analytics*, *2*(1), 5. doi:10.118641044-016-0018-9

Tromp, E., Pechenizkiy, M., & Gaber, M. (2017). Expressive modeling for trusted big data analytics: Techniques and applications in sentiment analysis. *Big Data Analytics*, *2*(1), 5. doi:10.118641044-016-0018-9

Waterman, K., & Hendler, J. (2013). Getting the Dirt on Big Data. *Big Data*, *1*(3), 137–140. doi:10.1089/big.2013.0026 PMID:27442195

Weber, C., Königsberger, J., Kassner, L., & Mitschang, B. (2017). M2DDM – A Maturity Model for Data-Driven Manufacturing. *Procedia CIRP*, *63*, 173–178. doi:10.1016/j.procir.2017.03.309

Yang, J., & Yecies, B. (2016). Mining Chinese social media UGC: A big-data framework for analyzing Douban movie reviews. *Journal Of Big Data*, *3*(1), 3. doi:10.118640537-015-0037-9

Yu, C., Yurovsky, D., & Xu, T. (2011). Visual Data Mining: An Exploratory Approach to Analyzing Temporal Patterns of Eye Movements. *Infancy*, *17*(1), 33–60. doi:10.1111/j.1532-7078.2011.00095.x

KEY TERMS AND DEFINITIONS

DM: Data mining or information mining is the route toward discovering plans in full instructive records including techniques at the union of machine learning, estimations, and database systems. An interdisciplinary subfield of software engineering, it is principal methodologies wherein adroit methodologies are associated with remove data designs the general goal of which is to isolate information from an educational file and change it into a reasonable structure for encouraging use. Aside from the unrefined examination step, it incorporates database and data organization points, data pre-taking care of, display and construing thoughts, interesting quality estimations, multifaceted nature considerations, post-getting ready of discovered structures, recognition, and web-based refreshing. Information mining is the examination adventure of the "learning disclosure in databases" process or KDD. The term is a misnomer, in light of the way that the goal is the extraction of precedents and gaining from a great deal of data, not merely the extraction (mining) of data.

HPDA: High-performance data analytics with data examination the methodology utilize HPC's usage of parallel taking care of to run notable logical programming at places higher than a teraflop or (a trillion skimming point assignments for each second). Through this methodology, it is possible to quickly investigate extensive enlightening lists, influencing conclusions about the information they to contain. Some examination remaining tasks at hand enhance the circumstance with HPC rather than standard figure structure. While some "gigantic data" errands proposed to executed on thing hardware, in "scale out" designing there are certain conditions where ultra-brisk, high-limit HPC "scale up" approaches are favored. It is the space of HPDA. Drivers consolidate a delicate time portion for examination (e.g., continuous, high-repeat stock trading or exceedingly complex examination issues found in legitimate research).

Chapter 61
Big Data Analytics in Higher Education

Tanveer H. Shah
University of Azad Jammu and Kashmir, Pakistan

ABSTRACT

This chapter reviews the literature on the use of business analytics in higher education. Universities have large datasets available to predict future direction and generate actionable information. An important type of analytics used to improve management processes and to make informed decisions is big data business analytics. State university executive leaders may improve the effectiveness of their decisions by integrating business analytics in the decision-making models. However, there is a need to examine the use of big data business analytics in the decision-making process at the executive leadership level of the selected state universities. Especially in the context of how descriptive, predictive, prescriptive, decisive and basic analytics, and data collection influence the decision-making process at the executive leadership level of the state universities in terms of student retention and graduation rates.

INTRODUCTION

The range of challenges that state universities face today is vast and continuously expanding. These challenges are political, economic, societal, and cultural. Higher educational leaders are struggling to meet these challenges and compete in a highly competitive environment. Universities have taken several initiatives to meet these challenges. One of these initiatives is the use of analytics to make informed decisions at the executive leadership level. Universities have large datasets available to predict future direction and generate actionable information. The integration of big data business analytics in decision-making processes at the executive leadership level of state universities may result in their increased effectiveness. Delen and Demirkan (2013) stated that big data analytics offer a great potential to provide much needed information for effective decision-making. In order to use big datasets and analytics effectively, it is important to understand what is big data and what is analytical process.

DOI: 10.4018/978-1-6684-3662-2.ch061

BACKGROUND

The term big data referred to large datasets first coined in the 1990s. The definition of these large datasets had been changing over time. In the 1980s, this term referred to a size of data that was so large that magnetic tapes were required to store it. In the 1990s, big data referred to any size of data that was beyond the limitations of Microsoft Excel and desktop PC. Currently, big data refers to any data that is too large to place and analyze in a desktop relational database and such data require specialized software and computing techniques (Jacobs, 2009).

Diebold et al. (2012) claimed that big data emerged from statistics, econometrics, and computer science disciplines. Big data utilized knowledge, skills, and techniques of these disciplines in a coordinated manner. John Mashey at a lunch table in Silicon Graphics Inc. coined the term big data and elaborated on its use. Diebold et al. (2012) further claimed that Mashey, Weiss and Indurkhya, Diebold, and Laney were among the earlier contributors to the term big data. Diebold concluded that big data had emerged as a discipline of its own.

Buhl (2013) indicated that there was a lot more to come in the field of big data such as sensor-generated data. The term big data did not only refer to traditional data but it also included the analysis of huge amounts of data. Analysis provided new opportunities to improve the management and decision-making processes. Big data provided more options for decision-making, but it also added complexity to this process. Therefore, besides knowing big data itself, knowing how to use big data was equally important (Buhl, 2013).

Buhl, Röglinger, Moser, and Heidemann (2013) claimed that big data was multidiscipline and evolved from the combination of emerging technologies of data storage and data processing. The characteristics of big data include volume, velocity, variety, and veracity of data. Veracity meant maintaining the quality of data.

According to Davenport, Barth, and Bean (2013), in big data, data flows were more important than data stocks. In a big data environment, quick analysis, decisions, and actions were required. It was important to keep pace with the emerging trends in data flows that kept changing continuously. Observing trends was useless unless leaders took specific actions identified by recognizable trends (Davenport et al., 2013).

Davenport further explained that big data environment needed data scientists instead of data analysts. These professionals possessed multidisciplinary skills of information technology, analytics, social network sociology, statistics, communication, and programming skills (Davenport et al., 2013).

In the journal *Strategic Direction*, the publishing director Tony Roche (2013) pointed out important differences between big data and traditional data. It was not only size but also the form of data that mattered. Big data was not just storage of historical data like traditional data rather it was constant, current, live, dynamic data that flew through an organization. It forced the organization to change information management systems in order to take advantage of these qualities of big data. Big data was not meant to be buried within the computers. Rather, it had to go to decision-makers who could use it to act quickly. The process of using big data would make the core functions of organizations appear completely different (Direction, 2013).

Schermann, Hemsen, Buchmüller, Bitter, Krcmar, and Markl (2014) elaborated the big data definition further. According to their study, big data referred to technologies used to provide right information to the right persons in the right volume and the right quality at the right time.

Daniel and Butson (2014) while describing features of big data added that beside volume, velocity, veracity, and variety, big data entailed features like verification and value. These six Vs represent fundamental characteristics of big data:

- Volume refers to challenging size of data.
- Velocity means ever rising speed of flow of data in an institution.
- Veracity explains quality of data.
- Variety means that big data includes numerous types of format including both structured and unstructured.
- Verification is authenticity and security of data.
- Value depicts whether data generates useful insights and benefits for management processes (Daniel & Butson, 2014).

Daniel et al. pointed out two additional important features of big data:

- Validity refers to accuracy of data.
- Volatility refers to how data changes constantly.

Therefore, these eight 'Vs' representing key characteristics of big data elaborate the importance and complexity of big data and how organizations used it for value creation. Following Figure is adapted from (Daniel & Butson, 2014) by adding two more Vs and renaming it as Eight Vs of Big Data. Figure 1 elaborates eight characteristics of big data.

Manyika et al. (2011) noted that big data offered great potential to leadership in organizations to generate value by improving their management of human and material resources. In addition, data management increased efficiency, accountability, and transparency, and added opportunities for creativity and innovation. Many sectors including education could benefit from the use of big data. The use of big data could bring efficiency and transparency to different departments of academic institutions. According to Manyika, in the public sector institutions, employees consumed 20% of their time searching for information from non-digital sources and travelling and walking from point to point in order to obtain information.

Manyika et al. (2011) studied how individuals shared large amounts of data on social websites and expressed their opinions, needs, and preferences that could inform decision-making and make management more scientific. Leaders in data driven organizations could make hypotheses before reaching their decisions. They could test those hypotheses with this large amount of data by designing experiments, using control groups, and analyzing quantitative results. Academic research had proven advantages for informed decision-making (Manyika et al., 2011).

Robust analytics would help leadership improve their decision-making process in the educational sector. This could minimize risks and help administrators and policy makers discover critical hidden aspects needed to create value (Manyika et al., 2011).

Manyika observed that there was a productivity difference among the units with the same organization at different locations in spite of using same work processes. Sharing the same information at different locations and among similar organizations could minimize this variability in performances without any other incentive. Employees could match their performances with employees of other units.

Figure 1.
This figure was adapted from (Daniel & Butson, 2014) and work by Buhl, Röglinger, Moser, and Heidemann (2013). Two Vs
were added and renamed as 'Eight Vs of big data'

A major hurdle in using big data in educational institutions was systemic-barriers, which once removed, would result in greater productivity. One potential area was measuring teacher performance in the form of student achievement (Manyika et al., 2011). Leaders who were able to interpret large datasets could find ways to remove barriers between divisions and improve in productivity, innovation, and competitiveness.

Organizations were under enormous pressure, because of the continued recession of 2010 and higher education felt the impact of technology (Picciano, 2012). After all, higher educational institutions also depended on political and economic systems within the country. Leadership in universities needed to cope with the problems of retention and graduation rates that demanded higher educational institutions find creative solutions to these problems.

Informed decision-making helped university management to generate innovative solutions to student retention problems. Picciano (2012) concluded that informed decision-making entered into a new era when big data offered new opportunities to expand options that helped develop strategies to resolve problems in low retention and graduation rates (Picciano, 2012).

Organizations in this era of information have tremendous access to data, but it is very challenging to convert this data into knowledge that ultimately will inform decisions to generate positive results. It is important to develop capacity and capabilities to analyze and use data to make informed decisions.

An important aspect is to develop skills to gather and clean relevant data (Thomas, Jeanne, David, & Alvin, 2001).

The first step towards informed decision-making is to develop analytical ability in an organization. Factors like transactional data environment and supportive top management play a critical role in creating analytical capacity, an ability to convert data into meaningful insights. These analytical capacities through technology help the institutions in converting analysis into informed decisions (Thomas et al., 2001).

Drigas and Leliopoulos (2014) noted that big data could help in shaping educational systems and make them more dynamic, optimized, and modernized to benefit each student. Big data helped to make good educational decisions and could provide educational leaders and teachers with new tools to use in their decision-making. Drigas et al. further said that there was a need to create an environment where educational leaders, teachers, and students could use these tools for desired results.

Luan (2002) noted that as a result of increasing competition and economic constraints, leaders at higher educational institutions have to proactively look for probable students. Leaders in higher education institutions need to design academic programs that address needs and demands of students instead of forcing the students into programs that did not consider what students wanted. Luan (2002) recommended that data mining techniques to determine students' needs be used in exploratory and predictive data analysis methods. Data mining processes could predict student desires for education by identifying patterns and underlying meanings in the large datasets available in institutions and online. These data mining techniques could forecast probable student entrants, likely graduates, and assist in decision-making by analyzing student data stored within an institution and online.

Similarly, leaders in higher educational institutions could also utilize big data to meet their challenges and to create evidence based decisions. Most of these institutions already had large datasets that they could use to predict future challenges. These challenges existed at different levels including institutional, teacher, and student levels (Daniel & Butson, 2014). For instance, mining unstructured and informal information produced by students on social media with motion sensors and location-based data could provide beneficial facts and patterns not uncovered before. This information could relate to retention of students and be useful as an input for policy-making.

Phillips-Wren and Hoskisson (2015) concluded that there was increasing evidence for organizations to gain strategic competitive advantage by using big data analytically. However, due to lack of human capital, leadership with strategic vision, and big data platforms, mid and small sized organizations were facing challenges in benefiting big data potentials.

According to Zhang (2015), big data silently entered into universities and gradually took roots. Characteristics of big data like volume, velocity, variety, veracity, and value revealed the impact of big data on different aspects of management of modern universities including management, classrooms, and teaching models. These influences have revolutionized internal management systems of universities (Zhang, 2015).

Daniel (2015) proclaimed that the environment in which universities functioned usually posed mounting pressure and high competition for students. Using big data could enable universities to cope with these challenges and respond to a need to increase students in certain academic areas, equip students with skills required at real work, and guarantee they meet both national and international standards. Daniel further claimed that big data offered tremendous opportunities to use data analysis for informed decision-making by efficiently aggregating and correlating large datasets to generate repetitive patterns of behavior and provide meaningful insights. However, he noted that there was limited research conducted on big data in higher education.

Daniel (2015) stated that there were three stages of implementing big data in any organization including data collection, analysis, and visualization and application. Data collection was about recognizing data that could generate valuable information. Data analysis generated actionable information after analyzing complex and diverse data by linking, correlating, and connecting different datasets. Visualization and application was about presenting information to relevant receivers in interpretable form so that they abled to integrate into existing processes of decision-making.

Thomas et al. (2001) noted that although organization leaders had incredible access to data, it was hard to generate useful information to inform decisions and achieve valuable outcomes. In many cases, personnel became confused because of the availability of abundant data. Currently, organizations needed to develop the capacity to combine, analyze, and use data to inform decisions and enable personnel to take quick actions and create true value.

Thomas et al. (2001) presented a model for converting transactional data into valuable information and outcomes. This model had three basic elements including context, transformation, and outcomes. Context included aspects related to strategies, organizational culture, organization, skills, technologies, and data. Transformation was where data were analyzed and used for the decision-making. Outcomes included the changes adopted from decision-making. These outcomes could alter behaviors, programs, and finances (Thomas et al., 2001).

According to Thomas et al. (2001) most personnel within an organization focused on technology and data and ignored other critical factors of organizational structure, culture, level of skills and experience. Contextual elements were important to design successful strategies for a particular environment. Experts who analyzed data needed to know the business processes, statistics, and communication skills so that they could present information in a useful way for decision-makers.

Thomas et al. (2001) claimed that in order to create a data driven culture, management needed to learn faster and be smarter with the use of information. The proper use of data required continuous improvement. The success of this analytic capability depended on a data driven culture across an organization that promoted the importance of data analysis and informed decision-making. Leadership in organizations needed to differentiate between automated transaction systems and analytics that required high involvement of personnel and their human insights.

Keeping in view strategies, skills and experience, structure, culture, and technological level of an organization, data transformed into knowledge influenced policies through interrelated phases of analysis and decision-making (Thomas et al., 2001).

Thomas et al. (2001) concluded that automated basic business procedures generated transactional data and there was a need to convert this data into valuable knowledge. Some decision-making processes required less human intervention but complex and unstructured processes required skilled humans using analytics.

Harris, Craig, and Light (2011) claimed that making full use of analytics required the integration of analysis and data processes throughout an organization. Furthermore, those who advocated for analytics had to be people with the right analytical skills, and capable to change a culture, process, and behavior at an organizational level. Finding right opportunities to implement analytics was important in order to get maximum output.

Kiron et al. (2011) found that organizations gained substantial competitive advantage by integrating analytics into strategies and processes. Organizations achieved sophistication in analytics by acquiring mastery in analytical skills and tools, robust information management practices, creating a data driven environment, and by improving those who lagged behind. Organizations without reasonable analytics strategies remained uncompetitive and their future was at risk. A continuous emerging and widening gap of competitive advantage was found between organizations that used analytics and those that did not (Kiron et al., 2011).

According to LaValle, Lesser, Shockley, Hopkins, and Kruschwitz (2011), organizations that used field related information, insights, and analytics in their decisions and strategies in day-to-day functioning performed better than those who did not. There was a strong correlation between use of analytics-driven leadership and performance. The use of analytics provided an organization with efficiency, progression, and competitive advantage. LaValle et al. recommended to start with the biggest and most significant challenge. The use of diagrams and available data could elaborate processes and applications and demonstrate where and how analytics would be most effective. For example, in the case of universities, retention of students was a major challenge and analytics could visualize and group issues related to retention.

Kiron and Shockley (2011) claimed that organizations that developed integrated data-driven environment across the organization gained the maximum potential from analytics. A data-driven culture required a strategic use of analytics, leadership supportive for analytics, availability of information, and insights for those who needed guidance in future decisions.

Beside creating a data-oriented culture, transformed organizations managed information and analytics in an excellent way (Kiron & Shockley, 2011). The mastery of analytics required talent, tools, and technology. Good information management provided the right information at right time to the right people. Robust data governance and data management practices delivered strong information management (Kiron & Shockley, 2011).

Barneveld, Arnold, and Campbell (2012) stated that data driven decision-making, another term for informed decision-making, was a process to provide critical data and support in decision-making for managerial and financial processes.

According to Picciano (2012), because of the recent 2008 recession, higher education like all other sectors found itself under tremendous pressure. Universities needed to find the means and ways to retain students, and have them complete their degrees. Many universities already used big data analytics in order to inform their decision-making, and to identify and evaluate strategies that could improve student retention (Picciano, 2012).

Rajesh (2013) elaborated that big data analytics were valuable for all organizations that wanted to make sense out of huge databases available on internet and on their networks. These organizations used analytics to improve their decision-making to compete with their competitors.

Kiron, Ferguson, and Prentice (2013) claimed that big data analytics would influence all decisions in coming years, and serve as an important driving force. They further elaborated that leaders could benefit from analytics by considering data as a core asset, by challenging the status quo, and by opening their minds to new thinking. They called it rethinking or reimagining.

Macfadyen, Dawson, Pardo, and Gasevic (2014) noted that education, as compared to all other sectors was much slower in utilizing the potential of big data analytics. This situation persisted in educational institutions all over the world, because of a lack of capacity to collect, manage, and analyze big data, effectively. Macfadyen et al. (2014) explained further that big data analytics provided educators with a useful alternative to get rid of time-consuming longitudinal and personalized assessment along with their ever-increasing workload.

Baer and Duin (2014) claimed that universities needed to rethink, readjust, and reinvent their institutional policies and practices to focus on student success. They insisted that a complete paradigm shift would result in a new model and culture to exploit the power of big data analytics.

Daniel (2015) observed that although the use of data in higher educational institutions grew in recent years, most of data were still stored across desktop computers in different departments making the integration and retrieval of data difficult for analysis. One important factor in using big data analytics in higher education institutions was how data sharing was implemented. Security of sensitive information was another key consideration. Daniel insisted that there was a need to define processes to store, retrieve, and secure information, and to authorize employees to access data.

MAIN FOCUS OF THE CHAPTER

There are many types of big data analytics that can be used in higher education for addressing different challenges. One of these analytics are business analytics that can provide solutions for informed decision-making to the leaders at higher educational institutions.

Business Analytics

In business, value creation was a major driving force behind the development of business analytics. This development occurred in all related fields including organizational processes and advanced technologies. One single focus of all this development was satisfaction and fulfillment of customer needs. Customer needs were driving force in making these technologies more accessible, reliable, and user-friendly. Gradually, data gathering, storing, and analyzing technologies became an integral part of almost every organizational process with a promise to generate actionable information that would produce business value (Kohavi, Rothleder, & Simoudis, 2002).

Eckerson (2006) claimed that organizational leaders would get an advantage from using information in their decision-making processes. He used examples of scorecards and dashboards that provided relevant information to make effective decisions and achieve strategic goals. These systems were capable of generating visual data to view an overall picture and analysis of operational data for actionable information. These instruments also enabled managers to monitor the performances of employees and keep track of the execution of their strategic objectives.

Research in business analytics continuously progressed over decades, and resulted in development of powerful analytical and performance management tools. In order to inform decisions, complex systems like expert systems, decision support systems, and data mining systems were devised to unearth complicated patterns and relationships in order to generate actionable information (Baars & Kemper, 2008).

According to Chaudhuri, Dayal, and Narasayya (2011), gradually, the business intelligence field progressed both in research and practice. One reason for this development was the availability of data and easy access to larger datasets. More diversity in the data, and the availability of text data resulted in systems to analyze data more intelligently. Beside availability of data, unprecedented advancement in computer technologies, and reduction in their prices also helped create technologies like cloud computing. These technologies were the backbone of business intelligence and business analytics. Chaudhuri et al. (2011) further hinted that the use of continuously advancing smartphone technologies would create further opportunities for business intelligence and business analytics in different fields and professions.

Watson (2011) argued that in spite of great potential, success of business analytics depended on how leaders made essential organizational and technological changes, and how much value they created from the use of these technologies.

Viaene and Van den Bunder (2011) reported that business analytics accompanied uncertainty and changes in requirements that required special skills for managers to lead in this field. New managers should expect changes in their starting plan at any phase in the progression of the project. These business analytics leaders were capable of involving all the concerned parties in the description and justification for new expectations. They strongly believed in experimentation based on iterative trial and error process and meaningful insights. This intelligent experimentation started with clear objectives, followed by a four-step cycle comprised design, build, run, and analyze (Viaene & Van den Bunder, 2011).

Klatt et al. (2011) noted that less bureaucratic organizations performed better in business analytics. There was a need for a clear and target-oriented strategic communication system, assignments, and actions. Success of business analytics depended on the planning style of analytical leadership. Successful organizations in implementing business analytics distributed across-the-board rational data analysis (Klatt et al., 2011).

Hsinchun, Chiang, and Storey (2012) observed that business analytics became an emerging trend in academia and business in the last two decades. Educational institutions need a new vision for information systems to use emerging analytical skills meet the needs of their traditional students.

According to Shanks and Bekmamedova (2012), organizations required a state of art technological and data setup for success in business analytics. Business analytics should be imbedded into different organizational process and required real-time relevant data feeds. Moreover, business analytics needed to advance continuously to give competitive advantage to institutions.

Delen and Demirkan (2013) claimed that business analytics became famous faster than any other management practice because of their potential to provide relevant information for effective decision-making. Delen et al. described that business analytics consisted of three types of analytics including descriptive, predictive, and prescriptive. Descriptive analytics or business reporting used data to pinpoint problems and business opportunities. Predictive analytics used mathematical modeling techniques on data to generate patterns to predict relationships between input and output. Predictive analytics accurately forecasted future events and reasoning behind them. Prescriptive analytics used different mathematical algorithms to provide different courses of actions or decision alternatives (Delen & Demirkan, 2013).

Kumar (2014) claimed that there was a fourth type of business analytics that was called decisive analytics. Decisive analytics used modeling techniques and visual analytics to support decisions and reasoning. According to Kumar, business analytics consisted of four types of analytics: descriptive, predictive, prescriptive, and decisive.

Descriptive Analytics

Descriptive analytics provided answers to questions like what happened and what is happening. These analytics were called business reporting (Delen & Demirkan, 2013). According to Delen et al. to identify well-defined business opportunities and problems, descriptive analytics generated different types of reports including periodic, on-demand, and interactive reports. Business reporting, data warehousing, dashboards, and scorecards were used to identify business opportunities and deficiencies (Delen & Demirkan, 2013).

Baer and Duin (2014) noted that higher education institutions rarely used information from data buried in their networks. Fewer people used this information for basic reporting and even less people used the data in their decision-making processes. Using these analytics enabled personnel in educational institutions to use past data of student enrollment records, types of admissions, and courses with high dropouts and failures to know where the problems rose and what was happening (Baer & Duin, 2014).

Kumar (2014) stated that descriptive analytics provided management with information from historical data to make their decisions more informed. Descriptive analytics used data from separate sources to integrate and generate accurate information of occurrence of past events.

Dashboards were enablers of descriptive analytics and used to present information to management in visual form including icons, graphs, text, and charts. This consolidated information presented a clear overview on a screen for monitoring and building further details (Santiago Rivera & Shanks, 2015).

Wilder and Ozgur (2015) suggested that skills and knowledge required for descriptive analytics were the abilities to describe and communicate past events in an effective manner within a variety of formats. Personnel using these analytics employed several techniques including descriptive statistics, frequency distributions, discrete distributions, continuous distributions, sampling distributions, and statistical inference (Wilder & Ozgur, 2015).

In the context of higher education, Daniel (2015) stated that descriptive analytics described and analyzed historical data of students, teachers, policies, administration, and academic activities including research and teaching. This analysis generated patterns to identify present trends on student enrollment, graduation and retention rates. Descriptive analytics enabled higher education institutions to look into frequency of student logins into certain pages, page views, course completion rates, activities of successful students compared to those of less successful students, and what material they searched for (Daniel, 2015).

Predictive Analytics

According to Agosta (2004), efforts in data mining technologies gave birth to predictive analytics. These analytics discovered patterns in data to make a hypothesis about future events. It was important to acknowledge that data itself was not information because it did not have qualities like organization, consistency, and conceptual constructs. Predictive analytics informed data with meaning.

Hair (2007) reported that predictive analytics used correlations of data and explanatory variables to predict chances of occurrence and relationships. Predictive analytics and data mining shared an interactive process. Data mining identified prospective correlations and patterns in past data including but not limited to text, numbers, visual data, and web clicks. Predictive analytics utilized confirmed relationships to identify future patterns, behaviors, events, and tendencies. Data mining examined large datasets in two phases. The first phase identified high value hidden relationships in valuable datasets that could potentially create knowledge to improve decision-making. This phase used automated machine learning processes to identify patterns of information. The second phase verified and identified correlations to confirm or reject by hypotheses (Hair, 2007).

Predictive analytics used these confirmed correlations for wide-ranging data analysis. These analytics used predictive, descriptive, and decision models with different statistical methods. Predictive models predicted the occurrence of a behavior in the future based upon the analysis of historical data. Abrupt patterns identified a risk or opportunity. Descriptive models grouped customers and events by describing correlations in data. Often descriptive models categorized individuals based on their choices, behaviors, and age levels. Decision models explained different aspects critical for a decision including explaining data, correlations, decision itself, and effect of the decision after implementation (Hair, 2007).

Jalonen and Lönnqvist (2009) claimed that observation, analysis, and optimization were basic factors of the predictive analysis process. Observation provided answers to questions such as, what happened, how much, how often, and where. Analysis was about why something happened and what would happen next. Whereas, optimization was about what was best to happen and what actions needed to be taken next. Jalonen and Lönnqvist (2009) claimed that predictive process could reveal the processes behind even unsystematic incidents.

Harris et al. (2011) identified that in order to improve retention of employees in an organization, knowing their preferences was crucial. Data could determine what employees like most. An analytical model based on data related to their preferences would predict actions to improve retention of employees. However, to tap maximum potential across the board, integration of data analysis and of analytical processes was mandatory.

Delen and Demirkan (2013) described that predictive analytics discovered patterns like tendencies, relations, and similarities by using data. These patterns represented integral relations between data inputs and outputs. Predictive analytics responded to queries like what and why something would happen. Techniques like data mining, text mining, web mining, and media mining helped in finding answers to these queries.

According to Waller and Fawcett (2013), predictive analytics was a subgroup of data science that used both qualitative and quantitative methods for forecasting. Besides predicting the future, these analytics were used to explore questions like what would happen in the past under a number of different conditions. Predictive analytics were very fast and a cost-effective way of drawing conclusions using processes of deductive mathematics. This was done through estimating relations between different variables.

Holsapple, Lee-Post, and Pakath (2014) noted that predictive analytics engaged sources to predict what would happen. The global consulting company Capgemini presented the threefold taxonomy of analytics in 2010. This taxonomy was comprised of descriptive, predictive, and prescriptive dimensions. Holsapple et al. (2014) also hinted about the fourth dimension of evaluation that would be discussed under decisive analytics.

Baer and Duin (2014) noted that predictive analytics could provide a plan to achieve optimum student learning while considering both individual and collective needs of students. Predictive analytics could play a vital role in students' readiness, advisement, continuous training of teachers, learning needs of students, and scheduling courses for students' success. As Baer and Duin (2014) observed, predictive analytics would enable educational intuitions management to track the progress of students. It was important to know where students were, where they were supposed to be, and how they would reach their goal.

Gandomi and Haider (2015) stated that predictive analytics employed several techniques to forecast results using past and present data. Almost all disciplines could utilize predictive analytics to predict outcomes of actions. Predictive analytics identified patterns and relations in data. A basic technique used in predictive analytical process was moving averages on historical data and their extension to the future to predict outcome variables. Another technique was linear regression in which interdependent relations between explanatory and outcome variables were identified and used to make predictions. This forecasting differed from traditional data analysis whose sample size was much less than the population. In predictive analysis sample size reffered to a majority if not the whole population (Gandomi & Haider, 2015).

Wilder and Ozgur (2015) emphasized the skills and knowledge for predictive analysis and how to exploit the outcomes of this analysis. They noted how to comprehend a problem, conduct analysis, and communicate the outcomes in simple language. Analytical techniques employed in predictive analysis included ANOVA, regression, correlation, time series, and nonparametric approaches (Wilder & Ozgur, 2015).

Daniel (2015) insisted that predictive analytics provided organizations with valuable insights derived from data analysis that would lead further actions. These analytics would forecast events by identifying trends and patterns in data, and acknowledging relations between different variables. This analysis would identify any opportunity or threat in the future. In contrast to descriptive analytics, predictive analytics would uncover unseen relations such as completion rates and demographic changes. They could also forecast behaviors of students earlier in their academic programs that would result in their failure or exit from programs. This would help educators make informed decisions for future courses of actions (Daniel, 2015).

Prescriptive Analytics

Evans (2012) described that optimization techniques were used in prescriptive analytics to select best available option to act upon in order to achieve certain goals such as maximizing retention rate of students in a university or minimizing dropouts in an academic program. Several processes of organizational management could benefit from prescriptive analytics including but not limited to operations, finance, and marketing. Mathematical and statistical techniques used in predicative analytics together with optimization techniques could result in informed decisions that accounted for the uncertainty of data (Evans, 2012).

Delen and Demirkan (2013) stated that prescriptive analytics obtained a set of valuable alternatives for taking actions or decisions to improve organizational performance. Algorithms used in prescriptive analysis could employ data in reliable processes. Simulation, optimization, multi-criteria decision modeling techniques, and expert systems could enable these analytics to produce best decisions and actions under certain situations and constraints. Prescriptive analytics provided answers to questions what and why one would do an action. Best possible decisions, actions, and transactions were outcomes of prescriptive analysis (Delen & Demirkan, 2013).

Power (2014) viewed prescriptive analytics as a planned quantitative analysis of real-time data capable of triggering events. Information generated through prescriptive analysis suggested desirable actions.

According to Kumar (2014), prescriptive analytics used results of both descriptive and predictive analytics to produce a set of actions. Organizational leaders used prescriptive analytics to get a reliable course of action to solve problems.

Wilder and Ozgur (2015) suggested that the successful use of prescriptive analytics required skills and knowledge of calculus, simulation, and optimization. Experts in these analytics needed skills to recognize patterns within a problem and interpret them using good communication skills. Prescriptive analytics helped analysts recommend what should happen.

Daniel (2015) stated that universities used prescriptive analytics to select alternatives. These alternatives were created through authentic and reliable predictions of events. Prescriptive analytics used analytical outputs of descriptive and predictive analytics to seek and establish a new course of action to achieve desired goals in a given situation within constraints. These analytics helped decision-makers in higher education to seek opportunities and identify threats in their future actions as well as act in time to take advantage of this foresight.

Decisive Analytics

Thomas and Cook (2005) stated that visual models were a multidiscipline analytical reasoning having interacting visual interfaces. Techniques used in visual models were analytical reasoning, data representation, and visual representation.

Analytical reasoning techniques empowered users to gain deep insights that directly facilitated evaluation, planning, and decision-making processes. The basic philosophy behind the use of visual models was to assist human judgment with limited time of analysis. These visual models enabled a quick analysis of past and present situations, trends and events that created current situations, and future probable courses of actions and their alarming signs. These techniques helped users to monitor occurrence of any alarming signs or any unexpected situations, helping analysts to determine a need to take an action, and supporting decision-makers in critical situations (Thomas & Cook, 2005).

Thomas and Cook (2005) stated that data representations and transformation techniques shaped conflicting and dynamic data in forms that supported visualization and analysis. These representations were in structured forms that existed already or derived from original data in order to fit in computer-based transformations. Production, presentation, and dissemination techniques used to communicate the results of an analysis in an appropriate perspective to a range of audiences (Thomas & Cook, 2005).

Visual representations and interaction techniques while taking advantage of the human eye's wide-ranging bandwidth path into the mind allowed users to see, explore, and comprehend large volumes of information immediately. Visual representations interpreted data in an observable form that underlined important features, including commonalities and abnormalities. These visual representations made it easy for users to identify significant characteristics of their data swiftly. Enhancing the cognitive reasoning process with perceptual reasoning through visual representations allowed the analytical reasoning process to act faster and be more attentive (Thomas & Cook, 2005).

According to Chang et al. (2007) visual analytical models could confront problems that were stubborn because of their size and complexity. These complex problems needed a combined human and machine analysis for their solution. Kielman et al. (2009) reported that visual analytical models employed advanced techniques for analytical reasoning, communication, data transformations, and representations. These techniques used computation, visualization, analytic reporting, and technology transition. Visual models derived from collaborative work of several scientific and technical communities in computer science, information visualization, cognitive and perceptual sciences, interactive design, graphic design, and social sciences. Visual models employed tools like geographic maps, info graphics, heat maps, spark lines, and fever charts (Kielman et al., 2009).

Holsapple et al. (2014) considered that there were two major taxonomies of business analytics including a threefold and alternative fourfold model. In 2010, a global consultation company Capgemini presented threefold taxonomy comprising descriptive, predictive and prescriptive dimensions. Steps involved in the fourfold taxonomy of business analytics included how to sense a situation, make predictions, make evaluations, and take decisive action (SPED). SPED taxonomy enabled management to do evidence based problem solving through sensing, predicting, and evaluating. Problem solving was a broader term not necessarily always decisional. Making sense was more related to understanding the problems rather than making decisions (Holsapple et al., 2014).

Hargreaves and Ding (2014) recommended construction of a decision agent within the business analytics framework. This agent's work would be based on recorded effects of recommended decisions that were accepted by a user and performed recommended actions. Recording this impact would be the only update that required human involvement. An evaluation agent would evaluate future decisions by comparing current choices and conditions with recorded impacts of past decisions. The evaluative agent acted only when an effect of a decision was recorded.

According to Kumar (2014) fourth a type of business analytics was decisive analytics. Managers used decisive analytics to create visual models to support their decisions and reasoning. Visual analytics supported human decisions with virtual representations of expressed reasoning.

CONCLUSION

Higher educational leaders are struggling to meet these challenges and compete in a highly competitive environment. Retention of students is one of the important challenges that state universities face today. Retaining students is crucial for universities not only for their financial resources but also for their reputation. One of the initiatives to address this issue is to make informed decisions is the use of big data analytics. Universities have large datasets available to predict future direction and generate actionable information. An important type of analytics used to improve management processes and to make informed decisions is big data business analytics. State university executive leaders may improve the effectiveness of their decisions by integrating business analytics in the decision-making models.

However, there is a need to examine the use of big data business analytics in the decision-making process at the executive leadership level of the selected state universities. Especially in the context of how descriptive, predictive, prescriptive, decisive and basic analytics, and data collection influence the decision-making process at the executive leadership level of the state universities in terms of student retention and graduation rates.

REFERENCES

Agosta, L. (2004). Data Mining is Dead-Long Live Predictive Analytics! *Information & Management*, *14*(1), 37.

Alavi, M., Yoo, Y., & Vogel, D. R. (1997). Using information technology to add value to management education. *Academy of Management Journal*, *40*(6), 1310–1333. doi:10.2307/257035

Astin, A. W. (1997). How good is your institutions retention rate? *Research in Higher Education*, *38*(6), 647–658. doi:10.1023/A:1024903702810

Avolio, B. J., Jung, D. I., Murry, W., & Sivasbramaniam, N. (1996). Building highly developed teams: Focusing on shared leadership process, efficacy, trust, and performance.

Baars, H., & Kemper, H.-G. (2008). Management Support with Structured and Unstructured Data— An Integrated Business Intelligence Framework. *Information Systems Management*, *25*(2), 132–148. doi:10.1080/10580530801941058

Baer, L., & Duin, A. H. (2014). Retain Your Students! The Analytics, Policies and Politics of Reinvention Strategies. *Planning for Higher Education*, *42*(3), 30.

Basham, L. M. (2010). Transformational and transactional leaders in higher education. *International Review of Business Research Papers, 6*(6), 141–152.

Bryman, A. (2007). Effective leadership in higher education: A literature review. *Studies in Higher Education, 32*(6), 693–710. doi:10.1080/03075070701685114

Buhl, H. U. (2013). Interview with Martin Petry on Big Data. *Business & Information Systems Engineering, 5*(2), 101–102. doi:10.100712599-013-0253-9

Buhl, H. U., Röglinger, M., Moser, F., & Heidemann, J. (2013). Big Data. *Wirtschaftsinformatik, 55*(2), 63–68. doi:10.100711576-013-0350-x

Burns, J. M. (2003). *Transforming leadership: A new pursuit of happiness* (Vol. 213). Grove Press.

Chang, R., Ghoniem, M., Kosara, R., Ribarsky, W., Yang, J., Suma, E., . . . Sudjianto, A. (2007). Wirevis: Visualization of categorical, time-varying data from financial transactions. *Paper presented at the IEEE Symposium on Visual Analytics Science and Technology VAST '07.*

Chang, R. M., Kauffman, R. J., & Kwon, Y. (2014). Understanding the paradigm shift to computational social science in the presence of big data. *Decision Support Systems, 63,* 67–80. doi:10.1016/j.dss.2013.08.008

Chaudhuri, S., Dayal, U., & Narasayya, V. (2011). An overview of business intelligence technology. *Communications of the ACM, 54*(8), 88–98. doi:10.1145/1978542.1978562

Daniel, B. (2015). Big Data and analytics in higher education: Opportunities and challenges. *British Journal of Educational Technology.* doi:10.1111/bjet.12230

Daniel, B., & Butson, R. (2014). Foundations of Big Data and Analytics in Higher Education. Retrieved from http://engineering.nyu.edu/files/ICAS2014-Proceedings-Publication.pdf

Daniel, B. K., & Butson, R. (2013). Technology enhanced analytics (TEA) in higher education. *Paper presented at the Proceedings of the International Conference on Educational Technologies.*

Davenport, T. H., Barth, P., & Bean, R. (2013). How 'big data' is different. *MIT Sloan Management Review, 54*(1).

Delen, D., & Demirkan, H. (2013). Data, information and analytics as services. *Decision Support Systems, 55*(1), 359–363. doi:10.1016/j.dss.2012.05.044

Dhar, V., & Sundararajan, A. (2007). Information Technologies in Business: A Blueprint for Education and Research.

Diebold, F. X., Cheng, X., Diebold, S., Foster, D., Halperin, M., Lohr, S., & Pospiech, M. (2012). *A Personal Perspective on the Origin (s) and Development of "Big Data".*

Direction, S. (2013). So, are the geeks inheriting the earth?: Big Data, big decisions and best practice for information management. *Strategic Direction, 29*(9).

Drigas, A. S., & Leliopoulos, P. (2014). The Use of Big Data in Education. *International Journal of Computer Science Issues, 11*(5), 58.

Dupin-Bryant, P. A., & Olsen, D. H. (2014). Business Intelligence, Analytics And Data Visualization: A Heat Map Project Tutorial. *International Journal of Management & Information Systems*, *18*(3), 185–200.

Dziuban, C., Moskal, P., Cavanagh, T., & Watts, A. (2012). Analytics that Inform the University: Using Data You Already Have. *Journal of Asynchronous Learning Networks*, *16*(3), 21–38.

Eckerson, W. W. (2006). Deploying dashboards and scorecards. The Data Warehouse Institute, 1-24.

Evans, J. R. (2012). Business analytics: the next frontier for decision sciences.

Franks, E. E. (2014). *State of the art analytics and managers in the defense industry*. CAPELLA UNIVERSITY.

Fullan, M. (2011). *Change leader: Learning to do what matters most*. John Wiley & Sons.

Fullan, M., & Scott, G. (2009). *Turnaround leadership for higher education*. John Wiley & Sons.

Gandomi, A., & Haider, M. (2015). Beyond the hype: Big data concepts, methods, and analytics. *International Journal of Information Management*, *35*(2), 137–144. doi:10.1016/j.ijinfomgt.2014.10.007

Hair, J. F. Jr. (2007). Knowledge creation in marketing: The role of predictive analytics. *European Business Review*, *19*(4), 303–315. doi:10.1108/09555340710760134

Hargreaves, C. A., & Ding, L. (2014). Business Analytics as a Framework for an Evolving Multi-Agent System. *Journal on Computing*, *2*(3).

Harris, J. G., Craig, E., & Light, D. A. (2011). Talent and analytics: New approaches, higher ROI. *The Journal of Business Strategy*, *32*(6), 4–13. doi:10.1108/02756661111180087

Harrison, L. M. (2011). Transformational leadership, integrity, and power. *New Directions for Student Services*, *2011*(135), 45–52. doi:10.1002s.403

Holsapple, C., Lee-Post, A., & Pakath, R. (2014). A unified foundation for business analytics. *Decision Support Systems*, *64*, 130–141. doi:10.1016/j.dss.2014.05.013

Hopkins, M. S. (2011). Big Data, analytics and the path from insights to value. *MIT Sloan Management Review, 52*(2), 21-22. Retrieved from http://0-search.ebscohost.com.library.dowling.edu/login.aspx?direct=true&db=buh&AN=57750727&site=ehost-live

Hsinchun, C., Chiang, R. H. L., & Storey, V. C. (2012). Business intelligence and analytics: from big data to big impact. *Management Information Systems Quarterly*, *36*(4), 1165–1188. Retrieved from http://0-search.ebscohost.com.library.dowling.edu/login.aspx?direct=true&db=lxh&AN=83466038&site=ehost-live

Jacobs, A. (2009). The pathologies of big data. *Communications of the ACM, 52*(8), 36–44. doi:10.1145/1536616.1536632

Jagadish, H. V., Gehrke, J., Labrinidis, A., Papakonstantinou, Y., Patel, J. M., Ramakrishnan, R., & Shahabi, C. (2014). Big Data and Its Technical Challenges. *Communications of the ACM, 57*(7), 86–94. doi:10.1145/2611567

Jalonen, H., & Lönnqvist, A. (2009). Predictive business – fresh initiative or old wine in a new bottle. *Management Decision, 47*(10), 1595–1609. doi:10.1108/00251740911004709

Kielman, J., Thomas, J., & May, R. (2009). Foundations and Frontiers in Visual Analytics. *Information Visualization, 8*(4), 239–246. doi:10.1057/ivs.2009.25

Kiron, D., Ferguson, R. B., & Prentice, P. K. (2013). From value to vision: Reimagining the possible with data analytics. *MIT Sloan Management Review, 54*(3), 1.

Kiron, D., & Shockley, R. (2011). Creating business value with analytics. *MIT Sloan Management Review, 53*(1), 57.

Kiron, D., Shockley, R., Kruschwitz, N., Finch, G., & Haydock, M. (2011). Analytics: The widening divide. *MIT Sloan Management Review, 53*(3), 1–22.

Klatt, T., Schlaefke, M., & Moeller, K. (2011). Integrating business analytics into strategic planning for better performance. *The Journal of Business Strategy, 32*(6), 30–39. doi:10.1108/02756661111180113

Knapp, M. S., Swinnerton, J. A., Copland, M. A., & Monpas-Huber, J. (2006). *Data-Informed Leadership in Education*. Center for the Study of Teaching and Policy.

Kohavi, R., Rothleder, N. J., & Simoudis, E. (2002). Emerging trends in business analytics. *Communications of the ACM, 45*(8), 45–48. Retrieved from http://0-search.ebscohost.com.library.dowling.edu/login.aspx?direct=true&db=buh&AN=11863428&site=ehost-live doi:10.1145/545151.545177

Kumar, B. S. (2014). Business Analytics: A way forward to Decision Making.

Lau, L. K. (2003). Institutional factors affecting student retention. *Education-Indianapolis Then Chula Vista, 124*(1), 126–136.

LaValle, S., Lesser, E., Shockley, R., Hopkins, M. S., & Kruschwitz, N. (2011). Big Data, Analytics and the Path from Insights to Value. *MIT Sloan Management Review, 52*(2), 21-32.

Luan, J. (2002). Data mining and its applications in higher education. *New Directions for Institutional Research, 2002*(113), 17–36. doi:10.1002/ir.35

Macfadyen, L. P., Dawson, S., Pardo, A., & Gasevic, D. (2014). Embracing big data in complex educational systems: The learning analytics imperative and the policy challenge. *Research & Practice in Assessment, 9*(2), 17–28.

Manyika, J., Chui, M., Brown, B., Bughin, J., Dobbs, R., Roxburgh, C., & Byers, A. H. (2011). Big data: The next frontier for innovation, competition, and productivity.

March, J. G., & Simon, H. A. (1958). Organizations.

Marsh, J. A., & Farrell, C. C. (2015). How leaders can support teachers with data-driven decision making A framework for understanding capacity building. *Educational Management Administration & Leadership, 43*(2), 269–289. doi:10.1177/1741143214537229

Murtaugh, P. A., Burns, L. D., & Schuster, J. (1999). Predicting the retention of university students. *Research in Higher Education, 40*(3), 355–371. doi:10.1023/A:1018755201899

Nandeshwar, A., Menzies, T., & Nelson, A. (2011). Learning patterns of university student retention. *Expert Systems with Applications, 38*(12), 14984–14996. doi:10.1016/j.eswa.2011.05.048

OReilly, K., & Paper, D. (2012). Want Value from Big Data? Close the Gap between the C-Suite and the Server Room. *Journal of Information Technology Case and Application Research, 14*(4), 3–10. doi :10.1080/15228053.2012.10845709

Phillips-Wren, G., & Hoskisson, A. (2015). An analytical journey towards big data. *Journal of Decision Systems, 24*(1), 87–102. doi:10.1080/12460125.2015.994333

Picciano, A. G. (2012). The Evolution of Big Data and Learning Analytics in American Higher Education. *Journal of Asynchronous Learning Networks, 16*(3), 9–20.

Power, D. J. (2014). Using Big Data for analytics and decision support. *Journal of Decision Systems, 23*(2), 222–228. doi:10.1080/12460125.2014.888848

Rajesh, K. (2013). Big Data Analytics: Applications and Benefits. *IUP Journal of Information Technology, 9*(4), 41.

Ravishanker, G. (2011). Doing academic analytics right: Intelligent answers to simple questions. *Research Bulletin (Sun Chiwawitthaya Thang Thale Phuket)*, 2.

Rogers, D. L. (2000). A paradigm shift: Technology integration for higher education in the new millennium. *AACE Journal, 1*(13), 19–33.

Santiago Rivera, D., & Shanks, G. (2015). A Dashboard to Support Management of Business Analytics Capabilities. *Journal of Decision Systems, 24*(1), 73–86. doi:10.1080/12460125.2015.994335

Senge, P. M. (2014). *The dance of change: The challenges to sustaining momentum in a learning organization*. Crown Business.

Shanks, G., & Bekmamedova, N. (2012). Achieving benefits with business analytics systems: An evolutionary process perspective. *Journal of Decision Systems, 21*(3), 231–244. doi:10.1080/12460125.2 012.729182

Thomas, D., Jeanne, G., David, W., & Alvin, L. (2001). Data to Knowledge to Results, Building an Analytic Capability. *California Management Review, 43*(2).

Thomas, J. J., & Cook, K. A. (2005). Illuminating the Path: The R&D Agenda for Visual Analytics National Visualization and Analytics Center.

Tinto, V. (2006). Research and practice of student retention: What next? *Journal of College Student Retention, 8*(1), 1–19. doi:10.2190/4YNU-4TMB-22DJ-AN4W

Tinto, V. (2007). *Taking student retention seriously*. Syracuse University.

Tucker, B. A., & Russell, R. F. (2004). The influence of the transformational leader. *Journal of Leadership & Organizational Studies, 10*(4), 103–111. doi:10.1177/107179190401000408

van Barneveld, A., Arnold, K. E., & Campbell, J. P. (2012). Analytics in higher education: Establishing a common language. *EDUCAUSE learning initiative, 1*, 1-11.

Viaene, S., & Van den Bunder, A. (2011). The secrets to managing business analytics projects. *MIT Sloan Management Review*, *53*(1), 65–69.

Waller, M. A., & Fawcett, S. E. (2013). Data science, predictive analytics, and big data: A revolution that will transform supply chain design and management. *Journal of Business Logistics*, *34*(2), 77–84. doi:10.1111/jbl.12010

Watson, H. (2011). Business analytics insight: Hype or here to stay? *Business Intelligence Journal*, *16*(1), 4–8.

Whitchurch, C. (2004). Administrative managers–A critical link. *Higher Education Quarterly*, *58*(4), 280–298. doi:10.1111/j.1468-2273.2004.00274.x

Wilder, C. R., & Ozgur, C. O. (2015). Business Analytics Curriculum for Undergraduate Majors. *INFORMS Transactions on Education*, *15*(2), 180–187. doi:10.1287/ited.2014.0134

Zhang, K. (2015). Four Changes of Modern Universities from the Perspective of "4V" of Big Data. *Canadian Social Science*, *11*(3).

This research was previously published in Maximizing Social Science Research Through Publicly Accessible Data Sets; pages 38-61, copyright year 2018 by Information Science Reference (an imprint of IGI Global).

Chapter 62
Implementation of Big Data Analytics for Government Enterprise

Namhla Matiwane

Cape Peninsula University of Technology, South Africa

Tiko Iyamu

iD https://orcid.org/0000-0002-4949-094X

Cape Peninsula University of Technology, South Africa

ABSTRACT

Within the South African government, there is an increasing amount of data. The problem is that the South African government is struggling to employ the concept of big data analytics (BDA) for the analysis of its big data. This could be attributed to know-how from both technical and nontechnical perspectives. Failure to implement BDA and ensure appropriate use hinders government enterprises and agencies in their drive to deliver quality service. A government enterprise was selected and used as a case in this study primarily because the concept of BDA is new to many South African government departments. Data was collected through in-depth interviews. From the analysis, four factors—knowledge, process, differentiation, and skillset—that can influence implementation of BDA for government enterprises were revealed. Based on the factors, a set of criteria in the form of a model was developed.

INTRODUCTION

Big data has attracted attention, not only from private organisations, but major governmental organisations as well (Cao, 2017). As with other sectors of the economy, large amounts of data have been generated by government of many countries (Archenaa & Anita, 2015). Big data is defined as large data sets with characteristics of high volume, variety, and velocity that cannot be easily stored, captured, managed, analysed effectively with traditional database storage software and methods (Ridge et al., 2015). The rate at which data is growing around the world is at a projected rate of 40% per year (Al Nuaimi et al.,

DOI: 10.4018/978-1-6684-3662-2.ch062

2015). According to Berg (2015), big data presents challenges to organisations because of data that are too vast, growing at a very high rate that make it very hard to manage, and difficult to analyse using traditional methods and tools.

The concept of BDA refers to "*the use of advanced data analytic techniques on vast data sets (Big Data) to discover patterns and meaningful use of information*" (Bamiah et al., 2018:231). Thus, it is through the implementation of BDA tools (application) that organisations and government enterprises can derive value and insights from these voluminous datasets (Mehta & Pandit, 2018). (Bumblauskas et al., 2017:703) defined big data analytics (BDA) as "*the ability to analyse meaningful and relevant data and convert data to information, knowledge, and ultimately action in time to favourably influence an organisation is a key competitive differentiator*". The BDA concept also presents government enterprises with opportunities of analysing the increasing amount of data in its repositories thereby enhancing its operations and decision-making processes (Medaglia, 2014). This includes BDA tools such as Hadoop, HDFS, MapReduce, Cassandra, and PIG to mention the few (Zakir et al., 2015).

This is compounded by the need to integrate the variety of separate legacy systems (silos). Insufficient funding is another challenge that is encountered in attempts to implement the concept in many governments' enterprises. Kim et al. (2014) explained that owing to the expensive nature of some information technology (IT) solutions such as the concept of big data, success is always threatened. Another major challenge pertains to the lack of technical expertise in the areas BDA because of its newness in many countries, particularly in developing world.

Furthermore, implementation of BDA tools requires stable and reliable IT infrastructure (Al Nuaimi et al., 2015). This includes components such as storage, networks, and telecommunications capabilities of these components (Kache & Seuring, 2017). Various organisations, including governments' enterprises have implemented BDA in their environments for various purposes, and with varying degrees of success. For example, countries such as Australia have implemented BDA tools to improve services in the education sector (Bamiah et al., 2018). This has led to enhanced learner performance, improved teaching and assessment methods and techniques (ibid). Whilst there are benefits to implementation of BDA tools, there are challenges from aspects of privacy and confidentiality issues (Hardy & Maurushat, 2017).

The aim of this study was to develop a criteria, which can be used to guide implementation of BDA within the South African government enterprises. In achieving the aim, two objectives were formulated: (1) to understand how big data within government enterprise is analysed; and (2) to examine and understand the factors that can facilitate the implementation of BDA.

CONTEXTUALISING THE RESEARCH PROBLEM

Globally, government enterprises are among the largest and influential companies in an economy (Kowalski et al., 2013). These enterprises occupy key and strategic sectors of the economy and become pillars of national economies whilst having economic, political and social responsibilities (Liu & Zhang, 2016). In South Africa, these enterprises play a vital in the economy and in the delivery of services in energy, transportation and telecommunications sectors (Thomas, 2012). Further, Thomas (2012) discusses that South African government enterprises aim to develop the country by reducing income inequalities, increase employment, and contribute to the development of the country. However, these enterprises have been exposed for their inefficiencies because of corruption, poor governance among the challenges which in turn are a burden to the same economy they seek to vitalize.

Some organisations have benefited from implementing BDA tools in various ways. Adrian et al. (2018) discussed how some organisations incorporated their strategic planning processing in order to enhance organisational performance by shifting their decision-making processes to be data-driven. This has also positively impacted the capabilities of the IT infrastructure by making them sharable and integrated (ibid). However, whilst some organisations have reaped the benefits of implementing BDA tools, many organisations have not been successful, including government enterprises.

The implementation of BDA in many governments' enterprises and agencies have been met with several challenges, such as poor IT infrastructure, bureaucracy, and poor data quality (Adrian et al., 2017). Some of the challenges relate to lack of clear understanding of the benefits and business implications of BDA implementation (Marco, 2016). On the other hand, there is lack of expertise in the area of BDA (ibid).

The South African government is beginning to understand the importance of BDA. However, there is a problem of know-how, in the selection and application of the BDA for government purposes, in improving service delivery (Cervone, 2016). Also, the lack of know-how affects BDA implementation (Al-Sai et al., 2017). Know-how is critical for innovation, and exploring traditional platforms including infrastructure that will be able to process BDA and generate meaningful information for better decision-making (Lui et al., 2016).

LITERATURE REVIEW

A review of literature was conducted, focusing on the core aspect of the study, which are government as an enterprise, big data analytics and implementation of big data analytics.

Government as an Enterprise

Like other countries, the South African government is well aware that its enterprises are vital to the economy, as they play an important roles in service delivery, such as: electricity, transportation and telecommunications (Adèle, 2012). Furthermore, Kanyane and Sausi (2015) argued that government enterprises are key drivers of the economy, as they play a very big role in economic growth as the major entities that deliver several social goods and facilities to certify the needs of South African citizens. Daiser et al. (2017) mentioned that public sector enterprises frequently take on the duty of providing the citizens with utility facilities, such as water, energy, health, and education.

As with other sectors of the economy, large amounts of data (big data) have been generated by government, and its agencies (Archenaa & Anita, 2015). According to Berg (2015), big data presents challenges to organisation because of data sets that are too vast, growing at a very high rate that make it very hard to manage, and difficult to analyse using traditional methods and tools. Thus, for organisation to gain value from the dataset, the implementation of BDA becomes a necessity. Furthermore, Kim et al. (2014) explained big data as original challenges relating to difficulty, safety, and threats to confidentiality, including a necessity for modern technology equipment and human services. This information supports real time decision-making for the public sector.

The public sector has begun to derive useful information from large volumes of data derived from different sources (Kim et al., 2014). Working on extracting meaningful information from big data that is generated quickly and straightforwardly is challenging. Therefore, analytics has developed to be inextricably vital to comprehend the full value of big data to advance the organisation's performance and service delivery (Zakir, 2015). Archenaa and Anita (2015) discussed the importance of BDA from the viewpoint that it would help government in improving service delivery in the areas of quality education, and to reduce unemployment rate.

Big Data Analytics

Big data analytics are tools (application) used to derive useful information, patterns, or conclusions from big data in making purposeful and quality decisions (Adrian et al., 2017). Gandomi and Haider (2015) explain analytics as methods employed to examine and obtain intellect from big data. Therefore, analysis of big data may be seen as a sub-process of the general process of 'insight extraction' from big data. Furthermore, BDA has the ability to empower organisations with opportunities from the perspectives of operations and effective utilization for useful information, business processes, and enhancement of analytical capabilities, to derive deeper meaningful insights (Mohanty et al., 2013).

The concept has the capacity to manage volumes of incongruent datasets, to permit organisations to implement BDA (Wang & Hajli, 2017). An indication that BDA has competence for improvement is shown through business value should include rapidity of insights, which enable the business to convert raw data into useful information. According to Batarseh et al. (2017), BDA aim to return the intellect and attentive version of big datasets, to deliver rapid insights into information, and assistance with conception and decision-making. The process of analysing big data employs certain methods, such as breaking down the data into 5 different categories: text, audio, video, and predictive analysis. Hence, different BDA tools are used to retrieve insights from different kinds of data (Gandomi & Haider, 2015).

The concept of BDA is employed by government in various areas such as health education, and transport and logistics, to maintain patterns, reveal trends, and ultimately improve services (Raghupathi & Raghupathi, 2014). This means that the concept is crucial in decision-making (Batarseh et al., 2017). In the midst of this premise some organisations have reaped the benefits of implementing BDA tools, while many others have not been successful, including government enterprises. With big data numerous attractive opportunities, there are several challenges organisations encounter in BDA implementation in both private and public sector organisations. BDA has a challenge when a large scale of data need to be analysed in a short period, and with a sensibly decent performance (Cheng et al., 2016). Furthermore, the rapidity of generating big data, leads to fast change of content because the content in big data changes with time, so is BDA targets (Ibid). Challenges on BDA also include inconsistency of data and partial finished, scalable, timeless and safety (Khan et al., 2014).

In the practice of big data analytics, different enterprises are able to derive insights about their businesses to improve the performance of services with data driven decision-making (Lee et al., 2017). This has over the years encouraged many private enterprises to employ data-driven decision-making, and that has an outcome of advancements in big data profits (Adrian et al., 2018). Government facilities might be significantly enhanced through the implementation of BDA in its enterprises as those enterprises are among the largest and influential companies in an economy of a country (Joseph & Johnson, 2013). South African government enterprises encounter challenges when it comes to some factors that could influence the implementation of BDA.

Implementation of Big Data Analytics

Implementation of BDA contains procedure, error handling, competences, capitals, and transforming big data into valuable information (Adrian et al, 2018). *"The model is developed based on three dimensions, performing data strategy (organisation), collaborative knowledge worker (people), and executing data analytics (technology)"* (Adrian et al, 2018:23). Ability to quickly process big data and implement analytics enables an organisation to take well-informed choices in a short period compared to the competitors (Comuzzi & Patel, 2016). Furthermore, to improve excellence of service an organisation should analyse big data effectively to answer new challenges through the information retrieved from those voluminous data sets (Archenaa & Anita, 2015).

The BDA implementation has the ability to benefit strategic long-term planning to support the organisation's growth that will consequently lead to enhanced organisational performance (Adrian et al., 2017). Archenaa and Anita (2015) discussed advantages of implementing BDA in government enterprises, which includes government services provided being reached by all citizens and without unnecessary delays. The factors that may influence implementation of BDA in organisations, include: technology capabilities, human capability, analytics capability, organisation capability, and information quality (Adrian et al., 2018). The Seoul government analysed big data generated from health, transport and residence and produced meaningful information, the benefit to the Seoul government was being able to recognize the patterns and strains, which led to upgraded midnight public services (Lim et al., 2015).

Technology capability in BDA refers to the capability of IT structures and platforms that could be used to analyse data to derive insights form big data for decision making (Adrain et al., 2017). Organisation capability refers to the organisation's readiness with resources to pursue implementation of BDA (Chen et al., 2015). Human competences are the technical IT skill and the managerial skills to coordinate the activities related to methods used in the analysis of big data (Agrawal, 2015). Information quality is capability to be able to make speed decisions from predictive analytics (Adrain et al., 2018).

RESEARCH METHODOLOGY

The qualitative method, case study approach and semi-structured interview technique were applied in this study. The qualitative method was selected primarily because it helps induce an understandings about the phenomenon being studied (Moser & Krostjens, 2017), which was highly needed to get to know better how the implementation of BDA is done in a government enterprise. Qualitative method is based on opinions and includes examining and reflecting on less physical features of the research focus (Neville, 2007). In achieving the aim of this study, it was critical to understand the reasons, opinions and motives from individuals and groups perspectives, why and how BDA tools are implemented within government enterprises. The case study approach was selected because it allows in-depth understanding of the phenomenon being studied (Kumar, 2011). A government enterprise was selected as a case in the study.

In this study, one organisation was selected as a case. In the process of selecting an organisation there was a criteria that was used. The organisation needed to be one of government enterprises either small, medium or big organisation. Secondly, it had to be an organisation that implements BDA. The selected organisation was not the only organisation that met the criteria that was used but due to time limitations the researcher had to use one organisation as a case for this study. After the organisation was selected, there had to be participant's selection for the study.

The semi-structured interview technique was elected primarily because it allows flexible conversation with the interviewee (Moser & Krostjens, 2017). In the collection of data, the semi-structured technique was used to interview participants on one-on-one basis. The number of interviews was reached at the point of saturation. The interviews were tape-recorded with the permission of the interviewees. Note were also taken in the process of interviews. The hermeneutics technique was used to analyse the qualitative data. Hermeneutics is explained as interpretation of text, or finding meaning in written words by Byrne (2001).

The participants that were selected to participate in this study were a total number of four from the organisation. Also, a certain criteria was followed in selecting who can be a participant. For an individual to be a participant needed to be someone who is currently working in the organisation and must be part of the team that implements BDA. To collect data from the participants there was a data collection technique that was used. The process that took place in data collection was requesting meetings with the participants, then participants responded about their availability. In the meetings that the researcher had with the participants, there were notes taken and recordings of the interview. The records were then transcribed and coded before analysis process of the data commenced.

DATA ANALYSIS

In the analysis of the data, the hermeneutics approach was used following the interpretivist approach. The analysis was done following two objectives as a guide to analyse the data that was collected. The primarily focus was to understand how big data is analysed within government enterprise, and to examine the factors that can facilitate the implementation of BDA. The code of analysis is as follows: participant_codename, page#: line#. EDU_01, Pg2: 3-5 – means that participant 1, page 2 of interview transcript: from line 3 to 5. The organisation that was selected as a case is EduCentre.

How Big Data is Analysed Within Government Enterprise

In EduCentre, big data consists of large volume of data-sets. According to Wielki (2013), big data is not only about size, it include velocity, variety, and volume, often referred to as 3Vs. Volume means the amount or size of data-sets used and managed by the organisation. Variety: the different types of data-sets, which include images, videos, text, and they come from various sources. Velocity: this is the frequency at which the data-sets are accessed or travel between different sources. In EduCentre there are some differences in understanding of big data and whether they do have big data or not. This maybe a contribution to not having same understanding on big data concept.

The first two participants understand that for data to be named as "big data" it has to meet all three Vs. But the other participant seems to have a different understanding on the concept of big data as he explains it as only Volume. These irregularities may affect how the organisation go about analysing the data and the selection of analytics tools. For big data to be useful or add value to the organisation, it needs to be analysed. The method of analysing big data is through the use of analytics tools. There are different types of analytics tools, which include predictive, descriptive, and prescriptive. Predictive analytics tools analyse data-sets using various techniques such as statistics and data mining to predict the future. Descriptive analytics tools are used to describe the past "what has happened?" by analysing data-sets. Prescriptive goes beyond just describing what has happened to go to make some recommendations.

In EduCentre there is not much of analytics that are done as they are still new in big data concept. For now, it is only the IT department that is involved in the big data and analytics and two other people who are not from the IT department. According to Batarseh et al. (2017), government enterprises are still beginning to understand the benefits of BDA that may drive to the direction of better service delivery, enhanced operations and well-informed decision making. The organisation only apply analytics in IT department. The datasets that are analysed are only for the IT department to make better decisions on how they manage and deliver their services in the organisation. In the department they grouped themselves into different sections, and conducted analysis of datasets differently. There are three sections. Section 1: Analyse big data for service delivery. Section 2: Works with organisation applications and do analysis on that. Section 3: analysis students' data and system performance.

The first section apply big data to assess their service delivery to all of its system users. To achieve that the section analysis logs calls or incidences that were reported. Where a certain user calls for assistance in something that the department need to resolve for that individual. That incident will then be sent to the relevant team and assigned to a person to attend it. There are different teams that belong to the section: blackboard team; desktop support team and the printing team. The incidents need to be stored and managed after they have been logged-in to observe and monitor progress of the activities.

In the second section, the organise make use of big data to manage students' special needs. The aim of the organisation is to accept first-time entering students and register them, then make sure that the student graduates as quick as possible. In this section the analysis are done using Splunk analytics tool. To ensure that students graduate, the data analysis is carried out to monitor to students' performances. The organisation also checks other factors such as the students' profile and background to understand the reasons of sudden change in marks.

On the other hand, there is system datasets analysis that is done for system management and security. For EduCentre to ensure the institution's data-sets are secured in various system they need apply analytics on how the systems operate. The organisation consists of various systems that produce log files. Whenever there is an event on each system, the event is recorded on a patchy server. Then from those log files that is where the analysis of big data comes in. They analyse system log files to be able to detect when something unusual happens in their systems.

The third section use big data to develop reports and analytics from the data that is stored in the databases of the organisation. They get requests from different stakeholders to develop reports on certain data that they need to understand and make decisions from. As the organisation have different application which include academic applications and bursary applications. Those applications are analysed to understand the applicant's by groups. For instance, to know how many applications were from local applicants by province or by region and even by nationality.

The Factors That can Facilitate the Implementation of Big Data Analytics

The implementation of BDA is based on three aspects: Organisation, people and technology. The organisation to perform data-sets strategy. People which includes managers and personnel that co-operate with their knowledge on the concept. The technology part of it is where BDA are executed (the platforms). Adrian et al. (2018) described implementation of BDA as procedures of handling BDA capabilities, capitals, and transforming big data valuable information.

There are different factors that contribute to successfulness of the implementation of BDA. These factors include: Knowledge; Skills; Experience; Management support and Access to various data-sets.

People or workers need to have at least basic IT skills for them to be able to implement BDA. The understanding of the BDA concept is the most crucial part. As the organisation need to have knowledge on how big data is implemented, the techniques used and analytics tools.

When it comes to experience, the personnel that implements BDA must have a background of working with various databases and using the analytics tools. Management support: the management has to have an understanding on the concept as they are the ones that are responsible to make sure that the analytics are done appropriately. They need to also understand the techniques that are used for BDA to benefit the organisation. Furthermore, the management has to gather all needed resources for implementation of BDA.

The success of BDA implementation is measured by its benefits to the organisation, to help the organisation make better well-informed decisions. For the organisation to reap the benefits of BDA, the organisation itself has to be ready financially and technically. Financial readiness of the organisation means that it will be able to buy license for the analytics tools needed for them to analyse the datasets. Also, the organisations personnel may need more knowledge, skills, and experiences on how to implement the analytics tools. Therefore, the organisation has to invest in its personnel by funding them on short courses and trainings that maybe needed.

FINDINGS AND DISCUSSIONS

Based on the analysis that was done. Four factors were identified. These factors include Knowledge; Process; Differentiation and Skill set.

Knowledge

Knowledge is explained as facts, information and skills. It can be gained by individual's experience or being educated about the subject (Simpson & Weiner, 2015). In EduCentre there are some irregularities when it comes to their knowledge of big data. This is because the organisation is still new on the concept of big data. They are still trying to understand it and its benefits. For an organisation to be able to implement Big Data needs to first understand what is meant by big data. Having full understanding of the concept includes knowledge on how big data can benefit the organisation. Have knowledge on how to achieve those benefits. This leads to understanding the analytics part of it.

The data-sets need to be analysed for them to make sense and be informative. So, it is important for an organisation to also understand BDA. This includes awareness of different analytics tools and how those tools are used. Also, have understanding about the factors that may facilitate the implementation of BDA for them to be successful and gain the benefits of big data.

The full understanding of BDA is very critical. As knowledge is one the factors that contribute in BDA implementation being successful. The successfulness of BDA implementation is measured by gaining its benefits. These benefits of BDA includes being able to make data driven decisions for the organisation. Being able to predict the future. And see where the organisation needs improvements in its service delivery. But if an organisation does not have knowledge on how to turn the data-sets that come in high velocity to meaningful information. That means they will never gain the benefits of big data stored in their databases.

Process

Process is a series of actions taken to achieve desired results at the end (Simpson & Weiner, 2015). For uniformity, there has to be some procedures followed. Having procedures in place helps everyone understand the process and techniques used in BDA. Also, understand the flow of events from one stage to the other. And be able categorize big data for analysis. When there is no process followed, then the intended results will not be achieved.

In EduCentre there is process followed in selecting the analytics tools. They are only using the analytics tools that are available to them. The tools that they are using come as package with the applications that they have as the organisation. For example, the Power BI analytics tool that they use is part of the package of MicroSoft Enterprise suit that the organisation use. And they are still using the demo of the analytic and they still to understand how the tool works. Because it is still a demo, it has limited features.

Differentiation

Differentiation is an action of being able to distinguish between two more subjects (Simpson & Weiner, 2015). It is crucial to be able to differentiate between big data and small data. If the organisation does not understand the difference. There will be impletions in analysing big data. Because, Small Data and Big Data are analysed differently.

Small Data is only about volume. The high quantity of data generated by an organisation and stores in its databases does not make it big data. For "data" to be categorised as big data it has meet the basic 3Vs at least, Volume; Variety and Velocity. This takes us back to the knowledge of big data being a critical factor in BDA implementation. When the organisation understands what makes data to be called big data. Having full understanding of the characteristics of big data. Which are normally called the 3Vs, Volume, Velocity and Variety. This helps an organisation to be able differentiate between Small Data and Big Data.

Skill set

Skill set is an individual's range of abilities (Simpson & Weiner, 2015). It is not easy to get highly skilled people in concept of BDA. As this concept of big data and analytics is new more especially in government enterprises including EduCentre. The skill set needed in BDA implementation includes knowledge and experience. The skills are crucial because for an individual to be able to implement BDA. They need to have some understanding and experience in working databases. Also, be able to understand how to implement the analytics tools. For them to achieve the desired results as an organisation.

CRITERIA FOR THE IMPLEMENTATION OF BIG DATA ANALYTICS

As discussed above, four factors, Knowledge; Process; Differentiation and Skill-set were found to influence the use of BDA tools within the South African government enterprises. The criteria were further interpreted by following the interpretivist approach, which allows research to be subjective in his or her reasoning (Sullivan, 2016).

In order to use BDA tools for improved usefulness and purposefulness, so as to gain results of value, the organisation must have achieved certain level. That level is defined by the factors that influence the use of the tools, which were revealed in this study. There are different, which are determined by the influencing factors and Key Indicators.

The criteria for using the analytics tools are depict in Table 1. The weights are associated with value: 5 as highest, and 1 being the lowest. The weights are briefly defined in the Table.

Table 1. Criteria for Big Data analytics tools

Weight	5	4	3	2	1
Knowledge	Understand BDA tools and able to use the tools	Understand how the BDA tools work but not using them	Understand few BDA tools and have knowledge on how to use the tools	Have basis understanding of the tools but do not know how to apply them	Do not understand the concept of BDA
Process	There is a procedure for selecting tools. it describes the goal and criteria for organisational purposes.	The goal is described with no criteria put in place in selecting BDA tools.	There is no procedure followed in selecting BDA tools. Make use of available BDA tools	Described the goal but do not know how to select the suitable BDA tools	There is no procedure and no BDA tools used
Differentiation	Understands the difference between Small data and Big Data.	Understand characteristics of big data.	Have average understand of big data.	Have little understanding of big data.	Do not understand the difference.
Skill-set	Understands BDA tools. Have experience of using BDA tools.	Understands BDA tools with only basic experience.	Understands BDA tools with no experience.	Have little understanding of BDA tools with no experience.	Do not understand BDA tools.
Total	20	16	12	8	4

Key Indicator

This is calculation of the weights that are associated to the influencing factors. The indications are divided into three categories, Advance, Intermediary, and Foundation as shown in Table 2.

Table 2. Key Indicator for use of big data analytics tools

Score	Level	Description
16 – 20	Above Average	Advanced in an understanding of BDA tools and implementation. Minimal or error free implementation.
10 – 15	Average	A good understands of BDA tools. Errors and challenges are easily detected and resolved.
0 - 9	Below Average	Have little or no understanding of the BDA tools. Errors and challenges take long or are hardly resolved.

How to employ the criteria:

1. The organisation assesses or evaluates itself in accordance to the set of criteria.
2. The weight is added, and the total score is reached.
3. The total score is aligned with the Key Indicator as described above.
4. Based on the alignment, a decision is reached.

CONCLUSION

This study explores an area that is vital to both government enterprises and private organisations, in that the phenomenon studied can add value to their processes and activities towards improved sustainability and competitiveness. To be more specific, the findings will help government employees in gaining an understanding of the challenges that they are faced with, in their attempts to employing BDA. Also, the study will assist data scientist in their designs as well as formulating policy and standard, to ensure appropriate use of BDA tools in their organisations. In addition, IT managers can draw their references from the study when developing employee retention strategy in the use of BDA tools. Another area of contribution is that the study adds to the existing literature, particularly, from developing countries perspective.

REFERENCES

Adrian, C., Abdullah, R., Atan, R., & Jusoh, Y. Y. 2017, July. Factors influencing to the implementation success of big data analytics: A systematic literature review. *2017 International Conference on Research and Innovation in Information Systems (ICRIIS)*, 1-6. 10.1109/ICRIIS.2017.8002536

Adrian, C., Abdullah, R., Atan, R., & Jusoh, Y. Y. (2018). Conceptual model development of big data analytics implementation assessment effect on decision-making. *Technology*, 23–24.

Al Nuaimi, E., Al Neyadi, H., Mohamed, N., & Al-Jaroodi, J. (2015). Applications of big data to smart cities. *Journal of Internet Services and Applications*, *6*(1), 25. doi:10.118613174-015-0041-5

Archenaa, J., & Anita, E. A. M. 2015. A Survey of Big Data Analytics in Healthcare and Government. *2nd International Symposium on Big data and Cloud Computing (ISBCC' 15)*, 408–413. 10.1016/j.procs.2015.04.021

Batarseh, F. A., Yang, R., & Deng, L. (2017). A comprehensive model for management and validation of federal big data analytical systems. *Big Data Analytics*, *2*(1), 2. doi:10.118641044-016-0017-x

Bumblauskas, D., Nold, H., Bumblauskas, P., & Igou, A. (2017). Big data analytics: Transforming data to action. *Business Process Management Journal*, *23*(3), 703–720. doi:10.1108/BPMJ-03-2016-0056

Byrne, M. (2001). Hermeneutics as a methodology for textual analysis. *AORN Journal*, *73*(5), 968–968. doi:10.1016/S0001-2092(06)61749-3 PMID:11378953

Cao, L. (2017). Data Science: A Comprehensive Overview. *ACM Computing Surveys*, *50*(3), 1–42. doi:10.1145/3076253

Cervone, H. F. (2016). Organisational considerations initiating a big data and analytics implementation. *Digital Library Perspectives*, *32*(3), 137–141. doi:10.1108/DLP-05-2016-0013

Chen, D. Q., Preston, D. S., & Swink, M. (2005). How the use of big data analytics affects value creation in supply chain management. *Journal of Management Information Systems*, *32*(4), 4–39. doi:10.1080/07421222.2015.1138364

Cheng, S., Zhang, Q., & Qin, Q. (2016). Big data analytics with swarm intelligence. *Industrial Management & Data Systems*, *116*(4), 646–666. doi:10.1108/IMDS-06-2015-0222

Comuzzi, M., & Patel, A. (2016). How organisations leverage big data: A maturity model. *Industrial Management & Data Systems*, *116*(8), 1468–1492. doi:10.1108/IMDS-12-2015-0495

Daiser, P., Ysa, T., & Schmitt, D. (2017). Corporate governance of state-owned enterprises: A systematic analysis of empirical literature. *International Journal of Public Sector Management*, *30*(5), 447–466. doi:10.1108/IJPSM-10-2016-0163

Gandomi, A., & Haider, M. (2015). Beyond the hype: Big data concepts, methods, and analytics. *International Journal of Information Management*, *35*(2), 137–144. doi:10.1016/j.ijinfomgt.2014.10.007

Garlasu, D., Sandulescu, V., Halcu, I., Neculoiu, G., Grigoriu, O., Marinescu, M., & Marinescu, V. (2013, January). A big data implementation based on Grid computing. *2013 11th RoEduNet International Conference*, 1-4.

Hardy, K., & Maurushat, A. (2017). Opening up government data for Big Data analysis and public benefit. *Computer Law & Security Review*, *33*(1), 30–37. doi:10.1016/j.clsr.2016.11.003

Joseph, R. C., & Johnson, N. A. (2013). Big data and transformational government. *IT Professional*, *15*(6), 43–48. doi:10.1109/MITP.2013.61

Kache, F., & Seuring, S. (2017). Challenges and opportunities of digital information at the intersection of Big Data Analytics and supply chain management. *International Journal of Operations & Production Management*, *37*(1), 10–36. doi:10.1108/IJOPM-02-2015-0078

Kanyane, M. H., & Sausi, K. (2015). Reviewing state-owned entities' governance landscape in South Africa. *African Journal of Business Ethics*, *9*(1). Advance online publication. doi:10.15249/9-1-81

Khan, N., Yaqoob, I., Hashem, I. A. T., Inayat, Z., Ali, M., Kamaleldin, W., Alam, M., Shiraz, M., & Gani, A. (2014). Big data: Survey, technologies, opportunities, and challenges. *TheScientificWorldJournal*, *2014*, 2014. doi:10.1155/2014/712826 PMID:25136682

Kim, G. H., Trimi, S., & Chung, J. H. (2014). Big-data applications in the government sector. *Communications of the ACM*, *57*(3), 78–85. doi:10.1145/2500873

Kowalski, P. Büge, M., Sztajerowska, M. & Egeland, M. 2013. State-Owned Enterprises: Trade Effects and Policy Implications. *OECD Trade Policy Papers*, 147.

Kumar, R. (2011). *Research methodology: A step-by-step guide for beginners*. Sage Publications Limited.

Lee, H., Kweon, E., Kim, M., & Chai, S. (2017). Does Implementation of Big Data Analytics Improve Firms' Market Value? Investors' Reaction in Stock Market. *Sustainability*, *9*(6), 978. doi:10.3390u9060978

Lim, C., Kim, K. J., & Maglio, P. P. (2018). Smart cities with big data: Reference models, challenges, and considerations. *Cities (London, England)*, *82*, 82. doi:10.1016/j.cities.2018.04.011

Liu, X., & Zhang, C. (2016). Corporate governance, social responsibility information disclosure, and enterprise value in China. *Journal of Cleaner Production*, 1–10.

Mehta, N., & Pandit, A. (2018). Concurrence of big data analytics and healthcare: A systematic review. *International Journal of Medical Informatics*, *114*, 57–65. doi:10.1016/j.ijmedinf.2018.03.013 PMID:29673604

Mohanty, S., Jagadeesh, M., & Srivatsa, H. (2013). *Big data imperatives: Enterprise 'Big Data' warehouse, 'BI' implementations and analytics*. Apress. doi:10.1007/978-1-4302-4873-6

Moser, A., & Korstjens, I. (2018). Series: Practical guidance to qualitative research. Part 3: Sampling, data collection and analysis. *The European Journal of General Practice*, *24*(1), 9–18. doi:10.1080/138 14788.2017.1375091 PMID:29199486

Neville, C. (2007). *Introduction to research and research methods*. Bradford: Effective learning service.

Raghupathi, W., & Raghupathi, V. (2014). Big data analytics in healthcare: Promise and potential. *Health Information Science and Systems*, *2*(1), 3. doi:10.1186/2047-2501-2-3 PMID:25825667

Ridge, M., Johnston, K. A., & O'Donovan, B. (2015). The use of big data analytics in the retail industries in South Africa. *African Journal of Business Management*, *9*(19), 688–703. doi:10.5897/AJBM2015.7827

Sullivan, H. (2016). Interpretivism and Public Policy Research. Interpreting Governance High Politics and Public Policy, 184-204.

Thomas, A. (2012). Governance at South African state-owned enterprises: What do annual reports and the print media tell us? *Social Responsibility Journal*, *8*(4), 448–470. doi:10.1108/17471111211272057

Thomas, A. (2012). Governance at South African state-owned enterprises: What do annual reports and the print media tell us? *Social Responsibility Journal*, *8*(4), 448–470. doi:10.1108/17471111211272057

Wang, Y., & Hajli, N. (2017). Exploring the path to big data analytics success in healthcare. *Journal of Business Research*, *70*, 287–299. doi:10.1016/j.jbusres.2016.08.002

Wielki, J. (2013, September). Implementation of the big data concept in organisations-possibilities, impediments and challenges. *2013 Federated Conference on Computer Science and Information Systems*, 985-989.

Zakir, J., Seymour, T., & Berg, K. (2015). Big Data Analytics. *Issues in Information Systems*, *16*(2).

Chapter 63
Public Administration Curriculum–Based Big Data Policy–Analytic Epistemology:
Symbolic IoT Action–Learning Solution Model

Emmanuel N. A. Tetteh

iD https://orcid.org/0000-0003-3931-1634

Norwich University, USA & Action Learning, Action Research Association, USA

ABSTRACT

The equilibration that underscores the internet of things (IoT) and big data analytics (BDA) cannot be underestimated at the behest of real-life social challenges and significant policy data generated to redress the concerns of epistemic communities, such as political policy actors, stakeholders, and the citizenry. The cognitive balancing of new information gathered by BDA and assimilated across the IoT is at the crossroads of ascertaining how the growing increases of such BDA can be better managed to transition from the big data state of disequilibration to reach a more stable equilibrium of policy data usefulness. In the quest for explicating the equilibration of policy data usefulness, an account of the curriculum-based MPA policy analysis and analytics concentration program at Norwich University is described as a case example of big data policy-analytic epistemology. The case study offers a symbolic ideology of an IoT action-learning solution model as a recommendation for fostering the stable equilibration of policy data usefulness.

ORGANIZATION BACKGROUND

This section provides an introductory viewpoint of the background on the case history of the organization underscoring the experiential learning context of the curriculum-based Master of Public Administration (MPA) Policy Analysis and Analytics (PAA) concentration program at Norwich University (NU). Since

DOI: 10.4018/978-1-6684-3662-2.ch063

its inception in 1819, NU, founded by Captain Alden Partridge, a former United States Military Academy Superintendent, has remained well-committed to the philosophy of experiential learning for preparation of traditional-age and nontraditional-age students in a Corps of Cadets and as civilians to advance future societal leadership, service professionalism, and business industries (Norwich University, 2014a). Building upon the works of Dewey, Lewin, and Piaget, Kolb (1984) made a significant contribution to the experiential learning theorization model. According to Kolb, experiential learning fosters the creation of knowledge through critical thinking and persistent adaptation to community engagement, as can be attested to or derived by the process of concrete experience, and also modified by reflective learning, conceptual evaluation, and active investigation (Bergsteiner, Avery, & Neumann, 2010; Kolb, 1984).

By simplifying Kolb's theorization, the experiential learning model has been conceptualized as "an experience or problem situation; a reflective phase in which the learner examines the experience and creates learning from his/her reflection; and an application phase in which the new knowledge or skills are applied to a new problem or situation" (National Institute of Food and Agriculture, 2017, p. 1). As a coeducational institution of experiential learning pedagogy and andragogy in Northfield, Vermont, as well as one of America's six senior military institutions of higher learning and the initiation of the Reserve Officers' Training Corps (ROTC), NU offers various traditional learning and distance-learning baccalaureate and graduate degree programs to approximately 3,500 students (Norwich University, 2015).

Recognizing its enormous contribution to the ROTC, along with its training of military officers and non-military learners for various careers in the business enterprise, government agencies, and military service, as well as for the pursuit of academic degrees, NU has evolved in many significant ways over its almost 200 years. In 2014, it began the *Forging the Future* initiative in preparation for its bicentennial celebration in 2019 (Norwich University, 2010, 2014a). This five-year campaign for the bicentennial celebration is geared toward fostering an increased level of innovative learning atmosphere through high-tech pedagogical and restructuring of top-notch facilities to contribute to the university's vitality of service innovation to the nation (Norwich University, 2014a).

In keeping with the *Forging the Future* campaign initiatives and in alignment with its mission mandate, NU's College of Graduate and Continuing Studies (CGCS) has resoundingly remained more committed to providing lifelong learners with dynamic experiential learning model. This dynamic experiential learning paradigm is structured on the balance between learners' real-life challenges and the application of:

- A collaborative action-learning model;
- Action research modalities;
- Knowledge and process management protocols;
- Public service leadership via the traditional face-to-face teaching/learning model and the open and distance learning (ODL) framework of fostering pragmatic learning (Norwich University, 2014b).

Accredited by the New England Association of Schools and Colleges, the University's Board of Trustees adopted its mission mandate as:

To give our youth an education that shall be American in its character–to enable them to act as well as to think–to execute as well as to conceive–'to tolerate all opinions when reason is left free to combat them' – to make moral, patriotic, efficient, and useful citizens, and to qualify them for all those high responsibilities resting upon a citizen in this free republic. (Norwich University, 2010, p. 22)

By way of operationalizing this mission mandate, the essential linkages between the NU mission mandate and its organizational governance structure are to stimulate core objectives, as well as to facilitate effective decision making, policy-making process, career capacity building, functioning systems development, public service values' enhancement, and translation of these initiatives into the most effective and efficient delivery of services. It thus goes to show that the management of organizational core objectives and relationships within levels of management, task performances, and adaptation to the organization's changing environment could coordinate the dynamic dimensional structures of the organizational functioning systems to shape its governance structure. An organization's functioning systems reflect the dynamic dimension of its symbolic governance structure involving the hierarchical or democratic pattern of activities and behaviors, the relationships among the levels of people in authority, the reporting system that shapes task performances, and adaptation to its changing environment (Fuller, 2008).

As opposed to a hierarchical government structure, NU organizational culture is characterized by shared governance (Norwich University, 2014b) as epitomized by a democratic governance structure model in keeping with its strategic mission mandate. A hierarchical government structure model entails a president-to-management decision-making process, whereas the context of accountability, authority, and information-sharing model is mainly a one-way flow from the top that works downward. The democratic governance structure model, however, fosters a participatory form of the information-sharing model and promotes a circular-structure accountability model of disseminating the decision-making process (Tetteh, 2004). Thus, there is a higher level of equilibration in the decision-making process within the democratic governance structure model.

As the CGCS embarks upon disseminating NU mission mandate, one of the seven MPA program concentrations, the PAA concentration, has been developed in recognition of the need to equip graduate-level students with the knowledge base and technical know-how regarding the methods of policy analysis for handling Big Data policy-analytic epistemology via the Internet of Things (IoT) ecosystem platform of the ODL framework. Epistemology generally deals with the questions concerning the nature, scope, and sources of the systems of adequate and inadequate knowledge that shape the reality of human worldviews. The Big Data policy-analytic epistemology is, therefore, an intended inquiry into ways that the large ever-increasing Big Data across the epistemic communities can be better explored using data analysis software tools via the IoT ecosystem framework to shape a public policy decision-making process. Unlike the other six MPA program concentrations (i.e., Criminal Justice, Public Works, Municipal Governance, International Development and Influence, Nonprofit Management, Fiscal Management), the PAA concentration is unique in that it has an accompanying web-based data analytic lab for the facilitation of Big Data analytics (BDA).

SETTING THE STAGE

This section provides an overview of the case vignette into the data epistemology that shapes the MPA curriculum-based BDA of the IoT ecosystem framework. With the appointment of Dr. Rosemarie Pelletier, MPA and Information Security and Assurance Program Director, and under the collaborative support of Dr. William Clements, Vice President and Dean of College of Graduate and Continuing Studies (CGCS), the PAA concentration were developed with unique curriculum-based BDA methods of policy analysis. The MPA curriculum-based BDA methods of policy analysis involve a wide range of data analysis software tools and data analysis methodologies (Pelletier & Tetteh, 2015) employed in the analysis of public policy data epistemology.

Public Policy Data Epistemology

The public policy data epistemology recognizes the power of the IoT ecosystem framework for which the equilibration of the BDA is facilitated. This allows for the continuum of evolving Big Data of the multifaceted public, organizational, and humankind problems or situational needs that permeate and transcend all fabric of the human society to be tackled for problem resolution. By way of tackling such an array of complex issues, the MPA curriculum-based BDA focuses on extensive methods of policy analysis at the systems level of the epistemic communities and the interactions of system-level decisions on public policy and its effects. The policy-related research is thus intended to explore BDA epistemology of policy structure, analytic process, and policy outcomes related to organizational service delivery systems as funded by public and nonprofit sources.

Equilibration of BDA Epistemology of the Epistemic Communities

The BDA epistemology entails fostering the equilibration of coherent and consistent policy data analysis that structure the analysis of Big Data shaping the uncultivated data and the cultivated data via the use of data analytics software tools across the IoT ecosystem framework to aid in the symbolic ideology of IoT action-learning solution. The equilibration of coherent and consistent policy data analysis focuses on the accessibility of policy decision making, the acceptability of policy decision, the availability of policy, and the usability of policy initiatives. It also includes distributive policy channels, cost-benefit analysis of policy initiatives, efficiency, and effectiveness of policy initiatives. It cites the use of quantitative and qualitative approaches as suitable methods of inquiry to redress policy dilemmas and urban planning problems of the epistemic communities. It thus indicates that the identification and analysis of policy problems involve a comprehensive understanding of the complex policy issues of the epistemic communities and the applicable policy analysis methods for handling multidimensional policy data cases. Therefore, the would-be public administrators and/or policy analysts are expected to possess a working knowledge of the various software tools for the facilitation of BDA epistemology toward problem resolution and policy decision making in the public sector and nonprofit arena of the epistemic communities (Tetteh, Core Faculty Lead, Policy Analysis and Analytics concentration, 2015c).

CASE DESCRIPTION

Device Entities to Support the IoT Ecosystem Framework of the Epistemic Communities

In this case study chapter, the importance of emerging data analytic relevance of ranking job functions and data analysis software tools structured as device entities to support the IoT ecosystem framework of the epistemic communities are explored. The means by which such data analysis software tools are used via the IoT ecosystem framework of the epistemic communities in policy data analysis within the age of BDA to account for an innovative curriculum-based PAA program model in public administration are also explored. The IoT ecosystem framework encompasses cross-domain of all components of data analytics software tools, tech-enabled systems or systemic technologies, and techno-politics data of the epistemic communities. The IoT ecosystem framework enables governments, businesses, and consumers to create BDA values by connecting to their IoT devices using the systemic technologies, including cloud computing, application layers, remotes, dashboards, data storage, networks, gateways, analytics, and security infrastructures (Farooq & Kunz, 2017; Zdravković et al., 2018).

Epistemic Communities

The seminary work of Adler and Haas (1992) and Haas (1992) underscored the definitional orientation of the epistemic communities as a network of political policy actors, stakeholders, citizenry, and service professionals with inherent capabilities whose ethos of shared knowledge are shaped by policy-relevant knowledge, policy coordination, policy analytic data, policy innovation, a shared set of principled belief systems, mutual expectations, social action, and shared interpretations. For Haas (1992), the epistemic communities play an essential role in explaining the network of policy-relevant cause-and-effect relationships, elucidate the intricate connection between policy issues, delineate policy self-interest, and aid in the policy-relevant formation. In recent years, the legal profession and related sectors for career advancement (e.g., legal occupations, tech businesses, public service careers, government, state and city jobs) have all called for the emerging workforce of the epistemic communities to be prepared for data analytic relevance of ranking job functions in the age of BDA (EY Building a Better Working World, 2014; Frey & Osborne, 2017).

Data Analytic Relevance of Ranking Job Functions in the Epistemic Communities

Data analytic relevance of ranking job functions in the epistemic communities include analytic data networking for legal coding, the hermeneutics of data analysis, the depiction of data visualization, data process management, and automated concept or subject indexing text and classification for retrieval (Francesconi & Peruginelli, 2007; Koniaris, Anagnostopoulos, & Vassiliou, 2017; Zhang & Koppaka, 2007). An *analytic data network for legal coding* engages in strategic data coding of litigation analytics to unlock data-driven perceptions into case litigation and associated case laws, historical insights, and trends toward strengthening case strategy and managing client expectations for case outcomes (Koniaris et al., 2017). The *hermeneutics of data analysis* focuses on the utilization of various data analysis methods and interpretations to shape public policy decision making and stakeholder insight of data findings' usefulness.

The *depiction of data visualization* involves the efforts of policy data analysts and decision makers to help stakeholders to understand the significance of data findings using data visualization software to create mind maps, concept mappings, graphical mappings, pie charts, data tables, and infographics to understand policy data to aid in streamlining a policy decision-making process. *Data process management* entails the management of procuring, authenticating, loading, guarding, and processing required policy data to ensure user-friendliness, dependability, and data usefulness for stakeholder administrative process. *Automated concept or subject indexing text and classification for retrieval* is conceptualized as:

Denotes non-intellectual, machine-based processes of subject indexing as defined by the library science community: derived and assigned indexing using both alphabetical and classification indexing systems, for the purposes of improved information retrieval. The rationale for combining them into one entry is the fact that the underlying machine-based principles are rather similar, especially when it comes to application to textual documents. (Golub, 2017, para. 12)

Other functional areas include symbolism of data simulations, semantics-based legal citation network viewers, legislation network construction, a network of instrument data analytic citation, and policy codification of network data analysis of legal basis (Francesconi & Peruginelli, 2007; Koniaris et al., 2017; Zhang & Koppaka, 2007). The *symbolism of data simulations* involves data modeling, mapping, and simplifying, using the executions of a system of symbolism, depictions, and those of metaphorical constructs to convey data findings' reports. The *semantics-based legal citation network viewer* involves the use of legal research tools to generate citation relevance between policy cases and issues within the legal and judicial field of practice to enable the legal professionals identify broad-range of case citations more efficiently and streamlined legal case research for attorneys, legal scholars, and judges (Zhang & Koppaka, 2007). *Legislation network construction* is comprised of the legal collection, classification, and analysis of a several normative-focused policies, issues-based information gathering, and legal case documents derived from legal document databases that are cross-referred to one another to aid in the promulgation of laws by legislators and policymakers (Francesconi & Peruginelli, 2007; Koniaris et al., 2017).

The *network of instrument data analytic citation* focuses on deploying the predictive data analytics of a broad range methods to identify patterns and distinctive trends in data to attain increased valuation concerning ways to operationalize BDA to drive strategic organizational analysis of value propositions and forecast trends for embedded data analytics across organizational culture, technical dimensions, and data analytics infrastructure (Chen, 2013; Halper, 2014). Thus, predictive data analytics for a network of instrument data analytics citation is instrumental in predicting functional data, operational strategies, cultural dynamics, and forecasting future trends for organizational vitality. The *policy codification of network data analysis of legal basis* provides policy analytic data procedure of application framework guidelines for the adoption of network security, reliability rules, interoperability, operational procedures, suspected control system vulnerabilities, and network codes that are embedded into regulatory data structures.

Additional areas of data analytic relevance for career functions in the epistemic communities include concept-based searching, ranking, and analytic indexing techniques; equilibration of knowledge-based data epistemology and analytic management systems; network of regulations analyst and data pragmatism; representation model for legal case data analysis; and comprehensive legal ontology of authority data codification (Ashley, 2009; Karmakar & Swarnakar, 2017; Koniaris et al., 2017; Mazzega, Bourcier, & Boulet, 2009). *Concept-based searching, ranking, and analytic indexing techniques* entail data search engine indexing of the accurate information retrieval storage system, along with document clustering to optimize speed and performance during search queries for relevant documents (Karmakar & Swarnakar, 2017). The *equilibration of knowledge-based data epistemology and analytic management system* focuses on the strategic inquiry of the leveraging of cloud-based BDA and the balancing of premeditated exploration to successfully gather and handle BDA and information management that can be readily made accessible for enhanced decision making in organizations (Shorfuzzaman, 2017).

The *network of regulations analyst and data pragmatism* involves data information asset management; regulations concerning the construction, design, and production of work equipment; and compliance framework. The *representation model for legal case data analysis* focuses on the quality of representation and legal services provided to clientele shaped by information-rich data analysis of case law model and application. The *comprehensive legal ontology of authority data codification* involves the process of arranging laws or rules according to established precedence, critical functional systems of judicial rulings, cross-case analogies, case-based legal reasoning, and representative decision justifications' application (Ashley, 2009; Bagby & Mullen, 2007).

Daunting Challenges of the Equilibration of Data Deontological and Teleological Hermeneutics

The importance of data analytics that considers the IoT ecosystem in the period of Big Data can be, in part, reminiscent to the growing concern that public policy problems and associated data analytic software devices are becoming increasingly enormous, but the policy decision makers' quest for data management solutions is also becoming somewhat more elusive. The linkages between IoT data analytic demand and policy data supply are thus faced with daunting challenges for policy decision makers who want to gain some degree of hermeneutical insight into the data analytical viewpoints and vice versa. The public policy analysis that implicates the policy decision-making framework, however, might require the equilibration of data deontological and teleological hermeneutics being shaped by the epistemological inquisition into the BDA (Ashley, 2009). The equilibration of data deontological hermeneutics tends to focus on the balance between the ontology of analogical BDA and the means by which the rightness or wrongness of data analytics might be conceived to implicate the sense-making process of the BDA to aid a formidable data interpretation.

The equilibration of data teleological hermeneutics focuses on the alignment between the fitness or suitability of challenging policy data interest interpretation and the ontological interpretation of analogical BDA epistemology. It thus follows that one way to make a better sense of the BDA is to know the best ways to handle the immense knowledge intended to be made from the data analytic stimulations (Kettl, 2018). The ontological interpretation of analogical BDA is therefore structured on the premise that no one has a monopoly on the epistemology of knowledge inquisition, and that "the *gap* between what we [*may*] *know*—and what we can agree that we [*might*] *know*—and what we [*might*] *need* to *know* is [becoming increasingly] enormous" (emphasis added, Kettl, 2018, p. 2). Thus, due to its unique, cutting-edge program innovation, the PAA concentration offered through the ODL dashboard in the MPA degree program at NU is discussed to account for the importance of BDA as a framework for the symbolic ideology of IoT policy action-learning solutions' mechanism of the epistemic communities.

PUBLIC ADMINISTRATION BIG DATA EPISTEMIC COMMUNITY POLICYMAKING

Gaps in Data-Driven Policies of the Epistemic Community in Public Administration Field

More than two decades ago, Thomas (1997) argued that the epistemic community idea had not made inroads into the field of public administration. There appears, however, to be an emerging paradigm shift in the domain of public service management for which Big Data are being generated to tackle public policy issues of the epistemic communities (Cinquegrani, 2002; Dunlop, 2017; Wu & He, 2009). The enterprise of the prefix "public" in public administration (PA) is highly diverse, multitask-oriented, and shaped by variation of sectors whose spheres of operation encompass agencies, public policy creativities, and service policy delivery systems publicly funded with the transactional resources of the city, state, government, and citizenry of the epistemic communities (Basu, 2016; Fard, 2012; Van Der Waldt, 2014).

The service policy delivery systems are characterized by data-driven policies and service-linkages rooted in the public values and stakeholder interests, as well as the balance between the political ideology and technical dimensions of system changes geared toward providing policy-based services and programs to the epistemic communities (Melaville, Blank, & Asayesh, 1993). It thus follows that the domain of the "public" in PA is not only at the *heart* of PA, but it is also shaped by the data epistemology and ideology of politics and social values of service functionality, policymaking, and budgetary resources to serve the public good. This data epistemology that structures the public good is operationalized in stakeholder ideals to which societal civility, democratic governance systems, interest groups, public service, values of the citizenry, situational needs of society, and functional systems of a democratic society can be said to shape the public policy decision-making processes.

Dynamic Challenges in the Data-Driven Policymaking Process

The functional systems of a democratic society tend to reflect the operationalization of dynamic policymaking process that shapes democratic governance systems, organizational governance structure, and the socio-economic sectors, including education, nonprofit, for-profit or the proprietary sectors. The dynamics of a policymaking process involve deeply held values, different perceptions regarding the causes of social problems, and appropriate service policy impact that is responsive to those problems within the domain of the political propositions or the ideological policy needs of the epistemic communities. Deficiencies in the data-driven policies as shaped by the imposition of public service values, for which the service policy delivery systems are operationalized to meet the needs satisfaction of the epistemic communities, can thus create problems for the public policy decision-making processes. In other words, the dynamics of data-driven policies generated to shape important policy development and implementation processes can be productive while some aspects might be ineffective in addressing the desirable goals of the epistemic communities' policy interests.

Contextual Equilibration Challenges Structuring Data-Driven Policymaking Functionality Process

The political proposition of a data-driven policy dynamic might introspect sound as atypical concerning the equilibration challenges that structure the ideological values, perceptions, and beliefs of the epistemic communities. The policymaking processes, however, might occasionally seem to be self-centered toward gaining egocentric policy agendas of the epistemic communities. It may be argued otherwise, but the explicit representation of the data-driven policy interests inherent within the epistemic communities might show adversary policy interests that often undermine the potential strength of the citizenry's various needs. The context of this adversarial relationship, while posing a threat to the data-driven policy interests of the epistemic communities, may also revolutionize the service policy delivery systems toward meeting the citizenry's satisfaction. Therefore, the crucial goal is to bridge the growing gap between the productive elements of the data-driven policies and the climate of service operation toward forecasting collaborative service policies and decisions to satisfy the needs of the society at large. Figure 1 illustrates the dynamics of equilibration that structure the PA domain of the Big Data-driven policy perception that impacts social action of public policy decision-making processes within the epistemic communities.

The contextual working capabilities of the "public" in PA are administered or executed by the "administration" component of the Big Data-driven policies in the PA, so it can also be said that it is this "administration" aspect of the PA that gives the soul of PA its systemic administration functionality. However, the systemic "administration" functionality of PA often gets caught up in the multiplicity of data-driven epistemic community policies due to the competing needs of the public and interfaces with budgetary resource limitations. This tends to raise questions regarding the ways to ensure that the budgetary resource limitations are adequately and equitably used to meet the variations of stakeholders' policy interests or to satisfy the public needs of the epistemic communities. Response to such needs-based questions calls for the equilibration of BDA epistemology as a symbolic ideology of the IoT action-learning solution model that structures the connections between the "public" and "administration" components in the PA of the epistemic communities. The equilibration of BDA epistemology as the symbolic ideology of the IoT action-learning solution model is thus characterized by the contextual and topological data analytic paradigms that shape the instrumentality framework of data management.

Figure 1. Domain of data-driven policy perception impacting social action of public policy decision-making processes in the epistemic communities

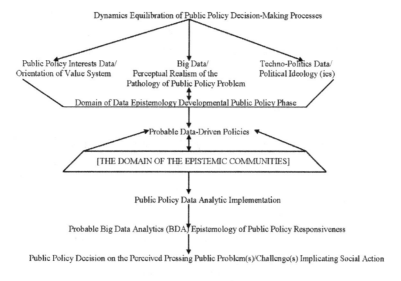

Contextual Instrumentalities of Topological Data Analytic Paradigms of the Internet of Things

In the policymaking, analysis, and implementation processes depicted in Figure 1, both qualitative textual data analysis and quantitative statistical data analysis rely upon contextual and topological data analytic paradigms of political ideology and policy action-learning data management instrumentality framework. The topological data analytic paradigms are intended to transport data understanding beyond the "plain meaning" of words to diagnose that words or the worldviews of the epistemic communities can mean many things. Those meanings surrounding the words or worldviews, however, must be consistent and coherent to shape policy data such that the meaning of a specific word or worldview might need to be shaped by the other words around it (Fard, 2012; Krim, Gentimis, & Chintakunta, 2016). Probably the best known standard topological data analytic paradigm is the use of symbolic data isomorphic interactions of metaphorical computation or metaphorical concept mapping, which is an implied comparison that uses a word or phrase figuratively applied to one object to convey something different (Bench-Capon & Gordon, 2009; Tetteh, 2010, 2015a). Metaphors are used in the qualitative data analysis as symbolic data isomorphic interactions to serve as: (i) data-condensing or data-reducing devices, (b) pattern-making or data-building devices, (c) decentering or symbolic kaleidoscopic devices, and (d) the means or vehicles for connecting data to theory (Miles, Huberman, & Saldaña, 2014).

As a core, lead faculty, and senior lecturer since the inception of the development of the data analytics courses in the PAA concentration at NU, Tetteh (2015b) has always held the notion that the décor of the symbolic ideology of IoT instrumentalities that may structure analytic data paradigms can be conceived by methods of action-learning solutions and policy data statistics to help mitigate the pressing social issues facing policy stakeholders. Moreover, the plethora of policy data generated through the policy-making process can make better sense to stakeholders if it is translated into policy statistics and descriptive policies to inform further action-learning solutions of policy implementation. Policymaking and planning can therefore be viewed as structured by complex bureaucratic contexts and cross-sector collaborations. To comprehend such policy complexity, the policy-student administrator must develop a policy capacity of bureaucratic expertise for data-based policy analysis in keeping with the values of public service governance. Pertinent to the capacity building of bureaucratic expertise, the would-be policy analyst is thus expected to gain practical knowledge and insight into the multifaceted issues and political ideologies that shape policy action learning, planning, formation, and dissemination processes.

CURRENT FOCUSED CHALLENGES

Curriculum-Based Big Data Policy-Analytic Epistemology Model in Norwich University MPA Policy Analysis and Analytics Concentration

Heuristic Epistemology of Big Data Analytics Framework

The Norwich MPA PAA concentration recognizes the role of Big Data analytics (BDA) epistemology as a framework for heuristic epistemology, wherein industry-based and community-based Big Data are made useful based on hands-on data analysis findings and reports to policy decision makers. For Armstrong (2009), the heuristic epistemology "comprises of three symbiotic and heuristic modalities, namely, the Triad of *Apperception, Appraisal*, and *Appropriation*, undergirded by the understanding that the notion of truth is a type of virtue" (emphasis added, p. 1). These "virtuous truth" data-driven policies can thus be conceived of as the equilibration of coherent and consistent data-generated knowledge of the contextual data triangulation structuring apperception, appraisal, and appropriation techniques that underscores the worldviews of the epistemic communities.

Therefore, through the facilitation of apperception, appraisal, and appropriation processes, such data triangulation techniques are intended to ensure that the equilibration of coherent validation and consistent cross-verification of the "virtuous truth" data-driven policies is generated from the epistemic communities' worldviews via the IoT ecosystem framework. Given the complexity of BDA epistemology for which such contextual data triangulation techniques are thus warranted, Armstrong (2009) asserted that the heuristic epistemology "seeks to bring to light the contributing causes of divergence and divisiveness over opposing truth claims, which, in turn, hinder the knowing process of moving from error or ignorance to truth appropriated" (p. 2). However, when valid "virtuous truth" is gathered from the epistemic communities' worldviews, it can offer credence to the equilibration of the data-driven policies.

Discrepant Policy Case Challenges of the Epistemic Communities

The challenge is that the discrepant policy cases inherent in the epistemic communities' data worldviews can offer information-rich viewpoints and thus should not be ignored if the "virtuous truth" data-driven policies are intended to meet the threshold of the coherent validation and consistent cross-verification processes. Consequently, the means by which the "divergence and divisiveness over opposing truth claims" can be handled to shape the public policy data are imperative for ensuring that all of the voices that shape the varied, competing, and complex self-interests of the epistemic communities are given careful consideration in the facilitation of the BDA epistemology as symbolic ideology of IoT action-learning solution model.

Equilibration of Apperception, Appraisal, and Appropriation Techniques

The *apperception technique* serves as a fulcrum for redirecting the discrepant policy cases that shape the divergence and divisiveness data in a manner that can complement the enrichment of the epistemic communities' data worldviews. For Armstrong (2009), the *appraisal technique* "diverts the object of enquiry to the subject [by] assessing one's level of apperception and appropriation in order to ensure that the other two modalities do not become static" (p. 3), but is instead useful in enhancing the policy data worldviews of the epistemic communities. The *appropriation technique* fosters data authentication process of the transfer of data-driven policies to the policy data know-how of shaping a policy decision-making process to implicate social action for the epistemic communities' shared interests.

In the quest of facilitating the equilibration of apperception, appraisal, and appropriation techniques, the emerging powerful computer-assisted software applications and the importance of IoT data mining, data matrix, data reconstruction, data filtering, data recording, data reduction, and data visualization techniques, to name just a few, can be resourcefully useful. With the increasing availability of substantial analytic databases, data analytics software and the computer-assisted software program applications are intended to create a framework for the Norwich MPA PAA concentration by providing a hands-on, cutting-edge innovation of online learning coupled with a data analytic tech-enabled lab known as the *virtual action learning big analytic data* (VAL-BAD) lab.

Virtual Action Learning Big Analytic Data and Computer-Assisted Software Application

Data mining entails "digging" around in large analytic databases to discover relationships among variables of interests, or sometimes until the researcher finds a statistical association that "demonstrates" something of value to demonstrate. *Data matrix* allows the use of computer-assisted software for storing information-rich Big Data to facilitate the coordination in locating of data, data filtering, data coding, data reduction, data reconstruction, data recording, and data visualization. The *data reconstruction* identifies, organizes, and manages the disconnect of intricate and integral data from the compressed sensed data using a network-coding-based file system to regenerate code as its distributed storage coding scheme and creates categorization that fits the coding boundary values and multi-layers of neural network to provide a streamline data summary report for policy decision makers (Chen, 2013; Li & Deng, 2014).

Data filtering involves the process of delineating, identifying, and rectifying outlier values and errors in the analytic data from big raw data to make the analytic data clean for further processing. The *data reduction* has been conceived as "an umbrella term for a suite of technologies—including compression, deduplication, and thin provisioning—that serve to reduce the storage capacity required to handle a given data set" (Pure Storage, 2018, para. 1). *Data visualization* represents the depiction of the data report using graphical models, mind-maps, concept mapping, and other visual portraits to aid data policy formulation and understanding for decision makers.

In the VAL-BAD lab, students begin to use data analysis tools such as Excel, SPSS, and R Statistical Analysis, and then move to explore the online-based Dedoose software application by utilizing relevant policy research methods for statistical analysis, policy planning, and policy problem resolution. The *SPSS* is a statistical data analysis software application for analyzing quantitative data and reporting systems. The *R statistical analysis* is free data analytic software that offers a wide range of statistical applications. The *Dedoose software* is a cloud-based data analytic computing application for collaborative data analysis of qualitative and mixed methods research. Data innovation, however, requires hands-on knowledge based on readily available state-of-the-art industry data analytic software, so students must also be exposed to emerging computer-assisted data analysis software such as NVivo, CAT (Coding Analysis Toolkit), NUDIST, HyperResearch, and Atlas-ti.

The *NVivo software* is an advanced data analytic application for analyzing qualitative and mixed methods research. *CAT* is a free web-based statistical data analytic tool. *NUDIST* and *HyperResearch* are powerful data analysis software used to analyze qualitative data. *Atlas-ti* is a cloud-based data analytic application for analyzing qualitative and mixed methods research. Throughout the PAA concentration, students are expected to work concurrently via the VAL-BAD lab, which is intended to expose them to the data analysis tools, as well as to policy research methods and data analysis techniques. The problems researched and analyzed in the VAL-BAD lab come from "real-world" work with community-based industries, corporations, various government agencies, and entities. Students, faculty, and representatives from "partner" organizations are expected to work together in the VAL-BAD lab to research and analyze data, write reflective reports and publish when required or become necessary to support stakeholders or policy decision makers.

Throughout the courses taken in the PAA concentration, students develop and keep an *Action-Learning Policy Data Analysis Casebook* (RALPDAC) of their hands-on action learning experiences of the VAL-BAD lab. Thus, the drafted RALPDAC is intended to showcase the interplay between course-based learning and work-based learning evident in students' functional resume and consolidation into a potential White Paper publication for career advancement. Students often pursue an education that does not translate into readily gained work industry experience concerning innovative ways of handling vast information. A function resume exposes students to the critical knowledge base on emerging theoretical propositions, as well as to the practical methods of handling trends in industry-led knowledge and data analysis experience. Table 1 provides synopses of the courses offered in the Norwich MPA PAA concentration.

Table 1. Summary of MPA 36-credit degree policy analysis and analytics curriculum-based Big Data policy analytic program model

AD 511: Foundations of Public Administration and Policy--(6 Credits) Among others, this course is intended to introduce students to the theories of public administration, administrative ethics, service accountability, leadership roles, democratic governance systems, organizational governance structure, strategic planning, policy research, critical analysis, and political ideology as implicated by data-driven policies.
AD 545: Politics, Policy, and Planning--(6 Credits) Among others, this course is designed to introduce students to the methods of policy-data analysis software applications such as Excel and SPSS to facilitate the analysis of policy statistics, policy planning, policy resolution, utilization of real-time policy data sets, and implications of politics and action learning in the policy-making process. *This course has an accompanying VAL-BAD lab.*
AD 555: Methods of Policy Analysis--(6 Credits) Among others, this course provides students the opportunity to explore in greater depths the methods of projection analysis, chi-square test, hypothesis testing, and policy analysis techniques using crosscutting research strategies, identifying and gathering data, data analysis, establishing evaluation criteria, and identifying alternatives. *This course has an accompanying VAL-BAD lab.*
AD 565: Policy and Policy Implementation--(6 Credits) Among others, this course is intended to examine data-driven policy complexities and functions at the organizational governance structure level, planning, formulation, iterative process, forecasting activities and effects, evaluation, and implementation, that implicate the behavior of policy actions and adoption. *This course has an accompanying VAL-BAD lab.*
AD 575: Tools for Policy Analysis--(6 Credits) Among others, this course is intended to utilize BDA software tools such as Excel, Dedoose, SPSS, and R applications in examining and analyzing policy cases of the nonprofit sector, sociopolitical environments, and at the federal, state, regional, and urban government levels to aid policy recommendations and implementations to support public policy decision-makers. *This course has an accompanying VAL-BAD lab.*
AD: 585 Economics and Decision Making--(6 Credits) Among others, this course is intended to introduce students to the data-driven policies that implicate a broader scope of administrative leadership, decision-making principles and strategies, financial management, and economic policies as might be utilized by public sector leaders and service industries to shape the state of the economy at both the domestic and global sectors of advancing service innovation. *This course has an accompanying VAL-BAD lab.*

Norwich University (2018). *Online Master of Public Administration Curriculum: Policy Analysis and Analytics Concentration.* Northfield, VT: Author. Retrieved from https://online.norwich.edu/academic-programs/masters/public-administration/overview.

SOLUTIONS AND RECOMMENDATIONS

Equilibration of Big Data Analytics Epistemology of Symbolic Ideology of the Internet of Things Action-Learning Solutions

Since the development of the policy analytics data courses of NU's PAA concentration, it can be conceived that the IoT ecosystem framework has become somewhat confronted with gigantic mountains of BDA epistemology for public administration. This is not, however, due to the discipline of public administration having a monopoly on knowledge (Van Der Waldt, 2014) regarding everything that must be done or whether this is the only field of inquiry that has the know-how (Kettl, 2018). Instead, common ground must be found concerning ways to engage in meaningful BDA epistemology of action-learning solutions. Policy makers are inundated with increasing heaps of Big Data (Kettl, 2018), but some known epistemology data, although not intended, might not only consist of data outliers, inaccurate observations, or perhaps illogical reasoning.

Equilibration of Idiographic and Nomothetic Explanations

It is necessary to make data analytic evidence and accuracy convey the equilibration of idiographic and nomothetic explanations. The idiographic explanation provides insight into the unique, peculiar, and distinctive causes of specific events, actions, or particular conditions of an individual or a single aspect of a situation within the epistemic community. The nomothetic explanation offers an overall or generalized insight into the causal factors among variables or the relationship between elements of conditions or events across the epistemic communities. Consistent with Armstrong's (2009) idea regarding "divergence and divisiveness over opposing truth claims" (p. 2), the data outliers, inaccurate observations, and illogical reasoning can thus be addressed using the equilibria triangulation of apperception, appraisal, and appropriation techniques.

Action Learning Solution

There is an oversupply of vast piles of Big Data across the IoT ecosystem framework (Kettl, 2018; Mohammadi, Al-Fuqaha, Sorour, & Guizani, 2018). It is perhaps for this that the equilibration of BDA epistemology must be shaped by the symbolic ideology of action-learning solutions of insightful precision for the restructuring of the right kind of questions to enable policy decision makers to reach reasonable policy problem resolutions. An action learning solution fosters collaborative methods of reflective practice inquiry, structured in policy data analysis of reflective thought processes and guided by the equilibration of data epistemology directed at tackling context-specific policy issues, capacity building, and coaching mechanism tailored to BDA epistemology of the epistemic communities.

Equilibration, Disequilibration, and Stable Equilibrium of Big Data Analytics Epistemology

Piaget conceived the three models of equilibration (i.e., state of equilibrium, state of disequilibration, more stable equilibrium or re-equilibration) (Boom, 2009; Piaget, 1985) for tackling all questions regarding human cognitive development. Such models can also be adapted to serve as alignment mechanisms for the symbolic ideology of IoT action-learning solution of BDA epistemology. Serving as alignment mechanisms implies that there must be a symbiotic relationship between the three models of equilibration, the triangulation of apperception, appraisal, and appropriation techniques, and the symbolic ideology of IoT action-learning solution of the BDA epistemology. The symbolic ideology of an IoT action-learning solution has become a framework for Big Data gathering, stimulation of techno-politics data, data learning device, and containment of data epistemology ideologies (Gutiérrez-Rubí & Sarsanedas, 2016; Kurban, Peña-López, & Haberer, 2017; Mohammadi et al., 2018).

Techno-politics data can be viewed as policy-based ideological data shaped and garnered by critical informants, political policy actors, citizenry, stakeholders, people, individuals, and/or functional intellectuals whose worldviews are aligned to the context of renewed self-interests, public spheres of politics, management of political action, and understanding of political communication dynamics (Dunlop, 2017; Gutiérrez-Rubí & Sarsanedas, 2016; Kellner, 1998). At the *equilibrium state level*, the modes of thought across the IoT that structure the epistemic communities' worldviews tend to shape techno-politics data.

The *disequilibration state level* tends to foster the identification of shortcomings inherent in the data outliers, inaccurate observation, or illogical reasoning that surfaced during the equilibrium state level to make data analytics evidence and accuracy convey the equilibration of idiographic and nomothetic explanations. This can then lead the epistemic communities to the more *stable equilibrium* or *re-equilibration levels*, at which point the elimination of shortcomings inherent in the data outliers, inaccurate observation, or illogical reasoning that surfaced during the equilibrium levels can bring about the symbolic ideology of IoT action-learning solution. The BDA epistemology ideologies can be conceived as being embedded into the conceptual scheme of political ideology orientation (Gutiérrez-Rubí& Sarsanedas, 2016; Kurban et al., 2017), so it is imperative that the models of equilibration should be aligned with the idealism of political ideology to better facilitate policy data coordination via the symbolic IoT action-learning solution of the BDA epistemology processes.

Conceptual Action-Learning Epistemologies of Political Ideology Scheme

In his 2000 work on *American Government,* Wilson provided a conceptual scheme of political ideology by operationally defining it as "A coherent and consistent set of beliefs about who ought to rule, what principles rulers ought to obey, and what policies rulers ought to pursue" (p. 73). From the standpoint of the Wilsonian operational definition, it can be deciphered that three action-learning epistemologies of conceptual scheme structure the idealism of political ideology: *who ought to rule*[1], *what principles rulers ought to obey*[2], and *what policies rulers ought to pursue*[3]. Consistent with the Wilsonian operational definition, Ball and Dagger (2014) conceptualized political ideology as:

A fairly coherent and comprehensive set of ideas that explains and evaluates social conditions, helps people understand their place in society, and provides a program for social and political action. An ideology, more precisely, performs four functions for people who hold it: the (1) explanatory, (2) evaluative, (3) orientative, and (4) programmatic functions. (p.5)

Thus, the policy data coordination requires the interplay of a coherent and consistent set of beliefs structuring the systemic "administration" functionality of executing and disseminating explanation, evaluation, policy orientation, and policy program initiation to satisfy the needs of the epistemic communities.

Five Action-Learning "P" Epistemology Orientations of the IoT Symbolic Ideology Framework

As depicted in Figure 2, the interplay of policy data coordination is also structured by the three political ideology schemes and triangulation techniques, as well as in responsive alignment with the equilibration, disequilibration, and stable equilibration levels, to aid the facilitation of the symbolic ideology of IoT action-learning solution of the BDA epistemology processes. The symbolic ideology of an IoT action-learning solution is also shaped by the transactional resources of symbolic capital power, which are characterized as a type of policy action, and the source, channel, substance, and directionality of policy initiatives (Fuller, 2008; Nataliia & Elena, 2015). By expanding upon the work of Kettl (2018), it is therefore essential to offer that the action-learning solutions should be reflective of the following five action-learning "P" orientations of the symbolic ideology of IoT ontology to facilitate the equilibration of BDA epistemology processes better:

1. **Policy-Focused Inquisition (PFI):** To what extent can the IoT action-learning solutions of techno-politics data and historical data shaping BDA teach about one's future policy actions?

2. **Prediction-Based Collaborative Inquisition (PBCI):** In what ways can the collaborative efforts of stakeholders make better policy decisions from the IoT action-learning solutions structuring the predictive BDA of techno-politics to shape knowledge production that implicates positive or constructive results?

3. **Production of Knowledge-Oriented Inquisition (PKOI):** To what extent has the positive implication of knowledge production been accomplished, and how can improvements be made with the IoT action-learning solutions that structure the productive techno-politics data in shaping policy actions?

4. **Potential Risk Management-Based Inquisition (PRMBI):** What, if any, are the potential symbolic ideologies of IoT action-learning solutions that structure techno-politic data challenges and undermine stakeholders' original intentions? Can these ideologies impede the action-learning solutions that shape policy data actions?

5. **Pliability-Focused Inquisition (PFI):** In what ways can the collaborative efforts of stakeholders' symbolic ideology of IoT action-learning solutions of data capacity building be improved? How can stakeholders recover when bad things unexpectedly happen to impede the action-learning solutions shaping policy data actions?

Figure 2. Equilibration schemes of political ideology facilitation of symbolic IoT action-learning solution of the big data analytics (BDA) epistemology of the epistemic communities

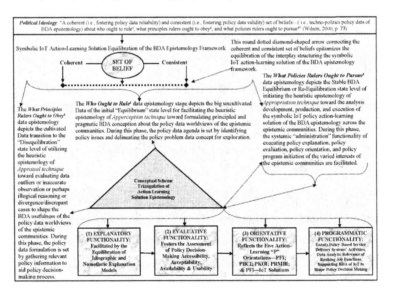

CONCLUSION

The dynamic power of the IoT ecosystem framework has become the most effective and efficient way for facilitating BDA as a channel by which people interact, learn, work, communicate, and do business with one another. Emerging data analytic software is becoming increasingly productive for policy analysts, researchers, students, and knowledge workers who design productive services and generate knowledge for organizations, governments, business enterprises, and industrial services for the benefit of epistemic communities. Epistemic communities have become knowledge-based technology service economies, with a growing number of companies and institutions attracting customers through the power of the IoT ecosystem framework.

The IoT ecosystem has created a framework of easy access to information-rich Big Data that are shaping the systemic way of analyzing data. The impact of the IoT ecosystem framework of delivery of teaching/learning across the institutions of higher education has offered knowledge acquisition that will better serve the career needs of the epistemic communities. In response to the Obama Administration's policy initiatives, institutions of higher education have been pursuing combinations of underlying assumptions regarding which educational options they should offer; how, where, and when they should offer them; and for whom they should be offered so they can prepare students for gainful employment. The PAA concentration is essential to core policy action-learning models across the epistemic communities of planning, analyzing, administering, managing policies, and preparing students for policy analytic jobs to redress pressing social issues inherent within the epistemic communities.

Of the related persistent public policy issue—whether one should consider the ramifications of political policy ideologies disseminated through television programs—such as news reports on Sony hacking, the White House hacking, the power going down around the DC area, or perhaps the 2016 Democratic National Committee email hacking, it is quite apparent that Big Data management, policy data creation, and data-driven cybersecurity threats are all interconnected. Governmental entities, corporations, non-profits all collect Big Data, but it has only recently come to light that these BDA have the potential to be used for something other than their primary purposes. Local governments continuously collect information, and social media gather information. What happens to the information gathered and how can such Big Data shape public policy decisions? Can public administrators use the information first to craft policy and then evaluate that policy in an iterative process? (Pelletier & Tetteh, 2015). These lead to the necessity and emergence of the PAA concentration regarding the use of data-driven policies to facilitate epistemological inquisitions into BDA to determine:

- Are the BDA epistemology securely held?
- Can the BDA epistemology be manipulated in such a way as to create new false records and cause harm?
- Can the public infrastructure be at risk due to the collection of BDA epistemology that is partially analyzed but not securely held?

Courses in the PAA concentration are thus designed to ensure that before moving onto the next seminar, all students understand and use the various quantitative statistical analysis software and qualitative computer-assisted software applications when exploring and examining the impact of politics on policy learning and action planning. Therefore, by using the symbolic ideology of IoT action-learning solution to facilitate the BDA epistemology processes, one can gather the policy data necessary to determine the outcome of public policy decision making for the benefit of epistemic communities.

REFERENCES

Adler, E., & Haas, P. M. (1992). Conclusion: Epistemic communities, world order, and the creation of a reflective research program. *International Organization, 46*(1), 367–390. doi:10.1017/S0020818300001533

Armstrong, M. C. C. (2009). Heuristic epistemology to limit divisiveness. *Journal of Dharma, 34*(2), 207–220. Retrieved from http://www.dharmaramjournals.in/ArticleDetails.aspx?AID=690

Ashley, K. D. (2009). Ontological requirements for analogical, teleological, and hypothetical legal reasoning. *Proceedings of the 12th International Conference on Artificial Intelligence and Law–ICAIL '09,* 1–10. 10.1145/1568234.1568236

Bagby, J. W., & Mullen, T. (2007). Legal ontology of sales law application to ecommerce. *Artificial Intelligence and Law, 15*(2), 155–170. doi:10.100710506-007-9027-3

Ball, T., & Dagger, R. (2014). Political ideologies and the democratic ideal (9th ed.). New York, NY: Pearson.

Basu, R. (2016). The discipline of public administration today: New perspectives. *The Indian Journal of Public Administration, 62*(1), 1–8. doi:10.1177/0019556120160101

Bench-Capon, T., & Gordon, T. F. (2009). Isomorphism and argumentation. *Proceedings of the 12th International Conference on Artificial Intelligence and Law–ICAIL '09,* 11–20. doi: 10.1145/1568234.1568237

Bergsteiner, H., Avery, G. C., & Neumann, R. (2010). Kolb's experiential learning model: Critique from a modelling perspective. *Studies in Continuing Education, 32*(1), 29–46. doi:10.1080/01580370903534355

Boom, J. (2009). Piaget on equilibration. In U. Müller, J. I. M. Carpendale, & L. Smith (Eds.), The Cambridge companion to Piaget (pp. 132–149). New York: Cambridge University Press. doi:10.1017/CCOL9780521898584.006

Chen, L. (2013). *Digital functions and data reconstruction: Digital–discrete methods.* New York: Springer. doi:10.1007/978-1-4614-5638-4

Cinquegrani, R. (2002). Futurist networks: Cases of epistemic community? *Futures, 34,* 779–783. doi:10.1016/S0016–3287(02)00020–4

Dunlop, C. A. (2017). The irony of epistemic learning: Epistemic communities, policy learning and the case of Europe's hormones saga. *Policy & Society, 36*(2), 215–232. doi:.2017.1322260 doi:10.1080/14494035

EY Building a Better Working World. (2014, April). *Big Data: Changing the way businesses compete and operate* (Insights on Governance, Risk and Compliance Report). Ernst & Young Global Limited. Retrieved from http://www.ey.com/us/en/home/library

Fard, H. D. (2012). Research paradigms in public administration. *International Journal of the Humanities, 19*(4), 55–108. Retrieved from http://eijh-old.modares.ac.ir/article_10524.html

Farooq, M. O., & Kunz, T. (2017). *IoT-RF: A routing framework for the Internet of Things.* Paper presented at the IEEE 28th Annual International Symposium on Personal, Indoor, and Mobile Radio Communications (PIMRC), Montreal, QC, Canada. Retrieved from https://ieeexplore.ieee.org/document/8292730/

Francesconi, E., & Peruginelli, G. (2007). Searching and retrieving legal literature through automated semantic indexing. *Proceedings of the 11th International Conference on Artificial intelligence and Law–ICAIL '07*, 131–139. 10.1145/1276318.1276343

Frey, C. B., & Osborne, M. A. (2017). The future of employment: How susceptible are jobs to computerisation? *Technological Forecasting and Social Change, 114*(1), 254–280. doi:10.1016/j.techfore.2016.08.019

Fuller, S. R. (2008). Organizational symbolism: A multidimensional conceptualization. *The Journal of Global Business and Management, 4*(2), 168–174. Retrieved from http://www.jgbm.org/page/ previous_V4-2.htm

Golub, K. (2017, October 16). *Encyclopedia of knowledge organization: Automatic subject indexing of text* [ISKO Version 1.0]. Retrieved from http://www.isko.org/cyclo/automatic

Gutiérrez-Rubí, A., & Sarsanedas, O. (2016, June 20). *Technopolitics and the new territories for political action* [Interview]. London, UK: Democracia Abierta/OpenDemocracy. Retrieved from https://www. opendemocracy.net/democraciaabierta/antoni-guti-rrez-rub-oleguer-sarsanedas/tecnopolitics-and-new-territories-for-poli

Haas, P. M. (1992). Introduction: Epistemic communities and international policy coordination. *International Organization, 46*(1), 1–35. doi:10.1017/S0020818300001442

Halper, F. (2014). Predictive analytics for business advantage [TDWI Best Practices Report]. *The Data Warehousing Institute (TDWI) Research*. Retrieved from https://tdwi.org/research/list/research-and-resources.aspx

Karmakar, S., & Swarnakar, S. (2017). New concept-based indexing technique for search engine. *Indian Journal of Science and Technology, 10*(18), 1–10. doi:10.17485/ijst/2017/v10i18/114018

Kellner, D. (1998). Intellectuals, the new public spheres, and techno-politics. In C. Toulouse & T. W. Luke (Eds.), *The politics of cyberspace* (pp. 167–186). New York, NY: Routledge.

Kettl, D. (2018). *Little bites of Big Data for public policy*. Thousand Oaks, CA: Sage.

Kolb, D. A. (1984). *Experiential learning: Experience as the source of learning and development*. Prentice–Hall.

Koniaris, M., Anagnostopoulos, I., & Vassiliou, Y. (2017). Network analysis in the legal domain: A complex model for European Union legal sources. *Journal of Complex Networks, 32*(1), 1–17. doi:10.1093/comnet/cnx029

Krim, H., Gentimis, T., & Chintakunta, H. (2016). Discovering the whole by the coarse: A topological paradigm for data analysis. *IEEE Signal Processing Magazine, 33*(2), 95–104. doi:.2015.2510703 doi:10.1109/MSP

Kurban, C., Peña–López, I., & Haberer, M. (2017, February). What is technopolitics? A conceptual scheme for understanding politics in the digital age. *IDP. Revista de Internet, Derecho y Ciencia Política, 24*, 3–20. Retrieved from http://edcp.blogs.uoc.edu/20170524-article-what-is-technopolitics-a-conceptual-scheme-for-understanding-politics-in-the-digital-age/

Li, K., & Deng, Y. (2014). Accelerating the reconstruction process in network coding storage system by leveraging data temperature. In C. H.Hsu, X. Shi & V. Salapura (Eds.), *Lecture Notes in Computer Science: Vol. 8707. Network and Parallel Computing* (pp. 510–521). Berlin: Springer.

Mazzega, P., Bourcier, D., & Boulet, R. (2009). The network of French legal codes. *Proceedings of the 12th International Conference on Artificial Intelligence and Law—ICAIL '09*, 236–237. doi: 10.1145/1568234.1568271

Melaville, A., Blank, M. J., & Asayesh, G. (1993). *Together we can: A guide for crafting a profamily system of education and human services.* Washington, DC: Center for the Study of Social Policy and the Institute for Educational Leadership.

Miles, M. B., Huberman, A. M., & Saldaña, J. (2014). *Qualitative data analysis: A methods sourcebook* (3rd ed.). Thousand Oaks, CA: Sage.

Mohammadi, M., Al-Fuqaha, A. I., Sorour, S., & Guizani, M. (2018, June 06). Deep learning for IoT Big Data and streaming analytics: A survey. In *IEEE Communications Surveys and Tutorials* (Early Access). Retrieved from https://ieeexplore.ieee.org/ document/8373692/

Nataliia, L., & Elena, F. (2015). Internet of things as a symbolic resource of power. *Procedia: Social and Behavioral Sciences, 166*, 521–525. doi:10.1016/j.sbspro.2014.12.565

National Institute of Food and Agriculture—United States Department of Agriculture. (2017, July 6). *Experiential learning model.* Washington, DC: Author. Retrieved from https://nifa.usda. gov/resources

Norwich University. (2010, July 31). *Norwich University 2010 NEASC self–study.* Northfield, VT: Author.

Norwich University (2014a, July). *NU2019 strategic plan update: Building on the past...strengthening our future.* Northfield, VT: Author.

Norwich University. (2014b). *College of Graduate and Continuing Studies (CGCS): Faculty Manual 2014–2015.* Northfield, VT: Author.

Norwich University (2015, August 15). *Interim/fifth year report.* Northfield, VT: Author.

Norwich University. (2018). *Online Master of Public Administration curriculum: Policy analysis and analytics concentration.* Northfield, VT: Author. Retrieved from https://online.norwich.edu/ academic-programs/masters/public-administration/overview

Pelletier, R. A., & Tetteh, E. N. A. (2015). *Policy Analysis and Analytics Concentration, Master of Public Administration Program, College of Graduate and Continuing Studies, Norwich University.* Northfield, VT: Norwich University.

Piaget, J. (1985). *The equilibration of cognitive structures: The central problem of intellectual development.* Chicago: University of Chicago Press. (Original work published 1975)

Pure Storage. (2018). *What is data reduction?* Retrieved from https://www.purestorage.com/fr/resources/ glossary/data–reduction.html

Shorfuzzaman, M. (2017). Leveraging cloud-based Big Data analytics in knowledge management for enhanced decision making in organizations. *International Journal of Distributed and Parallel Systems*, *8*(1), 1–13. doi:10.5121/ijdps.2017.8101

Tetteh, E. N. A. (2004). *Theories of democratic governance in the institutions of higher education.* New York: iUniverse.

Tetteh, E. N. A. (2010). *Communal photosynthesis: Metaphor-based heuristic study of service-learners' symbolic interactionism in security management.* Ann Arbor, MI: ProQuest LLC/UMI Dissertation.

Tetteh, E. N. A. (2015a). Communal–photosynthesis metaphor: Autobiographical action–research journeys and heuristic–action–learning frameworks of living educational theories. *ALARj*, *21*(1), 148–176.

Tetteh, E. N. A. (2015b). *Overview of AD 545 course: Politics, policy, and planning (Policy Analysis and Analytics Concentration, Master of Public Administration Program, College of Graduate and Continuing Studies, Norwich University).* Northfield, VT: Norwich University.

Tetteh, E. N. A. (2015c). *Overview of AD 555 course: Methods of policy analysis (Policy Analysis and Analytics Concentration, Master of Public Administration Program, College of Graduate and Continuing Studies, Norwich University).* Northfield, VT: Norwich University.

Thomas, C. W. (1997, April 1). Public management as interagency cooperation: Testing epistemic community theory at the domestic level. *Journal of Public Administration: Research and Theory*, *7*(2), 221–246. doi:10.1093/oxfordjournals.jpart.a024347

Van der Waldt, G. (2014). Public administration teaching and interdisciplinarity: Considering the consequences. *Teaching Public Administration, 32*(2), 169–193. doi: 14523285 doi:10.1177/01447394

Wilson, J. Q. (2000). *American government: A brief version* (5th ed.). Boston, MA: Houghton Mifflin.

Wu, X., & He, J. (2009). Paradigm shift in public administration: Implications for teaching professional training programs. *Public Administration Review,69*(s1), S21–S28. doi:10.1111/j.1540-6210.2009.02085.x

Zdravković, M., Zdravković, J., Aubry, A., Moalla, N., Guedria, W., & Sarraipa, J. (2018). Domain framework for implementation of open IoT ecosystems. *International Journal of Production Research*, *56*(7), 2552–2569. doi:10.1080/00207543.2017.1385870

Zhang, P., & Koppaka, L. (2007). Semantics–based legal citation network. *Proceedings of the 11th International Conference on Artificial intelligence and Law–ICAIL '07,* 123–130. doi: 10.1145/1276318.1276342

KEY TERMS AND DEFINITIONS

Data Deontological Hermeneutics: The interpretation of data regarding the means by which the rightness or wrongness of data analytics might be conceived to implicate the sense-making process of big data analytics.

Data Teleological Hermeneutics: The alignment, fitness, or suitability of challenging the interpretation of data structuring big data analytics.

Disequilibration: The unbalancing of big data analytics across the IoT created by the shortcomings inherent in the divergence or discrepant cases of data, data outliers, or inaccurate observation or illogical reasoning.

Equilibration: The balancing of big data analytics created by the initial stage of policy data analysis across the IoT.

Epistemic Communities: A network of the ethos of political policy actors, stakeholders, the citizenry, and professionals with the data capacity of shared knowledge, policy-relevant knowledge, policy analytic data, policy coordination, policy innovation, principled belief systems, mutual expectations, collective action, and shared interpretations.

Heuristic Epistemology: The equilibration of coherent and consistent data-generated knowledge of the data triangulation structuring apperception, appraisal, and appropriation techniques that underscores the worldviews of the epistemic communities.

Political Ideology: The balancing of a coherent and consistent set of policy beliefs and techno-politic data interest that implicates public policy data epistemology.

Public Policy Data Epistemology: The problem resolution continuum of evolving big data analytics of complex situational needs and public policy issues of organization and citizenry across the power of the IoT ecosystem framework of the epistemic communities.

Stable Equilibration/Re-Equilibration: The rebalancing of big data analytics created by the elimination of shortcomings inherent in the divergence or discrepant cases of data, data outliers, or inaccurate observations or illogical reasoning to contribute to the IoT action-learning solution.

This research was previously published in the Handbook of Research on Big Data and the IoT; pages 467-488, copyright year 2019 by Engineering Science Reference (an imprint of IGI Global).

Chapter 64
Bootstrapping Urban Planning:
Addressing Big Data Issues in Smart Cities

Ankur Lohachab

(iD) https://orcid.org/0000-0002-5291-7860

Kurukshetra University, India

ABSTRACT

Rapid growth of embedded devices and population density in IoT-based smart cities provides great potential for business and opportunities in urban planning. For addressing the current and future needs of living, smart cities have to revitalize the potential of big data analytics. However, a colossal amount of sensitive information invites various computational challenges. Moreover, big data generated by the IoT paradigm acquires different characteristics as compared to traditional big data because it contains heterogeneous unstructured data. Despite various challenges in big data, enterprises are trying to utilize its true potential for providing proactive applications to the citizens. In this chapter, the author finds the possibilities of the role of big data in the efficient management of smart cities. Representative applications of big data, along with advantages and disadvantages, are also discussed. By delving into the ongoing research approaches in securing and providing privacy to big data, this chapter is concluded by highlighting the open research issues in the domain.

INTRODUCTION

IoT envisages enormous number of smart devices and embedded systems which empowers physical objects with pervasive sensing, seeing, hearing, and communication with each other. As a result, IoT can be considered as a big outlook for future Internet which provides a new scope of opportunities. The promise of Smart Cities ensures the transformation in various areas of human life including transportation, education, health, and energy. Smart Cities led to the concept of smart communities in which distinct electronic devices are inter-connected with each other and generally produce high-quality two-way interactive multimedia content. This multimedia content along with colossal amount of incommensurable types of datasets generated by heterogeneous IoT devices are collectively termed as Big

DOI: 10.4018/978-1-6684-3662-2.ch064

Data. As compared with traditional data, Big Data contains more unstructured data that also require real-time analysis. Mainly, three aspects are used for characterizing Big Data: (a) it cannot be classified into regular relational database, (b) it is in enormous amount, and (c) it is captured, processed, and generated expeditiously. An observation from McKinsey & Company suggests that Big Data create productive, competitive, and economic value in the five core sectors. Record creation of data due to its deep detailing is eliciting attention of everyone.

Along with IoT, Cloud Computing is a major breakthrough technology which is used as an alternative for providing dedicated storage space, software, and even expensive hardware to the users according to their uses and needs. The reason for adoption of Cloud Computing among common users is that it minimizes infrastructure cost by providing virtual resources and parallel processing with anytime, anywhere user access, and efficient management (Bhushan & Gupta, 2018; Chen, Mao, & Liu, 2014; Bhushan & Gupta, 2017). The said advantages motivate organizations for using the virtualized environment in the Smart Cities scenario. The increasing popularity of IoT devices and personal digital assistants has taken the Cloud Computing concept to prominence peak due to their limited storage capacity, processing capability, and constrained energy resources. The concepts of Cloud Computing, IoT, and Big Data are coalescing as IoT provides users the convenience to interact with their physical objects, Cloud Computing provides the fundamental engine through the use of virtualization, and Big Data provides users the capability of using commodity computing for processing their queries in a timely and efficient manner.

Despite the fact that these smart connected objects are used for reducing traffic congestion, fighting crime, making local decisions more open, and foster economic development, they are creating the Big Data that require excessive amount of energy which is also responsible for increasing greenhouse gases. Researchers and industrialists see Big Data as an opportunity for developing new solutions and analyzing new problems. Big Data can be seen as one of the driving technology for drastic increase in development of machine learning algorithms (Labrinidis & Jagadish, 2012). For enhancement of Smart City services, Big Data is mined, processed, and stored efficiently in order to help managers for taking right decisions in real-time according to the provided information (Caragliu, Bo, & Nijkamp, 2011). Although analyzing datasets of network flows, logs, and system events is always considered as a problem, nevertheless this Big Data driven information security is utilized for forensics and intrusion detection.

The field of security and privacy has many standards and regulations, but the unprecedented value of Big Data exposes it to various security and privacy risks. In various authentication protocols, anonymized information is primarily used for hiding critical information, but recent studies show that this anonymized information can be easily breached by attackers in terms of privacy (Lohachab & Karambir, 2019). Usually in the process of data anonymization, removal of obvious identifiers is done, but attackers easily re-identify the information using spatial-temporal points in the processed datasets. Although cryptography is a powerful technique for privacy protection, various attacks motivate us to rethink the exact meaning of identification (Gupta & Quamara, 2018). Accordingly, communication privacy should also be explored in terms of Big Data. Privacy protection mechanisms can be classified into two major categories: content and interaction privacy.

Along with security and privacy issues, various issues regarding to Big Data including scalability, availability, transformation, data quality, heterogeneity, regulatory, governance, and data integrity should be addressed. Computational intelligence algorithms and Quality of Service (QoS) for maintaining the scalable, reliable, fault tolerant, and flexible Big Data are still facing many challenges. According to the growing demands of Big Data analysis for the development of new Smart City, services should be managed well for addressing the technological adoption of applications among common users. Figure

1 shows how Big Data and IoT collectively focus towards Smart Cities and their various services. Although, the age of Big Data also opens us to digital forensics investigation, but due to heterogeneous datasets, it is still considered as a challenging task (Cárdenas, Manadhata, & Rajan, 2013). Knowledge of this hype of Big Data analysis provides fine-grained, real-time control, and analysis for the governing bodies of the Smart Cities.

In this chapter, in depth analysis is done on the role of Big Data in Smart Cities. This chapter investigates the advantages of Big Data analysis in context of Smart Cities. Thereafter, it reviews the state-of-the-art of Big Data, and general background of the related technologies of Big Data. This chapter also examines the representative applications of Big Data including IoT, Smart Cities, Cloud Computing, and collective intelligence for presenting the big-picture to readers of this area. This chapter not only explores advantages of Big Data in relation to Cloud Computing and IoT, but also discusses various security and privacy challenges faced by the evolution of Big Data. This chapter also looks into the possibilities of Big Data forensics using secure data provenance mechanisms. How the issues like security and privacy of Big Data is affecting the use of widespread adoption of Big Data is also discussed. By delving into the on-going research approaches in securing and providing privacy to Big Data, this chapter concludes by highlighting the open research issues of Big Data and Smart City.

Figure 1. Impact of big data and IoT in rise of smart cities ecosystem

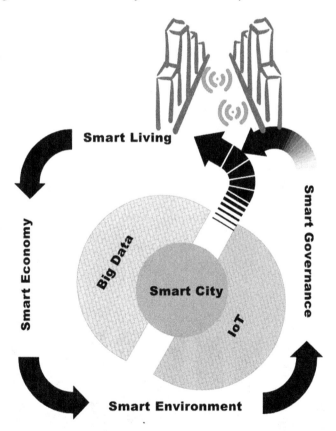

EVOLUTION, STATISTICS, AND MOTIVATION

This section summarizes evolutionary aspects of Smart Cities and Big Data and discusses their various aspects with the help of statistics along with motivation to work in the domain.

Historical Background

Although the synergic inter-connections between Smart Cities and Big Data are recognized by the recent developments made by IoT, their origin started in late 1990s after demands of smart growth. Since after its first appearance, the concept of Smart Cities springs its remarkable effects into various dimensions of our day-to-day lives (Zanella, Bui, Castellani, & Vangelista, 2014). The objectives of Smart Cities include Smart Mobility, Smart Environment, Smart Infrastructure, and Smart Utilities to their citizens. From an early understanding where the concept of Smart City gives emphasis only on Information and Communication Technology (ICT), now it also realizes the needs for connected physical infrastructure which assures better utilization of resources. Emerging technologies like Big Data and IoT make Smart Cities a responsive and effective inhabitant (Lazaroiua & Rosciab, 2012). Therefore, by reviewing the past events, it is more complacent for understanding their current state of importance. Table 1 summarizes the major events associated with the evolution of Smart Cities along with Big Data and IoT technologies.

Statistical Assessment

Most organizations and professionals believe that for making a plan more successful, data analytics plays a role of new frontier. Hence, during urban planning which is considered as the fundamental unit of Smart Cities, analysis of Big Data provides deeper insights. Big Data analysis can be done based on various requirements and levels. According to Intel research report in which they collected a broad range of data from top organizations for analyzing different types of data, they found that documents are still considered as the topmost data analytics source. Figure 2 summarizes the percentage of different kinds of sources that have been asked for analysis (Big Data Analytics, 2012).

Figure 2. Various sources for data analysis in organizations

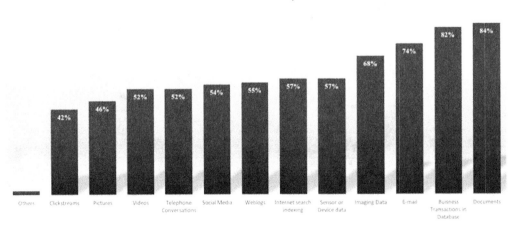

Table 1. Unfolding progress in the field of smart cities and the concept of Big Data

Year	Events
1949	Claude Shannon did research on punch cards and photographic data storage capacity and largest item stored was Library of Congress sized 100 trillion bits in Claude Shannon's list of items.
1980	Formulation of Parkinson's Law of Data
1986	1st Municipal open data provided by Greater London Council, Intelligent and Research Services.
1989	Business intelligence appears after an acceleration in Enterprise Resource Planning (ERP) systems.
1992	Agenda of "Smart Growth" discussed in United Nations (UN) Conference on Environment and Development, Rio.
1994	First digital city practice started in Amsterdam.
1997	Two NASA researchers David Ellsworth and Michael Cox used the term "Big Data" for the first time in their research paper.
1997	Concept of Smart communities" introduced in Global Forum World Foundation for Smart Communities and first literature evidence of virtual Smart Cities had recorded.
1999	First actual practice of Smart City started in Dubai.
1999	An approximate quantified report of data presented by Hal R. Varian and Peter Lyman and it tells that 1.5 Exabyte's of Information exists in the world. At the same time the term "IoT" was termed by Kevin Ashton.
2005	For processing large amount of unstructured datasets, Mike Cafarella and Doug Cutting introduced an open source solution namely "Hadoop".
2005	First literature evidence for eco city and also first ubiquitous city practice started in Dongtan, Hwaseong, South Korea.
2007	First European Smart City group is announced.
2008	CPU's around the world processed almost 9.57 trillion gigabytes of data, in which Google alone processed 20 petabytes of data on a single day.
2009	A report given by McKinsey estimates that, US company with an average of 1000 employees stores more than 200 TB of information and also UN Habitat Agenda Urban Indicators are declared.
2011	In few seconds, 4TB of data is analyzed by IBM's supercomputer Watson and first U.S Smart City group is introduced.
2013	Several Smart City standards are introduced and Dell EMC studies finds out that only 22% of the actual collected data contains semantic value.
2014	Gartner finds out that almost 4.9 billion connected things present in our surroundings.
2015	IEEE declares its first Smart City group and also every day in the world approximately 2.5 quintillion bytes of data is produced, of which google processes 3.5 billion requests every day.

It can be clearly seen from the Figure 2 that considerable amount of data has been asked for analysis. But in case of Smart Cities, these different kinds of data are collectively analyzed, since Smart City itself consists of various sources of data. Along with these heterogeneous types of data, various different sub-projects contribute their shares to Smart Cities. According to the Statista report 2017, various major sectors that represent the share in Smart Cities are shown in Figure 3 (IoT: smart cities projects share breakdown, 2017). Besides these sub-projects, comprehensive detail is given in Figure 4 which presents the number of installed IoT devices, particularly in Smart Cities within a time period from 2015 to 2018 (Smart cities total installed base of connected things 2015-2018, 2018).

Apart from general processing of information, enterprises use Big Data for security analytics. Security strategies adopted by enterprises are still not sufficient to prevent insider threats or hackers. There are various reasons that are responsible for these types of attacks including weak security infrastructure, malware, and many others. Hence, there are various companies who believe that re-designing the whole infrastructure is not an effective idea. Instead, if they implement preventive and defensive strategies based on the data analysis, then it would be a better option. Hence, to do this effectively, enterprises rely on various kinds of real-time and historical data for identifying various types of illegitimate behavior. Although this approach is not new, but the organizations still believe that this is an efficient way. Various kinds of data with their share that can be considered for security analysis are shown in Figure 5 (Balaganski & Sebastian, 2016).

Figure 3. Contribution of various sub-projects that collaboratively constitute smart cities

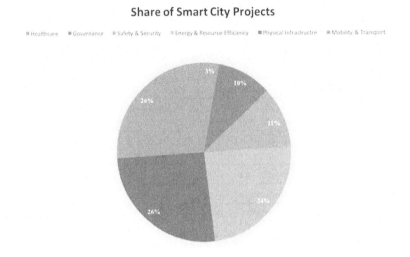

Figure 4. IoT devices installed within smart cities

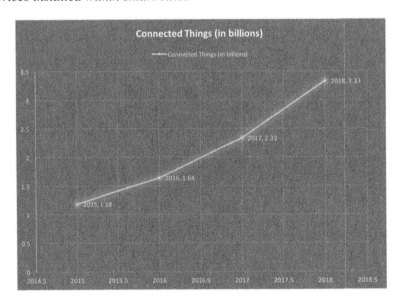

Figure 5. Various kinds of raw data used for security analysis

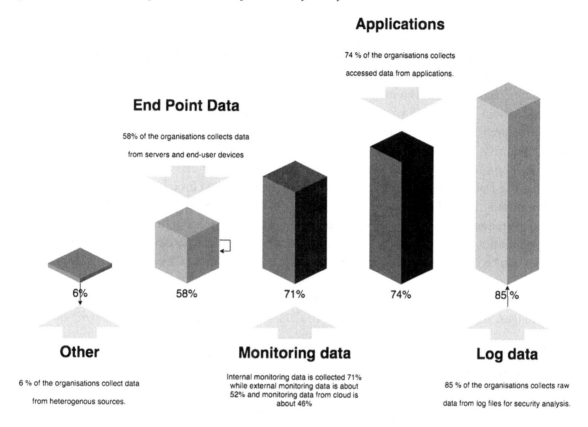

According to KuppingerCole report, 85% of the log data is used for security analysis despite the fact that the primary reason for keeping these files are auditing and compliance. Ponemon Institute conducted a survey on more than 750 organizations and found that various technologies are generally combined with Big Data analytics for detecting potential threats to their organizations and betterment of their security, as shown in Figure 6 (Big Data Analytics in Cyber Defense, 2013).

Figure 6. Various technologies integrated with big data analytics for security betterment

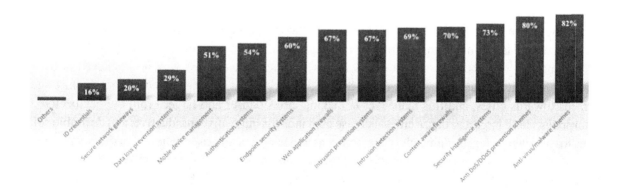

Motivation

As Smart Cities are equipped with various IoT and traditional digital devices, so due to the embellished nature of digital devices, Smart Cities produce enormous amount of data. For providing value added services, various applications take initiatives to integrate with IoT devices, such as street cameras, sensors, actuators, and so forth. The majority of these applications have the facility to provide real-time sensing and actions, resulting in voluminous data being produced. By considering this, a formal definition and structure for Smart Cities is required, so that a significant amount of development can be seen in the near future.

The structure of the Smart Cities requires all the capabilities for efficient urban planning. Despite the fact that Big Data analysis prescribes the best environment suited for taking decisive actions, it also faces various integration challenges with the Smart City. This is also a fact that huge portion of the Big Data contains redundant and noisy data that need to be converted into a fruitful state. Both Big Data and IoT capabilities help in the process of urban planning and Smart City development, so accordingly, smart cities can be grouped into various component areas. These Smart City components include smart governance, smart economy, smart healthcare, smart people, and so on. Thus, this chapter comes up with a detailed discussion of Big Data, its impact on Smart Cities, various Smart City components, and their challenges. After reading this chapter, the readers will be able to answer the following questions:

- How can Big Data and Smart City be conceptualized and defined?
- What is the roadmap for Big Data and Smart Cities development according to the historical documentation from literature?
- What are the significant impacts of collaboration Big Data analysis with Smart Cities?
- How can the process of Big Data and Smart City be classified?
- What is the meta-architecture for Smart Cities from Big Data point of view?
- What are the current concerns for Big Data and Smart Cities?

SMART CITIES AND BIG DATA: AN OVERVIEW

In this section, basic concepts of Smart Cities and Big Data are illustrated for providing more appropriate understanding of these concepts.

Concept of Smart Cities

The paradigm of Smart Cities has gained more popularity among international policies and scientific literature in the last two decades. Hence, to understand the concept of Smart Cities, there is a need to understand that why the concept of cities achieves so much concern and why it is believed to be the primary element for the future (Angelidou, 2015). 21st century witnesses a global trend of shifting of citizens towards cities, and this maneuver is making cities denser and large. From the perspective of enterprises, these large and dense cities increase demands for innovative, productive, and desirable solutions for overwhelming the demands of their citizens and hence, enterprises believe that they can increase their revenues by lavishing these cities with solutions (Letaifa, 2015). Along with the various advantages these cities bring, the expeditious increase of new citizens creates new challenges for the Governments in various aspects including traffic congestion, informal development, waste management, and crime. This scenario looks for a way to find out the best possible scenario to tackle these challenges. In this context, global cities start looking for the solutions that will provide high-quality services by making deep-rooted effects on the economy (Osman, 2019). The approach to smart urban planning based on astonishing technologies focuses towards the concept of Smart Cities. The concept of the term Smart City is not just limited to the applications related to cities. In fact, this concept proliferates itself in many areas, but with no settlement on unanimous definition. Although various definitions of the Smart Cities exist in the literature, with conceptual variants accomplished by replacing "smart" with "digital" or "intelligent". This suggests that Smart City is a fuzzy concept, as single framing of definition cannot fit all templates of its applications (Piro, Cianci, Grieco, Boggia, & Camarda, 2014). Despite the fact that the current ongoing discussion does not settle down on a single definition of Smart City, but Smart Cities can be generally defined as a conceptual development model which makes collective use of humans and technology for the expansion of collaborative urban development. Anthopoulos and Fitsilis discusses various other alternative definitions of Smart Cities based on their classes by doing an analysis over 34 Smart City projects (Winters, 2010). Although their classes are not exactly reflecting the representative definition of Smart City, but some of the useful classes and also new classes along with their representative cities are summarized in Table 2. As per Table 2, it can be seen that various representative cities come under different categories.

Table 2. Representative smart cities on the basis of different categories

Initiative Year	Categories	Representative Cities
2005	Ubiquitous City	Helsinki, Arabianranta, Finland
2005	Ubiquitous City	Dongtan, South Korea
2008	Ubiquitous City	Masdar, United Arab Emirates
2008	Ubiquitous City	Osaka, Japan
2008	Ubiquitous City	New Sondgo, South Korea
2010	Ubiquitous City	Manhattan Harbour, Kentucky, U.S.A.
1999	Smart City	Dubai, U.A.E
2000	Smart City	Barcelona, Spain
2004	Smart City	Taipei, Taiwan
2004	Smart City	Brisbane, Australia
2007	Smart City	Kochi, India
2007	Smart City	Tianjin, China
2007	Smart City	Malta
1995	Digital City	Austin, U.S.A.
1995	Digital City	Knowledge Based Cities, Portugal
2000	Digital City	Cape Town, South Africa
2000	Digital City	Hull, U.K
2003	Digital City	Trikala, Greece
2003	Digital City	Tampere, Finland

continues on following page

Table 2. Continued

Initiative Year	Categories	Representative Cities
1996	Virtual/Web City	Kyoto, Japan
1997		Bristol, U.S.A.
		Amsterdam, Netherlands
		America-On-Line (AOL) Cities
1994	Connected City	New York, U.S.A
		Geneva-MAN, Switzerland
1995		Helsinki, Finland
		Antwerp, Belgium
1997		Seoul, South Korea
1999		Beijing, China
2002		Kista Science City/Stockholm
2006		Florence, Italy

Architecture of Smart Cities

Smart Cities architecture contemplates various technological aspects and design principles including facilitating smart services, smart governance, smart infrastructure, smart environment, and smart living (Cardullo & Kitchin, 2018). This chapter proposes an architecture which defines the structure of the layers and relationship among them. The main significance of this proposed architecture is that it takes Big Data and IoT into account during its definition of layers. Along with this, the fundamental concept upon which this Smart City architecture design relies is that it apparently separates the layers according to their functionalities (Mohanty, Choppali, & Kougianos, 2016), (Pan, Qi, Zhang, Li, Wu, & Yang, 2013).

The purpose of designing a Smart City architecture is somewhat similar to various other architectures that it also provides end-users with refined and comprehensible structure of collection of different functionalities and components (Walravens & Ballon, 2013). Moreover, various other features that are provided by defining the architecture of the Smart City concept are as follows:

- A single "platform" is defined by the architecture.
- Various functional aspects are also described by the architecture.
- It also focuses on the description of the structure of the Smart City environment.
- It describes the inter and intra-relationships among various components of the prescribed layers.

Hence, in this regard, layers from left to right constitute the meta multi-layered architecture for the Smart Cities as shown in Figure 7.

- **IoT Devices Layer:** From the Smart Cities view, the main functionality of this layer is to collect information, object control, and perception. Since Smart Cities need a physical infrastructure which is able to provide smart and efficient services. Hence, for fulfilling these requirements, IoT devices are deployed all over the city according to the functionalities needed by the end-users. Various devices like Radio Frequency Identification (RFID), sensors, actuators, and many others are used in the IoT devices so as to provide connectivity along with smartness (Kohler & Specht, 2019).

- **Networking Layer:** Now after the successful deployment of the physical infrastructure, Smart Cities need ubiquitous networks which will be able to connect the end-user and service provider anytime and anywhere. It includes the core network, transport layer functionalities, and edge computing nodes. Core network is the basic network which provides access to the IoT devices according to the structure of the network. The reason of the integration of the edge nodes is that they are able to process the information locally and hence, decrease the latency in the network. They are also able to provide real-time processing in a much faster way and also reduce the load of the Cloud infrastructure. Moreover, the transport layer nodes are also integrated in this layer for resolving interoperability issues in the network (Muhammad, Lloret, & Baik, 2019). Heterogeneous protocol integration at this layer provides not only the reliability, but also provides energy efficient solutions to the IoT nodes.

- **Big Data Storage Layer:** Since the traditional database technologies are not reliable in case of Big Data storage, so in order for Smart Cities to incorporate the collected large scale data, Big Data storage mechanisms have to be promoted for the development of better and scalable infrastructure (Wang & Mao, 2019). Hence, according to the requirement of databases, file systems, and programming models, this layer provide the features.

Figure 7. Multilayer meta-architecture for the smart cities

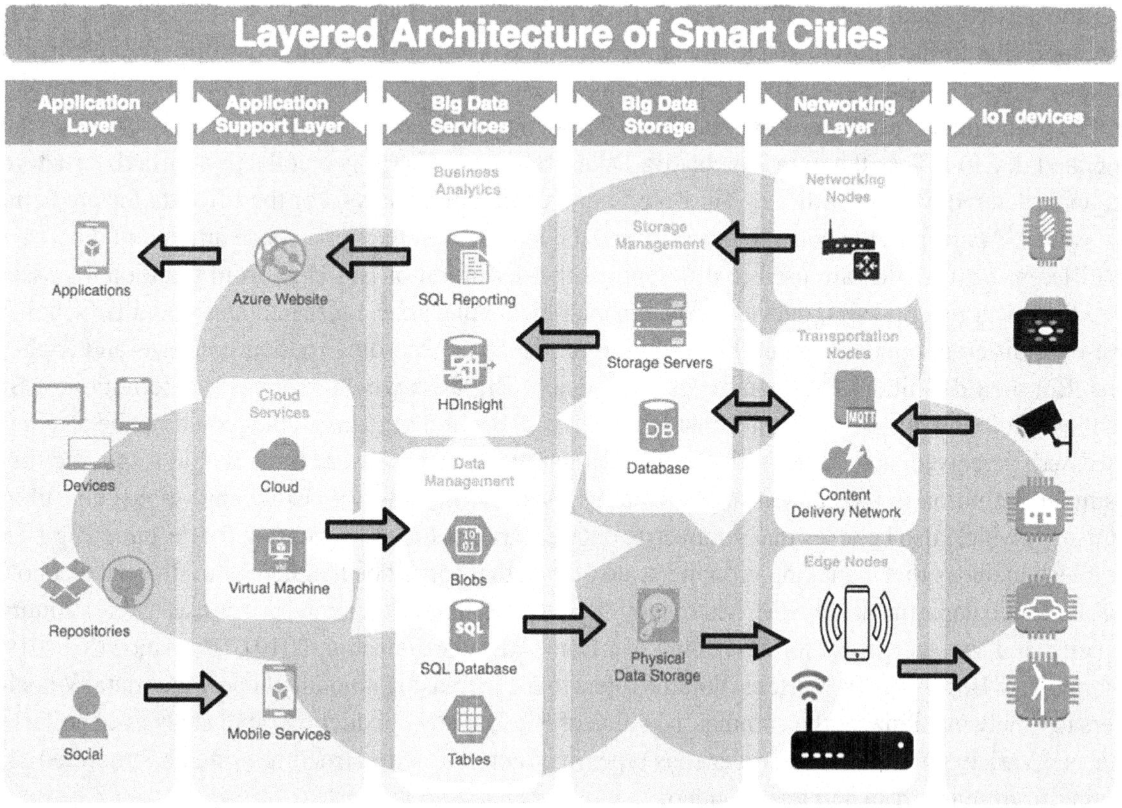

- **Big Data Services Layer:** After successful storage of Big Data, now comes the challenge of managing and analysis of Big Data. Hence, this layer supports the analysis and management of the Big Data (Yu, Yang, & Sinnott, 2018). The data collected from the IoT devices are managed by this layer.

- **Application Support Layer:** This is an advanced layer which collectively provides Big Data storage, management, and analysis in a cost efficient way. Basically, the need of this layer is that some enterprises build their own local Big Data infrastructure for storage and analysis purpose. But now-a-days, various organizations are shifting their data to the Cloud (Doku & Rawat, 2019). Hence, this layer supports the functionalities of Cloud Computing and various mechanisms are also included in this layer. So when Smart Cities based on the Cloud Computing are designed, this single layer has the capability to incorporate the functionalities of the immediate two right layers (Ejaz & Anpalagan, 2018). It concludes that this layer has the functionality which eliminates the need of Big Data storage and service layers as this layer support the features of the both.

- **Application Layer:** The application layer comes at the end of the Smart City architecture, but supports the most important functionalities in the meta-architecture (Solanki, Makkar, Kumar, & Chatterjee, 2018). During the whole process, this layer presents the analyzed data, directly interacts with the end-users, decides resource allocation, and selects the processed data. This layer gives the capability to the end-user to not only interact with the connected devices, but to understand the characteristics of the connected devices (Din, Paul, Hong, & Seo, 2019).

Concept of Big Data

Over the past 10 years, size of data has risen in an unprecedented way, and various technological areas are responsible for it. Amid different domains, IoT is the primary area, and according to an estimation given by Cisco, IoT is responsible for generating nearly 500 Zettabytes of data every year (Shridhar, 2019), (Luo, Huang, Kanhere, Zhang, & Das, 2019). The concept of Big Data is best suited for data generated due to IoT, as the core idea of Big Data itself states that it is a collection of both structured and un-structured data. In addition, Big Data improves in-depth analysis of the IoT data for predicting new values. Apart from the general idea of Big Data which states that it is a huge amount of data, there are different features that are used to differentiate the definition of Big Data from traditional massive data. Technical practitioners, data analysts, technological enterprises, research and scientific scholars, have their different opinions about the definition of Big Data according to their concerns and applications. But their definitions focus on the general idea of Big Data which explores the definition of Big Data in a profound manner and states that Big Data is collection of datasets that could not be acquired, processed, perceived, and managed by traditional hardware and software tools within a specific time. A similar definition in the context of Big Data is given by McKinsey & Company (global consulting company), which also believes that volumetric datasets are not the only criterion for defining Big Data, but it also includes that managing growing scale of data that cannot be handled by traditional technologies. Research departments of IBM, Microsoft, Gartner, and many other enterprises use "3Vs" (Volume, Velocity, and Variety) model for describing Big Data (Berry & Johnston, 2019), (Romanowski, 2019), (Fahmideh & Beydoun, 2019). Here, Volume refers to the increasing amount of enormous data, Velocity refers to timely maximizing the commercial value of Big Data by conducting rapid analysis of collected data, and Variety refers to the heterogeneous types of structured, semi-structured, and un-structured data ranging from sensor data and text to videos.

Value Chain in Big Data

By considering Big Data as raw material, the process of Big Data is categorized into four phases: (1) data generation (2) data acquisition (3) data storage, and (4) data analytics, in which data acquisition and data generation can be seen as exploitation processes, whereas data analysis can be considered as a production process, and data storage as a storage process, as shown in Figure 8.

Data Generation

In the process of Big Data, first step is generation of the data. Taking the example of IoT data, enormous amount of data is generated from the sensors, actuators, IoT smart devices, applications, and communication (Du, Wang, Xia, & Zhang, 2018). A close substantial connection between this generated data and people's daily lives has been found which includes low density and high value features of this data. Moreover, this generated data appends more characteristics when it comes from IoT based Smart Cities, as the data consists of medical care, industry, public departments, smart communities, agriculture, and transport. Due to heterogeneity of IoT devices, generated data possess various distinctive characteristics that are discussed below:

- **Correlation Between Space and Time:** In a broader manner, IoT devices that are responsible for acquisition of data are placed at distinct geographic locations. Since every packet of data has its own timestamp, that is why, space and time correlation are inter-related and important dimensions for statistical analysis of data.
- **Heterogeneity and Large Scale:** IoT acquisition devices collect heterogeneous forms of data from distributed sources and due to this, sometimes there is a need of large scale of data to be acquired for different kinds of analysis. Moreover, sometimes historical data has to be recalled for analysis in real-time. Hence, this historical data has to be stored in a certain amount of time, and due to this, real-time and historical data collectively needs huge amount of data storage.
- **Effective Data:** During the process of data generation and collection, various kinds of noises get intermixed with IoT data. This suggests that only a small portion of the original collected data is significant and rest of the data falls under the category of invaluable data. For instance, during the process of video capturing of traffic, only a few data are useful during its whole lifetime and the rest of the collected data is not useful at all.

Data Acquisition

After successful generation of Big Data, it needs to be collected, transmitted, and pre-processed in an efficient manner, and all these come under the data acquisition phase (Pang, Yang, Khedri, & Zhang, 2018). This phase of data acquisition consists of various processes for efficient transmission and storage. These processes have their own significance and are discussed below:

- **Data Collection:** The generated data needs to be collected in an appropriate manner, and this collection of data needs specific tools and techniques. One such way of collecting data is in the form of log files, that are record files and are automatically generated by the source digital device. These different file format recorded activities are used for subsequent analysis (Lohachab & Bidhan,

2018). Most popular use of log files is for stock indication and network monitoring. Sensory data (temperature, voice, automobile, weather, chemical, current, pressure, vibration) are collected at data collection point from the deployed IoT sensors by sending requests through wired or wireless medium to the base station. The IoT network data is collected using specific technology including zero-copy packet capture technology and Libpcap-based packet capture technology. IoT application data based on web pages is accomplished by the combination of index, task, and word segmentation system.

- **Data Transportation:** For processing and analysis of collected raw data, it should be transferred to storage infrastructure (Mohammadi, Fuqaha, Sorour, & Guizani, 2018). In case of Big Data, generally the infrastructure used for data storage are data centers. Hence, there is need for adjustment of data layout for facilitating hardware maintenance and improving computing efficiency. Data centers also facilitate internal transmission of data in two phases: Intra-DCN transmissions, and Inter-DCN transmissions. In the Intra-DCN transmissions, flow of data communication happens within the data centers. Communication mechanism (protocols, network architectures of data centers, internal memories, physical connection chips) are responsible for Intra-DCN transmissions. A typical data center contains various integrated server racks inter-connected by their internal networks (i.e., three-layer or two-layer structures, fat-tree). While on the other hand, inter-DCN transmissions utilize the physical network infrastructure for communicating data between data source and data center. The existing cost-effective, high rate, and volume optic fiber systems are able to fulfil the demands of rapidly increasing network traffic.

- Data pre-processing: During the process of data collection and transportation under some circumstances, data becomes redundant and noisy. For improving data quality and better data analysis, this meaningless data should be converted to useful data (Li, He, & Li, 2019). Pre-processing of data not only reduces expenses of storage, but also enhances analytical accuracy of analysis methods. Data cleaning, integration and redundancy elimination are some of the common methods of data pre-processing. In the current state of art, process of data integration acts as a keystone in commercial informatics. It provides consistent view of data to the end-users irrespective of the heterogeneity of data.

Data Storage

After the successful exploitation of data, now comes the challenge of how to store this enormous amount of data. In this storage phase, we focus on the storage of explosive amount of data. The concept of Big Data storage refers to the stricter requirements on management and storage of large-scale data by accomplishing the goals of reliability and availability. Unlike the traditional equipment of data storage where servers used structured Relational Database Management Systems (RDBMs) to store, lookup, manage, and analyze the stored data, various distinctive technologies are used for massive data storage management. These technologies can be categorized as Network storage, and Direct Attached Storage (DAS) (Aazam, Huh, & Hilaire, 2016). In the DAS storage peripheral equipment, generally hard disks and servers are directly connected for providing server-centric approach. This server-centric approach of managing data is good enough to inter-connect servers only at a mini scale where peripheral devices utilize definite number of input/output resources and are managed by distinctive application software. In general scenario of Smart Cities, DAS is insufficient to provide desirable results due to its limited scalability, expandability, and upgradeability. Storage Area Network (SAN) and Network Attached Stor-

Figure 8. Various processes involved in big data leading towards building smart cities

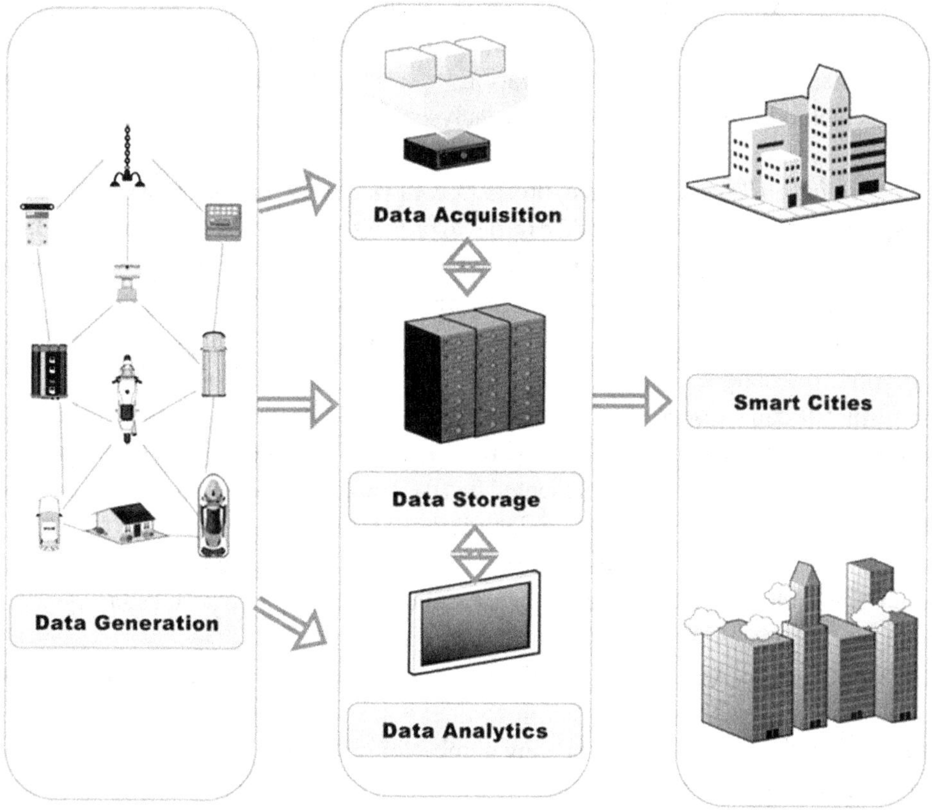

age (NAS) can be categorized under network storage. The basic concept behind network storage is that it utilizes network for providing storage to the end-users and it also provides consolidated interface for data sharing and access. NAS can be considered as an auxiliary storage device which is connected with network through switch or hub by using TCP/IP protocols. Although NAS is network-oriented service, but for providing specific services like scalability and bandwidth, SAN would be a preferable option for intensive networks. Basically, SAN provides independent data storage management by utilizing multipath based data switching among local area network (Mihovska & Sarkar, 2017).

Data Analysis

Most important and final phase in the process of Big Data is the analysis of Big Data which mainly involves providing analytical structure, methods, and software for Big Data. By the intention of extracting valuable records, contributing decisions, and suggestions, Big Data generates heterogeneous potential values of datasets. Data analysis creates a colossal impact on the development of various plans for Smart Cities as it helps to understand end-user's demands (Ferraro, King, & Shorten, 2018). Although there are various traditional data analysis methods that are rigorous in nature when dealing with Smart City data analysis, but Big Data analysis methods provide methods for Smart City data analysis that are much more helpful and precise. In the traditional data analysis methods, statistical methods are used for analyzing bulky data and to extract valuable data from hidden datasets. Cluster, correlation, factor, and regression analysis are some of the ways that are used in the traditional data analysis. Bucket testing and data mining algorithms are used as data extracting techniques in the traditional data analysis. Big Data analysis not only requires statistical analysis, but also various additional features that are provided by specific Big Data analysis methods. Some of the Big Data analysis/ processing methods are discussed as follows:

1. **Trie:** It is also called Triel, digital tree, prefix tree, or radix tree, and is mainly used for calculating word frequency statistics, and also makes retrieval process expeditious which makes it more suitable for Big Data. The basic concept of Trie is that it is considered as a kind of search tree which uses ordered data structure for storing·associative array or dynamic sets where strings are usually used as the keys for reducing comparison between strings and improving query efficiency (Ghasemi, Yousefi, Shin, & Zhang, 2019).

2. **Bloom Filter:** It can be seen as an alternative to various hashing techniques that use standard hash tables. These tables resolve collision by using open addressing. However, in bloom filter, arbitrary number of elements are represented by fixed size. The main principle behind bloom filter is that it uses series of hash functions and stores hash values by using a bit array (Luo, Guo, Ma, Rottenstreich, & Luo, 2018). Despite the fact that it has several disadvantages, (i.e., deletion and misrecognition) it has several features that are suitable for Big Data such as fast query processing and highly space efficient.

3. **Parallel Computing:** As compared to the traditional computing where complete resources are given for computing one task at a time, in parallel computing paradigm, simultaneous utilization of resources takes place for completing any number of given computing tasks. Basically, there are various mechanisms that are used in the parallel computing, but the fundamental concept remains the same (i.e., allocate distinctive processes to different tasks for their completion) (Gong, Wang, Zhang, & Fu, 2019). Hence, for accomplishing co-processing, some of the various classical models are discussed in Table 3 along with their comparison.

Table 3. Feature comparison of DRYAD, MPI, and MapReduce

Models → Features ↓	DRYAD	Message Passing Interface (MPI)	MapReduce
Deployment	In the same node Computing and data storage is arranged	Storage of data is separate from computing node	In the same node Computing and data storage is arranged
Programming	DryadLINQ, Dryad API, Scope	MPI API	MapReduce API, Pig, Hive, Jaql
Data Storage	NTFS, Cosmos DFS	NFS, Local file system	GFS (google), HDFS(Hadoop), KFS, Amazon S3
Task Partitioning	Automation	User manually partition the tasks	Automation
Communication	FIFOs, Shared-memory, TCP Pipes, Files	Remote memory access, Messaging	Files(Local FS, DFS)
Fault-Tolerant	Task re-execute	Checkpoint	Task re-execute

Big Data Open Source Tools

To accomplish the competitive nature of Big Data market, selecting the tools for data analysis and processing by considering the effectiveness and cost is always a primary concern. Along with these factors, multiple other aspects are also considered. For instance, what kind of analysis is required, quantity of data sets, quality of data, and so forth. Although there are various categories of tools that are available in the market for fulfilling the heterogeneous needs of organizations, this sub-section discusses the open source tools that have a possible future for adoption in the market. These are given are as follows:

- **Apache Hadoop:** Hadoop has created pronounce effect in the Big Data market with its colossal capability of processing large scale datasets efficiently. It is an open source tool which can run on an existing hardware or even on Cloud infrastructure.
- **Apache Spark:** This is also an open source tool which has created its image in the industry by fulfilling the concerns of Hadoop. It processes the data in a much faster manner, and is able to handle both real-time and batch data. It also provides flexibility to run on a single local system while working with various kinds of data formats.
- **Apache Storm:** For processing the data stream using the real-time distributed framework, Storm is useful. This tool supports various kinds of programming languages. It can also work with Hadoop's HDFS which makes it more useful in case of interoperability.
- **Apache Cassandra:** It provides distributed database which does not follow master-slave architecture. With no single point of failure, it is considered as the best open source tool for dealing with structured datasets.
- **MongoDB:** It is an open source tool which has built-in feature of interoperability among various platforms and hence, is ideal for providing real-time data processing with data-driven experiences.
- **RapidMiner:** It is an open source tool written in Java programming language and follows a client/server model for providing advanced analytical solutions.

STATE-OF-THE-ART OF BIG DATA FOR PLANNING IN SMART CITIES

After a detailed discussion about various aspects of Smart Cities and Big Data, this section will review the specific role of Big Data in Smart Cities. The main application of Big Data in Smart Cities is to improve the QoS in almost all characteristics related to Smart Cities. Different characteristics of Smart Cities along with their impact in urban living are summarized in Table 4.

Effective functioning of a Smart City requires persuasive communication, integration, coordination, and coupling among infrastructure and the services. Therefore, this needs new methods of database technology, new integration software, and many other things, so that Smart Cities are able to effectively balance equality by improving citizen's standards. There is quest going on for mastering the complexity of Big Data process for Smart Cities, and this quest suggests that there is a need for building a comprehensive system for data mining, acquisition, and querying (Mohammadi & Fuqaha, 2018). The process of Big Data analytics plays a major role in creating productive services for the Smart Cities, so it will have to support the following features:

Table 4. Taxonomy of smart city component features and affected sectors

Functionalities	Affected Sectors	Features Exploited
Smart Living	Quality and Security	Ease in cultural facilities
		Ease in Health monitoring
		Personal safety
		Increase in housing quality
		Social cohesion
		Education facilities and tourist attraction
Smart Environment	Sustainability and Efficiency	Better prediction of natural environment
		Better management of pollution
		Better management of natural resources
		Enhance protection of environment
		Flexibility in internal factors
		Smart disaster detection
Smart Mobility	Infrastructure and Mobility	Smart accessibility
		Innovation traffic system
		Safe international accessibility
		Safety in transportation
		Flexibility in travelling
		Sustainable mobility solutions
Smart Governance	Planning and Decision Making	Ease of public participation
		Transparency in governance
		Better political perspectives
		Flexibility in social services
		Ease in public services
		Electronic government
Smart People	Education standards	Increase in education qualifications
		Increase creativity
		Open minded people
		Increase in public engagement
		Flexibility in decisions
		Increase in learning
Smart Economy	Industry and Consumers	Entrepreneurship
		Increase in productivity
		Flexibility in markets
		Better lifestyle of labors
		Ability to transform
		International trademarks

- Dealing with Big Data by using distributed and incremental mining strategies for improving scalability.
- For exploring the behavior of models and patterns, resulting analytics have to be shown through visualization.
- Management and integration of heterogeneous data streams will be done into an intelligible database.
- Supports data transformation, and new definitions for observing relevant information.
- Management of distributed network analytics for seamless analysis of extracted patterns.
- Evaluation tools will have the quality of extracting patterns and models.

According to space and time complexity, there are various ways in which Big Data is analyzed in Smart Cities. So by considering this, two main categories for Big Data analysis are discussed as follows:

1. **Offline and Real-time Analysis (on the Basis of Timeliness Requirements):** From the security point of view, offline analysis is recommended as in this, by utilization of precise machine learning and recommendation algorithms, statistical analysis is performed. Through data acquisition, logs can be imported for conducting offline analysis based on which security measures can be taken into account (Lv, Song, Val, Steed, & Jo, 2017). In the context of social connections and online marketing, various Hadoop based Big Data analysis tools (like Scribe from Facebook, Kafka from LinkedIn, Timetunnel from Taobao) are used for better analysis of various connected nodes in order to increase efficiency of their products. Although these offline mechanisms meet the demand of data analysis with hundreds of MB per second, still these analysis methods are not well suitable for applications with requirements of fast response time. Along with offline data analysis, online data analysis also plays a crucial role in Smart Cities. The main feature of online analysis is that it does real-time analysis within a very short amount of time. HANA from SAP and Greenplum from EMC are two popular real-time analysis platforms that are capable for doing rapid data analysis (Faerber, Dees, Weidner, Baeuerle, & Lehner, 2015). In Smart Cities, since smart economy is seen as the major component, so by doing real data time analysis, better understanding of the finance data can be provided.

2. **Memory-Level, Massive, and Business Intelligent Analysis (on the Basis of Different Levels):** The memory-level analysis is best suited for the cases where volume of total memory of a cluster is larger than the total acquired data. It can be seen as an internal database analysis technique, as it believes that the crucial data still resides in the memory. With the recent developments in the Solid-State Drive technology, this memory-level architecture is best suited for real-time analysis and its representative architecture is MongoDB (Colombo & Ferrari, 2015). Massive analysis is used in the case where the capacity of data totally surpasses the existing relational database technology. According to the processing time of this analysis, it comes under the category of offline analysis (e.g., Map Reduce). Business intelligence analysis is used in the middle of both these cases, where data is not much bulky, but enough for analysis for making strategic decisions. This kind of analysis comes under the category of both offline and online analysis as in some cases, collected data demands immediate decisions (e.g., in finance sector) and sometimes data can be analyzed in an offline mode where data has to be analyzed deeply (online marketing) (Peng, Wang, & Xie, 2016).

Moreover, beyond this general categorization of Big Data analysis, there are various kinds of data that need to analyzed in a Smart City scenario for fulfilling the requirements of Smart City components. Hence, the various types of data fields that need to be analyzed are discussed below:

- **Personal Digital Assistant (PDA) Data Analysis**: With the massive growth of PDAs among users, now they are being used for building social communities, controlling devices, geographical coordination, and many other things. There are abundant number of applications that are specifically designed for every purpose, resulting of which generates PetaBytes (PB) amount of raw data. Considering as whole raw data of PDAs, analysis of data should be done for removing redundancy and noise. Mobile phones and smart watches are popular among other PDAs, since they support rich interactions among individuals or communities anywhere and anytime (Sarikaya, 2017). In fact, recent progress of IoT devices, specifically wireless sensors, enable end-users to create Body Area Network (BAN) for real-time monitoring of their health. Hence, analysis of medical data in context to smart health component of Smart Cities helps organizations to understand the physiological relations, time, and other health related features (He, Zeadally, Kumar, & Lee, 2016).

- **Smart City Network Data Analysis:** It involves quantitative analysis, sensors data analysis, and sociological network data analysis. Many Smart City network services include IoT devices, social networking, and enterprises network data. For detecting the behavior of network topology, peer nodes, and illegitimate behavior of network, concept of capturing the network data can be utilized. Recommendation, marketing, advertisement, security, and many other features are provided by the qualitative and quantitative analysis of network data (Jin, Wah, Cheng, & Wanga, 2015) .

- **Multimedia Data Analysis:** In the context of smart people component in Smart Cities, multimedia data analysis plays an important role for deciding the quality and content of data that is to be presented. Generally, it includes images, video, and audio from which richer information needs to extracted. But the process of analysis and extraction of data is not that simple, since it contains heterogeneous data with semantic differences (Zhu, Cui, Wang, & Hua, 2015). Hence, by considering this scenario in multimedia analysis, there are different sub-processes including multimedia annotation, multimedia summarization, multimedia suggestion, multimedia retrieval and indexing, and multimedia event detection. Extraction of embossed phrases and words is done during the process of audio data analysis for processing useful information. Both static and dynamic analysis can be performed during the video data analysis for finding the most adumbrative video sequence. In the multimedia annotation, labels are inserted for describing the contents of both video and audio at both semantic and syntax level. For conveniently providing assistance and description regarding information to the end users, multimedia indexing use five procedures. Now, the multimedia analysis after performing all sub-procedures looks forward for fulfilling its primary goal which is to recommend a specific content to the users according to their interests (Tous, Torres, & Ayguadé, 2015). The main benefit of this process is that citizens in the Smart Cities are able to personalize their services in an effective way. Collaborative-filtering based system and content based systems are the two existing systems that are popular among video data analysis.

- **Web Data Analysis:** For discovering fruitful knowledge from web documents, web data analysis can be seen as an effective field. Web usage mining, web content mining, and web structure mining are the persuasive fields of web data analysis. During the productive interaction with the web, the generated data including device and user registration data, proxy servers, queries, sessions, access logs, and other kinds of data are mined during the process of web usage mining (Mongeon

& Hus, 2015). Web content mining includes the database and information retrieval methods in which structured and unstructured data is mined and then knowledgeable data is extracted. For finding the various correlations and similarities between services, web structure mining is used. For instance, in case of websites, CLEVER and PageRank are used for finding relevant description and information regarding web pages (Riedy, 2016).

- **Structured and Text Data Analysis:** Although the structure and text data analysis is not very useful in the context to IoT devices, but regarding the Smart Cities, it plays an important role, specifically in the smart economy as it analyzes various text data documents along with structured data for making competitive economy (Chen, Hao, Hwang, Wang, & Wang, 2017). Powerful statistical mathematical algorithms are used for exploiting data flows, time, and space to make better interpretations. Natural Language Processing (NLP) is the powerful process when it comes to analyze text, and its method includes probabilistic context free grammar, lexical acquisition, part-of-speech tagging, and word sense disambiguation. For energy control and anomaly detection, structured data analysis provides knowledge structures driven by process mining.

Big Data Application in Smart Cities

Smart city services can be enhanced by processing information from data storage. Big Data applications are efficiently managing the Smart City data by helping decision makers during development of Smart City resources and services. For effective and efficient analysis of Smart City data, Big Data needs advance methods and tools to achieve its goals. Some of the involved tools and methods in the Big Data mechanism have been discussed in the above sections. Now, based on the methods and tools, various applications of Big Data in Smart Cities are discussed in this section. Table 5 summarizes various applications of Big Data in the Smart City scenarios that are discussed as follows –

- **Smart Economy:** Traditional economy refers to the way in which goods are produced and consumed in order to increase wealth and resources. In addition to all this, smart economy includes new way for increasing entrepreneurship, trademarks, innovations, productivity, and international markets. Hence, for increasing new and existing talents to come up with new solutions, there is need of the existing and real-time data analysis (Boes, Buhalis, & Inversini, 2014). Dealing with the labor and managing funds also need efficient and effective Big Data analysis methods.

- **Smart Grids:** For optimized consumption, supply, and generation of electric energy, the concept of smart grids integrate the traditional energy networks with next generation grids that are enabled with remote automation, communication, and computation. Big Data in smart grids is generated from various resources, such as (i) maintenance, management, and control data of power generation equipment's and devices, (ii) Financial data of energy market, (iii) energy consumption data collected by smart meters, and (iv) end-user's habits of power utilization. Hence, in this regard, Big Data analysis is used for efficient management of electricity to fulfill the supply demands of the end-users. Furthermore, collected Big Data from smart grids help decision makers for making specific objectives while deciding the pricing plans (Deng, Yang, Chow, & Chen, 2015).

- **Smart Healthcare:** Rapidly growing complex medical and healthcare data is potentially handled by the Big Data methods. In fact, the growth in the business of healthcare is profoundly influenced by the applications of healthcare Big Data. Big Data related to the healthcare sector facilitates the decisions behind the changes in the delivery system of medical services. Smart gadgets, homes, and vehicles constitute for providing the best medical facilities in order to cure diseases and predicting epidemics. By analyzing the patient's data along with preventable measures, it helps to understand the patient's behavior during their health issues. The primary purpose of the healthcare Big Data is to save lives as many as possible by detecting, curing, and taking preventive measures for the serious diseases (Hossain, 2016).

- **Smart Governance:** Every city has its own needs for managing its internal and external policies in order to fulfill the goals. Smart Cities need specific governance policies that are dynamic in nature. Hence, for making dynamic policies and finding the common goals of their citizens, Big Data analytics has the potential to lead forward for enabling smart governance (Lin, Zhang, & Geertman, 2015). Big Data analytics implements satisfactory development with collaboration between governing policies. Since Governments are already aware of the needs of their citizens in terms of employment, medical, education, and so forth, Big Data helps them in increasing the success ratio.

Table 5. Various Big Data applications in smart cities

Applications	Utilization	Involved IoT Devices	Possible Communication Technologies	Advantages	Limitations
Smart Economy	Digitalization of financial services	Smart phones, RFID cards, Sensors, Actuators	Wi-Fi, Bluetooth, ZigBee, MQTT, CoAP, and many others	Easy monitoring of financial activities, reduction in paper work	Security threats, dis-connectivity
Smart Grid	Manage power supply	Smart readers, Smart meters	Wi-Fi, Z-wave, ZigBee, 5G, MQTT, CoAP, and many others	Efficient power supply, Efficient manage of energy market	Currently costly, Security threats
Smart Healthcare	Flexible health monitoring	RFID cards, Cameras, smart wearable devices, sensors, smart vehicles	ZigBee, Bluetooth, 5G, CoAP, MQTT, and many others	Early diagnosis of diseases, easy monitoring, effective remote treatment	Lack of precision, Patients trust, Security Threats
Smart Governance	Smart, efficient and flexible policies	Cameras, Transportation, Smart phones, Sensors, Actuators	LoRaWAN, LTE-A, Bluetooth, WiMAX, Wi-Fi, LTE, and many others	Easy fulfillment of the needs of citizens	Heterogeneous data to be analyzed, security threats
Smart Transportation	Efficient traffic management	Smart vehicles, cameras, smart phones	5G, 4G, 3G, RFID and many others	Effective management of routes	Dis-connectivity, Security Threats
Information security	Protection against various advance threats and attacks	Various IoT sensors and actuators	Wi-Fi, Bluetooth, ZigBee, MQTT, CoAP, and many others	Effective actions for strengthening security	Big Data availability and integration

- **Smart Transportation:** In the traditional transportation system, governing parties are aware of the situations like traffic jam, but unable to take strict actions. The simple reason behind this is that they collect the raw data, but are unaware of what to do with the collected data. Big Data methods help transportation systems in the way that they predict patterns from the enormous amount of collected raw data. These patterns help to analyze the current situation for taking the decisive actions, such as suggesting alternative routes in order to minimize the traffic congestion. Moreover, various factors like finding the cause of any mishaps happened during movement of vehicles are recommended by Big Data analysis that certainly reduce number of accidents. Smart transportation also includes facilities like tracking of shipments. Hence, in order to reduce wastage of supply chain, Big Data improves the experience of end-users by suggesting more appropriate factors.

- **Information Security:** Along with various general purpose applications in Smart Cities, Big Data also brings efficient development in the information security mechanisms in Smart Cities. Big Data analysis helps to discover various potential security threats, and system loopholes. After analysis of the log files of the various connected devices, it develops specific intrusion detection systems. It can also easily identify various characteristics of attacks, loopholes, viruses, and characterizes them accordingly into various levels of security threats.

CONCERNS OF BIG DATA AND SMART CITIES

Despite the fact that age of Big Data made a significant impact on the concept of new value creation in Smart Cities, it has also opened various multi-dimensional challenges that can possibly require interdisciplinary perspectives to get addressed properly. Both Big Data and Smart Cities needs a comprehensive and holistic definition, structural model, and formal description of their integration. From commercial to academic research point of view, there is a need for scientific research than speculations (Lohachab, 2019). Big Data and Smart Cities confront various individual and combined challenges. However, ongoing research efforts done by organizations and researchers are also creating a significant impact in the domains. In the remainder of this section, current challenges of Big Data and ongoing research efforts are summarized.

- **Smart City Planning:** In the business model of Smart Cities, growing market of IoT and Big Data has gained attention for the future developments. In the planning of the Smart Cities, challenges are encountered in the form of building the combined control methodologies and master planning Big Data and IoT for the Smart Cities. To understand how Big Data can be used for designing the best model and guidelines for Smart Cities at minimal cost is still a challenge.
- **Sustainable Smart Cities:** How to establish communication and interaction with Big Data and IoT in a sustainable and resilient way with their full potential is still a challenge. Moreover, how to integrate the power of Big Data and IoT in Smart Cities for making them self-sustainable is still considered as a complex task. Scarcity of available resources in Smart Cities points towards lack of planning. Hence, to make a sustainable city by planning with the help of Big Data regarding IoT resources should be precise.
- **Smart City Costs and Sources:** Diversity in technologies can help the organizations for accelerating the process of services. However, on the other side, this diversity introduces challenges for consumers and markets. For instance, if a user utilizes various applications on daily basis, organizations face many difficulties in finding their interests. Another challenge for adoption of these heterogeneous technologies in a Smart City is that integration of different standards or components of these technologies will certainly increase the cost of infrastructure. Although there are

various open standards that are able to provide robust integration mechanisms through facilitating collaboration among different services, devices, products, and applications, these open standards have not been adopted in a comprehensive way.

- **Big Data Standardization:** For increasing computational efficiency of the collected data, there should be an improvement in the process of data analytics and evaluation. However, to increase these features, a unified benchmark for standardizing the process is required. To effectively evaluate the quality of data, process of screening and processing the data should be simplified. Another important characteristic of Big Data is that it is collected from diverse and heterogeneous data sources, which makes the conversion of data format more complex. Certainly if these data conversions can be more reliable and easier, the applications of Big Data can be increased in context of Smart Cities.

- **Performance of Big Data:** The performance of Big Data transfer involves Big Data storage, acquisition, and generation that arise new problems as compared to the traditional data analysis. High performance of Big Data has incurred higher costs, which coercion its use in a limited way. Moreover, real-time processing of Big Data requires vast amount of resources which limits its capabilities in resource-constrained environment (e.g., IoT environment). Hence, if effective utilization of the processes involved in Big Data is done during building real-time computation models in the Smart Cities, it will influence the overall development scenario.

- **Big Data Provenance:** The concept of data provenance is used from the data generation till its evolution in order to investigate the data. Since the value of an individual dataset is much lower than comprehensive Big Datasets, the process of data provenance faces more challenges in Big Data. Because the process of data provenance not only has to track the data generation and evolution, but the integration of various heterogeneous datasets is also to be tracked. However, the process of data provenance in Big Datasets helps in understanding the concept of Smart Cities more effectively as it gathers the integrated information from various datasets of different standards. Moreover, Big Data provenance suggests various security measures in accordance for taking decisive actions against various data security threats and attacks (Wang, Crawl, Purawat, Nguyen, & Altintas, 2015).

- **Big Data Privacy and Security:** The era of Big Data is confronted by two primary concerns which includes security and privacy of data. Although various traditional mechanisms are available for data protection, they are inefficient while dealing with Big Data security concerns. Privacy in Big Data may be breached in two aspects – first, privacy may be violated during acquisition of data, and second, violation of privacy may be done during storage, usage, and transmission of data. Big Data analysis provides seamless useful information. But at the same time, it opens challenges for its management. For instance, during the process of analysis, it mines sensitive information which if breached can lead to user's privacy at stake. In addition to the privacy challenges, Big Data also faces various security challenges. Mechanism of encryption in traditional dataset can be easily implemented. However, it faces challenges due to high diversity and large scale of Big Datasets. By looking into the performance of the traditional encryption methods on datasets, it can be seen that there is a need for developing effective Big Data encryption techniques. Goals of security including authentication, availability, and confidentiality should be implemented in unstructured datasets in an efficient manner (Lohachab & Karambir, 2019) .

CONCLUSION

In this chapter, in-depth analysis is done over the role of Big Data for efficient urban planning in Smart Cities. The chapter investigated the concepts of Big Data analysis including how it exploits the opportunities in Smart Cities, and also discussed the various possible applications of Smart Cities. The chapter also tried to find out the possible architecture of Smart Cities by integrating Big Data technology with it. The process of Big Data is also summarized along with the various components of the Smart Cities. Finally, the chapter is concluded by exploring the on-going research challenges faced by Smart Cities and Big Data.

REFERENCES

Bhushan, K., & Gupta, B. B. (2017). Network flow analysis for detection and mitigation of Fraudulent Resource Consumption (FRC) attacks in multimedia cloud computing. *Multimedia Tools and Applications, 78*(4), 4267–4298. doi:10.100711042-017-5522-z

Boes, K., Buhalis, D., & Inversini, A. (2014, December 27). Conceptualising Smart Tourism Destination Dimensions. *Information and Communication Technologies in Tourism,* 391-403.

Caragliu, A., Bo, D. C., & Nijkamp, P. (2011). Smart Cities in Europe. *Journal of Urban Technology, 18*(2), 65–82. doi:10.1080/10630732.2011.601117

Cárdenas, A. A., Manadhata, K. P., & Rajan, P. S. (2013). Big Data Analytics for Security. *IEEE Security and Privacy, 11*(6), 74–76. doi:10.1109/MSP.2013.138

Cardullo, P., & Kitchin, R. (2018). Being a 'citizen' in the Smart City: Up and down the scaffold of smart citizen participation in Dublin, Ireland. *GeoJournal, 84*(1), 1–13. doi:10.100710708-018-9845-8

Chen, M., Hao, Y., Hwang, K., Wang, L., & Wang, L. (2017). Disease Prediction by Machine Learning Over Big Data from Healthcare Communities. *IEEE Access: Practical Innovations, Open Solutions, 5,* 8869–8879. doi:10.1109/ACCESS.2017.2694446

Chen, M., Mao, S., & Liu, Y. (2014). Big Data: A Survey. *Mobile Networks and Applications, 19*(2), 171–209. doi:10.100711036-013-0489-0

Colombo, P., & Ferrari, E. (2015). Enhancing MongoDB with Purpose-Based Access Control. *IEEE Transactions on Dependable and Secure Computing, 14*(6), 591–604. doi:10.1109/TDSC.2015.2497680

Deng, R., Yang, Z., Chow, Y. M., & Chen, J. (2015). A Survey on Demand Response in Smart Grids: Mathematical Models and Approaches. *IEEE Transactions on Industrial Informatics, 11*(3), 570–582. doi:10.1109/TII.2015.2414719

Din, S., Paul, A., Hong, H. W., & Seo, H. (2019). Constrained application for mobility management using embedded devices in the Internet of Things based urban planning in Smart Cities. *Sustainable Cities and Society, 44,* 144–151. doi:10.1016/j.scs.2018.07.017

Doku, R., & Rawat, B. D. (2019). Big Data in Cybersecurity for Smart City Applications. *Smart Cities Cybersecurity and Privacy,* 103-112.

Du, M., Wang, K., Xia, Z., & Zhang, Y. (2018, April 24). Differential Privacy Preserving of Training Model in Wireless Big Data with Edge Computing. *IEEE Transactions on Big Data.*

Ejaz, W., & Anpalagan, A. (2018, October 13). Dimension Reduction for Big Data Analytics in Internet of Things. *Internet of Things for Smart Cities*, 31-37.

Faerber, F., Dees, J., Weidner, M., Baeuerle, S., & Lehner, W. (2015). Towards a web-scale data management ecosystem demonstrated by SAP HANA. In *2015 IEEE 31st International Conference on Data Engineering* (pp. 1259-1267). Seoul, South Korea: IEEE.

Fahmideh, M., & Beydoun, G. (2019). Big data analytics architecture design—An application in manufacturing systems. *Computers & Industrial Engineering*, *128*, 948–963. doi:10.1016/j.cie.2018.08.004

Ferraro, P., King, C., & Shorten, R. (2018). Distributed Ledger Technology for Smart Cities, the Sharing Economy, and Social Compliance. *IEEE Access: Practical Innovations, Open Solutions*, *6*, 62728–62746. doi:10.1109/ACCESS.2018.2876766

Ghasemi, C., Yousefi, H., Shin, G. K., & Zhang, B. (2019). On the Granularity of Trie-Based Data Structures for Name Lookups and Updates. *IEEE/ACM Transactions on Networking*, *27*(2), 777–789. doi:10.1109/TNET.2019.2901487

Gong, L., Wang, C., Zhang, C., & Fu, Y. (2019). High-Performance Computing Based Fully Parallel Security-Constrained Unit Commitment with Dispatchable Transmission Network. *IEEE Power & Energy Society*, *34*(2), 931–941.

Gupta, B. B., & Quamara, M. (2018). Multi-layered Cloud and Fog based Secure Integrated Transmission and Storage Framework for IoT based Applications. In *2018 5th International Conference on Signal Processing and Integrated Networks (SPIN)* (pp. 462-467). Noida, India: IEEE.

He, D., Zeadally, S., Kumar, N., & Lee, H. J. (2016). Anonymous Authentication for Wireless Body Area Networks with Provable Security. *IEEE Systems Journal*, *11*(4), 2590–2601. doi:10.1109/JSYST.2016.2544805

Hossain, S. M. (2016). Patient State Recognition System for Healthcare Using Speech and Facial Expressions. *Journal of Medical Systems*, *40*(12), 272. doi:10.100710916-016-0627-x PMID:27757715

IoT: Smart Cities projects share breakdown 2017, by type. (2017). Retrieved February 27, 2019, from The Statistics Portal: https://www.statista.com/statistics/784331/internet-of-things-smart-Cities-projects-by-type/

Jin, X., Wah, B. W., Cheng, X., & Wanga, Y. (2015). Significance and Challenges of Big Data Research. *Big Data Research*, *2*(2), 59–64. doi:10.1016/j.bdr.2015.01.006

Kohler, J., & Specht, T. (2019). Towards a Secure, Distributed, and Reliable Cloud-Based Reference Architecture for Big Data in Smart Cities. *Big Data Analytics for Smart and Connected Cities*, 38-70.

Labrinidis, A., & Jagadish, V. H. (2012). Challenges and opportunities with big data. *Proceedings of the VLDB Endowment International Conference on Very Large Data Bases*, *5*(12), 2032–2033. doi:10.14778/2367502.2367572

Lazaroiua, C. G., & Rosciab, M. (2012). Definition methodology for the Smart Cities model. *Energy, 47*(1), 326–332. doi:10.1016/j.energy.2012.09.028

Letaifa, B. S. (2015). How to strategize Smart Cities: Revealing the SMART model. *Journal of Business Research, 68*(7), 1414–1419. doi:10.1016/j.jbusres.2015.01.024

Li, S., He, H., & Li, J. (2019). Big data driven lithium-ion battery modeling method based on SDAE-ELM algorithm and data pre-processing technology. *Applied Energy, 242*, 1259–1273. doi:10.1016/j.apenergy.2019.03.154

Lin, Y., Zhang, X., & Geertman, S. (2015). Toward smart governance and social sustainability for Chinese migrant communities. *Journal of Cleaner Production, 107*, 389–399. doi:10.1016/j.jclepro.2014.12.074

Lohachab, A. (2019). A Perspective on Using Blockchain for Ensuring Security in Smart Card Systems. In B. B. Gupta & P. D. Agrawal (Eds.), *Handbook of Research on Cloud Computing and Big Data Applications in IoT* (pp. 418–447). IGI Global. doi:10.4018/978-1-5225-8407-0.ch019

Lohachab, A., & Karambir. (2019). ECC based inter-device authentication and authorization scheme using MQTT for IoT networks. *Journal of Information Security and Applications, 46.*

Lohachab, A., & Karambir. (2019). Next Generation Computing: Enabling Multilevel Centralized Access Control using UCON and CapBAC Model for securing IoT Networks. In *2018 International Conference on Communication, Computing and Internet of Things (IC3IoT)* (pp. 159-164). Chennai, India: IEEE.

Lohachab, A., & Bidhan, K. (2018). Critical Analysis of DDoS—An Emerging Security Threat over IoT Networks. *Journal of Communications and Information Networks, 3*(3), 57–78. doi:10.100741650-018-0022-5

Luo, L., Guo, D., Ma, B. T., Rottenstreich, O., & Luo, X. (2018, December 24). Optimizing Bloom Filter: Challenges, Solutions, and Comparisons. *IEEE Communications Surveys and Tutorials.*

Luo, T., Huang, J., Kanhere, S. S., Zhang, J., & Das, K. S. (2019, March 13). Improving IoT Data Quality in Mobile Crowd Sensing: A Cross Validation Approach. *IEEE Internet of Things Journal.*

Lv, Z., Song, H., Val, B. P., Steed, A., & Jo, M. (2017). Next-Generation Big Data Analytics: State of the Art, Challenges, and Future Research Topics. *IEEE Transactions on Industrial Informatics, 13*(4), 1891–1899. doi:10.1109/TII.2017.2650204

Mihovska, A., & Sarkar, M. (2017). Smart Connectivity for Internet of Things (IoT) Applications. *New Advances in the Internet of Things, 715*, 105–118.

Mohammadi, M., & Fuqaha, A. A. (2018). Enabling Cognitive Smart Cities Using Big Data and Machine Learning: Approaches and Challenges. *IEEE Communications Magazine, 56*(2), 94–101. doi:10.1109/MCOM.2018.1700298

Mohammadi, M., Fuqaha, A. A., Sorour, S., & Guizani, M. (2018). Deep Learning for IoT Big Data and Streaming Analytics: A Survey. *IEEE Communications Surveys and Tutorials, 20*(6), 2923–2960. doi:10.1109/COMST.2018.2844341

Mohanty, P. S., Choppali, U., & Kougianos, E. (2016). Everything you wanted to know about Smart Cities: The Internet of things is the backbone. *IEEE Consumer Electronics Magazine*, *5*(3), 60–70. doi:10.1109/MCE.2016.2556879

Mongeon, P., & Hus, P. A. (2015). The journal coverage of Web of Science and Scopus: A comparative analysis. *Scientometrics*, *106*(1), 213–228. doi:10.100711192-015-1765-5 PMID:25821280

Muhammad, K., Lloret, J., & Baik, W. S. (2019). Intelligent and Energy-Efficient Data Prioritization in Green Smart Cities: Current Challenges and Future Directions. *IEEE Communications Magazine*, *57*(2), 60–65. doi:10.1109/MCOM.2018.1800371

Osman, S. M. (2019). A novel big data analytics framework for Smart Cities. *Future Generation Computer Systems*, *91*, 620–633. doi:10.1016/j.future.2018.06.046

Pan, G., Qi, G., Zhang, W., Li, S., Wu, Z., & Yang, T. L. (2013). Trace analysis and mining for Smart Cities: Issues, methods, and applications. *IEEE Communications Magazine*, *51*(6), 120–126. doi:10.1109/MCOM.2013.6525604

Pang, Z., Yang, G., Khedri, R., & Zhang, T. Y. (2018). Introduction to the Special Section: Convergence of Automation Technology, Biomedical Engineering, and Health Informatics Toward the Healthcare 4.0. *IEEE Reviews in Biomedical Engineering*, *11*, 249–259. doi:10.1109/RBME.2018.2848518

Peng, S., Wang, G., & Xie, D. (2016). Social Influence Analysis in Social Networking Big Data: Opportunities and Challenges. *IEEE Network*, *31*(1), 11–17. doi:10.1109/MNET.2016.1500104NM

Piro, G., Cianci, I., Grieco, A., Boggia, G., & Camarda, P. (2014). Information centric services in Smart Cities. *Journal of Systems and Software*, *88*, 169–188. doi:10.1016/j.jss.2013.10.029

Riedy, J. (2016). Updating PageRank for Streaming Graphs. In *2016 IEEE International Parallel and Distributed Processing Symposium Workshops (IPDPSW)* (pp. 877-884). Chicago, IL: IEEE. 10.1109/IPDPSW.2016.22

Romanowski, A. (2019). Big Data-Driven Contextual Processing Methods for Electrical Capacitance Tomography. *IEEE Transactions on Industrial Informatics*, *15*(3), 1609–1618. doi:10.1109/TII.2018.2855200

Sarikaya, R. (2017). The Technology Behind Personal Digital Assistants: An overview of the system architecture and key components. *IEEE Signal Processing Magazine*, *34*(1), 67–81. doi:10.1109/MSP.2016.2617341

Shridhar, S. V. (2019). The India of Things: Tata Communications' countrywide IoT network aims to improve traffic, manufacturing, and health care. *IEEE Spectrum*, *56*(2), 42–47. doi:10.1109/MSPEC.2019.8635816

Smart Cities total installed base of connected things 2015-2018. (2018). Retrieved February 25, 2019, from The Statistics Portal: https://www.statista.com/statistics/422886/smart-Cities-connected-things-installed-base/

Solanki, K. V., Makkar, S., Kumar, R., & Chatterjee, M. J. (2018, December 31). Theoretical Analysis of Big Data for Smart Scenarios. *Internet of Things and Big Data Analytics for Smart Generation*, 1-12.

Tous, R., Torres, J., & Ayguadé, E. (2015). Multimedia Big Data Computing for In-Depth Event Analysis. In *2015 IEEE International Conference on Multimedia Big Data* (pp. 144-147). Beijing, China: IEEE. 10.1109/BigMM.2015.39

Walravens, N., & Ballon, P. (2013). Platform business models for Smart Cities: From control and value to governance and public value. *IEEE Communications Magazine, 51*(6), 72–79. doi:10.1109/MCOM.2013.6525598

Wang, J., Crawl, D., Purawat, S., Nguyen, M., & Altintas, I. (2015). Big data provenance: Challenges, state of the art and opportunities. In *2015 IEEE International Conference on Big Data (Big Data)* (pp. 2509-2516). Santa Clara, CA: IEEE. 10.1109/BigData.2015.7364047

Wang, N., & Mao, B. (2019). The Research on the Problems of Smart Old-Age Care in the Background of Smart City Construction. In *International Conference on Intelligent Transportation, Big Data & Smart City (ICITBS)* (pp. 151-154). Changsha, China: IEEE. 10.1109/ICITBS.2019.00043

Winters, V. J. (2010). Why are smart cities growing? who moves and who stays. *Journal of Regional Science, 51*(2), 253–270. doi:10.1111/j.1467-9787.2010.00693.x

Yu, H., Yang, Z., & Sinnott, O. R. (2018). Decentralized Big Data Auditing for Smart City Environments Leveraging Blockchain Technology. *IEEE Access: Practical Innovations, Open Solutions, 7*, 6288–6296. doi:10.1109/ACCESS.2018.2888940

Zanella, A., Bui, N., Castellani, A., Vangelista, L. Z., & Zorzi, M. (2014). Internet of Things for Smart Cities. *IEEE Internet of Things Journal, 1*(1), 22–32. doi:10.1109/JIOT.2014.2306328

Zhu, W., Cui, P., Wang, Z., & Hua, G. (2015). Multimedia Big Data Computing. *IEEE MultiMedia, 22*(3), 96–c3. doi:10.1109/MMUL.2015.66

ADDITIONAL READING

Cheng, B., Longo, S., Cirillo, F., Bauer, M., & Kovacs, E. (2015, June). Building a big data platform for smart cities: Experience and lessons from santander. In *2015 IEEE International Congress on Big Data* (pp. 592-599). IEEE. 10.1109/BigDataCongress.2015.91

Hashem, I. A. T., Chang, V., Anuar, N. B., Adewole, K., Yaqoob, I., Gani, A., ... Chiroma, H. (2016). The role of big data in smart city. *International Journal of Information Management, 36*(5), 748–758. doi:10.1016/j.ijinfomgt.2016.05.002

Sun, Y., Song, H., Jara, A. J., & Bie, R. (2016). Internet of things and big data analytics for smart and connected communities. *IEEE Access: Practical Innovations, Open Solutions, 4*, 766–773. doi:10.1109/ACCESS.2016.2529723

KEY TERMS AND DEFINITIONS

Big Data: Big data is collection of datasets that could not be acquired, processed, perceived, and managed by traditional hardware and software tools within a specific time.

Data Provenance: Data provenance is associated with the records of the inputs, systems, entities, and processes that influence the data of interest, and provide historical records of the data and its origins.

Internet of Things (IoT): IoT can be defined as the idea of envisaging enormous number of smart devices and embedded systems which empowers physical objects with pervasive sensing, seeing, hearing, and communication with each other.

Smart Cities: Smart cities can be generally defined as a conceptual development model which makes collective use of humans and technology for the expansion of collaborative urban development.

Smart Governance: Smart governance is about the use of technology and innovation for facilitating and supporting enhanced decision making and planning. It is associated with improving the democratic processes and transforming the ways that public services are delivered.

Smart Grid: For optimized consumption, supply, and generation of electric energy, the concept of smart grids integrates the traditional energy networks with next generation grids that are enabled with remote automation, communication, and computation.

Smart Healthcare: Smart healthcare can be defined as an integration of patients and doctors onto a common platform for intelligent health monitoring by analyzing day-to-day human activities.

Smart Transportation: Smart transportation is defined as the integration of modern technologies, innovations, and management strategies in transportation systems, that aim to provide enhanced services associated with different modes of transport and traffic management, and enable users to be actively informed regarding safe and smarter use of transport networks.

Urban Planning: Urban planning may be described as a specialized technical and political procedure which is concerned with the design and development of land usage and the built environment, which includes air, water, and the physical and virtual infrastructure passing into and out of urban zones, such as communication, transportation, and dissemination networks.

This research was previously published in Security, Privacy, and Forensics Issues in Big Data; pages 217-246, copyright year 2020 by Information Science Reference (an imprint of IGI Global).

Chapter 65
Big Data, Data Management, and Business Intelligence

Richard T. Herschel
Saint Joseph's University, USA

ABSTRACT

This paper examines big data and the opportunities it presents for improved business intelligence and decision making. Big data comes in multiple forms. It can be structured, semi-structured, or unstructured. The opportunity it presents is that there is so much of it and it is readily available to organizations. Organizations use big data for business intelligence (BI). They can apply analytics in BI activities to assess big data in order to gain new insights and opportunities for decision making. The problem is that oftentimes the data is of poor quality and it contains personal information. This paper explores these issues and examines the importance of effective data management in facilitating sound business intelligence. The Master Data Management methodology is reviewed and the importance of management support in its deployment is emphasized. With the advent of new sources of big data from IoT devices, the need for even more management involvement is stressed to ensure that organizational BI yield sound decisions and that use of data are in compliance with new regulations.

INTRODUCTION

Big data is one of the most commonly written about topics in todays press. In fact, today it has become a ubiquitous term. It is continuously transforming business, finance, healthcare, medicine, engineering, science, and society itself. Routinely we are provided with new information telling us much more data there is, how much more is now able to be captured, how many new sources it comes from, new ways to process it, and how it can be used in new and novel for decision making. It is a topic that is regularly discussed in boardrooms, business publications, and the mainstream media, because big data provides new insights into everything. Big data encompasses traditional sources of structured transaction data that is now supplemented by mass quantities of unstructured data. This data is processed by new, inexpensive, and faster hardware that is then scrutinized by new and more advance analytics that provide

DOI: 10.4018/978-1-6684-3662-2.ch065

organizations with more in-depth insight into their operational environment than ever before. And now, role of decision maker is increasingly being assumed by smart machines.

The goal of business intelligence [BI] is to extract value from data to better inform decision making. BI combines text, video, voice, location data, social media, and any other new source of data with traditional data sets in order to learn about, interact with, and predict what is happening so that the organization can respond as fast as possible to whatever it perceives is the opportunity that the data reveals. BI deals with imperfect data that is oftentimes ambiguous, but which is available on a vast scale. As a result, Mayer-Shonberger and Cukier (2014) assert that the effect is that the extraction of value from big data is analogous to a treasure hunt. That is, organizations are scrutinizing big data to learn what is happening, without necessarily needing to understand why. They argue that in a big data world, correlations supersede causality, because the data is simply used to discover patterns and correlations in the data that offer novel and invaluable insights. The more data you have the better the insights. The underlying premise for BI then becomes this: the more data an organization can capture, the better the data-driven probability of understanding what is happening, and the faster you can respond to this insight. This means then that actions taken in BI are often based on an organizational confidence level in the analytic assessment of what the data suggests without the necessity of a clear understanding of the root cause.

Big data would appear to many to be more about systems, and less about people. Certainly, people are important because they are themselves a major source of big data fodder and it is oftentimes people's behavior that big data is trying to affect. Nevertheless, big data also is dependent on people because people must inevitably be responsible for how data is used, how it is managed, and for the consequences of the decisions made when using it.

This paper is intended then to remind us that big data is not simply something that data, systems, and analytics make happen and that we are somehow divorced from it and not responsible for unintended consequences. Instead, prudence would require that since we have unleashed big data, we have to somehow insure to the best of our ability that if we can't control big data, we can at least use common sense in how we approach it and manage it. And, despite new technologies enabling machines to use big data to increasingly make decisions, people will not be able to divorce themselves from their decision-making responsibilities.

BACKGROUND

The amount of data in our world has exploded exponentially such that data, especially unstructured data, is now referred to as "big data". Where measures of data were once gradually evolving from megabytes to terabytes, the sudden phenomena of big data accelerated these measures to volumes expressed in petabytes (1,024 terabytes) or exabytes (1,024 petabytes). The new influx of data is derived from billions to trillions of records of millions of people—all from different sources (e.g. Web, sales, customer contact center, social media, mobile data and so on). The data is typically loosely structured and often incomplete.

Petrov (2019) states that in 2019, the big data market is expected to grow by 20 percent, with every person generating 1.7 megabytes of data in just a second. By 2020, he claims, there will be approximately 40 trillion gigabytes of data. He notes that 97.2 percent of organizations are investing in big data and artificial intelligence (AI), because automated analytics will become increasingly vital to big data by 2020.

Big Data is the natural result of four major global trends:

1. Mobile computing
2. Social networking
3. Cloud computing
4. Moore's Law [processing power doubles every 2 years]

A lot of big data is derived from cell phone traffic and social networks, with much of it being stored in the cloud. The amount of this information grows almost exponentially as people routinely interact with companies and each other via wireless and wired networks as a matter of course.

The data being transmitted and captured from these transactions has become a key basis of competition, underpinning new waves of productivity growth, innovation, and consumer surplus, according to research by MGI and McKinsey's Business Technology Office (Manyika, Chui, Brown, Bughin, Dobbs, Roxburgh, Hung Byers, 2011). From the standpoint of competitiveness and the potential capture of value, big data has had a substantial impact. Today, organizations leverage data-driven strategies to innovate, compete, and capture value from deep and up-to-real-time information. Hence, leaders in every sector are confronted with the need to grapple with the implications of big data in a quest to capture and harness its potential value.

The significance of big data to an organization falls into two categories: analytical use, and enabling new products. Big data analytics can reveal insights hidden previously by data too costly to process, such as peer influence among customers, revealed by analyzing shoppers' transactions, social and geographical data. Being able to process every item of data in reasonable time removes the troublesome need for sampling and promotes an investigative approach to data, in contrast to the somewhat static nature of running predetermined reports. Hence, big data expands BI's data-driven decision-making opportunities.

BIG DATA

In their book, "Big Data, Big Analytics: Emerging Business Intelligence and Analytic Trends for Today's Business", Minelli, Chambers, and Dhiraj (2013) present significant evidence supporting the value and justification for businesses to be 'big data-driven'. Minelli et al. define big data as data that goes beyond the traditional limits of data along three dimensions: volume, variety, and velocity. Volume is important because in the past, business use cases and predictive analyses were restricted because the data volume utilized was limited due to storage or computational processing constraints. However, with big data technology removing these constraints and allowing the use of unstructured data and more transaction data for larger data sets, Minelli et al., assert that organizations can now discover more subtle patterns that can lead to targeted actionable decisions, or allow them to factor in more observations or variables captured over a longer period of time into predictive models. Variety of data refers to the different types of data now available for analyses. Instead of simply using structured text or numbers, unstructured text, audio, images, geospatial information, and internet data are now captured and able to be analyzed. Velocity is about the speed at which data is created, accumulated, ingested, and processed. Minelli et al., state that since this data is now readily available, organizations pursue technologies to help them immediately process this information for real-time analytics-based decision-making.

IBM's Institute for Business Value (2013) added a fourth dimension to describe big data called *veracity*, or the uncertainty of data. They argue that the need to acknowledge and plan for uncertainty is a dimension of big data that has been introduced as executives seek to better understand the world around them. With data types changing constantly, and data collection increasing in quantity and speed, the quality of the data is a concern to be managed.

SAS Institute (2015) proposes two more dimensions as important to the understanding of big data:

1. **Variability.** In addition to the increasing velocities and varieties of data, data flows can be highly inconsistent with periodic peaks. Daily, seasonal and event-triggered peak data loads can be challenging to manage, but they are even more so with unstructured data involved.
2. **Complexity.** Data now comes from multiple sources. And it is still an undertaking to link, match, cleanse and transform data across systems. This requires that organizations increasingly focus on connecting and correlating relationships, hierarchies and multiple data linkages or data can quickly spiral out of control (SAS Institute, 2015).

In essence, big data has now become a new kind of capital. Because of its breadth, volume, richness, and timeliness, many firms see it as an important asset that when harnessed, can be used for creating new products and services. It is a capital on par with financial capital. Oracle (2015) asserts that for CEOs to realize its potential, they must secure access to big data and then increasingly exploit its use before their competition can.

Issues, Controversies, Problems

The rapid rise of the big data phenomena presents a plethora of new challenges for CEOs and their organizations. For example, IDG Enterprise Big Data research (IDG, 2014) conducted a survey with the goal of gaining a better understanding of organizations' big data initiatives, investments and strategies. Their key finding included the following:

*   Organizations are seeing exponential growth in the amount of data managed.
*   Companies are intensifying their efforts to derive value through big data initiatives.
*   CEOs are focused on the value of big data and are partnering with IT executives who will purchase/manage/execute the strategies.
*   Organizations are investing in developing or buying software applications, additional sever hardware, and hiring staff with analytics skills for big data initiatives.
*   Organizations are facing numerous challenges with big data initiatives, especially the limited availability of skilled employees to analyze and manage data.
*   Half of respondents indicated there is no clear thought leader in the big data solution space (IDG, 2014).

Today, big data is getting everyone's attention. That said, many firms are struggling to manage to manage it in order to harness its value.

Some of the challenges they face have been unanticipated. For example, access to mobile data, social media content, and location services information means that businesses are collecting an extensive amount of personal information about their customers. This means that:

*   Businesses now have the capacity to leverage more personally identifiable and sensitive information for competitive advantage.

- There is a dramatic surge in identity theft that has the potential to compromise secure transactions.
- Firms must address the development of sophisticated technology to exploit data security vulnerabilities.
- Consumers are increasingly aware and concerned about the collection, use, and disclosure of personal information.
- Legislators are responding to consumer concerns by restricting access to and the use of personal information. Europe's adoption of the General Data Protection Regulation (GDPR) is the best-known example of this. (Palmer, 2018).

An obvious conclusion is that big data can become a liability for organizations if they don't have a demonstrably effective plan to manage it. And, to enable this, firms will not be able to simply rely simply on software solutions, hardware fixes, or other IT initiatives. Instead, management will have to pursue organizational solutions that are designed to insure both data integrity and regulatory compliance.

SOLUTIONS AND RECOMMENDATIONS

To determine how well organizations were taking advantage of big data, the IBM Institute for Business Value (Balboni, Finch, Rodenbeck Reese, & Shockley, 2013) surveyed 900 business and IT executives from 70 countries. Their analysis of the survey results enabled them to establish nine levers that differentiated companies who are best able to derive value from big data from those who were not:

1. *Culture:* Availability and use of data and analytics within an organization
2. *Data:* Structure and formality of the organization's data governance process and the security of its data
3. *Expertise:* Development of and access to data management and analytic skills and capabilities
4. *Funding:* Financial rigor in the analytics funding process
5. *Measurement:* Evaluating the impact on business outcomes
6. *Platform:* Integrated capabilities delivered by hardware and software
7. *Source of value:* Actions and decisions that generate results
8. *Sponsorship:* Executive support and involvement
9. *Trust:* Organizational confidence (Balboni, Finch, Rodenbeck Reese, & Shockley, 2013).

This list affirmed that many of the issues surrounding big data are issues of organizational management. That is, organizational culture, expertise, finance, performance measurement, value creation, leadership, and trust are all traditional management concerns that affect value creation with big data as well.

What surprised management is the tension created from the sheer volume and availability of big data, the new technologies that are being created to acquire and process it, and the stress it is creating for firms to manage and react to it in an effective and timely manner. In essence, big data has become an aggressive, persistent, and pervasive irritant that is able expose organizational data management limitations. Therefore, one of the easiest ways to understand an organizations' shortcomings in the handling of big data would be to examine how capable they currently are in dealing with data management - period.

In his book on data management, Tony Fisher (2009) argues that data governance programs are essential for enterprises to experience success with business intelligence initiatives. As companies grow and look to incorporate additional data sources such as big data it is vital that they have an effective data governance processes in place. To assess this, Fisher created the Data Governance Maturity Model that encompasses four phases: Undisciplined, Reactive, Proactive, and Governed. Each phase represents a different risk versus reward profile and as a company progresses through the model, they increase their ROI for business intelligence while simultaneously reducing risk for the company. Each of these stages is defined below:

- Undisciplined: At the initial stage of the Data Governance Maturity Model, an organization has few defined rules and policies regarding data quality and data integration. The same data may exist in multiple applications, and redundant data is often found in different sources, formats and records. Companies in this stage have little or no executive-level insight into the costs of bad or poorly integrated data. About one-third of all organizations are at the Undisciplined stage.
- Reactive: A Reactive organization locates and confronts data-centric problems only after they occur. Enterprise resource planning (ERP) or Customer Relationship Management (CRM) applications perform specific tasks, and organizations experience varied levels of data quality. While certain employees understand the importance of high-quality information, corporate management support is lacking. Studies show that the largest share of all organizations – 45 to 50 percent – fall into this stage.
- Proactive: Less than 10% of all companies have reached this level. The Proactive organization adopts a more unified enterprise view of data, implementing and using customer data integration and product data management solutions. In this stage, management understands and appreciates the role of data governance and data is seen as a strategic asset. Here data stewards emerge as the primary implementers of data management strategy and work directly with cross-functional teams to enact data quality standards.
- Governed: At the Governed stage, an organization has a unified data governance strategy throughout the enterprise. Data quality, data integration and data synchronization are integral parts of all business processes. The organization has a comprehensive program that elevates the process of managing business-critical data (Dataflux, 2015).

These stages provide a framework for organizations to gauge how well the are progressing with their data governance, data quality, and data management efforts while also providing information as to how they can progress to improve to a higher level of Master Data Management [MDM] – a term commonly used in the marketplace to describe this framework. Informatica (2015) defines MDM this way:

Master data management (MDM) in effect turns the Data Governance Maturity Model from a framework to a methodology for improving data management. MDM, like the Maturity Model, has the goal of helping organizations to attain:

- **A single view of the data**—Creating a single, authoritative view of business-critical data from disparate, duplicate, and conflicting information.
- **A 360-degree view of the relationships**—establishing business rules that let firms identify the relationships among the data.
- **A complete view of all interactions**—Integrating the transactions and social interactions that have occurred with a product, customer, channel partner, or other data element to give the organization a complete view of that customer (Informatica, 2015).

Ali (2014) states that organizations who are able to effectively manage their data are better equipped to make time sensitive decisions, monitor emerging trends, react quickly to new business opportunities, and ultimately, maximize the ROI of real-time data better than ever before. If data is being dispersed throughout the enterprise, the ability to discover or to fully leverage analytics tools to gain value and insight from data is cumbersome and inaccurate. Employing an MDM provides a framework for better ensuring that the big data being employed in business intelligence analytics is relevant, timely and accurate. Inevitably then, executive support of MDM should be essential if the organization is going to employ big data for data-driven decision-making.

Eckerson (2014) argues that effective data governance programs must be enterprise-wide with effective programs combining both a top-down and bottom-up approach to data management. He argues that organizations must have a data governance methodology like MDM in place to enable this. Moreover, he recommends that senior management establish a data governance office (DGO) with a full-time staff and a data governance officer. Eckerson proposes that the DGO should work with a data governance steering committee and data stewards to manage and monitor the organization's data governance program. Data stewards are employees with specific subject matter expertise who assume responsibility for certifying data, managing exceptions, and applying controls to safeguard data and individual privacy. Their role is to ensure that the data management, data governance, and business and quality rules definitions are appropriate for different lines of business. Each data steward provides critical input into cross-enterprise data management policies and ensures that these policies are appropriate for the business processes and applications that support the specific lines of business that they represent. Because of the necessity for these interactions, Eckerson believes that data governance is mostly about communications and change management where many conversations are routinely occurring among many people in different parts of the organization to ensure that business processes flow smoothly and efficiently.

Brown, Court, and Willmott (2013) state that effective data management requires executive buy-in for data governance efforts to succeed, because capturing the potential of data analytics requires a clear plan that establishes priorities and well-defined pathways to business results and developing that plan requires leadership. This presumes that executives clearly understand and endorse the use of big data, that they comprehend what data governance is and how important their role is to ensure its adoption and diffusion, and that they fully comprehend that effective data governance comes at a cost: organizational change. This means that senior management must be intimately involved in crafting the blueprint that encompasses the vision, strategy and requirements for the organization's big data journey. This blueprint should define the scope of big data utilization and management within the organization, prioritize the key business challenges that big data will address, provide a schedule for dealing with these challenges, and provide a plan for developing or acquiring the people and technology resources needed to get the job done (Balboni, Finch, Rodenbeck Reese, & Shockley, 2013).

To be effective, big data solutions must be based on business requirements and address the infrastructure, processes, data sources, and skills required to support this business opportunity. To accomplish this, senior management must establish a plan and process that is consistent with the organization's culture and guiding principles such that these are subsequently reflected in the organizational data governance activities. Management must ensure that data governance is viewed as a continuous and systemic endeavor that is woven into the fabric of the organization's structure and processes.

Executive understanding and support of MDM-type big data governance processes should reflect the conscious realization that they will need to develop, acquire, and retain a strong core of human capital. Qualified data stewards, for example, must be identified and selected. These individuals, through their actions, reflect the values, policies, and procedural requirements that are derived from senior management. In a big data world, executive leadership is also needed to find, develop, and retain strong analytical talent. Analysts with strong mathematical, statistical and computer science roots, as well as familiarity or expertise in areas such as data mining, data visualization, optimization and simulation, text analytics, and predictive analytics are going to be required to harvest meaning and value from big data. The problem is that there is a severe shortage of this talent. Holak (2019) finds that because of big data and artificial intelligence (AI), demand for data science analytical skills is growing exponentially. He provides information showing a 29% increase in demand for data scientists year over year and a 344 percent increase since 2013. Clearly leadership is required to find creative means for acquiring the requisite BI talent that organizations need.

Dyché and Nevala (2015) assert that there are key issues where executives have to be careful in addressing big data and data management issues. These issues include failing to define what data governance is, not approaching big data and data management in a progressive and systematic manner, failing to design data governance teams properly, treating data management as a project, and overlooking organizational cultural issues. They note that issues needing to be addressed by data governance and big data are far-flung and pervasive, ranging from arbitration of cross-functional data usage to information privacy, security, and access policies. As a result, executives need to understand that if they look to implement data governance and other big data initiatives too quickly, the intended results may well be stymied quickly by role confusion, prioritization debates, project development problems, and resistance from the incumbent culture. And with new legislation like the EU's GDPR, executives can ill afford any mistakes or delays.

Whitler (2018) notes that without effective data governance, organizations will be overwhelmed by big data. Indeed, she notes, organizations are suffering from data saturation. The rapid rise in the ability to collect data hasn't been matched by the ability of many organizations to support, filter, and manage this data. Their data management infrastructure and processes are unable to keep up with the continuous deluge of big data. To deal with this issue, she reinforces the importance of effective data governance practices. She asserts that organizations need to:

- focus on identifying and understanding the key questions that you want to employ big data to help you to address,
- identify measures that will address these questions,
- develop a data governance council,
- map out a complete view of the data that identifies what data exists and who has rights to it, and
- identify the business intelligence tools that are best suited to analyzing the data for the issue being addressed.

Partner (2019) warns that the overall importance of data and information within organizations will continue to grow as will the demand for effective data management practices. She reports that there will be more than 20 billion connected sensors by 2020 that will only further aggravate the vast volume of big data. To compound this issue further, she states that organizations must also address the opportunity to take advantage of their other captured, but untapped information assets as well as new opportunities to analyze newly digitized analog assets.

FUTURE RESEARCH DIRECTIONS

Research into the impact of big data needs to expand its focus to explore in more depth how BI is affected by management's ability to cope with data governance, analytics talent recruitment, and other peripheral issues. MDM and data governance activities appear to be sensible techniques for managing data, but it is clear from statistics that not all of these practices are being effectively adopted and deployed. Understanding the rationale for the adoption and leveraging of data management techniques as well as its ability to affect business intelligence and decision making provides meaningful insight into management's competence in exploiting big data.

Managing big data requires common sense. Common sense is derived from thought, intuition, and experience. It incorporates such attributes as the ability to think rationally, to act purposefully, and to deal effectively with your environment. Common sense dictates that firms need to be conscientious with big data so as not to compromise BI efforts and data-driven decision-making. At the same time, however, common sense dictates that there are clear opportunity costs when business intelligence efforts are compromised because of poor big data management practices.

And data management acumen is only going to become more important. Foote (2018) reports that the accessibility of big data has provided a new generation of technology that enables businesses to focus even more on data-driven decision making. Foote believes that the continuous growth of the Internet of Things (IoT) will provide several new resources for big data, including the ability to combine streaming analytics with machine learning and the ability of artificial intelligence (AI) to process big data, thereby improving the efficiency of business intelligence.

CONCLUSION

Big data presents opportunity, but it is inherently filled with noise and uncertainty. It has tremendous potential if people approach it in the right way. It requires effective management, especially competent data management. What it offers is the prospect of gaining better business intelligence for decision making.

Ironically, there is the real potential that people may soon become less involved in business intelligence processes. Ramasamy (2019) predicts that in the next few years artificial intelligence, data analytics, and machine learning embedded in applications will become the primary consumers of data. That is, these technologies will replace people-oriented output such as reports and dashboards, because software will assume the burden of consuming and analyzing data.

This prediction poses the prospect of a fundamental challenge to our understanding about organizational decision making. Traditionally, decision making processes and procedures are assigned to specific individuals. Decisions are made by people. If machines assume these responsibilities, this perspective will necessarily have to shift. Analytics become a surrogate for human reasoning and the machine essentially becomes the decision maker. The problem, however, will be that people will probably remain accountable for the quality of the machine's decisions. In this scenario, it makes sense that one should control what they can control. They should implement effective big data management techniques that ensure data quality and they should employ business intelligence techniques that are grounded in sound reasoning relative to the issue being addressed. Hence, management's role should become one where they necessarily focus on data quality, the appropriateness of the analytics used to gain business intelligence, and the viability of both relative to the resultant decision-making outcomes.

REFERENCES

Ali, S. (2014). *Developing a Modern Data Management Strategy.* Retrieved April 1, 2015 from http://www.information-management.com/news/Data-Management-Strategy-10026378-1.html

Balboni, F., Finch, G., Rodenbeck Reese, C., & Shockley, R. (2013). *Analytics: A Blueprint for Value. IBM Global Services.* IBM Corporation.

Brown, B., Court, D., & Willmott, P. (2013) *Mobilizing your C-suite for big-data analytics.* Retrieved March 10, 2015 from http://www.mckinsey.com/insights/business_technology/mobilizing_your_c_suite_for_big_data_analytics

Dataflux. (2015). *The Data Governance Maturity Model: Establishing the People, Policies and Technology That Manage Enterprise Data.* Retrieved April 19, 2015 from http://www.sas.com/offices/NA/canada/lp/DIDQ/DataFlux.pdf

Dyché, J., & Nevala, K. (2015). *Ten Mistakes to Avoid When Launching Your Data Governance Program.* Retrieved March 21, 2015 from http://www.sas.com/resources/whitepaper/wp_63774.pdf

Eckerson, W. (2014). *Data Governance for the Enterprise - Trends in the Use of Data Quality, Master Data Management and Metadata Management.* TechTarget.

Fisher, T. (2009). *The Data Asset: How Smart Companies Govern Their Data for Business Success.* John Wiley & Sons, Inc.

Foote, K. (2018). *Big Data tends in 2019.* Retrieved May 12, 2019, from https://www.dataversity.net/big-data-trends-2019/

Holak, B. (2019). *Demand for data scientists is booming and will only increase.* Retrieved May 14, 2019, from https://searchbusinessanalytics.techtarget.com/feature/Demand-for-data-scientists-is-booming-and-will-increase

IBM Institute for Business Value. (2013). *Analytics: The real-world use of big data.* IBM Corporation.

IDG. (2014). *Research Reports: Big Data.* Retrieved April 11, 2015 from http://www.idgenterprise.com/report/big-data-2

Informatica. (2015). *What is Master Data Management?* Retrieved April 02, 2015 from https://www.informatica.com/products/master-data-management.html#fbid=s7qB_Q-sMY-

Manyika, J., Chui, M., Brown, B., Bughin, J., Dobbs, R., Roxburgh, C., & Hung Byers, A. (2011). *Big data: The next frontier for innovation, competition, and productivity.* Retrieved April 17, 2015 from http://www.mckinsey.com/insights/business_technology/big_data_the_next_frontier_for_innovation

Marr, B. (2015). Big Data: Using Smart Big Data Analytics and Metrics to Make Better Decisions and Improve Performance. Chichester, UK: John Wiley & Sons Ltd.

Mayer-Schonberger, V., & Cukier, K. (2014). *Big Data.* First Mariner Books.

Minelli, M., Chambers, M., & Dhiraj, A. (2013). *Big Data, Big Analytics: Emerging Business Intelligence and Analytic Trends for Today's Business.* John Wiley & Sons, Inc. doi:10.1002/9781118562260

Oracle. (2015). *Enterprise Big Data Predictions 2015.* Retrieved April 18, 2015, from http://www.oracle. com/us/technologies/big-data/big-data-predictions-2015-2421021.pdf

Palmer, D. (n.d.). *What is GDPR? Everything you need to know about the new general data protection regulations.* Retrieved May 7, 2019, from https://www.zdnet.com/article/gdpr-an-executive-guide-to-what-you-need-to-know/

Partner, L. (2019). *Top big analytics trends hold true well into 2019.* Retrieved May 13, 2019, from https://blog.pythian.com/top-seven-big-data-analytics-trends-2019/

Petrov, C. (2019). *Big data statistics 2019.* Retrieved may 15, 2019, from https://techjury.net/stats-about/big-data-statistics/

Ramasamy, K. (2019). *2019 data predictions: Demise of big data and rise of intelligent apps.* Retrieved May 14, 2019, from https://www.forbes.com/sites/forbestechcouncil/2019/02/22/2019-data-predictions-demise-of-big-data-and-rise-of-intelligent-apps/#68898422753c

SAS Institute, Inc. (2015). *Big Data: What it is & why it matters.* Retrieved March 30, 2015 from http://www.sas.com/en_us/insights/big-data/what-is-big-data.html

Whitler, K. (2018). *Why too much data is a problem and how to fix it.* Retrieved May 9, 2019, from https://blog.pythian.com/top-seven-big-data-analytics-trends-2019/

ADDITIONAL READING

Fisher, T. (2009). *The Data Asset.* John Wiley& Sons.

Kaldero, N. (2018). *Data Science for Executives: Leveraging Machine Intelligence to Drive Business ROI.* Lioncrest Publishing.

Marr, B. (2017). *Data Strategy: How to Profit from a World of Big Data, Analytics, and the Internet of Things.* Kogan Page.

KEY TERMS AND DEFINITIONS

Artificial Intelligence (AI): Is a wide-ranging branch of computer science concerned with building smart machines capable of performing tasks that traditionally required human intelligence.

Big Data: Is a popular term used to describe the exponential growth and availability of data, both structured and unstructured.

Business Intelligence (BI): Is a business management term which refers to applications and technologies which are used to gather, provide access to, and analyze data and information about their company operations.

Data Governance: Is a combination of people, processes and technology that drives high-quality, high-value information. The technology portion of data governance combines data quality, data integration and master data management to ensure that data, processes, and people can be trusted and accountable, and that accurate information flows through the enterprise driving business efficiency.

Data Steward: A data steward is a job role that involves planning, implementing and managing the sourcing, use and maintenance of data assets in an organization. Data stewards enable an organization to take control and govern all the types and forms of data and their associated libraries or repositories.

General Data Protection Regulation (GDPR): Is legislation designed to give European Union citizens more control over their personal data. It dictates laws that organizations must abide by in their acquisition and management of personal information.

Internet of Things (IoT): Refers to the billions of physical devices around the world thatare connected to the internet, collecting, and sharing data.

Master Data Management (MDM): Is a technology-enabled discipline in which business and IT work together to ensure the uniformity, accuracy, stewardship, semantic consistency, and accountability of the enterprise's official shared master data assets. Master data is the consistent and uniform set of identifiers and extended attributes that describes the core entities of the enterprise including customers, prospects, citizens, suppliers, sites, hierarchies, and chart of accounts.

Unstructured Data: Unstructured data (or unstructured information) refers to information that either does not have a pre-defined data model or is not organized in a pre-defined manner. Unstructured information is typically text-heavy, but may contain data such as dates, numbers, facts, or video content as well.

This research was previously published in the Encyclopedia of Organizational Knowledge, Administration, and Technology; pages 509-519, copyright year 2021 by Business Science Reference (an imprint of IGI Global).

Chapter 66
The Use of Big Data in Marketing Analytics

Chai-Lee Goi
🆔 https://orcid.org/0000-0003-0131-2818
Curtin University, Malaysia

ABSTRACT

Big data has broken through the public imagination, has revolutionised the process through which business find innovative ways, and has transformed the data into valuable information that will shape business intelligence and gain business insights to make better decisions. The purpose of this study is to review the development of big data, architecture, and the use of big data in marketing analytics. From the analysis of literature reviews, a big data in marketing analytics model has been proposed. In using big data in marketing, marketers need balanced analytics and then identify opportunities for improvement based on reporting or analysing past and present big data to predict and influence the future.

INTRODUCTION

Big data analytics have been embraced as a disruptive technology that will shape business intelligence and to gain business insights to make better decision making (Fan et. al, 2015). The term of big data has been first used in 1989 by Erik Larson (Marr, 2015) and then being popularised by John R. Mashey in 1990s (Mashey, 1998). Big data is not just about the buzzword, it is a movement (Sarjana & Sanjana, 2013). Big data analytics has been around since 1663, when John Graunt dealt with overwhelming amounts of information using statistics to study the bubonic plague (Foote, 2017). Our current lives are filled and surrounded by all kinds of data and this data never sleeps (Domo, 2019). Chen et. al (2012) commented that it is also a step forward 'from big data to big impact'. Big data has broken through the public imagination (Baer, 2013), has revolutionised the process through which business find innovative ways (Baig et. al, 2019), and has transformed the data into valuable information that could make the difference between business success and failure (Kauffmann et. al, in press).

DOI: 10.4018/978-1-6684-3662-2.ch066

In marketing, as discussed in New Gen Apps (2017), big data can be used for several purposes. This includes market identification, trend analysis, understanding the consumer, markdown optimisation, market prediction, measuring influencers' impact and improving cross-selling. Customer Analytics, operational analytics, fraud and compliance, new product and service innovation, and enterprise data warehouse optimisation are use cases in sales and marketing. Also, Customer Value Analytics (CVA) is making it possible for marketers to deliver consistent omnichannel customer experiences across all channels (Columbus, 2016). Lozada et. al's study (2019) discussed the use of big data and its incorporation into the core of the processes associated with innovation management and along with the strategy, including value co-creation initiatives. To contribute to digital marketing success, Saran (2018) highlighted that big data helps marketers to design better marketing campaigns, to have better pricing decisions, and to show appropriate web contents.

Marketing analytics is the ticket to better decisions and stronger results, however many marketers still struggle with shoring up that foundation. When it comes to making the most of data, marketers must get the information in order if they want to turn insights into action (Carey, 2017). The major problems and challenges of big data are handling of data; security, privacy and regulation; lack of skilled staff; technology development is too fast; and financial resources. The summary of these challenges can be found in Table 1. There is a need for systematic planning in big data to be used in marketing analytics. Thus, the purpose of this study is to review the development of big data, architecture and the use of big data in marketing analytics. From the analysis literature reviews, a model will be proposed in relation to the big data in marketing analytics.

Note:

1. Vaghela (2018)
2. Bekker (2018)
3. Yakimova (2019)
4. PieSync (2020)
5. Hamilton and Sodeman (2020)

Overall, this chapter covers three main sections. Big data section discusses the overview of big data, characteristics of big data, sources of big data, content formats of big data, and types of marketing data. The second section discusses about big data architecture and the third section involves big data in marketing analytics discussion. In addition, the final section of this book chapter suggests the future research directions of big data in marketing analytics.

BIG DATA

What is Big Data?

Big data possess a suite of key traits, volume, velocity and variety, as well as exhaustivity, resolution, indexicality, relationality, extensionality and scalability. Big data as an analytical category needs to be unpacked, with the genus of big data further delineated and its various species identified through ontological work that we will gain conceptual clarity about what constitutes big data, formulate how best to make sense of it, and identify how it might be best used to make sense of the world (Kitchin & McArdle, 2018)

Table 1. Problems and challenges of big data

Problems and challenges					
Handling of data	**1**	**2**	**3**	**4**	**5**
Handling a large amount of data/ Complexity of managing data quality	Ö	Ö			
Real-time can be complex	Ö				
False equivalencies and bias			Ö		
Data silos				Ö	
Inaccurate data/ Reliability and validity				Ö	
Finding the signal in the noise				Ö	
Tricky process of converting big data into valuable insights		Ö			
Troubles of upscaling		Ö			
Security, privacy and regulation					
Data security/ Vulnerability to security breaches and unauthorized access	Ö	Ö	Ö		
Legal and ethical concerns					Ö
Lack of international standards for data privacy regulations			Ö		
Skilled staff					
Shortage/ Lack of skilled staff	Ö			Ö	
Insufficient understanding and acceptance of big data		Ö			
Technology development					
Technology moves too fast				Ö	
Confusing variety of big data technologies		Ö			
Financial resources					
Big data adoption projects entail lots of expenses		Ö			

The evolution of big data can be sub-divided into three main phases, phase 1, phase 2 and phase 3. In phase 1, data analysis, data analytics and big data originate from the longstanding domain of database management. In phase 2, HTTP-based web traffic introduced a massive increase in semi-structured and unstructured data. Finally, in phase 3, mobile devices analyse behavioural data and give the possibility to store and analyse location-based data (Big Data Framework, 2019). The summary can be referred to in Table 2.

Characteristics of Big Data

The major characteristics and also the mainstream of definition of big data involve Laney's (2001) three Vs – volume, velocity and variety. SAS (n.d) has added another two additional Vs, variability and veracity. In terms of data mining, Fan & Bifet (2012) proposed new technologies and frameworks to visualise the results from big data analysis. Oguntimilehin & Ademola (2014) defined big data in terms of five Vs (volume, velocity, variety, variability and value) and a C (complexity). Vorhies (2013) discussed 8 characteristics (volume, variety, velocity, value, veracity, variability, viscosity and virality) that define big data. Khan et. al (2014) provided a brief survey study of 7Vs of big data (volume, velocity, variety, veracity, validity, volatility and value) in order to understand big data and extract value concept. Borne

(2014) added another new three Vs (volume, variety, velocity, veracity, validity, value and variability, plus venue, vocabulary and vagueness), making it a total of 10 characteristics of big data. Overall, 14 Vs and a C of big data have been concluded in Table 3.

Table 2. Big data Phases

Phase 1	Phase 2	Phase 3
1970 – 2000	2000 – 2010	2010 – present
DBMS-based, structured content: · RDBMS & data warehousing · Extract transfer load · Online analytical processing · Dashboards & scorecards · Data mining & statistical analysis	Web-based, unstructured content · Information retrieval and extraction · Opinion mining · Question answering · Web analytics and web intelligence · Social media analysis · Social network analysis · Spatial-temporal analysis	Mobile and sensor-based content · Location-aware analysis · Person-centered analysis · Context-relevant analysis · Mobile visualization · Human computer interaction

Source: Adopted from Big Data Framework (2019)

Sources of Big Data

Raghupathi & Raghupathi (2014) highlighted that big data can come from internal and external sources, often in multiple formats (flat files, .csv, relational tables, ASCII/text, etc.) and residing at multiple locations (geographic as well as in different providers' sites) in numerous legacy and multiple applications (examples transaction processing applications, databases etc.). Sources and data types include:

- Web and social media data
- Machine to machine data
- Big transaction data
- Biometric data
- Human-generated data

Content Formats of Big Data

Data is generated in structured, unstructured and semi-structured forms (Moharm, 2019). Taylor (2018) highlighted that structured data is in a format created to be captured, stored, organised and analysed. It's neatly organised for easy access. Semi-structured data is related to information that does not reside in a relational database but does have organisational properties that make it much easier to analyse, examples XML and HTML documents (Chen et. al, 2016). Unstructured data can be divided into typical human-generated and machine-generated unstructured data as discussed below:

- Typical human-generated unstructured data includes:
    - Text files: Word processing, spreadsheets, presentations, email, logs.
    - Email: Email has some internal structure thanks to its metadata, and we sometimes refer to it as semi-structured. However, its message field is unstructured and traditional analytics tools cannot parse it.

- ◦ Social Media: Data from Facebook, Twitter, LinkedIn.
- ◦ Website: YouTube, Instagram, photo sharing sites.
- ◦ Mobile data: Text messages, locations.
- ◦ Communications: Chat, IM, phone recordings, collaboration software.
- ◦ Media: MP3, digital photos, audio and video files.
- ◦ Business applications: MS Office documents, productivity applications.

Table 3. Characteristics of big data

Characteristic	Description
Volume	Volume of big data refers to the size of data being created from all the sources including text, audio, video, social networking, research studies, data, images, reports, forecasting and natural disasters etc. (Khan, 2014). As data volume increases, the value of different data records will decrease in proportion to age, type, richness, and quantity among other factors (Kaisler et. al, 2013). Increases in data volume are handled by purchasing additional storage. As data volume increases, the relative value of each data point decreases resulting in poor financial justification of incrementing online storage (Laney, 2001).
Velocity	It is about the speed or velocity of data. The speed of feedback loop that takes data from input through to the decision (Khan, 2014). Data velocity management is much more than a physical bandwidth and protocol issue are implementing architectural solutions (Laney, 2001).
Variety	Data comes in all types of formats – structured, numeric data in traditional databases to unstructured text documents, emails, videos, audios, stock ticker data and financial transactions (SAS, n.d). No barrier to effective data management will exist than the variety of incompatible data formats, non-aligned data structures and inconsistent data semantics (Laney, 2001).
Variability	In addition to the increasing velocities and varieties of data, data flows are unpredictable. Businesses need to know when something is trending in social media, and how to manage daily, seasonal and event-triggered peak data loads (SAS, n.d). The challenges of big data involve dynamic, evolving, spatiotemporal data, time series, seasonal, and any other type of non-static behaviour in data sources, customers, objects of study etc. (Borne, 2014).
Veracity	Veracity refers to the quality of data. Due to data comes from so many different sources, it's difficult to link, match, cleanse and transform data across systems. Businesses need to connect and correlate relationships, hierarchies and multiple data linkages (SAS, n.d).
Visualisation	One of the main tasks of big data analysis is how to visualize the results (Fan & Bifet, 2012).
Value	Commercial value, any new sources and forms of data that can be added to the business and scientific research (Oguntimilehin & Ademola, 2014).
Viscosity	The latency or lag time in the data relative to the event being described (Vorhies, 2013).
Virality	The rate at which the data spreads, how often it is picked up and repeated by other users (Vorhies, 2013).
Validity	Validity means the correctness and accuracy of data with regard to the intended usage. Data may not have any veracity issues but may not be valid if not properly understood. Same set of data may be valid for one application or usage and then invalid for another application or usage (Khan et. al, 2014).
Volatility	We can easily recall the retention policy of structured data that we implement every day in businesses. Once retention period expires, we can easily destroy it (Khan et. al, 2014).
Venue	The challenges of big data involve distributed, heterogeneous data from multiple platforms, from different owners' systems, with different access and formatting requirements, private vs. public cloud (Borne, 2014).
Vocabulary	The challenges of big data involve schema, data models, semantics, ontologies, taxonomies, and other content- and context-based metadata that describe the data's structure, syntax, content, and provenance (Borne, 2014).
Vagueness	The challenges of big data involve confusion over the meaning of big data and what are the tools should be used (Borne, 2014).
Complexity	Data comes from multiple sources and it is still an undertaking to link, match, cleanse and transform data across systems. It is necessary to connect and correlate relationships, hierarchies and multiple data linkages or your data can quickly spiral out of control (Oguntimilehin & Ademola, 2014).

- Typical machine-generated unstructured data includes:
  ○ Satellite imagery: Weather data, land forms, military movements.
  ○ Scientific data: Oil and gas exploration, space exploration, seismic imagery, atmospheric data.
  ○ Digital surveillance: Surveillance photos and video.
  ○ Sensor data: Traffic, weather, oceanographic sensors.

In semi-structured data, the information that is associated with a schema is contained within the data, or so-called self-describing (Buneman, 1997). Table 4 gives an overview of comparison between unstructured, fully structured and semi-structured.

Table 4. Comparison between unstructured, fully structured and semi-structured content

	Unstructured	Structured	Semi-Structured
Technology	character and binary data	relational database tables	XML/ RDF
Transaction management	no transaction management, no concurrency	matured transaction management, various concurrency techniques	transaction management, adapted from RDBMS, not matured
version management	versioned as a whole	versioning over tuples, rows, tables etc.	not very common, versioning over triples or graphs is possible
flexibility	very flexible, absence of schema	schema-dependent, rigorous schema	flexible, tolerant schema
scalability	very scalable	scaling DB schema is difficult	schema scaling is simple
robustness		very robust, enhancements since 30 years	new technology, not widely spread
query-performance	only textual queries possible	structured query allows complex joins	queries over anonymous nodes are possible

Adopted from Sint et. al, 2009

Types of Marketing Data

The marketing world is dynamic and ever-changing due to trends, technology development and tactics Hubspot, n.d). Mehl (2015) highlighted 14 types of data that can enhance marketing activities. The summary can be referred to in Table 5.

BIG DATA ARCHITECTURE

Researchers are increasingly involved in studies combining big data and analytics, cloud, Internet of things, mobility or social media (Akoka et. al, 2017). Overall, these studies cover areas such as architecture design and selection of technologies; links between big data, programmatic marketing and real-time processing; big data solutions; forecasting model; marketing and consumer analytics for marketing problem solving; the potential of value creation embedded in the big data paradigm; and big data and

Table 5. Types of marketing data

Type of data	Description
Web analytics	· What are the prospects searching for and how does that vary based on customer segments? · What content makes customers come back again and again to the web site and convert? · Which pages of the site are most likely to attract customers? · Which pages turn them away?
Third party data	· What do the prospects and customers read? · What do customers purchase and from whom do the buy?
Intent data	· Which prospects are in the market to buy right now? · What content do customers read?
Predictive analytics	· What messages and content are likely to move customers further down the purchase cycle? · How does that vary by customer segments?
Multivariate and A/B testing data	· What are the messages, designs and offers that drive the most results?
Social media analytics	· What do customers say about the company, brands and products? · What are their concerns, likes and dislikes? · Who are the top influencers shaping opinions in the market?
Attitudinal/survey data	· How do customers feel about the products? · How likely are they to consider or purchase and which levers can better motivate them?
Best customer modeling	· Which prospects have similar characteristics as the best customers?
IP resolution data	· What companies visited the web site? · Where are the people in those companies located? · How does this stack up against the target accounts and VIP customers?
Call tracking data	· What times of the day and the week should we staff up the sales reps? · What companies called the company in the off hours but did not leave a message?
Semantic phone call analytics	· Which sales calls with prospects were missed opportunities that could have resulted in a sale?
Call centre analytics	· What is the optimal number of times a sales rep should try calling a prospect before moving on to another one?
CRM analytics	· Where exactly in the sales process are you losing prospects? · How much revenue is in the pipeline now? · Which sales reps are most successful at converting prospects into sales?
Conversations with customers	· How should the company talk to customers?

Source: Adapted from Mehl (2015)

business sustainability. This trend has created a revolution in marketing that has makes the 1960's style 4Ps increasingly obsolete (Rust, in press).

Pääkkönen & Pakkala's (2015) research involved technology independent reference architecture for big data systems, which is based on analysis of published implementation architectures of big data use cases.

An additional contribution is the classification of related implementation technologies and products/services. The reference architecture and associated classification are aimed for facilitating architecture design and selection of technologies when constructing big data systems. Jabbar et. al (2019)'s research encompasses appropriate big data sources and effective batch and real-time processing linked with structured and unstructured datasets that influence relative processing techniques. Also, along with directions for future research, they have developed interdisciplinary dialogues that overlay computer-engineering frameworks such as Apache Storm and Hadoop within B2B marketing viewpoints and their implications for contemporary marketing practices.

Although the review conducted by Amodo et. al's (2019) found that many studies have been conducted about big data and marketing, however, there is still a research gap related to big data solutions. Kumar et. al's (in press) research improves the demand-driven forecasting model to create a picture of accurate future demand prediction and calculates the diminishing returns of advertising effects. The selection of a forecasting technique among various available methods is based on accuracy, repeatability, automated and capacity to handle big data set.

Elia et. al (in press) studies the gap existing between the potential of value creation embedded in the big data paradigm. Eleven distinct value directions (market positioning, market responsiveness, customer loyalty enhancement, skill development, revenue growth, productivity gain, cost savings, decision making support, knowledge discovery, organizational benefits and IT infrastructure improvement) have been identified and then grouped in five dimensions (Informational, Transactional, Transformational, Strategic, Infrastructural Value), which constitute the pillars of the proposed framework.

Kauffmann et. al's (in press) highlighted previous studies on marketing and consumer analytics. The challenge is to transform the data and how marketers can use it to solve problems. Quach et. al's (2019) reviewed the current extent of research on marketing and consumer. The review revealed four basic components, listening to customers and the market, leveraging data for customer segmentation and profiling, co-creating value through relationship development with customers and external partners, and linking customer-oriented measures to organisation performance. France & Ghose (2019) presented a review of marketing analytics that primarily covers the topics of visualisation, segmentation and grouping, and class prediction.

To understand the business use of participatory web tools to achieve business sustainability to enable B2B organisations to become profitable, operations and marketing have been mapped against sustainability dimensions (economic, social and environmental) (Sivarajah et. al, 2019).

Galster & Avgeriou (2011) and Pääkkönen & Pakkala (2015) discussed an empirically-grounded architecture should be created based on six-step-wise approach. The procedure consists of defining a type for the reference architecture, selecting of a design strategy, empirical acquisition of data, construction of reference architecture, enabling variability, and finally evaluation of the reference architecture. Alley (2019) commented that big data architecture varies based on a company's infrastructure and needs, however it usually involves data sources, real-times message ingestion, data store, batch process and real-time processing, analytical data store, analysis tools, and automation. As discussed by Pan (2016), modern analytics need a plurality of systems, Hadoop clusters, in-memory processing systems, streaming tools, NoSQL databases, analytical appliances and operational data stores, among others. Also, four types of software products have been usually proposed for implementing the unifying component, BI tools, enterprise data warehouse federation capabilities, enterprise service buses, and data virtualisation .

BIG DATA IN MARKETING ANALYTICS

Using big data in marketing, marketers need an analytic assortment that is balanced and then to identify opportunities for improvement based on reporting or analysing the past and present big data and predicting and influencing the future (SAS, n.d).

Big data that has been processed and analysed can be used to develop a marketing plan based on six processes of using Smith's (2019) SOCTAC. It is an extension of the SWOT analysis. It is important to understand marketing and customer trends, so that marketers able to plan for marketing decision making in terms of customer engagement, personalisation, targeted dynamic advertisement activities and product life-cycle management (Svilar et. al, 2013). SOCTAC marketing model is developed by PR Smith in 1990s to help marketers develop marketing plans (Smith, 2019). Further explanation of SOCTAC can be referred to in Table 6. Furthermore, Fan et. al (2015) proposed a marketing mix framework (see Figure 1) to manage big data for marketing intelligence and provided guidelines for marketing decision-making based on big data analytics. Based on this framework, data from various sources are retrieved and utilised to generate vital marketing intelligence, analytics methods are applied to convert raw big data to actionable marketing intelligence, and finally data and methods are combined to support marketing applications.

Table 6. SOCTAC

Stage	Description	Further explanation
Stage 1: Situation analysis	Where are we now?	Performance Customer insight Market trends Competitor analysis Internal capabilities and resources
	This stage covers:	
	· Understanding of customers	How the customers interact with the brand?
	· SWOT analysis	Strengths, weaknesses, opportunities and threats to the business.
	· Competition analysis	Try to identify the competitors, observe how they act, what strategies they carry out and look at the main differences.
	· Channels landscape	The digital channels used and evaluate success of the brand.
Stage 2: Objectives	Where do we want to be?	5 Ss (sell, serve, sizzle, speak and save)
	SMART objectives	
	· Specific	The objective must be clearly defined.
	· Measurable	The objective must be measurable and quantified the benefit.
	· Actionable	The goal that we set is with our reach.
	· Relevant	Define what we are going to achieve the goal with.
	· Time-related	How long do we think it will take us to accomplish the goal?
Stage 3: Strategy	How do we get there?	STOP (Segments, target markets, objective and positioning) & SIT (Sequence, integration, and targeting and segmentation)
	It is a stage where we plan to get there in terms of fulfilling the objectives set. The strategy should identify which segments of the market we aim to target with the plan.	Strategy refers to the path you plan to follow until you achieve the established objectives. Once we have an objective and know how to get there, creating a strategy consists of drawing a road map that indicates the path we will follow.
Stage 4: Tactics	Which tactical tools do we use to implement strategy?	Marketing mix Content plan Contact plan
	Tactics cover the specific tools of marketing mix that we plan to use to realise the objectives of marketing plan.	Tactics cover the specific tools of the digital mix (examples SEO, PPC campaigns, affiliate marketing and email marketing) we plan to use to achieve the objectives of the marketing plan.

continues on following page

Table 6. Continued

Stage	Description	Further explanation
Stage 5: Action	Which action plans are required to implement strategy?	Responsibilities and structures Processes and systems Internal resources and skills External agencies
	The marketing planning is focused on how to bring the plan to life.	To bring your plan to life and take proper action based on answering 5 basic questions - who, what, where, where and how
Stage 6: Control	Did do we manage the strategy process?	Web analytics User experience review Conversion rate optimisation Frequency of reporting Process reporting and action
	The stage is to layout how we plan to monitor and measure the performance based on the objectives set at stage 2.	This phase focuses on analysis and KPIs. Indicators are usually chosen based on the type of campaign we launch and depend on the objective.
Source: Chaffey & Smith (2017), Smith (2019) and Swan (2019)		Source: Antevenio (2019)

Based on the literature review, we have proposed a big data in marketing analytics model. This proposed model can be referred to in Figure 2. The proposed model covers three main sections. The first section is about big data management. This includes sources of big data, characteristics of big data, types of big data, and finally content formats of big data. In this first section, marketers need to identify what data is best used to analyse the current trends and customers' behaviour. Section two discusses the big data architecture. The proposed architecture is adopted based on Pan's (2018) big data analytics platform. The modern analytics need a plurality of systems, which are one or several Hadoop clusters, in-memory processing systems, streaming tools, NoSQL databases, analytical appliances and operational data stores. The section three encompasses marketing analytics. The first part of this section is a further SWOT analysis. Thus, Smith's (2019) SOSTAC has been proposed to be used in this model. After SWOT analysis, marketers can use the results from marketing analytics to design marketing strategies, such as indicated by Svilar et al. (2013), customer engagement, personalisation, targeted dynamic advertisement, and product life cycle management.

CONCLUSION

Big data research is an important study because of the evolution of big data development grew rapidly in the 1970s and accelerated with the advent of web, mobile and sensor-based content in the 2000s. Based on big data in marketing analytics, marketers are able to understand marketing and customer trends, so that marketers able to plan for marketing decision making

This research literature analysis focused on an overview of big data, especially sources of big data, characteristics of big data, types of big data and content formats; big data architecture and finally big data in marketing analytics. Based on the analysis of literature reviews of these three aspects, we have proposed a big data in marketing analytics model.

Figure 1. A marketing mix framework for big data management
Source: Fan et. al (2015)

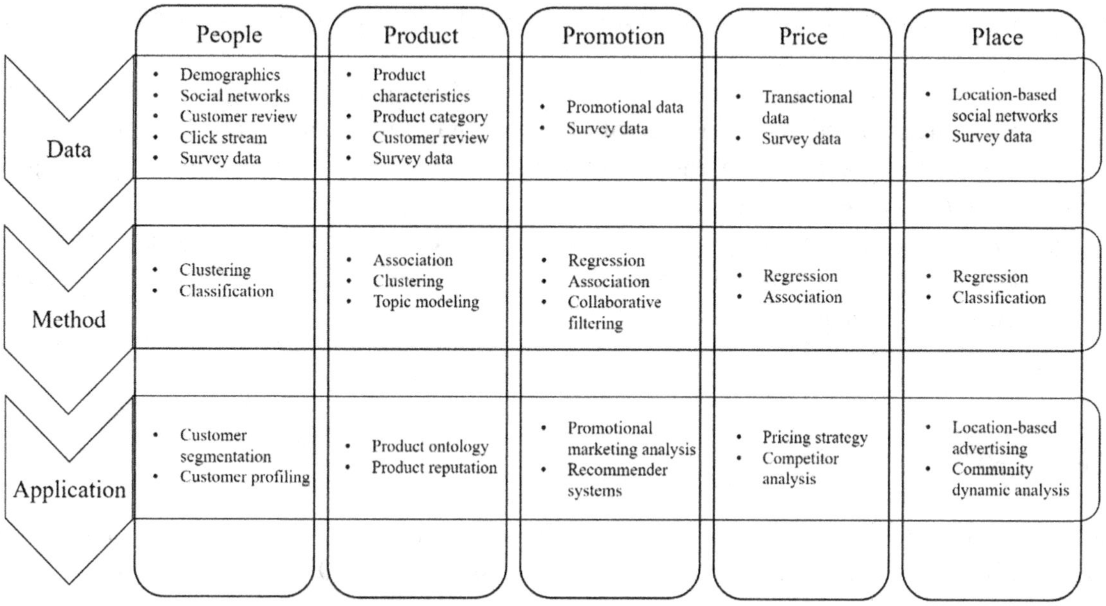

People
Product
Promotion
Price
Place
Data
Method
Application
Demographics
Social networks
Customer review
Click stream
Survey data
Product characteristics
Product category
Customer review
Survey data
Promotional data
Survey data
Transactional data
Survey data
Location-based social networks
Survey data
Clustering
Classification
Association
Clustering
Topic modeling
Regression
Association
Collaborative filtering
Regression
Association
Regression
Classification
Customer segmentation
Customer profiling
Product ontology
Product reputation
Promotional marketing analysis
Recommender systems
Pricing strategy
Competitor analysis
Location-based advertising
Community dynamic analysis

Figure 2. Marketing big data architecture

Big Data
Sources
Internal
External
Multiple formats
Multiple locations
Multiple applications
(Raghupathi and Raghupathi, 2014)
Characteristics
Volume
Velocity
Variety
Variability
Veracity
Visualisation
Value
Viscosity
Virality
Validity
Volatility
Variability
Venue
Vocabulary
Vagueness
Complexity
(SAS, n.d; Laney, 2001; Vorhies, 2013; Oguntimilehin & Ademola, 2014; Khan et. al, 2014; Borne, 2014)
Types of marketing data
Web analytics
Third party data
Intent data
Predictive analytics
Multivariate and A/B testing data
Social media analytics
Attitudinal/survey data
Best customer modelling
IP resolution data
Call tracking data
Semantic phone call analytics
Call centre analytics
CRM analytics
Conversations with customers
(Mehl, 2015)
Content formats
Structured data
Unstructured data
Semi-structured data
(Moharm, 2019)
Big Data Architecture
Sensor data
Machine data (logs)
Social data
Clickstream data
Internet data
Image and video
Enterprise content (unstructured)
Enterprise applications
Cloud applications
Sqoop
ETL
CDC
Real-time data access (On-demand/ streaming)
Tez Map Red
Hive
Spark Drill Impala
Storm
HBase
Solr Hunk
Hadoop YARN/ Workload Management
HDFS
Big data
EDW
In-memory (SAP Hana,...)
Analytical Appliances
ODS
Cloud DW (Redshift,...)
NoSQL
Data warehouse
Data search & discovery
Data federation
Data transformation
Data abstraction
Data services
Optimisation
Security
Governance
Data Caching
Data virtualisation
Real-time decision management
Alerts
Scorecards dashboards
Reporting
Data discovery self-services search
Predictive analytics
Statistical analytics
Text analytics
Data mining
(Pan, 2018)
Big Data in Marketing Analytics
SOSTAC ®
Situation analysis
Objectives
Strategy
Tactics
Actions
Control
(Smith, 2019)
From Big Data to marketing outcomes
Customer engagement
Personalisation
Targeted dynamic advertisement
Product life-cycle management
(Svilar et. al, 2013)

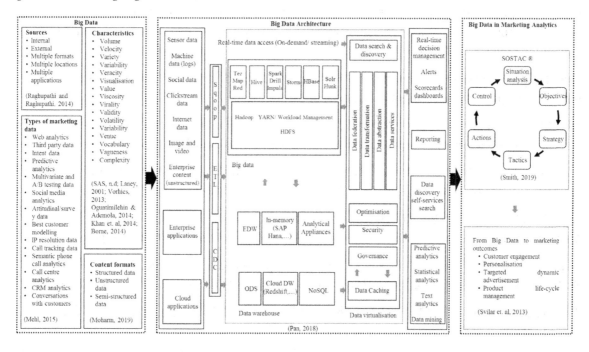

FUTURE RESEARCH DIRECTIONS

Based on the proposed model, we highlight future research directions of big data in marketing analytics.

- The use of big data enables us to predict a better decision making in marketing. It is important to identify data source that is in line with the big data in marketing analytics that can provide the most value to marketing decision-making. Future research in the area of identifying big data source needs to have a strategy
- However, as discussed by Amado et. al (2018), big data research is still in its infancy as volumes of data keep piling up. It is a very dynamic subject, implying the results presented may need updating in a narrow time window.

REFERENCES

Akoka, J., Comyn-Wattiau, I., & Laoufi, N. (2017). Research on big data – A systematic mapping study. *Computer Standards & Interfaces*, *54*(2), 105–115. doi:10.1016/j.csi.2017.01.004

Alley, G. (2019). What is big data architecture? *DZone*. Retrieved from https://dzone.com/articles/what-is-big-data-architecture

Amado, A., Cortez, P., Rita, P., & Moro, S. (2018). Research trends on Big Data in Marketing: A text mining and topic modeling based literature analysis. *European Research on Management and Business Economics*, *24*(1), 1–7. doi:10.1016/j.iedeen.2017.06.002

Baer, T. (2013). Process big data at speed. *Computer Weekly*. Retrieved from https://www.computer-weekly.com/feature/Process-big-data-at-speed

Baig, M. I., Shuib, L., & Yadegaridehkordi, E. (2019). Big data adoption: State of the art and research challenges. *Information Processing & Management*, *56*(6), 1–18. doi:10.1016/j.ipm.2019.102095

Big Data Framework. (2019). *Where does 'big data' come from?* Retrieved from https://www.bigdataframework.org/short-history-of-big-data

Borne, K. (2014). Top 10 big data challenges – A serious look at 10 big data V's. *MapR Technologies*. Retrieved from https://mapr.com/blog/top-10-big-data-challenges-serious-look-10-big-data-vs

Buneman, P. (1997, May). *Semistructured data*. Paper presented at the sixteenth ACM SIGACT-SIGMOD-SIGART symposium on Principles of database systems, Tucson, AZ. 10.1145/263661.263675

Chaffey, D., & Smith, P. R. (2017). *Digital marketing excellence - Planning, optimizing and integrating online marketing*. Routledge.

Chen, H., Chiang, R. H., & Storey, V. C. (2012). Business intelligence and analytics: From big data to big impact. *Management Information Systems Quarterly*, *36*(4), 1165–1188. doi:10.2307/41703503

Chen, Z., Zhong, F., Yuan, Y., & Hu, Y. (2016, March). *Framework of integrated big data: A review.* Paper presented at 2016 IEEE International Conference on Big Data Analysis (ICBDA), Hangzhou, China. 10.1109/ICBDA.2016.7509815

Choi, T. M., Wallace, S. W., & Wang, Y. (2018). Big data analytics in operations management. *Production and Operations Management, 27*(10), 1868–1883. doi:10.1111/poms.12838

Columbus, L. (2016). Ten ways big data is revolutionizing marketing and sales. *Forbes.* Retrieved from https://www.forbes.com/sites/louiscolumbus/2016/05/09/ten-ways-big-data-is-revolutionizing-marketing-and-sales/#629168fa21cf

Domo. (2019). *Data never sleeps 7.0.* Retrieved from https://www.domo.com/learn/data-never-sleeps-7

Doszkocs, T. E., Hill, G., Lindgren, F., Yashinsky, N., Linthicum, D. L., & Giza, M. (n.d.). *XML (Extensible Markup Language).* Retrieved from https://whatis.techtarget.com/definition/XML-Extensible-Markup-Language

Elia, G., Polimeno, G., Solazzo, G., & Passiante, G. (in press). A multi-dimension framework for value creation through big data. *Industrial Marketing Management.*

Fan, S., Lau, R. Y. K., & Zhao, J. L. (2015). Demystifying big data analytics for business intelligence through the lens of marketing mix. *Big Data Research, 2*(1), 28–32. doi:10.1016/j.bdr.2015.02.006

Fan, W., & Bifet, A. (2012). Mining big data: Current status, and forecast to the future. *SIGKDD Explorations, 14*(2), 1–5. doi:10.1145/2481244.2481246

Foote, K. D. (2017). A brief history of big data. *DATAVERSITY.* Retrieved from https://www.dataversity.net/brief-history-big-data

France, S. L., & Ghose, S. (2019). Marketing analytics: Methods, practice, implementation, and links to other fields. *Expert Systems with Applications, 119*, 456–475. doi:10.1016/j.eswa.2018.11.002

Galster, M., & Avgeriou, P. (2011, June). *Empirically-grounded reference architectures: a proposal.* Paper presented at the 7th International Conference on the Quality of Software Architectures and the 2nd International Symposium on Architecting Critical Systems, Boulder, CO.

Haire, L. (n.d.). *Customer value analysis: Definition & example.* Retrieved from https://study.com/academy/lesson/customer-value-analysis-definition-example.html

Hashem, I. A. T., Yaqoob, I., Anuar, N. B., Mokhtar, S., Gani, A., & Ullah Khan, S. (2015). The rise of "big data" on cloud computing: Review and open research issues. *Information Systems, 47*, 98–115. doi:10.1016/j.is.2014.07.006

Hubspot. (n.d.). *The ultimate list of marketing statistics for 2019.* Retrieved from https://www.hubspot.com/marketing-statistics

Ippolito, P. P. (2019). Big data analysis: Spark and Hadoop. *Medium.* Retrieved from https://towardsdatascience.com/big-data-analysis-spark-and-hadoop-a11ba591c057

Jabbar, A., Akhtar, P., & Dani, S. (2019, September). Real-time big data processing for instantaneous marketing decisions: A problematization approach. *Industrial Marketing Management*. Advance online publication. doi:10.1016/j.indmarman.2019.09.001

Kaisler, S., Armour, F., Espinosa, J. A., & Money, W. (2013, January). *Big data: Issues and challenges moving forward.* Paper presented at the 2013 46th Hawaii International Conference on System Sciences, Wailea, Maui, HI. 10.1109/HICSS.2013.645

Kauffmann, E., Peral, J., Gil, D., Ferrández, A., Sellers, R., & Mora, H. (2019, August). (in press). A framework for big data analytics in commercial social networks: A case study on sentiment analysis and fake review detection for marketing decision-making. *Industrial Marketing Management*. Advance online publication. doi:10.1016/j.indmarman.2019.08.003

Khan, M. A., Uddin, M. F., & Gupta, N. (2014, April). *Seven V's of big data understanding big data to extract value.* Paper presented at the 2014 Zone 1 Conference of the American Society for Engineering Education, Bridgeport, CT. 10.1109/ASEEZone1.2014.6820689

Kitchin, R., & McArdle, G. (2016). What makes big data, big data? Exploring the ontological characteristics of 26 datasets. *Big Data & Society*, 3(1), 1–10. doi:10.1177/2053951716631130

Kumar, A., Shankar, R., & Aljohani, N. R. (2019, June). A big data driven framework for demand-driven forecasting with effects of marketing-mix variables. *Industrial Marketing Management*. Advance online publication. doi:10.1016/j.indmarman.2019.05.003

Laney, D. (2012). Application delivery strategies. *META Group*. Retrieved from https://blogs.gartner.com/doug-laney/files/2012/01/ad949-3D-Data-Management-Controlling-Data-Volume-Velocity-and-Variety.pdf

Lozada, N., Arias-Pérez, J., & Perdomo-Charry, G. (2019). Big data analytics capability and co-innovation: An empirical study. *Heliyon*, 5(10), 1–7. doi:10.1016/j.heliyon.2019.e02541 PMID:31667393

Marr, B. (2015). A brief history of big data everyone should read. *World Economic Forum*. Retrieved from https://www.weforum.org/agenda/2015/02/a-brief-history-of-big-data-everyone-should-read

Mashey, J. R. (1999, January). *Big data and the next wave of InfraStress problems, solutions, opportunities.* Paper presented at 1999 USENIX Annual Technical Conference, Monterey, CA.

Mehl, B. (2015). 14 types of data that can boost your marketing and sales. *Boundless Markets*. Retrieved from https://boundlessmarkets.com/14-types-of-data-that-can-boost-your-marketing-and-sales

Moharm, K. (2019). State of the art in big data applications in microgrid: A review. *Advanced Engineering Informatics*, 42, 1–13. doi:10.1016/j.aei.2019.100945

Muse, D. (2017). Structured data. *Datamation*. Retrieved from https://www.datamation.com/big-data/structured-data.html

New Gen Apps. (2017). *Bringing analytics in design: 7 novel ways of using big data in fashion*. Retrieved from https://www.newgenapps.com/blog/7-ways-using-big-data-in-fashion-industry-retail-merchandising

Oguntimilehin, A., & Ademola, E. O. (2014). A review of big data management, benefits and challenges. *Journal of Emerging Trends in Computing and Information Sciences*, 5(6), 433–438.

Pääkkönen, P., & Pakkala, D. (2015). Reference architecture and classification of technologies, products and services for big data systems. *Big Data Research*, 2(4), 166–186. doi:10.1016/j.bdr.2015.01.001

Pan, A. (2016). Logical architectures for big data analytics. *Data Virtualization and Modern Data Management*. Retrieved from http://www.datavirtualizationblog.com/logical-architectures-big-data-analytics

Quach, S., Thaichon, P., Lee, J. Y., Weaven, S., & Palmatier, R. W. (2019, December). (in press). Toward a theory of outside-in marketing: Past, present, and future. *Industrial Marketing Management*. Advance online publication. doi:10.1016/j.indmarman.2019.10.016

Raghupathi, W., & Raghupathi, V. (2014). Big data analytics in healthcare: Promise and potential. *Health Information Science and Systems*, 2(3), 1–10. doi:10.1186/2047-2501-2-3 PMID:25825667

Rust, R. T. (in press). The future of marketing. *International Journal of Research in Marketing*.

Saran, J. (2018). How can big data contribute to digital marketing success? *Forbes*. Retrieved from https://www.forbes.com/sites/theyec/2018/11/08/how-can-big-data-contribute-to-digital-marketing-success/#619e7f8c1ca8

Sarjana, S., & Sarjana, S. (2013). Big data: It's not a buzzword, it's a movement. *Forbes*. Retrieved from https://www.forbes.com/sites/sanjeevsardana/2013/11/20/bigdata/#727bead81129

SAS. (n.d.). *History of big data*. Retrieved from https://www.sas.com/en_in/insights/big-data/what-is-big-data.html

Schooley, S. (2019). SWOT analysis: What it is and when to use it. *Business New Daily*. Retrieved from https://www.businessnewsdaily.com/4245-swot-analysis.html

Sint, R., Schaert, S., Stroka, S., & Ferst, R. (2009, June). *Combining unstructured, fully structured and semi-structured information in semantic wikis*. Paper presented at 4th Semantic Wiki Workshop (SemWiki 2009) at the 6th European Semantic Web Conference (ESWC 2009), Hersonissos, Greece.

Sivarajah, U., Irani, Z., Gupta, S., & Mahroof, K. (2020, April). Role of big data and social media analytics for business to business sustainability: A participatory web context. *Industrial Marketing Management*, 86, 163–179. doi:10.1016/j.indmarman.2019.04.005

Smith, P. R. (2019). *SOSTAC® Guide to your perfect digital marketing plan 2019*. PR Smith.

Svilar, M., Chakraborty, A., & Kanioura, A. (2013). Big data analytics in marketing. *ORMS-Today*, 40(5). Retrieved from https://www.informs.org/ORMS-Today/Public-Articles/October-Volume-40-Number-5/Big-data-analytics-in-marketing

Swan, S. (2019). A SOSTAC® plan example. *Smart Insights*. Retrieved from https://www.smartinsights.com/digital-marketing-strategy/sostac-plan-example

Taylor, C. (2018). Structured vs. unstructured data. *Datamation*. Retrieved from https://www.datamation.com/big-data/structured-vs-unstructured-data.html

Vorhies, B. (2013). How many "V"s in big data – The characteristics that define big data. *Data Magnum*. Retrieved from https://data-magnum.com/how-many-vs-in-big-data-the-characteristics-that-define-big-data

Wedel, M., & Kannan, P. K. (2016). Marketing analytics for data-rich environments. *Journal of Marketing*, *80*(6), 97–121. doi:10.1509/jm.15.0413

ADDITIONAL READING

Batistič, S., & Van der Laken, P. (2019). History, evolution and future of big data and analytics: A bibliometric analysis of its relationship to performance in organizations. *British Journal of Management*, *30*(2), 229–251. doi:10.1111/1467-8551.12340

Comm, C. L., & Mathaisel, D. F. X. (2018). The use of analytics to market the sustainability of "Unique" products. *Journal of Marketing Analytics*, *6*(4), 150–156. doi:10.105741270-018-0038-6

Erevelles, S., Fukawa, N., & Swayne, L. (2016). Big Data consumer analytics and the transformation of marketing. *Journal of Business Research*, *69*(2), 897–904. doi:10.1016/j.jbusres.2015.07.001

Iacobucci, D., Petrescu, M., Krishen, A., & Bendixen, M. (2019). The state of marketing analytics in research and practice. *Journal of Marketing Analytics*, *7*(3), 152–181. doi:10.105741270-019-00059-2

Isson, J. P. (2018). *Unstructured data analytics: How to improve customer acquisition, customer retention, and fraud detection and prevention*. Wiley. doi:10.1002/9781119378846

Thompson, C. J. (2019). The 'big data' myth and the pitfalls of 'thick data' opportunism: On the need for a different ontology of markets and consumption. *Journal of Marketing Management*, *35*(3/4), 207–230. doi:10.1080/0267257X.2019.1579751

Xu, Z., Frankwick, G. L., & Ramirez, E. (2016). Effects of big data analytics and traditional marketing analytics on new product success: A knowledge fusion perspective. *Journal of Business Research*, *69*(5), 1562–1566. doi:10.1016/j.jbusres.2015.10.017

KEY TERMS AND DEFINITIONS

Big Data: Big data refers to the situation when the dataset exhibits several characteristics, such as high volume, high variety, and high data processing velocity (Choi et al., 2018).

Customer Value Analytics: Customer value analysis refers to a research method that is used to identify how an organisation is perceived by consumers of an organisation and their competitors (Haire, n.d.).

Extensible Markup Language (XML): Extensible Markup Language (XML) is used to describe data. The XML standard is a flexible way to create information formats and electronically share structured data via the public Internet and corporate networks (Doszkocs et al., n.d.).

HyperText Markup Language (HTML): HyperText Markup Language (HTML) is a computer language devised to allow website creation.

Marketing Analytics: Marketing analytics involves collection, management, and analysis such as descriptive, diagnostic, predictive, and prescriptive of data to obtain insights into marketing performance, maximize the effectiveness of instruments of marketing control, and optimize firms' return on investment (Wedel & Kannan, 2016).

SWOT Analysis: SWOT analysis is a compilation of a company's strengths, weaknesses, opportunities and threats. SWOT analysis helps a company to develop a full awareness of all the factors involved in making a business decision (Schooley, 2019).

This research was previously published in the Handbook of Research on Innovation and Development of E-Commerce and E-Business in ASEAN; pages 62-78, copyright year 2021 by Business Science Reference (an imprint of IGI Global).

Chapter 67
Use of Big Data Analytics by Tax Authorities

Brendan Walker-Munro
https://orcid.org/0000-0001-5484-1145
Swinburne University, Australia

ABSTRACT

This chapter provides a thematic analysis for the Australian context of the legality and challenges to the use of big data analytics to identify risk, conduct compliance action, and make decisions within the tax administration space. Recent federal court jurisprudence and research is discussed to identify common themes (i.e., privacy/opacity, inaccuracy/bias, and fairness/due process) currently influencing the legal treatment of big data analytics within the tax administration and compliance environment in Australia.

INTRODUCTION

Computers and smart devices continue to play an increasingly significant role in our daily lives. The seamless integration of computers, smartphones, tablets and internet-enabled devices into our society has facilitated the rise of 'big data', the notion that near-infinite storage and fast computer processing has permitted the mass collection and storage of information regarding all aspects of our lives. Yet having access to enormous amounts of data is one thing; the ability to derive useful connections and observations from such data is what has fueled significant growth in another field: 'big analysis'. Also known as analytics or data profiling, the growth of Big Analysis enables analysis of massive datasets and identification of trends, issues and risks invisible to human observation (Cohen, 2012). Fertik and Thompson (2015, p. 5) explains the difference between 'big data' and 'big analysis' as "knowing that you [a]re sitting on a gold mine [and] actually getting it out of the ground and turned into bullion".

Nowhere is this concept becoming more prevalent than in the labyrinthine, complex public administration and enforcement of tax statutes. Incorporation of technology into the tax process has always been somewhat of a *fait accompli*—technological innovations in the tax system foster improved connections between the tax authority and consumers, as well as reduce the opportunity for tax evasion (Maciejewski,

DOI: 10.4018/978-1-6684-3662-2.ch067

2016). In a world where computer programs can mine personal, social, economic or law enforcement information and then use this data to make informed, evidence-based predictions on individuals' or classes of individuals' likely actions and risks (Pasquale, 2011), it is not surprising such programs are attractive to tax authorities.

The objective of this chapter is to examine the use of big data analytics by tax administrations as represented by the Australian Taxation Office (ATO) from the following thematic perspectives:

- Inaccuracy
- Privacy
- Opacity
- Due process
- Fairness/bias

These themes are considered important as they are distilled from the Administrative Review Council (ARC) 2004 report into technology-assisted decision making (TADM) (Attorney-General's Department, 2004), and synthesized with more recent observations emerging from both regulatory (OAIC, 2018b) and academic literature (Houser & Sander, 2016; Hogan-Doran, 2017; Veit, 2019). Thus, the pervasive use of information technology, data collection and storage provides substantial datasets of interest and utility to the tax authorities in protecting the public revenue. Yet these data sets are unwieldy and un-informative without powerful and speedy means by which the data can be analyzed, transformed and distilled into practical insights. The purpose of this chapter therefore is to scrutinize this tax use from the thematic perspectives of inaccuracy, privacy, opacity, due process, and fairness/bias and identify the challenges and opportunities for future use.

BACKGROUND

Since their invention, computers have been an invaluable tool for public service agencies (Savas, 1969). The ATO (like many other tax administrations) has certainly been using computers in its compliance activities since the 1970s. Though originally seen as a more powerful typewriter and then as a medium for entering and storing greater amounts of public information, growth in computing power has witnessed an increase in computer use for the purpose of decision-making, where there is a clear niche for computers to assist delegates in making the correct and preferable decision. The 2004 ARC report noted that numerous government departments of the time were already using TADM without a suitably strong oversight or review framework. To fill this void, the Department of Finance and Deregulation published a better practice guide to assist with TADM in 2007, which sought to ensure the ARC principles were implemented in a way that was practical and based on good sense (AGIMO, 2007).

But the ARC report and subsequent better practice guide highlight that TADM involves providing support and guidance to a delegate or decision-maker. Under Australian law, this follows an approach permitted by the principles set down in *Carltona Ltd v Commissioners of Works* (1943), where the English Court of Appeal determined a person in whom decision-making power is reposed has implied authority to authorize another to exercise that power on their behalf. This is especially so in government, where "ministers have so many functions and powers, administrative necessity dictates that they act through duly authorized officials" (*Carltona Ltd v Commissioners of Works*, 1943, p. 563). The computer algorithms and programs used under the auspices of TADM do not – of themselves – make decisions.

Going a step beyond TADM is where a computer program makes a decision on behalf of a human decision-maker, often without the input of a human being (what this author terms 'automated decision-making' or ADM). ADM emerged first in the marketing sector in the early 2000s in the guise of behavioral targeting – users are presented with advertisements for products or services that demonstrate linkages with a set of perceived interests based on their browser history (Brotherton, 2012). The correctness of these linkages is not checked, analyzed or validated by a human being. In 2012, the retail giant Target was criticized after its ADM programs sent coupons to women whose buying patterns suggested they might be pregnant (Hill, 2012). As business became more *au fait* with the use of big data and analytics, the financial services sector also used ADM programs to assess the creditworthiness of finance applicants. In the recent case of *ASIC v Westpac Banking Corporation* (2019), the Federal Court found that a decision made by a bank computer to either reject or accept home loan applicants based on an assessment of living expenses was not in breach of the *National Consumer Credit Protection Act 2009* (Cth).

The use of ADM in government is now commonplace. Under Australian Commonwealth law, there are 29 Acts which explicitly permit ADM. These Acts predominantly govern decisions made in relation to social security, but are also present in other Ministerial portfolios such as migration and citizenship, digital health records and customs, and biosecurity (Elvery, 2017). In these fields, specific statutory permissions often exist to allow computer programs to make delegated decisions, such as s. 6A of the *Social Security (Administration) Act 1999* (Cth):

6A Secretary may arrange for use of computer programs to make decisions

(1) The Secretary may arrange for the use, under the Secretary's control, of computer programs for any purposes for which the Secretary may make decisions under the social security law.

There are no similar provisions to s. 6A explicitly permitting ADM in any of Australia's taxation laws. This is despite the obvious benefits of using data analytics to protect the public revenue, where taxation data-matching has specific statutory and policy dynamic. Sections 6 and 7 of the *Data-matching Program (Assistance and Tax) Act 1990* (Cth) outline how the Education, Social Services, Veterans' Affairs and Human Services Departments may share information with the ATO for them to conduct data matching cycles and identify data that relates to particular individuals. At a policy level, the Australian Law Reform Commission (ALRC) noted that the former federal Privacy Commissioner described data matching as "the large-scale comparison of records or files … collected or held for different purposes, with a view to identifying matters of interest" (ALRC, 1998, para 14.94). More recently this definition has been clarified by the Office of the Australian Information Commissioner's (OAIC) 2014 guidance that data matching comprises "the bringing together of at least two data sets that contain personal information, and that come from different sources, and the comparison of those data sets with the intention of producing a match" (OAIC, 2014, Key Terms section).

In 2008, the Australian National Audit Office (ANAO) published a report on the ATO's use of data-matching which had been in place since the 1970s (ANAO, 2008). The ANAO observed that the ATO used data to help service customers and identify compliance risks and "[i]n many cases it generates automatic correspondence to tax payers. It can also bring to notice discrepancies in the information provided by taxpayers in their tax returns and authoritative relevant third-party data" (ANAO, 2008, p. 46). According to the ATO this usage has continued to today (Australian Taxation Office, 2019, p. 1):

Data helps us get things right from the start—meaning we can address issues quickly, before they escalate. It also helps us to find taxpayers who are not doing the right thing. Data-matching is a powerful administrative and law enforcement tool.

It is important to observe that this data-matching by the ATO is not strictly ADM, as there is no specific decision being made. Because of Australia's self-assessment system for taxation, taxpayers carry the onus of proving the returns they lodge with the ATO comply with the relevant laws. Therefore, data analytics can assist the Commissioner and their staff in determining how and to what extent taxpayers comply with this onus (Veit, 2019).

Unfortunately for the ATO, the Full Federal Court recently ruled that in the absence of an enabling provision like s. 6A, the general tax jurisprudence does not support ADM. In *Pintarich v Deputy Commissioner of Taxation* (2018) (Pintarich case), a 2-1 majority held that the computerized issue of a "bulk template letter" (*Pintarich v Deputy Commissioner of Taxation*, 2018, para. 18) by the ATO did not involve a decision by a delegate of the Deputy Commissioner to remit general interest charges (GIC), and so granted the appeal.

So whilst ADM is not explicitly permitted in the taxation laws, there are grounds for it to be. Though in the minority judgment, His Honor Justice Kerr stated in Pintarich that technology is rapidly changing what it means to make a decision (*Pintarich v Deputy Commissioner of Taxation*, 2018, para. 47-49):

What was once inconceivable, that a complex decision might be made without any requirement of human mental processes is, for better or worse, rapidly becoming unexceptional. Automated systems are already routinely relied upon by a number of Australian government departments for bulk decision making... This trend is not restricted to government. Automated share trading is at the heart of international commerce. Machines make contracts with machines... The legal conception of what constitutes a decision cannot be static; it must comprehend that technology has altered how decisions are in fact made and that aspects of, or the entirety of, decision making can occur independently of human mental input.

More recently Veit (2019) claimed that the use of data analytics embeds and expands existing practices in tax administration, but now staff have the capacity to utilize more data to make their decisions in a more timely and accurate manner.

The next step in computerized decision-making is the integration of a simple business rules program into a machine learning or artificial intelligence (AI) program (that is, one that can learn from its previous mistakes and adapt itself to the need to make these decisions). Under these circumstances, AI may become so advanced that the capability for such a program to make reasoned, calculated decisions based on all relevant factors may match or even exceed the decision-making capability of human beings.

Though closely allied to the process of TADM, ADM and even AI, data analytics is not the same concept and faces a slightly more nuanced series of legal challenges. Data analytics (at least for the purposes of this chapter) is the mining, research or examination of large-scale datasets to yield evidence pertaining to past, present or future behavior (Maciejewski, 2016):

1. **Historical:** Datasets are mined to examine trends and fluctuations in certain behaviors or observable characteristics over time. For example, tax administrations may examine previously lodged returns for a given taxpayer to identify anomalies in reporting (e.g., increased or decreased income) or the lodgement or claiming basis of a whole class of taxpayers (e.g., the number of particular occupations which claim certain work-related expense deductions).

2. **Real-time:** Data is examined either as it is submitted to the administration or after a short delay (which, in turn, is limited by the sophistication of the monitoring technology or process) to identify in real-time the types of behaviors or conduct of interest. For a tax administration, this can, for example, give detailed information on changes in asset ownership, share trading or preferential deals which may be relevant to declaring a particular tax position.

3. **Predictive:** Data is examined to identify and link observed characteristics to particular behaviors of interest, and make reasoned and evidence-based predictions of future behavior. In tax administrations, predictive analytics can be utilized to identify potential indicators of criminal behavior (e.g., money laundering, tax evasion, fraud or under-declaration of income), as well as allowing the deployment of proactive tools to prevent non-compliance (e.g., behavioral insight tools known as 'nudges').

Unsurprisingly, the use of computers in decision-making (including under the taxation laws) and particularly in arenas involving compliance and enforcement, has raised concerns among scholars and civil libertarians, especially given the scope of data analytics work enables tax administrations "to shift surveillance from 'targeting a specific suspect to categorical suspicion of everyone'" (Nunn, 2003, p. 457). Professor Roger Brownsword, a world-renowned expert in the field of technological regulation, explains that the concepts of choice, transparency and accountability can be undermined by the data analytics concept (Brownsword, 2004; Brownsword & Yeung, 2008; Brownsword & Harel, 2019). Therefore, data analytics can potentially be subject to the same corruption, bias, incorrectness and difficulty as many of our existing bureaucratic processes (Lepri, Staiano, Sangokoya, Letouze & Oliver, 2017).

CONCERNS ASSOCIATED WITH THE USE OF DATA ANALYTICS

Importantly, the focus of this chapter excludes certain challenges to data analytics which have been identified in the literature and appear to apply solely to the use of big data in the private sector. Some of these suggested challenges in relation to data analytics set out in academic and journalistic writings are ameliorated or even eliminated by the legal status of the tax administration as an organ of the State. For example, there is no tension in choosing between 'profit' and 'social need' as drivers for the use of 'big data' in an environment where tax administrations have no requirement to earn money for their shareholders. Because tax administrations are accountable to parliaments or congresses (and, thereby, the taxpayers themselves) and not shareholders, there is no conflict of interest between data collection and its ultimate use—the whole of society benefits when administrations reduce the number of tax cheats. Furthermore, the likely conflicts of competing interests involving fundamental human rights around privacy and interference with information are less likely to be 'ignored' by tax administrations' use of data analytics, not only because governments have a vested interest in maintaining legitimacy with their own privacy legislation, but also because the State has substantial interest in protecting the rights of those accused of crimes including those alleged to have engaged in tax evasion and fraud (Fellmeth, 2005). Instead, the five major domains of concern with big data analytics appear to come from:

- **Inaccuracy:** Analytics of large datasets is not always an indicator of future behavior.
- **Privacy:** Analytics moves tax surveillance from specific taxpayers to the systemic scrutiny of every taxpayer.
- **Opacity:** As the source code of data analytics programs is not publicly available, it is difficult to determine whether the program is operating correctly.
- **Fairness/Bias:** Corrupted, biased or incomplete data will likely produce corrupted, biased or incomplete decisions.
- **Due process:** It is difficult to challenge a tax decision where the steps in the decision (i.e., made by an analytical program) are not clear.

Inaccuracy

The first problem with big data analytics is the concept of inaccuracy. As a concept, inaccuracy has a number of definitions which are largely dependent on where the inaccuracy has arisen in the dataset to be analyzed, and whether the inaccuracy is inadvertent or deliberate. For example, the data may have been inaccurate when first recorded at its source. Government departments are not without error and tax administrations may count themselves included—it is a relatively simple mistake to add an 'e' to someone's surname where none exists, or to incorrectly record a birthdate of 1 February (1/2) as 2 January ('2/1'). Mistakes may also have been deliberately recorded at the source. Fraudulent actors in the taxation space may see great and obvious benefit in inaccurately recording their birthdate, address, income or other statistics, in turn helping to obfuscate or confuse the data-matching powers of the tax administration. Deliberate mistakes may also be engaged in by otherwise wholly law-abiding taxpayers for legitimate personal reasons. Consider the following:

- A taxpayer may post on their Facebook page a picture of a high-powered sports car with a caption implying they have just purchased it, which may be picked up by data analytics as evidence the taxpayer is living outside their means. However, the post was done only to impress their friends or perhaps as a joke.
- A taxpayer creates a webpage indicating they are operating a business and may, therefore, have undisclosed income not reported in their tax returns. However, the webpage could have been created in the name of artistic expression, satire, or could represent a moment of boredom with no real intent to follow through.
- A taxpayer changes their LinkedIn profile to state they work in a high-profile job at a law firm when, in fact, they are unemployed or drawing a pension or unemployment benefit. Whilst this may raise a red flag for a tax auditor, the taxpayer is simply trying to project a more socially acceptable digital identity.

These forms of deliberate misinformation being promulgated in open source or public websites/blogs were found in a recent survey by the Australian Communications and Media Authority (ACMA) to be undertaken by almost half of Australians as a form of "defensive inaccuracy" designed to protect a digital identity (ACMA, 2013, p. 6). Whilst these mistakes or exaggerations may seem inadvertent and minor, when looked at through the lens of mass data-matching and big data analytics it becomes feasible a taxpayer may have their own, wholly compliant records matched with that of a serial fraudster as a result of a simple mistake.

Inaccuracy may also arise in the linkage between certain observed behaviors with corresponding risk factors (that is the use of data analytics requires an inherent acceptance of causal *if-then* links between an observed behavior and a risk posed). Consider the following scene from the popular movie *Minority Report* (Twentieth Century Fox, 2002):

WITWER: *'But it's not the future if you stop it. Isn't that a fundamental paradox?'*
ANDERTON: *'Yes, it is. You're talking about predetermination, which happens all the time.'*
(Anderton rolls the ball towards Witwer who catches it just as it's about to go off the table).
ANDERTON: *'Why did you catch that?'*
WITWER: *'Because it was going to fall.'*
ANDERTON: *'You're certain?'*
WITWER: *'Yes.'*
ANDERTON: *'But it didn't fall. You caught it. The fact that you prevented it from happening doesn't change the fact that it was going to happen.'*

Therefore, a taxpayer who fails to disclose the income they earned from being an Uber or Lyft driver in their spare time must surely have decided to intentionally hide that from the tax administration (*Uber BV v Commissioner of Taxation*, 2017). Correspondingly, the taxpayer who over-claims their allowable deductions despite being warned by a computer program they were at risk of being audited justifies a higher penalty. Additionally, a taxpayer who has defaulted on three previous payment arrangements will surely default on a fourth. Unfortunately, these kinds of predictions can be wrong, irrespective of whether historical or future analytics are undertaken. The behaviors observed by the tax administration may be linked to risky behavior such as tax avoidance, but they also may not be, as current analytics programs usually take no notice of psychological motivations or narratives (Rouvroy, 2012). Analytics also requires the correct inputs be selected and validated in order to produce proper outputs, a concept widely recognized by the computer science maxim 'garbage in-garbage out'. In Australia, the ATO's focus on work-related expenses can and often do produce substantial amendments to pre-lodgement claims for work-related expenses, but require the taxpayer to select the correct occupation code, otherwise the analytics risks comparing the deductions of butchers with hairdressers, or doctors with miners (Veit, 2019).

The consequences of incorrect data matching, analytics and predictions can be catastrophic. In Australia, the social security agency, Centrelink, launched a new Online Compliance Intervention (OCI) system in 2016 to assist in recovering debts of overpaid allowances. Client data held by Centrelink payments was matched with historical tax information supplied by the ATO to identify where Centrelink clients were earning a wage whilst earning a disability or unemployment payment. In such cases, a debt was automatically raised and processed for collection via Centrelink's powers under Australia's social security laws. However, the OCI failed in a number of respects to correctly verify income with taxpayers and resulted in certain absurd circumstances such as the pursuit of debt owed by a deceased taxpayer and pursuit of debts that had been fully repaid (Commonwealth Ombudsman, 2017).

In Australia, judicial scrutiny of inaccuracy in tax analytics has been scant—the Commissioner is not required to identify how he or she came to select a taxpayer for audit (*Industrial Equity Ltd v Deputy Commissioner of Taxation*, 1990), nor are they required to give reasons for what information is selected or checked (*Federal Commissioner of Taxation v Citibank*, 1989) and they may obtain such information from any parties they see fit (*Southwestern Indemnities Ltd v Bank of New South Wales & Federal Commissioner of Taxation*, 1973). Furthermore, the Commissioner has significant evidentiary powers in proceedings, where certain documents produced under s. 350-10 of sch. 1 of the *Taxation Administration Act 1953* (Cth) are considered *prima facie* evidence that the matters are correct. Despite this, there is some obiter in *Denlay v Commissioner of Taxation* (2011), *Deputy Commissioner of Taxation v Bonaccorso* (2016) and *Deputy Commissioner of Taxation v Armstrong Scalisi Holdings Pty Ltd* (2019), where the Court accepted evidence from a taxation officer relating to the use of data analytics within the course of their normal duties which may have evidenced certain inaccuracies relevant to the course of the litigation. However, in counterpoint to these cases, in *Sgardelis and Commissioner of Taxation* (2007), the Administrative Appeals Tribunal seemed to accept that an "audit" under s. 995-1 of the *Income Tax Assessment Act 1997* (Cth) had commenced once the ATO case officer had downloaded a case from an Automated Work Allocation (AWA) system, and no further inquiry was deemed to be necessary by the learned Tribunal. Perhaps in such circumstances what is needed is an acceptance by the tax administration that observations of potential risks need to be validated through the use of different datasets, or perhaps just an acknowledgement that the findings of the algorithm are informative rather than probative.

The Honourable Justice Melissa Perry (2019, p. 4) wrote extra-judicially that we must:

Be cautious of the human tendency to trust the reliability of computers... Legal advisers and decision-makers must therefore be alert to the risk of assuming the correctness of information provided by automated processes and to take steps to ensure an understanding of the way in which such material has been produced. It may not be enough to assume that the "bottom line" is correct.

Privacy

Privacy is a substantial challenge for data analytics, where the concepts pertaining to big data already create tensions between both individual and collective privacy on the one hand, and the potential benefits to the greater good of society on the other. These tensions are important when considering individual and collective privacy can be interfered with when tax administrations are conducting big data analytics, either in a direct way (e.g., an individual's tax records being reviewed by an algorithm where no officer has formed a reasonable suspicion of wrongdoing) or in an indirect way (e.g., where the inadvertent disclosure of non-tax information, such as on social media or blogs, permits inferences to be drawn regarding taxable affairs).

Therefore, it is important to recognize privacy is a substantial concern when massive amounts of data are being collected, stored, matched and analyzed by government agencies (especially the tax administrations) in circumstances where the individual to whom that information relates may not have consented or even been aware of the information becoming available. There are also substantial protections in place relating to the privacy of tax information—in Australia, these are recognized in both the *Privacy Act 1988* (Cth) (the Privacy Act) and the *Taxation Administration Act 1953* (Cth). Similar protections exist in the US (e.g. *Internal Revenue Code of 1986* [US] §. 6103) and the United Kingdom (UK) and Europe (e.g. statutory tax acts but, more broadly, the General Data Protection Regulation 2016/679 (GPDR)).

In the European Union (EU), one of the widespread data protections enshrined in the GPDR was first enunciated by Viviane Reding, the European Commissioner for Justice, Fundamental Rights and Citizenship when she described the "right to be forgotten" (Rosen, 2012, p.89). The Commissioner described the right to be forgotten falling under circumstances where "[if] an individual no longer wants his personal data to be processed or stored by a data controller, and if there is no legitimate reason for keeping it, the data should be removed from their system" (Rosen, 2012, p. 89). In the literature, Commissioner Reding's sentiments are reflected in the academic commentary that establishes generally accepted requirements for information collection and privacy involve notice and consent—that is, the individual must be aware their information is being collected and the purpose/s for collection, and be given the opportunity to consent or refuse consent for those purposes (Cate & Mayer-Schonberger, 2013; Solove, 2013).

Both of these concepts (the right to be forgotten and the awareness/consent paradigm) have relevance to Australia because of the "growing power asymmetries between institutions that accumulate data, and the individuals who generate it" (Campolo, Sanfilippo, Whittaker & Crawford, 2017, p. 28). The OAIC has clearly recognized this connection, having made several submissions to government and regulatory discussion papers which call for recognition of the EU's approach to the right to be forgotten in the age of data analytics (OAIC, 2019a; OAIC, 2019b). The right to be forgotten and awareness/consent also speak directly to obligations imposed on entities under Australia's privacy framework, which at a Commonwealth level is regulated by the Privacy Act containing the Australian Privacy Principles (APP). Compliance with the Privacy Act is overseen by the OAIC. Each of the States and Territories handles the protection of personal information in different ways which creates a somewhat difficult patchwork of laws to navigate.

Under s.6 of the Privacy Act, personal information is defined as:

information or an opinion about an identified individual, or an individual who is reasonably identifiable (a) whether the information or opinion is true or not; and (b) whether the information or opinion is recorded in a material form or not.

Entities covered by the Act (including Commonwealth agencies and organizations) must comply with the APPs, including APP1 (open and transparent management of personal information), APP5 (notification of the collection of personal information) and APP6 (use or disclosure of personal information). Generally, small businesses with an annual turnover of less than $3 million are exempt for the Act. These obligations impose a number of obligations in a tax environment generally discharged by obtaining consent from taxpayers during lodgment or physical interaction, having open and public data handling and processing procedures, and allowing human intervention to correct errors (whether taxpayer-initiated or audit-initiated).

However, consent can be a nebulous or even moot issue when it comes to the administration of public revenue due in many instances to tax administrations having lawful rights to access the information they do. Under Australian law, the Commissioner of Taxation is permitted full and free access to any documents and places for the purposes of the taxation laws (*Taxation Administration Act 1953* (Cth), div. 353, sch. 1), and similar sweeping access provisions exist in other common law jurisdictions (e.g., §. 7602 of the *Internal Revenue Code* (US) or the HMRC's automatic exchange of information agreements).

From a taxation perspective at least, there is a presumption for taxation administrations to have access to the information they need to protect the public revenue (see *Bloemen v Commissioner of Taxation*, 1980; *Deputy Commissioner of Taxation v Richard Walter Pty Ltd*, 1994; *Commissioner of Taxation v Futuris Corporation Ltd*, 2008). This has been reflected in common law in cases such as *Commissioner of Taxation v Warner* (2015), where the statutory duty of a liquidator to keep records confidential unless ordered by the Court is overridden by the Commissioner's right to free and full access to documents.

In the US, third-party sellers such as eBay and PayPal have been ordered to turn over records of sales to catch taxpayers out in under-declaring their income (*Orellana v Commissioner*, 2010; *U.S. v Wilson*, 2014). In the UK, a proposal is currently underway to consider whether to remove requirements for approval by the First-tier Tribunal (Tax Chamber) before Her Majesty's Revenue and Customs (HMRC) can issue compulsory information-gathering notices to financial institutions (HMRC, 2015; Register & Adams, 2017). In *Deputy Commissioner of Taxation v Zeqaj* (2019), the Victorian Supreme Court rejected allegations that the Commissioner had improperly violated the appellant's privacy by seeking, and subsequently using, information from Victorian Police regarding his alleged involvement in the cultivation of cannabis. Finally, and most recently, in *Glencore International AG & Ors v Commissioner of Taxation of the Commonwealth of Australia & Ors* (2019), the High Court established the Commissioner may, in the course of his or her duties of assessing the taxation liabilities of any person, use whatever material which happens to come to the ATO or be in the public domain, including material which may have been gathered illegally or subject to legal professional privilege.

There may be valid reasons for privacy considerations being waived or ignored in a number of contexts in the taxation administration. First, the mere knowledge of scrutiny can be sufficient to change behavior. If a person is notified or informed they are being investigated, this may be enough to cause them to shift their behavior—particularly the case for serious offences involving theft, money laundering, tax evasion or fraud. This type of behavior was clearly contemplated by Zarsky (2013, p. 1555) when he stated that, "with full transparency [of analytics], monitored individuals will sidestep proxies even while still engaging in risk-generating behavior". This perhaps stands as an answer to why certain approaches, such as the release of certain source codes of analytical programs to public websites under a black box tinkering model, are considered to be inappropriate in ensuring transparency of state-sanctioned data analytics (Perel & Elkin-Koren, 2017).

Even where we have given consent to the collection, use or disclosure of our personal information, there are still circumstances where we remain blind to the effect of inadvertent disclosures and the effects on our privacy. For example, when we sign up for rewards programs in retail stores, we agree to marketing agencies potentially selling our data; we eSign collection statements on websites without reading them; and we agree that our phones can store our passwords in keychains or virtual lockers (van Dijsck, 2014). Zuboff (2015, p. 75) called this phenomenon "surveillance capitalism", the idea that we appear more than happy to trade our individual privacy for monetary gain, non-financial rewards or some other kind of convenience. There is no strict legislative barrier preventing a tax administration, either under a statutory information-gathering power or by purchasing the dataset on the open market, from obtaining this information for tax administration purposes. On this point, Professor Karen Yeung (2016, p. 56) was acerbic in her comments when she stated that "we suspend our privacy rights in return for new technology built with our data and the convenience and efficiency that they offer".

Privacy considerations also come to the fore in circumstances where tax administrations overstep their bounds in relation to compliance or audit activity—often taxpayer sentiment is quick to question whether a tax administration that does not have its own house in order should have the right to access such confidential information. Whilst, thankfully, these instances are relatively few in number, they go a long way in undermining the legitimacy of administrations and the credibility to engage in what may otherwise be lawful compliance activity. Globally, Houser and Sanders (2016) detail the politicization of the Internal Revenue Service (IRS) audit by previous Presidential administrations, and Freedman and Vella (2011) discuss the common law treatment of the HMRC where auditors have acted contrary to the principles of good administrative decision-making and either acted *ultra vires* or contravened a legitimate expectation. Thankfully, Australia's experience with similar instances appears brief. A recent review by the Inspector-General of Taxation (IGT) was conducted into the ATO's use of garnishee notices, a powerful debt recovery tool forcing entities that may owe a taxpayer money to pay those funds to the Commissioner instead, and is usually used to "dock" earnings of taxpayers who do not meet their debt obligations and have the capacity to repay them (Inspector-General of Taxation, 2019b). Whilst found no misconduct by the ATO was found, the IGT nevertheless concluded there were several improvements that could be made to the ATO's garnishee and debt recovery program.

The privacy landscape also changes if the shift in data analytics pushes tax assessments towards source-based rather than taxpayer-based assessments of income. Where the tax administration can obtain information on matters such as wages, contractor payments, deductions, sales taxes and other financial data directly from retailers or employers (Ibrahim & Pope, 2011), this reduces the need to directly obtain information from the taxpayer. Income can be verified with the entity that pays it, rather than requiring the taxpayer to prove the income and calculating revenue on that basis. In the UK, the HMRC is already transitioning to a fully pre-filled system of data analytics and employer-obligation reporting which would see individual taxpayers not needing to lodge a tax return—they would simply receive a notice of assessment indicating whether a debt or refund has been raised. Under these circumstances, tax administrations are relying on third-party information which may have been gathered without the taxpayer's notice or consent. This raises potential concerns regarding the disclosure obligations of third-parties of that information, but also whether the taxpayer has a right to provide information that may change their tax assessment prior to such a determination being made.

Privacy will likely remain a key consideration for tax administrations well into the future. However, the individual rights of privacy appear largely undisturbed by big data analytics, where it seems to have effected a change more in form than in substance. Privacy regulators may have concerns with the expansion of programs into areas of data being used for taxation purposes (OVIC, 2018; OAIC, 2018a; OAIC, 2018b; OAIC, 2019c; OAIC, 2019d), but it appears on evidence that these actions are consistent with the ATO's broader statutory mandates to protect public revenue. Even in circumstances where the Commissioner or his or her delegates are engaging in a fishing expedition and hoping to catch an errant taxpayer, there are grounds to consider the collection of such personal information for assessing a tax liability is within the scope of legal authority.

Opacity

Opacity is an interlinked, but distinct, concept from privacy and covers the "black box" nature of analytics programs (Pasquale, 2016). For example, opacity occurs when we cannot answer questions such as how do tax administrations' analytics programs reach the conclusions they do? How do these programs weigh or assess the data they are fed? What things/situations/facts do they consider more relevant than others? Opacity, therefore, is a term with two potential meanings, as follows:

- *Opacity-by-understanding*. This concept describes opacity relating to the technical know-how needed to read computer code and data science, to interpret what the code does and how it works.
- *Opacity-at-law*. This form of opacity creates a blanket of secrecy over the data analytics program, either by reference to the tax information the program deals with or the analytics program code itself (opacity-by-law).

Opacity-by-understanding hinges on the basis of a technical argument—that is, the skills to decipher complex coding languages are highly complex, and even the creators of algorithms can struggle to define how they work (Burrell, 2015). However, this concern is somewhat temporal in nature. Whilst the skills of computer coding and data science are currently specialized, society is very quickly reacting to data analytics, algorithms and even AI, to the extent these skills are considered highly desirable by modern business recruiters and computer coding is now a common inclusion in most school curricula. There is also evidence to suggest opacity-by-understanding is limited only by the willingness of the party examining the analytics program. In 2019, investigative journalists successfully reversed-engineered a Chinese Government algorithm, proving it racially segregated the minority Uighur population for targeting by police and national security officers (Human Rights Watch, 2019). Opacity-by-understanding also has limited application to machine learning and AI programs, where even understanding of the algorithm itself will not necessarily demonstrate what it has learned and how it applies the requisite business rules to making decisions (Desai & Kroll, 2017). This is widely known in the computing community as the "interpretability problem", and requires that humans adopt alternative approaches more akin to psychology in dealing with machine learning or AI programs (Anannay & Crawford, 2018, p. 4).

Opacity-by-understanding also has the potential to exacerbate or contribute to substantial information asymmetries between governments and taxpayers. In the EU, the GPDR includes a somewhat limited right of explanation, under which an affected individual can seek explanations from governments as to how a computer program made decisions using their personal data and covers any entity that "controls" or "processes" personal data (GPDR, art. 4, 12 and 22). However, there is a growing concept in the academic and computing literature for explainability (Pasquale, 2017), where a black box algorithm becomes a "white box" and allows "people [to] scrutinise and understand how the algorithms make decisions, and judge the algorithms that judge us" (Loke, 2019, pp. 25). Explainability builds on the explicit or implicit requirements for entities conducting data analytics to provide reasoning for their decisions when those decisions are based on analytics, such as under the GPDR (Casey, Farhangi & Vogl, 2019).

Whilst Australia lacks a similar provision, there remains a requirement (and avenue of remedy) under the *Administrative Decisions (Judicial Review) Act 1977* (Cth) for aggrieved persons to seek the reasons for why a particular decision is made, including those made by a computer (*Re Minister for Immigration and Multicultural Affairs; Ex parte Palme*, 2003). There may also be valid reasons for information asymmetries between the regulator and regulated. Most regulators (including tax administrations) strive for more information than their subjects or targets, making their decisions more effective and better tailored to the regulated environment. In some cases, it can also enable covert assessments or activities which may catch offending red-handed (Lim, Hagendorff, & Armitage, 2016; Loftus, 2019).

On the other hand, opacity-by-law creates circumstances of secrecy or confidentiality around the workings of a data analytics program, and is often cited in the literature as a foreign entity to the principles of transparency, open government, and accountability (e.g., see the various works by Professor Brownsword referenced in this chapter). Opacity-by-law has an even greater scope of application in the taxation spaces due to the highly sensitive nature of taxpayer information such administrations deal with. Sandvig (2014, p. 9) and Burrell (2015, p. 4) describe a "right to look" as a claim by right of consumers to see and understand how algorithms used by private enterprise receive, sort, assess and rank data to ensure the results are not being unfairly skewed by players in given markets.

In the Australian tax administration space, there are strong provisions regarding the disclosure of information related to the tax affairs of an individual, which is generally considered as protected information (see *Taxation Administration Act 1953* (Cth), subdiv. 355-B, sch. 1). However, the source code for a data analytics tool which simply reads or analyses this protected information and produces an output may not necessarily be protected in and of itself. Yet other agencies have had some judicial consideration of their own approach to data analytics and the use of algorithms. In *Cordover v Australian Electoral Commission* (2015), the Administrative Appeals Tribunal determined the Australian Electoral Commission (AEC) was correct in its decision not to hand over the source code for vote-counting software known as 'Easycount'. The Tribunal accepted the grounds that the software was a "trade secret", that is it met the terms under *Searle Australia v PIAC* (1992) of having commercial value and steps being taken to limit or control its dissemination and also having commercial value that would be destroyed if disclosed.

However, the aforementioned 'right to look' is not as relevant in a tax administration context. There are valid reasons why data analytics and algorithms assessing various forms of taxpayer behavior should remain hidden (or, at least, the nature of the algorithm's internal workings). As described earlier, when taxpayers are aware of the 'red flags' their behavior can trigger with tax administrations, they are more likely to modify their behaviors to avoid detection. It would also be hard to argue a person or class of people suspected of being involved in a criminal enterprise has a 'right to look' at the algorithms which may detect them. Assume for a moment the ATO builds an algorithm to analyze a series of inputs (e.g., banking information, travel documents, social media posts) and provides a single output—that is, an individual's risk score of engaging in tax evasion. If the precise nature of the inputs was made public, it would be possible to game the algorithm by tailoring behavior to avoid detection via those inputs. Yet, in this circumstance, the penalty is not defaulting on a loan but a substantial risk to the public revenue. There are also certain classes of criminal investigation that occur in the taxation world which are only possible under a blanket of secrecy, cast either by the tax statutes themselves or associated legislation relating to terrorism, money laundering, serious organized crime or national security (e.g., the ATO's experience in Project Wickenby; see also Numerato, 2016; Baldwin & Gadboys, 2016). These tensions between an open society and secret government have always involved the balance between rights of citizens engaging in lawful activity and "foreign spies, terrorists and criminals when they pry, plot and steal" (Moore & Rid, 2016, p. 9).

However, the purpose of this chapter is not to argue that data analytics should be shrouded in absolute secrecy. Instead, what is necessary is a careful reframing of our arguments around secrecy. One option is to utilize open-source software as the algorithmic base, but then to vary the inputs to information only available to law enforcement. The actual work being undertaken by the algorithm in terms of ranking and sorting can easily be understood, but the dataset on which the algorithm runs remains (rightfully) secret. Buiten (2019) proposes perhaps a more useful version of transparency, one that considers transparency on the inputs (what data is fed to the algorithm), transparency of the decision-making process and transparency of the outcomes (where counterfactuals, being the measurement of different outcomes based on a single variable input, become relevant in assessing accuracy). Another option would be the establishment of an effective governance-within-governance framework, such as oversight by an ombudsman-style body or review by a judge. This type of overview is already contemplated in the Australian context, including the IGT established under the *Inspector-General of Taxation Act 2003* (Cth), the Commonwealth Ombudsman established by the *Ombudsman Act 1976* (Cth), as well as Parliamentary scrutiny via the House of Representatives Standing Committee on Tax and Revenue and the Senate Standing Committee on Economics. In this manner, the secrecy of an algorithm could remain protected whilst providing opportunities for independent review, investigation and amendment.

Bias

The use of analytics can also suffer from bias. Although analytical programs as computer constructs are inherently bias-neutral, they also currently lack the relative insight of an objective human decision-maker who may take into account certain matters not easily interpreted by data. Barocas and Selbst explain that, depending on where in the decision-making process a term of bias arises, data analytics create the potential for a "disproportionately adverse impact on protected classes" (2016, p. 5). In taxation administration, these can be substantially problematic, especially when data analytics may be used for assessments of qualitative rather than quantitative matters. For example, how does an analytical program determine if someone is "fit and proper" in the terms used in s. 126A(3) of the *Superannuation Industry (Supervision) Act 1993* (Cth) (SISA)? Though there are pathways for disqualification for contraventions of the SISA, subs. 126A(3) permits that "the Regulator may disqualify an individual if satisfied that the individual is otherwise not a fit and proper person". How does the analytics program properly evaluate qualitative matters for honesty, knowledge and ability as set out in Australia's seminal cases of *Hughes and Vale Pty Ltd v State of New South Wales* (1955) and *Australian Broadcasting Tribunal v Bond & Ors* (1990)?

Assuming it can do so, how do analytics weigh honesty, knowledge and ability against other matters which may count against them? Indeed, the Courts have stipulated that for such matters there is no "neat arithmetical algorithm or a guide which is able to be used mechanically" (*Australian Securities & Investments Commission v Lindberg*, 2012, para. 89).

Data analytics can therefore be biased on a number of different counts. First, the data being used for analysis may have been deliberately or inadvertently swayed due to pre-existing bias in the data collection. The deployment of predictive policing analytics in the US has been marred in several states by predilections of over-representation of risk scores for African-American and Latino communities (Ferguson, 2017). Data analytics based on policing data may be drawing correlations based on arrests made as far back as the 1950s, a time in which racial profiling and segregation by police was a common sight. Chiao (2019, p. 129) describes this effect as follows: "where upstream decisions exert significant influence over downstream ones, if for no other reason than that they determine the profile of the population over which downstream decisions operate". For gang membership, persons of color inevitably associate with other race-similar groups, feeding "associational suspicion" amongst minority members of the target population. Geographically-oriented analytics programs used by police have also associated high crime risks with poor socio-economic neighborhoods which disproportionately feature these same African-American and Latino communities, leading to increased policing scrutiny (and, of course, more policing data, reinforcing the vicious cycle; Ferguson, 2017). In tax administration, certain classes of individuals may be targeted for audit either deliberately or inadvertently on the basis of certain misconceptions regarding how their wealth may have been accrued or how those classes respond to taxation audits (Sharkey & Murray, 2016; Henricks & Seamster, 2017). As outlined earlier, the IGT review into the ATO's use of garnishee notices found a number of small businesses were disproportionately targeted for the issue of enduring garnishee notices, resulting in the IGT making recommendations regarding the way the ATO analytics selected taxpayers for the issue of enduring garnishee notices (Inspector-General of Taxation, 2019a).

The data itself may also be the source of bias, where the data may have been preferentially selected, collected, entered or transformed prior to analysis. For example, if tax auditors over-select their targets from 'working professionals' and achieve a 100 per cent strike rate for over claiming a certain deduction, this may permit the inference that all working professionals are over claiming (even though there is actually no correlation between those two characteristics). If the datasets used are not sufficient, complete or lack cohesive detail, the analytics program may be selecting characteristics that have no bearing on the behavior sought to be regulated. This can result when the datasets reflect existing social biases (e.g., a data analytics program which selects on wages earned will preferentially select men, because women earning high wages are underrepresented in the target population). Where a test environment is used to train a data analytics program (e.g., an algorithm or machine learning system) which is not representative of the wider society, the selection will necessarily be biased. In a recent study, an algorithm was built to distinguish huskies from wolves and worked perfectly under laboratory settings but failed to work in field tests (Ribeiro, Singh, & Guestrin, 2016). After further work it was found the algorithm, which had been trained on photographs of wolves and huskies, was selecting on the presence or absence of snow in the backgrounds. In tax administration, there is a body of work showing young taxpayers between the ages of 18 to 30 are disproportionately represented in tax audits due to their *laissez faire* attitudes to tax obligations and reporting requirements (see an excellent example in Braithwaite, Reinhart, & Smart, 2010).

The linkages between entities (particularly in the context of tax administration) may also be of questionable veracity. Associational analytics can be used to identify co-actors in complex networks of interrelationship; yet, when these types of associational analytics are used in practice—such as by police to identify gang membership—they inevitably tar innocent individuals with the same brush based on loose connection. US police in the cities of New Orleans, Kansas City, Chicago and New York City used similar programs to identify people they believed were involved in gang violence or gun crime, and implemented risk treatment strategies for those with top scores according to their risk models, even if these persons had never been the subject of police attention previously (Ferguson, 2017). Where associational analytics is used in tax administrations, such as in analyzing the relationship between egregious taxpayers and tax advisors or agents who offer them advice on how to avoid or evade their lawful obligations, innocent taxpayers who also use that advisor or agent may be caught up by the audit or enforcement activity. In much the same way, credit card companies have been known to limit or downgrade the credit scores of individuals on the basis they visited the same establishments as others who demonstrated a poor repayment history (Lepri et al., 2017).

The questions on how analytics might respond to biased data requires a nuanced response. The first step is to recognize that analytics programs, at least at the level currently utilized, should be considered indicative and not probative without further review. A set of human eyes is always important in validating whether the selections of the dataset are achieving the aims for which the analytics program was initially established. Second, where data analytics programs show a tendency towards bias or unfair weightings, this must be incorporated into feedback structures to foster continuous improvement of the selection models. Third, data analytics based on associational dynamics between individuals should be carefully managed to ensure that racial, social or sexual biases do not arise inadvertently. Finally, analytics programs can be designed (particularly in a tax administration context) to utilize multiple decision trees to identify and minimize the occurrence of bias.

Fairness and Due Process

Where decisions are made by computer programs—even relatively simple decisions such as which taxpayers to audit, or which taxpayer debts may be more easily recovered—and the source code of the data analytics is not publicly available, it can be difficult to challenge how that decision was made in a court or tribunal. Fairness and due process challenges in analytics can present in two interesting scenarios:

(1) an algorithm is not as objective as a human being; and (2) an algorithm is diametrically opposed where analytics are *too* objective, and interprets the data with no interpretation of the subjective 'vibe' of the matter.

Legally, the protections for fairness and due process in data analytics are difficult to articulate. Generally, there is a long line of authority dictating administrative decision-makers must afford "procedural fairness" to those whose interests are or may be affected by their decisions (see *X v The Minister for Immigration & Multicultural Affairs*, 1999, para. 92). However, from a tax perspective, where analytics may have been used to find a tax liability, there appears little ground for legal challenge to the tools employed. Rather, the focus is usually on the basis of the Commissioner's assessment and there remains an equally long line of clear authority for the proposition that recovery of tax owed is preferable to considering a taxpayer's challenge to the Commissioner's assessment (see *Deputy Commissioner of Taxation v Mackey*, 1982; *Uratoriu v Commissioner of Taxation*, 2008; *Queensland Maintenance Services Pty Ltd v Commissioner of Taxation*, 2011; *Rossi v Commissioner of Taxation*, 2015). It is worth noting that an element of caution is necessary. For example, as the Full Federal Court decided in the Pintarich case that a decision by computer lacked "both a mental process of reaching a conclusion and an objective manifestation of that conclusion" (*Pintarich v Deputy Commissioner of Taxation*, 2018, [140]), there is no confidence that Australian jurists would be willing to entertain data analytics decisions without a decision from a superior court.

Fairness is also a double-sided concept, as binding on the Commissioner as on the taxpayer. In circumstances where the tax authority has access to much greater, more accurate and more real-time reporting of data from taxpayers and third parties, the window for error is reduced. Taxpayers will (quite understandably) be more likely to hold tax administrations to account if their information is wrong or outdated, and trust in the ATO will be eroded as taxpayers' dispute more and more of their individual assessments. Given the extensive use by the ATO for data analytics for debt, lodgement, refunds, compliance activities and future strategic planning of tax policy, there is an equally binding obligation on the ATO to use this information fairly, honestly and as transparently as the legislation permits. Should the ATO (or any other tax administration) seek to move to fully automated tax reporting and completely remove the need for an individual or small business taxpayer to lodge a return by pre-filling and by third-party data validation, this would be a considerable savings initiative and reduce a substantial amount of regulatory burden. However, there are a number of downstream effects on professional advisors to give tailored and specific advice, as well as on the ATO to ensure it continued its focus on taxpayer assistance rather than taxpayer deterrence such that fairness under tax algorithms is "a right they will pursue in Australia, to ensure global competitive equality" (Bentley, 2019, p. 712).

The additional challenges to analytics in tax regulation and enforcement involving issues of wrong or unfair decisions could also be ameliorated by the adoption of constant feedback and self-orientation. Zweig, Wenzelburer & Krafft (2018) describe a need for algorithms in use in national security environments to be embedded in social oversight (either by systems internal to the security organization, or externally as a community ombudsman or other surveillant organization) as a way of ensuring quality decision-making and eliminating racial and ethnic bias. The constant feedback and repositioning required in a systemic design framework would inevitably need this degree of algorithmic tweaking to ensure ongoing accuracy and viability. Zweig et al. (2018) also describe a need for effective counterfactuals and being transparent about where algorithms or analytics feed predictions into decision-making.

CONCLUSION

The prospect of data analytics, particularly in the arena of tax administration, is an exciting development in the fields of data science and governmental regulation. In Australia, where tax liability is determined and pursued by the Commissioner of Taxation and the ATO, data analytics has enabled taxation officers to make decisions with better access to evidence and more processing power to make the correct calculations of tax liability. However, the use of powerful analytical programs to mine the gems out of 'big data' raises a series of interrelated and complex concerns relating to privacy, opacity, inaccuracy, fairness, bias and due process which apply to individuals as well as whole classes of taxpayers across entire segments of society. Additionally, the tax policy and regulatory environment is changing every day and requires adaptation of data analytics programs to both support the Commissioner's statutory objectives and align with contemporary societal values.

On individual cases, there is a danger to accept that a computer program will detect more than the human eye, a danger that will only increase as we develop ever more sophisticated models of analytics which blur the line between algorithms, machine learning and full AI. This danger extends well into the hazards of our own ignorance, engendered by a reliance on machines to do the work for us where law or policy does not clearly delineate where a machine may make a decision and where it cannot, or at what point in an automated decision-making tree a human should intervene to respond. Therefore, data analytics in tax administrations offer significant promise, as long as we respect that decision-making occurs "under condition of paying adequate respect to human rights, offering choice, providing for transparency, and adhering to accountability" (Leenes, 2011, p. 159).

Yet for all the risks, there are substantial benefits to be had. The use of data analytics, machine learning and AI will likely only increase in the future. Therefore, the potential issues regarding privacy, opacity, inaccuracy, fairness, bias and due process need to be duly considered when systems are designed to take advantage of our technological strength. Privacy can live side-by-side with compulsive investigation; opacity can exist with qualification; and, inaccuracy, fairness and bias can be appropriately managed and treated with proper respect for the checks and balances of the legal system, parliamentary debate and adherence to the commonality of human rights.

REFERENCES

Administrative Decisions (Judicial Review) Act 1977 (Cth).

Anannay, M., & Crawford, K. (2018). Seeing without knowing: Limitations of the transparency ideal and its application to algorithmic accountability. *New Media & Society, 20*(3), 981. doi:10.1177/1461444816676645

ASIC v Westpac Banking Corporation [2019] FCA 1244.

Attorney-General's Department. (2004). *Automated assistance in administrative decision making*. Canberra: Administrative Review Council.

Australian Broadcasting Tribunal v Bond & Ors (1990) 170 CLR 321.

Australian Communications & Media Authority (ACMA). (2013). *Managing your digital identity: Digital footprints and identities research short report*. Canberra, Australia: Commonwealth Government Printer. Retrieved from https://apo.org.au/node/36376

Australian Government Information Management Office (AGIMO). (2007). *Automated assistance in administrative decision-making: Better practice guide*. Canberra, Australia: Department of Finance and Deregulation.

Australian Law Reform Commission (ALRC). (1998). *Secrecy & open government in Australia* (Report 112). Retrieved from https://www.alrc.gov.au/publication/secrecy-laws-and-open-government-in-australia-alrc-report-112/14-frameworks-for-effective-information-handling/data-matching/

Australian National Audit Office (ANAO). (2008). *The Australian taxation office's use of data matching and analytics in tax administration*. Retrieved from https://www.anao.gov.au/work/performance-audit/australian-taxation-offices-use-data-matching-and-analytics-tax

Australian Securities & Investments Commission v Lindberg [2012] VSC 332.

Australian Taxation Office. (2019). *Australian tax gaps - an overview*. Retrieved from https://www.ato.gov.au/About-ATO/Research-and-statistics/In-detail/Tax-gap/Australian-tax-gaps-overview/?page=1#Tax_gap_research_program

Baldwin, F., & Gadboys, J. (2016). The duty of financial institutions to investigate and report suspicions of Fraud, financial crime, and corruption. In M. Dion, D. Weisstub, & J.-L. Richet (Eds.), Financial crimes: Psychological, technological, and ethical Issues (pp. 83-104). Cham, Switzerland: Springer. doi:10.1007/978-3-319-32419-7_4

Barocas, S., & Selbst, A. (2016). Big data's disparate impact. *California Law Review, 104*(3), 671–732.

Bentley, D. (2019). Timeless principles of taxpayer protection: how they adapt to digital disruption. *eJournal of Tax Research, 16*(3), 679-713.

Bloemen v Commissioner of Taxation (1980) 147 CLR 360.

Braithwaite, V., Reinhart, M., & Smart, M. (2010). Tax non-compliance among the under-30s: Knowledge, obligation or scepticism? In J. Alm, J. Martinez-Vazquez, & B. Torgler (Eds.), *Developing alternative frameworks for explaining tax compliance*. London, UK: Routledge.

Brotherton, E. A. (2012). Big brother gets a makeover: Behavioural targeting and the third-party doctrine. *Emory Law Journal, 61*(3), 555–558.

Brownsword, R. (2004). What the world needs now: Techno-regulation, human rights and human dignity. In R. Brownsword (Ed.), Global governance and the quest for justice: Volume 4 human rights (pp. 203-234). Oxford, UK: Hart Publishing.

Brownsword, R., & Harel, A. (2019). Law, liberty and technology: Criminal justice in the context of smart machines. *International Journal of Law in Context, 15*(2), 107–125. doi:10.1017/S1744552319000065

Brownsword, R., & Yeung, K. (2008). *Regulating technologies: Legal futures, regulatory frames and technological fixes*. Oxford, UK: Hart Publishing.

Buiten, M. (2019). Towards Intelligent Regulation of Artificial Intelligence. *European Journal of Risk Regulation*, *10*(1), 41–59. doi:10.1017/err.2019.8

Burrell, J. (2015, Jan.). How the machine "thinks": Understanding opacity in machine learning algorithms. *Big Data & Society*, 1–12. doi:10.2139srn.2660674

Campolo, A., Sanfilippo, M., Whittaker, M., & Crawford, K. (2017). *AI now 2017*. Retrieved from https://ainowinstitute.org/AI_Now_2017_Report.pdf

Carltona Ltd v Commissioners of Works [1943] 2 All ER 560.

Casey, B., Farhangi, A., & Vogl, R. (2019). Rethinking explainable machines: The GDPR's right to explanation debate and the rise of algorithmic audits in enterprise. *Berkeley Technology Law Journal*, *34*(1), 143–188.

Cate, F., & Mayer-Schonberger, V. (2013). Notice and consent in a world of big data. *International Data Privacy*, *3*(2), 67–73. doi:10.1093/idpl/ipt005

Chiao, V. (2019). Fairness, accountability and transparency: Notes on algorithmic decision-making in criminal justice. *International Journal of Law in Context*, *15*(2), 126–139. doi:10.1017/S1744552319000077

Cohen, J. E. (2012). *Configuring the Networked Self*. New Haven, CT: Yale University.

Commissioner of Taxation v Futuris Corporation Ltd (2008) 237 CLR 146.

Commissioner of Taxation v Warner (2015) FCA 659.

Commonwealth Ombudsman. (2017). *Centrelink's automated debt raising and recovery system*. Retrieved from https://www.ombudsman.gov.au/__data/assets/pdf_file/0022/43528/Report-Centrelinks-automated-debt-raising-and-recovery-system-April-2017.pdf

Cordover v Australian Electoral Commission (2015) AATA 956.

Data-matching Program (Assistance and Tax) Act 1990 (Cth).

Denlay v Commissioner of Taxation (2011) FCAFC 63.

Deputy Commissioner of Taxation v Armstrong Scalisi Holdings Pty Ltd (2019) NSWSC 129.

Deputy Commissioner of Taxation v Bonaccorso (2016) NSWSC 595.

Deputy Commissioner of Taxation v Mackey [1982] 13 ATR 547.

Deputy Commissioner of Taxation v Richard Walter Pty Ltd (1994) 183 CLR 168.

Deputy Commissioner of Taxation v Zeqaj (2019) VSC 194.

Desai, D., & Kroll, J. (2017). Trust but verify: A guide to algorithms and the law. *Harvard Journal of Law & Technology*, *31*(1), 1–64.

Elvery, S. (2017). How algorithms make important government decisions — and how that affects you. *ABC News*. Retrieved from https://www.abc.net.au/news/2017-07-21/algorithms-can-make-decisions-on-behalf-of-federal-ministers/8704858

Federal Commissioner of Taxation v Citibank [1989] 89 ATC 4268.

Fellmeth, A. (2005). Civil and criminal sanctions in the constitution and courts. *The Georgetown Law Journal, 94*(1), 1–15.

Ferguson, A. G. (2017). Illuminating black data policing. *Ohio State Journal of Criminal Law, 15*(2), 503–525.

Fertik, M., & Thompson, D. (2015). *The reputation economy: How to optimize your digital footprint in a world where your reputation is your most valuable asset*. Danvers, MA: New York Crown Business.

Freedman, J., & Vella, J. (2011). *HMRC's management of the UK tax system: The boundaries of legitimate discretion*. Oxford, UK: Oxford University Centre for Business Taxation. Retrieved from https://ora.ox.ac.uk/objects/uuid:869d0c16-7748-489d-9a74-

Glencore International AG & Ors v Commissioner of Taxation of the Commonwealth of Australia & Ors (2019) HCA 26.

Henricks, K., & Seamster, L. (2017). Mechanisms of the racial tax state. *Critical Sociology, 43*(2), 169–179. doi:10.1177/0896920516670463

Her Majesty's Revenue & Customs (HMRC). (2015). *Tax administration: regulations to implement the UK's automatic exchange of information agreements*. London, UK: HMRC. Retrieved from https://www.gov.uk/government/publications/tax-administration-regulations-to-implement-the-uks-automatic-exchange-of-information-agreements

Hill, K. (2012, February 16). How Target figured out a teen girl was pregnant before her father did. *Forbes*. Retrieved from https://www.forbes.com/sites/kashmirhill/2012/02/16/how-target-figured-out-a-teen-girl-was-pregnant-before-her-father-did/

Hogan-Doran, D. (2017). Computer says "no": Automation, algorithms and artificial intelligence in Government decision-making. *The Judicial Review, 13*, 1–39.

Houser, K., & Sanders, D. (2016). The use of big data analytics by the IRS: Efficient solutions or the end of privacy as we know it. *Vanderbilt Journal of Entertainment & Technology Law, 19*(4), 817–872.

Hughes and Vale Pty Ltd v State of New South Wales (1955) 93 CLR 127.

Human Rights Watch. (2019, 1 May). *China's algorithms of repression: Reverse engineering a Xinjiang police mass surveillance app*. Retrieved from https://www.hrw.org/report/2019/05/01/chinas-algorithms-repression/reverse-engineering-xinjiang-police

Ibrahim, I., & Pope, J. (2011). The viability of a pre-filled income tax return system for Malaysia. *Journal of Contemporary Issues in Business and Government, 17*(2), 85–89.

Income Tax Assessment Act 1997 (Cth).

Industrial Equity Ltd v Deputy Commissioner of Taxation [1990] 89 ATC 5316.

Inspector-General of Taxation. (2019a). *The future of the tax profession*. Canberra, Australia: Australian Government Printer.

Inspector-General of Taxation. (2019b). *Review into the Australian Taxation Office's use of garnishee notices*. Canberra, Australia: Australian Government Printer.

Inspector-General of Taxation Act 2003 (Cth).

Internal Revenue Code of. (1986). *Title 26*. USC.

Leenes, R. (2011). Framing techno-regulation: An exploration of state and non-state regulation by technology. *Legisprudence*, *5*(2), 159. doi:10.5235/175214611797885675

Lepri, B., Staiano, J., Sangokoya, D., Letouze, E., & Oliver, N. (2017). The tyranny of data? The bright and dark sides of data-driven decision making for social good. In T. Cerquitelli, D. Quercia, & F. Pasquale (Eds.), *Transparent data mining for big and small data* (pp. 2–22). Dordrecht, Germany: Springer. doi:10.1007/978-3-319-54024-5_1

Lim, I., Hagendorff, J., & Armitage, S. (2016). Regulatory monitoring, information asymmetry and accounting quality: Evidence from the banking industry. *EFMA 25th Annual Meeting*. Retrieved from https://efmaefm.org/0efmameetings/efma%20annual%20meetings/2016-Switzerland/papers/EFMA2016_0504_fullpaper.pdf

Loftus, B. (2019). Normalizing covert surveillance: the subterranean world of policing. *British Journal of Sociology*, *70*(5), 2070-2091. http://doi-org/ doi:10.1111/1468-4446.12651

Loke, S. (2019). *Achieving ethical algorithmic behaviour in the internet-of-things: A review*. Retrieved from https://arxiv.org/pdf/1910.10241.pdf

Maciejewski, M. (2016). To do more, better, faster and more cheaply: using big data in public administration. *International Review of Administrative Sciences, 83*(IS), 120-135. doi:10.1177/0020852316640058

Moore, D., & Rid, T. (2016). Cryptopolitik and the darknet. *Global Politics and Strategy, 58*(1), 7–38. doi:10.1080/00396338.2016.1142085

National Consumer Credit Protection Act 2009 (Cth).

Numerato, D. (2016). Corruption and public secrecy: An ethnography of football match-fixing. *Current Sociology, 64*(5), 699–717. doi:10.1177/0011392115599815

Nunn, S. (2003). Seeking tools for the war on terror: A critical assessment of emerging technologies in law enforcement. *Policing, 26*(3), 454–472. doi:10.1108/13639510310489494

Office of the Australian Information Commissioner (OAIC). (2014). *Guidelines on data matching in Australian Government administration*. Retrieved from https://www.oaic.gov.au/privacy/guidance-and-advice/guidelines-on-data-matching-in-australian-government-administration/

Office of the Australian Information Commissioner (OAIC). (2018a). *The ATO's administrative approach to the disclosure of tax debt information to credit reporting bureaus — submission to the Australian Taxation Office*. Canberra, Australia: OAIC.

Office of the Australian Information Commissioner (OAIC). (2018b). *Guide to data analytics and the Australian Privacy Principles*. Canberra, Australia: OAIC.

Office of the Australian Information Commissioner (OAIC). (2019a). *Artificial Intelligence: Australia's Ethics Framework – Submission to the Department of Industry, Innovation and Science and Data 61 discussion paper*. Canberra, Australia: OAIC.

Office of the Australian Information Commissioner (OAIC). (2019b). *Developing Standards for Artificial Intelligence: Hearing Australia's Voice — submission to Standards Australia*. Canberra, Australia: OAIC.

Office of the Australian Information Commissioner (OAIC). (2019c). *Handling of personal information — Department of Human Services PAYG data matching program*. Canberra, Australia: OAIC.

Office of the Australian Information Commissioner (OAIC). (2019d). *Handling of personal information — Department of Human Services NEIDM data matching program*. Canberra, Australia: OAIC.

Office of the Victorian Information Commissioner (OVIC). (2018). *Artifical intelligence and privacy: issues paper*. Melbourne: OVIC.

Ombudsman Act 1976 (Cth).

Orellana v Commissioner, No. 8950-08S, 2010 WL 1568447 [T.C. Apr. 20, 2010].

Pasquale, F. (2011). Restoring Transparency to Automated Authority. *Journal on Telecommunications & High Technology Law, 9*, 235–254. Retrieved from http://digitalcommons.law.umaryland.edu/cgi/viewcontent.cgi?article=2357&context=fac_pubs

Pasquale, F. (2016). *Black Box Society: The Secret Algorithms That Control Money and Information*. Harvard University Press.

Pasquale, F. (2017). Toward a Fourth Law of Robotics: Preserving Attribution, Responsibility, and Explainability in an Algorithmic Society. *Ohio State Law Journal, 78*, 1243–1255. Retrieved from https://kb.osu.edu/bitstream/handle/1811/85768/OSLJ_V78N5_1243.pdf

Perel, M., & Elkin-Koren, N. (2017). Black Box Tinkering: Beyond Disclosure in Algorithmic Enforcement. *Florida Law Review, 69*, 181–221. Retrieved from https://scholarship.law.ufl.edu/cgi/viewcontent.cgi?article=1348

Perry, M. (2019). iDecide: Digital pathways to decisions. *Federal Judicial Scholarship, 3*. Retrieved from http://www.austlii.edu.au/cgi-bin/sinodisp/au/journals/FedJSchol/2019/3.html

Pintarich v Deputy Commissioner of Taxation [2018] FCAFC 79.

Privacy Act 1988 (Cth).

Queensland Maintenance Services Pty Ltd v Commissioner of Taxation [2011] FCA 1443.

Re Minister for Immigration and Multicultural Affairs; Ex parte Palme [2003] 216 CLR 212.

Register, D., & Adams, H. (2017). Extending HMRC's civil information powers. *Tax Journal*. Retrieved from https://www.taxjournal.com/articles/extending-hmrc-s-civil-information-powers-30082018

Ribeiro, M. T., Singh, S., & Guestrin, C. (2016). Why should I trust you? Explaining the predictions of any classifier. *Proceedings of the 22nd ACM SIGKDD international conference on knowledge discovery and data mining*, 1135-1144. Retrieved from https://arxiv.org/pdf/1602.04938.pdf

Rosen, J. (2012). The right to be forgotten. *Stanford Law Review, 64*, 88–92. Retrieved from https://review.law.stanford.edu/wp-content/uploads/sites/3/2012/02/64-SLRO-88.pdf

Rossi v Commissioner of Taxation [2015] AATA 601.

Rouvroy, A. (2012). The end(s) of critique: data-behaviourism vs. due-process. In M. Hildebrandt & K. De Vries (Eds.), *Privacy, due process and the computational turn: Philosophers of law meet philosophers of technology* (pp. 142–168). Abingdon, UK: Routledge.

Sandvig, C. (2014). Seeing the sort: The aesthetic and industrial defense of the algorithm. *Journal of the New Media Caucus, 10*(3). Retrieved from http://median.newmediacaucus.org/art-infrastructures-information/seeing-the-sort-the-aesthetic-and-industrial-defense-of-the-algorithm/

Savas, E. S., Fite, H. H., Schumacher, B. G., Kanter, J., Bowen, H. R., & Mangum, G. L. (1969). Computers in public administration. *Public Administration Review, 29*(2), 225–231. doi:10.2307/973708

Searle Australia v PIAC [1992] 108 ALR 163.

Sgardelis and Commissioner of Taxation (2007) 68 ATR 963.

Sharkey, N., & Murray, I. (2016). Reinventing administrative leadership in Australian taxation: Beware the fine balance of social psychological and rule of law principles. *Australian Tax Forum*, 63.

Social Security (Administration) Act 1999 (Cth).

Solove, D. (2013). Privacy self-management and the consent dilemma. *Harvard Law Review, 126*, 1880–1893.

Southwestern Indemnities Ltd v Bank of New South Wales & Federal Commissioner of Taxation [1973] 73 ATC 4171.

Superannuation Industry (Supervision) Act 1993 (Cth).

Taxation Administration Act 1953 (Cth).

Twentieth Century Fox. (2002). *Minority Report*.

Uber BV v Commissioner of Taxation (2017) FCA 110.

Uratoriu v Commissioner of Taxation [2008] FCA 1531.

U.S. v Wilson, 593 F. Appendix 942 [11th Cir. 2014].

van Dijsck, J. (2014). Datafication, dataism and dataveillance: Big Data between scientific paradigm and ideology. *Surveillance & Society, 12*(2), 199–208. doi:10.24908s.v12i2.4776

Veit, A. (2019). Swimming upstream: leveraging data and analytics for taxpayer engagement - an Australian and international perspective. *eJournal of Tax Research, 16*(3), 474-499.

X v The Minister for Immigration & Multicultural Affairs [1999] 92 FCR 524.

Yeung, K. (2016, October). Algorithmic regulation and intelligent enforcement. In M. Lodge (Ed.), *Regulation scholarship in crisis? LSE discussion paper No 84* (p. 56). London: London School of Economics.

Zarsky, T. (2013). Transparent predictions. *University of Illinois Law Review, 4*, 1503–1570.

Zuboff, S. (2015). Big other: Surveillance capitalism and the prospects of an informal Civilization. *Journal of Information Technology, 30*(1), 75–89. doi:10.1057/jit.2015.5

Zweig, K., Wenzelburer, G., & Krafft, T. D. (2018). On chances and risks of security related algorithmic decision-making systems. *European Journal for Security Research, 3*(2), 181–203. doi:10.100741125-018-0031-2

ADDITIONAL READING

Coglianese, C., & Lehr, D. (2017). Regulating by robot: Administrative decision-making in the machine-learning era. *The Georgetown Law Journal, 105*, 1147–1223.

Danaher, J. (2016). The threat of algocracy: Reality, resistance and accommodation. *Philosophy & Technology, 29*(3), 245–268. doi:10.100713347-015-0211-1

European Commission. (2016). *General Data Protection Code, Regulation (EU) 2016/679 of the European Parliament and of the Council of 27 April 2016 on the protection of natural persons with regard to the processing of personal data and on the free movement of such data, and repealing Directive 95/46/ EC.* Retrieved from https://publications.europa.eu/en/publication-detail/-/publication/3e485e15-11bd-11e6-ba9a-01aa75ed71a1/language-en

Ferguson, A. G. (2017). *The rise of big data policing: Surveillance, race, and the future of law enforcement.* New York: NYU Press. doi:10.2307/j.ctt1pwtb27

Hannah-Moffat, K. (2018). Algorithmic risk governance: Big data analytics, race and information activism in criminal justice debates. *Theoretical Criminology, 13*, 1–20. doi:10.1177/1362480618763582

Hildebrandt, M., & Koops, B. (2010). The challenges of ambient law and legal protection in the profiling era. *The Modern Law Review, 73*(3), 428–460. doi:10.1111/j.1468-2230.2010.00806.x

Holzinger, L. A., & Biddle, N. (2016). *Behavioural insights of tax compliance: An overview of recent conceptual and empirical approaches.* Canberra, Australia: Crawford School of Public Policy.

Martin, F. (1991). The audit power of the commissioner of taxation: Sections 263 and 264 of the income tax assessment Act 1936. Queensland University of Technology Law Journal, 7, 67-80.

Organization for Economic Cooperation and Development (OECD). (2017a). *The changing tax compliance environment and the role of audit.* Paris, France: OECD. Retrieved from https://www.oecd.org/ctp/the-changing-tax-compliance-environment-and-the-role-of-audit-9789264282186-en.htm

Organization for Economic Cooperation and Development (OECD). (2017b). *Tax Administration 2017.* Paris: OECD. Retrieved from https://www.oecd.org/tax/administration/tax-administration-23077727.htm

Sales, N. (2007). Secrecy and national security investigations. *Alabama Law Review, 58*, 811–884.

Walker-Munro, B. (2019). Disruption, regulatory theory and China: What surveillance and profiling can teach the modern regulator. *Journal of Governance & Regulation, 8*(1), 23–40. doi:10.22495/jgr_v8_i2_p3

Yeung, K. (2018). Algorithmic regulation: A critical interrogation. *Regulation & Governance, 12*(4), 505–523. doi:10.1111/rego.12158

KEY TERMS AND DEFINITIONS

Analytics: The mining, research, or examination of large-scale datasets to yield evidence of past, present or future behavior.

Artificial Intelligence (AI): Any system of computing capable (in part or in whole) of simulating the decision-making capability of a human being.

Big Data: The concept that near-infinite storage and computer processing has permitted the mass collection and storage of information about every aspect of our lives.

Data Matching: The comparison of two or more data sets to identify matches and anomalies in both.

Machine Learning: Where a computer program or algorithm 'learns' how to select or filter input data by assessing previous cases or instances and making correlations or judgements.

Chapter 68
Big Data Analytics Driven Supply Chain Transformation

Mondher Feki
Lemna Research Center, France

ABSTRACT

Big data has emerged as the new frontier in supply chain management; however, few firms know how to embrace big data and capitalize on its value. The non-stop production of massive amounts of data on various digital platforms has prompted academics and practitioners to focus on the data economy. Companies must rethink how to harness big data and take full advantage of its possibilities. Big data analytics can help them in giving valuable insights. This chapter provides an overview of big data analytics use in the supply chain field and underlines its potential role in the supply chain transformation. The results show that big data analytics techniques can be categorized into three types: descriptive, predictive, and prescriptive. These techniques influence supply chain processes and create business value. This study sets out future research directions.

INTRODUCTION

Big data promises to trigger a revolution in supply chain management (SCM) (Waller & Fawcett, 2013). Fawcett and Waller (2014) argued that big data is one of the forces that will redefine supply chain design. The big-data-driven digital economy facilitates this change by capturing, analyzing and using big data to make evidence-based decisions. Thousands of exabytes of new data are generated each year on a variety of digital platforms such as social media, mobile devices and the Internet of Things. Many companies can capitalize on this big data by managing risks, reducing costs and improving supply chain visibility.

Big data is often characterized by the five Vs: Volume, Velocity, Variety, Veracity, and Value (Fosso Wamba, Akter, Edwards, Chopin, & Gnanzou, 2015). The volume of big data refers to the quantity of data, which is increasing exponentially. Velocity is the speed of data collection, processing and analyzing in real time. Variety refers to the different types of data collected. The data can be structured (e.g., data found in relational databases), semi-structured (e.g., Extensible Markup Language – XML), or

DOI: 10.4018/978-1-6684-3662-2.ch068

unstructured (e.g., images, audio, and video). Veracity represents the reliability of data sources. The variation in the data flow rates reflects the variability of big data, while the myriad of big data sources reflects its complexity. Finally, value represents the process of creating value from big data (Gandomi & Haider, 2015; Hashem et al., 2015; Kshetri, 2014). Fosso Wamba et al. (2015, p. 235) define big data analytics (BDA) as "a holistic approach to manage, process and analyze 5 Vs in order to create actionable insights for sustained value delivery, measuring performance and establishing competitive advantages."

Companies apply BDA in their supply chain to reduce cycle time, react faster to changes, optimize performance and gain insight into the future. A supply chain is defined as "a bidirectional flow of information, products and money between the initial suppliers and final customers through different organizations" (Nurmilaakso, 2008, p. 721); SCM includes planning, implementing and controlling this flow. BDA is expected to transform the supply chain (Fosso Wamba & Akter, 2015). Compared with traditional analytic tools, BDA could help companies to better understand customers' preferences and behavior and launch new products and services that are more customized (Duta & Bose, 2015). Several companies, such as Procter & Gamble, Walmart and Tesco, have benefited from the implementation of supply chain analytics (SCA), which enabled them to improve their operational efficiency and reduce costs (Chae, Olson, & Sheu, 2013). SCA refers to the use of supply chain data and analytical technologies and methods to improve operational performance (Chae et al., 2013). It represents the intersection of three academic disciplines: technologies (tools that support data processing), quantitative approaches (methods for analyzing data) and decision-making (tools used to support the decision-making process). These disciplines share a similar purpose: "…the improvement of business operations and decision making through the utilization of information, quantitative analyses, and/or technologies…" (Mortenson, Doherty, & Robinson, 2015, p. 585).

Three different aspects of analytics can be distinguished: (1) Descriptive analytics uses statistical methods and reports on the past; it is designed to answer the question "What happened?" (2) Predictive analytics uses models based on past data to predict the future and answer the question "What will happen next?" (3) Prescriptive analytics uses models to specify optimal behaviors and actions and answer the question "What should the business do next?" (Davenport, 2013; Lustig, Dietrich, Johnson, & Dziekan, 2010; Mortenson et al., 2015). Despite the benefits of BDA in SCM, companies may find it difficult to adopt the approach if they lack the capacity to make large investments, an analytic culture, executive support, a strong security framework, or analytic capability. In addition, creating business value from big data still represents a challenging and controversial mission as the steep growth curve of performance using analytics is flattening out (Kiron, Prentice, & Ferguson, 2014). Some scholars also describe the hype about big data as a myth, as it does not reflect innovative capability and improved firm performance (Manyika et al., 2011). Ross, Beath, and Quaadgras (2013, p. 90) state that "The biggest reason that investments in big data fail to pay off, though, is that most companies don't do a good job with the information they already have. They don't know how to manage it, analyse it in ways that enhance their understanding, and then make changes in response to new insights."

Motivated by this debate, the main objective of this research is to provide a comprehensive overview on BDA application in SCM and underscore its potential role in supply chain transformation. To this end, the author conducted a literature review to arrive at answers to the following questions:

- What big data analytic techniques are used in the supply chain field?
- How does big data analytics influence supply chain management?
- How can big data analytics create business value in supply chain?

The remainder of this paper is structured as follows. Section 2 presents a sample of business cases. Section 3 describes the big data analytic techniques used in the supply chain field and section 4 summarizes the supply chain analytics approaches. Section 5 and 6 presents respectively the impact of BDA on SCM processes and business value. Finally, section 7 sets out future research directions.

ILLUSTRATIVE EXAMPLES OF BIG DATA ANALYTICS APPLICATIONS

Big data has generated tremendous attention worldwide recently mainly due to its operational and strategic potentials. For example, Anaya et al. (2015) found that by applying data analytics tools into data accumulated by firms in various enterprise systems may lead to the extraction of new insights as well as innovative practices. Similarly, Kohlborn et al. (2014) argued that the firms could use of big data analytics capabilities to generate new insights "into business processes, improve organizational learning, and enable innovative business models". Table 1 shows the business value created by the world's Top 10 most innovative companies in big data (Fast Company, 2014).

Table 1. Business value of Top 10 most innovative companies in big data

Company	Business Value
1. General Electric	Big data help airlines to predict mechanical malfunctions and reduce flight cancellations.
2. Kaggle	Algorithms developed by its data scientists allow analyzing complex data and making big decisions.
3. Ayasdi	Visual approach of big data reveals new trends.
4. IBM	IBM was launched a new big data technology in the French city of Lyon, for predicting points of congestion to improve traffic flow.
5. Mount Sinai Icahn School of Medicine	It processes gigabytes of health data from more than 25000 patients in order to predict diseases and streamline electronic medical records.
6. The Weather Company	Analyzing millions of local climates to predict habits and behavior patterns of its digital and mobile users in worldwide.
7. Knewton	Through its digital platform, Knewton analyzes the progress of millions of students to create better test questions and personalized course goals.
8. Splunk	As a pure-play leader in the big data space, Splunk provides businesses with hundreds of homegrown apps to sniff out error files and keep things humming.
9. Gnip	Gnip provides and analyzes data from social media websites via API services in order to understand customer profile.
10. Evolv	Evolv provides workforce performance solutions to help employers better understand employees and job candidates by comparing their skills, work experience, and personalities.

Source: Fast Company (2014)

Big data promises to generate a revolution in supply chain management (Waller and Fawcett, 2013). A recent study by SCM World states that "64% of supply chain executives consider big data analytics a disruptive and important technology, setting the foundation for long-term change management in their organizations" (Columbus, 2015). Many companies can capitalize on big data analytics by managing risks, reducing costs and improving supply chain visibility and traceability. An Accenture research reveals that big data analytics helping some companies to "improve customer service and demand fulfillment, experience faster and more effective reaction time to supply chain issues, increase supply chain efficiency, and drive greater integration across the supply chain" (Accenture, 2014, p. 11). Table 2 presents the benefits of companies from the implementation of analytics in supply chain (Dell, 2014).

Table 2. Business value from using big data analytics in supply chain

Industry	Company	Business Value From Using Big Data Analytics
Food	McDonald's	"McDonalds tracks vast amounts of data in order to **improve operations** and **boost the customer experience**. The company looks at factors such as the design of the drive-thru, information provided on the menu, wait times, the size of orders and ordering patterns in order to optimize each restaurant to its particular market." (p.12)
	Coca-Cola Co.	"Coca-Cola uses an algorithm to **ensure that its orange juice has a consistent taste throughout the year**. The algorithm incorporates satellite imagery, crop yields, consumer preferences and details about the flavours that make up a particular fruit in order to determine how the juice should be blended." (p.29)
Retail	Nordstrom	"Nordstrom collects data from its website, social media, transactions and customer rewards program in order to **create customized marketing messages** and shopping experiences for each customer, based on the products and channels that customer prefers." (p.17)
	Procter & Gamble	"P&G uses simulation models and predictive analytics in order to **create the best design for its products**. It creates and sorts through thousands of iterations in order to develop the best design for a disposable diaper, and uses predictive analytics to determine how moisture affects the fragrance molecules in dish soap, so the right fragrance comes out at the right time in the dishwashing process." (p.27)
	Amazon	"With more than 1.5 billion items in its catalog, Amazon has a lot of product to keep track of and protect. It uses its cloud system, S3, to **predict which items are most likely to be stolen**, so it can **better secure its warehouses**." (p.32)
Transportation	Union Pacific Railroad	"With predictive analytics and tools such as visual sensors and thermometers, Union Pacific can detect imminent problems with railway tracks in order to **predict potential derailments days** before they would likely occur. So far the sensors have reduced derailments by 75 percent." (p.24)
	Kayak	"Kayak uses big data analytics **to create a predictive model that tells users if the price** for a particular flight will go up or down within the next week. The system uses one billion search queries to find the cheapest flights, as well as popular destinations and the busiest airports. The algorithm is constantly improved by tracking the flights to see if its predictions are correct." (p.38)
Oil	Shell	"Shell uses sensor data to map its oil and gas wells in order to **increase output and boost the efficiency of its operations**. The data received from the sensors is analyzed by artificial intelligence and rendered in 3D and 4D maps." (p.41)

Source: Dell (2014)

BIG DATA ANALYTIC TECHNIQUES IN SUPPLY CHAIN

Supply chain analytics refers to the use of supply chain data and analytical technologies and methods to improve operational performance (Chae et al., 2013). Below, the author presents the advanced analytics techniques founded in literature.

Data mining approaches incorporate statistical and analytical techniques such as classification, regression, clustering and semantic analysis (Z. Y. Chen et al., 2015; Chongwatpol, 2015; Kulkarni et al., 2014; Liao, Chu, & Hsiao, 2012). The inputs to these techniques are large amounts of structured or unstructured data which will be interpreted as useful information in a specific business context by identifying intrinsic models (Chongwatpol, 2015).

Data mining techniques allow users "to find the best predictive model and identify top predictors" (Ballings & Van den Poel, 2015, p. 249). Generally applied in the domains of retail, marketing and customer relationship management, these techniques make it possible to identify customer behavior patterns. For example, data mining allows data captured by RFID and data extracted from point-of-sale systems to be analyzed in order to predict consumer purchasing behavior and detect any changes in it (Chongwatpol, 2015).

Machine learning techniques allow for hierarchical representations to be learned automatically (Chen & Lin, 2014). These techniques include neural networks, Bayesian networks, genetic algorithms or programming, decision trees, support vector machines, and feature selection (Bose & Chen, 2009; Chen et al., 2015; Chongwatpol, 2015).

Advanced machine learning techniques enhance conjoint analysis capabilities and improve prediction performance, making it possible to better identify consumer preferences and relevant attributes (Chen et al., 2015; Maldonado et al., 2015). These techniques, which are frequently used in direct marketing (Chongwatpol, 2015), also allow business managers to make decisions concerning promotional and advertising campaigns and new product design. In addition, they enable managers to assess consumers' willingness to pay and decide on a pricing strategy (Maldonado et al., 2015).

Optimization methods use data with models and algorithms in simulations to solve optimization problems and to help make strategic decisions about operations. For example, in the gas industry, they can improve job scheduling and crew assignment (Angalakudati et al., 2014).

The classification of the examined literature by BDA techniques is summarized in Table 3.

Table 3. Literature references on big data analytics techniques in supply chain

Techniques	References
Statistics	Wang et al. (2016), Chae (2015), Hahn and Packowski (2015), Groves et al. (2014), Chae et al. (2014).
Data visualization approaches	Zhong et al. (2016), Duta and Bose (2015), Tan et al. (2015), Groves et al. (2014), Souza (2014)
Data mining	Krumeich et al. (2016), Chae (2015), Zhong et al. (2015), Tan et al. (2015), Hahn and Packowski (2015), Souza (2014), Kahn (2014), Kwon et al. (2014)
Machine learning	Zhong et al. (2016), Zhong et al. (2015), Chae (2015)
Social network analysis	Chae (2015), Tan et al. (2015)
Optimization methods	Wang et al. (2016), Hahn and Packowski (2015), Duta and Bose (2015), Souza (2014), Groves et al. (2014), Hazen et al. (2014), Chae et al. (2014)

SUPPLY CHAIN ANALYTICS APPROACHES

Big data analytics in supply chain focuses on the use of analytical techniques to drive decisions and actions regarding flows in the supply chain (Souza, 2014). These techniques, found from our literature review, can be categorized into three types: descriptive, predictive, and prescriptive (Souza, 2014; Hahn and Packowski, 2015; Wang, Gunasekaran, Ngai, & Papadopoulos, 2016).

The descriptive analytics bases on the use of statistics techniques to transform big data into meaningful information. Indeed, the GPS (Global Positioning System), RFID (Radio-Frequency Identification) technologies and sensors collect data on a real-time which will be summarized and converted into information relative to location and quantity of goods in supply chain (Groves et al., 2014; Chae, 2015). Thus, the manager can have real-time information, for example, on carrier's location or stock state and consequently, he can make adjustments concerning the delivery schedules or replenishment orders for instance (Souza, 2014). Thereby, the descriptive analytics provide information regarding "what has happened?" and "what is happening at the moment?" for reporting and monitoring purposes (Souza, 2014; Hahn and Packowski, 2015). Statistics techniques can be combined with visualization techniques in order to give an overview of data represented in form of performance scorecard with key performance indicator such as delivery deadline and sales growth (Duta and Bose, 2015).

The predictive analytics concerns the use of techniques such as data mining, machine learning and social network analysis. The data mining is a set of tools, including classification, clustering, association analysis, sentiment analysis and regression (Souza, 2014; Kahn, 2014; Chae, 2015; Zhong et al., 2015), to extract subjective information from big data (e.g., emotion, opinions) (Chae, 2015). The machine learning uses algorithms to discover knowledge and evolve behaviors (Chen and Zhang, 2014; Chae, 2015; Zhong et al., 2015). On the other hand, network analytics explores network-level characteristics (Chae, 2015). Other tools for forecasting are used such as time series methods and market basket analysis (Souza, 2014; Kahn, 2014; Hahn and Packowski, 2015). All these techniques allow to make predictions concerning the future intended from big data. So, predictive analytics in supply chain answer the questions "what will happen?" and "why will it happen?" (Souza, 2014; Hahn and Packowski, 2015).

The prescriptive analytics is based on descriptive and predictive analytics and optimization methods (Souza, 2014). This last tool includes mathematical models and simulation techniques (Groves et al., 2014; Hazen et al., 2014; Chae et al., 2014) to support decision and optimize process on a real-time (Souza, 2014; Duta and Bose, 2015). For example, by using this technique in outbound logistics, every order is analyzed with regard to the availability of stock in order to manage expeditions and determine the appropriate deadlines of delivery on a real-time, what allows to decrease the logistics cost, increase the efficiency and provide a better service to the customer (Duta and Bose, 2015). Accordingly, perspective analytics address the question "what should be happening?" (Souza, 2014; Hahn and Packowski, 2015).

Hahn and Packowski (2015) distinguish four types of use cases of analytics in supply chain management: (1) "monitor and navigate", (2) "sense and respond", (3) "predict and act", and (4) "plan and optimize". The first use case requires descriptive analytics and data visualization techniques. "Plan and optimize" use cases correspond to prescriptive analytics. By contrast, predictive analytics enable "sense and respond" and "predict and act" use cases.

Figure 1 presents three types of big data analytics approaches in supply chain with data examples and references.

BIG DATA ANALYTICS IN SUPPLY CHAIN PROCESSES

Big data can influence business processes in the context of SCM. To study processes concerned by big data-enabled supply chain transformation, the author uses SCOR (Supply Chain Operations Reference) model developed by the Supply Chain Council (www.supply-chain.org) as such a framework of classification. This model divides supply chain processes into six main areas: Plan, Source, Make, Deliver, Return and Enable. Table 4 presents the objectives of the SCORE model (Supply Chain Council, 2008).

Figure 1. Supply chain analytics approaches

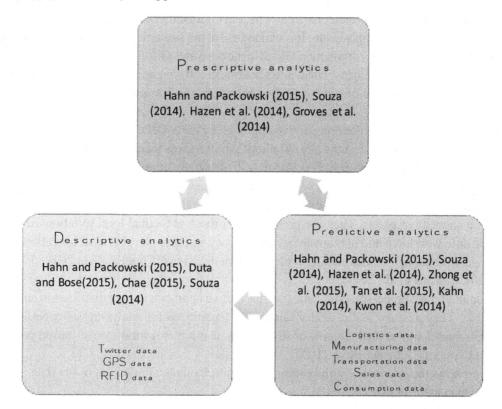

Table 4. Objectives of SCORE model

Processes	Objectives
Source	The ordering, delivery, receipt and transfer of raw material items, subassemblies, products and/or services
Make	The process of adding value to products through mixing, separating, forming, machining, and chemical processes
Deliver	Performing customer-facing order management and order fulfillment activities including outbound logistics
Return	Moving material from customer back through supply chain to address defects in product, ordering, or manufacturing, or to perform upkeep activities.
Plan	The process of determining requirements and corrective actions to achieve supply chain objectives.
Enable	Three distinct types of objectives: • Manage process performance • Manage process control data • Manage process relationships

Source: Supply Chain Council (2008)

With a huge increasing quantity of business data, consumption data and contextual, companies need to use analytics in order to make sense of big data so as to drive decisions and actions. The big data analytics use in supply chain was influenced SCOR areas.

For supply chain planning, companies use predictive approach such as time series, causal forecasting or data mining methods. Usually, they begin with data mining techniques such as clustering or market basket analysis for analyzing purchase models, knowing customers' perceptions with regard to products and services and determining demand factors. These factors will then be analyzed by using causal forecasting methods such as the regression to predict product demand. The demand prediction constitutes the main input of planning in supply chain. It is carried out at the strategic, tactical and operational levels to plan operations (procurement, production and distribution) and sales in order to synchronize demand with offer (Souza, 2014; Chae, 2015). Hahn and Packowski (2015) argue that strategic and operational planning is mainly based on prescriptive analytics approaches in particular on the use of optimization methods.

For the sourcing, companies use prescriptive approach by means of the analytic hierarchy process at strategic level to estimate and select the key suppliers and use game theory at the tactical level to define the rules of auction and prescribe contracts (Souza, 2014). Wang et al. (2016) argue that supply chain analytics allow managing the supply risks and optimizing the sourcing decision.

In make process, companies use prescriptive approach at strategic level such as genetic algorithms to determine the capacity of plants. They use predictive approach at tactical level to rationalize the product line, schedule workforce and plan inventory level. They also use algorithms at operational level for manufacturing scheduling and automating replenishment decisions (Condea et al., 2012; Souza, 2014; Tan et al., 2015; Zhang et al., 2017).

In deliver and return processes, companies use predictive approach to plan distribution and transport (Souza, 2014). They also use statics and visualization techniques for analyzing sales performance at various levels such as by zones, regions, or districts by using a real-time metric- based performance measurement system (Duta and Bose, 2015).

Table 5 presents the references of the examined literature on the application of big data analytics in supply chain management processes.

Table 5. Literature references by SCM process

Process	References
Plan	Krumeich et al. (2016), Wang and Zhang (2016), Chae (2015), Li et al. (2015), Hahn and Packowski (2015), Chae et al. (2014), Souza (2014), Kahn (2014)
Source	Wang et al. (2016), Li et al. (2015), Hahn and Packowski (2015), Souza (2014), Groves et al. (2014), Verdouw et al. (2013), Condea et al. (2012)
Make	Zhang et al. (2017), Wang et al. (2016), Ng et al. (2015), Tan et al. (2015), Zhong et al. (2015), Li et al. (2015), Hahn and Packowski (2015), Kwon et al. (2014), Groves et al. (2014), Hazen et al. (2014), Chae et al. (2014), Souza (2014), Verdouw et al. (2013)
Deliver	Wang et al. (2016), Chae (2015), Duta and Bose (2015), Hahn and Packowski (2015), Li et al. (2015), Groves et al. (2014), Souza (2014), Verdouw et al. (2013)
Return	Li et al. (2015), Souza (2014)

VALUE CREATION FROM BIG DATA ANALYTICS IN SUPPLY CHAIN

In supply chain management, the use of big data analytics enables to know customers' perceptions of offered products and services and discover their unobservable characteristics in order to understand market demands and anticipate future consumer product variety desires. The customer's knowledge enables to develop new products and services more customized and consequently improve their satisfaction (Ng et al., 2015; Chae, 2015).

Furthermore, the demand prediction through big data analytics enables to plan and execute supply chain so as to balance supply and demand and improve supply chain operations (Chae, 2015; Tan et al., 2015). Indeed, the combination of analytics techniques enables to optimize manufacturing processes, shop-floor management and manufacturing logistics (Hahn and Packowski, 2015; Groves et al., 2014) which allows producing new products in a more profitable way (Tan et al., 2015) and reducing logistics cost (Duta and Bose, 2015). Hahn and Packowski (2015) argue that the use sensor-based technology with analytics applications on a real-time involve substantial value potential of 10 to 25% in operating cost reductions.

In addition, big data analytics enables the management and control of manufacturing process on a real-time. Indeed, an advanced process management method developed for data mining allowed to follow and control stocks, manufacturing workflows and workers on a real-time, and consequently improving the productivity (Kwon et al., 2014). Therefore, the use of visualization techniques allows making real-time corrective actions. For example, RCL (Ramco Cements Limited) is an Indian company that mainly produces cement in the South of India. It has "5 cement plants, 3 grinding units, 2 packing plants, a dry mix plant and a ready-mix concrete plant spread all over India" and "six captive wind mill sites" (Duta and Bose, 2015, p. 297). Thanks to visualization techniques, RCL was able to adjust its marketing plan in some locations what increased its sales and market share (Duta and Bose, 2015). Indeed, the combination of analytical techniques such as data mining and visualization tools allow to generate relevant and viable information for decision-makers (Tan et al., 2015) in particularity production logistics (Zhong et al., 2015). The use of simulation with statistics and visualization techniques allows analyzing markets, production and sales data on a real-time and computing the key performance indicators relative to supply chain for developing strategic, tactical, and operational decision-making (Groves et al., 2014).

However, Chae et al. (2014) argue that for improving operational performance and increasing big data analytics value, it is necessary that supply chain analytics techniques be combined with SCM initiatives such as "Total Quality Management", "Just in time", and "Statistical Process Control" which can be used to monitor and control data quality in a supply chain (Hazen et al., 2014).

Table 6 presents the references of the examined literature on the business value of big data analytics in supply chain management.

Table 6. Literature references by business value

Business Value	References
Improving decision-making	Tan et al. (2015), Zhong et al. (2015), Duta and Bose (2015), Hahn and Packowski (2015), Groves et al. (2014), Souza (2014), Condea et al. (2012)
Creating new products and services	Addo-Tenkorang and Helo (2016), Chae (2015), Ng et al. (2015), Kahn (2014)
Enabling to discover needs and customization	Addo-Tenkorang and Helo (2016), Tan et al. (2015), Ng et al. (2015), Chae (2015)
Operational excellence	Addo-Tenkorang and Helo (2016), Ng et al. (2015), Duta and Bose (2015), Chae (2015), Li et al. (2015), Chae et al. (2014), Kwon et al. (2014), Condea et al. (2012)
Improving supply chain management	Zhong et al. (2016), Zhong et al. (2015), Hahn and Packowski (2015), Tan et al. (2015), Li et al. (2015), Duta and Bose (2015), Chae et al. (2014), Hazen et al. (2014)

FUTURE RESEARCH DIRECTIONS

This section presents potential future research questions based on our literature review in order to capitalize the research development of BDA applications in the SCM context.

Potential Future Research Questions on Methodology and Theories

The majority of the articles analyzed focused on a mathematical analysis, experiment, literature analysis or research derived from opinions, with no empirical evidence. This finding raises a challenge to use other methodologies such as qualitative research, surveys and quantitative research to study and measure the impact of BDA on operations and supply chain management, as well on supply chain performance and operational performance.

Our review of the articles revealed that several theories have been mobilized to study BDA in the supply chain. However, a number of other potentially useful theories, such as resource-based view theory, contingency theory and systems theory, could also be mobilized. The determination of which theories can usefully be mobilized to study big data in supply chains requires further study. Revisiting resource-based view theory could help determine other resources and capabilities for supply chain analytics.

Potential Future Research Questions on BDA in Supply Chain Processes

Big data can influence business processes in the context of SCM. It would be interesting to study the key processes concerned by big-data-enabled supply chain transformation. Table 7 presents the key processes of the SCORE model (Supply Chain Council, 2008).

Future work can study and identify SCORE areas, which are influenced by BDA.

- What is the impact of BDA on each SCORE area?
- Which SCORE area is the most influenced?
- What is the impact of BDA on each of the key processes of the SCORE model?
- What is the impact of BDA on supply chain processes' performance?

Potential Future Research Questions on BDA Techniques in Supply Chains

BDA in supply chains focuses on the use of statistics, data mining, and machine learning. The author notes the emergence of optimization methods. Future research on this type of analytical technique in the supply chain context should be encouraged. However, the author noticed from the analyzed articles that no study had been done on data visualization approaches and social network analysis. Case studies and/ or reports on experiments that explore these opportunities are recommended. Such studies can inform the community about these tools and demonstrate their potential benefits.

- What are the opportunities for and limitations on using data visualization approaches in a supply chain context?
- What are the potential benefits of using data visualization approaches in a supply chain context?
- What are the opportunities for and limitations on using social network analysis in a supply chain context?

- What are the potential benefits of using social network analysis in a supply chain context?

Potential Future Research Questions on Big Data Strategies in a Supply Chain Context

The development, implementation and management of big data strategies in the context of a supply chain cannot yet be discussed in any depth. Further research should be done to address those challenges:

- How should a big data strategy be developed in the supply chain context?
- What are the facilitators and inhibitors of BDA implementation for supply chains?
- What are the costs of implementing and driving big data applications and capabilities?

Table 7. Key processes of SCORE model

Source	Make	Deliver	Return	Plan	Enable
Schedule product deliveries	Schedule production, request and receive material from source and/or Make processes	Product, service and price quotations	Identification of the need to return a product or asset	Supply chain revenue planning/ forecasting	Manage business rules and monitor adherence
Receive, inspect, and hold materials	Manufacture, assemble/ disassemble and test product, package, hold/release product	Order entry and maintenance	Requesting and issuing return authorization	Materials requirement planning	Measure supply chain performance and determine corrective action
Issue material to Make or Deliver processes	Manage product quality and engineering changes	Order consolidation, picking, packing, labeling and shipping	Inspection and disposition decision-making	Factory, repair, maintenance facilities capacity planning	Manage risk and environmental impact
Supplier/vendor agreements	Manage facilities and equipment, production status workflow and capacity management	Import/export documentation	Transfer/disposition of product or asset	Distribution requirements planning	Manage the supply chain network and facilities
Vendor certification and feedback, sourcing quality	Manage work-in-process inventories	Customer delivery and installation	Manage return transportation capacity	Manage planning parameters	
Manage raw materials inventories		Logistics and freight management	Manage returned material inventories		
Freight, import/export documentation		Manage finished goods inventories			

Source: Supply Chain Council (2008, pp. 21, 25, 32, 37, 41)

Potential Future Research Questions on the Use and Impact of Big Data in a Supply Chain Context

There is a need to develop more exploratory research and build theories to explain the use of BDA in OSM at the intra- and interorganizational levels and assess its impact on supply chain performance. It would be interesting to identify the contingent factors that can moderate the effect of BDA on supply chain performance. The questions that arise are:

- How is BDA used in operations and supply chain management at the intra- and inter- organizational levels?
- What is its impact on supply chain performance?
- How can firms measure supply chain performance?
- What are the contingent factors that influence this effect?
- What is the impact of BDA on predictive maintenance?
- What is the impact of BDA on after-sales management
- What is the impact of BDA on pricing management?
- What is the impact of BDA on risk management in a supply chain context? How can BDA help with supply chain risk detection and disruption recovery?

Potential Future Research Questions on SCM Practices in a Big Data Context

SCM practices, such as total quality management, just-in-time and statistical process control, allow managers to monitor and correct manufacturing processes and performance (Chae et al., 2013). Chae, Yang, Olson, and Shen (2014) argue that supply chain analytic techniques must be combined with SCM practices to increase the value of BDA. The questions that then arise are:

- How can organizations integrate SCM practices into BDA programs?
- What is the impact of BDA on SCM practices?

Potential Future Research Questions on Big Data in Supply Chain Networks

The articles analyzed in our review tend to concentrate on the study of big data or business analytics in the supply chain of a company by assessing their positive impact on decision-making or forecasting and planning. Our review shows only intra-organizational transformation. However, SCM is concerned with integration of activities both within and between organizations. To our knowledge, no the studies have examined big data or business analytics within the interorganizational framework of a multi-level supply chain. In this context, companies involved in the supply chain network need to share data and interact with each other collaboratively. Thus, it would be interesting to study:

- How can one design a dynamic supply chain network using BDA?
- How should big data applications be aligned between the members of a supply chain network?
- Is potential of BDA different for the various members of a supply chain network?
- What is the differential impact on upstream and downstream members?
- How can BDA support supply chain coordination mechanisms?

- How is data shared between the members of a supply chain network?
- How do members of a supply chain network react to using BDA?

CONCLUSION

This study provides a comprehensive literature review on big data analytics in supply chain management. It describes BDA techniques and shows their influence on SCM processes and value creation. BDA has become necessary given the increasing number of data in SCM. It supports all the supply chain processes. BDA can play a critical role in supply chain management on a strategic, tactical and operational level (Souza, 2014). Wang et al. (2016) found that "Strategic supply chain analytics are important for sourcing, network design, and product design. Tactical and operational supply chain analytics are important for demand planning, procurement, production, inventory, and logistics." Tiwari, Wee and Daryanto (2018, p. 321). According to Akter, Wamba, Gunasekaran, Dubey, and Childe (2016), big data analytics has a big impact to enhance firm performance. Big data analytics can help managers to transform the supply chain management. However, a recent study by Accenture states that "while most companies have high expectations for big data analytics in their supply chain, many have had difficulty adopting it. In fact, 97 percent of executives report having an understanding of how big data analytics can benefit their supply chain, but only 17 percent report having already implemented analytics in one or more supply chain functions" (Accenture, 2014, p. 3). So why don't more firms embrace big data analytics (BDA) in SCM? Firms need to embrace a more sophisticated analytics culture so they can handle, manage, analyze, and interpret big data. There is considerable room for big data research in operations and supply chain by focusing on business process transformation, business strategy alignment, deployment and utilization of new technology etc.

REFERENCES

Accenture. (2014). Big data analytics in supply chain: Hype or here to stay? Retrieved from https://acnprod.accenture.com/_acnmedia/Accenture/Conversion-Assets/DotCom/Documents/Global/PDF/Dualpub_2/Accenture-Global-Operations-Megatrends-Study-Big-Data-Analytics.pdf#zoom=50

Addo-Tenkorang, R., & Helo, P. T. (2016). Big data applications in operations/supply-chain management: A literature review. *Computers & Industrial Engineering*, *101*, 528–543. doi:10.1016/j.cie.2016.09.023

Akter, S., Wamba, S. F., Gunasekaran, A., Dubey, R., & Childe, S. J. (2016). How to improve firm performance using big data analytics capability and business strategy alignment? *International Journal of Production Economics*, *182*, 113–131. doi:10.1016/j.ijpe.2016.08.018

Anaya, L., Dulaimi, M., & Abdallah, S. (2015). An investigation into the role of enterprise information systems in enabling business innovation. *Business Process Management Journal*, *21*(4), 771–790. doi:10.1108/BPMJ-11-2014-0108

Angalakudati, M., Balwani, S., Calzada, J., Chatterjee, B., Perakis, G., Raad, N., & Uichanco, J. (2014). Business analytics for flexible resource allocation under random emergencies. *Management Science*, *60*(6), 1552–1573. doi:10.1287/mnsc.2014.1919

Ballings, M., & Van den Poel, D. (2015). CRM in social media: Predicting increases in Facebook usage frequency. *European Journal of Operational Research, 244*(1), 248–260. doi:10.1016/j.ejor.2015.01.001

Barton, D., & Court, D. (2012). Making advanced analytics work for you. *Harvard Business Review, 90*(10), 78–83. PMID:23074867

Bose, I., & Chen, X. (2009). Quantitative models for direct marketing: A review from systems perspective. *European Journal of Operational Research, 195*(1), 1–16. doi:10.1016/j.ejor.2008.04.006

Chae, B. (2015). Insights from hashtag #supplychain and Twitter Analytics: Considering Twitter and Twitter data for supply chain practice and research. *International Journal of Production Economics, 165*, 247–259. doi:10.1016/j.ijpe.2014.12.037

Chae, B. K., Olson, D., & Sheu, C. (2013). The impact of supply chain analytics on operational performance: A resource-based view. *International Journal of Production Research, 52*(16), 4695–4710. doi:10.1080/00207543.2013.861616

Chae, B. K., Yang, C., Olson, D., & Sheu, C. (2014). The impact of advanced analytics and data accuracy on operational performance: A contingent resource based theory (RBT) perspective. *Decision Support Systems, 59*, 119–126. doi:10.1016/j.dss.2013.10.012

Chen, C. L. P., & Zhang, C. Y. (2014). Data-intensive applications, challenges, techniques and technologies: A survey on big data. *Information Sciences, 275*, 314–347. doi:10.1016/j.ins.2014.01.015

Chen, X. W., & Lin, A. X. (2014). Big data deep learning: Challenges and perspectives. *IEEE Access: Practical Innovations, Open Solutions, 2*, 514–526. doi:10.1109/ACCESS.2014.2325029

Chen, Z. Y., Fan, Z. P., & Sun, M. (2015). Behavior-aware user response modeling in social media: Learning from diverse heterogeneous data. *European Journal of Operational Research, 241*(2), 422–434. doi:10.1016/j.ejor.2014.09.008

Chongwatpol, J. (2015). Integration of RFID and business analytics for trade show exhibitors. *European Journal of Operational Research, 244*(2), 662–673. doi:10.1016/j.ejor.2015.01.054

Columbus, L. (2015). Ten ways big data is revolutionizing supply chain management. *Forbes*. Retrieved from http://www.forbes.com/sites/louiscolumbus/2015/07/13/ten-ways-big-data-is-revolutionizing-supply-chain-management/

Condea, C., Thiesse, F., & Fleisch, E. (2012). RFID-enabled shelf replenishment with backroom monitoring in retail stores. *Decision Support Systems, 52*(4), 839–849. doi:10.1016/j.dss.2011.11.018

Danaher, B., Huang, Y., Smith, M. D., & Telang, R. (2014). An empirical analysis of digital music bundling strategies. *Management Science, 60*(6), 1413–1433. doi:10.1287/mnsc.2014.1958

Davenport, T. H. (2013). Analytics 3.0. *Harvard Business Review, 91*(12), 64–72.

Dell. (2014). Big Data Use Cases. Retrieved from https://fr.slideshare.net/Dell/big-data-use-cases-36019892

Dobrzykowski, D. D., Leuschner, R., Hong, P. C., & Roh, J. J. (2015). Examining Absorptive Capacity in Supply Chains: Linking Responsive Strategy and Firm Performance. *The Journal of Supply Chain Management, 51*(4), 3–28. doi:10.1111/jscm.12085

Duta, D., & Bose, I. (2015). Managing a big data project: The case of Ramco Cements Limited. *International Journal of Production Economics*, *165*, 293–306. doi:10.1016/j.ijpe.2014.12.032

Fast Company. (2014). The world's Top 10 most innovative companies in big data. Retrieved from http://www.fastcompany.com/most-innovative-companies/2014/industry/big-data

Fawcett, S. E., & Waller, M. A. (2014). Supply chain game changers—mega, nano, and virtual trends—and forces that impede supply chain design (i.e., building a winning team). *Journal of Business Logistics*, *35*(3), 157–164. doi:10.1111/jbl.12058

Fosso Wamba, S., & Akter, S. (2015). Big data analytics for supply chain management: A literature review and research agenda. In *The 11th International Workshop on Enterprise & Organizational Modeling And Simulation* (EOMAS 2015), Stockholm, Sweden, June 8–9.

Fosso Wamba, S., Akter, S., Edwards, A., Chopin, G., & Gnanzou, D. (2015). How "big data" can make big impact: Findings from a systematic review and a longitudinal case study. *International Journal of Production Economics*, *165*, 234–246. doi:10.1016/j.ijpe.2014.12.031

Gandomi, A., & Haider, M. (2015). Beyond the hype: Big data concepts, methods, and analytics. *International Journal of Information Management*, *35*(2), 137–144. doi:10.1016/j.ijinfomgt.2014.10.007

Groves, W., Collins, J., Gini, M., & Ketter, W. (2014). Agent-assisted supply chain management: Analysis and lessons learned. *Decision Support Systems*, *57*, 274–284. doi:10.1016/j.dss.2013.09.006

Hahn, G. J., & Packowski, J. (2015). A perspective on applications of in-memory analytics in supply chain management. *Decision Support Systems*, *76*, 45–52. doi:10.1016/j.dss.2015.01.003

Hashem, I. A. T., Yaqoob, I., Anuar, N. B., Mokhtar, S., Gani, A., & Khan, S. U. (2015). The rise of "big data" on cloud computing: Review and open research issues. *Information Systems*, *47*, 98–115. doi:10.1016/j.is.2014.07.006

Hazen, H. T., Boone, C. A., Ezell, J. D., & Jones-Farmer, L. A. (2014). Data quality for data science, predictive analytics, and big data in supply chain management: An introduction to the problem and suggestions for research and applications. *International Journal of Production Economics*, *154*, 72–80. doi:10.1016/j.ijpe.2014.04.018

Hofmann, E. (2015). Big data and supply chain decisions: The impact of volume, variety and velocity properties on the bullwhip effect. *International Journal of Production Research*. doi:10.1080/00207543.2015.1061222

Hogarth, R.M., and Soyer, E. (2015). Using Simulated Experience to Make Sense of Big Data. *MIT Sloan Management Review,* (spring), 5-10.

Issacs, L. (2013). Rolling the Dice with Predictive Coding: Leveraging Analytics Technology for Information Governance. *Information & Management*, *47*(1), 22–26.

Kahn, K. B. (2014). Solving the problems of new product Forecasting. *Business Horizons*, *57*(5), 607–615. doi:10.1016/j.bushor.2014.05.003

Kemp, R. (2014). Legal Aspects of Managing Big Data. *Computer Law & Security Review, 30*(5), 482–491. doi:10.1016/j.clsr.2014.07.006

Kiron, D., Prentice, P. K., & Ferguson, R. B. (2014). The analytics mandate. *MIT Sloan Management Review, 55*(4), 1–25.

Kohlborn, T., Mueller, O., Poeppelbuss, J., & Roeglinger, M. (2014). Interview with Michael Rosemann on ambidextrous business process management. *Business Process Management Journal, 20*(4), 634–638. doi:10.1108/BPMJ-02-2014-0012

Krumeich, J., Werth, D., & Loos, P. (2016). Prescriptive control of business processes. *Business & Information Systems Engineering, 58*(4), 261–280. doi:10.100712599-015-0412-2

Kshetri, N. (2014). Big data's impact on privacy, security and consumer welfare. *Telecommunications Policy, 38*(11), 1134–1145. doi:10.1016/j.telpol.2014.10.002

Kulkarni, S. S., Apte, U. M., & Evangelopoulos, N. E. (2014). The use of latent semantic analysis in operations management research. *Decision Sciences, 45*(5), 971–994. doi:10.1111/deci.12095

Kwon, K., Kang, D., Yoon, Y., Sohn, J. S., & Chung, I. J. (2014). A real time process management system using RFID data mining. *Computers in Industry, 65*(4), 721–732. doi:10.1016/j.compind.2014.02.007

Li, Q., Luo, H., Xie, P. X., Feng, X. Q., & Du, R. Y. (2015). Product whole life-cycle and omni-channels data convergence oriented enterprise networks integration in a sensing environment. *Computers in Industry, 70*, 23–45. doi:10.1016/j.compind.2015.01.011

Liao, S. H., Chu, P. H., & Hsiao, P. Y. (2012). Data mining techniques and applications – A decade review from 2000 to 2011. *Expert Systems with Applications, 39*(12), 11303–11311. doi:10.1016/j.eswa.2012.02.063

Lustig, I., Dietrich, B., Johnson, C., & Dziekan, C. (2010). The analytics journey. *Analytics Magazine*, November/December, 11–13.

Maldonado, S., Montoya, R., & Weber, R. (2015). Advanced conjoint analysis using feature selection via support vector machines. *European Journal of Operational Research, 241*(2), 564–574. doi:10.1016/j.ejor.2014.09.051

Malhotra, M. K., & Kher, H. V. (1996). Institutional research productivity in production and operations management. *Journal of Operations Management, 14*(1), 55–77. doi:10.1016/0272-6963(95)00037-2

Manyika, J., Chui, M., Brown, B., Bughin, J., Dobbs, R., Roxburgh, C., & Byers, A. H. (2011). *Big data: The next frontier for innovation, competition and productivity*. New York: McKinsey Global Institute.

Mortenson, M. J., Doherty, N. F., & Robinson, S. (2015). Operational research from Taylorism to terabytes: A research agenda for the analytics age. *European Journal of Operational Research, 241*(3), 583–595. doi:10.1016/j.ejor.2014.08.029

Ng, I., Scharf, K., Pogrebna, G., & Maull, R. (2015). Contextual variety, Internet-of-Things and the choice of tailoring over platform: Mass customisation strategy in supply chain management. *International Journal of Production Economics, 159*(0), 76–87. doi:10.1016/j.ijpe.2014.09.007

Ngai, E. W. T., & Wat, F. K. T. (2002). A literature review and classification of electronic commerce research. *Information & Management, 39*(5), 415–429. doi:10.1016/S0378-7206(01)00107-0

Nguyen-Duc, A., Cruzes, D. S., & Conradi, R. (2015). The impact of Global Dispersion on Coordination, Team Performance and Software Quality: A Systematic Literature Review. *Information and Software Technology, 57*, 277–294. doi:10.1016/j.infsof.2014.06.002

Nurmilaakso, J. M. (2008). Adoption of e-business functions and migration from EDI-based to XML-based e-business frameworks in supply chain integration. *International Journal of Production Economics, 113*(2), 721–733. doi:10.1016/j.ijpe.2007.11.001

Ranyard, J. C., Fildes, R., & Hu, T. I. (2015). Reassessing the scope of OR practice: The influences of problem structuring methods and the analytics movement. *European Journal of Operational Research, 245*(1), 1–13. doi:10.1016/j.ejor.2015.01.058

Ross, J. W., Beath, C. M., & Quaadgras, A. (2013). You may not need big data after all. *Harvard Business Review, 91*(12), 90–98. PMID:23593770

Sampler, J. L., & Earl, M. J. (2014). What's your information footprint? *Sloan Management Review, 55*(2), 95–96.

Shang, G., Saladin, B., Fry, T., & Donohue, J. (2015). Twenty-six years of operations management research (1985–2010): Authorship patterns and research constituents in eleven top rated journals. *International Journal of Production Research, 53*(20), 6161–6197. doi:10.1080/00207543.2015.1037935

Sodhi, M. S., & Tang, C. S. (2010). *A Long View of Research and Practice in Operations Research and Management Science.* US: Springer. doi:10.1007/978-1-4419-6810-4

Souza, G. C. (2014). Supply chain analytics. *Business Horizons, 57*(5), 595–605. doi:10.1016/j.bushor.2014.06.004

Supply Chain Council. (2008). SCOR Framework – Introducing all elements of the supply chain reference model: Standard processes, metrics and best practices. Available at supplychainresearch.com/images/SCOR_Framework_2.1.ppt

Tambe, P. (2014). Big data investment, skills, and firm value. *Management Science, 60*(6), 1452–1469. doi:10.1287/mnsc.2014.1899

Tan, K. H., Zhan, Y. Z., Ji, G., Ye, F., & Chang, C. (2015). Harvesting big data to enhance supply chain innovation capabilities: An analytic infrastructure based on deduction graph. *International Journal of Production Economics, 165*, 223–233. doi:10.1016/j.ijpe.2014.12.034

Tiwari, S., Wee, H. M., & Daryanto, Y. (2018). Big data analytics in supply chain management between 2010 and 2016: Insights to industries. *Computers & Industrial Engineering, 115*, 319–330. doi:10.1016/j.cie.2017.11.017

Verdouw, C. N., Beulens, A. J. M., & van der Vorst, J. G. A. J. (2013). Virtualisation of floricultural supply chains: A review from an Internet of Things perspective. *Computers and Electronics in Agriculture, 99*, 160–175. doi:10.1016/j.compag.2013.09.006

Waller, M. A., & Fawcett, S. E. (2013). Data science, predictive analytics, and big data: A revolution that will transform supply chain design and management. *Journal of Business Logistics*, *34*(2), 77–84. doi:10.1111/jbl.12010

Wang, G., Gunasekaran, A., Ngai, E. W., & Papadopoulos, T. (2016). Big data analytics in logistics and supply chain management: Certain investigations for research and applications. *International Journal of Production Economics*, *176*, 98–110. doi:10.1016/j.ijpe.2016.03.014

Wang, J., & Zhang, J. (2016). Big data analytics for forecasting cycle time in semiconductor wafer fabrication system. *International Journal of Production Research*, *54*(23), 7231–7244. doi:10.1080/00 207543.2016.1174789

White, M. (2012). Digital Workplaces: Vision and Reality. *Business Information Review*, *29*(4), 205–214. doi:10.1177/0266382112470412

Zhang, Y., Ren, S., Liu, Y., & Si, S. (2017). A big data analytics architecture for cleaner manufacturing and maintenance processes of complex products. *Journal of Cleaner Production*, *142*, 626–641. doi:10.1016/j.jclepro.2016.07.123

Zhong, R. Y., Huang, G. Q., Lan, S., Dai, Q. Y., Xu, C., & Zhang, T. (2015). A big data approach for logistics trajectory discovery from RFID-enabled production data. *International Journal of Production Economics*, *165*, 260–272. doi:10.1016/j.ijpe.2015.02.014

Zhong, R. Y., Lan, S., Xu, C., Dai, Q., & Huang, G. Q. (2016). Visualization of RFID-enabled shopfloor logistics big data in cloud manufacturing. *International Journal of Advanced Manufacturing Technology*, *84*(1–4), 5–16. doi:10.100700170-015-7702-1

This research was previously published in Business Transformations in the Era of Digitalization; pages 106-124, copyright year 2019 by Business Science Reference (an imprint of IGI Global).

APPENDIX

Table 8. Summary of highlights and key findings of some reviewed articles

Authors	Highlights and Key Findings
Angalakudati et al. (2014)	• The resource allocation problem of scheduled and unpredictable tasks is addressed in the gas industry. • "The goal is to perform all the standard jobs by their respective deadlines, to address all emergency jobs in a timely manner, and to minimize maintenance crew overtime" (p. 1552). • This study use models and heuristics to develop a decision support tool.
Ballings and Van den Poel (2015)	• This study assesses the feasibility of predicting increases in Facebook usage frequency. • Six classification algorithms are evaluated and the importance of many predictors is assessed. • The top-performing algorithm is Stochastic Adaptive Boosting. • The top predictor is the deviation from regular usage patterns. • Facebook can use this approach to customize its service (advertisements, recommendations).
Barton and Court (2012)	• To benefit from big data, a firm has to build prediction and optimization models and develop the ability to use advanced analytics to improve its performance.
Chae, Olson, and Sheu (2013)	• The impact of supply chain analytics on supply chain planning satisfaction and operational performance is studied. • From the perspective of a resource-based view, supply chain analytics consists of three types of resources: data management resources, IT-enabled planning resources, and performance management resources. • The analysis of data collected from 537 manufacturing plants shows that data management resources are a stronger predictor of performance management resources than IT planning resources. • The deployment of advanced IT-enabled planning resources occurs after acquisition of data management resources. • All three sets of resources improve supply chain planning satisfaction and operational performance. • "Manufacturers with sophisticated planning technologies are likely to take advantage of data-driven processes and quality control practices" (p. 1).
Z. Y. Chen, Fan, and Sun (2015)	• A hierarchical ensemble learning framework is proposed for behavior-aware user response modeling using diverse heterogeneous data. • A data transformation and feature extraction strategy is developed to transform large-scale, multi-relational data into customer-centered high-order tensors. • "An improved hierarchical multiple kernel support vector machine (H-MK-SVM) is developed to integrate the external, tag and keyword, individual behavioral and engagement behavioral data for feature selection from multiple correlated attributes and for ensemble learning in user response modeling" (p. 422).
Chongwatpol (2015)	• An RFID-enabled traceability framework is proposed to improve information visibility at the exhibition industry. • RFID allows exhibitors to track attendees' movements and activities during their entire exhibition visit. • The integration of RFID data and business analytics improves exhibitors' understanding of customers' purchasing behavior. • The key findings provide feedback to business analysts to promote follow-up marketing strategies.
Danaher et al. (2014)	• This study uses a "panel data on digital song and album sales coupled with a quasi-random price experiment to determine own- and cross-price elasticities for songs and albums" (p. 1413). • A "structural model of consumer demand to estimate welfare under various policy relevant counterfactual scenarios" (p. 1413) is developed. • Guidance on optimal pricing and marketing strategies for digital music is provided. • The results show that "tiered pricing coupled with reduced album pricing increases revenue to the labels by 18% relative to uniform pricing policies traditionally preferred by digital marketplaces while also increasing consumer surplus by 23%" (p. 1413).
Davenport (2013)	• The evolution of analytics is presented. • Ten requirements are proposed for capitalizing on analytics 3.0. • The impact of analytics in creating value is discussed.
Hofmann (2015)	• The potential of big data to improve supply chain processes is studied. • The potential of big data characteristics (velocity, volume and variety) to mitigate the bullwhip effect is assessed. • The operationalization of big data in control engineering analyses is presented. • Velocity has the greatest potential to enhance performance.

Authors	Highlights and Key Findings
Kulkarni, Apte, and Evangelopoulos (2014)	• The use of the Latent Semantic Analysis technique is presented. • The implementation of Latent Semantic Analysis is explained and illustrated. • The field study of operations management is presented in the area of big data.
Maldonado, Montoya, and Weber (2015)	• Advanced machine learning techniques enhance conjoint analysis capabilities to better identify consumer preferences. • Feature selection procedure pools information across consumers while identifying individual preferences. • Applications on experimental data and on two empirical studies show that the proposed approaches outperform traditional techniques for conjoint analysis.
Mortenson, Doherty, and Robinson (2015)	• The lack of research into analytics in the operational research field is underscored. • The histories of operational research, analytics and a range of related disciplines are presented and their relationships are discussed. • Avenues for future research are proposed by combining several key themes related to analytics and operational research.
Ranyard, Fildes, and Hu (2015)	• Results of a global survey of operational research practices are presented. • The scope of operational research practices has been extended via problem structuring methods and business analytics. • The gap between academic research and practice is emphasized. • Business analytics and operational research overlap, presenting challenges and opportunities that must be addressed.
Sampler and Earl (2014)	• This study deals with the information assets a company has to have in order to generate economic value.
Tambe (2014)	• "This paper analyzes how labor market factors have shaped early returns on big data investment using a new data source—the LinkedIn skills database" (p. 1452). • Hadoop investments to complement workers' technical skills were associated with 3% faster productivity growth.

Chapter 69
Exploring Factors Influencing Big Data and Analytics Adoption in Healthcare Management

Sampson Abeeku Edu
Cyprus International University, Cyprus

Divine Q. Agozie
Cyprus International University, Cyprus

ABSTRACT

Demand for improvement in healthcare management in the areas of quality, cost, and patient care has been on the upsurge because of technology. Incessant application and new technological development to manage healthcare data significantly led to leveraging on the use of big data and analytics (BDA). The application of the capabilities from BDA has provided healthcare institutions with the ability to make critical and timely decisions for patients and data management. Adopting BDA by healthcare institutions hinges on some factors necessitating its application. This study aims to identify and review what influences healthcare institutions towards the use of business intelligence and analytics. With the use of a systematic review of 25 articles, the study identified nine dominant factors driving healthcare institutions to BDA adoption. Factors such as patient management, quality decision making, disease management, data management, and promoting healthcare efficiencies were among the highly ranked factors influencing BDA adoption.

INTRODUCTION

Recent deliberations and developments on Big Data and Analytics and (BDA) have primarily resulted in many firms gaining leverage on data utilization due to availability of big data (Trieu, 2016; Popovic, Hackney, Coelho, & Jaklic, 2012; Visinescu, Jones, & Sidorova, 2017). Business Intelligence and Analytics capabilities have therefore provided a lot of opportunities for organizations operations and quality in decision making (Popovic, Hackney, Tassabehji, & Castelli, 2106; Wang & Hajli, 2017; Hagel,

DOI: 10.4018/978-1-6684-3662-2.ch069

2015; Agarwal & Dhar, 2014). For example, BI capabilities implementation results in creating business values (Wang & Hajli, 2017). Business values are, therefore, categorised into "organizational benefits, operational benefits, IT infrastructure benefits, managerial benefits and strategic benefits" (Wang & Hajli, 2017). Popovic, Hackney, Tassabehji and Castelli (2016) also indicated that application of BDA enhances business performance. Innovations in Business and Analytics through visual analytics have indeed improved how information is reported through dashboards and scorecards for quick decision making by managers (Turban, Ramesh, Delen, & King, 2011). Also, BDA tools like data mining have given organizations a lifeline to improve customer relationship and resolve intricate organization problems (Persson & Riyals, 2014).

The healthcare sector has also seen a tremendous growth of adopting BDA due to the enormous opportunities it offers (Chen, Chiang, & Storey, 2012; Denaxas & Morley, 2015; Wang & Hajli, 2017; Costa, 2014; Raghupathi & Raghupathi, 2014). Studies over the past decades have demonstrated that the integration of BDA with other health systems such as Electronic health (E-Health) systems, Telehealth systems and health care ecosystems, in general, improve healthcare (Luo, Wu, Gopukumar, & Zhao, 2016; Mehta & Pandit, 2018). Arguably, the healthcare sector is perceived to generate large volumes of data ranging from patient records, biomedical data and administrative records which are difficult to manage through traditional storage applications and analytical tools (Sakr & Elgammal, 2016). For example, data aggregation through BDA have enhanced healthcare data to be standardized (Shah & Pathak, 2014) and the agility to decision making (Wixcom, Yen, & Relich, 2013). Quality decision making in healthcare management is tremendously improved through the use of BDA (Chen et al., 2012). It is therefore essential to note that healthcare sectors efforts in the adoption of Big data and Business Intelligent provides business values (Wu, Li, Cheng, & Lin, 2016). Other studies revealed that the level of digitization of healthcare systems and continuous reliance of information technology to provide safe healthcare mostly contributed to BDA adoption (Agarwal, Gao, DesRoches, & Jha, 2010; Nicolini, Powell, Conville, & Matinez-Solano, 2008).

Albeit all the many successes BDA offers to the healthcare sector, it hinges on several factors or the intention of deployment and usage. These factors, when neglected, would lead to failure or undermine the sole purpose for BDA adoption in healthcare. The present study from IS literature posits several factors that regularly affect the benefits accrued to any new technology adopted by organizations. For example, Hung, Huang, Lin, Chen, and Tarn (2016) addressed specific factors influencing BDA adoption in no small extent. More importantly, healthcare preparedness and knowledge towards BDA implementation and application. Besides, there is lack of understanding of these factors from literature specifically attributed to BDA adoption for healthcare institutions (Murdoch & Detsky, 2013; Shah & Pathak, 2014; Watson, 2014) and evidence indicates that 60% failed in the quest (Deloitte Centre, 2015). Even though, these factors have resulted in some level of benefits firms could derive from new technology, Angeles (2013) emphasised a need for a clear direction for firm's technology to align to the new demands with innovations. Tornatzky and Fleischer (1990) have argued that firm's preparedness for new technology adoption is often by the level of technical abilities the firm has, characteristics of the organization and environmental context within which the firm operates. BDA adoption is, therefore, considered as new IS technological innovation that comes with its challenges and factors in its implementation, especially, for healthcare management (Safwan, Meredithand & Burst, 2016). There is, therefore, the need to explore further the factors leading to the success or failure of BDA adoption among healthcare institutions and more importantly, how developing countries can leverage from established healthcare institutions.

The motivation for this paper is to identify and report on empirical research findings on the factors influencing healthcare institutions decision to adopt BDA. Mainly, to provide insights from developed countries perspectives for such motivating factors and how healthcare institutions in developing economies could be aware of these findings for BDA adoptions as well. The study would also classify these critical factors for BDA adoption in healthcare management. The classification of these vital factors will enhance further discussions towards implication for practice and theory of BDA in Healthcare management. The study significantly used a systematic review of relevant literature on BDA adoption in healthcare.

This paper focused on:

1. Review of factors that influence Big Data and Analytics adoption in Healthcare.
2. Identifying dominant factors into classifications.
3. Rating factors mostly influencing Big Data and Analytics adoption in Healthcare.

The rest of the paper is organised into three sections: From E-Health to BDA application and implication in Healthcare, the methodology adopted for the study, Discussion of Literature findings and Conclusion of the study.

FROM E-HEALTH TO BIG DATA AND ANALYTICS ADOPTION

Increasingly, the drive to improve healthcare delivery has also seen technology applications such as BDA by healthcare institutions (Mehta & Pandit, 2018). From their review, Blayer, Fraser and Holt (2010) suggested how healthcare institutions are taking advantage of information communication and technology (ICT) in general, and related platforms to improve healthcare delivery. Over the last decade, significance reliance on ICT for healthcare delivery are ascribed to Electronic Health systems (e-health) (Edworthy, 2001; Alpay, Henkemans, Otten, Rovekamp, & Dumay, 2010; Christensen, Reynolds, & Griffiths, 2011). Primarily, e-health systems and applications are to promote health delivery services to improve patients care (Ramtohul, 2016). Ganesh (2004) pointed health policy, customer choices and technological capabilities as a driving force for e-health adoption. Other issues such as the characteristic of health institutions, that is, public, private or referral hospitals and peculiar needs also influence e-health adoption (Kesse-Tachi, Asmah, & Agbozo, 2019). The adoption of e-health is also due to responding to policy directions to effectively managed ambulatory care. For example, a study by Dunnebeil, Sunyaev, Blohm, Leimeister, and Krcmar (2012), revealed how healthcare policies towards telemedicine in Germany gradually influenced physicians to use e-health applications for ambulatory care. From a developing economies context, e-health adoption is also as a result of the need to meet both rural and urban health services. Miah, Hasan, and Gammack (2017) evaluated the success of e-health systems enabled through cloud platforms supporting medical doctors and healthcare workers to cure non-communicable infections in isolated communities in Bangladesh. In the case of Sub-Saharan countries, Adenuga, Iahad, and Miskon (2017) studied the motivating issues for telemedicine adoption in Nigeria by government hospitals. The study concluded on matters such as facilitating conditions, reinforcement issues and performance expectancy affecting clinicians' attitudes towards telemedicine adoptions. A survey conducted by Kesse-Tachi et al. (2019) further suggested that healthcare practitioners' characteristics have a significant influence on e-health adoption. Healthcare practitioners' characteristics such as educational level, age and gender, were among the influencing factors for e-health adoption.

Notably, from the views above, several decisions drive health institution towards e-health adoption. However, the nature of healthcare delivery services has changed significantly as a result of the large volumes of data generated through electronic medical systems, technology innovation, patients demands and real-time response for healthcare delivery services. The continuous implementations of e-health systems and other health platforms such as Mobile health have also contributed to an exponential amount of data generation. Consequently, these developments have potentially contributed to the adoption of BDA by healthcare institutions (Bates, Saria, Ohno-Machado, Shah, Escobar, 2014). The extraction, providing insights and knowledge creation through these large volumes of structured and unstructured data is complicated and therefore, the need for BDA adoption by healthcare. Accordingly, Sonnati, (2017), and Al-Qahtani and Al-Asem (2015) explored the prospects and usefulness health institutions derive through BDA adoption. A synthesis report by Gu, Li, Li and Liang (2017) further revealed a tremendous growth in BDA adoption in health informatics between 2003 to 2016 by healthcare institutions. Majority of these healthcare institutions were mainly from a developed country context, showing a lack of BDA adoption in developing countries.

Big data and analytics application have transcended beyond just a term which affects organizations' agility to decision making. The multiplicity that BDA applications offer has been described as the *"Game changer"* to improving an institution's efficiency and effectiveness (Wamba et al., 2016). Undeniably, the adoption and right attitude towards BDA implementation have provided a competitive advantage to most organizations. Liu (2014) proposed that, with BDA deployment and usage, differentiating high performing organizations from low performing organization is made easier through the level of revenues and cost of responding to customers.

Deploying Big data technologies has also introduced discussions towards Business Intelligent and applications. To some extent, it is just a "buzzwords" that describe the integration of analytical tools, architectures, applications, databases and methodologies towards transforming data to actionable results (Turban, Ramesh, Delen & King, 2011). The consequences for organizations adopting BDA & BI hinges on specific needs and factors that influence the decision towards embracing it. Some of these factors are prevailing market conditions, consumer demands, technology and societal pressure (Hung et al., 2016). The extent to which these factors influence organization decisions is categorized into several theoretical frameworks through empirical and exploratory studies in IS literature. Key among them is Technology Acceptance Model (TAM) (Davis, 1989; Davis, Bagozzi & Warshaw, 1989), Technology, Organization and Environmental framework (TOE) (Tornatzky & Fleischer, 1990), the Institutional theory (Dacin, Goodstein, & Scott, 2002) and the Diffusion of Innovation theory (Rogers, 2003). The effect of these factors on technology adoption differs from industry-specific depending on the exact need of the organization (Sun, Cegielski, Jia, & Hall, 2016).

To a large extent, these factors may not differ from the adoption of BDA application by Healthcare sectors. Implementation of BDA adoption has resulted in several prepositions from literature. Many studies have suggested its advantages or opportunities health institutions derive from its application (Denaxas & Morley, 2015; Sonnati, 2017). According to Wu et al. (2016), BDA capabilities have become the "promising future" for healthcare delivery. Consequently, this has influenced the level at which the healthcare sectors are adopting BDA to leverage healthcare delivery.

METHODOLOGY

Research Design

The research design is an exploratory approach that focused on describing findings from extant studies in the context of the study (Cresswell, 2014). In achieving this goal, the study adopted a systematic review approach to extract explicit academic journal in IS. Systematic review approach identified the step by step criteria in identifying journals to address the main aim of the study. The plan focused on the "inclusion and exclusion criteria" (Jesson, Matheson, & Lacey, 2011) to sort relevant articles identified. The search strategy was to identify related studies based on BDA adoption, appraise the quality of the journal and summarize evidence that distinguishes other articles. Academic Journals used for the search were from the following databases: Web of Science, Taylor and Francis, Elsevier, Scopus, IEEE, Emerald and Ebscohost.

Procedure and Sample selection

The search used keywords such as "big data", AND "business intelligent" AND "analytics" AND "critical factors OR influences", "adoption OR implementation", AND "healthcare OR hospitals". The keywords for the search revealed 952 articles. Some articles were dropped from the search due to duplication from other databases and also, a review of abstracts. The study adopted systematic and snowballing techniques to identify 150 articles which were selected because they met specific indicators for the study. A final sample of 25 articles was decided on using the inclusion and exclusion criteria approach through the systematic review concept in Table 1 below. These articles were critically considered based on the specific criteria adopted for this study.

Table 1. Inclusion and Exclusion Criteria

Criteria	Inclusion	Exclusion
Types of articles	Published Peer-reviewed journals	Articles not peer-reviewed
Literature Focus	BDA adoption in the health sector	Different sectors with BDA adoption
Language	Journal wrote in English	Non-English study
Year of study	2010 to 2017	Articles outside this study periods.

Results from Data Extraction and Literature

Articles extracted for the study categorised the name of the author, year of publication, the title of the article, name of journal and factors influencing adoption in Healthcare. Table 2 below shows the taxonomy of 25 articles systematically reviewed using the inclusion and exclusion criteria. According to Chawla and Davis (2013), Zhu and Cahan (2016), and Casselma, Onopa, and Khansa (2017), tracking and managing of patients' disease and care in real-time response based on data available through wearable devices are improving through BDA applications and tools. The literature review also revealed an improvement in healthcare efficiencies through the use of BDA in areas such as securing patient data and financial management (Sonnati, 2017), quality of care (Fosso, Anand, & Carter, 2013) and predicting specific patients for re-admission (Bates et al., 2012). In their review, Fosso et al. (2013) observed that the use of RFID applications provide enamours data to support the use of BDA to support healthcare services. Indeed, this has led to the use of BDA to personalized patients care in real-time (Chawla & Davis, 2013). Big data analytics and business intelligence applications have also harness data for precise decision-making to improve patients' outcomes (Ashrafi et al., 2014). Specifically, BDA adoption among healthcare institutions is mostly by factors such as quality decision making, managing patient data, and improving healthcare efficiency (Foshay & Kuziemsky, 2014). Identifying the promises and potential BDA offers, Raghupathi and Raghupathi (2014) indicated further insights such as data visualization BDA provides to healthcare practitioners. Ghosh and Scott (2011) also disclosed the "antecedent and catalysts for developing healthcare capability" and concluded that BDA capabilities are improving data visualization during surgical procedures. A systematic review by Thakur and Ramzan (2015), tracking disease pattern for specific treatment and patient care is through BDA and Hadoop applications. Findings from Bates et al. (2015) further revealed that BDA is becoming useful for monitoring, identifying and predicting high-risk patients for specific treatment among healthcare institutions. A review on BDA in "health informatics" by Kumar and Singh (2015) provided insight on how healthcare industries are adopting big data capabilities mainly for data management and quality decision- making. From the perspectives of telehealth in care management, Zhu and Cahan (2016) argue that wearable technologies have become the conduit for large data generation from patients. Big data analytics capabilities, therefore, leverage on telehealth and wearable technologies to manage and provide real-time analysis to respond to patients with a chronic illness before readmission. Casselma, Onopa, and Khansa (2107) pointed out that due to high demand for wearable technologies by patients, BDA applications have become essential for analysing, tracking and managing patients' diseases. Spriut, Vroon, and Batenburg (2014), on the other hand, emphasized BDA usefulness to improving patient's satisfaction through quality care and operational efficiency among health institutions in the Netherlands. Significantly, Ward, Marsolo and Froehle (2014), pointed out the continuous improvement of healthcare efficiency through the adoption of BDA in modern healthcare systems globally. Also, Zailani, Iranmanesh, Nikbin and Beng (2015) and Jee and Kim (2013) suggested recent healthcare operations, mostly from developed countries, are as a result of massive adoption of BDA. Big data and analytics are, therefore, are at the infant stages of approval or implementation in the developing countries. Finally, other studies show that the adoption of BDA has assisted in managing fraud in medical payments and reducing the cost of healthcare services (Sonnati, 2017).

From the above synthesis of the usefulness of BDA adoption from the 25 articles reviewed, Tables 2 to 5 further classified and conceptualised the various uses of BDA into nine (9) prevailing factors. As shown in Tables 2 to 5, these factors include Quality Decision Making, Patient Care Management, Medicine Tracking, Disease Tracking, Data Management, Data Visualization, Healthcare Efficiency, Securing Patient Data and Financial Management. Towards the aspect of improving the decision-making process, healthcare institutions, especially clinicians, rely on data generated from patients' medical records for real-time responses to emergency services. Also, BDA offers various visualization reports in a more user-friendly manner to support decision making by clinicians (Chan, Esteve, Fourniols, Escriba,

& Campo, 2012). Other healthcare institutions were also leveraging on Data Visualization capabilities such as Dashboards and Scorecards in the surgical wards by Physicians and additional related financial or bill payment reporting. Data generated from wearable technologies also support medical carers with quick notification for real-time decision-making processes, especially for social health welfare (Wu, Li, Liu, & Zheng, 2017). Foshay and Kuziemsky (2014), Ashrafi, Kelleher and Kuilboer (2014), and Wang and Byrd (2017) also advocated that healthcare institutions and practitioners deploy BDA to generate insights from such data are critical to improving quick and concise diagnostics response to patients. For example, improving infant safety and health tracking through integrating wearable healthcare devices and big data platforms (Casselma et al., 2017). Another critical factor to BDA adoption in healthcare delivery is Patient management. From the review, healthcare institutions are harnessing the vast majority of data daily about the patient and eventually been used to manage and guarantee patient outcomes. Also, healthcare efficiency and improving productivity are driving the healthcare sector into BDA adoption. As a result, BDA is improving inventory management, financial management, quality healthcare at a low cost and confidence in decision making by healthcare practitioners.

Furthermore, the factors identified were ranked to indicate the most influencing factor(s) for BDA adoption by health institutions. Table 6 demonstrates that Patient care management is a critical factor for most healthcare institutions to monitor patients with exceptional cases such as diabetics patients, mental health cases and elderly care (Bellazsi, Dagliti, Sacchi, & Segani, 2015; Saravana, Eswari, Sampath & Lavanya, 2015). Big data and analytics re therefore used to respond to the critical needs of patients in real-time to prevent fatal occurrences. Disease management ranked as the second factor influencing healthcare sector decision to adopt BDA. With the aid of wearable devices or actuating devices which collect and share patient's health report in real-time, monitoring and tracking the level of infections for the physician for quick diagnostics at the early stages. The next factor influencing BDA adoption is decision making. A significant advantage of combining BDA and Hadoop tools is the high level of data processing without any human interaction, thereby reducing the level of errors in reports generated (Manikandan & Ravi, 2014). Ultimately, health practitioners depend on these reports to make a precise and quality decision. Most studies have also shown that the ultimate concerns for BDA adoption by healthcare institution is to improve efficiency in healthcare delivery. Accordingly, this factor is ranked fourth from the 25 literature articles reviewed which seek to promote the future of healthcare delivery at a low cost. Using BDA for data management is also rated to be important as an influencing factor from this study. As espoused by other studies, the healthcare sector is one of the most significant contributors of data and the adoption of BDA provides support and managing data accordingly. Factors such as Medicine tracking, Data visualization, securing patients data and financial management were the least factors for BDA adoption, as shown in Table 6.

The results from the systematic review also show that most of these factors identified are mainly due to changes in technological advancements and patients need. Thus, the motivation for most healthcare institutions to adopt BDA is through technological innovation to manage and monitor Patients care, quality healthcare and quality in decision making. The findings further identified the use of Radio Frequency Identification Device (RFID), Wearable devices and gesture-based technologies as the most common devices facilitating data gathering for BDA tools to provide critical information for quick decision-making processes.

Table 2. Results from Literature Review

Name of Author	Year	Title of Article	Name of Journal	Use of BDA in Healthcare	Factors Conceptualization
Foshay and Kuziemsky	2014	Towards an implementation framework for business intelligence in healthcare	International Journal of Information Management	1. Impacts of information quality to the decision-making process. 2. Impact of Personnel issues. 3. Decision Timeliness 4. Decision Confidence	Quality Decision Making
Fosso et al.	2013	A literature review of RFID-enabled healthcare applications and issues	International Journal of Information Management	5. Identification of Blood bags for blood type Matching. 6. Medicine Tracking. 7. Detecting tampered Drugs. 8. Inventory Utilization. 9. Patience Management	Patient Management Medicine Tracking
Chawla and Davis	2013	Bringing Big Data to Personalized Healthcare: A Patient-Centred Framework	Journal of General Internal Medicine	10. Personalised healthcare by consumers through wearable devices.	Patient Management
Ashrafi et al.	2014	The impact of business intelligence on healthcare delivery in the USA	Interdisciplinary Journal of Information, Knowledge and Management	11. Harnessing data for precise decision-making to help improve patient outcomes, reduce costs, and ensure the future of the healthcare industry. 12. Streamline data and improve population health. 13. Instant guarantee to knowledge by Healthcare providers to deliver quality care at a low cost.	Quality Decision Making Data Management Healthcare Efficiency

Table 3. Results from Literature Review

Name of Author	Year	Title of Article	Name of Journal	Use of BDA in Healthcare	Factors Conceptualization
Zailani et al.	2015	"Determinants of RFID Adoption in Malaysia's Healthcare Industry: Occupational Level as a Moderator"	Journal of Medical Science	14. BI tools help to improve the security of data 15. BDA tools increase efficiency and productivity in healthcare and support staff delivery. 16. BDA tools in the Health Management Information System improve healthcare services offered to patients. 17. BDA tools are user-friendly for knowledge creation and reporting.	Securing Patient Data Healthcare Efficiency Data Visualization
Zhu and Cahan	2016	"Wearable technology and Telehealth in care management for chronic illness."	Health Information Management Systems	18. Notification of Health Emergency Services using wearable devices and BDA	Patient Management
Casselma et al.	2017	"Wearable Healthcare: Lessons from the past and a peek into the future."	Telematics and Informatics	19. Customer Demand for Wearable health device 20. For Infant safety and health tracking	Patient Management Disease Tracking
Amirian et al.	2017	"Using Big Data Analytics to extract disease surveillance information from the point of care diagnostics machines."	Pervasive and Mobile Computing	21. BDA supports d	Disease Tracking
Jee and Kim	2013	"Potentiality of Big Data in the Medical Sector: Focus on How to Reshape the Healthcare System"	Healthcare Informatics Research	22. For Healthcare Efficiency improvement 23. Disease Treatment	Healthcare Efficiency

Table 4. Results from Literature Review

Name of Author	Year	Title of Article	Name of Journal	Use of BDA in Healthcare	Factors Conceptualization
Chan et al.	2012	"Smart wearables systems: current status and future challenges."	Artificial Intelligence Medicine	24. For Real-time collection of healthcare data	Data Management
Lin, Brown, Yang, Li, and Lu	2011	"Data mining large-scale electronic health records for clinical support."	IEEE Intelligent System	25. To Identifying different diseases	Disease Tracking
Ward et al.	2014	"Application of business analytics in healthcare."	Business Horizons	26. For quality and efficient healthcare	Healthcare Efficiency
Wu et al.	2017	"Adoption of Big data and analytics in the mobile healthcare market: an economic perspective."	Electronic Commerce Research and Applications	27. For improving Social health welfare	Patient Management
Wang and Byrd	2017	"Business analytics-enabled decision-making effectiveness through knowledge absorptive capacity in healthcare."	Journal of Knowledge Management	28. For improving decision making effectiveness	Quality Decision Making
Ghosh and Scott	2011	"Antecedent and Catalysts for developing healthcare capability."	Communications of the Association for Information Systems	29. For Healthcare analytic capabilities 30. For visualization of surgical procedure	Data Visualization
Ferranti et al.	2010	"Bridging the gap: leveraging business intelligence tools in support of patient safety and financial effectiveness."	Journal of the American Medical Informatics Association	31. For improving patient's safety	Patient Management
Bardhan, Oh, Zheng and Kirksey	2014	"Predictive Analytics for Readmission of Patients with Congestive heart failure."	Information Systems Research	32. For monitoring a patient's readmission rate	Patient Management
Al-Qahtani and Al-Asem	2015	"Business Analytics in Healthcare: Opportunities and Challenges"	Information and Knowledge Management	33. For Diseases control 34. Tracking Patients healthier behaviours. 35. Mobile health for monitoring and treating patients timely	Disease Tracking Patient Management

Table 5. Results from Literature Review

Name of Author	Year	Title of Article	Name of Journal	Use of BDA in Healthcare	Factors Conceptualization
Sonnati	2017	"Improving Healthcare Using Big Data Analytics"	International Journal of Scientific and Technology Research	36. Detecting Fraud in Medical Payments. 37. Securing Patients Medical records. 38. Disease Management	Disease Tracking Data Management Financial Management
Bates et al.	2014	"Big Data in Healthcare: Using Analytics to Identify and Manage High-Risk and High-Cost Patients"	Health Affairs	39. Monitoring and predicting specific patients for readmission.	Disease Tracking Patient Care Management
Thakur and Ramzan	2015	"A Systematic Review on Cardiovascular disease using Big-Data by Hadoop."	Cloud system and big data engineering, IEEE	40. Tracking Disease pattern for appropriate treatment.	Disease Tracking
Raghupathi and Raghupathi	2014	"Big data Analytics in Healthcare: Promise and Potential."	Health Information Science and Systems	41. Gaining insight from Clinical Data.	Data Visualization
Tremblay, Hevner and Berndt	2012	"Design of an information Volatility measure for Healthcare decision making."	Decision Support Systems	42. Patient care and managing diseases	Patience Care Management
Spruit et al.	2014	"Towards Healthcare Business Intelligence in long-term care: an exploratory case study in the Netherlands."	Computer in Human Behaviour	43. Quality of care 44. Patient Satisfaction Healthcare improvement.	Disease Tracking Patient Management Healthcare Efficiency
Kumar and Singh	2017	"Review paper on Big Data in healthcare informatics."	International Research Journal of Engineering and Technology	45. Improvement in Patient Safety 46. Responding to Patients health needs	Data Management Disease Tracking Decision Making

Table 6. Rating of BDA Influencing Factors from 25 Articles

Factors	Frequency of Adoption	Ranking
Patient Management	12	1
Disease Tracking	8	2
Quality Decision Making	6	3
Medicine Tracking	1	7
Healthcare Efficiency	5	4
Financial Management	1	7
Data Management	4	5
Data Visualization	2	6
Securing Patient Data	1	7

CONCLUSION

The study presented a systematic review of existing studies in BDA adoption among health institutions. Significantly, this is as a result of the universal application of new technologies to enhance and improve healthcare delivery quality, efficiency and Patients monitors. With the level of extensive data generated from biomedical data, patient's data and health-related data, BDA has emerged as the frontier to provide insight to improve healthcare delivery. Generally, the paper sought to explore emerging issues advancing the adoption of BDA by healthcare institutions. Also, to classify these issues into prevailing factors and to provide an overview of the most common factor affecting BDA adoption. Relevant issues advancing BDA adoption ranges from improving patient's safety, securing patients records, monitoring and predicting. Other essential uses of BDA are specific for patients before readmission, using BDA to track disease patterns, harnessing data for precise decision making and an overall improvement in healthcare efficiency.

The issues identified from the review were classified into nine key factors influencing the level of BDA adoption. Among the nine discovered, patient care management revealed as the most recurring factor prompting healthcare institutions to deploy BDA to improve quality of care. Disease tracking management is the second factor affecting BDA adoption. Such arrangements are possible through RFIDs and wearable devices attached to patients' bodies for data collection. Respectively, quality decision making, improving healthcare efficiency, data management, data visualization, financial management, and securing patients data were among other factors promoting BDA adoption in healthcare. Through the systematic review, these factors provide clear strategies for healthcare institutions towards BDA to improve quality of healthcare more importantly for developing countries.

Interestingly, majority of the papers reviewed indicated that BDA adoption in healthcare is mostly from the developed economies which signify the continuous promotion of the study of BDA in emerging economies. In addition to further provide empirical research underpinning potentials for BDA deployment and usage in healthcare management, more importantly, to support patient's safety and cost-effectiveness. Finally, the study echoes the need for healthcare institutions to define a clear scope for BDA applications to maximise the value of its adoption.

REFERENCES

Adenuga, K. I., Iahad, N. A., & Miskon, S. (2017). Towards reinforcing telemedicine adoption amongst clinicians in Nigeria. *International Journal of Medical Informatics, 104*, 84–98. doi:10.1016/j.ijmedinf.2017.05.008 PMID:28599820

Agarwal, R., & Dhar, V. (2014). Editorial—big data, data science, and analytics: The opportunity and challenge of IS research. *Information Systems Research, 25*(3), 443–448. doi:10.1287/isre.2014.0546

Agarwal, R., Gao, G., DesRoches, C., & Jha, A. K. (2010). Research Commentary-The Digital Transformation of Healthcare: Current status and the Road Ahead. *Information Systems Research, 21*(4), 661–101. doi:10.1287/isre.1100.0327

Al-Qahtani, N., & Al-Asem, S. A. (2015). Business Analytics in Healthcare: Opportunities and Challenges. *Information and Knowledge Management, 5*(12).

Alpay, L., Henkemans, O. B., Otten, W., Rövekamp, T. A. J. M., & Dumay, A. C. M. (2010). E-health Applications and Services for Patient Empowerment: Directions for Best Practices in The Netherlands. *Telemedicine Journal and e-Health, 16*(7), 787–791. doi:10.1089/tmj.2009.0156 PMID:20815745

Angeles, R. (2013). Using the Technology-Organization-Environment framework and Zuboff's concepts for understanding environmental sustainability and RFID: Two case studies. *International Journal of Social, Management. Economics and Business Engineering, 7*(10), 1605–1613.

Ashrafi, N., Kelleher, L., & Kuilboer, J.-P. (2014). The Impact of Business Intelligence on Healthcare Delivery in the USA. *Interdisciplinary Journal of Information, Knowledge, and Management, 9*.

Bardhan, I., Oh, J., Zheng, Z., & Kirksey, K. (2014). Predictive Analytics for Readmission of Patients with Congestive heart failure. *Information Systems Research, 26*(1), 19–36. doi:10.1287/isre.2014.0553

Bates, D. W., Saria, S., Ohno-Machado, L., Shah, A., & Escoba, G. (2014). Big Data in Healthcare: Using Analytics to Identify and Manage High-Risk and High-Cost Patients. *Health Affairs, 33*(7), 1123–1131. doi:10.1377/hlthaff.2014.0041 PMID:25006137

Bellazsi, R., Dagliti, A., Sacchi, L., & Segani, D. (2015). Big Data Technologies: New Opportunities for Diabetes Management. *Journal of Diabetes Science and Technology, 9*(5), 1119-1125. . doi:10.1177/1932296815583505

Casselma, J., Onopa, N., & Khansa, L. (2017). Wearable Healthcare: Lessons from the past a peek into the future. *Telematics and Informatics, 34*(7), 1011–1023. doi:10.1016/j.tele.2017.04.011

Chan, M., Esteve, D., Fourniols, J. E., Escriba, C., & Campo, E. (2012). Smart wearable systems: Current status and future challenges. *Artificial Intelligence in Medicine, 56*(3), 137–156. doi:10.1016/j.artmed.2012.09.003 PMID:23122689

Chawla, N., & Davis, D. (2013). Bringing Big Data to Personalized Healthcare: A Patient-Centred. *Journal of General Internal Medicine, 28*(S3), 660–665. doi:10.100711606-013-2455-8

Chen, H., Chiang, R., & Storey, V. (2012). Business intelligence and analytics: From big data to big impact. *Management Information Systems Quarterly, 36*(4), 1165–1188. doi:10.2307/41703503

Christensen, H., Reynolds, J., & Griffiths, K., M. (2011). The use of e-health applications for anxiety and depression in young people: challenges and solutions. *Early Intervention in Psychiatry, 5*(1), 58-62. doi:10.1111/j.1751-7893.2010.00242

Costa, F. F. (2014). Big data in Biomedicine. *Drug Discovery Today, 17*(4), 433–440. doi:10.1016/j.drudis.2013.10.012 PMID:24183925

Cresswell, J. W. (2014). Research Design: qualitative, quantitative and mixed methods approach (4th ed.). Sage Publication Inc.

Dacin, M., Goodstein, J., & Scott, W. (2002). Institutional theory and institutional change: Introduction to the special research forum. *Academy of Management Journal, 45*(1), 45–56. doi:10.5465/amj.2002.6283388

Davis, F. (1989). Perceived usefulness, perceived ease of use and user acceptance of information technology. *Management Information Systems Quarterly, 13*(3), 318–339. doi:10.2307/249008

Davis, F., Bagozzi, R., & Warshaw, P. (1989). User acceptance of computer technology: A comparison of two theoretical models. *Management Science, 35*(8), 982–1003. doi:10.1287/mnsc.35.8.982

Deloitte Centre for Health Solution. (2015). *Health system analytics: The missing key to unlock value-based care*. Deloitte Development LCC.

Denaxas, S. C., & Morley, K. I. (2015). Big Biomedical data and Cardiovascular disease research: potentials and challenges. *European Heart Journal - Quality of Care and Clinical Outcomes, 1*(1), 9-16. doi:10.1093/ehjqcco/qcv005

Dunnebeil, S., Sunyaev, A., Blohm, I., Leimeister, J., & Krcmar, H. (2012). Determinants of physicians' technology acceptance for e-health in ambulatory care. *International Journal of Medical Informatics, 81*, 746-760. . doi:10.1016/jijmedinf.2012.02.002

Edworthy, S. M. (2001). Telemedicine in developing countries. *BMJ (Clinical Research Ed.), 323*(7312), 524–525. doi:10.1136/bmj.323.7312.524 PMID:11546681

Ferranti, J. M., Langman, K., Tanaka, D., McCall, J., & Ahmad, A. (2010). Bridging the gap: Leveraging business intelligence tools in support of patient safety and financial effectiveness. *Journal of the American Medical Informatics Association, 17*(2), 136–143. doi:10.1136/jamia.2009.002220 PMID:20190055

Foshay, N., & Kuziemsky, C. (2014). Towards an implementation framework for business intelligence in healthcare. *International Journal of Information Management, 34*(1), 20–27. doi:10.1016/j.ijinfomgt.2013.09.003

Fosso, S. W., Anand, A., & Carter, L. (2013). A literature review of RFID-enabled healthcare applications and issues. *Journal of International Management, 33*, 875–891. doi:10.1016/j.ijinfomgt.2013.07.005

Ghosh, B., & Scott, J. E. (2011). Antecedent and Catalysts for developing healthcare capability. *Communication of the Association for Information Systems*, 395-310.

Gu, D., Li, J., Li, X., & Liang, C. (2017). Visualizing the knowledge structure and evolution of big data research in healthcare informatics. *International Journal of Medical Informatics, 98*, 22–38. doi:10.1016/j.ijmedinf.2016.11.006 PMID:28034409

Hagel, J. (2015). Bringing analytics to life. *Journal of Accountancy, 219*, 24–25.

Hung, S. Y., Huang, Y. W., Lin, C. C., Chen, K. C., & Tarn, J. (2016). Factors Influencing Business Intelligence Systems Implementation Success in the Enterprises. Association for Information Systems.

Jee, K., & Kim, G.-K. (2013). The potentiality of Big Data in the Medical Sector: Focus on how to Re-shape the Healthcare Sector. *Healthcare Informatics Research, 19*(2), 79–85. doi:10.4258/hir.2013.19.2.79 PMID:23882412

Jesson, J., Matheson, L., & Lacey, F. M. (2011). *Doing your Literature Review: Traditional and Systematic Techniques*. London: Sage Publications.

Kesse-Tachi, A., Asmah, A. E., & Agbozo, E. (2019). Factors influencing the adoption of eHealth technologies in Ghana. *Digital Health, 5*. doi:10.1177/2055207619871425

Lin, Y., Brown, R., Yang, H., Li, S., & Lu, H. (2011). Data mining large-scale electronic health records for clinical support. *IEEE Intelligent Systems, 23*, 87–90.

Liu, Y. (2014). Big data and predictive business analytics. *The Journal of Business Forecasting, 33*, 40–42.

Luo, J., Wu, M., Gopukumar, D., & Zhao, Y. (2016). Big Data Application in Biomedical Research and Healthcare: A Literature Review. *Biomedical Informatics Insights, 8*, 1-10. doi:10.4137/Bii.s31559

Manikandan, S. G., & Ravi, S. (2014). Big Data Analysis Using Apache Hadoop. *2014 International Conference on IT Convergence and Security (ICITCS)*, 1-4. 10.1109/ICITCS.2014.7021746

Mehta, N., & Pandit, A. (2017). Concurrence of big data analytics and healthcare: A systematic review. *International Journal of Medical Informatics, 114*, 57–65. doi:10.1016/j.ijmedinf.2018.03.013 PMID:29673604

Miah, S. J., Hassan, J., & Gammack, J. G. (2017). On-Cloud Healthcare Clinic: E-health consultancy approach for remote communities in a developing country. *Telematics and Informatics, 34*(1), 311–322. doi:10.1016/j.tele.2016.05.008

Murdoch, T., & Detsky, A. (2013). The inevitable application of big data to healthcare. *Journal of the American Medical Association, 309*(13), 1351–1352. doi:10.1001/jama.2013.393 PMID:23549579

Nicolini, D., Powell, J., Conville, P., & Matinez-Solano, L. (2008). Managing knowledge in the healthcare sector: A review. *International Journal of Management Reviews, 10*(3), 245-263. doi:10.1111/j.1468-2370.2007.00219

Persson, A., & Riyals, L. (2014). Making customer relationship decisions: Analytics v rules of thumb. *Journal of Business Research, 67*(8), 1725–1732. doi:10.1016/j.jbusres.2014.02.019

Popovic, A., Hackney, R., Coelho, P., & Jaklic, J. (2012). Towards Business Intelligence Systems Success: Effects of Maturity and Culture on Analytical Decision Making. *Decision Support Systems, 54*(1), 729–739. doi:10.1016/j.dss.2012.08.017

Popovic, A., Hackney, R., Tassabehji, R., & Castelli, M. (2106). The impact of big data analytics on firms' high-value business performance. *Information Systems Front*, 3-14. doi:10.1007/s10796-016-9720-4

Raghupathi, W., & Raghupathi, V. (2014). Big data Analytics in Healthcare: Promise and Potential. *Health Information Science and Systems*, 2(3), 2–10. doi:10.1186/2047-2501-2-3 PMID:25825667

Ramtohul, I. (2016). Identifying the Adoption Process for Electronic Health Services: Qualitative Study. In H. Albach, H. Meffert, A. Pinkwart, R. Reichwald, & W. von Eiff (Eds.), *Boundaryless Hospital. Springer*. doi:10.1007/978-3-662-49012-9_15

Rogers, E. (2003). *Diffusions of Innovations*. New York: Free Press.

Safwan, E. R., Meredithand, R., & Burst, F. (2016). Business Intelligence (BI) system evolution: A case in a healthcare institution. *Journal of Decision Systems*, 25(1), 463–475. doi:10.1080/12460125.2016.1187384

Sakr, S., & Elgammal, A. (2016). Towards a Comprehensive Data Analytics Frameworks for Smart Healthcare Services. *Big Data Research.*, 4, 44–58. doi:10.1016/j.bdr.2016.05.002

Saravana, K., N., M., Eswari, T., Sampath, P., & Lavanya, S. (2015). Predictive Methodology for Diabetic Data Analysis in Big Data. *Procedia Computer Science, 50*, 203-208. doi:10.1016/j.procs.2015.04.069

Shah, N., & Pathak, J. (2014). Why healthcare may finally be ready for big data. *Harvard Business Review*.

Sonnati, R. (2017). Improving Healthcare using Big Data Analytics. *International Journal of Scientific and Technology Research*, 6(3), 142–146.

Spruit, M., Vroon, R., & Batenburg, R. (2014). Towards Healthcare Business Intelligence in long-term care: An exploratory case study in the Netherlands. *Computers in Human Behavior*, 30, 698–707. doi:10.1016/j.chb.2013.07.038

Sun, S., Cegielski, C. G., Jia, L., & Hall, D. J. (2016). Understanding the Factors Affecting the Organizational Adoption of Big Data. *Journal of Computer Information Systems*. doi:10.1080/08874417.2016.1222891

Thakur, S., & Ramzan, M. (2015). A Systematic Review on Cardiovascular disease using Big-Data by Hadoop. Cloud system and big data engineering, IEEE, 351-355.

Tornatzky, L., & Fleischer, M. (1990). *The processes of technological innovation*. Lexington Books.

Tremblay, M., Hevner, A., & Berndt, D. (2012). Design of an information Volatility measure for Healthcare decision making. *Decision Support Systems*, 52(2), 331–341. doi:10.1016/j.dss.2011.08.009

Trieu, V.-H. (2016). Getting value from Business Intelligence systems: A review and Agenda. *Decision Support System, 93*(2017), 112-124. doi:10.1016/j.dss.2016.09.019

Turban, E., Ramesh, S., Delen, D., & King, D. (2011). Business Intelligence: A Managerial Approach (2nd ed.). Pearson Education, Inc.

Visinescu, L. L., Jones, M., & Sidorova, A. (2017). Improving Decision Quality: The Role of Business Intelligence. *Journal of Computer Information Systems*, 57(1), 58–66. doi:10.1080/08874417.2016.1181494

Wamba, S. F., Anand, A., & Carter, L. (2013). A literature review of RFID-enabled healthcare applications and issues. *International Journal of Information Management, 33*(5), 875–891. doi:10.1016/j.ijinfomgt.2013.07.005

Wamba, S. F., Gunasekaran, A., Akter, S., Ren, S., Dubey, R., & Childe, S. J. (2016). Big data analytics and firm performance: Effects of dynamic capabilities. *Journal of Business Research, 70*(2017), 356-365. doi:10.1016/j.jbusres.2016.08.009

Wang, Y., & Byrd, T. A. (2017). Business analytics-enabled decision0making effectiveness through knowledge absorptive capacity in healthcare. *Journal of Knowledge Management, 21*(3), 517–539. doi:10.1108/JKM-08-2015-0301

Wang, Y., & Hajli, N. (2017). Exploring the path to big data analytics success in healthcare. *Journal of Business Research, 70*, 287–299. doi:10.1016/j.jbusres.2016.08.002

Ward, M., Marsolo, K., & Froehle, C. (n.d.). Application of business analytics in healthcare. *Business Horizon, 57*(5), 571-582. doi:10.1016/j.bushor.2014.06.003

Watson, H. J. (2014). Tutorial: Big data analytics: Concepts, technologies, and applications. *Communications of the Association for Information Systems, 34*(1), 1247–1268.

Wixcom, B., Yen, B., & Relich, M. (2013). Maximizing value from business analytics. *MIS Quarterly Executive, 12*(2), 111–123.

Wu, J., Li, H., Liu, L., & Zheng, H. (2017). Adoption of Big data and analytics in the mobile healthcare market: An economic perspective. *Electronic Commerce Research and Applications, 22*, 24-41. doi:10.1016/j.elerap.2017.02.002

Wu, J., Li, L., Cheng, S., & Lin, Z. (2016). The promising of healthcare services: When big data meet wearable technology. *Information & Management, 53*, 1020–1033. doi:10.1016/j.im.2016.07.003

Zailani, S., Iranmanesh, M., Nikbin, D., & Beng, J. K. (2015). Determinants of RFID Adoption in Malaysia's Healthcare Industry: Occupational Level as a Moderator. *Journal of Medical Systems, 39*(1), 172. doi:10.100710916-014-0172-4 PMID:25503418

Zhu, X., & Cahan, A. (2016). Wearable technologies and telehealth in care management for chronic illness. *Healthcare Information Management Systems*, 375-398.

This research was previously published in the Handbook of Research on Managing Information Systems in Developing Economies; pages 413-428, copyright year 2020 by Business Science Reference (an imprint of IGI Global).

Chapter 70

An Article on Big Data Analytics in Healthcare Applications and Challenges

Jaimin Navinchandra Undavia

🆔 https://orcid.org/0000-0002-6854-3904

Smt. Chandaben Mohanbhai Patel Institute of Computer Applications, India

Atul Manubhai Patel

Smt. Chandaben Mohanbhai Patel Institute of Computer Applications, India

ABSTRACT

The technological advancement has also opened up various ways to collect data through automatic mechanisms. One installed mechanism collects a huge amount of data without any further maintenance or human interventions. The health industry has been confronted by the need to manage the big data being produced by various sources, which are well known for producing high volumes of heterogeneous data. A high level of sophistication has been incorporated in almost all the industry, and healthcare is also one of them. The article explores the existence of a huge amount of data in the healthcare industry, and the data generated in the healthcare industry is neither homogeneous nor simple. Then the various sources and objectives of data are highlighted and discussed. As data come from various sources, they must be versatile in nature in all aspects. So, rightly and meaningfully, big data analytics has penetrated the healthcare industry, and its impact is highlighted.

INTRODUCTION

Huge amount, high speed, versatility converts traditional database into Big Data. These characteristics make big data more difficult and challenging for compilation. The techniques used to compile traditional data; it cannot be used to compile such big data as it is not always collection of structured data (Jaimin & Undavia, 2018). Such informative mass of data prove crucial for purpose of analytics.

DOI: 10.4018/978-1-6684-3662-2.ch070

This is because of availability of sophisticated data storage, which stores this huge amount of data. You cannot imagine a world without such data store where versatile information like details of person, organization, transaction performed, etc. are stored. This data can be used to extract valuable information and knowledge for the growth of the particular organization or improved activity. In the recent time, all aspects of information is available related to a customer. It ranges from customer name, its details about the purchase, his social connection, professional association, etc., This proves that, in current time data is the founding stone and vital element of any organization (Elragal, 2014).

The way Big Data is defined is changed against its aspect of application. In the recent time it is characterized as a collection of data elements whose size, speed, type and complexity is changed frequently (Belle, 2015). These frequent changes makes one to seek, adopt and invent new hardware and software mechanisms to manage, store, visualize and analyse these form of data.

The three Vs are Velocity, variety and volume, playing very important role in all various applications of such data. Healthcare is one of the prime user of this Big Data technology. In health care, data is widely spread among multiple health care systems, health insurers, researchers, government entities etc (Manyika, 2011). The data repositories are not always sophisticated enough which can provide platform of transparency for global data. As these kind of data have huge size, versatility in variety and rapid changing in nature, new type of data analytics, well-structured storage and accurate analysis methods are required. This huge amount of data then can be analysed properly and desired information can extracted from them.

Application of the Big Data technology in healthcare has large number of positive outcomes and such outcomes have life-saving phenomenon. Like other fields, in healthcare also, vast quantities of data and information is created/generated through digitization, automatic sensor data, etc. and then these mass have to consolidated and analysed by some specific technologies (Rehermann, n.d.).

The technological advancements have also inferred the way healthcare systems work. Treatment models, data capturing of population or a person, deciding the treatment once a disease is diagnosed, the model of diagnosis, etc. have changed drastically with the advent use of the recent technologies. This all changes are taking place based on the data collected of the same domain so that proper corrective and improved steps can incorporated in recent and newer technologies. Most of these changes are data driven so the healthcare domain also become conscious about the data collection and storage. For the physician who are treating their patients, they always eager to know as much as possible about his patient. This early stage of detection will help the doctors to decide mode of the treatment especially in case of some serious illness or disease. It is already proved that curing of such critical illnesses in early stage is more effective and less expensive as well.

When healthcare industry attempt to use the big data comprehensively, micro level analysis can be done for patient as huge amount of versatile data will be made available about the patient's history, way of treatment of other patients of same decease, other related parameters to cure this decease.

A tailored package of the data can be provided to doctors for better life-saving outcomes.

In past not only in healthcare, but in all industry gathering, storing and maintaining of data was very costly and time consuming too. Now in current time, there is availability of improved technology, it becomes very easy and providing very critical insight of data which can offer better understanding and usage of stored data.

The core purpose of healthcare data analytics is listed as under:

- Collect, maintain and store huge amount data;
- Collect critical insights from that stored data;
- Explore and evaluate ways of better care through historical data;
- Use data-driving findings to solve some critical problems;
- Assess methods and offer faster treatment;
- Maintain better track of inventory.

So, the technology Big Data Analytics in healthcare is the recent application of big data technology which is emerged as an enhancement in the field of healthcare. The data available of healthcare domain is in extraordinarily high volume, moves at high velocity and highly variable in nature. These 3 Vs are the founding stone of Big Data in Healthcare (Healthcare Big Data and the Promise of Value-Based Care, 2018).

BACKGROUND

The main objective of the article is to show case various applications of Big Data analytics especially in the field of healthcare. The article also highlights the insights of the challenges and applications of the Big Data analytics in the domain of Healthcare.

BIG DATA AND HEALTHCARE

As described in the introduction section, Big Data technology has impact in almost all types of industries. The healthcare is also one of them. When Big Data in healthcare is focused, basically it focuses the data from hospitals, pharmacist, druggist, pathologist, automatic data generated through sensors and web based applications which are responsible to manage healthcare data (Raghupathi, 2014). Describing Big data technologies used in healthcare refers to healthcare data that is available online or electronically in large amounts such as terabytes and petabytes, which makes it almost impossible to maintain the data using traditional hardware or software. The main challenge for big data in healthcare is the volume of data as well as the diversity of data types along with the accuracy and speed at which it needs to be managed (Anantharam, n.d.).

Objective of penetration of the big data analytics in the area of healthcare varies across the aspect and nature of the application. Healthcare is substantially become costly over the year and so as the cost can be one of the prime objective of the research (Rehermann, n.d.).

The healthcare is system, which is multidimensional in nature, and the primary objective of the healthcare system is to prevent, diagnosed and find best suitable treatment for health-related issues (Dash, 2019). The major components are responsible to generate and provide data for this health-related repository, which can be used for further use of data analytics. Mainly these components are health facilities like hospitals, medical stores, pharmacists, treatment technologies, doctors, etc. The health professionals belong to various health sectors like dentistry, medicine, midwifery, nursing, psychology, physiotherapy, and many others. Healthcare is required at several levels depending on the urgency of situation (Dash, 2019).

Traditional health analysis was carried out before the advent of computers and other recent technologies. Before the big data technology, the traditional health analysis was carried out where healthcare industry had to be dependent on another industry for the big data analysis purpose. The stack holders of healthcare industries now become more inclined towards the results generated through such big data analysis. Like other industries, healthcare is also facing the challenge to handle huge amount of data, which is versatile and dynamic in nature, and it is increasing at rapid speed. In this situation, big data analytics is proved to be one of the most prominent solution to handle this dynamicity of data with power to find some interesting patterns within it. Data stored in hard copies of healthcare industries are required to be digitized for the defined purpose of analytics (Sunil Kumar, 2019).

Following figure explains more insights in the field of big data analytics in the domain of healthcare.

Figure 1. Insight of Big Data in healthcare

LITERATURE REVIEW

Many researchers have indulge in the field of Big data analytics and later many of them have explore their research in the area of healthcare:

- Ashwin Belle and many have published their article titled "Big Data Analytics in Healthcare" and they have concluded that the data in healthcare is structured, semi-structured and unstructured. The data source which provides such collection of variety data is going to play vital role in future for healthcare practices in future. They have focused especially medical image analysis, physiological signal processing and integration of physiological and genomic data (Belle, 2015);
- Nada Elgendy and Ahmed Elragal have claimed in their article named "Big Data Analytics: A Literature Review Paper" that effective data source can help for the betterment in predictive analysis and other analytical purposes (Elragal, 2014);

- In McKinsey Global Institute, James Manyika and others have highlighted importance of big data in their article titled "Big Data: The Next Frontier for innovation, competition and productivity. The team of authors have narrated that how big data creates values in several ways. Authors have also shown the way to enable experimentation to discover needs, expose variability and improve performance. Segmenting populations to customize actions were also narrated in the article (Manyika, 2011);

- A book chapter titled "Security Issues and Challenges Related to Big Data" in the book series titled "Big Data Management and the Internet of Things for Improved Health Systems" narrated security issues while implementing big data in healthcare systems (Jaimin & Undavia, 2018);

- Aishwarya Anantharam wrote in the article titled "Explore the Applications of Big Data Technologies in Healthcare" that Big data analytics in healthcare is evolving by improving the cost reductions involved in the projects. The author to represent the real-time models that are being utilized in industries to provide patients with better treatment and keep track of these humongous amounts of data in an orderly manner conducted a case study (Anantharam, n.d.);

- Journal research paper titled "Improving Healthcare Using Big Data Analytics" authored by Revanth Sonnati contains details of possible improvements in the field healthcare. The paper claimed that geographic location is also important to analyse healthcare data. Moving towards the big data analytics makes the system more reciprocal, effective and efficient when it comes in the healthcare domain (Sonnati, 2017);

- A recent research article by Abhilash Shukla and Atul Patel explained the image segementation technique to detect bone cancer from the images of MRI and X-ray. They have also narrated Image segmentation technique like sobel, prewitt, canny, K-means and Region Growing are described in this paper which can be stimulated for X-Ray and MRI image interpretation (Abhilash Shukla, 2020).

These are the brief of the survey papers referred by us to find use case of the big data analytics in healthcare industry. Following figure, also depict the same to narrate the use cases.

Figure 2. Use cases of Big Data Analytics in healthcare

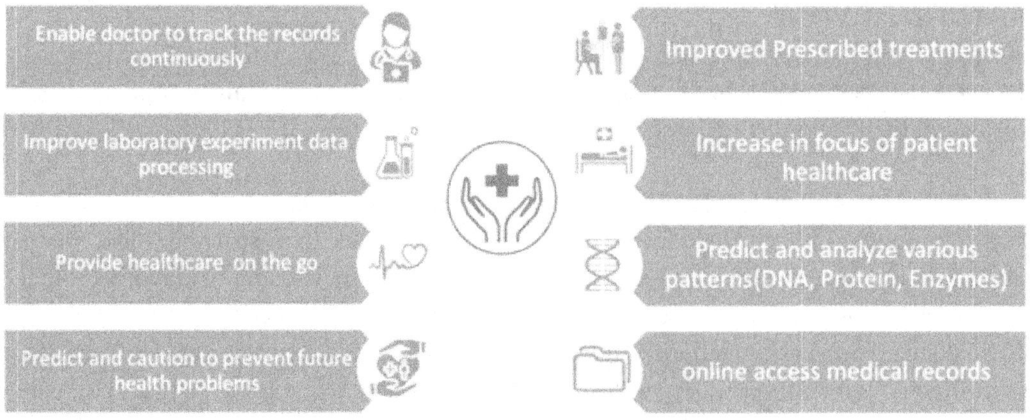

USE CASE OF BIG DATA ANALYTICS IN HEALTHCARE

Applications of big data analytics can improve the patient-based service, to detect spreading diseases earlier, generate new insights into disease mechanisms, monitor the quality of the medical and healthcare institutions as well as provide better treatment methods.

As discussed in previous sections, big data has use cases in almost all the industry and it has very crucial use cases in healthcare domain too.

There are many computing solutions available, which are feasible through big data technology in healthcare domain. The main objective of this combination of healthcare and big data analytics is to find new insights of this big data analytics, expand research horizon in the field of healthcare, offer measurable benefits in the outcome of healthcare research, offer better and improved healthcare facilities to the society, etc. As a concluding point of this, the abstract aim of this combination is to benefit the society with the advent use of advanced technology to improve and enhance healthcare (Sonnati, 2017).

There is a wide spectrum of Big Data applications in healthcare domain. Currently big data analytics is used to predict the possible effect of the given treatment against the historical data of the patient, to find best suitable medication, decide treatment plan of the patient, etc. However, to manage this complex data of healthcare domain is again a challenge itself (Sunil Kumar, 2019) (Abhilash Shukla, 2020). In this section, general methods have been discussed which has impact of big data analytics in the healthcare domain (Anantharam, n.d.) (Sunil Kumar, 2019):

- Medical Signal Analytics:
  - To keep track of patient's health over a period, reaction against the various medicine, etc., are belong to Telemetry and Physiological signal monitoring system;
  - Such automated data generation systems produce huge amount of data of wide variety. These heterogeneous data requires high analytical end to analyse it for its meaningful use (Dash, 2019);
- Prediction in Healthcare:
  - Regardless to the nature of the business, analytics become an integral part of all type of business to predict the future trends of the business. This predictive analysis in the healthcare industry is very important use case of big data analytics;
  - As discussed in preceding sections, healthcare industry too generating wide range of data, which is maintained by computer systems. These big data can be subject to various analytics techniques like text mining, video mining, data mining, clustering of data, association rule mining to find out interesting insight of data, which is useful for future;
  - In recent times, machine learning and deep learning techniques can also be applied over these data. Current trend, future trend and past trend can be compared and analysed with the help of these techniques;
- Machine Learning/Deep Learning in Healthcare:
  - In recent times the techniques used in data mining is now inclined with machine learning techniques. These techniques are again responsible to discover hidden patterns from the huge amount of data;
  - In machine learning, the machine alters the execution of the program by learning from the hidden patterns within the data (Herland et al., 2014);

- EHR (Electronic Health Records):
  - Electronic Health Records means the health related data, which is stored and maintained electronically for future purpose;
  - Such sophisticated record keeping helps the healthcare related resources to be more accurate and predictive. Such records can be shared in public and private sector for its effective use;
  - Once the data is available, there are versatile ways to use it against more sophisticated applications of Big Data analytics (Mike, 2014);
- Image Processing of Healthcare Data:
  - Image processing is an integral technology used in medical science where way to treatment, nature of the treatment, intensity of the decease, area of infected area, etc are to be determined and decided and disease states is considered;
  - Under the image processing, mostly used techniques is image segmentation. Such image segmentation techniques are used to detect bone cancer through the image of MRI and X- ray (Abhilash Shukla, 2020);
  - Image enhancement is also used to get details of a particular disease and decide the mode and plan of treatment. Such healthcare data are kept as electronic health record (EHR). Such data can be kept for future use in order to improve overall healthcare system;
- Big Data Genomics:
  - AS human genes are great in number, so it is not possible to treat or maintain them through traditional database system;
  - So big data is a very good option to handle such huge amount of data, which is ultimately from the healthcare industry. Therefore, GeneBank, Gene Structure prediction is part of Big Data Genomics, which has a good power and potential in terms of healthcare applications. Such gene analysis is required sophisticated big data analytics techniques.

CONCLUSION

In this article, we have highlighted application areas of big data analytics in healthcare industry. Like other industries, healthcare is also producing huge amount of data through either manual process or automatic data capturing machines. Such huge amount of data is considered as big data as it possesses all the characteristics of it. Over this data, big data analytics techniques are used to get very useful insight of the data. Such hidden patterns and other outcomes are useful for stockholders of this healthcare industry. It is also highlighted that for a specific use, customized architecture can be developed for finite set out outcomes. Further, healthcare is directly in the human life and its survival, such important data insights are used for overall social welfare.

REFERENCES

Abhilash Shukla, A. P. (2020). Bone Cancer Detection from X-Ray and MRI Images through Image Segmentation Techniques. *International Journal of Recent Technology and Engineering*, 8(6), 273–278. doi:10.35940/ijrte.F7159.038620

Anantharam. (n.d.). *Explore the applications of big data technologies in healthcare.* Academic Press.

Belle, . (2015). Big Data Analytics in Healthcare. *Journal of Biomedicine & Biotechnology*, 2–37.

Dash. (2019). Big data in healthcare: management, analysis and future prospects. *Journal of Big Data,* 1-25.

Elragal, N. E. A. (2014). Big Data Analytics: A Literature Review Paper. *Springer International Publishing Switzerland, 2014*, 214–227.

Healthcare Big Data and the Promise of Value-Based Care. (2018). Available: https://catalyst.nejm.org/doi/full/10.1056/CAT.18.0290

Herland, T. M. K. R. M., Khoshgoftaar, T. M., & Wald, R. (2014). A review of data mining using big data in health informatics. *Journal of Big Data, 1*(1), 2. doi:10.1186/2196-1115-1-2

Jaimin, & Undavia. (2018). Security Issues and Challenges Related to Big Data. In *Big Data Management and the Internet of Things for Improved Health Systems* (pp. 86–101). IGI Global. doi:10.4018/978-1-5225-5222-2.ch006

Manyika. (2011). *Big Data: The next frontier for innovation, competition, and productivity.* Academic Press.

Mehmood, G. G. R., & Graham, G. (2015). Big data logistics: A healthcare transport capacity sharing model. *Procedia Computer Science, 64*, 1107–1114. doi:10.1016/j.procs.2015.08.566

Mike. (2014). Available: http://ihealthtran.com/iHT2 BigData 2013.pdf

Raghupathi. (2014). Big data analytics in healthcare: promise and potential. *Health Information Science and Systems, 2*(1).

Rehermann. (n.d.). *Datapine.* Available: https://www.datapine.com/blog/big-data-examples-in-healthcare/

Sonnati, R. (2017). Improving Healthcare Using Big Data Analytics. International Journal of Scientific & Technology Research, 6(3).

Sunil Kumar, M. S. (2019). Big Data Analytics for Healthcare Industry: Impact, Applications, and Tools. Big Data Mining and Analytics, 2(1).

This research was previously published in the International Journal of Big Data and Analytics in Healthcare (IJBDAH), 5(2); pages 58-64, copyright year 2020 by IGI Publishing (an imprint of IGI Global).

Chapter 71
Big Data Classification and Internet of Things in Healthcare

Amine Rghioui

Research Team in Smart Communications-ERSC–Research Centre E3S, EMI, Mohamed V University, Rabat, Morocco

Jaime Lloret

https://orcid.org/0000-0002-0862-0533

Integrated Management Coastal Research Institute, Universitat Politecnica de Valencia, 46370 Valencia, Spain

Abedlmajid Oumnad

Research Team in Smart Communications-ERSC–Research Centre E3S, EMI, Mohamed V University, Rabat, Morocco

ABSTRACT

Every single day, a massive amount of data is generated by different medical data sources. Processing this wealth of data is indeed a daunting task, and it forces us to adopt smart and scalable computational strategies, including machine intelligence, big data analytics, and data classification. The authors can use the Big Data analysis for effective decision making in healthcare domain using the existing machine learning algorithms with some modification to it. The fundamental purpose of this article is to summarize the role of Big Data analysis in healthcare, and to provide a comprehensive analysis of the various techniques involved in mining big data. This article provides an overview of Big Data, applicability of it in healthcare, some of the work in progress and a future works. Therefore, in this article, the use of machine learning techniques is proposed for real-time diabetic patient data analysis from IoT devices and gateways.

DOI: 10.4018/978-1-6684-3662-2.ch071

1. INTRODUCTION

The Internet of Things (IoT) is a computing concept that describes a future where every day physical objects will be connected to the Internet and be able to identify themselves to other devices. This paper presents a review of literature on the subject of the IoT technologies and their applications domains and the futuristic research areas. Several research studies have addressed and developed this topic with detailed studies synthesis about the fields of application of internet of things, and general visions (Gubbi, Buyya, Marusic, & Palaniswami, 2013). Other papers summarize the applications of IoT in the healthcare industry and identify the intelligentization trend and directions of future research in this field (Yin, 2016).

Over the last two decades, we have seen an enormous amount of growth in data. The data has been doubling every two years since 2011. As a result of this technological revolution, big data is becoming an important issue in the sciences, governments, and enterprises increasingly. Big Data is a data set, which is difficult to capture, store, filter, share, analyze and visualize on it with current technologies (Young, Min, Wenixa, & Depeng, 2015).

By understanding, processing and utilizing the knowledge and information hidden in Big Data concerning health issues and disease trends in certain population, we can find solutions, with which, we can live longer and healthier (Lloret, Parra, Taha, & Tomás, 2017, 2017). Big data analytics improve health care insights in many aspects shown in Figure 1.

Figure 1. Benefits in healthcare

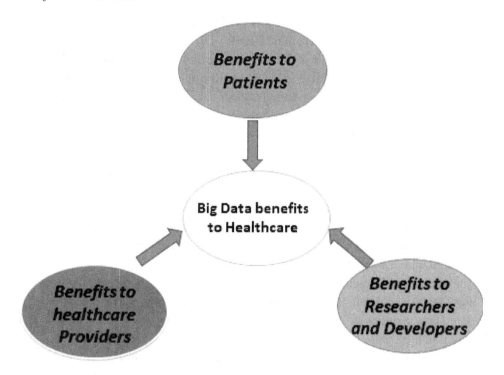

Benefits to Patients: Big Data in healthcare is being used to predict epidemics, cure disease, improve quality of life and avoid preventable deaths. With the world's population increasing and everyone living longer, models of treatment delivery are rapidly changing, and data are driving many of the decisions behind those changes. Big data can help patients make the right decision in a timely manner. From patient data, analytics can be applied to identify individuals that need "proactive care" or need a change in their lifestyle to avoid health condition degradation. For example, patients in early stages of some diseases (e.g., heart failure often caused by some risk factors such as hypertension or diabetes) should be able to benefit from preventive care thanks to Big data.

Benefits to Researchers and Developers (R & D): R & D contribute to new algorithms and tools, such as the algorithms by Google, Facebook, and Twitter that define what we find about the health system. Google, for instance, has applied algorithms of data mining and machine learning to detect influenza epidemics through search queries. R & D can also: Enhance predictive models to produce more devices and treatment for the market, and can give statistical tools and algorithms to improve the clinical trial design and patient recruitment to better match treatments to individual patients, thus reducing trial failures and speeding new treatments to market.

Benefits to healthcare Providers: can analyze disease patterns and tracking disease outbreaks and transmission to improve public health surveillance and speed response, Turning large amounts of data into actionable information that can be used to identify needs, provide services, and predict and prevent crises, Capture and analyze in real-time large volumes of fast-moving data from in-hospital and in-home devices, for safety monitoring and adverse event prediction, also providers can Apply advanced analytics to patient profiles to identify individuals who would benefit from proactive care or lifestyle changes, for example, those patients at risk of developing a specific disease (e.g., diabetes) who would benefit from preventive care (Sendra, Parra, Lloret, & Tomás, 2018).

The rising costs of health care and the increasing availability of new personal health devices are the ingredients of the vision of the IoT in the connected healthcare. The vision of connected healthcare is growing because of the availability of new technological tools. By the application of the IoT and new technologies, it is possible to create a health application that appears every morning to request reading the level of glucose in the blood and collects data from the patient automatically (Bennett, Savaglio, Lu et al., 2014). In the vision of connected healthcare, patients are those who take control of their health and being in good physical and mental health due to this application. In addition, this leads to a good responsibility and control of heath by allowing a real scenario for the IoT in healthcare. IoT will help doctors to respond quickly in emergencies and allow them to cooperate with international hospitals to track the status of a patient. There are also other applications of IoT such as patient identification; this application aims to reduce adverse events for patients, maintenance of comprehensive electronic medical records (Rghioui, Sendra, Lloret, & Oumnad, 2016).

The contour of the contributions of this paper compared to other documents from the field survey, this survey provides a deeper summary of the Big Data in Healthcare, which allows us to know what the value of Big Data analytics in Healthcare is in details. We also present the different algorithms of data classification in healthcare fields.

The remainder of this article is structured as follows: Section II presents and explaining other surveys on big data in Health care. Section III contains concept of Big Data in healthcare, their technologies, architecture, and applications. The Big Data tools and platforms are discussed in Section IV, section V present the Benefits of Big Data to Healthcare. HealthCare Big Data Sources are described in Section

VI, and Section VII explains Big Data Initiatives in Healthcare. We will then present our use case in Data Classification with Weka tool. Finally, some remarks conclude the paper.

2. RELATED WORK

In this part, we are going to show the main research areas considered by most surveys published in the field of the Internet of Things and Big Data in Health-care.

There are many related works in the literature about Big Data and IoT and their useful applications in many life aspects including healthcare. Not neglecting the important issue of classification data, a predictive Big Data analytics in Healthcare is proposed in (Reddy & Kumar, 2016). This paper gives an overview of storing and retrieval methods, Big Data tools, and techniques used in healthcare clouds.

There are several documents published survey covering different aspects of Big Data technology. For example, the survey by (Thara, Premasudha, Ram, & Suma, 2016) presents the review of various research efforts made in healthcare domain using Big Data concepts and methodologies. In (Wang, Kung, & Byrd, 2018), the authors examine the historical development, architectural design and component functionalities of big data analytics. In (Dogaru & Dumitrache, 2017), the authors present big data from the perspective of improving healthcare services and offers a holistic view of system security and factors determining security breaches. A baseline for assessing the rapid growth of the implementation of big data analytics into healthcare and life science aspects that assists in the understanding the big data applications and its impacts presented in (Zayeri, 2017). In (Moreira, Rodrigues, Furtado et al., 2018), the authors use of a machine learning technique, known as averaged one-dependence estimators, is proposed for real-time pregnancy data analysis from IoT devices and gateways. The authors (Sterling, 2017) provide an overview of big data analytics for healthcare.

The IoT big-data management and knowledge discovery is a key research challenge for the real-time industrial automation applications. Therefore, we study some existing system, models, or frameworks that are implemented in IoT big-data management and knowledge discovery perspective. The IoT big-data management includes several managerial activities such as data collection, integrations, cleaning, storage, processing, analysis, and visualizations that have been implemented through various systems, models, and frameworks (Zhou, Hu, Wang, Lu, & Zhao, 2013) (Mozumdar, Shahbazian, & Ton, 2014).

In addition, (Lee, 2017) share some successes in healthcare, defense, and service sector applications through innovation in predictive and big data analytics through the modeling and computational advances in integer programming. A framework to help organize and guide the understanding of the application of big data technologies for processing health and healthcare data presented in (Sheeran & Steele, 2017). Examination of the concept of big data in healthcare, its benefits, and attendant challenges and implementation of big data in healthcare presented in (Olaronke & Oluwaseun, 2016). A probabilistic data collection mechanism and the correlation analysis of those collected data is given by (Sahoo, Mohapatra, & Wu, 2016). The use of Artificial Neural Networks (ANN) model based on clinical and biochemical variables in patients with moderate to severe traumatic injury. Is presented in (Gholipour, Rahim, Fakhree, & Ziapour, 2015). In (Moudani, Hussein, AbdelRazzak, & Mora-Camino, 2014), a proficient methodology for the extraction of significant patterns from the Coronary Heart Disease warehouses for heart attack prediction has been presented, and they propose to validate the classification using Multi-classifier decision tree to identify the risky heart disease cases.

The work in (Gazal & Kaur, 2015) gives a brief research direction in data management and knowledge discovery prospective in IoT big-data management platform, in which three activities are mainly associated, that is, data association, inference, and knowledge discovery.

3. BIG DATA IN HEALTHCARE

Doug Laney, an analyst of META (presently Gartner), defined challenges and opportunities brought about by increased data with a 3Vs model. (Gartner, 2012) (Figure 2).

In the "3Vs" model, Volume means, with the generation and collection of masses of data, data scale becomes increasingly big; Velocity means the timeliness of big data, specifically, data collection and analysis, must be rapidly and timely conducted; Variety indicates the various types of data, which include semi-structured and unstructured data such as audio, video, webpage, and text, as well as traditional structured data.

Figure 2. Big Data: The three V's

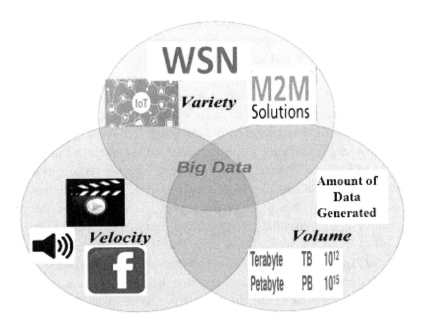

We explain the meanings of the 3 Vs that characterize Big Data and motivate their relevance to health care data:

- **Volume:** Health care data grows dramatically. Health care systems data require terabytes and petabytes. These systems include information such as personal information, radiology images, personal medical records, 3D imaging, genomics, and biometric sensor readings. Healthcare systems can now have the potential to manage and analyse this complex data structure. Thanks to the use of cloud computing, manipulation, storage and use of such a complex data is now made possible.

According to KPMG report, the volume of healthcare data reached 150 Exabyte's in 2013, and it is increasing at a prominent rate of 1.2 - 2-4 Exabyte's a year;

- **Variety:** Health care data sources and complexity, this dimension represents a big challenge because of the variety of data: structured, unstructured and semi-structured. Structured information, such as clinical data, are easy to manipulate, store and analyse by machine. However, most of health care data, such as office medical records, doctor notes, paper prescriptions, images, and radiograph films, are unstructured or semi-structured. The most challenging aspect of big data in health care consists-of-combining traditional data with new forms of data to get the closer to the right solution for a specific patient;

- **Velocity:** Big data analytics the information stored in health care systems is often correct, but not always even if it is updated on a regular basis. Thus, big data must be retrieved, analysed and compared to make time and accurate decisions based on real-time data processing. Life or death of patients can rely on real time data. Therefore, big data analytics must be done to prevent and detect infections as early as possible to make better decisions and consequently save lives.

Big data has advanced not only the size of data but also creating value from it. In other words, big data, that becomes a synonymous of data mining, business analytics and business intelligence, has made a big change in BI from reporting and decision to prediction of results. In healthcare, this value can be translated into understanding new diseases and therapies, predicting outcomes at earlier stages, making real-time decisions, promoting patients' health, enhancing medicine, reducing cost and improving healthcare value and quality (Stankovic, 2014).

3.1. Existing Technologies

The Big Data technologies involve commercial and open source platforms and services for storage, security, access and processing of data, many of them are based on the widely used open-source Hadoop framework. It is an open-source framework designed to deal with large-scale data using clusters of commodity hardware. It consists of a distributed storage component: Hadoop Distributed File System (HDFS) and a processing component: MapReduce programming model. Hadoop Distributed File System (HDFS) is a distributed file system and data engine designed to handle extremely high volumes of data in any structure. Hadoop is an independent Java-based programming framework that enhances the computation of large data sets in a distributed computing environment. Hadoop has two components (Narayan, Bailey, & Daga, 2012):

- Hadoop distributed file system
- Map Reduce

HDFS is a distributed file system that provides high-performance access to data distributed in Hadoop clusters. Like other technologies related to Hadoop, HDFS has become a key tool for managing Big Data pools and supporting analytic applications. HDFS is usually deployed on low-cost so-called convenience servers. Breakdowns are frequent. The file system is therefore designed to be extremely fault-tolerant, while facilitating fast data transfer between system nodes. When HDFS collects data, the system segments the information into several bricks and distributes them on several nodes of the cluster, which allows parallel processing. The file system copies each data brick several times and distributes the copies on each of the nodes, placing at least one copy on a separate server in the cluster. As a result, the data, stored on failed nodes, can be found elsewhere in the cluster. Treatment can continue despite the breakdown. HDFS is developed to support applications with large volumes of data, such as individual files whose quantity can be counted in terabytes (Ilakiyaa & Nalini, 2017).

MapReduce is one of the most adopted frameworks in the field of batch processing, is a programming model in which a MapReduce program can have two functions: the map and the reduction, which requires moving data across the nodes. The map and the reduction, each defining a mapping of one set of key-value pairs to another. MapReduce is an efficient solution for one-pass computation but when it comes to multi-pass computation, Map Reduce is inefficient due to the high latency of disk operations. MapReduce programs can be written in various languages; Java, Ruby, Python, and C++. These functions work the same for any data size, but the execution time depends on the data size and the cluster size. Increasing data size causes increased execution and increasing cluster size decreases the execution time (Shah, Shukla, & Pandey, 2016).

3.2. Big Data Architecture

In this section, we present the proposed Big Data architecture as shown in Figure 3. Given the challenges of Big Data analysis, there is a clear need to aggregate and organize this data to facilitate analysis. To this end, the proposed architecture is designed to make this analysis simpler, allowing for focus on analytics rather than data management, storage and collection (Din, Ghayvat, Paul et al., 2015):

- **Data collection:** Data collection is to utilize special data collection techniques including data sensing using medical sensors, data acquisition, and data buffering.to acquire raw data from a specific data generation environment;
- **Data storage:** The storage system functions as a decision model in the proposed scheme, because the storage system checks whether the data is real-time data or offline data.

Figure 3. Big data architecture

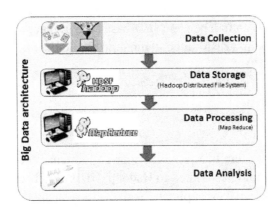

In the case of real-time data, the data is transmitted to a filtration system. Filtration requires a special algorithm that filters the data, so it is necessary to pre-process the data since the real-time data arrives quickly in the system. Therefore, the filtration system helps eliminate unwanted data. Apparently, if the data is offline data, the data is sent to the storage server. The storage server is used to store a massive volume of data. The storage server performs the following tasks:

- Provide server storage capabilities;
- Sharing the massive amount of data;
- Equal distribution of data between different processing servers;
- Queuing of processing efficiency improving data.
- **Data processing:** Is a fundamental component that receives sequence files from the collection unit. It processes the data while performing necessary statistical calculations based on the nature of the data. For Big Data, to accomplish high efficiency, the overall data are disassembled into small pieces, and each of the pieces is separately processed in parallel using HDFS and MapReduce. Therefore, in order to enable effective data analysis, we shall pre-process data under many circumstances to integrate the data from different sources, which cannot only reduce storage expense but also improve analysis accuracy;
- **Data analysis:** Data analysis is the final and the most important phase in the value chain of big data, with the purpose of extracting useful values, providing suggestions or decisions. This layer delivers connectivity to the end-user to access various facilities, such as hospitals, emergency treatment. Furthermore, doctors can also monitor the patient by continuous analysis of his or her medical history. These services enable a doctor to connect to a facility to obtain a patient's present health status.

Different levels of potential values can be generated through the analysis of datasets in different fields.

4. BIG DATA PLATFORMS

There are thousands of Big Data tools out there, we have compiled a list of a few of data tools in the areas of extraction, storage, cleaning, mining, visualizing, analysing and integrating. Here are the top open source tools for big data.

Table 1 gives the different platforms and corresponding tools in handling the big data (import.io, 2015).

There are other tools used in large data, namely Hortonworks, hypertable, CouchDB, Grid Gain. It is used to improve the various factors in the development of large data and functionality of a computer system.

Below is comparison Table 2, consisting of various Big Data tools and the key features or facilities they support. We note that all Big Data tools are open source except Cloudera, as all these tools are scalable, so it differs just with the programming language and data storage format.

Table 1. Platforms and tools for big data

Platform/Tool	Description
Hadoop Distributed File System (HDFS)	Hadoop has the potential to process extremely large amounts of data mainly by allocating partitioned data sets to numerous servers (nodes)
MapReduce	Originally developed by Google, a software framework for distributed processing of large data set on computing clusters of commodity hardware. MapReduce provides the interface for the distribution of sub-tasks and the gathering of outputs, the sequence of the name MapReduce implies, the reduce job is always performed after the map job.
Cassandra	Developed by Facebook, and built on Amazon Dynamo and Google BigTable, it's designed to handle large amounts of data across many commodity servers. It works on distributed servers where it requires reliable service and no failure.
MongoDB	A cross-platform document-oriented database that supports dynamic schema design. It's a NoSQL database with document-oriented storage and full index support. MongoDB can be used as a file system. It's good for managing data that changes frequently or data that is unstructured or semi-structured.
Zookeeper	Open source service for maintaining and configuration service for large distributed systems. ZooKeeper provides an infrastructure for cross-node synchronization and can be used by applications to ensure that tasks across the Hadoop cluster are serialized or synchronized. A ZooKeeper server is a machine that keeps a copy of the state of the entiresystem and preserves this information in local log files.
Hive	Hive was initially developed by Facebook but is now being used and developed by other companies like Netflix and Amazon. It is a query language it runs on Hadoop architecture, their creation, called Apache® Hive™, allows SQL developers to write Hive Query Language (HQL) statements that are similar to standard SQL statements, but it is built on top of Hadoop and MapReduce for providing data summarization, query, and analysis operations with several key differences.
Cloudera	Cloudera creates a commercial version of Hadoop with some additional services. They can help your business create a corporate data center so that people in your organization can access the data you store. Cloudera is mainly and a business solution to help companies manage their Hadoop ecosystem. Although Hadoop is a free and open source project for storing large amounts of data on inexpensive computing servers, the free version of Hadoop is not easy to use.
HBase	Traditional databases are row-oriented database management systems but HBase is a column-oriented. HBase provides random, real time access to your data in Hadoop. It is known for providing strong data consistency on reads and writes, which distinguishes it from other NoSQL databases. It combines the scalability of Hadoop by running on the Hadoop Distributed File System (HDFS), with real-time data access as a key/value store and deep analytic capabilities of Map Reduce.

Table 2. Big data tools comparison table

Big Data Tool	Open Source	Programming Language	Scalable	Data Storage Format
Hadoop Distributed File System (HDFS)	Yes	Java	Yes	Structured/Semi-Structured
MapReduce	Yes	Java/C#/C++	Yes	Structured
Cassandra	Yes	Java	Yes	Structured/Semi-Structured/ Unstructured
MongoDB	Yes	C++	Yes	semi-structured/ unstructured
Zookeeper	Yes	Java	Yes	Structured
Hive	Yes	SQL	Yes	Structured/Unstructured
Cloudera	No	Python	Yes	Semi-Structured
HBase	Yes	Many Language	Yes	Structured

5. HEALTHCARE BIG DATA SOURCES

Healthcare big data is a revolutionary tool in the healthcare industry and is becoming vital in current patient-centric care. Diverse data sources have been aggregated into the healthcare big data ecosystem. These data sources are discussed below:

1. **Physiological data:** These data are huge in terms of volume and velocity:
   a. **Volume:** A variety of signals is collected from heterogeneous sources to monitor patient characteristics, including blood pressure, blood glucose, and heart rate;
   b. **Velocity:** The growth rate of data generation from continuous monitoring requires these data to be processed in real-time, for decision-making. Efficient and comprehensive methods are also required to analyze and process the collected signals to provide useable data to the healthcare professionals and other related stakeholders;
2. **EHRs:** Or electronic medical records (EMRs) are digitized structured healthcare data from a patient. The EHRs are collected from and shared among hospitals, and insurance companies. Security, integrity and privacy violations of these data can cause irremediable damage to the health, or even death, of the individual and loss to society. Thus, big healthcare data security is now a key topic of research;
3. **Medical images:** These images generate a huge volume of data to assist healthcare professionals for identifying or detecting disease. Medical imaging techniques such as X-ray scan play a crucial role in diagnosis. Owing to the complication, dimensionality and noise of the collected images, efficient image processing methods are required to provide clinically suitable data for patient care;
4. **Sensed data:** Collected from patients using different wearable or implantable devices. Sensed data must be collected, pre-processed, stored, shared and delivered correctly in a reasonable time to be of use to healthcare providers when making clinical decisions. It is a challenge to collect and collate multimodal sensed data from multiple sources at the same time;
5. **Clinical notes:** Its claims, recommendations, and decisions constitute one of the largest unstructured sources of healthcare big data. Owing to the variety in format, reliability, completeness, and accuracy of the clinical notes, it is challenging to ensure the health care provider has the correct information. Efficient data mining and natural language processing techniques are required to provide meaningful data.

6. BIG DATA INITIATIVES IN HEALTHCARE

There are several initiatives utilizing the potential of Big Data in healthcare. Some of the examples are listed below:

- **Asthmapolis:** Launched in 2010 to help find a solution by leveraging the advances in sensor technology (and the reduced costs of producing said sensors) and mobile data monitoring to help people manage their asthma more effectively, in turn reducing the costs both for those suffering from asthma and for the U.S. healthcare system itself.

When a patient is suffering from an asthma attack and is required to use his or her inhaler, the little device records the time and place that the inhaler was used and transmits this information to a web site. This data is then combined with information available through the Center for Disease Control (CDC).

- **Battling the Flu:** The Big Data analysis has become a weapon for the CDC to fight the flu, which claims millions of lives a year. Each week, the CDC receives over 700,000 reports on influenza. These reports include details about the disease, the treatment that was given and whether the treatment was unsuccessful. The CDC has made this information available to the general public under the name Flu View, an application that organizes and analyzes this vast amount of data to give doctors a clearer picture of the spread of the disease in near real-time. In addition to providing the precise location of patients who are struggling with the flu (Marjani, Nasaruddin, Gani et al., 2017);
- **GNS Healthcare and Aetna:** GNS Healthcare is a privately held data analytics company based in Cambridge. Has come together with the health insurance company Aetna to help combat people at risk or already with metabolic syndromes. Founded in 2000 by Cornell physicists Colin Hill and Iya Khalil, GNS Healthcare uses proprietary causal Bayesian network modeling and simulation software to analyze data for clients in the pharmaceutical, biotechnology, healthcare provider, health insurance, pharmacy benefit management and health informatics industries;
- **Diabetes and Big Data:** Diabetes is a major public health problem affecting more than 400 million people worldwide and causes 1.5 million deaths each year, according to the World Health Organization (WHO). With more than 9% of the adult population now living with diabetes, the recent WHO World Diabetes Report calls for more initiatives to improve the management and treatment of this disease. Diabetes patients can also benefit from the Big Data revolution in health care. A company named Common Sensing has produced GoCap, a cap for prefilled insulin pens that can not only record the amount of insulin administered daily but also the specific times the dosages were administered. This information is then transmitted either to a mobile phone where an application records this data or to a connected glucometer. This data is then easily available to healthcare professionals and allows them to identify problems before they become severe and to tweak dosages if required;
- **USC Medical Monitor:** Computer scientists at the University of Southern California (USC) are teaming up with neurologists, kinesiologists and public health experts to fight against Parkinson's disease. The team uses various devices to track the movement of the patient and gather large amounts of data including data from 3D sensors of Microsoft Kinect, patient's smartphone, and additional body sensors. Then the data is fed into an algorithm that analyzes the data to identify any significant changes in movement and monitor disease progression and the effectiveness of treatments in real-time." The team hopes to extend this technology beyond Parkinson's disease in the future.

7. CLASSIFICATION DATA IN HEALTHCARE

Data classification is a process with many types of existing data sets for analysis, the development of classification technology has made great achievements. In general, we can classify them into two categories: one is the use of statistical principles, such as KNN, support vector machine, regression model, maximum entropy model Bayesian networks and other methods; Another is based on the principle of classifying certain rules, such as rough set theory, association rules, and decision trees and so on.

Diabetes comes from no communicable diseases (NCDs), and many people suffer from them. Nowadays, for developing countries like Morocco, diabetes has become a big health problem. Diabetes is one of the critical diseases that has associated long-term complications and also follows with various health problems. With the help of technology, it is necessary to build a system that stores and analyzes diabetes data and to predict possible risks accordingly. This work will be able to predict what types of diabetes are prevalent, future risks related and depending on the level of risk of the patient, the type of treatment can be provided.

There are six main classification models integrated in recent Weka tools; namely, decision tree, ripper rule, neural networks, naive Bayes, k-nearest neighbor and support vector machine:

1. Decision Tree (J48) is one of the tree classification techniques in which a particular tree will be generated as attributes, leaves as classes and edges as test results;
2. Ripper Rule (JRIP) is used to generate various rules by adding repetitive datasets until the rules cover all data configurations according to the set of learning data. In addition, once all the rules are generated, some of them will be merged to reduce the size;
3. Neural Networks (MLPs - Multilayer Perceptron) have a distinctive feature as a three-layer feed-forward neural network: an input layer, a hidden layer, and an output layer. In order to link each node in each level, it may include additional weight to properly adjust the traversing path selection process;
4. Naïve Bayes is derived from Bayes' theorem by applying the probabilistic learning knowledge for classification, assuming that the predictive attribute is conditionally independent according to each individual class;
5. k-Nearest-Neighbor (IBK) is used to perform the classification considering k subsets of data, each of them has similar characteristics by applying the Euclidean distance to understand the group, and here, IBK is the one of the k-Nearest-Simplified-Neighbor Classifiers;
6. Vector Support (Sequential Minimal Optimization (SMO)) is basically a linear classifier (two classes) used to determine the largest distance between two sets, and SMO is the minimum sequential optimization algorithm for SVM training using polynomial or Gaussian kernels.

7.1. Use Case

Continuous glucose monitors (CGMs) generate data streams that have the potential to revolutionize the possibilities of reducing extreme blood glucose levels (BGs) that characterize blood sugar levels in diabetes mellitus. These data, however, are both large and complex, and their analysis requires an understanding of the physical and physical, biochemical and mathematical principles involved in this new technology. According to the International Diabetes Federation (IDF), in 2015, 418 million people had Diabetes Mellitus (DM) in the world.

As shown in Figure 4, the Glucose sensor is used to sense the glucose values in the blood of the diabetic patient, and transfer the sensed data over short-range wireless communication to the patient's Android smartphone. The smartphone then aggregates and stores the sensed data, provides the healthcare monitoring interface to the patients for logging and also sends the physiological data to the medical

Figure 4. Illustration of blood glucose measurement

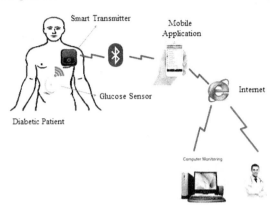

server at a specified time interval whereby the physicians can directly have access for further analysis, diagnosis and intervention.

A glucose concentration value ≤70 mg/dl is defined as hypoglycemic and a glucose concentration value ≥180 mg/dl is defined as hyperglycemic. If ever the threshold set is reached, an alarm is triggered whereby the patient will receive a warning message on his mobile phone and similarly the physician will receive a warning message on the remote server.

5.2. Tool Used

WEKA 3.6.12 (Hall, Frank, Holmes et al., 2009) is used for analysis purpose; this tool provides a large range of classifiers like Bayes, Functions, Meta, and Tree-based. It can be also used for clustering and association of data. WEKA processes ".arff" files in its explorer to perform classification. It also provides different test options such as percentage split, cross-validation. and it also generates the graphical results like visualized classifiers errors, visualized margin curve.

The main limitation of this study is the data source is mostly here in Morocco, the national hospitals do not contain any database relating to the diabetic patient. Also, the challenges of the health care industry is that uses information technology in a manner generally inferior to that of other industries, making it difficult to find these data. The dataset measured with CGM is used as data to test the individual and ensemble classifier. This study enrolled 20 diabetes men who were at least 45 years old with 3 measurements per day, for 20 days. The format of this dataset contains five columns designated by Date, Day, Glucose Level, and Request. The Glucose dataset is implemented and tested on four classifiers. Three out of four classifiers are individual classifiers, namely: the NaiveBayes classifier, the J48 classifier, ZeroR classifier and the BayesNet classifier.

These results prove that the used classifiers give good results of classification as well as attest the beneficial use of Trees Random Forest compared to Random Trees. The ROC curve is often used to determine the optimal threshold in classification problems. The area under the ROC curve (AUC) gives a good estimate of the system's rejection capability, figure 5 and 6 show the ROC curve (%) for the True and False Classifiers.

Figure 5. Comparison of true classifiers based on area under ROC, PRC area, and precision

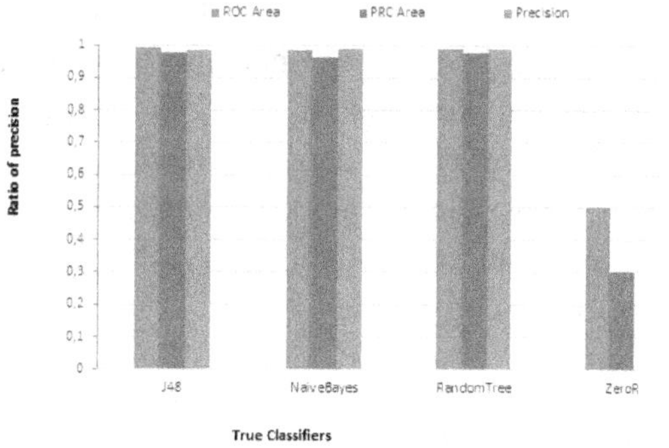

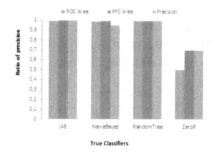

The ROC which is receiver operating characteristic curve for the too high which indicate good performance of the techniques, therefore, it can be used for prediction, Figure 6 shows the comparison of False Classifiers Based on Area under ROC, PRC Area, and Precision of ROC Area, for J48, NaivBayes, RandomTree, and ZeroR algorithms.

Figure 6. Comparison of false classifiers based on area under ROC, PRC area, and precision

When the dataset is tested on four classifiers, we obtain the precision and F-measures summarized in Table 3 using the "recall" approach. The accuracy of the NaiveBayes classifier is 88.78%, the accuracy of the J48 classifier is 99.21%, the accuracy of the BayesNet classifier is 93.48%, and the accuracy of the ZeroR classifier is 69.6078%.

Table 3. Accuracy of classifications algorithms

Algorithms	Correctly Classified Instances	Incorrectly Classified Instances	F-Measure	Precision
Naïve Bayes	88.78%	11.22%	0,970	0,946
BayesNet	93.48%	6.52%	0,994	0,993
ZeroR	69.60%	30.40%	0,821	0,696
J48	99.21%	0.79%	0,994	0,992

The precision corresponds to the average success percentage for k iterations (Moreira, Rodrigues, Kumar et al., 2018). In practice, cross-validation with k equal to ten is the most commonly used method. This study also used the F-measure for indicating the imbalance among the classes. Table 4 compares the performance of the proposed method with similar works in literature. All these studies used the same database, but with different treatments for the data. The results show that for the leading indicator, namely the F-measure, the method proposed in this work provides excellent performance in comparison with other methods in literature. Regarding precision, the BayesNet algorithm has a performance that is very close to that of the J48 tree-based classifier.

Table 4. Precision and F-measure values in recent research using the diabetes database

Authors	Method	F-Measure	Precision
Habibi, Ahmadi, & Alizadeh, 2015	J48	0,705	0,717
Sa'di, Maleki, Hashemi et al., 2015	BayesNet	0,767	0,768
	J48	0,786	0,771
Rghioui, Sendra, Lloret, & Oumnad, 2016	BayesNet	0,994	0,993
	J48	0,994	0,992

The graphs representation in Figure7 shows the difference of correctly and incorrectly classified instances using four algorithms. The four algorithms are Naïve Bayes, BayesNet, ZeroR, and J48. We found that the J48 algorithm was the best as it had 99.21% correctly classified instances and only 0,79% were incorrectly classified instances.

Figure 7. The graph of correctly and incorrectly classified instances of algorithms

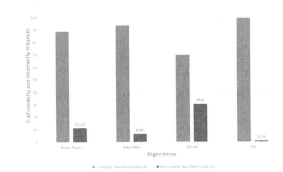

Figure 8 shows the time graph of various classification algorithms. The longest time is taken by ZeroR consuming a time of 0.05 seconds and the shortest time is taken by RandomTree consuming 0.01 seconds only.

Figure 8. The graph for training time for top four classifiers

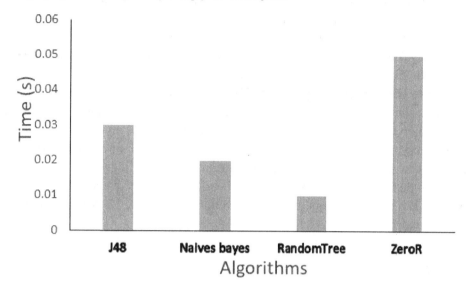

Figure 9 shows an example of Weka's visualization of a decision tree regarding the seed-size attribute from the Glucose Level.arff file. Once the information has been classified with the Weka algorithm J4.8, the decision tree shown in Figure 9 was obtained at the output.

Figure 9. Visualize tree with random tree

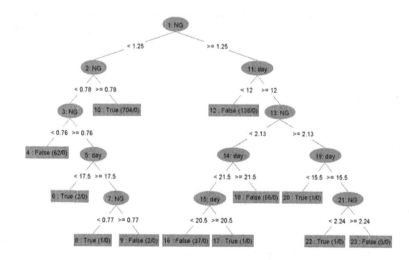

6. CONCLUSION

Today the healthcare industry is just beginning to understand all the innovative things that can be done with Big Data. The intersection of data from multiple sources, tools, and technologies will promote informative extrapolations of Big Data, allowing the information to generate new and innovative solutions to healthcare. While Big Data technologies are improving day by day this also means that, the volume of data along with the rate at which data is flowing into enterprises today is increasing. The healthcare system today is on a trajectory that is unsustainable. In this paper, classification techniques are used for prediction on the dataset of patient's data, to analyze overall diabetic performance and predict some relative's disease. In this study, among all data, mining classifiers J48 performs best with 99.21% accuracy and therefore J48 proves to be potentially effective and efficient classifier algorithm. The main contribution of this study is that it provides the possibility of handling a large amount of data to find useful results that support health experts in the decision-making process. In the future, some new factors can be applied to improve the patient's performance and results can be obtained based on station data. In addition, more data mining techniques such as k-means, clustering algorithms and other classification algorithms can be applied to this data. Thus, a focus in the future should be on preventive care as well as population health management and overall wellness. With Big Data, health management of a population can be understood better.

REFERENCES

Bennett, T. R., Savaglio, C., Lu, D., Massey, H., Wang, X., Wu, J., & Jafari, R. (2014, August). Motion-synthesis toolset (most): a toolset for human motion data synthesis and validation. In *Proceedings of the 4th ACM MobiHoc workshop on Pervasive wireless healthcare* (pp. 25-30). ACM.

Dogaru, D. I., & Dumitrache, I. (2017, June). Holistic perspective of big data in healthcare. In *Proceedings of the 2017 E-Health and Bioengineering Conference (EHB)* (pp. 418-421). IEEE.

Gartner. (2012). 3D Data management controlling data volume velocity and variety. Retrieved from https://blogs.gartner.com/doug-laney/files/2012/01/ad949-3D-Data-Management-Controlling-Data-Volume-Velocity-and-Variety.pdf

Gazal, & Kaur, P.D. (2015). A survey on big data storage strategies. In *Proceedings of the 2015 International Conference on Green Computing and Internet of Things (ICGCIoT)* (pp. 280-284). IEEE.

Din, SGhayvat, H., Paul, A., Ahmad, A., Rathore, M. M., & Shafi, I. (2015). An architecture to analyze big data in the Internet of Things. *9th International Conference on Sensing Technology (ICST)*.

Gholipour, C., Rahim, F., Fakhree, A., & Ziapour, B. (2015). Using an artificial neural networks (ANNs) model for prediction of intensive care unit (ICU) outcome and length of stay at hospital in traumatic patients. *Journal of Clinical and Diagnostic Research: JCDR*, *9*(4), OC19.

Gubbi, J., Buyya, R., Marusic, S., & Palaniswami, M. (2013). Internet of Things (IoT): A vision, architectural elements, and future directions. *Future Generation Computer Systems*, *29*(7), 1645–1660.

IHTT. (2013). *Transforming Health Care through Big Data Strategies for leveraging big data in the health care industry*.

Ilakiyaa, R. N., & Nalini, N. J. (2017). Supervised Learning Based HDFS Replication Management System. In *Proceedings of the International Conference on Technical Advancements in Computers and Communications (ICTACC)* (pp. 116-120). Academic Press. 10.1109/ICTACC.2017.38

import.io. (2015). All the best big data tools and how to use them. Retrieved from https://www.import.io/post/all-the-best-big-data-tools-and-how-to-use-them

Lee, E. K. (2017, December). Innovation in big data analytics: Applications of mathematical programming in medicine and healthcare. In *Proceedings of the 2017 IEEE International Conference on Big Data (Big Data)* (pp. 3586-3595). IEEE.

Liu, J., Li, Y., Chen, M., Dong, W., & Jin, D. (2015). Software-defined internet of things for smart urban sensing. *IEEE Communications Magazine*, *53*(9), 55–63.

Lloret, J., Parra, L., Taha, M., & Tomás, J. (2017). An architecture and protocol for smart continuous eHealth monitoring using 5G. *Computer Networks*, *129*, 340–351.

Marjani, M., Nasaruddin, F., Gani, A., Karim, A., Hashem, I. A. T., Siddiqa, A., & Yaqoob, I. (2017). Big IoT data analytics: Architecture, opportunities, and open research challenges. *IEEE Access: Practical Innovations, Open Solutions*, *5*, 5247–5261.

Moreira, M. W., Rodrigues, J. J., Furtado, V., Kumar, N., & Korotaev, V. V. (2018). Averaged one-dependence estimators on edge devices for smart pregnancy data analysis. *Computers & Electrical Engineering*.

Moreira, M. W., Rodrigues, J. J., Kumar, N., Al-Muhtadi, J., & Korotaev, V. (2018). Evolutionary radial basis function network for gestational diabetes data analytics. *Journal of Computational Science*, *27*, 410–417.

Moudani, W., Hussein, M., AbdelRazzak, M. & Mora-Camino, F. (2014). Heart disease diagnosis using fuzzy supervised learning based on dynamic reduced features. International Journal of E-Health and Medical Communications, 5(3), 78-101. doi:10.4018/ijehmc.2014070106

Mozumdar, M., Shahbazian, A., & Ton, Q. (2014). A big data correlation orchestrator for Internet of Things. In *Proceeding of the IEEE World Forum on Internet of Things (WF-IoT '14)*, 304–308. 10.1109/WF-IoT.2014.6803177

Narayan, S., Bailey, S., & Daga, A. (2012, November). Hadoop acceleration in an openflow-based cluster. In *Proceedings of the 2012 SC Companion: High Performance Computing, Networking Storage and Analysis* (pp. 535-538). IEEE.

Olaronke, I., & Oluwaseun, O. (2016). Big Data in Healthcare: Prospects, challenges and resolutions. In *Proceedings of the Future Technologies Conference (FTC)*. Academic Press. 10.1109/FTC.2016.7821747

Reddy, A. R., & Kumar, P. S. (2016, February). Predictive big data analytics in healthcare. In *Proceedings of the 2016 Second International Conference on Computational Intelligence & Communication Technology (CICT)* (pp. 623-626). IEEE.

Rghioui, A., Sendra, S., Lloret, J., & Oumnad, A. (2016). Internet of things for measuring human activities in ambient assisted living and e-health. *Network Protocols and Algorithms*, *8*(3), 15–28.

Sa'di, S., Maleki, A., Hashemi, R., Panbechi, Z., & Chalabi, K. (2015). Comparison of data mining algorithms in the diagnosis of type II diabetes. *International Journal on Computational Science & Applications*, *5*(5), 1–12.

Sahoo, P. K., Mohapatra, S. K., & Wu, S. L. (2016). Analyzing Healthcare Big Data with prediction for future Health condition. *IEEE Access, 4,* 9786–9799. doi:10.1109/ACCESS.2016.2647619

Sendra, S., Parra, L., Lloret, J., & Tomás, J. (2018). Smart system for children's chronic illness monitoring. Information Fusion, 40, 76-86.

Shah, M., Shukla, P. K., & Pandey, R. (2016). Phase level energy aware map reduce scheduling for big data applications. In *Proceedings of the International Conference on Signal Processing, Communication, Power and Embedded System (SCOPES),* pp. 532-535. 10.1109/SCOPES.2016.7955884

Sheeran, M., & Steele, R. (2017). A framework for big data technology in health and healthcare. *IEEE 8th Annual Conference Ubiquitous Computing, Electronics and Mobile Communication (UEMCON).*

Stankovic, A. J. (2014). Research directions for the internet of things. *IEEE Internet of Things Journal, 1*(1), 3–9.

Sterling, M. (2017, October). Situated big data and big data analytics for healthcare. In *Proceedings of the 2017 IEEE Global Humanitarian Technology Conference (GHTC).* IEEE.

Thara, D. K., Premasudha, B. G., Ram, V. R., & Suma, R. (2016, December). Impact of big data in healthcare: A survey. In *Proceedings of the 2016 2nd International Conference on Contemporary Computing and Informatics (IC3I)* (pp. 729-735). IEEE.

Hall, M., Frank, E., Holmes, G., Pfahringer, B., Reutemann, P., & Witten, I. H. (2009). The WEKA Data Mining Software: An Update. *SIGKDD Explorations, 11*(1), 10–18. doi:10.1145/1656274.1656278

Habibi, S., Ahmadi, M., & Alizadeh, S. (2015). Type 2 diabetes mellitus screening and risk factors using decision tree: Results of data mining. *Global Journal of Health Science, 7*(5), 304–310. PMID:26156928

Wang, Y., Kung, L., & Byrd, T. A. (2018). Big data analytics: Understanding its capabilities and potential benefits for healthcare organizations. *Technological Forecasting and Social Change, 126,* 3–13.

Yuehong, Y. I. N., Zeng, Y., Chen, X., & Fan, Y. (2016). The internet of things in healthcare: An overview. *Journal of Industrial Information Integration, 1,* 3–13.

Zaveri, C. (2017, February). Use of big-data in healthcare and lifescience using hadoop technologies. In *Proceedings of the 2017 Second International Conference on Electrical, Computer and Communication Technologies (ICECCT)* (pp. 1-5). IEEE.

Zhou, J., Hu, L., Wang, F., Lu, H., & Zhao, K. (2013). An efficient multidimensional fusion algorithm for IoT data based on partitioning. *Tsinghua Science and Technology, 18*(4), 369–378.

This research was previously published in the International Journal of E-Health and Medical Communications (IJEHMC), 11(2); pages 20-37, copyright year 2020 by IGI Publishing (an imprint of IGI Global).

Index

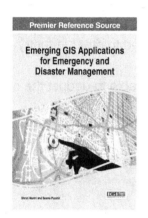
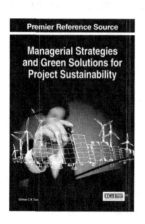

www.igi-global.com

Publisher of Peer-Reviewed, Timely, and
Innovative Academic Research Since 1988

IGI Global's Transformative Open Access (OA) Model:
How to Turn Your University Library's Database Acquisitions Into a Source of OA Funding

Well in advance of Plan S, IGI Global unveiled their OA Fee Waiver (Read & Publish) Initiative. Under this initiative, librarians who invest in IGI Global's InfoSci-Books and/or InfoSci-Journals databases will be able to subsidize their patrons' OA article processing charges (APCs) when their work is submitted and accepted (after the peer review process) into an IGI Global journal.

How Does it Work?

Step 1: **Library Invests in the InfoSci-Databases:** A library perpetually purchases or subscribes to the InfoSci-Books, InfoSci-Journals, or discipline/subject databases.

Step 2: **IGI Global Matches the Library Investment with OA Subsidies Fund:** IGI Global provides a fund to go towards subsidizing the OA APCs for the library's patrons.

Step 3: **Patron of the Library is Accepted into IGI Global Journal (After Peer Review):** When a patron's paper is accepted into an IGI Global journal, they option to have their paper published under a traditional publishing model or as OA.

Step 4: **IGI Global Will Deduct APC Cost from OA Subsidies Fund:** If the author decides to publish under OA, the OA APC fee will be deducted from the OA subsidies fund.

Step 5: **Author's Work Becomes Freely Available:** The patron's work will be freely available under CC BY copyright license, enabling them to share it freely with the academic community.

Note: This fund will be offered on an annual basis and will renew as the subscription is renewed for each year thereafter. IGI Global will manage the fund and award the APC waivers unless the librarian has a preference as to how the funds should be managed.

Hear From the Experts on This Initiative:

"I'm very happy to have been able to make one of my recent research contributions *freely available* along with having access to the *valuable resources* found within IGI Global's InfoSci-Journals database."

— **Prof. Stuart Palmer**,
Deakin University, Australia

"Receiving the support from IGI Global's OA Fee Waiver Initiative *encourages me to continue my research work without any hesitation.*"

— **Prof. Wenlong Liu**, College of Economics and Management at Nanjing University of Aeronautics & Astronautics, China

For More Information, Scan the QR Code or Contact:
IGI Global's Digital Resources Team at eresources@igi-global.com.

Printed in the United States
by Baker & Taylor Publisher Services